ADVERTISING AND PROMOTION MANAGEMENT

McGraw-Hill Series in Marketing

ADVERTISING AND PROMOTION MANAGEMENT

John R. Rossiter

The New South Wales Institute of Technology

Larry Percy

HBM/CREAMER

McGRAW-HILL BOOK COMPANY

New York   St. Louis   San Francisco   Auckland   Bogotá
Hamburg   Johannesburg   London   Madrid   Mexico   Milan   Montreal   New Delhi
Panama   Paris   São Paulo   Singapore   Sydney   Tokyo   Toronto

This book was set in Times Roman by Monotype Composition Company (ECU).
The editor was Sam Costanzo;
the production supervisor was Friederich Schulte;
the cover was designed by James Handloser.
Project supervision was done by Caliber Design Planning.
Photo research by Lorinda Morris/Photoquest®, Inc.
Arcata Graphics/Halliday was printer and binder.

ADVERTISING AND PROMOTION MANAGEMENT

ISBN 0-07-053907-3

1 2 3 4 5 6 7 8 9 0 H A L H A L 8 9 2 1 0 9 8 7

Library of Congress Cataloging-in-Publication Data

Rossiter, John R.
  Advertising and promotion management.

  Bibliography: p.
  1. Advertising. 2. Sales promotion. I. Percy,
Larry. II. Title.
HF5821.R65   1987   659.1   86-27381
ISBN 0-07-053907-3

ABOUT THE AUTHORS

JOHN R. ROSSITER is an ''Aussie'' with 15 years of United States marketing experience. Now Principal Lecturer in Marketing at The New South Wales Institute of Technology in Sydney, Australia, where he teaches marketing management, consumer behavior, and advertising management. He was previously Assistant Professor of Marketing at The Wharton School, University of Pennsylvania, and then Associate Professor of Business in the Graduate School of Business at Columbia University in New York.

Dr. Rossiter has coauthored three other books and has contributed more than 50 conference papers and journal articles, with his work appearing in the *Journal of Consumer Research,* the *Journal of Marketing Research,* and the *Journal of Advertising Research*. He has been a marketing and advertising consultant to Ogilvy & Mather advertising agency and to numerous client companies in the United States and Australia.

LARRY PERCY is Corporate Research Director at HBM/CREAMER advertising agency in Pittsburgh, and Adjunct Professor at the University of Pittsburgh's Graduate School of Business. He began his advertising career at Young & Rubicam in New York and then became director of advertising research for several other leading agencies before joining HBM/CREAMER and admitting that his heart was with the Pittsburgh Steelers.

Mr. Percy has taught at Carnegie-Mellon University and currently teaches marketing theory and advertising management at the University of Pittsburgh. Coauthor and coeditor of two previous books on advertising theory, he has contributed over 30 conference papers and journal articles to the field. He has served as a Director of the Association for Consumer Research and sits on the editorial board of a number of journals, including the *Journal of Marketing Research*. He has also conducted numerous executive seminars across the United States on advertising and promotion management.

CONTENTS

PREFACE

This book presents a completely new approach to the management of advertising and (sales) promotion. A prepublication review pleased us greatly by describing the book as being "light years ahead" in terms of theory and practical implications for advertising and promotion. The book is written for:

- MBA students taking a single course in advertising management, and undergraduate students in managerial rather than descriptive advertising courses
- Managers in client companies and advertising agencies who wish to update and advance their on-the-job planning for advertising and promotion

Whereas this book is conceptual in its approach, its orientation *from* the concepts is applied and managerial. Throughout, we discuss what to do and when, and most of all why. The book's aim is to assist the manager to make, and to be able to justify, the best decisions in the overall advertising and promotion plan.

The main point of difference in our text versus other texts is the central theme of *advertising communication models,* although we don't use the term "models" until the end of the book. Advertising and promotion both are forms of marketing communication, and it therefore follows that correct specification of the communication process for the brand is essential for their success. Here, we believe, we have made a significant advance by identifying the major alternative advertising communication models and by specifying how to select an appropriate advertising communication model for the brand. The advertising communication model selected for the brand—the company, store, product, or service being advertised—flows from the target audience action objectives, dictates the communication objectives, and then guides the creative strategy, promotion strategy, and media strategy.

Although the approach is new, the book covers all the standard, major topics in advertising and promotion management. Questions covered in the eight parts of the book include: What are the purposes of advertising and promotion? How should the manager plan for advertising and promotion? (Introduction) How do advertising and promotion contribute to profit? Should the emphasis be on sales or on competitive market share? (Marketing objectives) How does a target audience differ from a market segment, and how is the target audience selected? Should the behavioral objective for the campaign be purchase action or should it be prior, purchase-related action? (Target audience action objectives) What specific communication objectives have to be addressed to produce the desired action? How is the target audience decision maker to be made aware of the brand; and which benefits should be emphasized, which benefits should be mentioned, and which perhaps omitted in the brand's advertising? (Communication objectives) Do ads have to be believable and likable in order to be effective? When should creative techniques such as comparative advertising, a special presenter, or humor be used? (Creative strategy) How can promotion campaigns be designed not only to create short-term sales increases but also to contribute to long-term sales? Which promotion techniques work best for stimulating trial and which work best for maintaining usage of the brand? (Promotion strategy) Which primary and secondary media should be selected for consumer, retail, industrial, corporate, or direct response campaigns? Why is effective reach, based on effective frequency, so important in media scheduling? (Media strategy) How can qualitative research be used in conjunction with quantitative research to develop an advertising strategy for the brand? How should ads and promotion offers be tested, and how should campaigns be monitored and evaluated? (Advertising research) We discuss and recommend answers to all these questions, and many more, in the text. At the end of the book, to summarize our approach, we have provided an advertising and promotion checklist for use by managers.

In this book, we believe we have put together a comprehensive yet new approach to advertising and promotion management. The new ideas have been extensively tested in the real world and in the classroom prior to publication, and for this assistance we owe many acknowledgments.

Broad acknowledgment goes to the many advertising management students— at The Wharton School, Carnegie-Mellon University, the University of Pittsburgh, Columbia University, and, more recently, The New South Wales Institute of Technology in Sydney, Australia—whose comments on early drafts of the text helped to refine the principles and clarify the presentation.

Professor Robert Donovan, first at New York University and later in Australia, was responsible for improving many of our ideas, especially by testing them in advertising research projects. To him we are greatly indebted.

Professor Charles Schewe of the University of Massachusetts, consulting editor to McGraw-Hill for the original draft of the book, realized we had a very new and exciting approach and was instrumental in sharpening our communication of this approach to marketing executives and students.

Personnel at the Ogilvy & Mather advertising agency in New York and Australia made practical contributions to the book's development. Too many contributed to be listed here, but we would like to single out Lindsay Hardingham for her thorough evaluation of the book's principles in many campaign applications.

Our reviewers at McGraw-Hill were right behind the book from the start and counseled wisely during its development: Robert E. Burnkrant, Ohio State University; Philip Ward Burton, Indiana University; Ernest F. Cooke, Loyola College in Maryland; Lawrence J. Danks, formerly of Stockton State College and Atlantic Community College, New Jersey; William Keene, Truitt and Associates; Geoffrey Lantos, Stonehill College; Thomas Leigh, Pennsylvania State University; Edward Popper, Northeastern University; Bonnie B. Reece, Michigan State University; Charles Schewe, University of Massachusetts; and Richard Werbel, San Jose State University.

Donata Ellis of The New South Wales Institute of Technology did all of the word processing of the manuscript with speed and style. Donna Conte and Bill Haller of Caliber Design Planning supervised the copyediting and production with consideration and precision.

McGraw-Hill's College Division Marketing Editor, Sam Costanzo, kept the whole project moving and made thoughtful suggestions for the book's presentation.

John R. Rossiter
Larry Percy

PART **ONE**

INTRODUCTION

Chapter 1 Advertising and Promotion Management

ADVERTISING AND PROMOTION MANAGEMENT

This chapter defines the general nature and purpose of advertising and (sales) promotion[1] and shows how they fit into the general process of marketing management. It then introduces a six-step advertising and promotion plan for the manager to follow. After reading this chapter you should be able to:

- Distinguish the basic differences between advertising and promotion
- Understand the relative roles of advertising and promotion in marketing management
- Learn the four steps constituting the buyer response sequence in the six-step plan
- See how the manager proceeds "from the top down" in formulating the advertising and promotion plan

ADVERTISING AND PROMOTION DEFINED

Advertising and promotion are increasingly being viewed by marketing managers as highly interrelated yet distinctly specialized means of informing customers about products and services and persuading them to buy. Advertising and promotion are highly interrelated because they both rely on marketing communication processes for their effects and are so often used together. Yet they are specialized because of the respective effectiveness of the techniques available for each.

The differences and similarities between advertising and promotion can be defined from a conceptual perspective and from a practical perspective.

TABLE 1-1 LATIN ORIGINS OF THE TERMS "ADVERTISING" AND "PROMOTION"†

Promotional term	Latin origin	Functional translation
Advertising	*Advertere* = to turn toward	Advertising aims at turning the buyer or consumer's mind toward purchase.
Promotion	*Promovere* = to move forward or advance	Promotion aims at immediately stimulating purchase.

† As far as we can tell, the famous marketing research and former Harvard professor of advertising, Daniel Starch, was the first to mention advertising's Latin root as a means of explaining the term (D. Starch, *Principles of Advertising,* Chicago: A. W. Shaw, 1926. The notion of advertising "turning the *mind* toward" purchase was suggested by Dirksen and Kroeger (C. J. Dirksen and A. Kroeger, *Advertising Principles, Problems, and Cases,* Homewood, IL: Irwin, 1960).

Conceptual Perspective

The basic conceptual difference between advertising and promotion is suggested by the Latin origins of the two terms (Table 1.1).

- *Advertising* is often regarded as a process of relatively indirect persuasion, based on information about product benefits, which is designed to create favorable mental impressions that "turn the mind toward" purchase.
- *Promotion* is often regarded as a more direct form of persuasion, based frequently on external incentives rather than inherent product benefits, which is designed to stimulate immediate purchase and to "move sales forward" more rapidly than would otherwise occur.

Various writers have described other conceptual differences between advertising and promotion. However, the differences are relative rather than absolute. Some of these can be studied in Table 1.2 along with exceptions that illustrate the relative nature of the differences.

TABLE 1-2 RELATIVE DIFFERENCES BETWEEN ADVERTISING AND PROMOTION

Differences	Advertising	Promotion
1. Directness of emphasis on purchase behavior	*Indirect.* Exceptions: Direct mail, retail newspaper ads, and direct response TV ads	*Direct.* Exceptions: PR-type promotions such as corporate sponsorship of sports events
2. Scope of non-price-related information presented	*Broad.* Exceptions: Retail newspaper ads often list only the brand name, store, and price; emotional ads, e.g., for cosmetics, often give very little information	*Narrow.* Exceptions: Promotion offers for new brands often list brand benefits along with the promotion
3. Timing of presentation	*Before purchase.* Exceptions: Point-of-purchase (p-o-p) and on-package ads	*With purchase.* Exceptions: Promotion offers placed in ads or distributed by mail or door to door

Conceptual similarities between advertising and promotion become even greater when we realize that both can be used to achieve the same objectives. As we shall see later, advertising and promotion can both be used to generate awareness, establish or change attitudes, and stimulate purchase intentions. Both advertising and promotion have the potential for building a "consumer franchise," or relatively permanent preference for a brand, as well as for creating "non-franchise" effects, in the form of temporary preference for a brand.[2]

Practical Perspective

In practice, advertising and promotion are most readily distinguished in terms of *types* and *techniques*.

Advertising can be categorized into at least 11 different types based on who is advertising, within the marketing channel, and to what target the advertising is directed (Figure 1.1). Marketers and distributors advertise; and the targets can be distributors, usually retailers, or end-users of industrial or consumer products. Promotion consists of three main types: trade promotion (marketer to distributor); retail promotion (distributor to consumer); and consumer promotion (marketer to consumer or industrial user). The "by whom, to whom" basis of these types of promotion can also be distinguished in the figure.

In terms of techniques, advertising uses eight different approaches depending on its brand awareness objective (brand recognition versus brand recall) coupled with its brand attitude objective and strategy (four combinations of low- versus high-involvement purchase decisions and informational versus transformational purchase motivations) as we will explain later in the book. Promotions use one or more of 10 easily identifiable techniques: direct price-offs, indirect price-offs, sampling, coupons, trade coupons, bonus packs, in/on packs, premiums, sweepstakes or contests, and continuity programs.

Advertising and promotion are often used as combined means of reaching the respective target customers in the consumer, industrial, trade, and retail channels. Although the techniques differ, advertising's and promotion's general purposes are the same. Both work, via communication, to produce target customer action in the marketplace.

Advertising and Promotion Expenditures

Overall Expenditures   Accounting practices make it difficult to directly compare expenditures for advertising and promotion. The accounting difficulty is caused by the dual practices, on the one hand, of frequently placing promotions in advertisements or in advertising media, and on the other, of frequently including advertising messages in promotion offers. The exhibit for Arm & Hammer Baking Soda (Figure 1.2) is a good illustration of these dual practices. Is it an ad or is it a promotion offer?

```
┌──────────┐                                                          ┌──────────┐
│ Marketer │                                                          │Consumers │
└──────────┘     ┌──────────────────────────────────────────┐        └──────────┘
                 │ 1.  Consumer (national and local): "Buy our brand;
                 │     use our service."
                 │ 2.  Corporate: "We're a good company."
                 │ 3.  Institutional: "Help our cause."
                 │ 4.  Public Service: "Do this, it's good for all of us."
                 │ 5.  Professional: "Come to us for your legal,
                 │     medical (etc.) needs."
                 │ 6.  Classified: "Hire me; buy this from me."
                 └──────────────────────────────────────────┘

                          ┌──────────────┐
                          │ Distributors │
                          └──────────────┘
   ┌─────────────────────────┐          ┌─────────────────────────┐
   │ 7.  Trade: "Stock and   │          │ 9.  Retail: "Buy it     │
   │     promote our products."│        │     at our store."      │
   │ 8.  Professional Trade: │          │ 10. Cooperative (joint retail-
   │     "Recommend or       │          │     consumer): "Buy our brand in
   │     prescribe our products."│      │     this store."        │
   └─────────────────────────┘          └─────────────────────────┘

                                                          ┌──────────────┐
                                                          │  Industrial  │
                                                          │    Users     │
                                                          └──────────────┘
   ┌─────────────────────────┐
   │ 11. Industrial: "Use our │
   │     supplies and services."│
   └─────────────────────────┘
```

FIGURE 1.1   Channel-related typology of advertising and promotion. (*Adapted from C.H. Sandage and V. Fryburger, Advertising Theory and Practice, 9th ed., Homewood, IL: Irwin, 1975, by permission.*)

By most accounts, overall expenditures for advertising and promotion are approximately equal. Table 1.3 lists estimated expenditures in advertising media (about $93 billion annually). But this figure includes promotion offers placed in advertising media. Similarly, Table 1.4 lists estimated expenditures for promotion by major categories (about $91 billion annually). But this figure includes advertising messages appearing in promotion offers.

Reasons for Increased Use of Promotion   There has been a dramatic increase in the use of promotion in recent years. Some of the reasons for the increased

Help us find 1001 uses for Arm & Hammer® Baking Soda.

Arm & Hammer Baking Soda does more jobs than just about any other product you can buy. It absorbs refrigerator and freezer odors, deodorizes cat litter, helps keep septic tanks trouble-free, freshens laundry, and softens your skin in the bath – just to name a few.

Arm & Hammer Baking Soda may have 1001 uses – uses even we don't know about. That's why we're running this sweepstakes. Tell us your favorite use for Arm & Hammer Baking Soda – and you could win one of the fabulous prizes on the opposite page. No purchase necessary.

Six popular ways you can use Arm & Hammer Baking Soda.

A fresh box every 2 months helps keep refrigerators fresh and clean smelling.

Absorbs freezer odors that can spoil the taste of ice cubes and ice cream.

A cup down the toilet weekly helps keep septic tanks odor- and trouble-free.

Leaves skin feeling soft and smooth – naturally.

Keeps cat litter boxes fresh for days and days.

Helps give your laundry a sweeter, cleaner smell.

Win one of 1001 prizes!

Grand Prize: 1980 Oldsmobile 98 LS.
2 Second Prizes: Week for two in London or Hawaii.
5 Third Prizes: G.E. Video Cassette Recorder and G.E. 25" Color TV.
25 Fourth Prizes: G.E. Microwave Ovens.
100 Fifth Prizes: Hamilton Beach Food Processors.
868 Sixth Prizes: Imported Simulated Pearl Ropes.

Sweepstakes open to U.S. residents over 18. Void where prohibited. All prizes will be awarded. Offer expires 12/31/79. For a list of winners, send a self-addressed stamped envelope to Scharer Assoc. Inc., P.O. Box 1329, Great Neck, N.Y. 11023.

OFFICIAL ENTRY FORM

$1001 cash bonus awarded to Grand Prize winner if official entry form is accompanied by the red circle from Arm & Hammer® Baking Soda box top. Or, on a separate 3" x 5" card, draw a red circle and hand letter the words Arm & Hammer Baking Soda.

Send to Arm & Hammer Baking Soda
1001 Uses Sweepstakes
P.O. Box 700, Flushing, N.Y. 11390

I use Arm & Hammer to deodorize and freshen my freezer ☐ cat litter ☐ septic tank ☐
My favorite use not listed is _____

Name _____
Address _____
City _____ State _____ Zip _____

Nothing says fresh & clean like Arm & Hammer Baking Soda – naturally.

FIGURE 1.2   Arm & Hammer Baking Soda exhibit. This is an advertised promotion. But how would you classify the exhibit: as an advertisement or as a promotion offer? (*Arm & Hammer is a registered trademark of Church & Dwight Co., Inc. This ad was reproduced with the permission of Church & Dwight Co., Inc.*)

TABLE 1-3   ADVERTISING (INCLUDING IN-AD PROMOTION) EXPENDITURES BY MEDIA TYPE†

Rank	Medium	Expenditure	Percent
1	Newspaper	$27 billion	29
2	TV	20	21
3	Direct mail	13	14
4	Magazine	8	9
5	Radio	6	6
6	Outdoor	1	1
7	Miscellaneous media	18	19
		$93 billion	100

† Advertising expenditures taken from estimates in *Advertising Age*, Jan. 5, 1981, p. 56 (by permission), and projected to 1987. Percentages in the table actually add to 99 due to rounding.

TABLE 1-4   PROMOTION EXPENDITURES BY TYPE†

Promotion type	Expenditure	Percent
Industrial (business-to-business) promotions	$37 billion	40
Trade promotions	26	29
Consumer promotions	18	20
Retailer promotions	10	11
	$91 billion	100

† Promotional expenditures based on estimates from various sources, including *Advertising Age,* Jan. 4, 1982, p. 32 (by permission), and projected to 1987.

and now essentially equal status of promotion vis-à-vis advertising have been suggested by Strang:[3]

1 Promotion techniques have come to be regarded as less gimmicky and more legitimate in the eyes of top management.

2 Expanding use of the product manager system has brought increasing emphasis on visible short-term results which promotion offers can help to deliver.

3 Escalating media costs for advertising, as well as advertising "clutter," have increased the attractiveness of promotional alternatives.

4 Slowdowns in the economy make many consumers more price-sensitive and thereby increase the effectiveness of price-oriented techniques.

5 In the face of proliferating brands and the battle for shelf space, retailers rely on promotional inducements from manufacturers in deciding which brands to stock and display.

Management Time Expenditures

It is clear that marketing managers are increasingly regarding advertising and promotion as interrelated means of selling products and services. Interestingly, though, time expenditure for the actual *management* of advertising continues to considerably outweigh time expenditure for the management of promotion. For example, in 1977, a typical year for the U.S. economy, the top 40 consumer packaged goods advertisers spent 90 percent of management funds on advertising and only 10 percent on promotion, despite the fact that advertising and promotion, in total, had similar overall budgets.[4]

Management's lesser attention to promotion probably reflects the belief that promotion techniques are more "empirical" and require less planning and theorizing than advertising techniques. (To some extent this is true. But there have been several major theoretical breakthroughs in promotion that most managers have not yet heard about. These are described in Part Six.)

Another reason for lower *internal* management expenditure on promotion is due to the widespread practice of hiring outside sales promotion services who provide external program management in contrast with more direct client management of advertising programs.

ADVERTISING AND PROMOTION AND STRATEGIC MARKETING MANAGEMENT

Marketing Strategy Principles

It is useful to approach advertising and promotion by reviewing their role in the strategic marketing management process as a whole. Marketing management can be conceptualized in a strategic framework that identifies four basic principles (Figure 1.3).[5]

FIGURE 1.3 Marketing strategy framework. The outer boxes show the four strategy components, linked by four strategy principles, to form the overall marketing strategy.

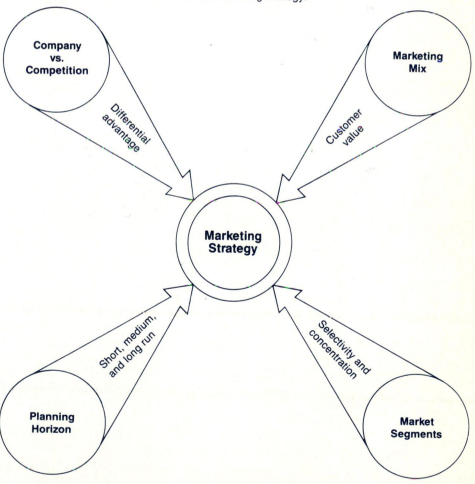

First, the manager makes an assessment of *company resources*—financial, technical, and managerial—versus principal competitors' resources. The strategy principle in this assessment is to identify *differential advantages,* relative to the competition, which can be parlayed into superior marketplace performance and financial success. The competitive orientation is frequently as vital to success as the much-heralded customer orientation which underlies "the marketing concept."[6] A great deal of advertising and promotion planning is competitor-oriented rather than customer-oriented, and in competitive situations, the manager does not have to generate the best (or ideal) plan but rather a plan that is better than those of competitors. Most managers have to simultaneously adopt a customer orientation and a competitor orientation.

Second, the manager reviews the controllable inputs to the market: most importantly the company's product or products, but also the other three "P's" which together make up the famous "4 P's" of the *marketing mix*: price, place (distribution), and promotion. The strategy principle underlying marketing mix management is the provision of *customer value,* which is a set of utilities or benefits represented by the 4 P's: product and service attributes, price-value and payment terms; distribution convenience and store image; and promotional factors.[7]

Third, customer value is "packaged" to appeal to particular *target markets*. Target markets include trade distributors as well as ultimate buyers and consumers. This introduces the third facet of marketing strategy: target market selection. The strategy principle here is *selectivity* (market segmentation) *and concentration* (of financial and marketing resources) on markets that represent the best profit potential. The marketing mix, one for each target market, is fine-tuned to deliver maximal customer value to the target market.

Fourth, marketing strategy must be formulated in relation to a particular *planning horizon.* Short-run (usually a year or less), medium-run (1 to 5 years), and long-run (5 to 10 or more years) objectives and strategies must be planned in terms of anticipated changes in the uncontrollable future environment. Technical, economic, political, legal, and socio-cultural trends must be estimated while adhering to the three principles of differential advantage versus competitors, customer value in the marketing mix, and selectivity and concentration in target markets.

Advertising and promotion planning, as part of marketing strategy, should be conducted in accordance with the four basic principles of strategic marketing management. General illustrations are as follows:

1 *Differential Advantage* Advertising budgets and superior advertising creativity are sources of differential advantage for the firm. So too are promotion budgets and the correct selection of promotion techniques for new and existing products.

2 *Customer Value* Advertising can provide customer value by informing customers about product and service benefits and availability, by signifying brand reliability, or by conferring a desired image or status upon the user. Promotion can provide customer value by providing rewards for immediate purchase, most often monetary in the form of discounts or savings, but also participatory rewards as in promotional contests and sweepstakes.

3 *Selectivity and Concentration* Advertising is most often selectively aimed at target customers who are prospectively or currently "loyal" to the brand. Promotion is most often aimed at target customers on the "fringe" of the loyal segment to induce them to try or occasionally buy the brand.

4 *Time Factor* Advertising generally has a longer planning (and effects) horizon than promotion, although both can be used as elements of short-, medium-, and long-run marketing strategies.

These are the general strategic considerations for advertising and promotion planning. In the next several sections, we examine more specific considerations.

Promotion Sub-Mix Management

Advertising and promotion are strategic inputs to the marketing mix, specifically, to the promotion sub-mix (Figure 1.4). The elements of the promotion sub-mix are listed in order of aggregate expenditures: personal selling, advertising, promotion, and public relations. This book does not cover personal selling because this is typically a specialized marketing function outside the direct control of most advertising managers.[8] Public relations ("PR") strategy is similar in many respects to advertising strategy. The implementation of PR differs from advertising, however, and is too detailed to include in this book. Our focus is on advertising and promotion.

FIGURE 1.4   Advertising and promotion within the marketing mix and promotion sub-mix. Note the broad use of the term "promotion" when referring to the sub-mix, and the narrow use (sales promotion) within the sub-mix.

Overall Emphasis The overall emphasis on advertising and promotion within the promotion sub-mix differs by type of business. An early study by Udell[9] asked managers to judge the importance of advertising and promotion relative to personal selling, which is the other major component of the promotion sub-mix. Udell's results indicated that industrial product managers place less importance (31 percent) on advertising and promotion than on personal selling; that consumer durable goods managers place about equal emphasis (52 percent) on advertising and promotion and personal selling; and that, as expected, for consumer packaged goods managers, advertising and promotion are more important (62 percent) than personal selling.

Relative Emphasis The foregoing differences in overall emphasis are still very general and do not really reflect the relative use of advertising "versus" promotion from the manager's viewpoint. The following sections address relative use by managers. Much of our coverage draws on the recent study by Strang which, although based on interviews with consumer packaged goods managers, contains implications of relevance for all advertising and promotion managers.[10]

Product Life Cycle

The main factor that determines the use of advertising and promotion over the longer term is stage in the product life cycle (PLC).[11] As conceptualized in Figure 1.5, the product life cycle consists of four major stages: introduction, growth, maturity, and decline.[12]

FIGURE 1.5   Product life cycle (PLC) stages.

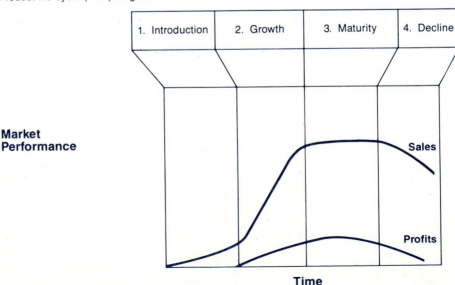

Advertising and promotion expenditures in the *introduction* stage typically are *both* high (Table 1.5). A high level of advertising is needed to make people aware of the newly introduced product and to communicate its benefits for prospective buyers' considerations. A high level of promotion, also, is needed to further build awareness and to induce people to try the new product.

Advertising and promotion strategy in the *growth* stage may differ depending on whether the brand is (a) either the market share leader or well-differentiated from other brands in the product category, versus (b) an imitative "me-too" brand. In the former instance, advertising is emphasized as a means of maintaining brand identity and differentiation. In the latter instance, with a me-too product or brand, advertising can be lower because the imitator can capitalize on the leader's advertising. Correspondingly, promotion is higher so as to induce trial of, and switching to, the me-too brand. Thus, the relative roles of advertising and promotion may be reversed depending on the brand's positioning in the growth stage of the PLC.

Advertising and promotion strategy in the *maturity* stage may also differ, this time depending upon whether the brand has managed to engender (a) high brand loyalty or (b) low brand loyalty. Brands with high loyalty usually will emphasize advertising to maintain the successful brand "image." Brands with a low degree of loyalty, on the other hand, will usually have to emphasize promotion as a means of attracting and holding buyers.

Advertising and promotion in the *decline* stage of the product life cycle are phased out as the manager tries to minimize marketing costs. Advertising is discontinued. Promotion, however, is continued at a low level—to distributors—to keep the product in stock while the manufacturer's inventory is reduced to zero.

Other Factors Affecting Relative Use of Advertising and Promotion

A number of other marketing factors[13] can be identified as affecting the relative use of advertising versus promotion (Table 1.6).

TABLE 1-5 RELATIVE ROLES OF ADVERTISING AND PROMOTION ACCORDING TO PRODUCT LIFE CYCLE (PLC) STAGES†

PLC stage	Advertising	Promotion
1. Introduction	High	High
2. Growth		
(a) Leader or differentiated	High	Low
(b) Me-too product	Low	High
3. Maturity		
(a) High brand loyalty	High	Low
(b) Low brand loyalty	Low	High
4. Decline	None	Low (trade)

† After R. A. Strang, *The Promotional Planning Process*, New York: Praeger, 1980, p. 82, by permission.

TABLE 1-6   OTHER FACTORS AFFECTING THE RELATIVE USE OF ADVERTISING AND PROMOTION†

Advertising emphasized	Promotion emphasized
High quality brand	Low quality brand
High price brand	Low price brand
Differentiated brand	Commodity brand
High risk product	Low risk product
When store brands have greater than 25% share	(No equivalent recommendation)
Direct competitor increases advertising	Direct competitor increases promotion

† After R. A. Strang, *The Promotional Planning Process*, New York: Praeger, 1980, Chapters 6 and 7, by permission.

A high quality brand will tend to emphasize advertising to communicate its quality benefits and maintain its "quality image." A low quality brand will tend to use promotional inducements to persuade buyers to "trade down." Quality generally relates to price, so the second factor in the table correspondingly finds high priced brands emphasizing advertising to justify their higher price and lower priced brands emphasizing promotion, usually price promotion, to appeal to buyers on a "value" basis.

Differentiated brands have a stronger reason for advertising—to inform buyers about unique benefits. In contrast, "commodity" brands are perceived as similar and tend to compete on a promotion basis. Brands can be differentiated on the basis of obvious attributes, such as taste, but also on the basis of attributes that the consumer never really sees, such as fluoride in a toothpaste. As long as a brand is *perceived* as different, then advertising can have a greater effect than promotion.

High risk products tend to employ advertising to reassure prospective buyers that they are making a good brand choice. Low risk products may go straight for promotion, tempting the buyer to "try the brand and see." Actually, this distinction is a little artificial—there is a proper type of advertising for high risk (high involvement) brands and a proper type for low risk (low involvement) brands, as well as appropriate types of promotion for each. These are described later in the book.

A rule of thumb for many brands is to increase advertising when store brands (private labels or generics) attain greater than 25 percent share of the product category's sales. Store brand competition usually forces the higher-priced national brands to justify their price differential, and thus to deemphasize price, through increased advertising which stresses high quality. Of course, this may not work for a national brand that is already low-priced; it must usually meet the store brand's price or lose sales.

The final factor in the table reflects the competitor orientation. If a direct competitor increases its advertising, most managers will want to increase their advertising too, for fear of losing sales. Likewise, if a direct competitor goes "on special" or otherwise increases promotion, most managers usually will increase their promotion to try to prevent the competitor from gaining an edge in sales.

Altogether, then, we have seen that marketing managers make strategic use of *both* advertising and promotion. It is not sufficient to regard advertising and promotion as independent promotional tools. Rather, advertising and promotion embrace sets of specialized techniques to achieve related marketing purposes with the decisions centering on relative emphasis according to the factors we have outlined.

THE SIX-STEP EFFECTS SEQUENCE

Advertising and promotion have one ultimately desired effect—to contribute to company profits. A firm would not, or should not, spend money on advertising and promotion unless the expenditure more than pays for itself by ultimately increasing profit. Things are not as simple as this, however. Advertising and promotion have to produce a series of *prior* effects which, if successfully accomplished, *lead to* profit.

Our approach identifies a six-step effects sequence (Figure 1.6): exposure → processing → communication effects → target audience action → sales or market share → profit. The six steps can be explained as follows:

1 *Exposure* In order for advertising or promotion to be successful, the prospective buyer must first be *exposed* to the advertisement or the promotion offer. This means that the ad or promotion offer must be placed so that the

FIGURE 1.6   Six-step effects sequence. The effects are in upper-case and lower-case letters. The level at which the effect operates is shown in parentheses in lower case.

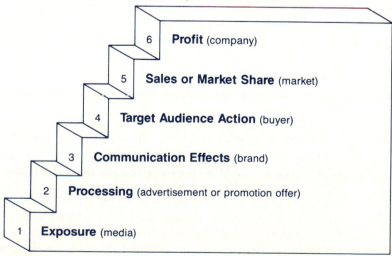

prospective buyer can see, read, or hear it, as appropriate. Exposure takes place via advertising or promotion media. Step 1 is exposure (via media).

2 *Processing* Exposure alone is not sufficient. The prospective buyer must next *process* (respond to) one or more elements in the advertisement or promotion offer if it is to have an effect. Processing consists of immediate responses to elements of an ad or promotion offer, such as attention, learning, acceptance, and emotional responses. Step 2 is processing (of the ad or promotion offer).

3 *Communication Effects* Immediate responses to an ad or promotion offer have to produce more permanent responses—associated with the *brand*. These more permanent, brand-connected, responses are called *communication effects*. Two universally necessary communication effects are brand awareness and brand attitude. We will meet other communication effects later. Step 3 is communication effects (connected to the brand).

4 *Target Audience Action* Communication effects, as brand associations, are elicited in the decision situation when the prospective buyer—a member of the *target audience* for the advertising or promotion—decides whether or not to take *action* with regard to the brand, such as purchasing the brand. More broadly this is called buyer behavior, although in an advertising or promotion context it is target audience buyer behavior that the campaign is specifically seeking. Step 4 is target audience action (by each prospective buyer).

5 *Sales or Market Share* The actions of individual buyers of the brand cumulate to produce *sales*. In comparison with the sales of competing brands in a category or market, sales can be expressed as *market share*. Step 5 is sales or market share (in a market).

6 *Profit* From the company's standpoint, sales are worthwhile only insofar as they lead to profit. If advertising and promotion are supposed to produce sales, then they must be accountable for producing *profit* too. Step 6 is profit (for the company).

Briefly, these are the six steps comprising the six-step effects sequence for advertising and promotion. We now examine the application of these steps in more detail.

BUYER RESPONSE SEQUENCE

The first four steps (exposure → processing → communication effects → target audience action) constitute the *buyer response sequence* (Figure 1.7). All advertising and promotion campaigns attempt to influence this sequence of steps. An example will help to illustrate why the four buyer response steps are necessary for advertising or promotion to be successful.

Exposure, processing, communication effects, and action are the steps that you yourself go through when you buy a product as a result of advertising (or promotion). Think of the TV campaign for Diet Coke not too long ago.

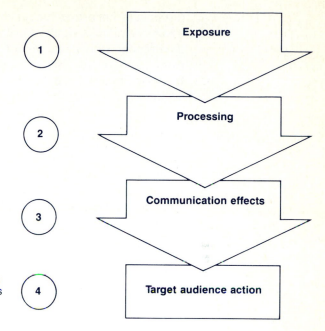

FIGURE 1.7   Buyer response sequence. Note that these are the first four steps of the overall six-step effects sequence.

1 *Exposure* With regard to the first of the steps in the buyer response sequence, unless you were an absolute non-TV watcher, you were undoubtedly *exposed* to one or more commercials for Diet Coke. The Coca-Cola Company ran a very heavy TV media campaign for this brand.

2 *Processing* With regard to the second step, you probably paid attention to some parts, such as the music or visuals, of at least one of the commercials. In other words, you *processed* the Diet Coke advertising to some, or perhaps a considerable, degree.

3 *Communication Effects* The third step is communication effects. There are usually several effects. If you learned the brand name from the advertising, "Diet Coke," and remembered what the new brand looks like, you have attained one of the communication effects (brand awareness). If you also formed an opinion for or against Diet Coke, you attained another communication effect (brand attitude). Brand awareness *plus* a favorable brand attitude would largely determine whether you have taken the final step intended for the target audience—action.

4 *Target Audience Action* The relevant target audience action for Diet Coke is purchase. This is the fourth and final step in the buyer response sequence. If you have purchased Diet Coke, then the advertising has influenced you successfully via the four steps in the buyer response sequence.

Of course, advertising is rarely responsible, by itself, for purchase. The rest of the marketing mix contributes too: product performance, such as taste (especially important for repeat purchase following trial of the brand); price, assuming price is similar to other colas; distribution, assuming you could find the brand in stores; and other forms of promotion, such as favorable comments from your friends. But the advertising undoubtedly has played a large part. Because of all the people who purchased Diet Coke, it is now the third-largest selling soft drink in the United States.

Repetition and the Buyer Response Sequence

Advertising in most cases has to *repeatedly* influence the buyer response sequence in order to initiate purchase and maintain repeated purchases of the brand. Promotion offers, too, have to repeatedly influence the buyer response sequence if they are to maintain repeat purchase.

No Repetition   The one exception to this repetition or "recycling" of the buyer response sequence is direct response advertising or a one-time promotion offer (Figure 1.8). In panel 1 of the figure, we see that the direct response ad or one-time promotion offer (which are very often combined) goes through the sequence once, then terminates with action in the form of a single purchase.

Communication Repetition   Most advertising situations, however, require repetition. For example, you may have had to have been exposed to Diet Coke commercials several times before you processed them sufficiently to acquire communication effects (mainly brand awareness and brand attitude) that were strong enough for you to make your first purchase of Diet Coke. This communication repetition is illustrated in panel 2.

Purchase Repetition   After you have purchased Diet Coke for the first time, the advertiser wants you to purchase it again and become a regular buyer of Diet Coke. This generally requires repeated exposures to the advertising and also, perhaps, to promotions, if they are offered. Panel 3 illustrates the purchase repetition situation.

Note that the purchase repetition situation is different in one important way from communication repetition. You now have *direct experience* with the brand, which will affect your exposure, processing, and communication effects (notably brand attitude, which is now based on experience) the next time around. If you liked Diet Coke, fine. But if you disliked it, this direct experience would prevent positive processing, lead to negative communication effects (a loss of brand awareness and a change to a negative brand attitude) and, of course, prevent you from taking action and purchasing Diet Coke again.

The Ideal: Eventual Independence from Advertising and Promotion   Panel 4 of the figure illustrates where advertisers would like their customers to be, eventually, and that is: independent of the need for further advertising and promotion. For example, after buying Diet Coke a number of times with the

1. Direct response ad or one-time promotion offer:

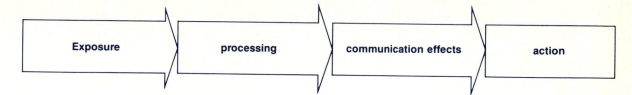

2. Communication repetition prior to action:

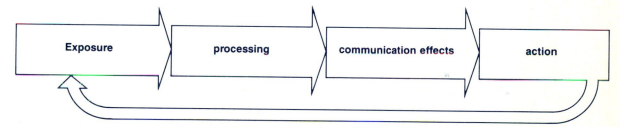

3. Purchase repetition following action:

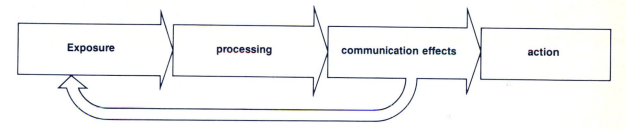

4. Ultimate ideal (continued purchase without advertising or promotion):

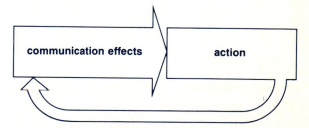

FIGURE 1.8   Repetition and the buyer response sequence. Four situations are illustrated here and discussed in the accompanying text.

help of advertising and promotion, you should have quite firmly established communication effects (you are well aware of the brand and have a highly favorable attitude toward it) such that you will continue to buy it without further aid from advertising or promotion.

In this ideal case, steps 1 and 2, exposure to and processing of further advertisements and promotion offers, become unnecessary and you simply recycle on steps 3 and 4. Subjectively, this means that you think of Diet Coke automatically and favorably when you want a soda and you therefore buy it again.

Not many brands can survive without advertising or promotion for too long a period or "hiatus," however. Communication effects become weaker or "interfered with" by advertising and promotion for competing brands, thus breaking the ideal two-step cycle. The advertiser then has to create new advertising or promotion that brings you back to exposure, then through the full four-step buyer response sequence anew, so that you will remain a regular buyer.

To summarize, there are four steps in the buyer response sequence. Advertising and promotion must positively influence each of the four steps: (1) exposure (media); (2) processing (ad or promotion offer); (3) communication effects (brand); and (4) target audience action (buyer). If any one of these steps is not influenced positively, and not only positively but often enough as well, the advertising or promotion won't work; and, going beyond the buyer response sequence, the advertising or promotion therefore will not contribute to (5) sales or market share and (6) profit. All four buyer response steps must be attained successfully if sales, market share, and profit are to increase.

THE SIX STEPS FROM THE MANAGER'S VIEWPOINT

The manager views the six-step effects sequence in reverse. Going back to Figure 1.6 earlier, the manager must plan from the "top down," beginning with step 6 (profit) and concluding with step 1 (exposure). This is because objectives at the top end must be set before strategies at the lower end can be devised. To put it plainly, you don't advertise first and then devise a purpose for the advertising later!

The *manager's planning stages* are depicted in Figure 1.9. As the figure illustrates, the manager goes "down" the six steps, in reverse, in five main stages. These are explained next. Also, the five stages correspond to the way this book is laid out.[14]

Marketing Objectives

In planning for advertising and promotion, the manager first has to consider the marketing objectives for the brand.[15] Marketing objectives encompass the profit, sales, and market share objectives (steps 5 and 6) established for the brand in its marketing plan. In fact, the manager has to do more than just "consider" these. In establishing the overall advertising and promotion budget, the manager is, in effect, estimating advertising's and promotion's exact contribution to sales, market share, and profit.

The advertising manager for Diet Coke, for example, would expect Diet Coke's advertising to contribute to profit; otherwise the brand would have to

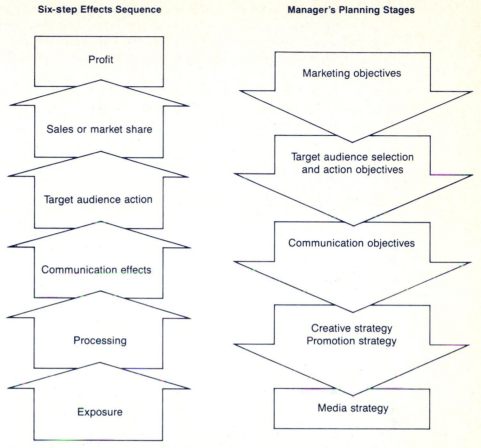

FIGURE 1.9 The six steps as seen from the manager's viewpoint. The manager proceeds from the "top down," in five main stages, to develop the advertising and promotion plan.

be marketed without advertising! This is possible for some store brands and generic items, but not for a national brand like Diet Coke hoping to do well in the fiercely competitive cola market.

The manager would also have to estimate Diet Coke advertising's contribution to sales (or, alternatively, market share). The Coca-Cola company, for its soft drinks overall, has an advertising-to-sales ratio of about 4 percent, which is right on average for the 100 leading U.S. advertisers.[16] This can be interpreted to mean that advertising is expected to contribute about 4 percent of sales.[17] When Diet Coke was first launched, its (estimated) advertising-to-sales ratio would probably have been much higher than 4 percent, because it was a new brand, with heavy introductory advertising and low initial sales.

Budgeting on the basis of advertising's expected contribution to market share is much more difficult, because it depends on how "market share" is defined. Does Diet Coke compete in the total beverage market, in the soft drink market, in the cola market, or in the diet cola market? The concept of market share must be very carefully thought through by the manager. It depends on what consumers perceive as the market, that is, on the brands that consumers regard as purchase alternatives.

In Part Two we show how advertising and promotion are planned to fit marketing objectives, and how overall budgets can be set in relation to profit, sales, or market share.

Target Audience Selection and Action Objectives

The manager now has to consider "where sales are going to come from" in response to advertising and promotion. The question of who is most likely to respond—*to* advertising or *to* promotion—is the question of target audience selection. Concurrent with target audience selection is the step of setting behavioral action objectives (step 4) for advertising and promotion. Depending on the target audience, the action objectives will normally be trial or repeat usage (for distributors as well as consumers) although other behavioral objectives may be set consisting of purchase-related actions that are converted to purchase by the rest of the marketing mix.

In the Diet Coke example, our manager faces a considerable task in selecting a target audience for the brand. The manager must have expected that Diet Coke would "cannibalize" some of Coca-Cola's other diet cola—Tab's—sales and indeed Diet Coke now outsells Tab. But was Diet Coke also intended to appeal to *regular* Coke drinkers (of either Coca-Cola Classic or "new" Coke) who were thinking of switching to diet drinks?

Advertising can be instrumental in "positioning" a brand toward the desired target audience. For non-users of Diet Coke, the action objective would of course be trial. For those who've tried it, the action objective would be continued usage in the form of repeat purchase.

In Part Three we show how to select target audiences and how to set behavioral action objectives for advertising and promotion.

Communication Objectives

Advertising and promotion work via communication effects (step 3) to cause action. The manager, in the third stage of planning, has to determine which communication effects (brand associations) need to be established "in the prospective buyer's mind" in order to cause him or her to take action. In determining the relevant communication effects, the manager sets communication *objectives* for advertising and promotion. Communication objectives are selected from options within the basic five communication effects: category need, brand awareness, brand attitude, brand purchase intention, and purchase facilitation.

When Diet Coke was first launched, the manager probably set multiple communication objectives for the advertising:

1 The introductory advertising probably tried to stimulate the diet soda category as a whole, since Diet Coke would benefit from an increase in ''primary demand'' for diet soda (category need).

2 Potential new consumers of Diet Coke have to learn the new beverage's name, ''Diet Coke,'' and learn to recognize the new container, a white can with red lettering, in stores (brand awareness).

3 Further, before trying Diet Coke, potential new consumers would have to develop a favorable (if tentative before trial) opinion of the brand (brand attitude).

4 Also, a definite intention to try it at the first opportunity would be a likely advertising communication objective (brand purchase intention).

5 Potential consumers would know where to buy it, so the fifth communication effect (purchase facilitation) would *not,* in this case, be an advertising objective.[18]

In Part Four we describe these communication effects and show the manager how to set appropriate communication objectives for advertising and promotion.

Creative Strategy and Promotion Strategy

Once the communication objectives for an advertising or promotion campaign have been determined, the manager next has to devise (if in an agency) or approve (if in a client company) a creative strategy or a promotion strategy that will achieve the communication objectives. This involves designing individual advertisements or promotion offers and ensuring, through testing, that they are processed (step 2) by the target audience in the intended manner to produce the desired communication effects.

In our advertising example for Diet Coke, the manager probably had several creative strategies offered by the agency, McCann-Erickson, for Diet Coke.

Note that there are *many possible creative strategies* that could achieve the desired communication effects for Diet Coke (category need, brand awareness, brand attitude, and brand purchase intention). On brand attitude, for instance, the agency could have proposed a creative emphasis on the low calorie benefit (much as Diet Pepsi did with its ''Only one calorie'' campaign). Or the creative strategy could have focused on the taste benefit. These or a considerable number of other creative strategies could each potentially deliver the required communication objectives.

The creative strategy for Diet Coke (''Just for the taste of it'') that appeared on TV in a set of related commercials probably delivered better on the communication objectives, by an advertising pre-test, or more closely met management's approval than alternative creative strategies.

Diet Coke probably was launched with promotion as well as advertising. There would have been introductory promotions to retailers if not to consumers.

Promotion offers, too, help the brand deliver on its communication objectives, notably by increasing brand awareness and brand purchase intention, which lead to the final buyer response step of purchase action.

Promotion strategies, like creative strategies, potentially are numerous. The promotion strategy for Diet Coke has to meet the brand's communication objectives and, of course, increase trial or repeat purchase of the brand.

In Part Five we discuss creative strategy. Part Eight shows how to test advertisements in relation to their communication objectives (and also explains the overall procedure of advertising research). Part Six discusses promotion strategy and promotion testing.

Media Strategy

Finally, the manager has to plan how best to expose (step 1) the advertisements or promotion offers to the target audience. This fifth and final management stage centers on media strategy. In this stage the manager makes two main decisions: media selection (*where* to most efficiently reach the target audience) and media scheduling (*how often* the target audience needs to be reached to produce the intended communication and action results).

Our Diet Coke manager, for example, had to select and then schedule media for Diet Coke. The Coca-Cola Company does most of its consumer advertising on TV, so this would be the primary medium selected for Diet Coke. However, there are also "back-up" or secondary media to be selected, for instance, radio and outdoor signs.

The second media strategy decision, media scheduling, is quite complicated. How many times would the Diet Coke advertising have to be exposed to the non-user of Diet Coke to entice him or her to try the brand? And once tried, assuming a favorable opinion of the product, how often, between typical soft drink purchase occasions, would the "continuing" advertising have to be seen or heard in order to keep the trier aware of and interested in the brand?

The media budget then has to be allocated in accordance with these media strategy decisions.

In Part Seven we show the manager how to select a media strategy (which must fit the communication objectives and creative strategy) in constructing the media plan.

To summarize: The six-step effects sequence is the sequence in which advertising and promotion operate to produce profit for the firm. Managers, on the other hand, plan in reverse, in five main stages. Profit is considered first and then objectives and strategies are formulated "down" the effects sequence.

SUMMARY

Advertising and promotion are best regarded practically as alternative sets of techniques, often used in combination, to meet the same marketing objectives.

Advertising *tends* to take an indirect ("turn the *mind* toward" purchase) longer-term approach to gain customers, whereas promotion *tends* to take a direct ("buy now") shorter-term approach to gain customers. However, advertising and promotion both are forms of marketing communication designed to make prospective buyers aware of the brand, create or change brand attitudes, and stimulate purchase intentions.

The real differences between advertising and promotion lie in their relative emphasis in strategic marketing management. We have seen how the emphasis differs, in the longer term, according to the brand's stage in the product life cycle and, most immediately, in terms of quality and price positioning and response to competition.

Advertising and promotion work via a six-step sequence: (1) Exposure (via media); (2) processing (of the ad or promotion offer); (3) communication effects (connected to the brand); (4) target audience action (by the buyer); (5) sales or market share (resulting from cumulative buyer actions in a market); leading to (6) profit (for the company).

The first four of these steps are called the buyer response sequence. Each prospective buyer of the brand in response to advertising or promotion must be exposed via media, process the ad or offer in the manner intended by the advertiser, acquire communication effects associated with the brand, and based on these, take action and buy the brand.

Repetition of advertising or promotion is necessary in most cases to either initiate purchase or to cause repeat purchase. Repetition occurs in several ways within the buyer response sequence. Direct response advertising or promotion goes through the sequence once and may not require repetition. But most advertising requires communication repetition (repeating steps 1 to 3) prior to purchase, and purchase repetition (repeating steps 1 to 4) to cause further purchases. Ideally, "automatic" recycling on steps 3 and 4 eventually will occur whereby further advertising and promotion are no longer needed in order to maintain purchase for an extended period.

The manager plans according to the six steps, but in reverse, and in five main stages. Marketing objectives are considered first (profit, sales, and market share), then target audience selection and action objectives, then communication objectives, then creative strategy and promotion strategy, and then media strategy. This hierarchical "top down" process progressively narrows down the alternatives until a complete plan is constructed.

In Appendix A to this book, a checklist advertising and promotion plan is provided. But how is the checklist filled out? That is the subject of the rest of the book.

NOTES

1 Promotion throughout this book refers to *sales* promotion, except for one section in this chapter where we discuss the overall promotion mix. Promotion is widely accepted as a shorthand way of referring to sales promotion.

2 R.M. Prentice, How to split your marketing funds between advertising and promotion, *Advertising Age,* January 10, 1977, p. 41.

3 R.A. Strang, *The Promotional Planning Process,* New York: Praeger, 1980.

4 F. Lemont, Presentation to the American Marketing Association, New York Chapter, Biltmore Hotel, April 17, 1979.

5 The strategic framework owes a debt to various marketing theorists, including Peter Drucker and Abe Shuchman. This version is used in Columbia University's marketing management course.

6 For a worthwhile assessment of why the competitor orientation is equal in importance to the customer orientation, see A.R. Oxenfeldt and W.L. Moore, Customer or competitor: which guideline for marketing?, *Management Review,* 1978, *67* (8), 43–48. A broader view of the importance of competitive advantage in business strategy is given in R.S. Achrol and D.L. Appel, New developments in corporate strategy planning, *AMA Marketing Educators Conference Proceedings,* Chicago, IL: American Marketing Association, 1983, pp. 305–310.

7 James Culliton, of Harvard, in the 1940s began referring to the business executive as a "mixer of ingredients." The idea was borrowed by his colleague, Neil Borden, who popularized the term "marketing mix." If the chemical analogy is followed closely, the marketing mix is really a "marketing compound," since the elements of the mix (such as advertising and promotion) interact with each other to produce the final result. See N.H. Borden, *Advertising Text and Cases,* Homewood, IL: Irwin, 1964.

8 A survey of *Fortune 500* companies found that advertising managers most frequently do *not* plan advertising and promotion strategy jointly with sales managers, contrary to textbook wisdom. See A.J. Dubinsky, T.E. Barry, and R.A. Kerin, The sales-advertising interface in promotion planning, *Journal of Advertising,* 1981, *10* (3), 35–41.

9 J.G. Udell, The perceived importance of the elements of strategy, *Journal of Marketing,* 1968, *32* (1), 34–40.

10 R.A. Strang, *The Promotional Planning Process,* New York, NY: Praeger, 1980.

11 The product life cycle concept was introduced by Columbia University's business economics professor Joel Dean. See J. Dean, Pricing policies for new products, *Harvard Business Review,* 1950, *28* (6), 45–53. For a more specific breakdown of PLC stages, see C.W. Hofer and D. Schendel, *Strategy Formulation: Analytical Concepts,* St. Paul, MN: West, 1978.

Some writers have expressed doubts about the product life cycle phenomenon. For a convenient summary of the main issues and main references, see G.S. Day, The product life cycle: analysis and applications issues, *Journal of Marketing,* 1981, *45* (4), 60–67. However, in a comprehensive review across industries, it has been shown that the classic PLC curve is the most common; see D.R. Rink and J.E. Swan, Product life cycle research: a literature review, *Journal of Business Research,* 1979, *7* (3), 219–242.

An important article by D.F. Midgley demonstrates that both the classic PLC curve and exceptions to it, such as the cycle-recycle pattern, can be closely predicted by separating sales into first-time purchases and repeat or replacement purchases; the curves can be predicted for product classes, product forms, and brands. See D.F. Midgley, Toward a theory of the product life cycle: explaining diversity, *Journal of Marketing,* 1981, *45* (4), 109–115.

The classic PLC holds almost universally for product classes, very well for product forms, but less often for particular brands, largely because brand managers try to manage their way *out* of the life cycle, especially in the late growth and decline stages. Claims that some brands "last forever" are usually deceptive. For example, M. Lubliner compared the top 25 consumer package goods brands from 1923 and found that 19 were still brand leaders in 1983 ("Old standbys hold their own," *Advertising Age,* September 19, 1983, p. 32). However, these results conceal the many model (product form) changes within the brand names. For instance the leading Gillette razor "brand" in 1923 is not the same as Trac II, the leading Gillette razor on the market now.

12 Here we are addressing not just the absolute emphasis on advertising and promotion but also the relative use of advertising "versus" promotion during the product life cycle. For a review of factors affecting the absolute emphasis on advertising and promotion, see P.W. Farris and R.D. Buzzell, Why advertising and promotion costs vary: some cross-sectional analyses, *Journal of Marketing,* 1979, *43* (4), 112–122.

13 These factors are discussed further in R.A. Strang, *The Promotional Planning Process,* New York: Praeger, 1980.

14 In the manager's planning sequence, and in theory, creative strategy and promotion strategy occur together. In this book, and most often in reality, creative strategy precedes promotion strategy.

15 Throughout the book we will use the term "brand" to refer to any advertisable or promotable entity which the manager is responsible for. Most often, this will indeed be a brand—of either a product or service. However, a brand could also be a company, as in corporate image advertising or public relations; an institution, such as Red Cross; or even a person, such as a political candidate, or an idea, such as free enterprise. Sometimes, too, an unbranded commodity, such as produce or raw materials, may be the focus of advertising or promotion. It is convenient to use the term "brand" unless otherwise stated.

16 Advertising expenditure as a percentage of sales for Coca-Cola's soft drinks in 1982 was 4.1 percent. The average advertising-to-sales ratio for the 100 leading national advertisers in the United States in 1982 was 4.2 percent, with a range from 0.2 percent (IBM, interestingly) to 18.9 percent (Noxell Corporation, for toiletries and cosmetics). These are publicly reported figures in *Advertising Age,* September 8, 1983.

17 See Chapter 3. The 4 percent is advertising's actual contribution to sales. In budgeting, an advertising-to-sales ratio usually is set on the basis of advertising's (estimated) contribution to *expected* sales. For example, if you budget $4 million for advertising at the beginning of the year and you expect $100 million in sales by the end of the year, the (estimated) advertising-to-sales ratio is 4 percent. Advertising actually may produce (contribute to) more or less sales than the $100 million forecast, which would result in a different (actual) advertising-to-sales ratio at the end of the year.

18 Although purchase facilitation, which addresses potential problems with the other "4 P's" of the marketing mix, would not be a communication objective for consumers, it may well have been an advertising communication objective for the *trade,* to aid the brand's distribution. Heavy introductory consumer advertising often is used to try to "pull" the brand through the distribution channel. See any introductory marketing management text for a discussion of "push" versus "pull" promotion in distribution strategy.

DISCUSSION QUESTIONS

1.1 Look at the Arm & Hammer Baking Soda exhibit again (Figure 1.2):
   a Given the conceptual definition of advertising as (indirectly) "turning the buyer

or consumer's mind toward purchase," which elements of the message execution seem to do this, and why?

b Given the conceptual definition of promotion as (directly) trying to "immediately stimulate purchase," which elements seem to do this, and why?

c Overall, how would you classify the exhibit? Pick a ratio to summarize your conclusion, for example, 50% A and 50% P.

1.2 You are probably already quite familiar with marketing strategy, but it is worthwhile to emphasize that advertising and promotion must be consistent with marketing strategy principles. Some refresher questions:

a What are IBM's differential advantages in the computer market?

b What customer value or values do "designer" label clothes offer for their premium price?

c Which demographic market (or markets) appears to have been selected for concentrated efforts by Michelob beer? Miller High Life?

d "Avon ladies" selling Avon cosmetics door to door do not seem to be as prevalent as they once were. Do you think this represents a change in planning by the company, and if so, how and why?

1.3 Why do you think industrial product managers, in general, rely less on advertising than managers of consumer goods?

1.4 Visit a local supermarket and look at the brand displays for (a) detergent and (b) paper towels. What is the proportion of brands in each category using in-store promotions? Relate your findings to the discussion of product life cycle and "other factors" that affect the relative use of advertising versus promotion.

1.5 There are six steps in advertising and promotion. They can be regarded as forming three sequences. Explain each of the three sequences one by one, noting first its purpose and then using a different product example to illustrate the steps or stages in each.

1.6 What was your personal experience with the TV advertising for Diet Coke? Write a two-page description of how you personally remember going through the four buyer response steps, concluding with whether you purchased Diet Coke or not, and why.

1.7 A more difficult question following on from question 1.6: Could Diet Coke have been launched successfully *without* any advertising or promotion? How could the four buyer response steps be achieved by using *other* elements of the marketing mix, that is, product, price, distribution, and personal selling (exclude publicity or PR).

1.8 If advertising causes purchase, why is it that *repetition* of advertising is not always necessary for purchase to occur? Note that this question has two separate answers.

FURTHER READING

Association of National Advertisers, Inc. *How Major Packaged Goods Companies Classify Promotion Expenditures for Accounting and Budgeting Purposes*. New York, 1980.

This booklet surveys and discusses the problem of distinguishing advertising and promotion and shows how variable the accounting criteria are across companies.

Drucker, P.F. *Management: Tasks, Responsibilities, Practices*. New York: Harper & Row, 1973.

Contains an excellent and highly readable discussion of basic principles in strategic marketing management, including differential advantage, customer value, and selectivity and concentration.

Hofer, C.W. and Schendel, D. *Strategy Formulation: Analytical Concepts*. St. Paul, MN: West, 1978.

A concise review of business strategy options, including a very useful summary of strategy options in detailed stages of the product life cycle.

Kotler, P. *Marketing Management*. Englewood Cliffs, NJ: Prentice-Hall, 5th edition, 1984.

We expect that many readers will have read this leading marketing textbook. It provides a handy reference for terms in our first chapter (such as marketing mix, market segmentation, planning, and product life cycle) as well as marketing concepts used later in our text.

Colley, R.H. *Defining Advertising Goals for Measured Advertising Results*. New York: Association of National Advertisers, Inc., 1961.

The classic DAGMAR approach to advertising (an acronym from the title) is worth reading although the specific steps in Colley's approach do not exactly match the steps utilized in our book.

Strang, R.A. *The Promotional Planning Process*. New York: Praeger, 1980.

Landmark survey of strategic factors determining managers' use of advertising "versus" promotion. Although based on consumer packaged goods companies, the findings have general relevance to all advertising and promotion managers.

PART TWO

MARKETING OBJECTIVES

PROFIT, SALES, AND MARKET SHARE OBJECTIVES

This chapter has one aim, but it is a major one: to show how advertising and promotion fit into the product's marketing plan. After reading this chapter you should be able to:

- Know when to set broad objectives versus more specific quantified goals
- Understand that there are three ways in which advertising and promotion can affect profits
- Decide when to use sales objectives
- Decide when to use market share objectives, and know how to identify the brand's "true" market
- Realize why there may be limits to a brand's market share

In terms of the six-step effects sequence, this chapter covers steps 5 and 6. For the manager's planning sequence, it is the first stage of the advertising and promotion plan.

The Importance of Objectives

Before we begin our examination of objectives, it is worthwhile to consider a basic question: Why is it important to set objectives? The philosophy of "management by objectives" has been widely accepted as preferable to "seat-of-the-pants" or intuitive management. But is there any proof that management by objectives actually *is* better than intuitive management?

There are two considerations that support the importance of management by objectives: better performance, and improved planning and evaluation.

Better Performance   The limited evidence that is publicly available suggests that companies that set explicit objectives for advertising and promotion repeatedly tend to be more successful than those that do not set objectives.[1] While the direction of cause and effect is not clear from these studies, the likelihood is that the companies were successful because of explicit objectives rather than that success led them to set objectives or that objectives and success were simply the correlated products, one trivial and the other vital, of good management.

The causal relationship between objectives and performance is supported by several studies.[2] One study, by Ansoff and his colleagues, assessed corporate performance over a 20-year period. Companies classified as explicit planners early in the period averaged a 4.5 percent increase on 21 measures of corporate performance compared with a 2.2 percent increase for non-planners. That is, explicit planners had double the "bottom line" success rate.

Improved Planning and Evaluation It is quite likely that better "external" performance by companies who set objectives is due in large part to better "internal" performance. Objectives greatly facilitate internal planning and evaluation. In the case of advertising and promotion, this is evidenced in three areas:

1 *Company Coordination* Managers in other functional areas—such as finance and production—are able to coordinate with their advertising and promotion manager much more effectively if all managers are working with a common, written set of marketing objectives for the product.

2 *Agency Coordination* Similarly, many disputes and errors can be avoided if everyone within the advertising agency concerned with the account—account executives, researchers, creative group, and media planners—has the same set of client-approved objectives to work toward.

3 *Performance Evaluation* The presence of written objectives makes performance evaluation—both by the company and the agency—much less ambiguous, particularly if the objectives are expressed as goals.[3]

OBJECTIVES AND GOALS

An extremely useful distinction for the advertising and promotion manager can be made between objectives and goals: an objective is a broad aim, whereas a goal is an objective made specific as to *degree* and *time*.[4] (For other useful definitions, see Table 2.1.) A typical objective for advertising and

TABLE 2-1 DEFINITIONS FOR ADVERTISING AND PROMOTION PLANNING

Strategic planning	= formulation of objectives (ends) and strategies (means) for attaining them
Objective	= broad aim or general description of desired outcome
Goal	= an objective made specific as to *degree* and *time*
Strategy	= broad plan of action with an objective or goal in mind
Tactics	= specific details or subcomponents of a strategy showing how the strategy can be implemented

promotion is "to increase profit." This can be expressed as a goal by specifying degree and time, such as "to contribute 10 percent to pre-tax profit for fiscal year 19XX."

Some examples of the difference between an objective and a goal are provided in Table 2.2 for the subjects of this chapter: profit, sales, and market share. The goals are from recently published figures in the business press. The first column shows how these goals would be expressed as broad objectives had the figures not been known.

Appropriateness of Goals versus Objectives

It should be evident that goals provide more precise performance targets for managers to aim for and, for this reason, goals are preferable to objectives. However, it is not always possible to estimate all types of performance precisely and thereby to set goals. Similarly, an overly precise goal does not mean much unless the company is willing and able to *measure* goal attainment.

When goal estimation is not possible, or when goal attainment is not measurable, it is still worthwhile to set objectives. Although objectives are broad aims that do not specify either the degree of performance required or the expected attainment period, objectives can still serve as general guides for management. These general guides are better than no guides at all. For example, knowledge that the company is trying to increase sales rather than hold sales at their present level (two possible objectives) provides a useful guide for managers even though the amount and timing of the targeted sales increase are not specified.

Objectives, Goals, and the Six-Step Effects Sequence

The distinction between objectives and goals becomes relevant for our six-step effects sequence. This is because advertising and promotion effects can be caused, on the one hand, by an individual ad or promotion offer, and cumulatively, on the other, by particular advertising or promotion campaigns, and then, overall, by total advertising and promotion expenditures. Indeed,

TABLE 2-2 EXAMPLES OF OBJECTIVES VERSUS GOALS†

Product	Objective	Goal
High-volume copiers (e.g., Xerox)	Increase profits	Increase pre-tax profit margin from current 20% to 40% after costs of introduction have been covered
Sears stores	Increase sales	Increase sales by 7 to 10% (in constant dollars) in fiscal 1982
Anheuser-Busch	Increase market share	Increase company's share of U.S. beer market to a long-run expected peak of 40% (now 29%)

† The goals are from *The Wall Street Journal*, April 10, 1981, p. 27; January 15, 1981, pp. 10 and 25 (by permission).

we might think of a continuum of "planning levels" from micro (an individual ad or promotion offer) to macro (the total advertising and promotion budget). Typical relationships are shown in Table 2.3.

Individual Ad or Promotion Offer   Commencing at the top left-hand corner of Table 2.3, it can be seen that an individual ad or promotion offer can be held accountable for a specific level of exposure (for example, reaching 40 percent of the target audience) and message processing (for example, 35 percent pay attention to the ad or offer); but that beyond this, the effect of an individual ad or promotion gets merged with other communication effects. Thus, from step 3 onwards, we can usually set only broad objectives for individual ads and promotion offers.

Cumulative Campaign   The middle section of Table 2.3 indicates that precise goals are appropriate at the level of a cumulative advertising or promotion (or combined advertising and promotion) campaign. Campaign effects can be measured in terms of definite communication goals (for example, 20 percent of the target audience acquire brand awareness *plus* a favorable brand attitude) and result in precise levels of target audience action (for example, 5 percent trial). Depending on how significant the campaign is in relationship to the total advertising and promotion effort, goals may also be feasible for effects beyond the action step, such as sales. However, we have shown these subsequent campaign effects as objectives, under the assumption that the campaign is but one of several advertising and promotion efforts for the brand over the course of the planning period.

Total Advertising and Promotion Budget   The lower right-hand corner of Table 2.3 shows that goals are appropriate for the ultimate marketing effects steps of sales, market share, and profit—but only at the extreme macro level of the total advertising and promotion budget for the entire planning period (usually 1 year). Note, for example, that an advertising-to-sales ratio is essentially a goal, not just a broad objective. An A/S ratio specifies the degree

TABLE 2-3   TYPICAL OBJECTIVES AND GOALS FOR THE SIX-STEP EFFECTS SEQUENCE BY LEVEL OF ADVERTISING AND PROMOTION PLANNING

| | MICRO | | MACRO |
	Individual ad or promotion offer	Cumulative campaign	Total advertising and promotion budget
1. Exposure	GOALS	Objectives	Objectives
2. Processing	GOALS	Objectives	Objectives
3. Communication effects	Objectives	GOALS	Objectives
4. Target audience action	Objectives	GOALS	Objectives
5. Sales or market share	Objectives	Objectives	GOALS
6. Profit	Objectives	Objectives	GOALS

of sales that are expected to result from a given advertising budget in a specific time period, usually 1 year. It is meaningful to set goals at these ultimate effects steps for overall advertising and promotion budgets, but this level of planning usually is too broad to set goals for it at the earlier steps.

To summarize on objectives and goals:

1 Objectives (at minimum) should always be set at all levels of advertising and promotion planning and for all six effects steps.

2 Goals (preferably) should be set whenever they are meaningful and measurable—for individual ads and promotion offers at steps 1 and 2 (exposure and processing); for campaigns at steps 3 and 4 (communication effects and target audience action); and for total advertising and promotion budgets at steps 5 and 6 (sales or market share, and profit).

The manager begins from the "top down" with step 6: profit objectives. Profit is always an advertising and promotion objective; and for the total advertising and promotion budget, it can become a goal.

PROFIT OBJECTIVES

Three Ways in Which Advertising and Promotion Can Contribute to Profit

Generally defined, total profit = (price − cost) × unit sales. From this we see there are three potential ways in which advertising and promotion can contribute to the product's profit objectives:

1 By maintaining or increasing the brand's *price differential* (through advertising especially)

2 By *lowering costs* (through both advertising and promotion)

3 By *increasing sales* at constant price and cost (through both advertising and promotion)

Let us consider each of these avenues in turn, recognizing that combinations also are possible.

Price and Profit

The higher price avenue to profit is more the province of advertising than it is of promotion. Absolute or overall price levels for a product category may or may not be raised by advertising. However, *relative* prices for brands (price differentials) within a product category are often positively related to brand advertising.[5]

Advertising can support a higher price for a product by creating or maintaining what consumers refer to as a "name brand." Such brands carry an implicitly or explicitly guaranteed quality image for which consumers are often willing to pay a higher price. For example, supermarket shoppers pay, on average, about 14 percent more for nationally advertised brands than they do for "store" brands.[6] During the inflationary period of the late 1970s and early 1980s, this differential increased even further so that shoppers buying nationally advertised brands paid an exceptionally high 26 percent premium over "store" brands and a 37 percent premium over "generic" products.[7]

"Name brands" also tend to be less resistant to loss of sales following price increases. Their less "elastic" demand, supported by advertising, means that price may be increased to increase profit without losing sales.

On a broader scale, advertising may also support higher prices by creating or maintaining a strong "corporate image." A study conducted for Bozell & Jacobs, a New York advertising agency, suggests that corporate advertising has a small (4 percent) but significant and positive effect on company stock prices.[8] Corporate advertising also has a low relative cost and can be an efficient way to add to company profit.

Cost and Profit

The cost avenue to profit can be assisted by advertising and also by promotion. There are two major ways in which cost reductions can be achieved through advertising and promotion.

One way in which advertising and promotion can reduce costs is by increasing sales which may subsequently allow the firm to achieve economies of scale and realize a higher profit for a given sales volume.[9] A related mechanism underlies the concept of an "experience curve" whereby faster unit sales allow the firm to attain not only economies of production but also economies gained from experience in marketing the product. This experience translates into greater efficiency and lower overall costs.

A recent study of 200 leading companies by Buzzell indicates that some degree of cost reduction appears to be a general rule for industrial products and consumer durables.[10] However, it should be noted that economies of scale and experience are hard to demonstrate for all industries,[11] and have not been widely proven for fast-turnover consumer products. Accordingly, cost reduction should be *directly investigated* rather than loosely assumed. Nevertheless, cost-reduction objectives are often part of the purpose in heavy advertising and promotion spending behind new products to generate fast sales growth.

A second way in which advertising and promotion can reduce costs is by "pre-selling" the product to buyers and thereby saving on introductory sales calls. The average cost of an industrial sales call, for example, is currently about $200 and has risen more than 250 percent in terms of constant 1969 prices. Business advertising rates in terms of cost per thousand have risen by only about 100 percent in the same period and can deliver "aware" prospects at a much lower cost.[12] Similarly, promotions, especially trial offers, can reduce selling costs by saving on sales demonstrations.

Advertising and promotion may therefore contribute to profit objectives through the avenues of price differentials and cost reduction. Perhaps the main role of advertising and promotion in contributing to profit, however, is through contribution to sales.

Sales and Profit

Before we consider sales objectives in detail, it is worthwhile to review the classical economic relationship of sales to profit[13] (Figure 2.1). To the extent that a product's economic performance follows these classic patterns, and most should be assumed to unless there is evidence to the contrary, it can be seen that the advertising and promotion expenditure level that maximizes sales is not the same level that maximizes profit.

FIGURE 2.1   Maximum profit usually occurs *before* the peak of sales at a *lower* level of advertising and promotion expenditure than the level that maximizes sales. (*Reprinted by permission from the Journal of Advertising Research, March 1961.*)

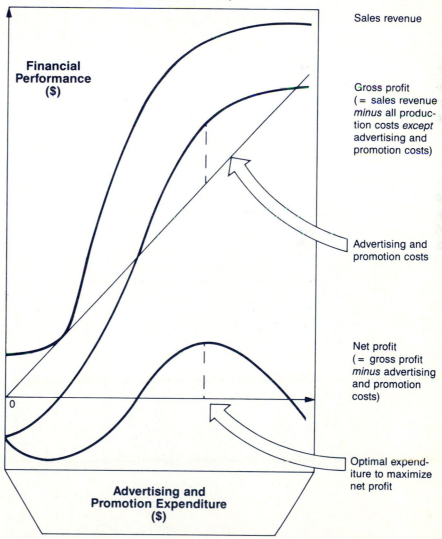

In fact, the maximum profit point usually is reached *before* sales have reached their maximum. This fits the concept of the product life cycle (see Chapter 1) where profits begin to get squeezed during the maturity or maximum sales phase when product category growth has stabilized and flattened and competition is most intense. Simon and Arndt[14] also provide strong evidence for a diminishing rate of sales increase as advertising and promotion expenditures increase, which supports the conclusion that maximum profits are reached below the level of maximum sales.

Remember, too, that profit margins may be deliberately sacrificed in the short run in the quest for market share and experience-curve cost reductions, with the intention of attaining higher long-run profits. This is not incompatible with the importance of setting profit objectives for advertising and promotion; it simply means that the short-run profit objective might be negative, zero, or low in conjunction with a deliberate market share objective.

Profit Measures

If profit objectives are to be expressed as goals, the level of profit must be measured. There are numerous ways to measure profit and only two of the more important ones will be mentioned here (see Further Readings at the end of this chapter for more information).

1 *Internal Rate of Return* This measure of profit takes into account the cost of capital and the time value of money through the application of a discounted rate of return. It is advocated by leading consultants such as Booz-Allen & Hamilton. The return may be calculated on sales, on assets, or on equity, for which various accounting procedures may be applied.

2 *Profit Contribution* A profit measure of more specific value to the manager's determination of the profitability of a particular product in the product line is the contribution method. A product's contribution (also called "gross margin") is simply the difference between its unit revenue or selling price (received by the seller) and its unit direct cost (also called "cost of goods sold"). The difference or margin is then multiplied by the number of units sold to obtain an overall contribution, that is,

$$\text{Contribution} = (\text{revenue} - \text{direct cost}) \times \text{units sold}$$

This "cash contribution" is then available to cover any fixed costs that may be allocated to the product, such as part of the production equipment cost, fixed sales force salaries—and also the advertising and promotion budget. A product's profit or "profit impact" is thus

$$\text{Profit} = \text{contribution} - \text{fixed-cost allocation}$$

A new product may, of course, experience a negative profit (that is, a loss) until sales reach a level sufficient for the cumulative contribution to cover fixed costs. The sales level at which a product's contribution equals its fixed cost allocation is known as the "break-even" level of sales. When sales increase further such that the product becomes profitable, it still has to cover the opportunity loss of its own investment, that is, the amount that could have been earned had its expenditures been invested elsewhere. The time taken from initial development of a product to recovery of its own investment is known as the "payback period," and thereafter realized profits begin.

SALES OBJECTIVES

When to Use Sales Objectives

The fifth step in our effects sequence leading to profit is described as sales or market share. The *or* is deliberate in this instance because, depending on circumstances, a company may wish to focus on sales, or market share, or both. Sales objectives—sometimes called "volume" objectives—are not the same as market share objectives, however. Sales objectives exist independently whereas market share objectives are entirely a relative concept, dependent on how one defines a market and on what the competitors' sales are in that market.

Growing versus Declining Markets   The distinction between sales objectives and market share objectives is most easily seen in growing versus declining markets (that is, in growing or declining product categories). In growing markets—which occur during the introduction and growth stages of the product (category) life cycle—it is quite possible for a brand to have increasing sales but a declining market share. This happens when competitors' sales are growing faster than yours are growing. Conversely, in a declining market it is quite possible to have declining sales with an increasing share, as competitors leave the category. The two terms, sales and market share, cannot be used interchangeably.

Always Set Sales Objectives   The best recommendation, we believe, is to always set sales objectives regardless of whether market share objectives are also specified. This removes the problem of ambiguous market share objectives described below.

Sales Measures

Companies use lots of different methods of measuring sales. These can be placed in three categories:

1 *Exact Measures*
    a *Sales Receipts* Actual sales receipts are the most exact measure of sales. However, sales receipts are often very slow to reach the company and, since evaluation of advertising or promotion campaign effectiveness

often has to be made as early as possible, various other methods (below) are frequently used.

2 *Pre-Sales Measures*

a *Factory Shipments* This is the fastest measure but it has the problem of having to allow for returns, which are very hard to estimate for new products.

b *Warehouse Withdrawals* (monitored for example, by the A.C. Nielsen Company or by Selling Areas Marketing, Inc., known as "SAMI") This is a little better than factory shipments since warehouse withdrawals imply actual demand by retailers; this may not translate to consumer demand, however, as there is still the problem of returns.

c *Retail Store Audits* (for example, Nielsen, Audits & Surveys, Inc., Interactive Market Systems, National Retail Testing Institute) Audits are closer to the actual sale, but still not the same; also, they are limited to certain industries and types of stores such as food and drug outlets.

d *UPC Scanners* (for example, Nielsen's TestSight, Information Resources, Inc.'s BehaviorScan, Burke's AdTel) UPC scanners are as good as sales receipts but the use of these "cash register" devices is limited at present to certain markets and to food and drug outlets. Also they depend on consumer cooperation in using scanner cards for all purchases.

3 *Projected Measures*

a *Purchase Diary Panels* (for example, The National Purchase Diary Group, National Family Opinion, Inc., Market Research Corporation of America) These give fairly accurate projections from sample to actual sales; however, the diary method used to record most panel purchases suffers from some recording errors and a possible reporting bias toward national brands.

b *Surveys* (customized by most large marketing research firms) Surveys are less accurate because of more reliance on the consumer's memory than in the diary method, and again there is a possible reporting bias toward national brands.

c *Simulation Tests* (for example, IRI's Assessor; Yankelovich, Skelly & White; Erhart-Babic Group) These measure sales but only under "simulated store display" conditions; hence the unreliability of sales projections to actual stores may be substantial.

The *best* measure of sales is sales receipts (in units and in dollars). When other "faster" measures are used, they should be checked periodically for accuracy with sales receipts.

MARKET SHARE OBJECTIVES

When to Use Market Share Objectives

Market share is a measure of sales relative to competitors' sales—usually company or brand sales expressed as a percentage or proportion of total market sales. For example, Heineken beer has a market share of 2 percent (or 0.02) of the total U.S. beer market; Xerox has a market share of 5 percent (or 0.05) of the total U.S. copier market. Clearly, market share depends on how you define the competition, and thus the market. We will return to this essential point shortly.

Market Share Is Not Relevant for All Companies   Market share, unlike sales, is not a meaningful objective for all companies. Historical monopolies, for example, AT&T or the U.S. Postal Service, have had to think in terms of sales but not in terms of market share since there has been no direct competition. The outlook for monopolies is changing, of course, at least in the United States. With deregulation, companies such as MCI and Sprint are beginning to compete with AT&T for a segment of the telephone market, by offering long-distance business service. The postal service also has witnessed strong competition in the segment of small package delivery, from companies like Federal Express and Emery.

At the other end of the spectrum, too, many small companies do not think in terms of market share, and this concept does not really direct their advertising and promotion planning. The corner grocery store, for instance, makes its advertising and promotion decisions mostly on the basis of its own sales and profits, even though the store may compete for share with other nearby stores and supermarkets.

Market Share and Competitor Orientation   Market share is a relevant objective for most companies in between these extremes. Nearly all industrial and consumer companies compete for customers' dollars with several or many close rivals. While customer satisfaction, as expressed in "the marketing concept," is one proven route to sales and profit, there is an alternative route, called "competitor orientation," which underlies the emphasis of many companies (and managers) on market share.[15]

As shown in Figure 2.2, *both* the customer orientation and the competitor orientation can lead to increased sales and profit and, of course, the two approaches can be combined. Note particularly the boxes in the competitor orientation diagram that depict a key part of the strategy as taking customers from rivals and minimizing loss of customers to rivals. This is the essence of market share.

Market Share and Sales   Earlier we said that sales objectives should always be set regardless of whether market share objectives are also used. This is because market share performance alone can be uninformative depending on whether the category or market (in other words, the product life cycle, PLC, where the "product" refers to all closely competing brands) is growing or, alternatively, flat or declining:

1 *Growing markets (Introduction and Growth Stages of PLC)* Market share is *more important* than sales in growing markets because brand sales should

Means/End Chain for Customer Orientation

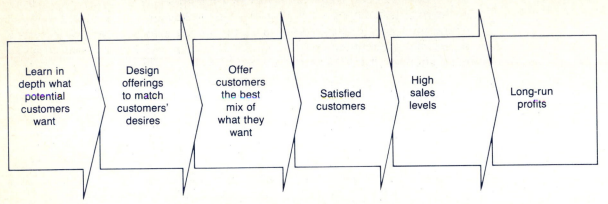

Means/End Chain for Competitor Orientation

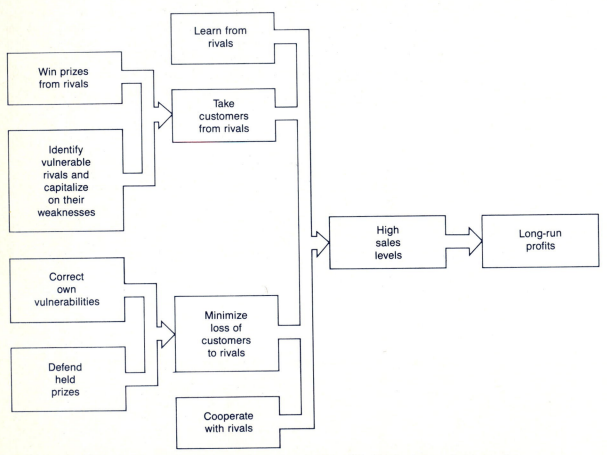

FIGURE 2.2   Customer orientation and competitor orientation. The models for markets underlying customer and competitor orientation differ substantially. Both are essentially valid. Since they are compatible, the issue is not which is right but how best to combine them. (*Reprinted by permission from Management Review, August 1978.*)

be increasing anyway as category sales increase; market share indicates whether the brand is growing faster than the competition.

2 *Flat or Declining Markets (Maturity and Decline stages of PLC)* Market share is *less important* than sales in flat or declining markets; of course, the only way sales can increase in a flat or declining market is by "taking share" away from the competition. One must be sure, however, that market share increases are not the spurious results of competitors leaving the market, and that *sales* are in fact increasing.

Market Share Measures

Because market share is simply relative sales, the sales measures described previously are also used to measure market share. In using these measures, the manager has to have access to competitors' or category sales against which to assess the brand's own sales.

Market share, like sales, can be measured in terms of product units sold or sales dollars received. The manager should use both measures. Market share in *units* reveals how well the brand is selling versus competing brands and is the basic measure of market share. Market share in *dollars* is additionally informative because it reflects the effects of selling price differentials, which are in turn usually related to profit. A brand pursuing the price differential avenue to profit, for instance, might be quite happy with a constant unit market share and an increasing dollar market share. The same dual consideration, of course, would apply to its sales trends in units and dollars.

MARKET DEFINITION AND PARTITIONING

The most critical component in setting market share objectives is correct definition of the market or product category in which the brand is *actually* (or, if a new brand, could *potentially* be) competing. Actual competition occurs when a substantial number of customers regard brands as close substitutes or purchase alternatives. Actual competition, and thus the "true" market, is not always easy to determine. For instance:

- Recall the example of Heineken beer. Heineken has a 2 percent market share of the U.S. beer market; however, it has a 40 percent share of the U.S. market for *imported* beers. But does Heineken just compete with imports or does it also compete with quasi imports such as Lowenbrau and super-premium U.S. beers such as Michelob? If so, Heineken's "true" market share is neither 2 percent or 40 percent but some figure in between.
- *Xerox copiers:* Does Xerox compete with all copiers, including cheaper desk-top models, or mainly against other expensive, high-speed, multiple-copy machines?
- *Sanka-brand coffee:* Does Sanka compete with all coffees, or just instant coffees, or just instant decaffeinated coffees?
- *Digital's computers:* Does Digital Equipment Corporation compete with

IBM for all types of computers, or is Digital's "true" market currently in mid-sized computers?

As these examples indicate, market share objectives can be statistically and *strategically* misleading if they are not based on an appropriate competitive market definition.

Partitioning the Overall Market to Find the True Market (Competitive Frame)

An analytical technique of great value to managers in deciding on the "true" market or "competitive frame" for a brand is known as "partitioning" or "hierarchical market definition."[16] As far as we can determine, The Hendry Corporation deserves major credit for developing this technique, although it has been applied in many ways by others.

The basic idea of partitioning is that the overall market or *product category* (often industry-defined) can be successively subdivided into partitions or sub-markets which increasingly approximate the true market for a *brand* or *brand-item* (as defined from the *consumer's* standpoint). As you go "down" the hierarchy of partitions, perceived substitutability increases, and actual brand or item switching behavior increases. This is shown in Figure 2.3.

Bases for Partitions The partitions that divide a market into sub-markets (in consumers' eyes) can be based on a number of factors. Most often these are:

1 *Product forms,* where there are distinct physical differences between products (for example, large, medium or mini-computers; margarine in sticks or cups)

2 *Benefits sought,* where products vary in the features they emphasize (for example, cavity prevention or fresh taste in a toothpaste; status or price-value in a pair of jeans)

FIGURE 2.3   Total market partitioned into sub-markets in which each brand or brand-item faces the most direct competition.

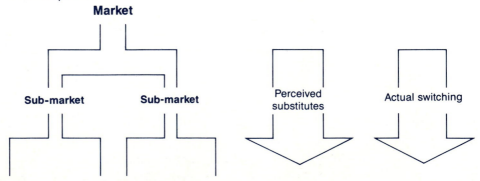

3 *Usage situations,* where benefits sought in the "same" product may vary over usage situations (for example, "special occasion" beers versus "regular" beers; family versus adult movies)

4 *Brand names,* where the brand name signifies a particular "image" or quality level and various items are available under that brand name (for example, Black & Decker versus Rockwell power tools; Macy's versus Saks Fifth Avenue department stores)

Partitioning and "Positioning"   Partitioning is one aspect of "positioning." A brand can be positioned, either deliberately or by consumer perception, in one sub-category or another of the total product category. For example, New Coke is positioned in the regular cola sub-category of the cola market and, more broadly, the soft drink market; Sprite is positioned in the regular lemon-lime sub-category.

Later, when we examine brand attitude, we will see that a brand can further be positioned *within* its sub-category with reference to *other brands* with which it competes. This is the second aspect of "positioning."

Here we will focus on the category-membership (competitive frame) aspect of positioning rather than the brand-differences aspect. Partitioning is relevant only to the former.

Determining the Order of Partitions   The "trick" in partitioning is deciding on the order of the partitions. For example, in choosing a yogurt, do consumers decide first on a brand name and then on a product benefit such as flavor? Or do they choose a flavor first and then a particular brand? In other words, the yogurt market could be partitioned in at least two different ways, as shown in Figure 2.4.

Note the importance of the different partition orders. If the yogurt market is partitioned by consumers in the manner shown in panel (a), Dannon's main advertising and promotion objective would be first to convince consumers to buy the Dannon brand, then offer flavors that suit "Dannon lovers." Alternatively, if the yogurt market is partitioned by consumers in the manner shown in panel (b), Dannon's main advertising and promotion objective would first be to appeal to, for example, "strawberry lovers," then convince these consumers that Dannon offers better strawberry yogurt than any other brand.

Fortunately, determination of the correct order of partitions need not be left to intuition. As we shall see at the end of this section, there are various consumer research measures that can identify the likely ordering by following the basic rule mentioned earlier: that perceived substitution and actual switching will be greater the *lower* the partition is in the hierarchy.

Implications of Partitioning for Setting Market Share Objectives

Implications of partitioning for setting market share objectives are best illustrated by a further example—this time with actual data (deliberately several years old to protect company confidentiality). Table 2.4 shows market share

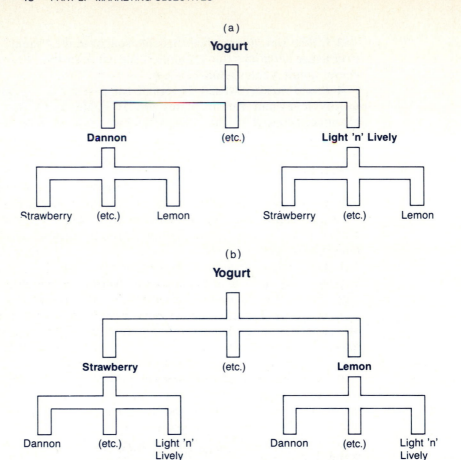

FIGURE 2.4   Alternative partitioning of the yogurt market. (a) Primary competition between brands followed by frequent switching between flavors. (b) Primary competition between flavors followed by frequent switching between brands.

TABLE 2-4   MARKET SHARES FOR PERSONAL DEODORANTS†

	1973 (%)	1976 (%)
1 Company shares		
Gillette	25	21
Bristol-Myers	13	20
Procter & Gamble	11	18
Carter-Wallace	14	9
2 Brand Shares		
Ban (B-M)	12	19
Right Guard (G)	20	17
Sure (P&G)	4	11
Arrid (C-W)	14	9

† The figures were compiled by Maxwell Associates and reported in *Advertising Age*, May 9, 1977, p. 68 (used with permission).

trends for the personal deodorant market several years ago.[17] Panel 1 shows market shares by company and panel 2 shows market shares by brand.

The company share trends are not very informative for the advertising and promotion manager responsible for an individual brand. But even more importantly, the brand share trends are not very informative either, unless the manager knows how the deodorant market is partitioned. It is the trends occurring *within the partitions* that are important for setting market share objectives.

Figure 2.5 shows a reasonable depiction of the (then) market partitioning for personal deodorants. The diagram indicates that the market for personal deodorants has its primary partition that separates consumers who prefer a spray-type deodorant and those who prefer a non-spray application. Consumers then choose a more specific type of applicator from within their preferred applicator category. Finally, they select a brand from within the specific applicator types.

Note that market share trends now depend crucially on market definition via partitioning. At the time between the market share measurements, 1973 and 1976, there was a major crackdown on aerosol spray containers because of fears of damage to the earth's ozone layer. Sprays lost a large share of market, from 75 down to 55 percent, despite the introduction of non-aerosol (pump) sprays which reversed some of this trend. Non-sprays benefited with a rise in market share from 25 to 45 percent. Non-spray subsidiary products,

FIGURE 2.5   Market structure for personal deodorants. Market share trends are shown in parentheses. First figure is 1973, second is 1976, and arrow shows trend.

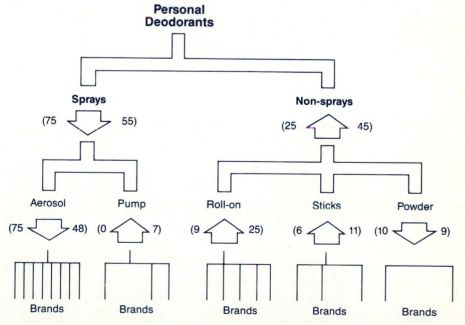

roll-on and stick deodorants, benefited simultaneously, although the other non-spray alternative, powders, remained fairly constant in usage.

What if you had been the advertising and promotion manager for Procter & Gamble's Sure brand in 1976?

Sure, a roll-on deodorant, should be setting its sights on a large increase in market share. This was not at all evident from panel 2 in Table 2.4, where Sure could not be sure that its rise from 4 to 11 percent did not represent a peak share for the brand. In fact, from Figure 2.5, Sure may have gained a lot of this increase anyway, with little advertising or promotion, simply by being in the growing category of roll-ons.

But Sure has a chance to dominate the roll-on category: Sure has 11 percent divided by 25 percent or a 44 percent share of the roll-on category. Sure should probably increase its advertising and promotion spending heavily rather than being content to ride the trend. Moreover, the message strategy, instead of solely focusing on the attributes of Sure, should also stress its roll-on product form and perhaps even comparatively remind consumers that it is not one of those "harmful" aerosols.

The market share objective and strategy for Sure (albeit hypothetical) would not be evident had we not known how the market was partitioned.

"De-partitioning" as a Strategy

Most product categories tend to have a maximum of four or five partition levels and frequently fewer.[18] It should be apparent that the more partition levels there are, the smaller the true markets at the bottom of the hierarchy become. Partitioning is essentially a sequential version of market segmentation. One could continue to segment until each individual customer had what he or she wanted, provided the firm could and would offer individualized "marketing mixes." This can be profitable in some industries, such as government contract work, but it is rarely profitable for most industries.

Consequently, a firm might try to proceed in reverse—by de-partitioning the market and thereby appealing to a larger group at the next highest partition level. Operationally, de-partitioning is "positioning" a brand more broadly to address two or more sub-categories simultaneously.

The reason that de-partitioning is not a frequent strategy is that it depends on being able to offer a *combination* of product forms or benefits by surmounting technological or psychological barriers. Technological combinations are usually the most difficult, but there have been some successful examples, such as Aim and Aqua Fresh toothpastes, which combined fluoride (cavity prevention) with the gel form (fresh taste) and gained fast market share as a result. Another interesting example is Michelob Light, which combined light beer with a super-premium "image" in an attempt to draw two sub-markets of the beer category together.

However, one must be sure that consumers indeed want the combination of forms or benefits, raising the possibility of psychological barriers. For example, in 1981, a new non-prescription pain reliever, called Gemnisyn, combined aspirin with acetaminophen (the Tylenol non-aspirin ingredient) in an attempt to appeal to consumers in both the aspirin and non-aspirin partitions of the pain remedy market. But how many consumers would want both ingredients after having learned from past advertising campaigns that aspirin and acetaminophen are so different? Another example that auto manufacturers have had problems with is the concept of a "luxury small car"; luxuriousness and smallness are almost impossibly contradictory to many car buyers.

De-partitioning, in summary, may be a tempting way to increase the potential market. However, there are often technological or psychological barriers preventing this option. And also, the firm must beware of alienating present segments of consumers who prefer the separate forms or benefits represented by the current partitioning.

Partitioning Markets for Durables

Most of our examples of partitioning have been for consumer packaged goods, for which consumers are frequently "in the market" and can perceive substitutes and switch brands as they wish. For consumer durables, such as TV sets or automobiles, or for industrial durables, such as equipment and machinery, brand switching is less meaningful because of the relatively long interval between purchases.

However, even for durables, customers do change brands or suppliers and, more pertinently, they are likely to confine their selections to a sub-set of similar offerings. Thus, it is still meaningful to partition markets for these less frequently purchased products so that the firm can identify where its true market is and who its real competitors are.

Durable goods partitioning examples include Savin, who has chipped away at Xerox by specializing in the small copier sub-market. Similarly, Midas has concentrated on the sub-market of auto muffler buyers who want firm quotations and brand name guarantees in the notoriously risky (overall) auto repair and service market.

Partitioning is, therefore, a relevant means of market definition for virtually any type of product or service. As we shall see shortly, the main difference with durables is that the partitioning measure is likely to focus on customer-perceived substitutability rather than, as for packaged goods, on brand-switching behavior.

THE POSSIBILITY OF LIMITS TO MARKET SHARE

It is comparatively easy to understand that there is a limit to sales of a *product category* (not everyone wants every product and those who do want it have some limit to consumption capacity), but it is rather revolutionary to contemplate that there may be a limit to a *brand's* market share of sales within the product-category sales level. After all, isn't it possible for the firm with the best brand to retain 100 percent of a market, if first in, or to gain 100 percent of it, if a later entry? If there are limits to retainable or attainable market

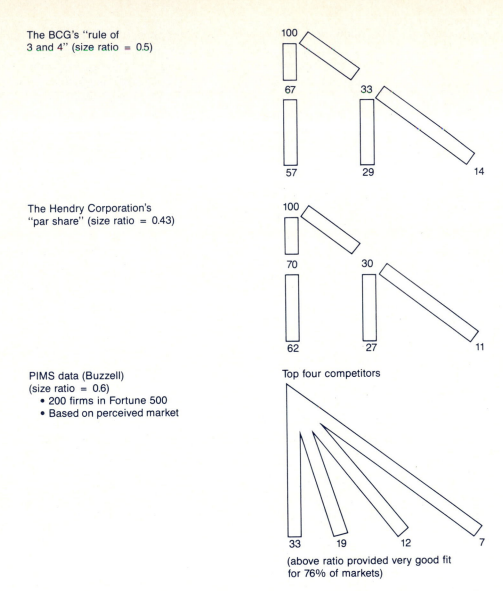

FIGURE 2.6   Alternative "natural rules" of market evolution and structure.

share, this would have significant implications for the establishment of market share objectives.

Several relatively recent lines of theory and evidence suggest that, for many product categories and probably a majority, there may indeed be "structural" limits to market share. The pattern of market shares for many product categories is remarkably consistent, leading some to propose "natural rules" of market evolution and structure (Figure 2.6). Two of the best-known rules are discussed next.

Boston Consulting Group's "Rule of 3 and 4"

Working primarily with industrial markets, the BCG[19] proposed the "rule of 3 and 4," which states that three major competitors will emerge and their market shares will tend to be distributed in the ratio 4:2:1. That is, following the first entrant, each successive entrant, up to the third, can expect to attain half the market share of its precursor (a "size ratio" of 0.5).

The BCG's principal explanation for their evolutionary market share rule centers on the "experience curve." Each subsequent entrant has less time to "ride down" the experience curve to lower costs; the leading firms dominate the market and thus further prevent smaller firms from reaching the low cost point, at least until the market itself changes through major innovation. Since the BCG has only occasionally published their supporting data, it is not possible to determine the extent of experience curve effects nor its generality as an explanation, although the BCG claims it is general in technological industries.

The Hendry Corporation's "Par Share" Concept

Working mainly with consumer packaged goods, The Hendry Corporation[20] developed a similar structural concept known as "par share." The first brand in a new category, obviously, will have 100 percent market share. According to the par share concept, the second brand entering can expect, on average (par), to gain a 30 percent market share. The third brand can expect 11 percent, and so on (a "size ratio" of 0.43). Each new brand changes the par share for the next brand and makes the market successively less vulnerable.

Market share, according to Hendry, therefore becomes harder and harder to attain as the number of brands in a market increases. In fact, virtually the only way a new brand entering late can attain a large share is for it to be so *substantially* different as to create another sub-market, that is, another *partition* or product category within the overall category. The Hendry Corporation claims to have substantiated the par share concept in many consumer packaged goods categories although these data are again proprietary and have not been published except in highly generalized form.

Hendry's explanation for market evolution and structure is quite different from the BCG experience curve explanation; it is consumer-based rather than based on company costs. The explanation is that consumers' preferences become progressively "polarized" either strongly for or strongly against each brand as they gain familiarity with a new category (although not part of the Hendry system, a possible reason for this is consumers' desire to simplify and "routinize" their purchases as much as possible; see Chapter 4). Early brands in the category have a better chance of picking up "loyals" whereas later brands find most consumers already committed to a new brand and less likely to try, or switch to, a new entry.

Most but Not All Markets Exhibit Market Share Structure

The best published evidence that markets frequently exhibit the size ratio type of descending share structure comes from a study by Buzzell.[21] The study was based on the PIMS data, contributed by 200 firms in the *Fortune* 500 list. Buzzell selected markets in which there were at least four significant competitors. This was done so there would be sufficient observations to fit a distribution to the data; but it introduces a bias, of unreported magnitude, by excluding markets dominated by fewer competitors.

Buzzell found that a size ratio of 0.6, predicting market shares of 33, 19, 12, and 7 percent for the top four competitors, fitted 76 percent of the markets extremely well (90 percent or higher confidence level). Of interest was the fact that the markets upon which market shares were computed were as judged by the reporting managers rather than predefined by industry codes. This makes it likelier that the market shares were close to consumer-defined markets which, as we have noted, are the only markets or competitive categories that count from a marketing strategy standpoint.

Caveat   About 24 percent of the markets in the Buzzell study (and possibly more given the selection process) did not follow the "natural" structure and it is important that the manager not assume this structure to be universally present. The advertising agency "market" is a good example: No U.S. agency has more than a 2 percent market share! This is partly due to the presence of many local accounts better serviced by smaller local agencies and also to the fact that agencies cannot take on competing accounts and thereby become overly specialized in an industry. Universities and business schools are another "market" where market share structures of the descending type do not occur.

Conclusion   Nevertheless, in the many markets where either or both the experience curve phenomenon (mainly technological markets) and the customer polarization process (consumer and also industrial markets) occur, the causal conditions for a structural evolution of market shares may be present. The idea of attainable *and* retainable limits to market share seems to be an important factor for managers to consider in setting market share objectives.

MARKET PARTITIONING MEASURES

There are two broad types of measurement methods for partitioning markets and thereby arriving at an appropriate definition of the "true" market and a reasonably sound basis for calculating market share: (1) perceived substitutability measures and (2) actual switching measures.

Whereas actual switching measures would at first appear to be superior, since they are based on behavior, this depends on the manager's purpose.[22] Actual switching measures are best for calculating market share in existing markets. However, a manager deciding how best to position a *new* product (perhaps even just a concept at this stage) will have to rely on perceptual measures since obviously there is no switching history yet established.

Both types of measures can be supplemented usefully with questions that ask consumers the *reasons* for their substitutability judgments or their brand-switching behavior. Diagnostic information of this type can help to "label" the partitions. Also, it can often suggest ideas for new products incorporating new or combined benefits.

Finally, we should note that although the partitioning structure requires greater perceived substitutability and more frequent switching as you go "down" the partitions (thus helping to determine the ordering of partitions), the ultimate ordering and lateral divisions must often be decided by management judgment. This happens when the measures are taken on small samples, making the substitution or switching figures somewhat unreliable, or when different consumer segments exhibit different patterns of perception or behavior which may generate a misleading "average" partitioning structure.

Perceived Substitutability

1 *Qualitative* These are focus groups or individual open-ended interviews in which consumers are asked about each brand's category membership; for example, "which brands of Scotch whiskey would you place in the very top quality category?" (for example, Howard[23]).

2 *Perceptual Mapping* A set of statistical techniques known loosely as "perceptual mapping" can provide indications of perceived substitutability based on similarities or preference judgments (for example, Green and Rao[24]); however, perceptual mapping does not directly provide the "tree" structure characteristic of partitioning.

3 *Dollar Metric or Price Sensitivity Method* Consumers are presented with pairs of brands at their regular prices and then asked by how much the other's price would have to be lowered to induce them to switch from the preferred alternative (for example, Pessemier[25]); although this method provides a range of substitutability coefficients, it often requires additional diagnostic questions to arrive at a meaningful partitioning.

Actual Switching

4 *Forced Switching* In simulated choice settings, one common method is to create "out of stocks" by successively removing the customer's first, second, third, etc. choices and observing which brands are chosen instead. Consumers can be post-interviewed to determine reasons for their switching behavior.

5 *Field Surveys* Panels and surveys are often used to track actual brand-switching behavior. Diary or scanner-purchase panels are the best methods (for established brands) because they are based on natural rather than forced choice, allowing for variety seeking, etc. Hendry partitioning measurement is often based on telephone surveys in which individual shoppers are asked which brand of "X" they bought last and which brand they bought the time before last (this measure assumes stationary switching probabilities and tentative prior definitions of the product category in which the brand competes which we cannot discuss adequately here).

6 *Competitive Market Structure Analysis* Using brand purchase records from panel studies, this method of analysis (developed by Fraser and Bradford[26]) deserves special mention. CMSA focuses on the household's time interval between brand purchases in the overall category. Brands bought close together in time are probably *not* competing but rather are preferred by different individuals within the household or else by the same individual for independent (situational) uses (for example, Crest and Ultra Brite). Brands bought at longer intervals, when the previous brand has had time to be used up, most likely *are* directly competing in that they are regarded as substitutes for each other (for example, Crest and Colgate). Purchase or usage interval analysis is an improvement over standard switching analysis in that the latter assumes that alternate purchase of two brands means they are competing whereas they may in fact be complementary or reflect independent preferences within the household.

SUMMARY

The first stage in the manager's planning sequence for advertising and promotion is to "fit in with" the marketing objectives for the brand. In our six-step effects sequence, this entails relating advertising and promotion to steps 5 and 6: sales or market share and profit.

The manager should do more than just "fitting in" in a general sense. By employing the concepts of *objectives* (broad aims), the manager can spell out in broad terms how advertising and promotion are expected to contribute to the brand's profit, as well as to the sales or market share levels that lead to profit. By employing the concept of *goals* (objectives made quantitatively specific by specifying the degree or amount of change, plus the time period), the manager can estimate the contribution of advertising and promotion to sales, or market share, or profit. The manager makes this goal estimation, for example, when budgeting in terms of an advertising-to-sales ratio, as we shall see in Chapter 3.

The use of objectives "versus" goals depends on the level of planning. Precise goals can be set: for individual ads or promotion offers at the first two steps of the effects sequence (exposure and processing); for an advertising or promotion campaign at the next two steps of the effects sequence (communication effects and target audience action); and for the total advertising and promotion budget at the final two steps of the effects sequence (sales or market share, and profit). Otherwise, broad objectives are stated.

Profit objectives—or goals—can be met by advertising and promotion in three ways: by maintaining or increasing the brand's price differential over other brands; by lowering production or marketing costs per unit sold; or by selling more units.

Sales objectives—or goals—should always be set for advertising and promotion because sales are the basic indicator of performance. Sales objectives are most relevant in a mature or declining market. Although the typical strategy is to "grab share" in mature or declining markets, market share increases can be spurious indicators of performance if share is increasing merely because competitors are leaving the category. Thus, sales is the important objective here.

Market share objectives (or goals) are appropriate when the company or brand chooses to adopt a competitive orientation and when sales alone cannot indicate how well the company or brand is performing against competitors. Market share objectives are most relevant in a growth market (introductory and growth phases of the PLC), where the brand's sales should be increasing faster than sales of competing brands.

The setting of a market share objective for the brand requires a correct definition of the true competitive market (actually a sub-market or sub-category) in which the share is to be attained.

The general method for identifying the competitive structure within an overall product category is known as market partitioning. Product categories generally exhibit several partitions or levels within the overall category. The primary partition reveals sub-markets or sub-categories between which large preference distinctions are made by consumers (for example, luxury cars versus mid-size versus compact cars) and thus very little perceived substitutability or actual competition occurs at upper levels. Lower-level partitions reveal closer and closer substitutes until small sets of brands (or brand-items) are left within which buyers, if they so desire, switch brands freely. The small set of brands is the brand's "true" market as currently perceived.

Market share can only be meaningfully defined in terms of market partitions. A brand can try for a larger share of its current market by gaining sales over other brands in its immediate competitive sub-category. Or it can try for a larger share of a bigger market by attempting to "de-partition" levels above it, by offering the combined benefits of its own and a neighboring sub-category (for example, a luxury compact car). Or a really different new brand can create a market partition of its own, for a while, until competitors enter.

To ignore market partitions is foolish, because buyers certainly don't ignore them: They use them as bases for brand choice within the overall product category.

Market share objectives also have to take account of another frequent possibility—the possibility of structural limits to the market share that a brand can attain (when entering a market or partition) or retain (when competing brands enter). There are two causes of structural limits to market share: the cost-reduction explanation, which applies especially to technological products; and the consumer-polarization explanation, which probably applies to all products.

Market structure and the nature of competition within an overall market or product category can be assessed through partitioning measures. For completely new products and for products purchased infrequently (many industrial products and consumer durables), measures of *perceived* substitutability are used. For frequently purchased products (most consumer packaged goods), measures of *actual* substitutability—brand switching—are usually used. Open-ended questions probing the reasons for substitute, complementary, and situational brand perceptions and usage help further to clarify the brand's competitive frame within which advertising and promotion have to operate.

This chapter concludes our examination of marketing objectives for the brand. In Chapter 3, we will see how the overall advertising budget can be set on the basis of the profit, sales, or market share objectives which have now been established.

NOTES

1 Evidence on the value of setting explicit advertising objectives comes from studies by: S.H. Britt, Are so-called successful advertising campaigns really successful? *Journal of Advertising Research,* 1969, *9* (2), 3–9; S. Majaro, Advertising by objectives, *Management Today,* 1970, January, 71–73; and D.C. Marshner, DAG-MAR revisited—eight years later, *Journal of Advertising Research,* 1971, *11* (27), 27–33.

2 H.I. Ansoff, J. Avner, R.G. Brandenburg, F.E. Portner, and R. Radosevich, Does planning pay? The effect of planning on success of acquisitions in American firms, *Long-Range Planning,* 1970, *3* (2), 2–7. Other studies showing that companies who make explicit plans (and set objectives) outperform companies in the same industry who don't plan formally are reviewed in J.S. Armstrong, The value of formal planning for strategic decisions: review of empirical research, *Strategic Management Journal,* 1983, *3* (3), 197–211.

3 Interestingly, too, individuals perform better when they are accountable to challenging, explicit objectives (i.e., goals). A review of 110 studies of goal-setting on individual performance found higher performance in 90 percent of the studies. See E.A. Locke, K.N. Shaw, L.M. Saari, and G.P. Latham, Goal setting and task performance, *Psychological Bulletin,* 1981, *90* (1), 125–152.

4 For further explanation of the distinctions between objectives and goals, see R.L. Ackoff, *A Concept of Corporate Planning,* New York, NY: Wiley-Interscience, 1970, and R.H. Colley, *Defining Advertising Goals for Measured Advertising Results,* New York, NY: Association of National Advertisers, Inc., 1961.

5 For excellent reviews of the relationship between advertising and (1) price levels and (2) price differentials, see R.L. Steiner, Does advertising lower consumer prices? *Journal of Marketing,* 1973, *37* (4), 19–26; P.W. Farris and M.S. Albion, The impact of advertising on the price of consumer products, *Journal of Marketing,* 1980, *44* (3), 17–35.

6 C. Anson and R.F. Silverstone, Supermarket strategy summary, in the Maryland Center for Public Broadcasting's *Consumer Survival Kit,* Owing Hills, MD: Maryland Center for Public Broadcasting, 1975.

7 Survey of generic products by Foot, Cone & Belding, Inc., reported in *The Wall Street Journal,* August 10, 1979, p. 6.

8 E.P. Schonfeld and J.H. Boyd, The financial payoff in corporate advertising, *Journal of Advertising Research,* 1982, *22* (1), 45–55.

9 Economies of scale are a well-known phenomenon in economics; see, for example, W.S. Comanor and T.A. Wilson, *Advertising and Marketing Power,* Cambridge, MA: Harvard University Press, 1974. The broader concept of an "experience curve," reflecting "expertise" efficiency as well as production efficiency, was popularized by The Boston Consulting Group, *Perspectives on Experience,* Cambridge, MA: The Boston Consulting Group, 1968.

10 R.D. Buzzell, Are there "natural" market structures? *Journal of Marketing,* 1981, *45* (1), 42–51.

11 M.E. Porter, *Competitive Strategy,* New York: The Free Press, 1980.

12 For many years, McGraw-Hill has been monitoring the cost of sales calls in relation

to the cost of advertising. These figures have been widely cited in advertisements on behalf of various advertising media to demonstrate their lower cost in contrast with personal selling.

13 The diagram is taken from an article by R.J. Jessen, A switch-over experimental design to measure advertising effect, *Journal of Advertising Research,* 1961, *1* (3), 15–22. It has been widely reproduced in similar form elsewhere.

14 J.L. Simon and J. Arndt, The shape of the advertising response function, *Journal of Advertising Research,* 1980, *20* (4), 11–28.

15 A.R. Oxenfeldt and W.L. Moore, Customer or competitor: which guideline for marketing?, *Management Review,* 1978, *67* (8), 43–48.

16 The term "partitioning" apparently was introduced by The Hendry Corporation in various industry presentations, some of which are compiled in a book by the company, *Speaking of Hendry,* New York: The Hendry Corporation, 1976. "Hierarchical market definition" is a more general term for the several techniques that have much the same purpose as partitioning; see G.L. Urban and J.R. Hauser, *Design and Marketing of New Products,* Englewood Cliffs, NJ: Prentice-Hall, 1980.

17 These data are taken from J.V. Lloyd, "Toiletries market growth only 6% in '76: Maxwell," *Advertising Age,* May 9, 1977, p. 68. The title refers to the research firm of Maxwell Associates, Richmond, VA, who compiled the figures.

18 G.L. Urban and J.R. Hauser, same reference as note 16.

19 The Boston Consulting Group, The rule of three and four, *Perspectives,* No. 187, Cambridge, MA: The Boston Consulting Group, 1976.

20 The Hendry Corporation, same reference as note 16.

21 R.D. Buzzell, same reference as note 10.

22 For a discussion of conditions of application of various measures of partitioning, see G.S. Day, A.D. Shocker, and R.K. Srivastava, Customer-oriented approaches to identifying product markets, *Journal of Marketing,* 1979, *43* (4), 8–19.

23 J.A. Howard, The concept of product hierarchy, working paper, Graduate School of Business, Columbia University, New York, 1981.

24 P.E. Green and V.R. Rao, *Applied Multidimensional Scaling: Comparison of Approaches and Algorithms,* New York: Holt, Rinehart and Winston, 1972.

25 E.A. Pessemier, *Product Management: Strategy and Organization,* Santa Barbara, CA: Wiley/Hamilton, 1972.

26 C. Fraser and J.W. Bradford, Competitive market structure analysis: principal partitioning of revealed substitutabilities, *Journal of Consumer Research,* 1983, *10* (1), 15–30.

DISCUSSION QUESTIONS

2.1 The use of objectives versus goals differs according to the level of advertising and promotion planning and the six-step effects sequence. Illustrate this with hypothetical objectives or goals for (a) a single Cherry Coke TV commercial; (b) a summer-length promotion campaign for Cherry Coke; and (c) the annual advertising and promotion budget for Cherry Coke.

2.2 Advertising and promotion can contribute to profit in three ways as well as in combinations of the three. Which avenues to profit do you think are most likely to be involved in these situations:

a Introduction of a new industrial component product expected to be useful to many different companies

b Stouffer's reaction to lower-priced imitations of its French Bread Pizza product c Introduction of Agree Shampoo by S.C. Johnson Company

d An investment brokerage house (like Bache or Smith-Barney) that decides to launch a mass media corporate advertising campaign.

2.3 How does sales differ from market share and why can't the two terms be used interchangeably? Answer with examples.

2.4 The U.S. total beer market is currently exhibiting low real (unit) growth. Do you think beer manufacturers, for their output in general, should be concerned with market share, sales, or both?

2.5 Interview three or four people, preferably of different backgrounds, about their toothpaste preferences over the past several years and also their reasons for preference. From their answers, and your own knowledge, construct a reasonable partitioning of the toothpaste market.

a How does your partitioning structure correspond to the following (historical) market share trends for toothpaste brands?

b What sales or market share objectives would you set if you were the brand manager for Ultra Brite?

Company	Brand	1973 (%)	1980 (%)
P&G	Crest	38	36
C-P	Colgate	22	19
Beecham	Aqua Fresh	0	⟶ 13
Lever	Aim	0	⟶ 10
Lever	Close-up	12	7
P&G	Gleem	7	3
C-P	Ultra Brite	7	3
Lever	Pepsodent	5	3

2.6 Assume there are two potential two-level partitioning structures for margarine: (a) form (cup or stick) then brand and, alternatively, (b) brand then form. Outline sample advertising copy for each partitioning structure.

2.7 One possible partition in the computer market would separate company computers from home computers. Where might this partition fit in a partitioning of the overall market for computers? (Sketch diagram.) How might a computer company attempt to "de-partition" the company versus home computer sub-markets?

2.8 The Dallas-Houston air travel market was dominated by two carriers in 1970, Braniff with about 70 percent share of passengers and Texas International with about 30 percent. A third carrier, Southwest Airlines, entered the market in June 1971. What market share goal could the new airline hope to attain and why?

FURTHER READING

Ackoff, R.L. *A Concept of Corporate Planning*. New York: Wiley-Interscience, 1970.

Chapter 2 provides a clear, elementary discussion of the difference between objectives and goals. Overall, a sensible introduction to planning, with lots of valuable management insights.

Gabor, A. *Pricing*. London: Heinemann, 1977.

Contains an excellent and readable account of factors affecting profit: price, costs, and sales. Also discusses cautions in interpreting price elasticity and in using break-even analysis.

Day, G.S., Shocker, A.D., and Srivastava, R.K. Customer-oriented approaches to identifying product-markets. *Journal of Marketing,* 1979, *43* (4), 8–19.

A useful review of the main methods of market partitioning. Contains a pointed warning for managers who arbitrarily define categories or markets, and ignore consumer input, so as to make their brand's market share look falsely impressive.

Urban, G.L. and Hauser, J.R. *Design and Marketing of New Products,* Englewood Cliffs, NJ: Prentice-Hall, 1980.

Discusses perceptual and actual measures for identifying market structure (with lots of examples). Also a worthwhile shelf reference in general.

CHAPTER 3

SETTING THE BUDGET

In this chapter we are concerned with setting the *overall* budget for advertising and promotion (allocation of the media budget specifically is covered in Part Seven). After reading this chapter you should:

- Know how to set the budget on the basis of advertising and promotion's expected contribution to profit, sales, or market share
- Appreciate the difference between the marginal method of budgeting and the task method of budgeting—and the need for both
- Have learned a useful procedure for improving management forecasts, which are always involved in budgeting
- See how the correct budget level depends on the sales response function

We view the overall budget-setting process as a logical conclusion to the process of fitting advertising and promotion into the brand's marketing objectives. It is up to the marketing manager whether the budget should be geared to a profit goal, a sales goal, or a market share goal (although all must be consistent with whichever is designated as the primary of these three goals). This chapter explains how budgeting should be done.

THE OVERALL ADVERTISING AND PROMOTION BUDGET

The establishment of an overall advertising and promotion budget for a brand requires that profit, sales, or market share now be considered as advertising and promotion *goals*. The manager has to estimate the contribution of advertising and promotion expenditures, to be fixed at the beginning of the planning year, to profit, sales or market share *expected* by the end of the year. The estimated contribution, is, by definition, an advertising and promotion goal since it specifies degree (for example, $X of advertising and promotion is expected to produce $[X + Y] of sales) as well as time (for example, over the course of 1 year which is the usual budgeting period).

Sales Forecast Necessary

Regardless of whether the company's objective is to attain a certain profit goal, sales goal, or market share goal, a sales forecast is always required. This is self-evident for a sales goal but it also applies to profit and market share goals. To set a profit goal, you have to estimate sales because profit is based on sales minus costs. Similarly, to set a market share goal, you have to estimate sales because market share is based on sales versus competitors' sales.

Sales for the coming year can never be known exactly and therefore require a managerial estimate or forecast. That is:

$$\text{Budget} = f \text{ (estimated sales)}$$

Setting the budget a year beforehand necessarily involves management judgment, which may range from total judgment (for a completely new product) to judgment supplemented with previous evidence (for an established product). We will return to this point about management judgment in our discussion of advertising and promotion contribution measures at the end of the chapter.

"How Much to Spend" (Marginal Method) versus "How to Spend It" (Task Method)

There are two methods required for advertising and promotion budgeting. The first is known as the *marginal method* and is the subject of this chapter. The marginal method is used, basically, to decide at the beginning of the planning period "how much to spend" on advertising and promotion.

The second method is known as the *task method*. The task method focuses on how to allocate the budget to *media* after subtracting the "up-front" costs of advertising research and creative production. That is, the task method is used to decide "how to spend" the budget in media. The task method gets its name from the "task" of moving prospective buyers through the buyer-response sequence: from step 1, exposure, to step 2, processing, to step 3, communication effects, to step 4, target audience action. It estimates the media expenditure (spent at the exposure step) needed to move as many prospects through to action as can be afforded. What can be afforded depends on the sales, market share, or profit objectives: steps 5 and 6. Therefore, the marginal method focuses on steps 5 and 6, whereas the task method focuses on steps 1 through 4 that *lead to* steps 5 and 6.

We will now describe the marginal method of setting the overall budget. We will defer discussion of the task method until Part Seven, where we take up the topic of media strategy.

THE MARGINAL METHOD

Recall our brief presentation of the contribution method of calculating profit: contribution = (revenue − direct cost) × units sold; the contribution is then available to cover any fixed cost allocated to the brand such that profit = contribution − fixed cost allocation. The advertising and promotion budget is one of the fixed costs, since it is fixed at the beginning of the planning period.

Two Types of Fixed Costs   Advertising and promotion expenditures at the beginning of the period are not *yet* fixed, however; at this point they still have to be estimated and are therefore discretionary.[1] Many other marketing costs fall into the "to-be-estimated" category also, and can be distinguished from "really" fixed costs that have already been allocated to the brand. Would-be fixed costs therefore break down as follows:

1 *Really fixed costs* that represent the proportion of overhead (plant and equipment, managers' salaries, etc.) assigned to the brand
2 *To-be-estimated costs* that include (typically) the following discretionary marketing inputs as means of influencing sales:

- **a** Product—short-term changes that could be made in quality, service, or packaging
- **b** Price—changes in the terms of sale at the trade or consumer levels
- **c** Distribution—changes in how widely or where the brand is sold
- **d** Personal selling—changes in the level of sales force effort behind the brand
- **e** Advertising—changes in the level of advertising (or promotion) expenditures for the brand

The Budgeting Procedure

Determination of the advertising and promotion budget now becomes a matter of choosing the best combination of to-be-estimated costs in relation to estimated sales. (It is much easier, by the way, to think of the advertising and promotion budget in terms of *advertising,* because managers can more readily envision how advertising would affect sales than how promotion—a mixed category anyway—would do so. Once the advertising budget is determined, the manager can later (using the *task* method) decide how this total should best be spent between advertising and promotion.)

The Marginal Concept   The combination of to-be-estimated or discretionary costs is where the "marginal" aspect enters. The manager has to think in terms of meaningful increases and decreases—marginal changes—in discretionary cost expenditures and their effects on sales revenue.

For a new product, this is like zero-based budgeting. Where could the first $100,000 most effectively be spent—for example, on distribution, on personal selling, or on advertising? And the next $100,000? And the next? And so on.

For an established product, what would an increase *or* decrease of $100,000 do to sales revenue and where should the change be applied—for example, to increased or decreased service, a price cut, increased or decreased advertising? And so on as above. This is what is meant by the marginal method.

The marginal method thus involves a *marginal cost* (all costs are compared in terms of one cost: money) and a *marginal effect* or effects. The target effects of the expenditure may be profit, sales, or market share, respectively. We will first present the general method and then show how it can be applied to these respective effects.

A Simplifying Assumption   The marginal method is fairly easy to apply if the various marketing inputs to be estimated do not interact. In reality, they usually do interact; for example, additional distribution and additional advertising will usually generate more sales than spending the same total on one of these two factors. This complicates the estimation procedure but, usually, this cannot be avoided.[2]

Let us simplify things for ourselves, however, by making the often realistic (for the advertising manager!) assumption that all other costs except the advertising budget are already allocated and are thus unalterable, really fixed costs. That is, no changes in product, price, distribution, or personal selling are planned for the budgeting period.

Figure 3.1 shows the manager's advertising budget estimation procedure schematically. For each potential level of advertising expenditure, the manager has to estimate or forecast what the sales revenue response would be (the same curve as unit sales if the selling price is not changed). We have also shown the contribution curve which, it will be remembered, is (sales revenue − direct costs) × units sold. However, it is much easier to think in terms of sales effects than contribution effects—and likewise advertising rather than advertising *and* promotion—when making these estimations.

The next three sections discuss budgeting to maximize profit, sales, and market share, respectively, using Figure 3.1 as an aid.

Budgeting to Maximize Profit

B_1 shows the advertising budget level that would maximize (expected) profit. Actually it maximizes expected *contribution* rather than expected profit per se. The amount of profit that this contribution yields depends on the amount of fixed cost allocated to the product, as explained in the next paragraph. Note that at B_1 the slope of the expected contribution curve is exactly parallel to the 45° line, which is another way of showing that profit maximization occurs when marginal cost equals marginal revenue.

We should note an important aspect here which is rarely mentioned in textbooks. In discussing where the advertising budget "comes from," it often is assumed that the money must come from the product's own sales revenue and cash contribution. Hence the profit-maximizing expenditure (B_1) in the figure subtracts the advertising cost (on the 45° line) in calculating profit.

However, this is neither necessary nor always desirable. For example, a

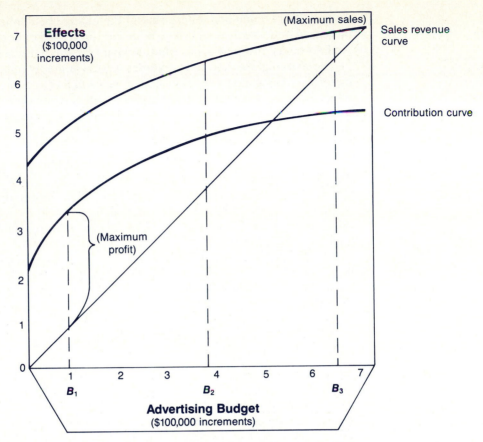

FIGURE 3.1   Estimating the effect of advertising budget levels on sales and profit.

struggling new brand's advertising could be financed from the contribution of one of the company's healthy existing brands. In this case the 45° line would not apply and the profit and contribution-maximizing point for the new brand would be at the maximum sales level (B_3) since there are no advertising costs to be subtracted for the new brand. In the next planning period, assuming the brand survives, costs can be allocated against its own contribution.

Budgeting to Maximize Sales

B_3 shows the advertising budget level that would efficiently maximize (expected) sales. This is where the marginal method becomes really useful.

Budgets larger than B_3 indicate *overspending*. Overspending would continue to maximize sales but, since sales are expected to peak or reach "saturation" at B_3, no additional revenue is created. Further advertising expenditures, at least within the current planning period, would then be useless and wasteful. An example of a brand apparently overspending in relation to sales (some years ago) is Budweiser beer, where the budget was reduced substantially for a while with no decrease in sales.[3]

The budget level B_2 indicates *underspending*. Expected sales are below their expected maximum. The marginal method would suggest an increase in advertising expenditure to B_3 if sales maximization is the goal.

Budgeting to Maximize Market Share

Budgeting to maximize market share is similar to budgeting to maximize sales in that we still have to estimate the sales curve. However, we also have to estimate our competitors' sales curves which, with ours, comprise the market. Estimating competitors' sales is much trickier because we have to guess at their advertising budgets and estimate how their sales will respond. This is possibly why so many false budgets are leaked to advertising trade publications, either a high budget to intimidate competitors altogether or a low budget to induce competitors to underspend.

If everyone's sales are similarly responsive to advertising, it follows that the only way to maximize market share is to outspend the competition—more precisely, to *outspend the leading competitor*. For the lesser goal of *maintaining* market share, a larger budget will be required if the market is growing than if it is flat or declining, because more sales will have to be generated to keep the same *share* of the growing category sales.

Share-of-Voice Budgeting Is Misleading   Many advertisers believe that to maintain market share, you have to keep your advertising budget at a constant ratio of expenditure with total advertising expenditure in the category, that is, keep your "share of voice" equal to your share of market. The corollary is that to increase market share to a desired percentage level, you have to increase your share of voice to the same percentage level (for example, 40 percent share of voice to attain 40 percent market share). Procter & Gamble reportedly uses this method and, in the fast food restaurant category, so do McDonald's and Wendy's.[4]

Share-of-voice budgeting is misleading because it is overly simplistic and likely to be wrong. In the first place. it ignores the possibility, discussed in Chapter 2, of a limit to attainable market share. For example, does anyone seriously believe that a brand with 10 percent market share could increase this to, say, 70 percent simply by spending 70 percent of the category's advertising dollars? Moreover, and somewhat relatedly, share-of-voice budgeting fails to consider the brand's sales response function (explained later in the chapter). For example, a brand with 10 percent share of voice that increased it to 20 percent might show a large, medium, small, or zero gain in market share depending on how its sales respond to increased advertising, that is, depending on its current position on its sales response curve for the quality of advertising it is currently doing. Far from being a solution, share-of-voice budgeting hides the problem of how best to maintain, increase, or maximize market share.

Conclusion   Market share budgeting requires much more complex sales forecasting than budgeting for sales (in isolation) or profit goals. Market share budgeting requires the manager to estimate not only the potential sales effects of the brand's own range of potential advertising budget levels but also how much competitors will spend and how their sales are likely to react. This is the sort of complex conditional judgment that makes the competitor orientation strategy so difficult and yet so challenging.

Quality of Advertising and Promotion Spending (Major Assumption)

The marginal method of budgeting is only concerned with deciding how much to spend on advertising and promotion and not how best to spend it. A little reflection should make it evident that sales results are dependent on the "quality" of spending as well as the quantity. Figure 3.2 shows this in highly simplified form.

Quality of spending is represented by factors such as accurate media placement (one budget may be partly wasted on non-prospects whereas another might be very accurately directed at the target audience) and of course the creative quality of the advertising or promotion itself (a great campaign versus an equally expensive but mediocre one). In fact, "quality" is a consideration all the way up the effects "ladder" to sales, that is, (1) accuracy of *exposure,* (2) correctness of *processing* of the ad or promotion offer, (3) attainment and appropriateness of *communication effects,* and (4) concentration on the right *target audience action.*

Quality considerations are much better addressed in the *task method* of budgeting, which arrives at an estimate of how best to spend the money in media given an expected creative (effectiveness) level of the campaign.

Quality of spending is a complicated phenomenon that we will address more fully under media strategy. It involves both media plan quality and creative quality in interaction. Briefly, low creative quality means a low incidence of conversion of target audience individuals from exposure to action; thus, the media plan will have to reach more prospects than with high quality creative to yield the same level of sales. However, media plan quality also depends on the frequency factor; creative executions, of any degree of quality, can be "choked" by too little frequency. Quality of spending, and therefore the quality of the campaign overall, depends both on media plan quality and creative quality.

The marginal method makes the *major assumption* that the advertising and promotion budget will be spent in a way that maximizes effectiveness—it holds quality of spending constant. As the *actual* quality of the campaign becomes revealed during its implementation, the overall budget may be revised radically downward or upward, as many advertising agencies have discovered to their annoyance or joy.

MEASURES OF ADVERTISING'S CONTRIBUTION

Budgeting involves making an estimate of advertising's contribution to sales for the forthcoming planning period. The estimate is essentially a conditional

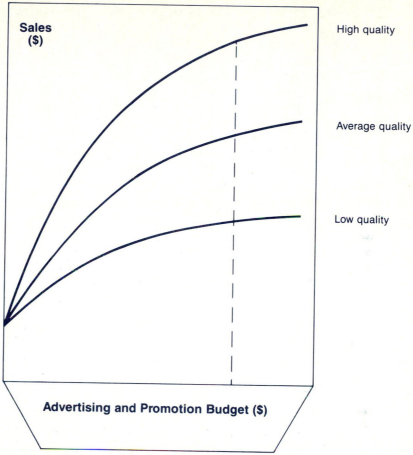

FIGURE 3.2   Sales effects of the same quantity of spending but different "quality" of spending. Although not shown in this simplified diagram, quality differences may occur all the way through the buyer response sequence leading to sales.

sales forecast: if we spend this much on advertising (including promotion) in 19XX, what sales level can we expect to achieve? As noted, a sales forecast of this type also is required when budgeting for market share (since sales are part of the market share calculation) or for profit (since profit is based on sales).

Three Ways to Measure Advertising's Contribution

There are three principal ways to estimate advertising's contribution to sales:

1 Marketplace experiments
2 Statistical projection
3 Management judgment

The three types of measures are ranked above in terms of cost and ease of application. All involve management judgment to some degree, but the third relies solely on it.

Other Factors Affecting Sales   Before describing the three contribution measures, it is worthwhile to review the major factors—beside advertising and promotion—that can affect sales. These have been mentioned in the two previous chapters and can be summarized conveniently here:

1 Product category trends
2 Brand competition and market structure
3 Carryover from previous periods' advertising and promotion (if any)
4 Other marketing inputs including
    a Product (quality, packaging, service)
    b Price
    c Distribution
    d Personal selling

The three contribution measures differ in the way in which these "other factors" are handled in assessing advertising's contribution relative to them, as outlined next.

Marketplace Experiments

The ideal way to estimate advertising's contribution to sales is to conduct a marketplace experiment or "investment spending" test. In this procedure, a set of typical and closely matched markets is selected for different levels of advertising spending (representing trial budget levels). Then the actual sales result in each is compared. The expenditure level that exhibits the highest sales, market share, or profit, depending on the firm's objectives, is then used as the budget for the total market.

Advantages   The experimental method controls for "other factors" (see list above) through randomization. If the trial budget levels are assigned randomly to markets, we can assume that other factors will average out, leaving advertising spending as the differentiating causal factor. Even if the assignment is not entirely random, differences in other factors can often be post-controlled statistically (for example, by analysis of covariance) thus allowing for a cleaner interpretation of the experimental results.

Disadvantages   Although marketplace experiments are the most valid way to estimate advertising's contribution to sales, they have several disadvantages that deter their widespread use: (1) cost—the best experiments use multiple markets for each spending level so as to better control for other factors, a step which few companies can afford and where risky compromises are often made; (2) time—the firm has to wait for the experimental results before setting the budget (hence experiments are often conducted for new brands while they are in test markets) and it becomes tempting to compromise on the length and thus the reliability of the experiment; (3) conservatism—many companies are reluctant to test extreme conditions, such as zero advertising or promotion, for fear of permanent or lasting damage to sales in those areas; (4) sabotage—competitors often realize when a test is being conducted and may try to sabotage it by altering their own spending or marketing inputs, thus "de-randomizing" the other factors in the experiment and making the results questionable.

An important but partial exception to the general disadvantages of market-place experiments is represented by the recent emergence of UPC scanner test markets (for example, Information Resources, Inc.'s BehaviorScan service, Burke's Adtel, or Nielsen's TestSight). Scanner test markets are a partial exception because, presently, they can be used only for consumer food or drug outlet products and for testing TV budgets rather than other types of media spending. By operating in test market areas wired for cable TV, the test service can select households at random, intercept cable transmissions, deliver different levels of a TV campaign to different households, and observe the effects of purchase through households' use of scanner ID cards at area food and drug outlets.

Although still in its infancy, the scanner test market measure potentially overcomes the first and third disadvantages above, but still is subject to the others, namely, delay and sabotage. The limitation to testing only TV advertising budgets for frequently purchased supermarket or drugstore products, as noted, precludes many advertisers from being able to use this method to set budgets.

Statistical Projection

For established brands, statistical projection of previous advertising-to-sales relationships to the forthcoming planning period can be an economical alternative to marketplace experiments. In this procedure, historical spending levels and historical sales levels are compared over time (years, quarters, or months) and a statistical technique (most often regression analysis) is used to compute the relationship between the two. The size of the relationship provides an estimate for determining the advertising budget size in relation to expected sales.

Advantages   Statistical projection controls for other factors statistically rather than experimentally, although they could be regarded as inputs to an "experiment over time" if their levels have been varied. A multiple regression equation can be developed, for example, which includes statistics on these other variables, such as distribution coverage and price levels, in addition to advertising and promotion. Regression techniques should be based on models which estimate not only within-period relationships but also carryover effects from previous periods.

Disadvantages   There are two main disadvantages of statistical projection techniques like regression analysis: (1) established brands only—obviously for new brands there are no historical advertising or sales trends from which to project; (2) assumed continuity—statistical projections assume that conditions that applied in the past periods will continue into the current budgeting period so that the relationship between advertising and sales will stay the same. This is a risky assumption if the market is volatile, with new brands entering or old brands leaving; however, the regression prediction can be modified by management judgment to take account of expected changes in market conditions.

Management Judgment

Advertising's contribution to sales can be estimated in all circumstances by using management judgment. This is the easiest and least expensive method (and thus the most widely used) but it also tends to be the least accurate.[5] There are three ways to improve the accuracy of management judgment:

1 Study others' results. The diligent manager should be constantly on the lookout for published studies, especially in the same or related product categories, of experiments and statistical analyses which report others' budgeting experiences.

2 Use graphical estimates. Although the A/S ratio is a "number" representing the budget against expected year-end sales, the manager should think instead of the A/S relationship as a "process" by sketching the estimated sales curve and considering its form as it "responds" to advertising and other inputs (graphical computer displays facilitate this considerably).

3 Use aggregated forecasts (as explained below).

Aggregated Forecasts   Managers' estimates of expected sales (or any other marketing or advertising outcome) can be improved considerably by using an aggregated forecast. Armstrong[6] has made an extensive study of the accuracy of the management judgment method of forecasting. The list below is a summary of his findings adapted to the advertising budgeting decision:

1 *Use 5 to 10 judges to make the forecasts.* You need 5 or 6 judges before errors start "canceling" and a more accurate forecast emerges, but beyond 10 judges the accuracy of forecasts does not improve much.

2 *The judges need not be advertising experts.* Surprising as it may seem, experts do no better than general managers in terms of forecast accuracy; anyone who is basically familiar with the product and the market can act as a judge.

3 *Provide the judges with a short list of the main factors affecting sales.* Better solutions to the complex task of sales forecasting emerge when the problem is broken into smaller components; however, only a short list should be used because judges will only rely on a small amount of information even if more is provided (our list earlier would be a good start: product category trends, brand competition and market structure, other marketing inputs, and the advertising carryover possibility).

4 *Remind the judges of potential interactions.* Experimental and statistical projection methods control for other factors affecting sales, through randomization and statistical analysis, respectively; in the management judgment method, managers must allow for or control for these other factors mentally. The judges should therefore be reminded that the factors in the list may be interdependent—particularly other marketing inputs.

5 *Obtain independent estimates and then average them to yield an aggregate forecast.* Do not use group discussion or feedback methods such as Delphi; these lead to group biases which destroy the random canceling effect and lead to a less accurate forecast. The simple average of independent estimates is best.

USING MANAGEMENT JUDGMENT TO SET THE BUDGET

Most companies will use management judgment to set the overall advertising budget. They should use the aggregate forecast procedure described above—but what should they actually be forecasting? The answer: the sales response function.

Estimating the Sales Response Function

The graphs in Figures 3.1 and 3.2 were examples—highly generalized—of sales response functions. These "sales curves" indicate how sales are expected to respond to various advertising budget amounts.

Experience in applying management judgments as inputs to mathematical models of budgeting[7] has shown that the sales response function for virtually any product (new or established) can be estimated reasonably well by asking managers to answer five questions:

1 What is the *current* level of advertising expenditure (established brand)? Or the *most likely* level of advertising expenditure (new brand)? ($A_{current}$)

2 What would sales be if advertising expenditure were *zero*? (A_0)

3 What would *maximum* sales be if you could spend as much as you wished on advertising and what would this expenditure have to be? (A_{max})

4 What would sales be if the current (or most likely) level of advertising were *halved*? ($A_{-50\%}$)

5 What would sales be if the current (or most likely) level of advertising were *increased* half as much again? ($A_{+50\%}$)

The sales levels estimated in response to these five questions allow five points on the sales response function to be plotted (Figure 3.3). Each point on the graph represents the average of all managers' sales forecasts for the five advertising budget amounts.

Of course, the sales response "curve" may not look exactly like the one shown in the figure (S-shaped). It may, for instance, be concave as in the first figure in this chapter (like the top part of an S). Similarly, for a new brand, sales may be estimated at zero with zero advertising; or, for an established brand, current advertising may be estimated as being above the maximum

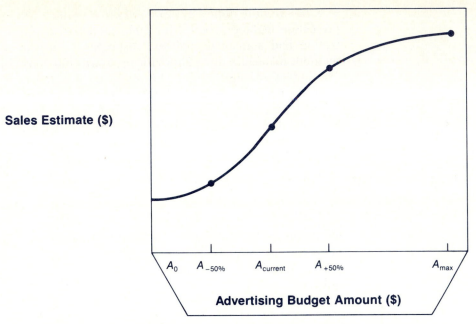

Sales Estimate ($)

A_0 $A_{-50\%}$ $A_{current}$ $A_{+50\%}$ A_{max}

Advertising Budget Amount ($)

FIGURE 3.3   Sales response function for advertising budget levels estimated from the "Five Questions" procedure.

spending needed to produce maximum sales. These situations are easily shown graphically.

The "Five Questions" procedure will yield enough data points to derive the brand's sales response function reasonably well. Whereas it might be contended that the resulting graph is "only based on judgment," it must be realized that it reflects managers' assumptions about reality. Each manager implicitly uses (his or her version of) this curve, often unknowingly, when making advertising budget recommendations. The questioning procedure simply makes the judgments explicit.

Deciding on the Budget

If the brand is being budgeted to maximize sales, the manager selects as the budget level the advertising amount that corresponds (on the bottom axis) with maximum sales (A_{max}). No more than this should be spent.

If the brand is being budgeted to maximize market share, the manager usually would *also* select A_{max}. Why? Because, in estimating the sales response of our brand to advertising, and if the judges used the "short list" of other factors that can affect sales as recommended above, then the influence of competing brands is most likely *already represented* in the sales response function. Alternatively, if market share is indeed the most important goal, as it may be for a new brand in a new product category, then managers could be asked the five questions in relation to market share rather than sales. This would produce an estimated *market share response function*. A_{max} *for* the market share maximum would be selected as the appropriate budget level.

If the brand is being budgeted to maximize profit, the sales response function should be estimated first, then the "cost of goods sold" (unit variable cost $\times$ volume), any additional fixed costs (such as a new factory to produce enough products), *and* the advertising cost should be subtracted out. Direct estimate of a "profit response function" is too difficult. The profit-maximizing budget is best derived by computation from the sales response function.

A Quick Note on Some Bad Budgeting Methods

Traditionally, overall advertising and promotion budgets are not set by the marginal method. (They should be. It's not too hard, as we've tried to illustrate in this chapter.) Instead, the budget is established by some other popular rule-of-thumb.

Among the more common of these rules-of-thumb are the percent-of-last-year's-sales method, the percent-of-this-year's-expected-sales method, and the competitive-parity method. Each of these methods is wrong and only by accident could they arrive at an appropriate budget.[8] The reason: They are all *static* methods. None of them takes into account how sales respond *dynamically* to different advertising levels.

A microcosm of the static methods' error is seen in the common practice of deciding on advertising allocations to various geographic markets[9] in relation to each market's Category Development Index (CDI) or Brand Development Index (BDI). CDI indicates the level of product category sales in the market and BDI indicates the level of our brand's sales in each market relative to the average for all brands.

CDI and BDI are static. CDI gives no clue as to where an increase in our brand's sales would be most likely to occur: A high CDI market might be full of strong competing brands, whereas a low CDI market might be hopeless for any brand. Nor does BDI tell us what level of advertising to use: a high BDI market, for instance, might require less advertising if we're advertising beyond A_{max} there, or more advertising if we are in fact somewhere below A_{max} on the sales response function for that market. You just can't tell.

Managers should use the marginal method to set the overall advertising and promotion budget, not rules-of-thumb.

SUMMARY

This chapter has decribed the recommended procedure for setting the overall budget for advertising and promotion, using the marginal method. Later we will see how to allocate the budget (and revise it if this seems necessary), using the task method.

The marginal method requires the manager to estimate the changes in sales that would result from a series of hypothetical changes (up or down) in advertising expenditure. (It is easiest to think in terms of "advertising" expenditure first, then break this down into advertising and promotion specifically during the budget allocation later.) The manager can then choose a budget level that is expected to maximize sales.

With some simple computations from the sales figures, the manager can alternatively choose a budget level that is expected to maximize market share (relative sales), or to maximize profit (roughly, sales minus costs). These three alternative budget levels will very likely differ, so the manager uses the one that fits the firm's marketing objectives for the brand.

Attention was given to the increasingly common practice of "share-of-voice" budgeting, which sets advertising spending proportional to the brand's desired market share. This method of budgeting is wrong. It ignores the possibility of limits to market share and it postulates an overly simplistic linear increasing sales response for an increase in the brand's advertising expenditure, for all brands in the market. Market share budgeting is much more complex than this. Also, market share budgeting is but one alternative; more important, in most cases, is budgeting to maximize profit.

There are three measures that can be employed in conjunction with the marginal method to estimate advertising's contribution to sales and thus to set the overall advertising and promotion budget: marketplace experiments, if you have the resources; statistical projection, but this measure cannot be used for new brands; and management judgment, which is the most widely used measure. Management judgment can be improved by using the aggregated forecast procedure outlined in the chapter.

Management judgment can be used with the marginal method to estimate the brand's sales response function and thereby set an appropriate budget. Sales response functions show how sales respond dynamically to alternative advertising budget levels. Other common rule-of-thumb budgeting methods are static, not dynamic, and should not be used.

NOTES

1 See P. Kotler, *Marketing Management: Analysis, Planning, and Control,* Englewood Cliffs, NJ: Prentice-Hall, 1980, pp. 251–253 for a discussion of costs.
2 BRANDAID, one of the more sophisticated mathematical models that can be used to set budgets for each input in the marketing mix, handles interactions between distribution, pricing, advertising, and promotion by indexing the current or, for a new product, expected level of spending for each input at 1.0 and then multiplying the indices to allow for the interactions. For example, advertising expenditure at 1.5 times the current level, combined with promotion expenditure at 1.2 times the current level, is expected to generate $1.5 \times 1.2 = 1.8$ times the current level of sales. The BRANDAID model, developed by J.D.C. Little (see note 5) is straightforwardly explained in G.L. Lilien and P. Kotler, *Marketing Decision Making: A Model-Building Approach,* New York: Harper & Row, 1983, chap. 18.
3 R.L. Ackoff and J.R. Emshoff, Advertising research at Anheuser-Busch, Inc. (1963–1968), *Sloan Management Review,* Winter, 1975, 1–15.
4 M.L. King, "Wendy's new management cooks up plans for growth and diversification," *The Wall Street Journal,* March 27, 1981, p. 34.

5 There are some very sophisticated management judgment procedures, using inter-active computer-aided models, that claim high accuracy. The best known of these models is BRANDAID, developed by J.D.C. Little [see *Operations Research,* 1975, *23* (3), 628–673]. General descriptions of these models are given in J.D.C. Little, Decision support systems for marketing managers, *Journal of Marketing,* 1979, *43* (3), 9–27, and their accuracy is discussed in J.D.C. Little and L.M. Lodish, Commentary on "Judgment based marketing decision models," *Journal of Marketing,* 1981, *45* (4), 24–29.

6 J.S. Armstrong, *Long-Range Forecasting: From Crystal Ball to Computer,* (2nd ed.) New York: Wiley-Interscience, 1985.

7 The "Five Questions" approach was developed by Professor Len Lodish of the Wharton School. It was first used in his CALLPLAN model of sales force allocation and later in Little's BRANDAID model (L.M. Lodish, personal communication). The approach has been slightly adapted for our purpose.

8 L.M. Lodish, *Advertising and Promotion: Vaguely Right or Precisely Wrong?* New York: Oxford University Press, 1986.

9 We treat geographic allocations by our version of the *task* method in media strategy. See Part Seven.

DISCUSSION QUESTIONS

3.1 What additional information would you need in order to evaluate the following two proposed advertising budgets? *Hint:* Lots of additional information (this question requires a comprehensive answer).

	Advertising budget ($ mill)	Expected sales ($ mill)	A/S ratio (%)
Company A	10	67	15
Company B	10	50	20

3.2 Explain "share-of-voice" budgeting in your own words and then describe its problems.

3.3 What major assumption does the marginal method of budgeting make? Illustrate with brands' advertising from a product category of your own choosing.

3.4 When should you use the marginal method of budgeting and when should you use the task method? Explain your answer clearly.

3.5 Assume that you have plenty of money to spend on research. Outline and explain an "investment spending" experiment designed to help set a sales-maximizing advertising budget for Diet Pepsi.

3.6 Assume that American Express currently is spending $50 million on advertising for Green Card and that current sales are $5000 million annually. In a team of five classmates, go through Armstrong's procedure and the "Five Questions" procedure and estimate the sales response function for Green Card. What should the advertising budget amount be, and why?

FURTHER READING

Armstrong, J.S. *Long-Range Forecasting: From Crystal Ball to Computer,* (2nd ed.) New York: Wiley-Interscience, 1985.

The easiest-to-read book on forecasting (including management judgment) ever written. Worthwhile shelf reference for any manager who has to make sales forecasts.

Farris, P. and Albion, M.S. Determinants of the advertising-to-sales ratio. *Journal of Advertising Research,* 1981, *21* (1), 19–27.

Identifies 11, sometimes overlapping, market conditions that affect advertising budgets (A/S ratios) in practice. Useful to compare their empirical findings and explanations with our shorter list of reasons why budgets should vary according to sales, market share, and profit objectives.

Simon, J.L. and Arndt, J. The shape of the advertising response function. *Journal of Advertising Research,* 1980, *20* (4), 11–28.

Review and discussion of numerous studies relating advertising to sales which concludes that the sales curve—in the typical operating range facing the manager—is not S-shaped (as in our "classical" Figure 2.1 or Figure 3.3 but rather is "little r-shaped" with sales increasing but at a diminishing rate until a peak or asymptote is reached (as in our Figures 3.1 and 3.2).

Lodish, L.M. *Advertising and Promotion: Vaguely Right or Precisely Wrong?* New York: Oxford University Press, 1986.

Written mainly for chief executives of companies, this book contains the best available discussion of how to set the overall advertising budget. As the author demonstrates, it's better to be vaguely right with the marginal method than to be precisely wrong with some other method.

PART **THREE**

TARGET AUDIENCE
ACTION OBJECTIVES

CHAPTER 4

TARGET AUDIENCE
SELECTION AND ACTION
OBJECTIVES

Where do additional sales (step 5) come from? They come from the purchase actions of individual buyers who, for advertising and promotion, comprise the target audience (step 4). This chapter describes the four general target audience options for advertising and promotion and the behavioral action objectives for each. After reading it you should:

- Know the nature of the four *prospective* target audiences for advertising and promotion and how one audience is selected as the *actual* target audience for a particular advertising or promotion campaign
- Understand trial and usage behaviors as action objectives and know to which target audiences they apply
- Appreciate the difference between purchase and purchase-related action objectives for trade and consumer target audiences
- Know how to measure these behaviors

FOUR BUYER GROUPS AS SOURCES OF SALES

In Chapter 3 we left the manager with sales objectives for the brand (which alternatively may be translated into market share objectives). To generate sales, obviously, people have to buy the brand. But which prospective buyers represent the best sales potential?

To determine which prospective buyers represent the best sales potential, it is useful to think of "our" sales as being dependent on product category sales as well as on our brand's performance in that category. We can see that our brand potentially could be purchased by any of four buyer groups:

1 New category users (NCU) who enter the category by buying our brand

2 Brand loyals (BL) who regularly buy our brand

3 Brand switchers (BS) who may occasionally buy our brand or could be induced to do so

4 Other-brand loyals (OBL) who regularly buy a brand other than ours

These potential buyer groups are shown schematically in Figure 4.1. Brand loyals are the "core" of our sales. Brand switchers are the "fringe" of our sales—when they include our brand in their brand-switching behavior. Sales also may be gained from attracting new category users to our brand and—an often difficult task—by drawing loyal customers away from other brands.

A good way to understand the four groups is to think of a well-known brand such as Maxwell House Instant Coffee. How would you classify yourself? You may be: (1) a non-category user who doesn't like instant coffee; (2) a loyal Maxwell House drinker who rarely drinks any other brand of instant coffee; (3) a brand switcher who drinks Maxwell House but also Nescafé or other brands; or (4) an other-brand loyal who primarily drinks some other brand but not Maxwell House.

FIGURE 4.1   Four buyer groups as sources of sales.

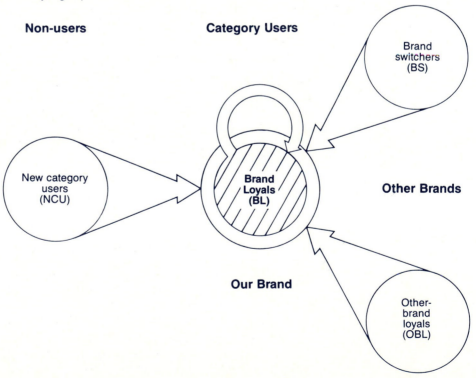

Brand Loyalty Is the Key

Our classification of buyer groups relies heavily on the phenomenon of brand loyalty. Brand loyalty can be defined as regular (repeat) purchase of the brand based on a favorable price- and promotion-resistant attitude toward it. Brand loyalty is therefore an attitudinal and behavioral concept.[1]

Why do we introduce attitudes here when our focus in this chapter is on buyer behavior? The answer is that the would-be buyer's attitude has to be known in addition to behavior in order to assess sales potential. Consider the following:

1 *New category users* may or may not represent good sales potential depending on their attitude toward the *category* and not just their attitude toward our brand. Note that behavior is not sufficient to assess the NCU's sales potential because those with favorable attitudes toward the category are no different behaviorally from those with neutral or negative attitudes (they all are non-buyers). We have to know their attitudes in order to assess NCU's sales potential.

2 *Brand loyals* already have a strongly favorable attitude toward our brand and are the core of our current and future expected sales. They may not, however, represent good potential for *increased* sales beyond the rate at which they are buying now.

3 *Brand switchers,* provided that they include our brand in their switching behavior, presumably have at least a moderately favorable attitude toward our brand; otherwise they would not buy it at all. We have to know their attitudes to see if they could be made loyal or whether they will always be just moderately favorable, attracted to our brand for variety or whenever it offers a promotion.

4 *Other-brand loyals* usually have the least sales potential because they are satisfied with, and are therefore committed attitudinally to, another brand. Although their behavior looks more promising than that of the NCU because they already purchase within the category, the attitudes of OBL's, which often are decidedly neutral or more often actively negative toward us, may make them our worst prospects.[2]

Sales Potential and the Product Life Cycle

The sales potential of the four buyer groups depends on market stages in the product life cycle (Figure 4.2). Here we relate sales strategy to our earlier discussion of market stages from Chapter 1.

1 In *growing* markets (introductory and growth stages of the product life cycle):

    a NCU's represent good sales potential because they are a larger group during these early stages and do not have strongly committed category and brand attitudes.

    b BL's are, as always, our mainstay; we want to develop brand loyalty as quickly and as widely as possible.

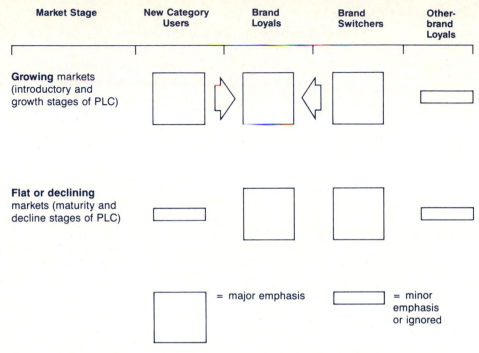

FIGURE 4.2   Sales strategy according to market stages in the product life cycle. All buyer groups except other-brand loyals usually are good prospects in growing markets. But in slowing markets the sales potential usually is reduced to two groups: brand loyals and brand switchers.

    c BS's also represent good sales potential in the early stages of the product life cycle because much of their brand switching may be "exploratory."[3] Many of the early brand switchers represent potential brand loyals, although others will remain relatively permanent switchers or become loyal to other brands.

    d OBL's still have some sales potential if they have not yet tried our brand, but almost zero sales potential if they have tried it and become loyal to another brand.

  2 In *flat or declining* markets (mature and decline stages of the product life cycle):

    a NCU's represent poor sales potential because most NCU's by now are aware of the product category and have decided, attitudinally, not to buy any brand in that category.

    b BL's, again, are our mainstay but not for an increased rate of sales unless we can find ways to increase their usage capacity.

    c BS's, by now, have relatively fixed attitudes and are "permanent," attitudinally committed brand switchers who, if they include our brand in their switching behavior, are moderately favorable toward it but do not see it as their first choice—they buy it for variety or when it is offered with a promotion. Depending on our brand's emphasis on promotion relative to advertising, BS's may nevertheless represent good sales potential.

d OBL's are essentially a "write-off" for us in the later stages of the product life cycle because nothing short of a massively expensive promotion would overcome their attitudinal commitment to another brand and probably not even that.

The Hendry "Bathtub" Explanation of Sales Potential

Another way of understanding the relationship between sales potential and the product life cycle is in terms of the Hendry Corporation's concept of a "bathtub" distribution of brand purchase potential.[4] Hendry's researchers noticed that purchase behavior for a brand, far from being distributed according to the familiar normal (bell-shaped) curve—with a few people buying it rarely or never (left rim), most buying it moderately (the bell), and a few people buying it often (right rim)—is usually just the reverse. The purchase distribution typically forms a bathtub shape (Figure 4.3).

Early in the introduction stage of the product life cycle [panel (a)] the "bathtub" will be fairly flat. Most consumers are trying the brand for the first time and are not yet loyal, or disloyal, to it. Note also the "shallow" bath, indicating the relatively small number of category users at this stage.

Later in the product life cycle [panel (b)] those early triers will now have had ample opportunity to decide whether or not they like the brand. The brand's buyers will become fairly rapidly "polarized" toward either end of the bathtub: either strongly loyal (buy it regularly) or strongly disloyal (buy it never) with fewer people undecided in the middle as brand switchers (buy it occasionally). The bath is also "fuller," as category users reach a peak.

This emerging bathtub pattern has been observed for hundreds of brands in many different product categories, although so-called "commodity products," by definition, would seem to be exceptions.

According to Hendry, whereas the best sales increase potential early in the product life cycle [panel (a) of Figure 4.3] presumably would include all except those near zero loyalty and thus possibly strongly loyal to another brand, later in the product life cycle the best sales increase potential is from those buyers who are 50 to 80 percent loyal [the shaded area in panel (b)].

Another aspect of the bathtub distribution is that the *100 percent loyal* group (the right-hand "height" of the bathwater) may be limited in size by the number of brands in the market. This follows from the concept of structural limits to market share explained in Chapter 2. Some recent research by Raj suggests that the "normal" incidence of brand loyals (those who say they bought solely this brand over the past year as a percentage of all *buyers* of the brand) by number of brands in the market should be: for 3 brands, 70 percent; for 6 brands, 45 percent; for 9 brands, 35 percent; for 12 brands, 32 percent; and for 15 brands, 30 percent; if there are more than 15 brands, a lower limit of 20 percent of consumers solely loyal to the brand is indicated.

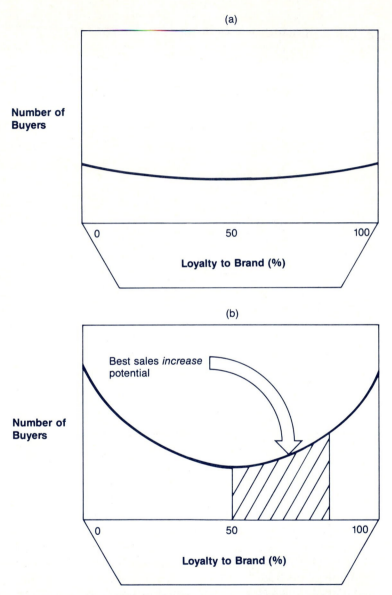

FIGURE 4.3   "Bathtub" distribution of brand loyalty: (a) early market stage; (b) later market stage. *Note*: The Hendry System measures the horizontal axis in terms of repeat purchase (behavioral) rather than brand loyalty (attitudinal as well as behavioral). Reasons for our use of brand loyalty are developed in this chapter.

Please note that these figures do *not* translate to the scale of brand loyalty (bottom axis) used by Hendry.[5] They relate to the right-hand height of the "bathwater."

THE FOUR GROUPS IN MORE DETAIL

The four groups—new category users, brand loyals, brand switchers, and other-brand loyals—are fairly broad and mask a number of specific sub-groups for more refined targeting. We elaborate on these here.

New Category Users

New category users are actually non-users of the product category and, as such, could be referred to as non-category users. We prefer to be optimistic. When targeting NCU's in advertising and promotion, we want them to be *new* category users, which they will be if our campaign works.

The term "new category user" includes several relevant sub-groups: those with a positive attitude toward the *category* (PNCU's); those who are unaware of the category and therefore have no attitude toward it as yet (UNCU's); and those who are negatively disposed toward the category (NNCU's). Positive new category users represent better prospects than negative new category users who have decided against the category. Unaware new category users fall somewhere in between, requiring "educational" advertising to make them aware of the category with the hope that their category attitude will become positive.

Brand Loyals

As Jacoby and Chestnut[6] and others have observed, it is possible for a buyer to be attitudinally and behaviorally loyal to more than one brand (though typically two or three brands at most). Multi-brand loyalty, of course, reduces sales to our brand loyals, so it is worth distinguishing from single-brand loyalty.

In brand attitude measurement, it is quite common to distinguish those buyers who regard the brand as their "single preferred brand" (single-brand loyals or SBL's) from those who regard it as "one of several preferred brands" (multi-brand loyals or MBL's). Behaviorally, because of out-of-stocks or the occasional desire for variety, purchases will fall a little behind attitude. Single-brand loyals will be devoting about 90 percent of their purchases to the brand, whereas multi-brand loyals will be buying it only about 30 to 80 percent of the time as one of their "regular" brands. Clearly, single-brand loyalty is the manager's desired status for the brand.

Brand Switchers

In most product categories, and especially consumer packaged goods categories, brand switchers are often the largest of the four potential sales groups. The size of the overall brand switcher group also expands during economic recessions. For example, in the lifestyle monitor surveys conducted by the Needham, Harper & Steers advertising agency,[7] the percentage of shoppers who agreed with the statement, "I try to stick with well-known brand names," fell from 76 percent in 1975 (a relatively good year for the economy) to 60 percent in 1980 (a recession year). Note that the 60 percent includes not just brand loyals but also brand switchers who switch between well-known brand names. Thus, generally, the proportion of brand switchers is very high. Similarly, in 1981, two-thirds of supermarket shoppers said they bought mainly according to price, thus indicating (in general) a further high incidence of brand switchers.[8]

There are two factors in terms of which brand switchers can be meaningfully distinguished into sub-groups: the first is related to market stage (of the PLC) and the second to whether their brand switching includes our brand.

Brand Switchers by Market Stage   We have already discussed the "experimental" nature of brand switching during early stages of the product life cycle. It is useful to designate this sub-group of brand switchers as *experimental* brand switchers (EBS). Later in the PLC, most continuing brand switchers are "hard-core" or *routinized* brand switchers (RBS). The EBS sub-group should be vulnerable to advertising and promotion, since their choices are not yet fixed, but the RBS sub-group will be responsive to price-related promotion only.[9]

Brand Switchers Who Include or Exclude Our Brand   Brand switchers, by definition, switch between a number of brands (usually many more than the multi-brand loyals, who focus on two or three preferred brands). Obviously, it makes a big difference whether brand switchers include our brand in their switching repertoire, or whether they exclude it, and switch between other brands. Thus it is worthwhile to distinguish *favorable* brand switchers (FBS), who include our brand, and those who exclude it and do their switching between *other* brands (OBS).

The reader will notice a continuity between multi-brand loyals (MBL's) as described previously and routinized brand switchers (RBS) of the FBS type. Both MBL's and favorable RBS's *buy* our brands, but MBL's buy only one or two other brands *and* have very positive attitudes toward them, whereas favorable RBS's buy three or more other brands and have more "switchable" attitudes toward these and our brand.

Brand switchers therefore can be distinguished into four sub-groups: EOBS (experimental other-brand switchers), EFBS (experimental favorable brand switchers), ROBS (routinized other-brand switchers), and RFBS (routinized favorable brand switchers). The size and importance of the overall-brand switcher group, for advertising and *also* promotion, justifies these sharper distinctions into four sub-groups.

Other-brand Loyals

Other-brand loyals (OBL) need no further categorization by the *number* of other brands to which they are loyal. From our brand's standpoint, it doesn't really matter whether an OBL is loyal to only one other brand or to several other brands, since our brand's share of purchases is zero in both instances. Other-brand loyals (OBL) are quite different from other-brand *switchers* (OBS, both EOBS and ROBS). We have a good chance to win over OBS's, notably with promotion, but very little chance to convert OBL's. The chance would seem to be greater in low-risk product categories but, remember, we are fighting against satisfied purchasers who have "been through the mill" in that category and who will be content to stay with their current choice.

If the manager does decide that other-brand loyals are a worthwhile target, then it is worth making a further division of OBL's into attitudinal sub-groups. (An OBL target might be chosen by a small-share brand in a mature market dominated by one or two large-share brands with many loyal customers. In this situation, there's little option but to attack the large OBL group.)

The OBL's should be distinguished in terms of their attitude toward *our* brand: favorable other-brand loyals (FOBL), neutral other-brand loyals (NOBL), and unfavorable other-brand loyals (UOBL). If the neutral or unfavorable brand attitudes are based on prior trial of our brand, then the second and especially the third sub-groups will be very difficult to convert and in most cases hopeless.

For convenience of reference, the various sub-groups identifiable from the four original prospect groups are summarized in Figure 4.4.

TARGET AUDIENCE SELECTION VIA LEVERAGE

Target Audience Defined

So far, we have avoided the term "target audience" for a very good reason. One or more of the four prospective sales groups (or sub-groups) becomes a *target audience* only when it is decided to direct advertising or promotion at that group (or sub-group).

A prospect group (or sub-group) becomes a *target* for advertising or promotion and, in the communication sense, becomes an *audience* for a particular advertising or promotion campaign. The term "target audience" distinguishes those *to whom a particular advertising or promotion campaign is directed,* whereas the term "target market" (see Chapter 1) refers to those to whom the entire marketing mix is directed. Typically, the target audience will be much smaller than the target market.

To repeat this important principle: The advertiser has a choice of four *prospect* groups (or, in more refined targeting, more numerous but smaller *prospect* sub-groups) to which to direct an advertising or promotion campaign. Usually only one prospect group (or two or three related prospect sub-groups) will be chosen as the *target audience* for a particular campaign.

Selecting a Target Audience via Leverage

Advertising or promotion directed to a particular prospect group must also consider the *cost* as well as the expected return. Another way of saying this is that each prospect groups's potential should be evaluated on the basis of its

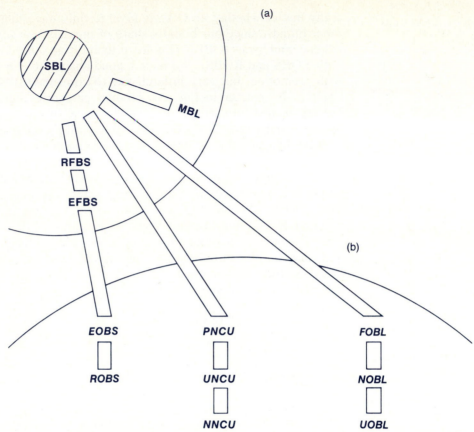

FIGURE 4.4   Sales sub-groups (potential target audiences) summarized. (a) Franchise (buying our brand); (b) non-franchise (not buying our brand). See text for explanation of each sub-group. The closeness of each sub-group to single-brand loyalty (hatched circle) approximately indicates its leverage.

advertising or promotion *leverage*: the expected increase in our brand's sales ($) divided by the advertising or promotion expenditure ($) we would have to make to get the increased sales.

The astute reader will note the identity between leverage and the marginal method of budgeting. Leverage refers to marginal sales in relation to marginal cost.

Let us consider the likely advertising and promotion leverage of the four general prospect groups:

1 *New category users* (NCU) have *decreasing* leverage as the product category matures. Early in the product life cycle, NCU's offer good sales potential but it also costs a considerable amount to get them to try our brand. By the maturity stage, NCU's have virtually zero leverage because their sales potential is now very small and the cost of converting them to buying a product (category) that they have already decided against would be very high, if indeed they could be converted at all. Leverage for NCU's therefore proceeds from *moderate to low* during the product life cycle.

2 *Brand loyals* (BL) have less and less potential for additional sales as the product life cycle advances—but they are also cheaper to retain. Since they like the brand, it will tend to "sell itself" without heavy additional advertising or promotion. The leverage for BL's is only *moderate* because additional advertising and promotion would not have a large additional sales effect.

3 *Brand switchers* (BS) have the largest potential for additional sales. Early in the product life cycle, when there are many experimental brand switchers, leverage will be high. But it also will be high later, too, in that routinized brand switchers can be held with less advertising (though continued promotion). Overall, the BS group has *high* leverage.

4 *Other brand loyals* (OBL) have very low sales potential. Those who are not fully 100 percent loyal to another brand may be converted temporarily by heavy promotion, but this would be at high cost. The OBL group therefore has *low* leverage.

Leverage also can be calculated for the specific prospect *sub-groups* described previously. Beyond the introduction stage of the PLC, the market becomes increasingly specialized, and it is worth assessing leverage for the specific sub-groups. The calculation method is the same.

Measuring Advertising or Promotion Leverage   Advertising or promotion leverage can be best grasped intuitively on a per capita basis. Think of how much of our brand the average individual in the group is buying now, for example, two packages a month at $2.00 a package = $4.00. Then think of by how much our advertising or promotion campaign could increase the sales level, for example, to three packages a month at $2.00 a package = $6.00; that is, an average per capita increase of $2.00. Overall leverage is then easily calculated by considering the number of buyers in the group and the cost of the advertising or promotion campaign. Thus:

$$\text{Advertising or promotion leverage} = \frac{\text{number of buyers in prospect group} \times \text{average per capita sales increase (\$)}}{\text{cost of advertising or promotion campaign (\$)}}$$

[Note that sales in the top right-hand term would be replaced by unit *profit* contribution if the objective is to increase profit rather than sales or market share (see Chapter 2)].

It should be obvious that we would only consider pursuing a prospect group as a target audience if its advertising or promotion leverage were larger than 1.0, that is, if the return outweighs the cost. The higher the leverage, the more attractive is the prospect group as a target audience.

Another Reminder: Money versus Strategy   As we emphasized in Chapter 3's discussion of budgeting, it is all too easy to fall into the trap of thinking that you can "buy" customers. Inexperienced business students nearly always think that if a brand increases its advertising or promotion expenditures, then increased sales will automatically follow. This type of thinking ignores the frequent possibility that a *qualitative change in strategy*—not simply more money—may be necessary.

On the one hand, it is true that many brands underspend on advertising and promotion (see The Hendry Corporation's book[10] for examples of this—or ask the opinion of any advertising agency!). On the other hand, a lot of advertising and promotion budgets are increased against poor strategies. Could any amount of money, short of paying people to drive one, have saved the Edsel? The rational general answer is that success is a matter of money as well as strategy.

SPECIFIC TARGET BEHAVIORS

Once the manager has selected the target audience for an advertising or promotion campaign, planning has to be narrowed down to specific target behaviors that form the target audience action objectives (or goals). There are three principal target behaviors:

1 Trial
2 Usage:
  a Repeat
  b Switching

Let us first see how these target behaviors relate to the four sales groups. Figure 4.5 shows the major stages of buyer behavior that a potential buyer can "go through." There are only three actual *behaviors* in the flowchart: trial, repeat, and switching (the latter two are specific forms of usage behavior). We have shown these three types of behavior in the context of sales groups so that you can see which sales groups the behaviors come from.

Trial

Trial is a target behavior for three buyer groups, depending on the sales strategy—new category users, buyers of *other* brands among brand switchers, and other-brand loyals. NCU's must try our brand. For NCU's, brand trial automatically includes category trial. For OBS's and OBL's, brand trial may be a first trial or a re-trial of the brand—the latter if they have tried the brand in the past and rejected it.

The strategy associated with trial is often known as "maximizing penetration" of the brand in the market, with the behavioral objective of getting more people to try it.

Examples Trial is a relevant buyer behavior objective for all types of products. For many expensive products (for example, some forms of insurance) and also fad products (for example, pet rocks), trial may be the sole objective, because most people buy once and never make a repeat purchase. Some

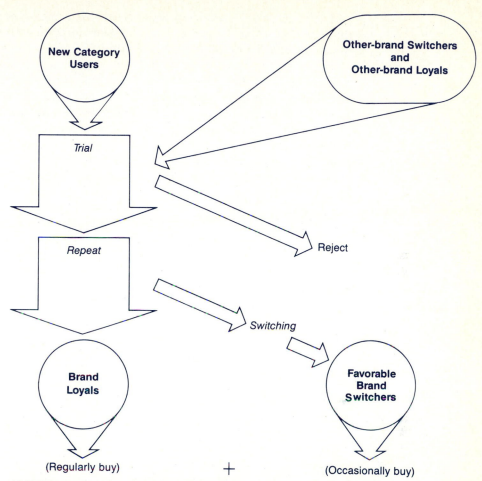

FIGURE 4.5   Target behaviors (italics) for each prospective target audience.

examples of trial: About 25 percent of households have bought microwave ovens; about 50 percent of adults have tried frozen pizza; surprisingly, only about 40 percent of adults have tried yogurt, and only 30 percent of adults classify themselves as users of the yogurt category.

Usage: (a) Repeat

Brand triers have two options: they can repeat, that is, buy our brand again, or they can reject our brand. These rejectors may drop out of the category altogether; or they may become loyal to another brand; or they may become switchers who do not include our brand. The rejectors therefore join the NCU or OBL groups or the OBS sub-group of brand switchers. To win them back, we would have to induce them to re-try the brand. But our focus here is on triers who repeat-purchase our brand.

The strategy associated with repeat purchase is often known as "maximizing the repeat rate" of the brand, with the behavioral objective of getting current buyers to buy the brand more frequently.

Examples   With the rare exceptions of one-time purchases, the success of all products depends on repeat purchase following trial. The appropriate time frame for calculating *rate* of repeat purchase will vary according to the nature of the product. For example, automobiles have a long interval between purchases whereas detergents have a relatively short interval between purchases. Rate includes not just frequency of purchase but also quantity purchased per occasion, which may vary with user characteristics (for example, larger families) and promotion activities (for example, bonus pack offers).

Managers can gauge how well their brand is doing by comparing its repeat rate with that of the product category as a whole—the rate for the "average" brand, statistically, in the category. Some examples: The average shopper buys toothpaste every 72 days or about once every 2 months; margarine every 36 days or about once a month; and instant coffee once every 21 days or about every 3 weeks.

Usage: (b) Switching

Following an initial repeat purchase or two, the manager now needs to consider the attitude-and-behavior concept of brand loyalty. This is because repeat purchase could be due either to a genuine preference for the brand (brand loyalty); or to a more temporary and circumstantial choice (brand switching) because of, for example, a low price or a promotion offer, or the unavailability of better alternatives.

The strategy associated with brand switching is to "maximize switching-in" (optimally by converting switchers to become brand loyals although this is not always possible) and to "minimize switching-out."

Examples   Almost everyone becomes a brand switcher eventually, except for expensive one-time purchases or fad products. For example, in the course of a 3-year period, about one in five adults will have changed banks. Brand switching for supermarket products is much higher, due to out-of-stocks, emergency trips to convenience stores, and occasional variety seeking.[11] This is why brand loyalty is so important: It encourages repeat purchase and low switching-out in spite of these external circumstances.

Most of the published examples of brand switching are for supermarket products. Nielsen[12] reports that out-of-stocks occur about three times in every 100 choices the typical shopper makes. When confronted with an out-of-stock on their preferred brand, 42 percent of shoppers will wait or shop elsewhere, presumably because of attitudinal brand loyalty, while 58 percent will switch brands, right then and there.

British data compiled by Ehrenberg[13] indicate that, for buyers of the average supermarket item, 15 percent will brand switch within a 1-week interval, 70 percent over 6 months, and 90 percent by the end of a year. Looked at another way, only 10 percent of the average supermarket brand's shoppers are "perfectly" loyal over the course of a year.

It has also been found that brand switching depends on the nature of the product. Products that involve real or imagined physiological consequences, such as coffee, cigarettes, over-the-counter drugs, and vitamins, tend to have high brand loyalty and very low brand switching.[14] Other products seem to involve little personal commitment and characteristically exhibit a high degree of brand switching. Examples include facial tissues and aluminum foil.

Advertising and promotion may be able to induce temporary brand switching in the form of trial of an alternative brand. But whether the switching is sustained in the form of high repeat purchase is mainly dependent on the nature of the product and the buyer's attitude toward the brand.

Relationship of Repeat and Switching to Sales and Market Share Objectives

Repeat and switching as behavioral action objectives (beyond trial) are related to the brand's marketing objectives of sales "versus" market share as discussed in Chapter 2:

1 Sales objectives (regardless of competitive sales) imply a repeat purchase emphasis whereby the purpose is to maximize the rate (and quantity) of our brand's purchase.

2 Market share objectives (our sales versus competitors' sales) imply a brand-switching emphasis—the target behavior is not just repeat purchase but rather repeat purchase due to switching from competitors' brands to maximize our *share* of purchases.

Speed of Response

The main behavioral action objectives are trial, repeat, and switching, with choice between the latter two depending on a sales orientation or a market share orientation. Another factor, speed of response, often accompanies these target behaviors.

Most often a *fast* response to advertising and promotion is desired. For example, from Chapter 2, both the experience-curve concept and the Hendry "bathtub" polarization process suggest that fast trial and repeat behavior are important when the firm and its competitors are launching entries into a new product category. Also, there may be exclusive distribution to be gained from speed of entry. At the other end of the product life cycle, or more generally, when trying to clear merchandise from stock, speed of exit becomes a relevant objective.

Sometimes, however, a *slow* response may be desired when there are benefits to be gained from extended payments and interest rates. Loans and mortgages would be examples where advertising and promotion often emphasize "years to pay." Sometimes, slower buyer behavior can benefit the firm financially.

ACTION OBJECTIVES FOR EACH TARGET AUDIENCE

It is useful at this point to identify the behavioral action objectives likely to be set for each of the potential target audiences. Table 4.1 identifies the likely behavioral action objectives for the specific sub-groups to whom advertising and promotion may potentially be directed. The table is self-explanatory.

Purchase and Purchase-Related Behaviors for Trade and Consumer Target Audiences

So far, we have focused on *purchase* behaviors as action objectives. Now we need to add more precision by realizing that advertising or promotion campaigns may have as action objectives *purchase-related* behaviors that lead to purchase.

Furthermore, nearly every advertising or promotion campaign has two types of "customers" who must be considered: trade (distributors and retailers) and consumers. Thus we can specify *trade behaviors* and *consumer behaviors* that a campaign may be designed to address.

This expanded consideration of action objectives is summarized in Table 4.2 and discussed next.

Trade behaviors   Before consumers can purchase the item, the item has to be accepted by the trade. In Table 4.2, trade acceptance has been labeled as "purchase" even though purchase may not be an accurate description, as with goods consigned to the trade. Trade acceptance, in turn, can be measured in

TABLE 4-1   ACTION OBJECTIVES FOR SPECIFIC TARGET AUDIENCES

Target audience	Action objectives
1 Negative new category users (NNCU)	Trial (including category trial) or re-trial (including category re-trial)
2 Unaware new category users (UNCU)	Trial (including category trial)
3 Positive new category users (PNCU)	Trial (including category trial)
4 Single-brand loyals (SBL)	Repeat
5 Multi-brand loyals (MBL)	Switching-in
6 Experimental other-brand switchers (EOBS)	Trial
7 Experimental favorable brand switchers (EFBS)	Repeat
8 Routinized other-brand switchers (ROBS)	Trial (or re-trial)
9 Routinized favorable brand switchers (RFBS)	Switching-in
10 Favorable other-brand loyals (FOBL)	Trial (or re-trial)
11 Neutral other-brand loyals (NOBL)	Trial (or re-trial)
12 Unfavorable other-brand loyals (UOBL)	Trial (or re-trial)

TABLE 4-2 PURCHASE AND PURCHASE-RELATED BEHAVIORS: TRADE AND CONSUMER TARGETS

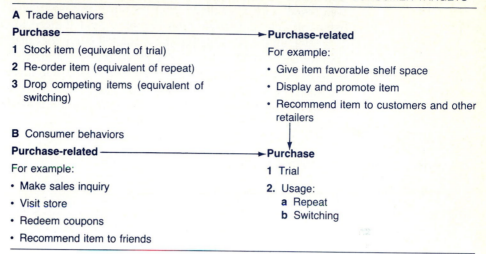

A Trade behaviors

Purchase ——————————————————→ **Purchase-related**

1 Stock item (equivalent of trial) For example:

2 Re-order item (equivalent of repeat) • Give item favorable shelf space

3 Drop competing items (equivalent of switching) • Display and promote item

  • Recommend item to customers and other retailers

B Consumer behaviors

Purchase-related ——————————————————→ **Purchase**

For example: **1** Trial

• Make sales inquiry **2.** Usage:

• Visit store   **a** Repeat

• Redeem coupons   **b** Switching

• Recommend item to friends

terms of our basic three buyer behaviors: trade trial (stocking the item in the first place), trade repeat (re-ordering the item), and trade switching (displacing competing items).

Usually, though, the marketer is interested not merely in trade acceptance but also in various purchase-related trade behaviors that help to sell the product by making it more available and salient to customers. The table lists some of these purchase-related behaviors, such as shelf space and special displays, for which advertising and promotion (to the trade) frequently play an important role. These purchase-related trade behaviors follow trade acceptance.

Consumer Behaviors For consumers, most of the important purchase-related behaviors precede purchase or precede repeat purchase. Table 4.2 shows some examples. Many advertisements for expensive products and services first invite a sales inquiry to the seller, who then relies on personal selling to close the sale by converting a favorable but tentative consumer attitude into purchase. Industrial products, automobiles, and life insurance are examples of this.

Similarly, retail advertising and retail promotion are often designed to generate store visits; store visits are purchase-related behavior which may lead to purchase of the advertised or promoted item and other items in the store as well. Redeeming coupons and recommending the item to friends via word of mouth are other purchase-related behaviors that may be targeted by advertising and promotion as lead-ins to purchase behavior.

All of these purchase-related behaviors on the part of consumers—as well as the purchase and purchase-related behaviors on the part of the trade—are aimed ultimately at increasing consumer-purchase behaviors (seen by following the arrows in Table 4.2). The marketer and advertiser are always ultimately concerned with consumer trial, repeat, and switching even though other behaviors may constitute vital purchase-related steps along the way.

Listing all the possible purchase-related behaviors that trade and consumers could engage in would not be a very productive exercise. Fortunately, there is an easier way. By constructing a *behavioral sequence model* as shown in the next chapter, the manager can easily identify those purchase-related behaviors and purchase behaviors that are most relevant to the advertising or promotion situation faced by the brand.

MEASURES OF TARGET AUDIENCE ACTION

Individual Buyer Measurement Required

The main realization to keep in mind regarding target audience action measures is that gross sales measures (sales receipts, factory withdrawals, or store audits) are not sufficient. To measure buyer behavior, the measures must be obtained at the *individual buyer level*. Remember, it is individual acts of buyer behavior that aggregate, or add up to, sales and it is the individual act of behavior, such as trial or repeat, that advertising is trying to influence. Sales measures do not tell you whether the observed sales level is due to many triers but few repeaters or few triers but many repeaters, thus obscuring the actual target audience action that has occurred.

Unless the firm has only a small number of buyers, as for some industrial firms and some large contracting firms, it will not be feasible to measure the buyer behavior of every customer. Accordingly, a sample is most often used, with the buyer behavior results from the sample being projected to the larger universe (population) of buyers.

Sample Considerations

Size and representativeness are important considerations when using a sample because these two factors affect the *reliability* or measurement "precision" of the results.

1 The *size* of the sample affects the degree of precision with which the sample results can be projected. Regardless of the size of the universe or population, the larger the sample, the more "numerically trustworthy" will be the figures. For example, if the sample size is 100 and we observe a trial purchase incidence of 10 percent among the sample, the projected trial rate (with 95 percent confidence) will be 10 ± 6 percent, that is, somewhere between 4 and 16 percent. We would need a sample of over 1000 to get the precision down to ± 1 percent. (Table 4.3 shows these plus-or-minus error rates for various sample sizes.)

2 The *representativeness* of the sample is assumed, but rarely realized, in the above calculations. A truly representative sample would be a randomly drawn sample from the universe or population. But we all know that some

TABLE 4-3 TWO USEFUL "LOOK-UP" TABLES FOR PERCENTAGES BASED ON SAMPLES OF DIFFERENT SIZES (95 PERCENT CONFIDENCE LEVEL)*

(a) Single Percentage

| Sample size | Plus-minus error when the percentage is close to: | | | | |
	10 or 90%	20 or 80%	30 or 70%	40 or 60%	50%
1000	2	2	3	3	3
500	3	4	4	4	4
250	4	5	6	6	6
200	4	6	6	7	7
150	5	6	7	8	8
100	6	8	9	10	10
50	8	11	13	14	14
25	12	16	18	19	20

Example: A reported percentage of 30%, based on a random sample of 200 consumers, has an error rate of plus-or-minus 6%. That is, we could be "95% confident" that the actual population percentage, had everyone been surveyed, is between 24 and 36%.

(b) Difference Between Percentages

| Average of the two Sample sizes | Difference needed when average of the two percentages is close to: | | | | |
	10 or 90%	20 or 80%	30 or 70%	40 or 60%	50%
1000	4	4	5	5	5
500	4	5	6	6	6
250	5	7	8	9	9
200	6	8	9	10	10
150	7	9	10	11	11
100	8	11	13	14	14
50	12	16	18	19	20
25	17	22	25	27	28

Example: Suppose a TV commercial day-after-recall test, based on a random sample of 200 viewers, indicates a recall score of 20%. You are disappointed. You decide to repeat the test with a new random sample of 100 viewers, and the commercial now obtains a recall score of 30%. Are these significantly different scores? The average of the two sample sizes is 150. The average of the two recall scores is 25%. The conservative difference needed is 10% (from the table at the intersection of the 150 row and the 30 column). Yes, you can be "95% confident" that the second recall score is significantly higher than the first.

* Tables compiled from more detailed tables in Newspaper Advertising Bureau, *The Audience for Newspaper Advertising*, New York: NAB, 1978, appendix.

buyers are hard to reach or refuse to be interviewed. Such departures from random inclusion or representativeness have the effect of expanding the plus-or-minus error rate to an unknown degree. Managers have to live with this and simply try to obtain as representative a sample as possible within the limitations of the research budget.

Apart from these reliability considerations there is the separate question of *validity*—the measure's "appropriateness" or "correctness." Does the measure record what it is supposed to? For example, does self-reported purchase provide a correct record of actual purchase? (A good way to distinguish validity from reliability is to think of validity as a "shotgun," which will appropriately hit the target, and reliability as a "rifle," which may or may not hit the target but will be very precise. One should look for validity first and then reliability— a measure should be like a *well-aimed* rifle.) We will comment on the validity question in the buyer behavior measures described below.

Measuring Trial and Repeat Purchase for New Products

New products pose several particular problems for buyer behavior measurement. The newer or more innovative the product, the more the manager needs care in interpreting buyer behavior results. The major considerations may be summarized as follows:

1 *Trial* Trial of new products can be inflated all too easily by promotion practices such as free samples where it is not clear whether the consumer actually tried the product after receiving it, or by introductory coupons or discounts that artificially aid trial. For this reason, some firms measure trial as the first "voluntary" purchase, a more conservative measure but one that better represents the product's natural penetration.[15]

2 *Repeat* With frequently purchased new products it is very important to measure the repeat rate based on at least four or five purchase opportunities. Many new product measuring services, and managers, only look at the first repeat purchase ("Of those who tried, what percentage repeated?"). As Tauber[16] points out, there are many reasons why consumers will repeat several times and then never buy the brand again: continued introductory promotions, eventual price resistance if highly priced, or simply the need to use or consume the product several times before finally deciding for or against it. For radically new products, social influence processes such as opinion leadership also may be operating, positively or negatively, and these processes take time to develop and to be adequately assessed. For most new products, multiple-purchase opportunities are required before the repeat purchase rate can be validly evaluated.

3 *Switching* If the new product is substantially innovative, switching behavior can be difficult to evaluate. This is because the product may be seen by consumers as a distinctly new category, that is, a category that does not compare readily with existing ones. Switching and, more broadly, market share, are essentially relative measures whose validity depends on competive category ("market") definition. The more innovative the product, the more difficult it is to categorize and the longer it takes to identify the competition.

It should be emphasized that new product purchase evaluation problems are basically problems of managerial interpretation, not problems with the measures themselves. The measures are considered next.

Purchase Behavior Measures

1 *UPC Scanners* (for example, Nielsen's Testsight, IRI's BehaviorScan, Burke's AdTel) Scanners are the most valid way of measuring purchase behavior because individual purchases (indexed by an I.D. punch card) are recorded mechanically at the cash register as they occur. However, as noted in Chapter 2 under sales measures, use of scanners is limited at present to certain store types and geographic markets. Limited market coverage also poses a representativeness (reliability) problem.

2 *Purchase-diary panels* (for example, NPD/HTI, NFO, MRCA) For frequently purchased products, and until scanners become widespread, purchase diary panels are the best method of measuring buyer behavior. Validity is relatively high due to respondents' recording of purchases in an easy-to-use diary soon after they occur, although there is still a tendency to inaccurately over-record nationally advertised brands and brands with large market shares. As far as reliability is concerned, the panel research services mentioned above all offer adequate sample sizes with the possibility of larger samples at client expense. Reliability in terms of representativeness is always a problem in that not everyone is willing to commit themselves to panel participation and, likewise, others drop out, making the panel sample less than random.

Purchase diary panels have one advantage over scanners: The diary can also be used to record associated buyer characteristics, such as demographics and media exposure. This has led to the emergence of scanner-plus-diary panels (for example, Information Resources, Inc.).

3 *Surveys* (customized by most large marketing research firms or conducted by the marketer or advertiser) Buyer surveys are the least valid method of measuring buyer behavior because they rely on the buyer's memory, which in most cases is incredibly faulty except for very recent purchases or for major and unusually salient durable purchases. Errors at the individual respondent or household level usually are intolerably extensive when compared with diary purchase records.[17] (Surveys are satisfactory for aggregate sales measures, as noted in Chapter 2, because the errors tend to cancel across respondents, providing much the same estimates as diary panel sales estimates.[18]) Surveys are not really satisfactory for purchase behavior measures, which require accuracy at the individual buyer level. However, in many instances there is no feasible alternative. Reliability, as with all other methods, depends on the survey's sample size and representativeness.

Despite the problem with survey measures of buyer behavior, surveys are probably the most widely used method and they are often the only available method. Typical survey questions to measure buyer behavior, here exemplified for the TV dinner category, include:

1 Have you ever bought a TV dinner?   (Category trial)
2 Which brands have you bought?   (Brand trial)
3 How many times in the past 3 months have you bought   (Repeat rate)
that brand?

4 Which brand did you buy (a) last time? (b) And the time   (Switching)
before that?

Kalwani and Morrison[19] have found that, for frequently purchased products, sample sizes of at least 400 category users (screened from question 1) and five purchase occasions per consumer are needed to obtain brand-switching estimates that are acceptably reliable (low plus-or-minus error in projection). Five purchases means a multi-wave survey to overcome memory problems, or continuous diary panel data, which largely avoids them, or scanner data, which avoids memory problems entirely.

For infrequently purchased durables and industrial products, a single-wave survey is sufficient. Here, as noted in Chapter 2, the manager is more concerned with perceived substitutability (not behavior) among buyers currently "in the market" for the product. The sample size of in-the-market buyers need be no larger than 200, usually, to obtain a reliable picture of perceived brand or brand-item substitutability.

Brand Loyalty Measures

Selection of a sales strategy and target buyer group depends heavily on the phenomenon of brand loyalty. There are numerous ways to measure brand loyalty, ranging from strictly behavioral measures (repeat purchase) to strictly attitudinal measures.[20] Our recommendation is a combination of behavior and attitude measures—focusing on the buyer's *attitudinal reasons* for behaviors such as trial, repeat, and switching or for *not* trying, repeating, or switching.

Attitude measurement is covered in Part Eight, but we can mention several points here:

1 Ideal for the marketer is a "top box" attitude score ("the best brand").
2 Next is an attitude rating indicating multi-brand loyalty ("one of several best brands"), especially if the buyer regards only two or three brands as being in the "best" category.
3 Less desirable are "just average," or "below average," or "one of the worst" ratings, indicating that the buyer normally would not consider buying the brand.

Note that there is no *deliberate* mention of price in these measures, although the buyer is free to use price as one factor in arriving at an attitude rating. Asking customers which brands are "best value" or "best for the money," thereby deliberately introducing an "external" price context, does not really get at their "internal" attitudinal commitment to the brand. Loyalty, as noted, implies an attitude that resists price and promotion factors.

SUMMARY

Sales, potentially, can come from any or all of four groups of buyers: new category users (NCU), brand loyals (BL), brand switchers (BS), or other-brand loyals (OBL). The sales potential of these groups varies over the product life cycle. Moreover, they can be broken down more finely into sub-groups that further indicate sales potential for the brand.

Selecting a *target audience* is a process of deciding which prospect group or sub-group will be *most responsive to advertising or promotion,* as the case may be, in relation to the *cost* of the advertising or promotion. The expected sales increase in relation to the cost of the advertising or promotion is known as leverage. Leverage is consistent with the marginal method of budgeting. A high-leverage prospect group or sub-group should be chosen as the target audience.

A particular advertising or promotion campaign usually is directed at a single target audience (one of the four prospect groups) or several related target audiences (prospect sub-groups). When there is a lesser leverage effect on other prospect groups or sub-groups, it sometimes is meaningful to designate a "primary" target audience and a "secondary" target audience to which the lesser prospects belong.

Action objectives must be established for the target audience to whom advertising or promotion is directed. The ultimate action desired is purchase behavior, in the form of trial of the brand or usage of the brand; usage, in turn, can be refined by regarding it as repeat purchase (a sales orientation) or brand switching (a market share orientation).

Purchase action objectives vary with each target audience. We saw that the prospect sub-groups have very specific purchase action objectives based on the three behaviors of trial, repeat, or switching.

Purchase-related behaviors also may be relevant action objectives for particular advertising or promotion campaigns. These are behaviors that are necessary for the potential target audience buyer to perform before purchase behavior itself can occur (such as visiting dealers, or redeeming coupons). Construction of a behavioral sequence model (Chapter 5), which identifies the decision maker, the nature of each behavioral step, and its location and timing, is of immense value in ordering the purchase-related behaviors and purchase behavior that the advertising or promotion campaign seeks to influence in favor of the brand.

Trade behaviors, too, are other very important action objectives that are prior to and thus purchase-related for consumer or buyer action objectives. Trade behaviors are similar, conceptually, to consumer behaviors in that the objective is to stimulate trade trial (stocking the brand in the first place), trade repeat (re-ordering), and trade switching (deleting other brands to give our brand favorable shelf position and display).

Measures of purchase behavior must be conducted at the individual buyer level. Increasingly, for supermarket products, this can be done with electronic scanners at the checkout counter. Most often, however, purchase panels, in which individual purchases are recorded in a diary, are used to measure purchase behavior. Survey interviews, asking people to recall past purchases, are another widely used though less reliable measure of purchase behavior that can be used to set action objectives for the target audience and the brand.

In the next chapter, we learn more about the target audience by "profiling" the typical decision maker in that audience in terms of personal characteristics that are useful to the advertiser in making the advertising message and its delivery more effective.

NOTES

1 G.S. Day, A two-dimensional concept of brand loyalty, *Journal of Advertising Research,* 1969, *9* (3), 29–35.

2 In a recent study it has been shown that consumers loyal to other brands (OBL's) can be vulnerable to brand switching if the product category is a "low risk" one (see also Chapter 11 regarding low involvement brand decisions). The product category studied was facial tissues. See R.C. Blattberg, T. Buesing, and S.K. Sen, Segmentation strategies for national brands, *Journal of Marketing,* 1980, *44* (4), 59–67.

3 See, for example, an experiment on new types of bread, in which the average number of brands examined fell from 5 to 2 over a 5-week period, in D.R. Lehmann and W.L. Moore, An investigation of self-reported search stage versus point of purchase information search behavior, in J.C. Olson (Ed.), *Advances in Consumer Research: Vol. 7,* Ann Arbor, MI: Association for Consumer Research, 1980, pp. 733–736.

4 The Hendry Corporation, *Speaking of Hendry,* New York: The Hendry Corporation, 1976.

5 For managers wishing to use these figures as "norms," care should be taken to use the *self-reported* brand loyalty measure (brands bought exclusively, most often, less often, or never over the past year) employed in this study, and then *exclude* the *never* group. Exclusive or sole loyalty measured by *diary* records is much lower, with only about 10 percent of consumers sticking with a single brand exclusively in a typical product category over a whole year. As long as the manager uses self-report surveys, the norms should be okay: the norms should be adjusted downward for lower-loyalty household products and upward for high-loyalty personal care products. More precise norms can be calculated from the article by S.P. Raj, Striking a balance between brand "popularity" and brand loyalty, *Journal of Marketing,* 1985, *49* (1), 53–59.

6 J. Jacoby and R.W. Chestnut, *Brand Loyalty Measurement and Management,* New York: Ronald Press, 1978.

7 Reported in R. Bartos, Ads that irritate may erode trust in advertised brands, *Harvard Business Review,* 1981, *59* (4), 138–140.

8 N. Giges, "Shoppers continue turn to price brands," *Advertising Age,* May 10, 1982, p. 82.

9 J.A. Howard, whose most recent work is presented in *Consumer Behavior: Application of Theory,* New York: McGraw-Hill, 1977, originated the term *routinized response behavior* to refer to those consumers or buyers who have settled on several acceptable brands and switch among them, buying a particular one at a particular time based on availability and relative price, on the day, at that store.

10 Same reference as note 4; see especially the data provided by A. Kershaw, pp. 36–45.

11 J.R. Rubinson, Brand strength means more than market share, *Journal of Advertising Research,* 1979, *19* (5), 83–87.

12 Marketing Research Group, A.C. Nielsen Company, Estimating the cost of out-of-stocks, *The Nielsen Researcher,* 1979, No. 2, 12–13.

13 A.S.C. Ehrenberg, *Repeat Buying: Theory and Applications,* Amsterdam: North-Holland Publishing Co., New York: American Elsevier, 1972.

14 See G.H. Brown, "Brand loyalty—fact or fiction?," *Advertising Age,* January 25, 1953, pp. 75–76; and also brand switching rates by product category compiled in 1968 by *Progressive Grocer* magazine, October 1968, and re-presented in D.I. Hawkins, K.A. Coney, and R.J. Best, *Consumer Behavior: Implications for Strategy,* Dallas, TX: Business Publications, Inc., 1980, pp. 484–485, Table 18-7, col. 5 (later editions of this excellent text omit column 5, which is the most general shopper base).

15 For a discussion of trial measurement, see G.L. Urban and J.R., Hauser, *Design and Marketing of New Products,* Englewood Cliffs, NJ: Prentice-Hall, 1980.

16 E.M. Tauber, Forecasting sales prior to test market, *Journal of Marketing,* 1977, *41* (1), 80–84.

17 J.H. Parfitt, A comparison of purchase recall with diary panel records, *Journal of Advertising Research,* 1967, *7* (3), 16–31.

18 Y. Wind and D. Lerner, On the measurement of purchase data: surveys versus purchase diaries, *Journal of Marketing Research,* 1979, *16* (1), 39–47.

19 M.U. Kalwani and D.G. Morrison, Sample size requirements for zero-order models, *Journal of Marketing Research,* 1980, *17* (2), 221–227.

20 For an excellent review of brand loyalty measures see J. Jacoby and R.W. Chestnut, same reference as note 6.

DISCUSSION QUESTIONS

4.1 If you were the advertising manager for Dr. Pepper, which sales group or groups would you concentrate on in your long-run sales strategy: NCU, BL, BS, or OBL? Rank the four groups in order of priority and explain your ranking.

4.2 How well do you think the Hendry "bathtub" process applies to brands in the following product categories, and why? (a) aspirin, (b) beer, (c) paper towels, (d) airlines. Conduct a few informal interviews if you're not a regular buyer of any of the categories.

4.3 In all, there are 12 sub-groups that can become target audiences for a brand: NNCU, UNCU, PNCU (among new category users); SBL, MBL (among brand loyals); EOBS, EFBS, ROBS, RFBS (among brand switchers); and FOBL, NOBL, UOBL (among other-brand loyals). For each of the following brands, classify yourself in 1 of the 12 sub-groups and explain how you decided on the classification:
  a Hewlett-Packard calculators
  b Gillette Dry Look hair spray
  c Helena Rubinstein mascara
  d Safeway (store brand) paper table napkins

4.4 Without looking back at the text, write out a definition of brand loyalty, then briefly describe your own loyalty status with respect to:
  a Beer brands
  b Your school or office cafeteria
  c Instant coffee brands
  d Paper towels

4.5 Visit two retail store managers and ask them to describe to you, in detail, how they would handle a request for a new brand introduction to the store (a) from a small, unknown manufacturer and, alternatively, (b) from a large manufacturer with whom they already do a lot of business. Probe the factors that would affect their decision in each case. Afterwards, write up a short report in which you identify from your interviews relevant purchase and purchase-related retailer behaviors.

4.6 You have recently launched a new brand of dishwashing liquid nationally, accompanied by heavy introductory promotion in the form of cents-off the purchase price. Results from a national consumer panel of 500 households indicate a trial incidence of 5% in the first month of the launch. Write a short memo to top management evaluating this result.

4.7 In which of the following instances, and why, would a single-wave consumer survey be an adequate substitute for multi-wave diary panel data:

   a Measuring trial-and-repeat purchase of GM automobiles
   b Measuring trial-and-repeat purchase of Green Giant frozen entrees
   c Measuring overall sales of Green Giant frozen entrees
   d Measuring brand switching between overnight airfrieght small package carriers (Federal Express, Emery, etc.) by large companies

FURTHER READING

Colley, R.H. *Defining Advertising Goals for Measured Advertising Results*. New York: Association of National Advertisers, Inc., 1961.

The DAGMAR approach outlined in Colley's classic text emphasizes that advertising (and by inference, promotion) may be directed at many types of buyer behavior. We have systematized these as trade and consumer purchase and purchase-related behaviors in this chapter.

Jacoby, J., and Chestnut, R.W. *Brand Loyalty Measurement and Management*. New York: Ronald Press, 1978.

The definitive account of brand loyalty. Clearly explains the attitudinal and behavioral basis of this concept, which is central to sales strategy and target audience definition. Very useful to the manager who wants to pursue the brand loyalty topic further.

McCann, J.M. Market segment response to the marketing decision variables. *Journal of Marketing Research,* 1974, *11* (4), 399–412.

Important article describing how to select a target audience based on size and purchase level as well as response to advertising or promotion (developed as "leverage" in this chapter). Readable though in a technical journal.

Wind, Y. Brand loyalty and vulnerability. In Woodside, A.G., Sheth, J.N., and Bennett, P.D. (Eds.). *Consumer and Industrial Buying Behavior*. New York: Elsevier North-Holland, 1977, pp. 313–319.

Expands on the importance of defining target audiences on the basis of behavior *and* attitude. This article shows why behavior alone (for example, usage) is insufficient to define a target audience for advertising.

CHAPTER 5

PROFILING THE DECISION MAKER

This chapter shows how to profile (describe) the decision maker within the target audience. The decision maker is the person to whom the advertising campaign or promotion campaign is *directly* addressed. After reading this chapter you should:

- Understand the various decision-making roles that target audience members can occupy and the specific action objectives that go with each role
- Be able to construct a behavioral sequence model for any product category or brand, which further refines action objectives for the decision maker
- Know why behavior and communication effects are the primary profile variables for describing the decision maker
- See how other personal characteristics are additionally useful in profiling the decision maker

Example   A brief example will help to preview the decision maker profiling process. Suppose you were advertising Hathaway brand men's shirts. First, you would have to decide to whom you would advertise: men or women. Hathaway's research shows that 68 percent of men's shirts are purchased by women.[1] This suggests women as the primary decision makers.

But what *decision-making role or roles* do women occupy? Are women the main deciders or do they simply carry out decisions already made by husbands or male friends? (Hathaway and its advertising agency, Ogilvy & Mather, apparently concluded that women play the main deciding role. They allocated two-thirds of the advertising budget to the women's audience.)

Second, what is the *purchase decision process* for men's shirts? Is the brand and item choice discussed at home prior to purchase, or is the entire purchase decision mainly made by women at the point of purchase? A behavioral sequence model denoting the "what," "who," "where," and "when" of men's shirt buying would greatly aid Hathaway in identifying aspects of the decision process that could be influenced by advertising.

Third, even if you assume that women are important decision makers for men's shirts, you would have to decide whether *all* women represent good targets for the advertising, or whether this depends on the particular woman's *prior behavior and current attitude* toward the Hathaway brand. Probably, women who have purchased Hathaway shirts before (brand behavior) and, taking into account their men's responses, were highly satisfied (brand attitude), would be better targets than women who have never even heard of the brand. The target audience definition could be narrowed to women who are "favorably disposed" toward Hathaway shirts.

Fourth, you have to decide how to "reach" favorably disposed women when advertising Hathaway shirts. You could take the shotgun approach and advertise broadly, hoping that women with favorable attitudes toward Hathaway will "self-select" in response to the ads. But this broad approach would be expensive and wasteful. A more efficient approach would be to gather additional profile information, beyond behavior and attitude, on the target audience. Profile information might include direct measurement of the target audience's *media exposure,* to help reach those women via media; and it might include *demographic variables* such as marital status and husband's occupation, *lifestyle variables* such as frequency of attending mixed-company social gatherings, and also *personality* variables, such as anxiety, that would help you select advertising message scenarios to more effectively persuade the decision maker.

Let us now consider the four steps in understanding the decision maker in more detail.

DECISION MAKERS' ROLES

Reaching Individual Decision Makers

Much has been made of the observation that, in both consumer and industrial buying, some purchase decisions are made by individuals whereas others are made by groups. This realization has led to the concept of a "decision-making unit" consisting of one *or more* individuals and the roles that they play in the decision. The decision-making unit can be one person or a group.

However, the emphasis on group decisions can be misleading. One does not advertise to a "family" or to a "company" but rather to *individuals* within these groups. Although the overall decision may be arrived at by group decision making—for example, choice of a vacation resort by a family or choice of a computer by a company—advertisements and promotion offers have to persuade individuals separately *before* they get together to make a group decision.

This is not to say that the advertiser can ignore group decision processes. It has been well documented that groups vary in their implicit or explicit decision rules, and the decision rule adopted by a particular group can radically affect whether or not our brand will be chosen. For example, husband-wife decisions may follow a "democratic consensus" rule, or the decision may be delegated "autocratically" to one spouse.[2] Organizational groups, similarly, may follow a variety of decision rules, including "majority vote" or "weighted participant importance" rules.[3]

But from an advertising and promotion standpoint, differences in group decision rules *merely shift the emphasis to be placed on various individuals in the group*. Group decisions do not change the fact that advertisements or promotion offers must persuade each person individually, beforehand. It is the persuaded individual that enters into the group decision. Whether the individual is re-persuaded in the group is beyond the direct control of advertising and promotion. What the advertiser must do is to target those individuals with the most weight (the most influential roles) in the decision.

Roles and Specific Action Objectives

With the foregoing point in mind, we are now ready to list the types of roles that individuals can occupy for purchase decisions. Each role should be regarded as involving a separate purchase-related or purchase action objective.

Table 5.1 presents a list of the most frequent decision roles that individuals occupy, along with the relevant specific action objective for each role.[4]

1 An individual in the *initiator* role gets the overall purchase decision started. From an advertising and promotion standpoint, the relevant specific action objective is whether or not our brand is *proposed* by the initiator. (*Example*: Child saying, "Mum, can I have Cheerios?")

2 An individual in the *influencer* role utilizes product information to either promote or retard the overall decision. The relevant specific action objective is whether or not the influencer *recommends* our brand. (*Example*: Father saying, "Cheerios are pretty low on sugar, I think they would be okay.")

3 The individual in the *decider* role makes the overall "go/no-go" decision. The relevant specific action objective is whether or not our brand is *chosen*. (*Example*: Mother saying, "All right, I'll buy Cheerios next time I'm at the supermarket.")

TABLE 5-1   DECISION-MAKING ROLES AND SPECIFIC ACTION OBJECTIVES

Role	Action objective
1 Initiator	Propose brand
2 Influencer	Recommend brand
3 Decider	Choose brand
4 Purchaser	Buy brand
5 User	Use brand

[handwritten note: initiator starts process - doesn't necessarily propose brand]

4 The individual in the *purchaser* role executes the decision. The relevant specific action objective is actual *purchase* of the brand—there may still be an opportunity for another brand to be considered and chosen at the point of purchase. (*Example*: Mother and child go to the supermarket. Mother is distracted by Total's on-package vitamin claims, but sees that Cheerios have only 1 g of sugar per 1 oz serving, versus 3 g for Total. She buys Cheerios.)

5 The individual in the *user* role is the actual consumer or user of the product. The relevant specific action objective is actual *use* of the brand, after purchase. (*Example*: Child nibbles at Cheerios but comments, "They're not sweet enough." Mother adds 1 g of sugar, with father's reluctant approval. . . .)

You can see the importance of these role definitions and actions for advertising and promotion. We advertise and promote to *individuals in role*: (1) to initiators to make them aware of our brand and propose it as a possible purchase candidate; (2) to influencers to communicate reasons why they should recommend our brand; (3) to deciders to persuade them to select our brand; (4) to purchasers to "lock in" the selection of our brand; and (5) to users to ensure that they actually use and, perhaps, more rapidly use our brand so that, if satisfying, our brand will be purchased again.

We have emphasized the roles of individuals in groups so as to prevent the fallacy of defining target audiences solely on a group basis. (Of course, many purchases are decided upon totally by one individual. In such cases, one person occupies all five roles. *Example*: You buying yourself a soda. Quite evidently, when the "decision-making unit" is an individual rather than a group of individuals, the advertiser's targeting job is much easier.) When the decision-making unit consists of a group, the advertiser must identify each individual's role and address the corresponding decision and action objective that accompanies that role.

CONSTRUCTING A BEHAVIORAL SEQUENCE MODEL

Alternative decision-making roles can most easily be identified by constructing a *behavioral sequence model* of the overall purchase decision process.

Stages, Roles, Location, and Timing

A behavioral sequence model utilizes a "flowchart" format to identify the target audience's required actions longitudinally in terms of (1) the major behavioral stages preceding, including, and following purchase—as well as (2) the decision roles, (3) location, and (4) timing of each stage. A useful "generic" behavioral sequence model is shown in Figure 5.1. It should be noted that although other writers have suggested similar stage models,[5] none of these models has combined the stage flow with decision roles, location, and timing. As we shall see, these additions are vital for advertisers.

Major stages:	Need arousal	Information search and evaluation	Purchase decision	Usage
Decision roles	• Initiator (proposes brand)	• Influencer (recommends brand) • Decider (chooses brand)	• Decider (chooses brand) • Purchaser (buys brand)	• User (uses brand)
Location	• Home • In store • etc.	• Media advertising • Word of mouth • Expert ratings • Point of purchase • etc.	• Pre-purchase • Point of purchase • etc.	• Private • Social • Business • etc.
Timing	t_1	t_2	t_3	t_4

FIGURE 5.1 A generic behavioral sequence model. The "generic" model shown here should be adapted to suit the particular target audience, product category and, usually, the particular brand.

Major Stages Our generic behavioral sequence model has four stages: need arousal, information search and evaluation, purchase decision, and usage. Some writers label the stages differently. For example, the first stage is sometimes called problem recognition (however, we doubt that buyers always are responding to "problems," unless the term is very broadly defined); the second stage may be separated into "internal" (memory) versus "external" (marketing environment) search and further into search versus evaluation (though we feel evaluation occurs simultaneously during search); and so forth. The labels do not really matter. The important thing is to get you, the manager, thinking about *points in the buyer's decision process at which advertising or promotion can be influential.*

Stages can be added, modified, or deleted to suit the particular target audience, product category, and even brand. For example, our brand loyal (BL) group will go through very little information search and evaluation, effectively deleting this stage; whereas a brand switcher (BS) will find this stage essential.

Furthermore, purchase in some product categories requires retail outlet selection as well as brand selection—for instance, grocery products, clothing—so that a *store decision stage* may be usefully added before or after (it depends!) the brand purchase decision.

In some instances, a particular brand may be bought differently from others in the same product category, necessitating a modified behavioral sequence model for the brand. For instance, people may buy Sears' brands more casually than they would others because of Sears' well-known liberal return policy. As in the brand loyal example above, but for a different reason, this may effectively delete the information search and evaluation stage for purchase of Sears' products.

As we said, the four stages shown in the figure are only a starting framework for a tailor-made behavioral sequence model for the target audience and the brand.

Decision Roles   The five decision roles fit logically into behavioral sequence models. Advertising and promotion are designed to influence individuals in particular decision roles. At the need arousal stage, the advertiser's purpose is to influence the brand proposal decision (initiator). At the information search and evaluation stage, the advertiser's purpose is to influence the brand recommendation decision (influencer) and brand selection (decider). At the purchase decision stage, the advertiser's purpose—this time especially through promotion at the point of purchase—is to further influence brand selection (decider) and actual purchase (purchaser). At the usage stage, the advertiser's purpose is to influence consumption rate and therefore the repeat purchase or switch-in rates (user). The behavioral sequence model is thus directly connected to target audience decision roles.

Location   The location of each stage in the behavioral sequence model is important in media planning—specifically, in media selection. The key question is: Where is the target audience decision maker likely to be making the decision?

Managerial attention to the location factor can result in some innovative media choices. For example, in 1980, R. J. Reynolds realized that many low-tar cigarette smokers were confused by the multitude of new low-tar brands and were perhaps overloaded with media ads for them. RJR shifted a sizable portion of their cigarette advertising budget to billboards, taxi cabs, buses, and point of purchase in an attempt to sway confused, last-minute deciders.

Locations may range from total in-home decisions, as in direct mail or catalog advertising, to total in-store decisions, as in a newly encountered point-of-purchase promotion offer. The location examples in Figure 5.1 hardly do justice to the wide variety of possible influence and decision situations, such as driving, commuting, restaurants, offices, parties, etc., that may be relevant to one or more stages in the particular behavioral sequence model for a target audience and brand.

Timing   The timing of each stage is important in media planning—specifically, in media scheduling. Examples of media timing in the behavioral sequence model stages include advertising to full-time homemakers in the initiator and decider roles during the morning hours prior to food shopping, for example, via morning radio, TV, or newspapers; or advertising Alka-Seltzer to *users* during holiday periods!

More generally, *overall* timing (from t_1 to t_4 in Figure 5.1) reflects the consumer's *purchase cycle*. Knowledge of the average purchase cycle for the target audience (their median inter-purchase interval) can be of considerable help to media planners for scheduling both advertising frequency and promotion offers. In Part Seven, where we analyze media strategy in detail, we will see the crucial importance of constructing an accurate behavioral sequence model for the target audience and brand to which the advertising or promotion is directed.

Measures for Constructing a Behavioral Sequence Model

"Measurement" for constructing a behavioral sequence model is more qualitative than quantitative. Accordingly, the best methods are qualitative and open-ended:

1 *Focus-Group Interviews (F-groups)*   The most efficient method of constructing a behavioral sequence model is through focus-group interviews in which consumers (or, of course, industrial decision makers) are asked to describe recent purchase processes from need arousal through to usage experiences. The group interview setting is more efficient than the next related method because people can remind one another of stages, roles, locations, and timing. A fast, composite picture of the behavioral sequence model usually emerges if the group consists of relatively homogeneous target audience individuals.

2 *Individual Depth Interviews (IDI's)*   If the product topic is sensitive, or if the researcher suspects substantial reporting bias in a group setting, individual open-ended interviews can be used instead. ("Open-ended" refers to the answers, not the questions, which might be quite structured; for example, "When did you first think about buying (the brand)?" "Where did you find out more about it?," and so forth. The same questions would be used in the F-group setting.)

The only "quantitative" aspect of constructing a behavioral sequence model is in ensuring that you have a representative sample of the target audience. If F-groups are used, it is wise to replicate over several groups. With F-groups, and with IDI's, the general rule-of-thumb is to keep interviewing until additional groups' or individuals' answers become repetitive, reaching the point of reasonable confirmation.

The timing (purchase cycle) element of the behavioral sequence model might be best confirmed with panel or survey data, since the exact cycle length is statistically important when used in media scheduling. However, use of a large survey or panel to derive the decision stages and roles themselves would, on the one hand, be overkill in relation to the number of people you need to interview; and, on the other, quite possibly invalid unless a properly trained interviewer is used. Behavioral sequence models require psychological interpretations of consumer decision processes which an untrained interviewer may be unable to elicit or detect.

THE DECISION MAKER'S INITIAL BEHAVIOR AND COMMUNICATION EFFECTS

It is convenient to refer to an individual in *any of the five roles* (not just the decider) as a *decision maker*. The next task in target audience profiling is to measure the decision maker's initial buyer behavior and communication effect status with regard to our brand. Only by knowing the decision maker's *current status* can we determine what has to be done to "move" the target audience to the *target* status, thereby attaining the communication and action objectives for the brand.

The Primacy of Behavior and Communication Effects as Advertising Segmentation (Target Audience) Variables

Market segmentation, as you know, is a process of dividing the overall market into prospective buyer groups. There are many ways this can be done. Traditionally viewed, market segmentation can be based on demographics, psychographics ("lifestyle"), personality, attitudes, or behaviors. Industrial and institutional markets, also, can be segmented by industry type, organizational "demographics" (number of employees, etc.), buyer attitudes, or buyer behaviors.[6] We will focus on consumer markets here although our reasoning applies to all markets.

Let us state our recommendation right at the outset: for *advertising,* the only *essential* way of segmenting the potential audience or market is by *current behavior and current communication effects* (primarily brand awareness and brand attitude). The behavior and communication effect status of the decision maker are primary. Other variables of the demographic and lifestyle variety are simply secondary, additional, target audience descriptors that enable us to reach and communicate to relevant behavioral–communication effect groups more effectively and efficiently *after* we have selected our target audience on behavioral and communication effect grounds.

The reason for the primacy of behavior and communication effect status in target audience definition is straightforward: The effects of more "distant" variables such as demographics (age, sex, etc.) are *already represented* in current awareness, attitudes, and behaviors toward the category and brand.[7]

Consider for example, the ad for Paco Rabanne men's cologne shown in Figure 5.2. A man is drawn to Paco Rabanne cologne only secondarily because he is a man, is in a particular age group, and is pursuing a given lifestyle (and perhaps a particular activity . . .). Assuming awareness of Paco Rabanne, he is drawn to the brand in a primary sense because of his attitude toward it, which in turn is conditioned by his behavior toward it; most notably, has he tried it before, does it "work"? Awareness, attitude, and behavior are primary.

Demographics and lifestyle information may help *additionally* to locate the favorably disposed buyer (via media) and perhaps even to communicate more effectively to him (via ads that portray his desired lifestyle and reinforce his brand awareness, brand attitude, and behavior). These are secondary, though obviously not unimportant, considerations.

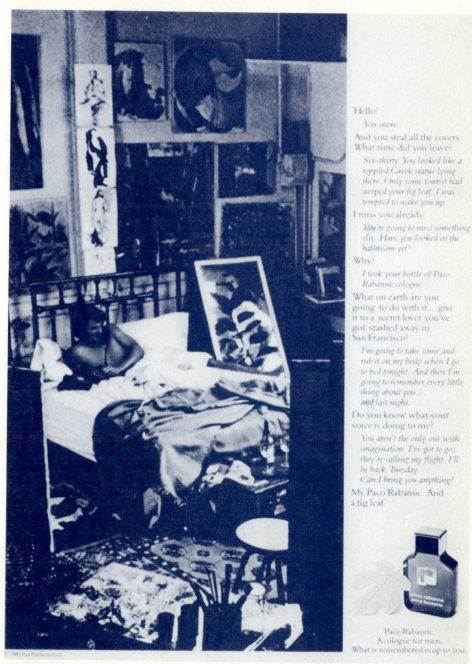

Hello?

You snore.

And you steal all the covers. What time did you leave?

Six-thirty. You looked like a toppled Greek statue lying there. Only some tourist had swiped your fig leaf. I was tempted to wake you up.

I miss you already.

You're going to miss something else. Have you looked in the bathroom yet?

Why?

I took your bottle of Paco Rabanne cologne.

What on earth are you going to do with it...give it to a secret lover you've got stashed away in San Francisco?

I'm going to take some and rub it on my body when I go to bed tonight. And then I'm going to remember every little thing about you... and last night.

Do you know what your voice is doing to me?

You aren't the only one with imagination. I've got to go; they're calling my flight. I'll be back Tuesday. Can I bring you anything?

My Paco Rabanne. And a fig leaf.

Paco Rabanne.
A cologne for men.
What is remembered is up to you.

FIGURE 5.2   Cologne ad showing (apparent) segmentation by demographics and lifestyle. But to whom does the ad actually appeal? (*Courtesy Paco Rabanne Perfumes.*)

New Products or New Brands Where There are No Behavior or Communication Effects

We chose the Paco Rabanne ad for a reason: It provides a difficult test for our contention that behavior and communication effects are primary. Suppose the advertiser's purpose is to reach consumers for whom Paco Rabanne is a new, untried brand. In this case, the consumer has "zero" brand behavior and "no" brand awareness or brand attitude. Nine out of 10 marketing students would probably say, "Well, our best bet would be men, single and youngish, with a 'swinging' lifestyle." That is, they would define the target audience on demographic and lifestyle grounds.

This would be a mistake. The mistake involves the *fallacy of backward segmentation,* that is, segmenting the market on some other variable or variables first, *then* seeing if that segment will, once aware, exhibit a favorable attitude and behavior toward the brand. It is easy to see why backward segmentation is a mistake. What if women buy a majority of men's cologne, as in the Hathaway men's shirt example earlier? What if older men, not just youngish men, are attracted by the brand's appeal? What if "mental swingers," not just actual swingers, are attracted to the brand?

A much better approach is to take a broad sample of people (we might rule out children, but this is a trivial and obvious prior "segmentation" step) and simply ask them directly what their awareness, attitude, and behavior toward Paco Rabanne are currently: Then, show them the ad and, now that they are aware, ask them to indicate their attitudes, and their likely behavior, based on what the ad says—or could say—about the brand. We would then avoid the backward segmentation fallacy described above.

The first part of this research procedure gives us the initial or *current* behavioral and communication effect status of everyone in the market. With this information, the total potential market can be divided into the four prospective target audience groups (or finer sub-groups) described in Chapter 4. In the second part, by assessing their response to the brand-as-advertised "concept," we then can set realistic *target* levels of communication effects and behavior for each potential target audience.

We reiterate: Behavior and communication effects are the primary basis of advertising segmentation and target audience definition. Even for new products or new brands, it is a mistake to seek other variables "first" as more promising candidates. If there are no current behaviors or current awareness or attitudes toward the brand, simply describe the brand to a broad sample of people, thus making them aware, and then ask them what their attitudes or behaviors *would be.* Those who exhibit the most favorable attitude and the most likely behavioral inclination to try the brand become the target audience, no matter what their demographic, lifestyle, or other personal characteristics may be.

ADDITIONAL PROFILE VARIABLES FOR ADVERTISING

It is often suggested that "other variables," such as demographic or lifestyle variables, can be used as *alternatives* to behavior and communication effects in segmenting a market for advertising and promotion. As we have pointed out, this is a fallacy. For example, if you were to segment a market by sex (a demographic variable), you would *still* have to know the product and brand-relevant behavior and communication effect status of men and women before you could put together an advertising or promotion strategy. "Other variables" *alone* are not sufficient to define a target audience for advertising or promotion.

Other variables such as media exposure, demographics, and lifestyles serve mainly to assist in more accurately reaching and in more effectively communicating to the target audience decision maker. After profiling the decision maker in terms of the all-important behavior and communication effects, these other variables then become *additional profile variables*.

Marketers and advertisers have a choice of many additional variables with which to profile the target audience decision maker. These variables can be grouped into the following categories: media exposure, demographics, psychographics (or lifestyle), personality traits, and personality states. It is not possible to describe fully the functions of all these variables without this chapter becoming a consumer behavior text! Instead, we will summarize the main purpose of each profile variable *for advertising* (Table 5.2).

Media Exposure

It is extremely useful for the manager to have a *direct* measure of target audience decision makers' media exposure—the TV shows they watch most often, the magazines they read, and so forth. Knowledge of decision makers' media exposure will enable advertising (and advertised promotions) to reach the target audience more accurately through media. This is vital for step 1, exposure, in the buyer response sequence.

As we shall see in Part Seven, direct measurement of the target audience decision maker's media exposure provides far superior media selection than does the usual indirect method, via demographics, discussed next.

TABLE 5-2   ADDITIONAL TARGET AUDIENCE PROFILE VARIABLES AND THEIR ADVERTISING APPLICATIONS

Profile variables	Advertising applications
Media exposure	• Media selection (direct matching) • Media scheduling (direct matching)
Demographics	• Media selection (demographic matching) • Message content (visual and verbal)
Psychographics (or lifestyle)	• Media vehicle selection • Message content (visual)
Personality traits	• Message content (verbal) • Media scheduling (repetition)
Personality states	• Media vehicle selection • Message content (verbal)

Demographics

Demographics are "societal location" characteristics of the individual. The most frequently utilized demographic variables are geographic region, age, sex, race, marital status, family size, occupation, education, and income, with combinations of the last three often used as an index of social class.

Demographics are used to *indirectly* reach the target audience via media. Media are primarily sold to advertisers on the basis of (numerical counts of) demographic profiles of viewers, listeners, or readers. If the advertiser also knows the demographic profile of the target audience, the advertiser can then try to "match" the medium's demographic profile with the target audience's demographic profile.

For example, if we are advertising Mercedes automobiles and our target audience is brand loyal Mercedes buyers (with the action objective of stimulating repeat purchase), and we know that the *target audience* is demographically mostly "upscale" men, who occupy all five decision roles as one person, then we could try to find a match with media or media vehicles whose *media audience* is also skewed toward "upscale" men, for example, golf tournaments on TV, *Fortune* magazine.

Demographic matching, though widely practiced, usually results in a poor "fit" because: (1) target audience definition usually is less than perfectly correlated with demographics; (2) media audience actualities usually are less than perfectly correlated with demographics; and therefore (3) the two sides of the "match" are far less than perfectly correlated with each other. Direct measurement of Mercedes brand loyals' media exposure, on the other hand, avoids problems 1 and 2 and results in a better match between the target audience and the media audience.[8] We want to reach Mercedes brand loyals no matter what their demographics are.

We will return to the role of demographics in media selection in Part Seven (media strategy). Here we will simply repeat that the most common use of demographics in advertising is in media selection, but that direct measurement of the target audience's media exposure is a better way.

A second and rather obvious advertising application of demographic variables is in choosing appropriate *message content*—both visual and verbal—for advertisements. For example, if the target audience's ethnic profile shows that most are Hispanic, then, visually, the advertisement is likely to feature Hispanic models (although one could think of exceptions) and Hispanic social settings. Also, verbally, the advertisement is likely to be bi-lingual. Target audience profiles by age, sex, and social class similarly affect the visual symbols and verbal copy wording likely to be effective with the particular demographic group.

Psychographics

Psychographic variables go "beyond" demographics by constructing a picture of the typical target audience decision maker's "lifestyle." Lifestyle reflects "the way a person lives."[9] It reflects personal expression and affects the way in which a person spends time and money. Lifestyle measurement is often based on the individual's general (not product-specific) activities, interests, and opinions. These are often referred to collectively as psychographic variables or simply "psychographics."

The value of going beyond demographics to psychographics is easy to illustrate. Two demographically identical individuals, neighbors or colleagues even, could have quite different lifestyles: One individual may lead a "modern" lifestyle and the other a "traditional" one. Knowledge of the target audience decision maker's typical lifestyle (if it *can* be typified) is of immense help to advertisers. Psychographic or lifestyle information helps:

1 In selecting *media vehicles* that portray lifestyles similar to those of the target audience (although, as explained in Part Seven, this may not be that important).

2 In deciding on advertising message content—particularly *visual content* in terms of appropriate types of people, settings, and *other* products, if any, to show in the advertisement (which *is* important for one type of advertising, as explained in Part Six).

For example, an automobile advertisement directed to our hypothetical "modern" man might be placed in *Hustler* magazine, which presumably appeals to contemporary men. The ad itself might portray a modern model (for example, Richard Gere) in modern settings (for example, outside a disco) with other modern products around him (for example, diamond-studded boots). Alternatively, an ad for the same automobile directed to our hypothetical "traditional" man might be placed in *National Review,* which presumably appeals to traditionalists. The ad itself might portray a traditionally dressed man (for example, William F. Buckley) in a traditional setting (for example, at the Yale Club) with other traditional products around him (for example, an American eagle wall plaque). It is easy to see why media planners appreciate— and copywriters love—psychographics.

Personality Traits

Personality traits are relatively enduring, often largely inherited, individual predispositions that produce a characteristic tendency to respond in a consistent way across situations.[10] Personality traits can be important profile variables for advertisers because certain traits affect the way an individual processes information including, especially, *verbal content* in, and *repetition* of, advertising messages.

Personality traits relevant to advertising include intelligence, trait anxiety, introversion-extraversion, and visual imaging ability.

Intelligence   Intelligence usually is measured indirectly and imprecisely in advertising through the demographic variable of education level instead of using a more valid I.Q. test. Intelligence is relevant to message complexity and the use of technical terminology in advertising. Intelligent individuals are better able to understand complex messages and also seem to be more "impressed," and persuaded, by technical wording in advertising.[11]

Also, for intelligent individuals, somewhat fewer repetitions should be needed to learn advertising messages whereas the opposite should be true for less intelligent individuals.[12]

Trait Anxiety   Trait anxiety refers to a relatively persistent or chronic level of anxiety (autonomic nervous system arousal) as opposed to temporary states of anxiety that we all experience occasionally. Trait anxiety needs to be interpreted carefully but seems relevant to advertising messages incorporating scare tactics or fear appeals, such as for many public service campaigns and for product categories such as aspirin and insurance.[13]

A "normal" fear appeal could be rejected as too frightening if the target audience contains a majority of individuals with high trait anxiety; likewise, it could be ineffectively tame if most of the individuals have low trait anxiety.

Introversion-Extraversion   Introverts exhibit a chronically high level of central nervous system (brain or cortical) arousal, whereas extraverts exhibit a chronically low level. British research on introversion-extraversion as a personality trait[14] suggests many intriguing implications for advertising. The main implications are for verbal message content and repetition.

Introverts should be more affected by negative appeals, such as fear or problem-solution appeals, whereas extraverts should be more affected by positive appeals, especially prestige or social reward appeals.

Introverts should learn advertising messages more rapidly than extraverts, thus requiring fewer repetitions of the ad, but should also be less brand loyal, as they are more easily distracted (their minds are "ticking over") by new messages for competing brands.

Unfortunately, no direct research in advertising has been conducted with this apparently powerful personality trait, but the implications are suggestive.

Visual Imaging Ability   Visual imaging ability is an interesting personality variable that relates to verbal message content and also visual content. Vivid visual imagers respond more strongly to concrete words in copy and also to pictorial advertising content that evokes imagery.[15]

Women, on average, have slightly greater visual imaging ability than men. Although controversial, for this and other reasons,[16] women may be *slightly* easier to persuade than men.

A Note on Personality Traits   Personality traits have not been widely used by advertisers as profile variables, for several reasons:

1 Personality tests are usually quite long and cannot always be justified in a time-consuming questionnnaire. Shortened versions of standardized personality measures can result in drastic loss of reliability, and possibly loss of validity through biased item-selection.[17]

2 Personality measures often prove disappointing because investigators use personality traits that are not theoretically and functionally related to consumer behavior, that is, to product behaviors and attitudes.[18]

3 Also, behavior and attitude *themselves* are often unreliably measured, for example, when a single purchase in a frequently purchased category is taken as the measure of behavior.[19] Unreliable measurement of the behavior and attitude variables tends to understate the predictive and perhaps explanatory value of personality variables that are related to them.

We believe there will be a resurgence of personality measurement in advertising as these problems are corrected.

Personality States

Personality states are, paradoxically, a contradiction in terms. Personality consists of enduring predispositions whereas states, obviously, are temporary. Personality states refer to the fact that, at some times and in some situations, we all experience physical or mental conditions that stimulate the corresponding personality trait.

For example, a severe hangover may render the best of us functionally unintelligent; transient events, such as a TV documentary on the threat of nuclear war, can make most of us anxious; at particular times of the day we may feel mentally alert whereas at other times we may feel tired and unwilling to think deeply; similarly, our visual imagery, an extreme form of which is "daydreaming," may fluctuate with the time and situation.

Personality states are a relevant consideration in *media vehicle selection* and, in this sense, can be regarded as specific refinements to our first profile variable, media exposure. For example, a person watching the early evening TV news may be in quite a different physiological and mental state than when watching a late-night movie in bed. A morning newspaper may be read in a different state than an evening one, and so forth. Many media planners take these audience states into account when selecting media vehicles. Personality-state variables allow advertisers to predict how the audience might differently respond to ads placed in different media vehicles.

Since personality states are functionally equivalent in the short run to personality traits, personality states, like traits, also should be relevant to *verbal content* selection in advertisements. This realization suggests, for example, the use of simpler messages when the audience is likely to be tired, emphasis on audio rather than video when the audience is likely to be inattentive, and other corresponding modifications of verbal message content to suit temporary personality states experienced during media exposure.

PROFILE MEASURES

Advertisers have two broad options in gathering profile information on the target audience decision maker, namely, custom surveys or syndicated media data. Custom surveys are preferable but more expensive; hence syndicated data often are used instead.

1 *Custom Surveys* Customized surveys allow the marketer or advertiser to include virtually any variables desired that might help to profile the decision maker. (Some consumer panel services allow customized surveys to be conducted on purchase panel members and, we expect, scanner services may offer this addition too. As noted in conjunction with buyer behavior measures in the previous chapter, panels and scanners generally provide more valid behavioral measures than surveys and are therefore a better starting point for target audience identification.)

A fully customized survey would include measures of brand awareness, attitudes, and behavior as well as measures of additional profile variables such as media exposure, demographics, psychographics, and personality traits and states.

2 *Syndicated Media Data* (for example, SMRB, VALS, PRIZM) Syndicated media data on audience profile variables offer a less expensive but much less satisfactory alternative to custom surveys.

Simmons Market Research Bureau (SMRB) is perhaps the most widely used service. Its main drawback is that its survey procedure provides no brand *attitude* measures (essential to our target audience definition). Other drawbacks include general rather than specific buyer behavior measures, and a limited and apparently unvalidated psychographic-cum-personality inventory. SMRB's main usefulness is for approximate matching of media audiences with product of brand user segments, but not with target audiences as we have defined them.

SRI International's Values and Lifestyles Survey (VALS) offers a fixed consumer typology based on a combination of *demographics and psychographics*. Nine consumer types are defined (theoretically, not statistically) in terms of a Maslow-type socioeconomic hierarchy crossed horizontally by the psychographic dimension of "outer" (traditional) versus "inner" (independent) value orientation. Unfortunately, the VALS system is not open to examination by objective experts, has been validated only anecdotally, needs a considerable amount of supplementary research before the decision maker can be properly understoood, and—in our opinion—has been "oversold" to advertisers. Furthemore, it commits the fallacy of backward segmentation by splitting the consumer population first and *then* seeing how they regard the brand. VALS does not fit our approach but potentially it is an additional way of profiling decision makers.

Claritas Corporation's Potential Rating Index by Zip Market (PRIZM) is useful for local media or direct mail marketers. PRIZM categorizes each zip code in the United States by *demographics,* such as age, income, and so forth, grouping zip codes into about 40 demographic types or clusters. If these demographics happen to be correlated with the target audience for a brand (quite unlikely) or with category users for a product (more likely), then "geo-demographic" services such as PRIZM can help to *locate* target audience decision makers.

Statistical Analysis of Profile Data   A number of statistical techniques are available to relate profile variables to the brand awareness, attitude, and behavior measures that define the target audience decision maker.

Academic researchers tend to employ multivariate statistical techniques such as multiple regression or discriminant analysis, but these can "strip" meaningful profile variables and often produce results that are difficult for the manager to interpret.[20]

Practitioners, on the other hand, tend to use simple cross-tabulations that often are redundant but are at the same time easy to interpret.

A useful compromise is offered by Bass[21]: Use regression or discriminant analysis first, to isolate important variables; then cross-tabulate on these variables to provide managerially interpretable results.

SUMMARY

This chapter has explained how to profile the target audience, selected from one of the four potential buyer groups or more specifically from the prospect sub-groups distinguished in Chapter 4. Profiling is instrumental in identifying the individual decision maker to whom the advertising or promotion is directed.

There are five roles that individual buyers or consumers who contribute to the purchase decision can play. Each has a specific action objective. The initiator proposes the brand for consideration. The influencer recommends the brand. The decider makes the final go/no go decision. The purchaser carries out the act of buying. The user is the actual user or consumer of the brand. Advertising and promotion may be directed to individuals in one or more of these roles, with the respective action objectives as described.

Many family purchases and industrial purchases are acquired by group decision. However, since advertising and promotion can't be "in" the group when the decision is made, advertising and promotion must attempt to influence the main individuals, in role, *before* they participate in the group decision. Personal purchases are simpler: The individual plays all five roles and there is only one decision maker to be reached.

The relevant decision maker (or decision makers) to be targeted in a campaign can be identified most easily by constructing a behavioral sequence model. Such a model, generated through qualitative (focus-group or individual depth interview) research with consumers, breaks the overall purchase decision process into stages, identifies the decision-making roles in each stage, and then specifies the location and timing of the decision stages as they evolve from initial need arousal through to purchase and usage. The behavioral sequence model shows which decision makers to target and where and when they can be reached.

The most important information the manager needs to know in profiling the target audience decision maker is his or her current behavior and communication effect status (notably brand awareness and brand attitude) with regard to the brand. If the target audience is unaware of the brand, this requires showing a cross-section of decision makers the brand and its advertised benefits, thus making them aware and asking them what their attitude and behavior would be.

Once the *current* behavior and communication effects status of the typical target audience member are known, the manager can then set objectives to reflect the *target* communication effects and action that the advertising or promotion seeks in the target audience.

Several additional profile variables (secondary to behavior and communication effects) help the advertiser to reach the target audience decision maker more effectively and efficiently. These are media exposure, which increases the accuracy of media selection and scheduling; demographics, a much less accurate but commonly employed way of matching target audiences with media audiences, and useful also for selecting appropriate visual and verbal message content; psychographics or lifestyle measures, which help in selecting suitable media vehicles and in selecting appropriate visual message content; personality traits, which affect verbal message content and also media scheduling via repetition; and personality states, which affect the decision maker during media vehicle exposure and thus also affect the choice of verbal message content.

So, we have selected the target audience, set action objectives, and gained a detailed understanding of the type of decision makers within the target audience to whom the advertising or promotion campaign is directed. Advertising and promotion work through communication, and it is to communication effects and communication objectives (step 3 in the effects sequence, preceding action) that we turn now in the next part of the book.

NOTES

1 R.Z. Chew, Hathaway paradox: shirts for men, ads for women, *Advertising Age,* October 31, 1977, p. 10.

2 H.L. Davis, Decision making within the household, *Journal of Consumer Research,* 1976, *2* (4), 241–260.

3 J.M. Choffray and G.L. Lilien, *Market Planning for New Industrial Products,* New York: Ronald Press, 1980.

4 It may be noted as an aside that industrial or organizational buyer behavior theorists often include another role, "gatekeeper," which is the role of screening incoming information. See, for example, F.E. Webster and Y. Wind, *Organizational Buying Behavior,* Englewood Cliffs, NJ: Prentice-Hall, 1972. We see the gatekeeping function as general to the first four roles rather than as a separate role. For example, a front-office secretary may screen sales calls but essentially the secretary is acting as a (negative) initiator and influencer.

5 See, for example, J.F. Engel, R.D. Blackwell, and P.F. Miniard, *Consumer Behavior* (5th ed.). Chicago: Dryden, 1985; D.I. Hawkins, R.B. Best, and K.A. Coney, *Consumer Behavior: Implications for Marketing Strategy* (rev. ed.). Dallas, TX: Business Publications, Inc., 1983; T.S. Robertson, J. Zeilinski, and S. Ward, *Consumer Behavior,* Glenview, IL: Scott, Foresman, 1984.

6 For a review of market segmentation variables and methods, see Y. Wind, Issues and advances in segmentation research, *Journal of Marketing Research,* 1978, *15* (3), 317–337. A convenient list is provided also in P. Kotler, *Marketing Management: Analysis, Planning, and Control* (5th ed.). Englewood Cliffs, NJ: Prentice-Hall, 1984, p. 256.

7 This point is well discussed in M. Fishbein, A theory of reasoned action, in H.E. Howe (Ed.), *Nebraska Symposium on Motivation,* Lincoln, NE: University of Nebraska Press, 1980, pp. 65–116.

8 The match is rarely perfect because to reach every member of the target audience, you'd have to advertise in at least one media vehicle that reaches each person. If target audience individuals have diverse media exposure, this could be prohibitively expensive. Thus, vehicles are chosen that a *majority* of target audience individuals are exposed to. See Part Seven for further explanation of the direct matching method of media selection.

9 The term "lifestyle" is attributed to the famous psychoanalyst, Alfred Adler. See, for example, A. Adler, *Understanding Human Nature,* London: George Allen & Unwin, 1962. Adler referred to "style of life" as the characteristic behavior patterns and attitudes that differentiate one person from another. Psychoanalytically, he regarded each person as "striving for superiority expressed in an individual way." Measurement of lifestyle is through psychographic questionnaire items. "Demographics" comes from the Greek words meaning "describing the people"; "psychographics," also from the Greek, means "describing the spirit, soul, or mind" of the person.

10 See, for example, R.B. Cattell, *The Scientific Analysis of Personality,* Baltimore, MD: Penguin Books, 1965; and H.J. Eysenck (Ed.), *A Model for Personality,* Berlin, GDR: Springer-Verlag, 1981.

11 Two interesting experiments on technical wording in ads are those by M.R. Lautman and L. Percy, Consumer-oriented versus advertiser-oriented language: comprehensibility and salience of the advertising message, in H.K. Hunt (Ed.), *Advances in Consumer Research,* Vol. 5, Ann Arbor, MI: Association for Consumer Research, 1978, pp. 52–56; and R.E. Anderson and M.A. Jolson, Technical wording in advertising: implications for market segmentation, *Journal of Marketing,* 1980, *44* (1), 57–66.

12 For example, Burke Related Recall norms, a rough measure of learning, indicate 20 percent lower scores, on average, for individuals who did not finish high school. See Burke Marketing Research, Inc., *Day-After Recall Television Commercial Norms,* Cincinnati, OH: Burke Marketing Research, Inc., 1979.

13 B. Sternthal and C.S. Craig, Fear appeals: revisited and revised, *Journal of Consumer Research,* 1974, *1* (3), 22–34. In their excellent review of fear appeals, Sternthal and Craig conclude that a relationship between fear level and trait anxiety has not been proven. However, a more recent, real-world study indicated that a high-fear promotion of a health maintenance organization (HMO) was differentially effective with older people, who may have more chronic anxiety about their health. See J.J. Burnett and R.E. Wilkes, Fear appeals to segments only, *Journal of Advertising Research,* 1980, *20* (5), 21–24.

14 H.J. Eysenck, same reference as note 10.

15 J.R. Rossiter and L. Percy, Attitude change through visual imagery in advertising, *Journal of Advertising,* 1980, *9* (2), 10–16; and J.R. Rossiter and L. Percy, Visual communication in advertising, in R.J. Harris (Ed.), *Information Processing Research in Advertising,* Hillsdale, NJ: Lawrence Erlbaum Associates, 1983, pp. 83–125.

16 W.J. McGuire discusses sex differences in persuasibility in his chapter, The nature of attitudes and attitude change, pp. 251–252, in G. Lindsey and E. Aronson (Eds.), *The Handbook of Social Psychology* (2nd ed.). Vol. 3, Reading, MA: Addison-Wesley, 1969, chapter 21, pp. 136–314.

17 G. Brooker, Representativeness of shortened personality measures, *Journal of Consumer Research,* 1978, *5* (2), 143–145.

18 H.H. Kasarjian, Personality and consumer behavior: a review, *Journal of Marketing Research,* 1971, *8* (4), 409–418.

19 This and many other excellent points are made by W.D. Wells, Psychographics: a critical review, *Journal of Marketing Research,* 1975, *12* (2), 196–213. For a demonstration of the dramatic effect of increasing the reliability of behavioral measures before relating them to personality, see S. Epstein, The stability of behavior: I. On predicting most of the people much of the time, *Journal of Personality and Social Psychology,* 1979, *37* (6), 1097–1126.

20 For an excellent discussion of this point, see W.D. Wells, same reference as note 19; and also W.D. Wells and D.J. Tigert, Activities, interests and opinions, *Journal of Advertising Research,* 1971, *11* (4), 27–35.

21 F.M. Bass, Analytical approaches in the study of purchase behavior and brand choice, in National Science Foundation, *Selected Aspects of Consumer Behavior,* Washington, D.C.: U.S. Government Printing Office, 1977, pp. 491–511.

DISCUSSION QUESTIONS

5.1 An example in the chapter mentioned men and women as alternative target audiences for Hathaway brand men's shirts. Based on the decision roles and specific action objectives identified in Table 5.1, prepare a more thorough account of the likely importance of men and women as target audiences for the brand's advertising *and* promotion.

5.2 Advertising to group decision makers, as is common in industrial buying, requires targeting decision makers in their individual roles. Imagine IBM is planning an advertising campaign for its personal computers for company, in-office use. Construct and discuss a likely behavioral sequence model that might aid IBM in its advertising plan.

5.3 One of the difficult realizations to communicate to marketing students is that you should segment *first* on behavior and communication effects and only *then* look at demographics, psychographics, etc. One of the better ways to assimilate a new viewpoint is to have to role-play arguing for it publicly. Prepare a short oral presentation to the class on how best to define the target audience for Stouffer's high-priced line of frozen entrees.

5.4 Summarize, with examples, the major advertising applications of the following profile variables: (a) television programs watched, (b) occupation, (c) liberated woman's lifestyle, (d) extraversion, (e) situational tiredness.

5.5 CBS Records uses four psychographic segments to profile the market for popular music: "Top 40's," "Sophisticates," "Straights," and "Uninterested." Based on the definition in this chapter, are these really psychographic segments; why or why not?

FURTHER READING

Percy, L. How market segmentation guides advertising strategy. *Journal of Advertising Research,* 1976, *16* (5), 11–22.

Fairly technical article by one of the present authors that emphasizes the primacy of attitudes in target audience definition and specifies what ideally needs to be known about the decision maker (we now emphasize behavior and other communication effects, notably awareness, as well, but this article presents a strong case for the attitude-alone viewpoint). Includes measurement details that may be of interest to technically sophisticated readers.

Wells, W.D. Psychographics: a critical review. *Journal of Marketing Research,* 1975, *12* (2), 196–213.

This and the earlier and less detailed Wells and Tigert article (note 20) should be studied by everyone who has used or is planning to use psychographic measures to profile a target audience. Also contains many practical pointers on validity, reliability, and interpretation of "high-powered" statistical results.

Wilkie, W.L., and Cohen, J.B. A behavioral science look at market segmentation research. In Wind, Y., and Greenberg, M. (Eds.). *Attitude Research Comes to a Head*. Chicago, IL: American Marketing Association, 1977, pp. 29–38.

Contrasts "academic" and "practitioner" approaches to market segmentation, with an extremely useful overview of alternative segmentation variables and how they fit together. Located in a somewhat obscure reference book but well worth finding.

COMMUNICATION
OBJECTIVES

CHAPTER 6

COMMUNICATION OBJECTIVES

Advertising and promotion cause action through the process of communication by establishing relatively enduring mental associations connected to the brand in the prospective buyer's mind, called communication effects. Communication *objectives* must be selected by the manager—from the five communication effects—when planning a specific advertising or promotion campaign. After reading this chapter you should:

- Become familiar with the five basic communication effects
- See how they translate to other decision maker roles
- Know how to select specific options from among these communication effects which become the communication *objectives* for the campaign

THE FIVE COMMUNICATION EFFECTS

There are five basic communication effects that can be caused, in whole or in part, by advertising and promotion. Definitions of each are provided in Table 6.1. The five basic communication effects are:

1 Category need
2 Brand awareness
3 Brand attitude
4 Brand purchase intention
5 Purchase facilitation

All potential buyers experience these effects "in their head" prior to purchase decisions. Decision makers in *other roles beside the purchaser role* also experience the communication effects; however, there is some modification

TABLE 6.1   THE FIVE BASIC COMMUNICATION EFFECTS DEFINED

1 Category need	Buyer's perception of requiring something (a product or service) to remove or satisfy a perceived discrepancy between the current motivational state and the desired motivational state.
2 Brand awareness	Buyer's ability to identify (recognize or recall) the brand within the category in sufficient detail to make a purchase.
3 Brand attitude	Buyer's overall evaluation of the brand with respect to its perceived ability to meet a currently relevant motivation (brand attitude consists of an "emotional" or affective motivation-related component which energizes brand choice and a "logical" or cognitive belief component which directs choice toward the particular brand).
4 Brand purchase intention	Buyer's self-instruction to purchase the brand or to take purchase-related action.
5 Purchase facilitation	Buyer's perception of other marketing factors (the "4 P's") that can hinder or stimulate purchase.

in the last two purchase-related effects since these other decision-making roles involve, not purchase, but rather proposing, recommending, choosing, or using the product (see Chapter 5). For convenience, we will focus on the *purchaser role* in this chapter.

The five communication effects are illustrated most easily with an "existential" example. The example is existential or introspective because we cannot directly see what goes on inside a potential buyer's head; we must infer the effects by seeing if they fit our own experiences in making purchase decisions.

Suppose you are exposed to an advertisement for the new Nissan 300 ZX automobile (Figure 6.1). What would have to happen "in your head" before you would buy this new car? Five communication effects would have to occur, approximately as follows.

1 *Category Need* First, you would have to be "in the market" for a new car. The Nissan 300 ZX advertisement could have some influence in stimulating this need (see need arousal stage in the behavioral sequence model in Chapter 5). Perhaps it reminds you that your present car is getting older or that it is less than contemporary-looking, or perhaps you are a potential new category user (NCU) seeking a first car and the ad reminds you of this perceived need.

At any one time, only about 7 percent of adults are definitely in the market for a new car, as measured by surveyed intentions to buy one in the next 6 months.[1] Perhaps an advertisement, such as the one shown in Figure 6.1—or a promotion, such as a rebate offer—could put you in the 7 percent. This would be a communication objective of the advertiser: to create or increase category need if it is not already previously established at action-taking strength.

2 *Brand Awareness* Of course, the marketer and advertiser do not want you to buy just any brand of new car; they want you to buy a Nissan 300 ZX.

FIGURE 6.1   Nissan 300 ZX advertisement used as the example in the communication effects overview. (*Courtesy Nissan Motor Corporation in U.S.A.*)

To consider a particular brand within the product category, you have to first be aware of it. You may have seen or heard about the Nissan 300 ZX before—or perhaps this ad, in this book, either made you aware or strengthened your awareness.

One of the primary functions of advertising is to create (for trial) and maintain (for repeat purchase) brand awareness. Promotion offers can do this, too. As we saw in Chapter 1, most new products are launched with an equally high ratio of advertising and promotion, with promotion taking the form of samples or demonstrations, rebates, trial coupons, etc.

Advertising, and attention-getting promotion offers, can create brand awareness widely, quickly, and efficiently. In this instance, advertising is aimed at people like you to generate brand awareness for the Nissan 300 ZX.

3 *Brand Attitude* Unless the product category is extremely inexpensive and low-risk, brand awareness alone will not be enough to induce purchase. The incidence of purchases based on brand awareness alone, without attitude, is so small as to be negligible. For purchase in virtually all product categories, prospective buyers have to develop a favorable *attitude* toward the brand before they will buy it.

It is unlikely that a single advertisement for the Nissan 300 ZX could, by itself, create a sufficiently favorable attitude for you to actively consider buying this car. If you are like most people, you would consult other information sources, such as friends, or car magazine ratings of automobiles, or you may even call a Nissan dealer for futher details of price and performance. However, there is no doubt that for most products, advertising (especially) and promotion (some types) can be highly instrumental in creating, increasing, maintaining, modifying, or changing brand attitude.

You may have noticed in the list of five basic communication effects, earlier, that the middle three carry a brand prefix. In contrast, the first communication effect, category need, by definition, is generic to the category, and purchase facilitation, the fifth communication effect, may be, as explained below.

Brand awareness, brand attitude, and brand purchase intention, the middle three communication effects, are brand specific and are usually competitive with awareness, attitudes, and intentions toward other brands.

Competing brand attitudes can be illustrated easily in the present example by exposing you to a competing advertisement for the Fiat Spider 2000 (Figure 6.2). Although you now have competing brand awareness for this other brand, Nissan hopes that your brand attitude toward the 300 ZX will be more favorable than your brand attitude toward the Fiat Spider 2000. The same would hold with regard to other automobile brands and models of which you may be aware.

Brand attitude, as we shall see in this chapter and in Chapter 7, is a complex communication effect with both logical and emotional components. For now, we will refer to it only in a general manner.

4 *Brand Purchase Intention* Consumer's heads are full of favorable brand attitudes that they don't seriously intend to do anything about by way of purchase action. What if the competing ad had been for a Rolls-Royce rather than a Fiat Spider? Most people have a highly favorable attitude toward Rolls-Royce automobiles—but very few seriously intend to buy one. This brings us to the fourth communication effect: brand purchase intention.

FIGURE 6.2 Fiat Spider 2000 advertisement exemplifying competing brand communication effects for the Nissan 300 ZX. (*Courtesy Fiat Auto U.S.A. Inc.*)

Promotion—in particular—plays a leading role in stimulating brand purchase intention. Recall the definition in Chapter 1 of promotion as "immediately stimulating purchase." A discount or rebate offer on the Nissan 300 ZX would probably hasten and increase your intention to buy the brand. With brand purchase intention stimulated to full strength, you would act immediately on the favorable brand attitude and plan to buy the car.

Advertising, too, can stimulate brand purchase intention. Perhaps you were already intending to visit a Nissan dealership regardless of any promotional inducement. Brand loyals (BL) often do not need promotional inducements, since their *re*-purchase intentions are already very high. However, promotional inducements—as well as attractive pricing terms as a marketing input—often are needed to get other target audiences to take purchase action, and sometimes are needed to get brand loyals up to the threshold of acting immediately, too. Usually, advertising and promotion function *together* to create or strengthen brand purchase intention.

5 *Purchase Facilitation* If the Nissan 300 ZX advertising has been successful to this point—increasing your category need, creating brand awareness, developing a favorable brand attitude, and increasing your brand purchase intention—there is still one more communication effect to be achieved. This we call *purchase facilitation*.

Purchase facilitation is mainly a result of other factors in the brand's (or the category's) marketing mix—the 4 P's described in Chapter 1. In relation to the Nissan 300 ZX, for example, you would probably have to be mentally satisfied (1) that the *product* looks good in the showroom and test-drives well; (2) that the *price* or payment terms are affordable; (3) that Nissan's *distribution* is reasonably convenient, both to visit the showroom in the first place, and for post-purchase service later; and (4) that the other aspects of *promotion,* namely, personal selling in the form of the salesperson's informativeness and fairness, and perhaps publicity about the Nissan 300 ZX in media or by word of mouth, are additionally positive.

Experienced advertising managers will recognize that these "other marketing factors" are often blamed as barriers to otherwise effective advertising. The advertising may be "effective" but, for instance, (1) the product doesn't meet consumer expectations; or (2) the distribution "pipeline" isn't filled in time to meet advertised or promoted demand; or (3) the price was higher than the consumer expected; or (4) the sales force muffed the sale.

We take a more positive view: Advertising and promotion must do everything possible to overcome these obstacles, when they exist. This is why we include purchase facilitation as a communication effect. In our Nissan 300 ZX example, we would target purchase facilitation by (1) only advertising believable and deliverable product (brand) attributes; (2) addressing possible price problems with judicious promotion offers *or* by creating a brand attitude that is so favorable that price is hardly considered; (3) indicating, in ads, where Nissan dealerships are and how to get there easily; and (4) in coordination with sales management, mentioning our informed and considerate sales personnel.

Our point is that purchase facilitation—though originally caused by other marketing factors—is a perceived (mental) effect in the buyer's mind to which, very often, advertising and promotion can substantially contribute.

We will now examine each of the communication effects in turn, discussing the options available to the manager in considering each communication effect for possible inclusion in the set of *communication objectives* for an advertising or promotion campaign.

1. CATEGORY NEED

Category Need Defined

Category need refers to the buyer's perception of requiring something (a product or service) to remove or satisfy a perceived discrepancy between the current motivational state and the desired motivational state. Category need is the *perceived connection*—which can be established by the advertiser—between a product category and a buyer motivation.

Buyer Motivation   Consumers are activated to buy products because they undergo any one of eight basic purchase motivations. As these product category needs or motives are also possible motives to which *brands* can be connected (via the brand attitude communication effect), we will defer detailed consideration of them for now. The motives, briefly, are: problem removal, problem avoidance, incomplete satisfaction, mixed approach-avoidance, and normal depletion (all negatively originated motives for action); and sensory gratification, intellectual stimulation, and social approval (all positively originated motives for action). A category need occurs when one of these motives is aroused *and* a general product category is perceived by the buyer as a way of resolving or satisfying the motive.

Primary Demand   By successfully establishing a perceived connection (a belief) between the product category and a relevant motivation, the advertiser can stimulate *primary demand,* that is, demand for the product category as a whole. Category need is the communication effect that causes primary demand. But note that category need, and its marketplace result, primary demand, apply to *all brands* in the category. To stimulate secondary or selective demand, the advertiser also must influence the brand-level communication effects: brand awareness, brand attitude, and brand purchase intention.

Managerial Options with Regard to Category Need

Category need has to be present at full strength before purchase of a brand within that category can occur. That is, the prospect has to be "in the market" for the product (category).

Category need is *not always* a communication *objective*. There are three options for the manager (Table 6.2): to assume that the category need is present, to remind the buyer of category need, or to "sell" category need.

Assume Category Need (Omit)   With frequently purchased products—and a category user (BL, BS, or OBL) target audience—category need is *not* a communication objective. Category need can be assumed to be present, and it does not have to be addressed in advertising or promotion.

An advertisement or promotion for any brand of a frequently purchased product—providing it is aimed at category users (that is, *not* at NCU's)—can assume category need to be present and omit this communication effect from its set of communication objectives.

Retail newspaper ads by supermarkets and drugstores are a prime example. They assume that category need is present and simply promote various brands to current product category users.

Reminder of Category Need   A second option, in which category need *is* an objective, is to remind the prospective buyer of a latent or forgotten (but previously established) category need. The Alka-Seltzer ad, "Will it be there when you need it," is a perfect example of "reminding" prospective buyers of the category need (Figure 6.3).

The reminder option applies mostly to product categories that are *infrequently purchased*, like pain remedies. The reminder option also applies to one-time-purchase products that are *infrequently used*, at least in the opinion of the advertiser. Ogilvy & Mather's well-known campaign theme for the American Express card, "Don't leave home without it," is a good example of the reminder objective for infrequent users.

Category need reminder campaigns usually can be achieved without detailed advertising content having to be devoted to category need. The purpose is merely to *re-establish* a previously learned connection between the product category and a motivation. This is in sharp contrast with the third option, which is to "sell" the category need.

TABLE 6-2   MANAGERIAL OPTIONS WITH REGARD TO CATEGORY NEED AS A COMMUNICATION OBJECTIVE

Buyer state	Communication objective
1 Category need already present	Category need can be *omitted* and is not an objective of the advertising or promotion.
2 Latent category need	Category need only has to be mentioned to *remind* buyer of previously established need.
3 No or weak category need	Category need must be addressed and "*sold*" using *category* communication effects.

FIGURE 6.3   Reminder of category need: a long-running ad for Alka-Seltzer. (*Courtesy Miles Laboratories, Inc.*)

Selling the Category Need   When the category need is not yet established in the prospective buyer's mind—as is the case with new category users—the advertising campaign, often with promotional support, has to "sell" the category need. The U.S. armed services recruitment campaign is a good example, selling this sort of career as the category need.

"Selling" category need is a communication objective for all new products and also for established products aimed at *new users* (NCU's). If the target audience has not bought within the category before, advertising or promotion must include selling the category need as a communication objective.

"Selling the category," from an advertising content standpoint, requires the selling of *category* benefits—the benefits that tie the product category to the purchase motivation. Selling the category involves creating, in the prospective buyer's mind, *category communication effects.*[2] Thus, when selling the category, it is meaningful to speak of category awareness, category attitude, and category purchase intention. When selling category need, these category-level communication effects must be addressed *in addition to* brand-level communication effects.

For example, when Campbell's introduced its "Soup is good food" campaign into test markets in California in 1980, sales of the prepared soup category increased 5.5 percent in the next 2 years and sales of the brand increased 2.6 percent. Clearly they had successfully addressed category communication effects as well as brand communication effects, selling the category as well as the brand.[3]

2. BRAND AWARENESS

Brand Awareness Defined

Brand awareness is the buyer's ability to identify (recognize or recall) the brand within the category in sufficient detail to make a purchase. Note that in decision maker roles other than the purchaser role, this definition is adapted to refer to identification of the brand in sufficient detail to propose, recommend, choose, or use the brand, respectively.

The "sufficient detail" aspect means that brand awareness does *not* always require identification of the brand *name,* as in brand name recall. For a child, or even an adult, brand awareness may consist of some other identifying stimulus such as package color (for example, "the red one" for Stouffer's) or an even more general stimulus such as location (for example, "the restaurant on the corner"). These identifications still enable brand choice to proceed even though no brand name is involved.

Moreover, *recall* of the name, color, etc., is not necessarily required. Instead, brand awareness may occur through brand *recognition*. When a package is recognized in a supermarket (for example, Birdseye) or when a retail store sign is recognized when on a shopping trip (for example, K mart), brand awareness does not require brand recall. We will return to this difference shortly, because brand recognition and brand recall are the two main options for brand awareness as a communication *objective*.

Brand Awareness Must Precede Brand Attitude

At the product category level, a person won't buy unless he or she has the category need. At the brand level, a person *cannot* buy unless he or she is first made aware of the brand. Thus, brand awareness takes *precedence* over the other brand-level communication effects, and in particular, over brand attitude.

The precedence of brand awareness is usually, and wrongly, overlooked by managers when conducting marketing or advertising research for a brand. Although this may seem like a technical measurement point better left to the chapters on advertising research, it is a vital point to emphasize here as well. In marketing and advertising research, interviewers generally ask consumers about their brand awareness, then make *all* consumers aware, asking all consumers about their brand attitude. This is okay as long as the two measures are analyzed properly, which usually they are not.

What usually happens is that a count is made of the "percent aware" and a *separate* count is made of the "percent with a favorable (or neutral or negative) attitude." Unless the two measures are compiled *together,* at the individual consumer level, the figures are meaningless. The manager needs to know the percent of individuals who have brand awareness *plus* a favorable brand attitude. A favorable brand attitude without prior brand awareness is useless, because the individual could not purchase the brand.

Recognition or Recall: An Essential Difference

Brand awareness is widely misunderstood and often wrongly measured, even by experienced managers. The difficulty relates to the essential difference between recognition and recall—a difference that is extremely relevant to advertising.[4] Brand recognition and brand recall are two different types of brand awareness. The difference depends on which communication effect occurs in the buyer's mind first: category need or brand awareness (see Table 6.3).

Recognition: Brand Awareness First In many decision-making situations, such as in a supermarket, the brand is literally presented to the consumer,

TABLE 6-3   BRAND AWARENESS: THE DIFFERENCE BETWEEN BRAND RECOGNITION AND BRAND RECALL

Brand recognition	
Brand is encountered first, e.g. (in supermarket), "That's Bounce"	Buyer then mentally checks category need, e.g., "Do I need fabric softener that works in the dryer?"
BA $\longrightarrow$	CN
Brand recall	
Category need is encountered first, e.g., "I have a headache"	Buyer then recalls brand, e.g., "Anacin"
CN $\longrightarrow$	BA

who *then* decides whether the relevant category need is present and whether to proceed with the decision. The sequence in the buyer's mind is: brand awareness (recognition) → category need. Thereafter, other communication effects are also elicited, notably brand attitude; that is, the buyer decides whether this is the best brand.

Note that the brand actually may fail a recall test—for example, in a consumer survey outside the context of the store—yet be recognized in the store precisely as intended (parodied in the cartoon in Figure 6.4). Reliance on the typical recall interpretation (unaided recall based on a product category cue, for example, "What fabric softeners have you heard of?") of brand awareness can be seriously misleading for the manager if the brand is not chosen by recall but by recognition.

The manager has to assess the *most likely decision situation* facing the buyer. A behavioral sequence model (see Chapter 5) is the best means of doing this unless the answer is intuitively apparent. For some product categories, brand awareness mostly occurs through recognition whereas for others, recall is the prevalent process.

Recall: Category Need First   In other decision-making situations, the brand is not present. A category need is experienced first, and the consumer must *recall* the brand or several brands from memory. In the example in Table 6.3, the would-be buyer gets a headache, then recalls (is aware of) the brand as a solution. Even better examples of recall-dominant decisions are airline reservations or courier services, such as Federal Express. Unlike the aspirin situation, where recall could be offset by recognition of another brand at the point of purchase, with product categories such as airline or courier services, where the purchase order is placed by telephone, the decision maker never visits the point of purchase or, perhaps in the airline situation, doesn't visit until after the brand choice is finalized. The first-recalled brand (given also a favorable attitude) will usually get the business.

Again the key is to assess the most likely decision situation for the brand.

FIGURE 6.4   A humorous example of brand recognition (Bounce Fabric Softener). The other type of brand awareness is brand recall, which occurs prior to the point of purchase. (*Drawing by C. Barsotti;* © *1981, The New Yorker Magazine, Inc.*)

This measurement can be made by questioning buyers (to develop a behavioral sequence model) or by common knowledge of how people buy the brand.

Managerial Options with Regard to Brand Awareness

Is it recognition or is it recall? One of these two types of brand awareness is relevant as a communication objective in *all* advertising and promotion situations. In all situations, the manager is trying to *create* or to *maintain* brand awareness so that the brand can be considered, by the prospective buyer, for purchase.

Whereas it might be argued that some target audiences are so fully aware of the brand that brand awareness could be omitted as a communication objective, this is not so, for two reasons. In the first place, it is impossible to have an "unbranded" ad or promotion offer. So as long as you're showing or mentioning the brand, you may as well do it in a way that maintains brand awareness. A second reason is the relative vulnerability of brand awareness. A brand can all too easily slip out of the buyer's "evoked set" if it is not given sufficient exposure.[5] Brand awareness is *always* a communication objective.

The managerial options for brand awareness as a communication objective therefore center on whether to emphasize brand recognition, or brand recall, or (only if necessary) both. These options are summarized in Table 6.4.

These options are important because they directly affect the choice of advertisement (or promotion) *content*. Several major differences are reviewed below, and details are left to Part Five's discussion of creative strategy.

Brand Recognition   When buyers identify the brand *at* the point of purchase, as with many supermarket products, advertisements and also promotional material should ensure that the buyer will be able to *recognize* the brand.

In most cases, this means showing packages in the advertising and (for a new brand especially) using exact package color. Close-ups of the package in TV commercials, and also in magazine ads, are the best type of advertising content for brand recognition. These ads must be in visual media (thereby excluding radio) and, again for a new brand, in color (thereby excluding newspapers unless a color insert is purchased).

TABLE 6-4   MANAGERIAL OPTIONS WITH REGARD TO BRAND AWARENESS AS A COMMUNICATION OBJECTIVE

Brand identification	Communication objective
1 *At* point of purchase	Brand *recognition*
2 *Prior* to purchase	Brand *recall*
3 Substantial proportions of the target audience use both of the above, or both on different occasions	*Both* brand recognition and brand recall

A slightly different case—easily detectable from the brand's behavioral sequence model—is brand *name* recognition when the brand name is *heard*. For example, when you say to a waiter in a restaurant "What types of beer do you have?," you have to recognize one of the names that the waiter gives you. Here we are dealing with *auditory recognition,* and for auditory recognition, an auditory medium (TV or radio) works best. In this one case, the advertising content is the same as for brand recall.

Brand Recall   When buyers must identify the brand *prior* to the point of purchase, the appropriate communication objective is brand *recall*.

Don't get brand recall confused with advertising recall—that is something quite different. The objective in brand recall is to get the buyer to recall the *brand,* regardless of whether he or she can recall the advertising.

Brand recall tactics are fairly obvious: Repeat the brand name in video and audio (TV) or in audio alone (radio) or in headlines and copy (print advertisements). It doesn't seem to matter whether buyers read or hear the brand name; when they read it they "hear" it in their minds anyway. Note, however, that for special audiences such as young children who can't read, or ethnic consumers who can't read English, *audio* repetition is required.

Both Brand Recognition and Brand Recall   The manager should think very carefully before emphasizing *both* brand recognition and brand recall. Reason: They require two different types of advertising content, and often, the use of more than one advertising medium, as outlined above, and this can be expensive.

The situations in which *both* brand recognition and brand recall become *dual* brand awareness communication objectives are as follows:

- For a *new brand,* when target audience consumers are likely to make a deliberate brand choice prior to purchase (by brand recall) and then have to *find* the brand from an often-crowded purchase display (by brand recognition). New brands sold in crowded supermarket or drugstore displays often have to achieve both types of brand awareness initially.
- When the typical target audience consumer—as an individual—in many *situations* chooses one way (for example, Pepsi recognized in a supermarket) and in many others chooses the other way (for example, Pepsi when recalling in a restaurant what to drink). If purchases in both situations are similarly important to the advertiser, then both types of brand awareness are appropriate.

Brand awareness is strictly a rote-learned connection between the brand and the category need. You don't have to be motivated to be aware of a brand, but you do have to be motivated to buy it. This is where brand attitude, the next communication effect, comes in.

3. BRAND ATTITUDE

Brand Attitude Defined

Like brand awareness which must precede it, brand attitude is also a necessary communication effect for purchase of the brand to occur. Brand attitude (even if only in a maintenance capacity) is *always* a communication objective. Potential buyers usually are aware of several to many brands in a given product category; they choose a particular brand based on brand attitude.

The term "attitude" has a long and distinguished history and has been defined in many ways. The definition that we favor is primarily pertinent to consumer behavior. Also, our definition fits advertising strategy better than other definitions.

Brand attitude refers to the buyer's overall evaluation of the brand with respect to its perceived ability to meet a currently relevant motivation. There are four important characteristics to be understood about brand attitude:

1 Brand attitude *depends on the currently relevant motivation*—if the buyer's motivation changes, so might the buyer's brand evaluation. It follows that it is essential, in assessing brand attitude, to identify the motivation that the brand is perceived to meet.

2 Brand attitude consists of a *cognitive* (or logical "belief") *component,* which guides behavior, and an associated *affective* (or emotional "feeling") *component,* which energizes behavior. These two components of attitude are explained below.

3 The cognitive component, in turn, may be made up of a number of specific *benefit beliefs*. These are not the attitude, but rather the *reasons for* the brand attitude. A brand attitude has one or more supporting benefit beliefs.

4 Brand attitude is a *relative* concept. In almost all product categories, it's a matter of which brand under consideration meets the motivation relatively better than alternative brands. If the motivation exists, the buyer will find *some* brand to meet it as best possible from those available. This will be reflected in our measurement recommendations, later.

Our purpose in this section is to explain brand attitude as a communication effect and to describe how brand attitude should be considered by the manager as a communication objective. Brand attitude is a complex and often subtle concept and it will require considerable space to elucidate it. We will defer the topic of how to *create and change* brand attitudes until the next chapter, where we examine brand attitude *strategy*. For now, we concentrate on brand attitude as a communication *objective,* that is, on the desired end result.

Brand Attitude Depends on the Currently Relevant Motivation

The first characteristic to be noted about brand attitude is that it depends on the buyer's currently relevant motivation (Figure 6.5). Failure to realize this has led to much confusion about the usefulness and predictiveness of brand attitude as a causal mediator of brand purchase and usage. Marketers often think of, and measure, brand attitudes "in a vacuum," for example, "How would you rate Xerox copiers?" or "Which is the best brand of soda?" Buyers or consumers will generally give an answer to such questions in an interview or survey setting. But they are really thinking, when it gets down to actual brand choice, "Well, it depends on what I need a copier for" or "It depends

FIGURE 6.5   The overall structure of brand attitude. Note the incomplete connection (dashed arrow) between the brand and the motivation, indicating that the brand may be evaluated as not completely delivering on (meeting) the buyer's current motivation. The advertiser's objective is to make this connection as substantial as possible (preferably a solid arrow). The brand attitude objective is achieved by establishing benefit beliefs in the buyer's mind (see Figure 6.8).

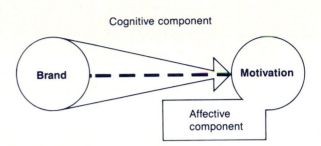

Cognitive component

Brand

Motivation

Affective component

on why I want a soda on this particular occasion.'' Generalized attitudes are practically meaningless.[6] Brand attitude is only meaningful in relation to the buyer's currently relevant motivation.

Brand Attitude: Cognitive and Affective Components

Brand attitude consists of two components: a ''logical'' (cognitive belief) component and an ''emotional'' (affective motivation-based) component. Whereas earlier theorists also believed that attitude has a ''conative'' (intention) component, recent evidence suggests that the cognitive-affective *bicomponent* construct of attitude is correct.[7] Intentions may or may not be present in the buyer's mind, as we shall see later, but cognition and affect always are.

Let us see how the cognitive and affective components of brand attitude fit together to form the overall attitude. Recall our definition of brand attitude as the buyer's overall evaluation of the brand with respect to its *perceived ability to meet* a currently *relevant motivation*. The cognitive and affective components of brand attitude pertain, respectively, to the underscored aspects of the definition.

1 *The cognitive (belief) component* represents the existence and strength of the perceived linkage between the brand and the motivation; that is, the ''perceived ability (of the brand) to meet'' the motivation. This belief or perception guides or *directs* the buyer toward the particular brand.

2 *The emotional (affect) component* is generated by the motivation itself; since it is ''currently relevant,'' the motivation is experienced as an emotional or ''felt'' deviation from the buyer's desired state. This emotion *energizes* the buyer to choose a brand.

The Order of Occurrence—and Some Examples   The cognitive (belief) and emotional (affect) components of brand attitude usually are experienced very closely in time in the buyer's mind. However, it is useful to ''stretch'' the normal experience to show how belief and affect operate. This can be done by considering the negative and positive origins of motivations.

With *negative* motivations—problem removal, problem avoidance, incomplete satisfaction, mixed approach-avoidance, and the mildly negative normal depletion—affect usually is experienced first, as the energizer, followed by belief, as the guide. The classic example of this is *problem-solution* advertising (Figure 6.6). The motivation (headache problem removal) is "hypoed" first, emotionally; then the brand (Panadol) is suggested, cognitively or "logically," as the solution. The "stretched" sequence is affect then belief, recognizing in reality that these two experiences may occur very closely in time.

With *positive* motivations—sensory gratification, intellectual stimulation, and social approval—belief usually is experienced first, as the guide, followed (almost simultaneously) by affect, as the energizer. The classic example of this is *straight reward* advertising (Figure 6.7). The brand (Tabu spray cologne) is suggested first, cognitively, followed by the promise of a reward (social approval) as the emotional energizer. The "stretched" sequence is belief then affect, again realizing that the two components are experienced very closely together.

Why Belief and Affect Are Jointly Important to Brand Attitude   So far, in explaining brand attitude, we've stressed theoretical reasons why two components, belief and affect, have to be considered. But there are practical reasons too. Firstly, belief without affect doesn't sell products. Take, for instance, "pro-social" advertising designed to encourage children to eat more nutritious foods. Studies have shown that children, almost upon starting school, *know* which foods are supposed to be "good for you" and which are supposed to be "bad for you."[8] However, children just can't get emotionally excited about this belief; instead, they stay with their sensory preferences, a completely different motivation, when choosing or requesting food. The belief-without-affect campaign doesn't work with children. Instead, it's up to parents to see that children eat nutritious food.

Conversely, affect without belief is of no help either. This means that the advertiser has aroused a motivation in the buyer but hasn't effectively instilled the brand as the choice that will meet the motivation. An example is when a hamburger advertisement reminds you that you're hungry but the hamburger looks awful. This is one reason, by the way, that food brand advertisers are so concerned about reproduction quality in various media. The brand belief has to be effectively instilled as the recommended choice to meet the buyer's motivation.

The Cognitive Component Consists of One or More Benefit Beliefs

Advertisers do not create a brand attitude by referring directly to the motivation. Rather, they connect the brand with the motivation, in advertising and promotion, through *benefits*. For example, an ad would not say: "Drink Sprite because it provides problem removal (the motivation)." Instead, ads for Sprite

FIGURE 6.6   An advertisement illustrating the affect-belief (problem-solution) sequence experienced with negatively originated motivations. (*Courtesy Sterling Drugs, Inc.*)

refer to its thirst-quenching taste (the benefit). Advertisements create *benefit beliefs* in the buyer's mind that *relate to* the underlying motivation.

Frequently, more than one benefit is necessary to cause the brand to be perceived as delivering on the motivation. The cognitive (brand delivery)

FIGURE 6.7   An advertisement illustrating the belief-affect (straight reward) sequence experienced with positively originated motivations. (*Courtesy Dana Perfumes Corporation.*)

component of brand attitude can consist of *one or more* benefit beliefs. The relationship of benefit beliefs to brand attitude is shown in Figure 6.8. Benefits are *specific beliefs* about the brand which are derived from the surface content of advertisements or promotion, whereas brand attitude is a *summary evaluation* that results, in the buyer' mind, from the benefit beliefs.

Another way of grasping this idea is to distinguish attributes, benefits, and motivations (Table 6.5):

- *Attributes* are what the brand *has*—objective characteristics such as ingredients, performance, or price—which may or may not be benefits to the buyer.
- *Benefits* are what the buyer *wants* from attributes—subjective rewards (more technically, positive and negative reinforcers) such as fresh taste, performance satisfaction, or money saving.
- *Motivations* are what the buyer wants the benefits *for*—to adjust his or her state of well-being via problem removal, sensory gratification, or one of the other eight motivations.

Benefits Must Be Linked to a Motivation   A vital point about benefits is that they must be linked to a motivation. As Fennell[9] has pointed out, benefits are *motivationally ambiguous*. It is therefore meaningless to nominate benefits in an advertising plan unless the underlying motivation, and thus the brand attitude to which the benefits contribute, is known and deliberately targeted.

For example, consumers might seek a toothpaste that delivers the benefit of "makes my mouth feel fresh." However, the motivations underlying this benefit could be quite different for different consumers. "Mouth freshness"

FIGURE 6.8   The relationship of benefit beliefs to brand attitude.

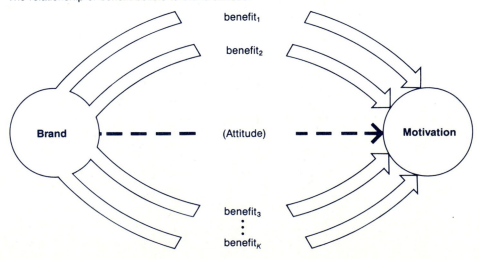

TABLE 6-5   ATTRIBUTES VS. BENEFITS VS. MOTIVATIONS

Attributes	Benefits	Motivations
Objective characteristics of the product ("what the product has")	Subjective rewards sought from attributes ("what the buyer wants")	Satisfaction of underlying motivation ("why the buyer wants it")

Examples (deliberately chosen to show frequent lack of one-to-one correspondence between attributes, benefits, and motivations)

Attributes	Benefits	Motivations
• Sugar (in food product)	• Taste	• Sensory gratification
	• "Extra energy"	• Problem removal (lack of energy)
	• Bad for teeth (negative)	• Problem avoidance (tooth decay)
• Heavy-duty (machine)	• Handles tough jobs	• Problem avoidance
	• Fewer breakdowns	
	• Shows that operator is "professional"	• Social status
• New (Rubik's Cube)	• Challenging leisure pursuit	• Intellectual stimulation
• Complex		
• Time consuming		• Problem removal (boredom)

could be sought in a toothpaste in response to several different motivations, such as:

- For sensory enjoyment (sensory gratification)
- To remove a bad taste (problem removal)
- Or in anticipation of social contact requiring fresh breath (problem avoidance)

The advertising scenarios for these three situations would be quite different, yet they all employ the same benefit! Benefits in advertising only work if they are linked to a motivation, and the advertiser has to know *which* motivation is relevant to the target audience.[10]

Let's take one more example to illustrate this basic point. Non-aspirin pain relievers, such as Panadol or Datril, advertise the benefit "gentle to the stomach." This benefit could be desired in response to several different motivations, such as:

- To reduce acute stomach pain (problem removal)
- As an additional guarantee of feeling well in case a headache, not a stomach ache, comes along (problem avoidance)
- Or even because it seems a "wise" version of the product to buy (intellectual stimulation)

Again, the advertising content would be quite different depending on which motivation the "gentle to the stomach" benefit is linked to.

Benefits, therefore, are *the surface means used in advertisements* (and also promotions) to connect the brand with the motivation—and thus to form or alter the consumer's brand attitude. The manager *has* to know the motivation before benefits can be employed to influence brand attitude. It follows that any advertising plan that simply lists benefits without referring to the motivation is incomplete and likely to fail.

Brand Attitude Is Nearly Always Relative

While it is possible to think of brand attitude in terms of the brand's perceived ability to "absolutely" meet the buyer's currently relevant motivation, the marketing manager is advised also to consider that, in competitive situations, brand attitude is "relative." There is rarely a brand that meets each individual buyer's motivation perfectly.

Almost always there are other brands out there trying to beat you in meeting buyer's needs. Even the virtual monopolist should adopt a relative stance toward brand attitude. For instance, several years ago, Xerox' share of the copier market slipped from a virtual monopoly of over 90 percent to just 46 percent in a 5-year span, largely lost to Japanese entrants. Xerox' management admits that the company took an absolute view toward its brand position.[11] Their lesson stands as a signal to all managers that the relative view is the prepared view.

More specifically, the best *measures* of brand attitude usually are those that rate competing brands relatively.[12] This makes sense when we realize that in most product categories the motivated buyer has multiple brands to choose from. In most product categories, it's a matter of *relative* perceived satisfaction when it comes to deciding on a brand on the basis of brand attitude.

Managerial Options with Regard to Brand Attitude

The managerial options when considering the brand attitude communication effect for a particular campaign comprise a set of alternative brand attitude *objectives*. In the next chapter, we examine the brand attitude strategies that have to be used to meet these objectives.

There are five alternative communication objectives for brand attitude (Table 6.6). The options are to create, increase, maintain, modify, or change the target audience's brand attitude.

Create Brand Attitude   The brand attitude objective is to *create* brand attitude when the target audience does not yet have an attitude toward the brand.

Brand attitude creation is most often relevant as the brand attitude objective for new category user target audiences. Unaware new category users (UNCU's) have no brand awareness and thus no brand attitude. However, it is possible that NCU's who are positively disposed toward the category (PNCU's) or negatively disposed (NNCU's) *will* be aware of the brand and *may* have a

TABLE 6.6   MANAGERIAL OPTIONS WITH REGARD TO BRAND ATTITUDE AS A COMMUNICATION OBJECTIVE

Buyer's prior attitude	Communication objective
1 No brand attitude (unaware)	*Create* attitude
2 Moderately favorable brand attitude	*Increase* attitude
3 Maximally favorable brand attitude	*Maintain* attitude
4 Any buyer (but usually moderately favorable brand attitude)	*Modify* attitude ("re-position" by linking to different motivation)
5 Negative brand attitude	*Change* attitude

correspondingly positive or negative attitude toward it that has been tentatively generalized from their positive or negative attitude toward the category. Consequently, an increase (PNCU's) or change (NNCU's) objective, not a creation objective, may be appropriate for these latter, specific target audiences.

Always, the manager has to determine the initial (prior) brand attitude status of the target audience before a brand attitude communication objective can be decided. This is reflected in the table.

Increase Brand Attitude   The brand attitude objective is to *increase* brand attitude when the target audience has only a moderately favorable attitude toward the brand.

A little thought will reveal that the target audiences for whom a brand attitude increase objective is applicable would be from several groups. First, positively disposed new category users (PNCU's) may be a target for brand attitude increase, as noted above, if they are aware of the brand and have a tentatively favorable attitude toward it. Second, favorable brand switchers during the early or "experimental" phase of the product life cycle (EFBS's) would certainly be a target for brand attitude increase.

Also, there are several "hard-core" attitude groups for whom an increase— if attainable—would be the objective. They are routinized favorable brand switchers (RFBS's), multi-brand loyals (MBL's), and other-brand loyals (OBL's). The objective would be to increase these groups' attitudes, if possible, toward single-brand loyalty (SBL) status.

Maintain Brand Attitude   The brand attitude objective is to *maintain* brand attitude when the target audience already has a maximally favorable brand attitude. This objective applies mainly to single-brand loyals (SBL's).

In light of the observation made above that brand attitude in most cases is relative (against competing brands) rather than absolute, the advertiser may be content to maintain the brand's relative (rank order) superiority over other brands rather than trying to make the brand be evaluated as providing perfect delivery on the motivation—that is, absolute maximum favorability. However, as the threat from competitors can always increase in the future, a maximum absolute brand attitude is a worthwhile if sometimes idealistic objective. Note that this would require an *increase* objective, even though the target audience is SBL's, unless the SBL's brand attitude is already at an absolute maximum rather than only relatively higher than the attitudes held toward other brands.

Modify Brand Attitude   We use the term *modify* to refer to the process of connecting the brand to a different motivation. The process is commonly known as "re-positioning" the brand. For example, American Express over the years has been repositioned from a utility (problem avoidance) to a prestige (social approval) card.

The motivation may be a new one for a new target audience, yet an old one for the brand. Johnson's Baby Shampoo has been repositioned using the same motivation of a mild shampoo (problem avoidance) for children to a mild shampoo (also problem avoidance because you can use it more frequently) for adults. Adults are a new target audience, being NCU's as far as baby shampoo for their own use is concerned.

Any target audience could potentially be the target for brand attitude modification. However, brand attitude modification is most likely to be tried on those groups with a moderately favorable attitude *when a brand attitude increase objective seems infeasible*. Advertisers have learned that if you can't increase an attitude, try a different attitude (a new motivation) for the brand.

Change Brand Attitude   Brand attitude *change* is the objective when the target audience holds a *negative* attitude toward the brand. Brand attitude change requires breaking a negative link between the brand and the motivation and replacing it with a positive link.

The shift from negative perceived delivery across the neutral point to positive perceived delivery is generally the hardest brand attitude objective for advertising to attain. In many cases, its infeasibility rules out prospective target audiences with a negative brand attitude completely. However, let us distinguish the possibilities.

Negative new category users (NNCU's) may be a feasible target for brand attitude change because their negative attitude may not yet be based on trial experience with the brand; first, however, you have to reverse their negative *category* attitude. Prospective target audiences who favor other brands—other brand loyals (OBL's) and other-brand switchers (OBS's)—may or may not be negative toward our brand in particular; if they are, as with unfavorable other-brand loyals (UOBL's) and routinized other-brand switchers (ROBS's), their attitude will be difficult to change because it is probably reinforced by negative trial or usage experience.

Brand Attitude Objectives: Summary   In selecting a brand attitude objective, the manager must first determine the *current brand attitude status* of the target audience. Initial attitude status dictates which brand attitude objective—create, increase, maintain, modify, or change—is needed for that target audience. The manager then has to consider the *feasibility* of attaining the *target attitude* *status* (inherent in the concept of target audience leverage) before finally selecting the brand attitude objective. To remind with just one illustration of feasibility, an increase objective may not be feasible for, say, other-brand loyals, so a modification objective may be selected instead.

4. BRAND PURCHASE INTENTION

Brand Purchase Intention Defined

Brand purchase intention is the buyer's *self-instruction* to purchase the brand (or to take other relevant purchase-related action). It is, in fact, a *conscious planning of the action step*. In other words, it's a conscious plan to complete the buyer response sequence. Depending on the decision maker targeted by the advertising, the intention could be to propose (initiator), recommend (influencer), choose (decider), buy (purchaser), or use the brand more often (user).

Delayed Versus Immediate Purchase Intentions

An intention must be conscious before the buyer will act; hence the emphasis on "self-instruction" to act.[13] An intention to buy must be conscious (the buyer literally thinks "I'll buy that") because otherwise people would behave like automatons or robots, which they don't. This much is straightforward.

The complicated part comes in considering just *when* the conscious purchase intention arises and also advertising's (or promotion's) function in producing the intention. Two advertising situations need to be distinguished:

1 There is one brand attitude strategy (see Chapter 7) where brand purchase intention does not seem to occur consciously until the last minute—*at the point of purchase* or point of decision.[14] This is called low involvement/transformational advertising. For this type of advertising, brand purchase intention is *omitted* as an objective.

2 For all other brand attitude strategies, a conscious purchase intention must occur *during advertising (or promotion) exposure*. Furthermore, it will occur only if the buyer has a current or soon-foreseen category need. You don't hear yourself saying "I'll buy that" when looking at, listening to, or reading an ad unless you're in the market for that type of product in general. Here, the objective is to *generate* brand purchase intention.

Thus we have two distinct advertising communication situations: one where brand purchase intention is *delayed,* and all others where it occurs *immediately,* if it is to occur at all. But why do the objectives differ in each case? This question is discussed next.

Managerial Options with Regard to Brand Purchase Intention

The options are to ignore (omit) or try to immediately stimulate (generate) brand purchase intention. These options are summarized in Table 6.7.

TABLE 6-7   MANAGERIAL OPTIONS WITH REGARD TO BRAND PURCHASE INTENTION AS A COMMUNICATION OBJECTIVE*

Brand attitude strategy	Communication objective
Low involvement/transformational: brand purchase is low-risk *and* the motivation is positive, specifically sensory gratification or social approval	*Omit* brand purchase intention (purchase intention forms later, at the point of purchase, not during exposure to advertising)
All others	*Generate* brand purchase intention (purchase intention forms during exposure to advertising or promotion, subject to category need)

* See Chapter 7 for further discussion of brand attitude strategies.

The Option to Omit Brand Purchase Intention   There is one type of brand choice via brand attitude that does not require that a conscious, prior intention to buy be formed during exposure to the brand's advertising. This we call low involvement/transformational brand choice (further discussed in Chapter 7). To preview this type of brand choice for present purposes, it relates to *low risk* brands that are purchased in response to either of two *positive* motivations[15]:

- *Sensory gratification,* for example, Coca-Cola, Mars bars
- *Social approval,* for example, Marlboro cigarettes, Moosehead beer

It would be inappropriate to expect, for instance, a Coca-Cola commercial to produce immediate purchase intention for the brand. Rather, after being seen and heard several times, the Coke commercial builds or reinforces an "image" (brand attitude) that comes into play in the form of a conscious purchase intention *only* when you are in the choice situation itself.[16]

Note that the buyer *does* form a brand purchase intention—not during advertising exposure, but *later,* when the purchase decision is being made. Brand purchase intention is not, therefore, a communication objective, in that the advertising is not expected to produce an immediate intention to buy (it is expected to produce category need, if relevant, and brand awareness and brand attitude, the two universal communication objectives, but not brand purchase intention).

Accordingly, for an "image" brand (purchased in response to sensory gratification or social approval) that is also low risk (low involvement), the manager should omit brand purchase intention as a communication objective.

The omit option applies only to *advertising* and not to promotion for the brand.

The Option to Generate Brand Purchase Intention   For all other types of brand choice, if the *advertising or promotion* is to work, it should generate brand purchase intention during exposure. Although the objective is to generate brand purchase intention, it must be realized that the intention will *only* occur

("I must try that" or "I'll buy that" or thoughts to this effect) *if* the buyer also has the category need.

Many advertisements and promotion offers, of course, are designed to remind or sell category need simultaneously with generating brand purchase intention. This is not surprising when we realize just how small a proportion of consumers are "in the market" for a particular product during advertising exposure. For example, in any given week, only about 20 percent of adults will be planning to buy detergent; only 2 percent will be planning to buy carpet cleaning products; and a very small proportion, 1/4 of 1 percent, will be planning to buy a new car that week.[17] Thus, most advertisements and promotion offers do *not* produce immediate purchase intentions, because they cannot if category need isn't there.

For an *advertisement* to generate brand purchase intention, the advertiser has the choice of "soft sell" (if the buyer will naturally *deduce* the intention to act, from brand attitude) or "hard sell" (if the buyer must be prodded or *induced* to act). All *promotion offers,* by their very nature, are "hard sell." These tactics we will meet further in later chapters.

To review, the options for brand purchase intention as a communication objective are to: *omit* it, for low risk, "image" advertising; or to *generate* brand purchase intention, for all other types of advertising and for promotions.

5. PURCHASE FACILITATION

Purchase Facilitation Defined

The fifth and final communication effect that the manager has to consider as a communication objective is purchase facilitation. Purchase facilitation can be defined as the buyer's perception of other marketing factors (the "4 P's") that can hinder or stimulate purchase. The other marketing factors that can hinder or stimulate purchase are product, price, place (distribution), and other forms of promotion, namely, personal selling and publicity.

A Positive Approach

Our viewpoint is that advertising and promotional planning is incomplete if it fails to take into account these other marketing factors *in advance*. The traditional viewpoint is to cry about marketing problems after the fact. The traditional viewpoint is expressed rather theatrically in the following comments by the late and great advertising expert, Rosser Reeves:

> You can run a brilliant advertising campaign, and sales go down. Why?
> (a) your product may not be right
> (b) your price may not be right
> (c) your distribution may not be right
> (d) your sales force may be bad

(e) your competitor may be outspending you five to one

(f) your competitor may be dealing you to death with one-cent sales and premiums and contests and special discounts to retailers.[18]

With modern market research input, there is little excuse for not anticipating most of these marketing factors that can "bomb out" an otherwise successful advertising campaign. Today's advertising manager has to take a comprehensive, marketing-oriented, and proactive (not reactive) stance. The advertising manager must work with full input from the manufacturing manager, marketing manager, sales manager, and other involved parties in preparing advertising and promotion campaigns.

The advertising agency, for its part, should do its homework before undertaking the campaign. With the exception of point (a) in Reeves' comments, the agency is obligated to do its best to communicate "over or around" any inherent marketing problems. [Concerning point (a): If the product *really* isn't right, the agency shouldn't take on the account in the first place.]

If the price isn't right, the agency should find out why, then try to create an adaptive campaign, for example, a "value" campaign if the price is exhorbitant.

If distribution isn't right, the agency should adapt its media location and timing to fit the available distribution. Either that, or the agency could suggest converting distribution of the brand to mail order, via direct response advertising, as has been done for several New England clothing manufacturers such as L. L. Bean or Talbot's, who sell their products nationally this way. Or customers could be brought to the store, as Atlantic City casinos have done with special buses for New York City and Philadelphia patrons. There is always a way to adapt.

If the sales force is bad, even this can be overcome (although this marketing problem should be corrected). For example, a campaign using "reverse psychology"—such as, "Our salespeople are such snobs" or "It's the product, not the seller"—might work to overcome a sales force problem.

And if a competitor is outspending you "5 to 1," this merely increases the agency's challenge to come up with a better message strategy and more effective and efficient media placement. Of course, the budget has to be adequate to justify advertising or promotion in the first place: The expected return has to be higher than for alternative use of the funds. Given this, it is the agency's mission to do the best job possible for the brand based on an understanding of the problems it may face.

Note, further, that we have positioned purchase facilitation as a communication effect, in the *buyer's* mind and not in the manager's mind. What this means is that even though the company may anticipate (for instance) a distribution problem, it really isn't a problem unless and until it is experienced by consumers. This realization can result in some creative and adaptive advertising and promotion that prevents (for instance) distribution problems from ever becoming salient to consumers.

It is the job of the advertising agency to be creative and adaptive. There is no excuse for advertising or promotion that fails to adapt to marketing constraints. It adapts via the communication effect of purchase facilitation.

Managerial Options with Regard to Purchase Facilitation

The manager has two broad options (see Table 6.8) in considering whether or not purchase facilitation should be a communication objective in a particular campaign:

Be assured that the rest of the marketing mix is coordinated and omit purchase facilitation. If the advertising and promotion were planned from the beginning as an integrated aspect of the marketing mix, then there should be no purchase facilitation problem. In this case, the manager can *omit* purchase facilitation from the set of communication objectives.

If a problem is present, adapt the advertising and promotion to minimize it (incorporate purchase facilitation in the campaign). Problems with the other "4 P's" shouldn't occur, but frequently they do. Consumer research prior to a campaign will often uncover marketing problems. Similarly, for new products, the marketing manager usually is aware of marketing factors that could become consumer problems. As we have described, the advertising and promotion should be actively adapted to address the problems through communication. The manager thereby *incorporates* purchase facilitation into the campaign as a communication objective.

SUMMARY

Communication effects are the focal purpose of advertising and promotion (the ultimate purpose is purchase action and thus sales and profit—but this is achieved, in advertising and promotion, through communication). Communication effects are mental associations or responses, connected to the brand, that are left "in the buyer's head" through advertising and promotion. They are subject to modification through experience with the product, word of mouth, and other marketing factors, as well as through further advertising and promotion.

TABLE 6-8   MANAGERIAL OPTIONS WITH REGARD TO PURCHASE FACILITATION AS A COMMUNICATION OBJECTIVE

Buyer state	Communication objective
1 No perceived problems with other marketing factors (and none anticipated by the manager)	*Omit* purchase facilitation as an objective; it has already been taken care of in the marketing plan
2 Perceived problem with other marketing factors	*Incorporate* purchase facilitation in campaign (adapt the advertising and promotion to minimize the problem)

Five communication effects (either pre-established or built by the campaign) are necessary for brand purchase to occur:

1 Category need
2 Brand awareness
3 Brand attitude
4 Brand purchase intention
5 Purchase facilitation

If these five communication effects are not already existent at "full strength" in the prospective buyer's mind, then advertising or promotion, or both, can be designed to "communicate to" these effects and thereby produce purchase action.

The purpose of advertising and promotion campaigns is to generate or maintain communication effects that as strongly as possible favor the advertiser's brand. To accomplish this, the manager selects communication *objectives* from options within the five communication effects. For convenience of reference, these options are summarized in Table 6.9.

Not all campaigns have to address all five communication effects. Rather, the manager has to decide, from consumer research with the target audience, which communication effects need to be brought up to full or sufficient strength to cause purchase action. It could be all five, for a new brand in a new product category, but more often selected effects, only, are relevant. In fact, there are only two communication effects that are always objectives, if only at a maintenance level: *brand awareness and brand attitude*. Other campaigns may omit particular communication effects.

TABLE 6-9   SUMMARY OF MANAGERIAL OPTIONS FOR THE FIVE COMMUNICATION EFFECTS WHEN SETTING COMMUNICATION OBJECTIVES

Communication effect	Communication objective options
1 Category need	• *Omit* if assumed to be present • *Remind* if latent • *Sell* if new category users are targeted
2 Brand awareness	• *Brand recognition* if choice made at point of purchase • *Brand recall* if choice made prior to purchase • *Both* if justified
3 Brand attitude	• *Create* attitude if unaware • *Increase* if moderately favorable • *Maintain* if maximally favorable • *Modify* if moderate with no increase possible • *Change* attitude if negative
4 Brand purchase intention	• *Omit* in advertising for low risk, image brand • *Generate* in all other advertising and in promotion
5 Purchase facilitation	• *Omit* if no problems with other 4 P's • *Incorporate* in campaign if problem

Up to this point in the six-step effects sequence, we have concentrated on *objectives* (the effects desired). The manager (in reverse order) has set communication objectives, target audience action objectives, sales or market share objectives, and profit objectives. Now, in our expansion of advertising and promotion's focal purpose, communication, we turn to *strategies and tactics* (the means for attaining the effects). Brand attitude, the most detailed communication effect, warrants a chapter of its own, and brand attitude strategies are considered next.

NOTES

1 Conference Board surveys summarized in *The Wall Street Journal,* June 8, 1979.
2 See J.A. Howard, *Consumer Behavior: Application of Theory,* New York: McGraw-Hill, 1977, for a discussion of category communication effects. Potential new users, to whom category need must be "sold," are characterized as being in a state of "extensive problem solving," with two problems to solve: (1) should I buy this category of product? and (2) if so, which brand should I buy? For these prospects, a campaign must establish category communication effects as well as brand communication effects.
3 Data from H.S. Schwerin, reported in *Marketing News,* February 3, 1984, p. 13.
4 For a discussion of the differing psychological processes underlying recognition and recall, see G.R. Loftus and E.F. Loftus, *Human Memory: The Processing of Information,* Hillsdale, NJ: Lawrence Erlbaum Associates, 1976. One of the few marketing texts to realize the major implications of brand recognition versus brand recall is J.R. Bettman, *An Information Processing Theory of Consumer Choice* Reading, MA: Addison-Wesley, 1979.
5 See J.A. Howard and J. Sheth, *The Theory of Buyer Behavior,* New York: Wiley, 1969.
6 E.M. Tauber, Reduce new product failures: measure needs as well as purchase interest, *Journal of Marketing,* 1973, *37* (3), 61–64.
7 R.P. Bagozzi and R.E. Burnkrandt, Attitude organization and the attitude-behavior relationship, *Journal of Personality and Social Psychology,* 1979, *37* (6), 913–929; P.M. Bentler and G. Speckart, Models of attitude-behavior relations, *Psychological Review,* 1979, *86* (5), 452–464.
8 M.E. Goldberg, G.J. Gorn, and W. Gibson, TV messages for snacks and breakfast foods: do they influence children's preferences? *Journal of Consumer Research,* 1978, *5* (2), 73–81.
9 G. Fennell, Consumers' perceptions of the product-use situation, *Journal of Marketing,* 1978, *42* (2), 38–47.
10 "Benefit segmentation," referred to in the next chapter, should more accurately be called "motivation segmentation." Segmentation on *benefits* is meaningless, because you'd end up with segments that are *not* homogenous: there would be different people wanting the same benefit for distinctly different reasons. Clearly, what is necessary is motivation segmentation. And note that for a given motivation segment, the advertiser may have to use *multiple* benefits (to put in ads) to meet the motivation.
11 *Business Week,* October 12, 1981.
12 Brand attitude measures are discussed in Part Eight where we review advertising research.

13 For a convincing analysis of why intentions must be consciously experienced if they are to cause action, see H.C. Triandis, Values, attitudes, and interpersonal behavior, in H.E. Howe and M.M. Page (Eds.), *Nebraska Symposium on Motivation 1979.* Lincoln, NE: University of Nebraska Press, 1980, pp. 195–259.

14 The advertising communication model developed by H.E. Krugman for TV advertising seems to propose unconscious intention. Our approach postulates unconscious intention prior to the purchase situation for a particular type of brand choice (low involvement/transformational—see Chapters 7 and 9) regardless of the advertising medium. Krugman's theorizing can be found in The impact of television advertising: learning without involvement, *Public Opinion Quarterly,* 1965, *29* (Fall), 349–356; and Why three exposures may be enough, *Journal of Advertising Research,* 1972, *12* (6), 11–14.

15 As discussed in Chapter 9, the other positive purchase motivation, intellectual stimulation, *does* require a purchase intention, even though it is classified as a transformational motivation in terms of brand attitude strategy.

16 The choice situation is usually the point of purchase; e.g., for Coke, in a supermarket or restaurant. However, it could also be the point of use (in the user role) which may be at home, while you're watching TV. In this case, a Coke commercial *could* produce an immediate action intention, by stimulating your *category need*. If you had Coke (or a similar beverage) in the refrigerator, you'd get up and get one. For some interesting evidence that even low level, possibly subliminal, advertising can stimulate category need by making you feel thirsty, see D.I. Hawkins, The effects of subliminal stimulation on drive level and brand preference, *Journal of Marketing Research,* 1970, *7* (3), 322–326.

17 These figures, and the point about how few people are usually "in the market" for a product on any given ad exposure, can be found in L. Bogart, *Strategy in Advertising,* New York: Harcourt Brace Jovanovich, 1967.

18 Reeves' quotation is cited in M. Mayer, *Madison Avenue U.S.A.,* Harmondsworth, Middlesex, U.K.: Penguin Books, 1961, p. 57. First published in hardcover in 1958, this book is a "classic" that should be read by everyone interested in advertising. Mayer's analysis of the issues facing managers and researchers in advertising provides a necessary historical perspective, yet it reads like an up-to-date account of the "agency business" today.

DISCUSSION QUESTIONS

6.1 You are the marketing manager for Fisher-Price preschooler toys.

    a You have an advertising campaign aimed at mothers (as NCU decision makers). Which of the five communication effects would your campaign address as communication objectives, and why?

    b If your Fisher-Price campaign is a TV campaign, children probably will be exposed to it too. What modifications would you make to the communication effects you've described for mothers? That is, what communication objectives would you like children to acquire for Fisher-Price toys?

6.2 (Difficult question) Can you think of any effect of advertising or promotion that meets the definition of a communication effect but does not fit well into one of the basic five? Which of the five is it closest to and how does it relate to purchase action?

6.3 Category need is obviously a communication objective whenever a new product category is advertised or promoted. But "selling the category" also may be an objective for established products. Under what circumstances is this true?

6.4 Brand awareness responses can take the form of brand recognition or brand recall. Which form of brand awareness response do you think would be more relevant for brands in the following product categories, and why?

   a Airlines that fly to Florida

   b TV dinners

   c Fast-food restaurants located on major highways

   d Elegant restaurants

6.5 a Although the two terms are often used interchangeably, the chapter makes a distinction between "attributes" and "benefits." What is this distinction and why is it especially important for marketers? Exemplify with respect to automobiles.

   b The chapter also makes a distinction between "benefits" and underlying "motivations." What is this distinction and why is it especially important for advertisers? Illustrate with respect to the benefits you identified for automobiles.

6.6 Find two advertisements—or an ad and a promotion offer—that clearly exemplify the cognitive and affective components of brand attitude: one that exemplifies the affect-belief sequence and another that exemplifies the belief-affect sequence. Write a short description of each, identifying elements in the ad or promotion offer that support your selection. Also, explain why both components of attitude are necessary.

6.7 Pick a category (such as men's cologne or women's perfume) and go through a magazine that advertises the category heavily (such as *Playboy* or *Cosmopolitan*). As you look at each ad, jot down your reaction toward the brand in a sentence or two. Now re-read the chapter's definition of brand purchase intention. Discuss the correspondence or lack of correspondence of your brand reactions with the definition of brand purchase intention and with the options for it as a communication objective.

6.8 Interview an industrial marketing executive about the "4 P's" associated with a product or service within the executive's responsibility. Ask how any problems with the 4 P's are addressed, if at all, in the product or service's advertising and sales promotion. Write up a short report that indicates how problems with the 4 P's are addressed or might be addressed effectively by incorporating purchase facilitation as a communication objective.

FURTHER READING

Bettman, J.R. Memory factors in consumer choice: a review. *Journal of Marketing*, 1979, *43* (2), 37–53.

One of the very few marketing theorists to realize the difference between recognition versus recall in brand choice, Bettmann describes concrete marketing and advertising implications of this overlooked but essential distinction. Brand recognition and brand recall are alternative objectives when targeting brand awareness.

Fennell, G. Perceptions of the product-use situation. *Journal of Marketing*, 1978, *42* (2) 38–47.

Forerunner to our typology of purchase motivations that underlie category need and brand attitude. A breakthrough article helping to clarify a perennial question: How do you motivate buyers?

Fishbein, M., and Ajzen, I. *Belief, Attitude, Intention and Behavior*. Reading, MA: Addison-Wesley, 1975.

Contains a good discussion of how benefit beliefs relate to (brand) attitude. However, these authors use a unitary definition of attitude which ignores motivation and is not well suited to advertising.

Greenberg, M.G. Occasion-based segmentation: five years later. Paper presented at the 12th Annual Research Conference, American Marketing Association, Hot Springs, VA, April 1981.

An excellent, clear presentation explaining how people can have more than one overall attitude toward a brand depending on the consumption occasion or "situation." Correctly groups benefits according to occasion-related needs (in our terminology, to motivations).

CHAPTER 7

BRAND ATTITUDE STRATEGY

We are now ready to examine the major strategies that can be employed to produce brand attitude. Correct selection of brand attitude strategy is vital because it affects the entire structure of the creative and media components of the advertising plan. After reading this chapter you should:

- Understand how the two dimensions of brand attitude (affective and cognitive) combine to constitute four brand attitude strategy quadrants
- Understand the motivational basis of brand attitude in more detail
- Further understand how benefits are selected to represent brand attitude
- Know what is meant by "positioning" a brand via advertising

In Chapter 6 we reviewed the options for brand attitude as a communication objective. We saw that the brand attitude objective in a particular campaign may be to create, increase, maintain, modify, or change brand attitude. But how is the brand attitude objective to be achieved? To answer this question of strategy, we have to look at four different types of brand attitude. (The decision by a particular target audience to buy a particular brand is based on *one* of the four types of brand attitude.) It is essential, when planning a campaign, for the manager to know which type of brand attitude the campaign must address. The four types of brand attitude, each requiring a separate brand attitude strategy, are the subject of the first part of this chapter.

In the second part of the chapter, we take a further look at benefits, this time from the particular standpoint of brand attitude strategy. Benefits, as explained in Chapter 6, are the means by which brand attitude is "accessed" via advertisements or promotion offers. Here, the question is: Which benefit or benefits will have the most influence on the buyer's brand attitude? We analyze benefit selection based on benefit importance, perceived delivery, and uniqueness. These three factors determine the contribution each benefit makes to the target audience's attitude toward the brand.

BRAND ATTITUDE STRATEGY QUADRANTS

A careful synthesis of the massive literature on brand attitude[1] shows that managers can broadly classify brand attitude strategies in terms of two major dimensions:

1 *Type of Decision* Brand attitude strategies depend on whether the target audience regards choice of the brand as either a "low involvement" (trial experience sufficient) decision or a "high involvement" (search and conviction required) decision. Involvement relates to the *cognitive* component of attitude, reflecting the perceived risk in deciding how well the brand "delivers" on the relevant motivation.

2 *Type of Motivation* Brand attitude strategies further depend on whether the target audience seeks the brand mainly for "informational" reasons (to reduce or turn off a negative motivation) or for "transformational" enhancement (to turn on a positive motivation). These two types of motives relate to the *affective* component of brand attitude.

Four fundamental strategies for brand attitude emerge from these two dimensions (Figure 7.1). Each of the two dimensions has two classifications: low involvement versus high involvement for the type of decision dimension and informational versus transformational for the motivational dimension. When we combine the two dimensions, four strategy *quadrants* are derived.

To lend some realism to the quadrants, we have inserted some *tentative* examples. Why are these tentative? They are tentative because the manager cannot safely classify either products or target audiences (see boxes in figure) without either doing first-hand research to select the brand attitude strategy or else having very astute intuition. A brief examination of the two dimensions will show why this is so.

Type of Decision: Low Involvement versus High Involvement

Involvement refers to the degree of *risk* perceived by the buyer in purchasing the brand.[2] There are two principal sources of perceived risk, and *either* source of perceived risk can contribute to purchase decision involvement[3]:

1 *Economic risk* includes consequences of incorrect brand choice such as money loss, performance problems, threats to physical safety, and also time or convenience loss.

2 *Psychosocial risk* includes psychological discrepancies between brand benefits and the buyer's own personal self-image, or social discrepancies affecting the buyer's social self-image caused by reference group disapproval of the brand.

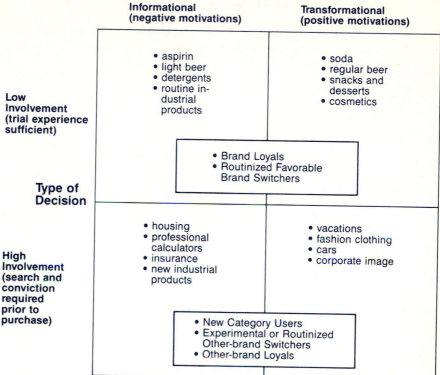

FIGURE 7.1   The four strategy quadrants for brand attitude. The product examples and target audience examples shown are *tentative only* (see text). In practice, the manager must assess how various target decision makers actually regard the brand purchase decision and also the actual motivation that will work best for the brand.

Low involvement occurs when the buyer perceives *neither* economic nor psychosocial risk in purchasing the brand. Wasson[4] has estimated that approximately 50 percent of consumers' dollar expenditures—but 90 percent of all decisions the consumer makes—are low involvement. Low-priced items in supermarkets contribute to the large number of low involvement purchases. But a high-priced item, also, can be low involvement for a *repeat purchaser* target audience.

High involvement occurs when the buyer perceives economic *or* psychosocial risk *or both* in purchasing the brand. This means that most high-priced purchases are high involvement because they involve economic risk. But a low-priced item, also, can be high involvement if it entails psychosocial risk, such as, for *first-time triers,* the choice of a brand of perfume or cologne, or the "right" tennis shirt like LaCoste or Polo.

Involvement therefore depends on the degree of risk perceived by the *target audience* in buying *this* brand on *this* purchase occasion.

Let us now see how the cognitive component of brand attitude (and thus the brand attitude strategy) differs by involvement.

Low Involvement Brand Attitude   A low involvement brand attitude operates when:

1 *First-time triers* of the brand regard trial—based on learning the *proposed* brand attitude from an advertisement or promotion offer—as the easiest way to evaluate the brand. That is, trial of the brand involves little or no economic or psychosocial risk, and the buyer simply decides to "try it and see."[5] Note that a low risk product category reduces the normally high involvement of triers to low involvement (thus overriding the tentative target audience classification shown earlier in Figure 7.1). For triers, the nature of the product category determines level of involvement.

2 *Repeat buyers* of the brand have tried the brand before and are satisfied with it. Thus, there is *no longer* any risk associated with its purchase. Note here that the target audience overrides the nature of the product. Satisfied repeat buyers of *any* product—that is, brand loyals (BL's) and *routinized favorable* brand switchers (RFBS's)—are making a low involvement decision when they repeat-buy the brand.

The economist Nelson[6] proposed the term "experience goods" to describe products for which consumers regard trial experience as sufficient[7] and therefore do not bother to search for detailed information prior to purchase. To this view of "experience products" we have added "experienced audiences," in that familiar repeat purchasers also do not have to search.

The brand attitude strategy implication of low involvement brand choice is that an *extreme favorable attitude* has to be created. McGuire[8] calls this the "ask more, get more" principle of persuasion. An extreme favorable brand attitude is needed because:

1 *First-time triers* must develop a *very favorable though tentatively held*[9] brand attitude to prompt them to try the brand; this tentative but extreme attitude is then confirmed or disconfirmed based on usage experience.

2 *Repeat buyers* already have a favorable attitude—thus only an extreme proposed attitude can possibly *increase* their attitude, although almost any advertising can *maintain* their attitude, if that is a sufficient objective.

We will encounter low involvement creative tactics in Part Five, Chapter 9, where we will see that extreme claims work best for this type of brand attitude.

High Involvement Brand Attitude   A high involvement brand attitude operates when the buyer perceives substantial economic or psychosocial risk in purchasing the brand. But what is "substantial" perceived risk? What cutoff or threshold puts the brand purchase decision into high involvement?

The concept of experience—or "try it and see"— purchases gives a very clear operational cutoff. If (in consumer research) the target audience decision maker would *not* be willing to pay the purchase price just to "try it and see," then the purchase decision is *high involvement*.

Nelson[10] calls risky products "search goods." For these types of products, buyers search for confirming information prior to purchase. The prospective buyer must be *convinced* of the brand's evaluation (brand attitude) *before* buying and trying it.

Again, however, we have to consider the *target audience* as well as the nature of the product. That is, we qualify "search goods" by the idea of a "search audience."

Thus, whereas high-priced products and conspicuously consumed products normally would be high involvement purchases for everybody, this is *not* generally true for *repeat buyers*. The "habitual" buyer of Rolls-Royces, for example, probably is not making a high involvement decision in buying another one. Only if the interval leading up to the repeat purchase is so long that the *category* may have changed, would repeat buyers (brand loyals and routinized favorable brand switchers) be thrown into high involvement when repeat-buying an expensive or conspicuously consumed brand.[11]

The brand attitude strategy implication of high involvement brand choice is that the buyer's *initial attitude*—prior to advertising or promotion offer exposure—*limits the final attitude* that can be obtained. This is known technically as the "latitude of acceptance" principle.[12] More colloquially, it can be described as the "ask only for a reasonable increase" principle of persuasion.

We will encounter high involvement creative tactics in Part Five, Chapter 10, where we will see that carefully tailored benefit claims work best.

Type of Motivation: Informational versus Transformational

There are eight basic ways in which purchase can be motivated (Table 7.1). We suggest, following and building upon Fennell's excellent analysis,[13] that all products and brands are purchased in response to one or more of eight basic motivations.[14]

Let us take a single product category—scotch whiskey—and show how each of the eight motivations may apply to purchase. The terms "informational" and "transformational" that we use to classify these motives will later become apparent.[15]

Negative Motivations   The first four motivations are negative in origin. They stem from the buyer's experience of an aversive stimulus or event. This aversiveness pushes the buyer's emotional state or "drive" below the equilibrium level, and the buyer will be motivated to remove the aversion or at least reduce it as far as possible toward equilibrium.

The first motivation, *problem removal*, stems from an actual problem *currently* experienced (for example, the buyer is simply "thirsty"). Product

TABLE 7-1   EIGHT BASIC MOTIVATIONS

Name of motive	Motivating process
Negative or aversive origin 1 Problem removal	*Drive reduction* Buyer experiences *current* problem: seeks a product that will *solve* the problem
2 Problem avoidance	Buyer anticipates a *future* problem: seeks a product that will *prevent* the problem from occurring
3 Incomplete satisfaction	Buyer is not satisfied with current product: *searches* for a better product
4 Mixed approach-avoidance	Buyer likes some things about product but dislikes others: tries to find product that will *resolve* the conflict
Mildly negative origin 5 Normal depletion	*Drive maintenance* Buyer is simply out of stock or running low: seeks to *maintain* regular supply of product
Positive or appetitive origin 6 Sensory gratification	*Drive increase* Buyer seeks extra (physiological) stimulation: to *enjoy* product
7 Intellectual stimulation	Buyer seeks extra (psychological) stimulation: to *explore or master* new product
8 Social approval	Buyer sees opportunity for social rewards: *personal recognition* through use of product

choice relates to the goal of *solving* the problem (that is, removing the thirst by drinking scotch). Whereas not all consumers may think of scotch as a thirst quencher, this is still a possible motivation for buying the product.

The second motivation, *problem avoidance,* occurs when a *future* problem is anticipated (for example, "I'm going to need a drink to get through the evening"). Product choice relates to the goal of *preventing* the actual problem, that is, avoiding it by drinking scotch and not allowing the problem to occur. Perhaps unfortunately, problem avoidance is quite a frequent motivation for buying and drinking scotch.

(The difference between problem removal and problem avoidance might be better expressed as "pain" versus "*fear* of pain." Fear is an extremely strong learned drive, and it may be learned without the person ever experiencing the problem itself, such as the fear of flying or fear of skydiving. Fear of problems can motivate just as well as actual problems.)

The third and fourth negatively originated motivations are a little more complex. The third motivation stems from *incomplete satisfaction,* with the incompleteness being aversive (insufficient positive reinforcement in technical terminology). Some scotch buyers may be motivated by this (for example, "I can't get a 'malty' enough scotch"). A product choice usually is made, but with a *continued search* for a more satisfactory product, which the astute marketer, if this motivation exists widely enough, might find worthwhile to address, by bringing out a high-malt scotch.

The fourth motivation, *mixed approach-avoidance,* stems from a conflict between one of the three negative motivations and one of the positive ones (for example, "I love scotch but it gives me a hangover") *or* between two of the three negative motivations when a product cannot satisfy both of the negative motivations simultaneously (for example, "Scotch helps me to overcome my shyness but it gives me a hangover"). Product choice then centers on *resolving* the conflict, such as seeking out a lighter (lower alcohol) scotch.

Mildly Negative Motivation Many purchases are prompted by a motivation that is best described as "mildly negative" in origin. No serious problem is experienced or anticipated, nor any dissatisfaction or conflict. Fennell[16] calls this motivation *normal depletion,* for which the buyer's goal is replenishment to *maintain* the current reasonably stable state (for example, buying a bottle of scotch to replenish the home bar).

However, whereas many *product category* purchases are motivated by normal depletion, *brand* choice, of course, may follow a different motivation. Normal depletion does, however, mean that the "normal brand" will be purchased each time, if the buyer is brand loyal.

Positive Motivations Completing the list of eight basic motivations are those that are positive in origin. They arise from the buyer's desire for positive or rewarding stimulation, where the person is motivated to *increase* the emotional state of "drive" above the current equilibrium level, to a *more* desirable state, at least temporarily.

The first of the positive motivations (the sixth· on the list) is *sensory gratification* (for example, "I just like the taste of scotch"). Here the product purchase goal is to *enjoy.* Many scotch drinkers consume the product purely for enjoyment.

The seventh motivation is *intellectual stimulation* (for example, some people may drink scotch to "free up the mind" or because it makes them feel "intellectual"). The product purchase or consumption goal in this instance is *exploration or mastery.* Note that this motivation may also fit the novice drinker who, out of curiosity, is trying scotch for the first time.

The eighth motivation is *social approval*[17] (for example, some people drink scotch because they perceive it to be a socially "in" drink; in France, it is reported, scotch on the rocks or straight has become a fashionable aperitif!). The product purchase goal is to achieve *personal recognition.* Conspicuously consumed products, like scotch, that "say something about the user," are strongly susceptible to social approval motivation.[18]

Social approval is classed as a positive motivation because it refers to the receipt of social rewards for buying and using the product. However, in cases where social approval is sought because of a prior state of *social anxiety,* the motivation is more properly *problem removal,* a negative motivation. The manager or researcher must be very careful to make this distinction. Social approval is the seeking of social rewards, without any strongly experienced prior anxiety problem.

"Informational" versus "Transformational" Motives

It is convenient when talking about brand attitude strategy to have a summary term for the negative motives and a summary term for the positive motives. We have borrowed, from William D. Wells[19], the terms "informational" and "transformational," respectively.

The negative motives should respond mainly to an informational or "reason why" style of advertising, in which the consumer is given information about brand benefits that will remove or avoid problems, meet an ideal, resolve consumption choice conflicts, or simply provide a convenient way to re-stock the brand.

The positive motives, on the other hand, should respond better to a transformational or "image" style of advertising, in which the consumer perceives that by using the brand, he or she can gain sensory, intellectual, or social rewards—that is, become positively "transformed" by using the brand.

Another good reason for introducing the terms informational and transformational is that they are an improvement on the traditional terms used to classify advertising: "rational" and "emotional." Our main objection to the older terms is that, whereas "rational" reasonably fits the informational approach, the description "emotional" is not very accurate because it applies to *both* informational and transformational advertising. Informational advertising focuses on *negative* emotions (to portray the negative motives of problem removal, problem avoidance, and so forth), and transformational advertising focuses on *positive* emotions (to portray the positive motives of sensory gratification and so forth). The eight motivations and the two summary classifications, informational and transformational, are a much more precise way of understanding the motivational factor in advertising.

The Quadrants in Practice

Notice that the two dimensions which form the brand attitude quadrants, involvement and motivation, are conceptualized as dichotomous, that is, low *or* high involvement decision, informational *or* transformational motivation.

In the case of involvement, it is really a continuous dimension in theory, but in practice it is dichotomous. The individual buyer either regards purchase of the brand to be a low enough risk to "try it and see" (low involvement) *or* regards it as requiring conviction before buying (high involvement). Generally, most individuals in the target audience will feel the same way, and so a majority classification can be made.

In rare cases where a substantial proportion of the target audience sees the purchase decision as low involvement and another substantial proportion sees it as high involvement, then the classification should be *high* involvement. As will be shown in Chapter 10, high involvement is the "safer" and more conservative assumption if classification is difficult.

Similarly, individual buyers can be characterized relatively easily according to whether their motivation for purchasing the brand is informational or transformational. Although individuals sometimes differ within target audiences, this is rare. Superficial research sometimes can give the appearance that there are many reasons for buying the brand. This usually means that the advertising research has not uncovered the real motivation or, in everyday language, has not identified the "buzz" that occurs when the consumer buys or uses the brand.

Occasionally, nevertheless, a brand may be found to be dually motivated— a true mixture of informational and transformational motivations. Here, *informational* motivation should be assumed as the more conservative classification.

Reasons for nominating high involvement and informational, respectively, as the "fallback" classifications for borderline cases will become evident when we consider creative tactics for each quadrant, in Part Five. Fortunately, in the great majority of advertising situations—with good research—the brand attitude of the target audience can be classified into *one* of the four brand attitude strategy quadrants.

SOME ADDITIONAL POINTS ABOUT MOTIVATION

Buyer motivations are such a vital aspect of advertising strategy that users of this book are very likely to be reading this section closely. For users such as managers formulating an advertising strategy or students doing an advertising project, these additional points about motivation may help.

Product Category Motivations and Brand Attitude Motivations

A product category, like a brand, can be linked to almost any of the eight motivations. Product category motivations underlie *category need* and are relevant when the advertiser has to *sell* category need. Brand purchase motivations underlie *brand attitude* and are relevant in *all* campaigns. Product and brand motivations may be the same or they may differ.

Single Motivation for Category and Brand   Many brands are governed by the same motivation as the product category within which the brand exists. That is, the motivation underlying category need and the motivation underlying brand attitude are the same. For example, most people buy aspirin products (the category) to get relief from pain (problem removal motivation). They also evaluate Anacin, Bayer, Excedrin, and similar alternatives (the brands) in terms of each brand's perceived ability to relieve pain (also problem removal). Motivation in this case is consistent for product and brands.

Category and Brand Motivations Differ   For many other products, the brand motivation may differ from the product category motivation. Let's consider our scotch whiskey example again. Whereas many consumers may buy scotch (the category) because they like scotch's taste (sensory gratification), they may then choose Chivas Regal, Johnny Walker, J&B, or similar alternatives (the brands) based on their prestige in social consumption situations (social approval). An advertiser targeting the NCU scotch drinker would therefore have to appeal to sensory gratification motivation, to sell category need, and also social approval motivation, to get the brand chosen via brand attitude.

Benefit Segmentation

In our discussion of partitioning in Chapter 2, we noted that one way of partitioning an overall market or product category was by "benefits sought." This is popularly called benefit segmentation.[20] It really should be called *motivation* segmentation because it is actually a way of "positioning" brands to fit people's differing motives for buying within the category. Each motive represents a *sub-category* or partition of the overall market.

Let us take Haley's toothpaste benefit segmentation study[21] as an example. This study is widely cited in marketing textbooks and has led to widespread use of the term "benefit segmentation." In the toothpaste product category, there are:

- "Worriers" who want an anti-decay toothpaste (problem avoidance motivation)
- "Sensories," including children, who want a nice-tasting toothpaste (sensory gratification)
- "Sociables" who want a breath-freshening and perhaps whitening toothpaste (social approval *unless* there is major anxiety)
- "Independents" who want a low-priced toothpaste (problem removal)

In addition to Haley's segments, and due to "de-partitioning" in the toothpaste market since his early research, we now could identify also an "all-in-one" segment who want all the above benefits in *one* toothpaste.

However, you cannot properly segment a market on benefits alone and you cannot design a brand attitude strategy on benefits alone. You have to know the *motive* to which the benefit is linked. For instance, Crest offers a decay-prevention benefit, which appears to relate to problem avoidance motivation. But is that why people really buy it? Crest has a very heavy upward socioeconomic "skew"—there's a lot of social approval motivation in buying this brand. Similarly, the nice-tasting benefit of Colgate could be sought for sensory gratification *or* it could be sought for its long-lasting nice taste for problem removal. The two motives for "nice taste" have quite different advertising implications.

The popular procedure of benefit segmentation is therefore incomplete according to the approach we advocate for understanding brand attitude. *Motivation* segmentation *within* an NCU, BL, BS or OBL target audience makes sense because it identifies people with different attitudes toward the product category or even toward the same brand. But *benefit* segmentation, without the motivational base, can be quite misleading for advertising strategy.

BENEFIT STRATEGY FOR BRAND ATTITUDE

Benefits are the "surface means," used in advertisements and promotion offers, to connect the brand with a motivation and thus to influence brand attitude. (This relationship was shown in Figure 6.8 earlier.) Now, we examine the relationship more closely, to decide on a benefit strategy for brand attitude.

The I-D-U Method of Benefit Selection

Benefits to be included in an advertising or promotion campaign should be selected according to three major considerations (Table 7.2):

1 Importance
2 Delivery
3 Uniqueness

These considerations constitute what can be called the "I-D-U method" of benefit selection. The abbreviation is fortunate in that it reminds the manager that the benefits you select must "identify (I.D.) *you* (U.)" among other brands in the category.

1 *Importance* Importance refers to the *relevance of the benefit to the motivation* that prompts the buyer to buy the brand. A benefit assumes importance *only if* it is instrumental in meeting the buyer's purchase motivation. For example, think about an expensive-looking label on a brand of coffee. An expensive-looking label probably has no importance when selecting a brand of coffee for everyday use (sensory gratification). But it may be very important when selecting a brand of coffee to serve to guests (social approval).

Importance of the benefit applies across *all* brands that could meet the motivation. Importance is general to the category or market partition (set of perceived competing brands) and not specific to any one brand. Thus, in the premium or "social occasion" coffee category, an expensive-looking label is important to Moccona, Andronicus, Robert Timms, and all other brands competing in the category.

TABLE 7-2   BENEFIT SELECTION CRITERIA FROM THE BUYER'S PERSPECTIVE (WITH THE MANAGER'S CONSIDERATIONS IN PARENTHESES)

1 *Importance:* "How *relevant* is this benefit?" (That is, how instrumental is the benefit in meeting the buyer's purchase motivation?)

2 *Delivery:* "How well does *this brand* provide this benefit?" (That is, how well is the brand perceived as delivering on the benefit?)

3 *Uniqueness:* "Does this brand provide the benefit *better than* other brands?" (That is, how relatively unique is this brand's delivery on the benefit?)

Benefit importance is often very difficult to measure accurately. However, we will defer the measurement issue to Part Eight (advertising research) and focus on the theory of benefit selection here.

2 *Delivery* Delivery refers to *the brand's perceived ability to provide the benefit*. Delivery is brand-specific. To continue the coffee example, benefit delivery reflects the extent to which *each* brand—Moccona, Andronicus, Robert Timms—is perceived as having an expensive-looking label.

Brand benefit delivery is always *perceptual*. It is based on the buyer's *belief* rather than fact. This is evident in the coffee label example, where the property of being "expensive-looking" is quite subjective—it depends on the consumer's perception.

Delivery, therefore, is the brand's *perceived* ability to provide (deliver on) the benefit. As we shall see in Part Eight, delivery is measured in terms of a brand benefit belief rating for each benefit that contributes to brand attitude.

3 *Uniqueness* Uniqueness refers to the brand's perceived ability to deliver on the benefit *relatively better* than other brands. In other words, it is not just delivery that counts, but rather, *superior delivery*. For example, Moccona may be perceived as having the *most* expensive-looking label, even though other competing brands also rate well on this benefit.

Uniqueness embodies what Myers and Alpert[22] call *determinant attributes* (in our terminology, determinant *benefits*). A benefit can be important—and indeed necessary to mention in the brand's advertising or promotion—yet not be determinant.

If two or more competing brands are seen as delivering equally well on a particular benefit, then this benefit cannot determine preference; the benefit provides no basis for discrimination or choice because the brands are "tied" on this choice factor. Therefore, one or more benefits that provide *differences* between brands—that is, allow "relative uniqueness"—must be *emphasized* in the brand's delivery.

For example, if the several brands of premium or "social occasion" coffees are perceived as being equal on taste appeal and price, then a relatively more expensive-looking label may well be the differentiating benefit that determines brand choice.

Uniqueness, in summary, is *differential* delivery. Uniqueness is considered third in benefit selection. A brand has to deliver (second consideration) on the important benefits (first consideration). But it also must deliver relatively uniquely *on at least one* of the important benefits (third consideration).[23] This point is illustrated next.

I-D-U for Each Prospective Target Audience

An I-D-U analysis of benefits must be conducted for *each* prospective target audience. The benefits that appeal to a brand's brand-loyal customers (BL's), for instance, usually will *not* be the benefits needed to attract other customers, for instance, other-brand loyals (OBL's). The importance, delivery, and uniqueness of benefits usually will differ for each prospective target audience.

This can be illustrated with the simple (and hypothetical) example of Colgate trying to attract customers from Crest. To simplify, although probably quite realistically, let us take just two benefits: cavity prevention and taste appeal to children.

(Toothpaste again, you say! But it's a well-known product category and it allows us to illustrate an earlier point about how benefit segmentation can be misleading. "Cavity prevention" and "taste appeal to children" do not represent *segments* of the toothpaste market. This is a common student error and many advertising researchers make it too. The proper segments are brand loyals and other-brand loyals. These two segments happen to want the two benefits, to varying degrees, as we shall see, but you can't "split" the market by these two benefits as a benefit segmentation approach would do. In fact, in this example there isn't even motivational segmentation. The predominant decision makers for these two brands, pretty obviously, are mothers trying to satisfy the *problem avoidance* motivation by buying a brand of toothpaste for their children that prevents cavities and, for one of the segments, also tastes good so children will use it without complaint.)

Figure 7.2 [panel (a)] shows how Colgate BL's might perceive the two competing brands' benefits. On cavity prevention, which is the most important benefit, Colgate BL's perceive Colgate and Crest as essentially *equal*. But on taste appeal to children, Colgate BL's perceive Colgate to be (relatively) unique. It is taste appeal to children that keeps Colgate loyals loyal. Colgate's advertising to its own brand loyals, therefore, would *mention* cavity prevention but *emphasize* its taste appeal to children.

Now contrast a different target audience: Colgate's *other-brand loyals* (presumed in this simplified example to all be loyal to Crest). In the figure [panel (b)] it can be seen that they attach the same order and degree of importance to the two benefits but that Crest brand loyals perceive parity on taste appeal to children and a substantial deficit on Colgate's ability to prevent cavities. Colgate's advertising to other-brand loyals, therefore, would be different from its advertising to its own loyals. Taste appeal to children would be *mentioned,* but the *emphasis* would shift to *cavity prevention,* where Colgate must improve its perceived delivery if it is to win over Crest customers.

(There are other benefit strategies that Colgate could adopt, as explained shortly, but these perceived *delivery* strategies are the most obvious ones.)

I-D-U analysis of benefit selection must be conducted for each prospective target audience because differential emphases on particular benefits, as illustrated in the Colgate-Crest example, are required to attract alternative groups of buyers to the brand.

The manager has to decide which audience—and thus which benefit strategy for brand attitude—provides the best *leverage*. It could well be, for example, that the cavity prevention-emphasis campaign directed to OBL's would win more new sales than might be lost by "slighting" the taste appeal desired by

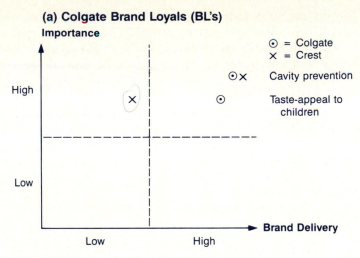

(a) Colgate Brand Loyals (BL's)

Colgate BL's see relative uniqueness in Colgate's taste-appeal to children.

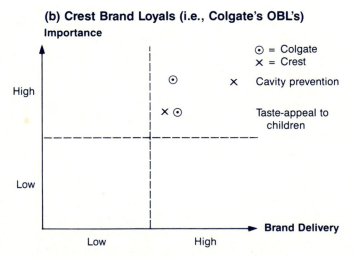

(b) Crest Brand Loyals (i.e., Colgate's OBL's)

Crest's BL's (Colgate OBL's) see a relative uniqueness *deficit* in Colgate's cavity prevention.

FIGURE 7.2   I-D-U benefit analysis for Colgate brand loyals [panel (a)] and Crest brand loyals, that is, Colgate's other-brand loyal prospects [panel (b)].

BL's. Also, of course, Colgate's BL's would presumably *know* that Colgate's taste appeals to their children, so sales among loyals may not decline at all, at least until new buyers of child-rearing age come into the market, seeking a brand with unique taste appeal, which Colgate would not now be emphasizing.

A "generic" version of the Importance-by-Delivery matrix shown in Figure 7.2 has been widely publicized.[24] A typical "application" of the matrix is shown in Figure 7.3. The matrix is, for our purposes, oversimplified because first, it collapses all prospective target audiences into one (you must construct a matrix for *each* prospective target audience, separately); and second, it ignores uniqueness[25] (we have seen how the brand must strive for one or more *differentially superior* benefits). The advice in the matrix is sound *if* it is used with these two provisions.

Putting Benefits Together: Benefit Composition Rules

There is one additional consideration that often arises in benefit selection, when there are multiple benefits to be included in a campaign. This is to discover and use the prospective buyer's (or decision maker's) *benefit composition rule*.[26]

Benefit composition rules describe how the prospective buyer *combines* benefits in mentally arriving at an attitude toward the brand. The composition rule assumed by most managers (even though they may not articulate it as such) is the *compensatory multi-attribute rule*. The best version of this rule is the *situational* one.[27] In our approach, "situation" refers to the particular *motivation* underlying brand attitude. The mathematical formula for the situational compensatory multi-attribute rule is

$$A_{bs} = \sum B_{bis} I_{is}$$

FIGURE 7.3   Simplified matrix showing "I-D" benefit strategy only. Uniqueness, "U," should also be considered and a matrix should be constructed for each target audience.

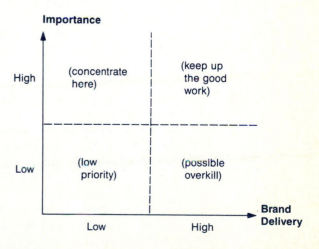

where

A_{bs} = (situational) brand attitude

b = brand

s = situation

B_{bis} = benefit belief (delivery) for the brand, on benefit "i," in situation "s"

i = benefits

I_{is} = relevance weight (importance) of benefit "i," in situation "s"

n = number of benefits

Uniqueness is indicated by the *variance* of B_{bis} across brands. If B_{bis} is equal across brands, there's no uniqueness on that benefit.

What this rule implies is that the brand's deficiencies on one benefit can be made up by advantages on any other benefit. In the toothpaste example, this would mean that, in attempting to win buyers from Crest, Colgate's lack of cavity prevention could be compensated by its taste appeal to children. But clearly this isn't true, which brings us to the role of alternative composition rules.

Composition Rules and Benefits There are many different composition rules that buyers may mentally use to combine benefits and arrive at a brand choice in different product categories. The best procedure is to make sure you understand how the target audience decision maker regards benefits within the category in which you are competing, then summarize with a *specific* composition rule.

In understanding how the decision maker combines benefits, the manager has to be alert to three types of benefits (only one of which, the second below, fits the compensatory multi-attribute rule)[28]:

1 *Necessary Benefits* Some benefits are such that if the brand doesn't meet a certain *threshold* of delivery, the brand will be rejected. (*Example:* Fluoride, that is, cavity prevention, in toothpastes purchased for children. If the brand is not perceived to have fluoride, it will be rejected—Ultra Brite, for instance. No other benefit can compensate for absence of fluoride in a children's toothpaste.) Advertising in a product category which has one or more necessary benefits *must mention* these benefits. If a brand is unique, that is, more above threshold than other brands, it should *emphasize* this benefit.

2 *More-the-Better Benefits* Many benefits are regarded by buyers as "the more, the better" (*Example:* Taste appeal in a toothpaste.) If a brand has *less* of the benefit than competing brands, this will have to be compensated by more of another more-the-better benefit. (*Example:* Generic or store brands of toothpaste may have less taste appeal, but they're also attractively low priced.) Advertising will, of course, *emphasize* the brand's *superior* (unique) more-the-better benefits.

3 *"Just Right" Benefits* Yet a third type of benefit is the "just right" benefit. With such benefits, more is *not* better, and less is not better either; it

TABLE 7-3   BENEFIT TABLE FOR CONSTRUCTING THE BENEFIT COMPOSITION RULE

Benefit	Necessary	More-the-better	Just-right	Inferred
1				
2				
3				
⋮				
K				

Composition rule example . . . Children's toothpaste bought by parents

Cavity prevention:	Necessary
Sweet to taste:	More-the-better
In-mouth texture:	Just right
Price:	Inferred slightly above average

has to be just right. Remember Goldilocks and the Three Bears. Her preferred porridge was not too hot, not too cold, but just right. (*Similar example:* The "hot taste" level of many breath-freshening toothpastes.) If the brand *uniquely* offers the just-right level, its advertising should *emphasize* this point. If it doesn't uniquely offer it, the best strategy might be to omit mention of the benefit altogether, as explained next.

4 *Inferred Benefits* What happens when an important benefit is *not* mentioned in advertising? This is an interesting case. Buyers who have *yet to try* the brand—and thus do not know how well the brand delivers on the "missing" benefit—will tend to infer a *slightly below average* level of delivery compared with other brands in the category.[29] (*Example:* "Hotness" is a salient or well-known characteristic of mouth-freshening toothpastes. Prospective triers will expect close-to-average hotness *for* mouth-freshening toothpastes if a brand that is new to them doesn't mention this benefit.) Advertising can therefore *omit* an important benefit *if* it is content for the brand to be assigned a slightly below average level prior to trial. (Omission is not possible for legally required disclosures, of course.) A brand with an inferior benefit will be quickly "found out" after trial; however, omitting mention of an inferior benefit can be effective if the benefit is *important but not necessary,* and provided that the brand has one or more *other* strong benefits.

Where does this detailed examination of benefits leave the manager? It gives the manager the ingredients for a proper composition rule for combining (the important) benefits (Table 7.3). How these benefits should be handled in advertising (or promotion) depends on the brand's delivery and uniqueness. Basically, the brand should:

- *Emphasize* its *unique* benefits
- *Mention* its *equal* benefits
- And *trade off* or *omit* its *inferior* benefits

These strategies apply only to the final set of *moderate to highly important* benefits. Low importance benefits, of course, would not be considered for inclusion in advertising. Also note that omitting an important benefit implies a favorable trade off after purchase in relation to the brand's other strong benefit or benefits if the brand is to be bought again.

Benefit Strategies Other than Brand Delivery

By far the most frequent benefit strategy employed to influence brand attitude is brand benefit delivery (brand benefit beliefs). The brand benefit delivery strategy is what we have been relying on to this point. The advertiser simply implies (in advertising or promotion) that the brand delivers—uniquely, or equally, or almost equally in the case of omission—on particular benefits when compared (in the buyer's mind) with other brands. The mental comparison, as will now be understood, occurs via the buyer's composition rule for benefits in that product category.

In *some* product categories, alternative strategies are possible for influencing brand attitude other than by benefit delivery. These are summarized in Table 7.4 (where the most common strategy, benefit delivery, is called strategy 1). Basically, the more established the product category, the *less* feasible these alternatives to the brand delivery strategy become. Let's consider some possible examples for toothpaste.

Increase the importance of a benefit on which the brand delivers uniquely. It's in Crest's best interest to try to increase the perceived importance of fluoride (cavity prevention) because Crest is regarded by most consumers as having superior delivery on this benefit. However, the importance of fluoride is well known to consumers. Remotely, if cancer scare rumours about fluoride increase, fluoride may become less important. Originally, of course, Crest was very successful in stressing fluoride importance.

TABLE 7-4   ALTERNATIVE BENEFIT STRATEGIES FOR ALTERING BRAND ATTITUDE

Strategy 1: *Increase the brand's perceived delivery on a benefit.* Most common strategy. Note, however, that some benefits have a threshold beyond which further increases are meaningless (e.g., a plastic toothpaste package can't be "more plastic") or there may be an ideal point beyond which increases would be worse (e.g., too much spearmint taste in a toothpaste).

Strategy 2: *Increase the importance of a benefit on which the brand delivers uniquely.* May be feasible in new product categories, but difficult to accomplish in established categories where benefits are well known.

Strategy 3: *Add a new benefit which is important and on which the brand delivers uniquely.* Typically requires a product improvement of an innovative and major nature; small improvements don't carry enough importance weight.

Strategy 4: *Weaken a competitor's perceived delivery on a benefit.* Can sometimes be achieved by comparative advertising (see Chapter 10) to increase the brand's relative uniqueness.

Strategy 5: *Alter the composition rule so as to favor the brand.* This amounts to altering benefit importance weights. As in the second strategy, this can be difficult except for relatively new product categories and thus an NCU target audience.

Add a new benefit which is important and on which the brand delivers uniquely. Aim achieved this by "adding" plaque removal as a benefit. Industry reports suggest that this benefit is moderately important, not alone enough to sustain the brand. New and *important* benefits for toothpaste become harder to find and await difficult technological innovation.

Weaken a competitor's perceived delivery on a benefit. Implicit comparisons, striving for uniqueness by relegating the competition to a lower level of perceived delivery, have been used for years by Crest ("You can't beat Crest for fighting cavities") and rival Colgate ("Only your dentist can give your teeth better fluoride protection than Colgate's"). Retaliation can limit effectiveness of a competitive benefit strategy.

Alter the composition rule so as to favor the brand. An "adult" toothpaste, such as Ultra Brite, could possibly gain an attitudinal advantage by trying to alter the composition rule used by most consumers, as follows: Fluoride has very little effect on *adult* teeth (which is true), so fluoride is *not* a necessary benefit (if you are an adult user). Cultural overlearning, however, probably would limit the feasibility of this strategy.

For *new* product categories, and *new category user* target audiences, however, many of these alternative benefit strategies may be feasible. This is because (1) benefit importance and the composition rule, (2) known brand delivery, and thus (3) uniqueness are not yet well established for NCU's. Thus, there is a good chance that one of these alternative strategies (if well thought out to favor the brand) will work.

"POSITIONING" DEFINED

It is perhaps fitting to conclude our examination of brand benefit strategy by offering a definition of "positioning." This concept is not emphasized in this book because of the multiplicity of meanings taken on by the term "positioning" in everyday advertising parlance. But now that we have covered all the necessary concepts, it is appropriate to consider the term because it is so popular that it virtually requires a definition.

The definition of positioning that we favor is one that several large advertising agencies use, Ogilvy & Mather among them, in which brand benefit strategy is the last of three components. The definition is as follows:

Positioning statement:

1 To (target audience),
2 ——is the brand of (category need),
3 that offers (brand benefit or benefits)

For example, the positioning statements for the toothpaste analysis discussed earlier might be, for Colgate's two target audiences:

- To Colgate brand loyals (target audience), Colgate is the brand of cavity-prevention toothpaste (category need) that tastes best for children (brand benefit).

- To *Crest* brand loyals, that is, to Colgate's other-brand loyals (target audience), *Colgate* is the brand of cavity-prevention toothpaste (category need) that fights cavities equally as well as any other fluoridated toothpaste (brand benefit).

The components of the three-part definition of positioning will now be examined.

Target Audience

Brands are always positioned *to* a specific target audience. In the example, we saw that Colgate is positioned *differently* depending on which target audience—its own loyals, or Crest loyals—it is trying to attract.

In theory, a brand can have as many positionings as there are target audiences to which it is directed. Only if the category need to which the brand is tied is the same across target audiences (quite likely) *and* the benefit or benefits emphasized across target audiences are identical (most *un*likely) would there be a single positioning statement for the brand.

Category Need

Category need must be defined specifically to reflect the category *partition* (Chapter 2) in which the brand competes. This in turn reflects the product category purchase motivation (Chapter 6). For example, notice that we framed the Colgate positioning statements, not in terms of the toothpaste category in general, but in terms of the cavity-prevention toothpaste sub-category, or partition, in particular.

As explained in Chapter 2, the brand's *true market* is defined as consisting of those brands that consumers (the target audience) perceive as being close substitutes. In agency parlance, these category-member brands comprise the "competitive frame" in which the brand must successfully compete. Note that a *necessary* benefit, such as cavity prevention, can define a sub-category, whereas a more-the-better benefit, such as tastes good to children, rarely does but is more likely to differentiate brands in the sub-category.

Note again that a brand could be positioned in different sub-categories. For example, Colgate many years ago was positioned in the mouth-freshening sub-category ("The Colgate ring of confidence"). To position it there today would be to push it to compete with another Colgate brand, Ultra Brite, an unlikely positioning but a possible one.

Accordingly, positioning requires *two* links: first, to the category need and, second, to the brand purchase motivation, discussed next.

Brand Benefit(s)

The second link, and the third component of the positioning statement, is the benefit or benefits that are *emphasized* by the brand's advertising (or promotion) when addressing the target audience. *Emphasized* benefits, as distinct from *mentioned* benefits, are those that crucially link the brand to the target audience's brand purchase motivation.

In the foregoing Colgate examples, the *category* purchase motivation was cavity prevention (problem avoidance). The *brand* purchase motivation for Colgate brand loyals was also problem avoidance but of a different form: getting children to *use* toothpaste (via the taste). The brand purchase motivation for Colgate's other-brand loyals was problem avoidance, too, and of the same form as the category motivation: cavity prevention. As noted in Chapter 6, the brand purchase motivation may or may not differ from the category purchase motivation—depending on which motivation happens to be most effective in selling the *brand* to the particular *target audience*.

As should by now be clear, a brand may have several positioning statements depending on whether it emphasizes different benefits, as it probably would if it is trying to gain sales from more than one target audience. For example, a brand could have an advertising positioning to brand loyals, and a promotion positioning, such as biggest discounts or best premiums, to brand switchers.

To summarize, positioning, in its best definition, incorporates specification of: (1) the target audience, (2) the category need to which the brand is linked via brand awareness, and (3) the brand benefit or benefits to be *emphasized* to that target audience as the means of favorably influencing their brand attitude.

SUMMARY

Brand attitude strategy considers the general means (not creative tactics, which come later) through which the brand attitude objective (create, increase, maintain, modify, or change) can be achieved.

Brand attitude strategy is decided at two levels: type of brand attitude, then selection of benefits to represent that attitude.

Type of brand attitude requires ascertaining which of four quadrants applies to the target audience's purchase decision regarding the brand. The quadrants reflect the degree of *involvement* (low or high) experienced by the target audience and the type of *motivation* (informational or transformational) underlying purchase of the brand. Thus, the brand attitude can be either: low involvement/informational, low involvement/transformational, high involvement/informational, or high involvement/transformational. In a genuinely mixed case, which is rare within a specific target audience, classification should conservatively lean towards high involvement, and informational motivation, respectively.

The involvement level for brand attitude depends on the nature of the product *and* the target audience. Generally, previous favorable triers of the brand (brand loyals and favorable brand switchers) will be making low involvement decisions to *re*-purchase, whereas non-triers or unfavorable triers (new category users, unfavorable brand switchers, and other-brand loyals) will be making high involvement decisions to purchase *unless* the product category itself is regarded as low risk.

The motivational basis for brand attitude depends on why target audience decision makers are considering buying the brand: Is it for solving consumer-experienced problems (informational motivation) or is it to enhance themselves in some way (transformational motivation)? Informational motivation includes the motives of problem removal, problem avoidance, incomplete satisfaction, mixed-approach avoidance, and normal depletion. Transformational motivation includes the motives of sensory gratification, intellectual stimulation, and social approval. A brand can be linked, via brand attitudes, to any of these purchase motives provided that enough target audience buyers have the respective motive.

Once the manager has ascertained the brand attitude type in terms of involvement and motivation, benefits have to be selected to "communicate to" the brand attitude in advertisements and promotion offers.

The I-D-U method of benefit selection is recommended. You should select benefits that are: important (I) to the target audience's motivation; upon which the brand can deliver (D) well; and, if possible, uniquely (U) well in comparison with competing brands. The more (relatively) unique the brand's delivery on an important benefit, the more that benefit will determine choice of the brand.

Unique-important benefits should be *emphasized* in the brand's advertising and promotion, whereas equally delivered or "parity" important benefits need only be mentioned. Inferior, or "below-parity," important benefits can, depending on the nature of the benefit and the knowledgability of the target audience, be traded off against other benefits or omitted in the hope that one or two deficits won't detract from the brand's stronger benefits.

The manager also has to be attuned to the way in which target audience decision makers put benefits together when multiple benefits are offered. Some benefits are necessary for all brands to have, at a satisfactory or threshold level; others are continuous "more-the-better" benefits; others have an ideal or "just-right" level; and still others are inevitably inferred by consumers even if they aren't mentioned. The description of how decision makers combine each important benefit is known as the benefit composition rule.

Most advertisements and promotion offers employ the benefit strategy of trying to increase or maintain the brand's perceived benefit delivery (brand benefit beliefs). However, other benefit strategies may be possible—especially in new product categories aimed at a new category user target audience. These alternative strategies include trying to alter benefit importance, adding a new benefit, trying to demean a competing brand's benefit delivery, or trying to alter the buyer's benefit composition rule—all in ways that favor the advertised brand.

NOTES

1 Special acknowledgment should be given to five major theorists whose work has variously influenced the synthesis presented in this chapter. Alphabetically, they

are J.T. Cacioppo, A.S.C. Ehrenberg, P. Nelson, R.E. Petty, and W.D. Wells. References to their work are given in later notes.

2 Perceived risk was introduced to marketing and consumer behavior by R.A. Bauer. For an excellent coverage of the topic, including papers by Bauer, see D.F. Cox (Ed.), *Risk Taking and Information Handling in Consumer Behavior,* Boston: Graduate School of Business Administration, Harvard University, 1967.

3 For evidence that economic and psychosocial risk can be operationally measured, see J.P. Peter and L.X. Tarpey, A comparative analysis of three consumer decision strategies, *Journal of Consumer Research,* 1975, *2* (1), 29–37.

4 C.R. Wasson, *Consumer Behavior: A Managerial Viewpoint,* Austin, TX: Austin Press, 1975, especially chap. 11.

5 J.C. Maloney, Curiosity versus disbelief in advertising, *Journal of Advertising Research,* 1962, *2* (2), 2–8.

6 P.E. Nelson, Information and consumer behavior, *Journal of Political Economy,* 1970, *78* (2), 311–329.

7 Similar theories in which trial experience is regarded as the easiest way to evaluate low risk purchases have been advanced by: A.S.C. Ehrenberg, Repetitive advertising and the consumer, *Journal of Advertising Research,* 1974, *14* (2), 25–34; R.J. Lutz and P.J. Reilly, An exploration of the effects of perceived social and performance risk on consumer information acquisition, in S. Ward and P. Wright (Eds.), *Advances in Consumer Research, Vol.1,* Ann Arbor, MI: Association for Consumer Research, 1974, pp. 393–405; D.W. Finn, Try it you'll like it: a case against the low involvement hierarchy, Working paper no. 6, M.J. Nealy School of Business, Texas Christian University, 1982; and R.E. Smith and W.R. Swinyard, Information response models: an integrated approach, *Journal of Marketing,* 1982, *46* (1), 81–93.

8 W.J. McGuire, The nature of attitudes and attitude change, in G. Lindzey and E. Aronson (Eds.), *The Handbook of Social Psychology, Vol. 3,* Reading, MA: Addison-Wesley, 1969, pp. 136–314.

9 T.S. Robertson, Low-commitment consumer behavior, *Journal of Advertising Research,* 1976, *16* (2), 19–26. For a more technical analysis of how extreme attitudes can be weakly held, see R.S. Wyer, *Cognitive Organization and Change: An Information Processing Approach,* Potomac, MD: Lawrence Erlbaum Associates, 1974, especially chap. 2.

10 P.E. Nelson, same reference as note 6.

11 J.A. Howard discusses this point in his theory of Extensive Problem Solving; see *Consumer Behavior: Application of Theory,* New York: McGraw-Hill, 1977.

12 The concept of latitude of acceptance comes from the assimilation-contrast theory of attitude formation and change advanced by M. Sherif, C.I. Hovland, and other Yale researchers, first announced in C.I. Hovland, I.L. Janis, and H.H. Kelley, *Communication and Persuasion,* New Haven, CT: Yale University Press, 1953. W.J. McGuire (note 8) provides an excellent summary of this theory.

13 G. Fennell. Consumer's perceptions of the product-use situation, *Journal of Marketing,* 1978, *42* (2), 38:47.

14 Early theories of motivation emphasized drive reduction as the governing principle. Modern theories emphasize both drive reduction (negative motivations) and drive increase (positive motivations). Sole emphasis on drive reduction would imply that people prefer to exist in a state of boring neutrality, whereas the dual emphasis recognizes that while people want to minimize pain, they want to maximize pleasure as well, to make life interesting and stimulating. This corresponds, in economics, to maximizing utility. For a discussion of drive-reduction and drive-increase

principles of motivation, see W.A. Wickelgren, *Learning and Memory,* Englewood Cliffs, NJ: Prentice-Hall, 1977, chaps. 5 and 6. For evidence that both negative and positive motivations are needed to account for human behavior, see P. Warr, J. Barter, and G. Brownbride, On the independence of positive and negative effect, *Journal of Personality and Social Psychology,* 1983, *44* (3), 644–651.

15 The informational vs. transformational distinction was introduced by William D. Wells, research director of Needham, Harper & Steers advertising agency, in several audio-visual presentations. A photocopied paper, "How advertising works," issued in 1981 is available from the agency. The only published article on the distinction at the time of writing is by C. Puto and W.D. Wells, Informational and transformational advertising: the differential effects of time, in T.C. Kinnear (Ed.), *Advances in Consumer Research: Vol. 11,* Provo, UT: Association for Consumer Research, 1984, pp. 638–643. Theorists should note that Dr. Wells applies the terms to advertisement types, whereas we apply them to brand purchase motivations. Thus, an advertisement might be inappropriately transformational for a brand that is informational, and vice versa. The advertisement should suit the *brand's* motivation.

16 G. Fennell, same reference as note 13.

17 Social approval is manifest in social rewards such as praise, envious looks, etc. However, as with the other motivations, it is the buyer's *perception* that counts, that is, a feeling of *personal* recognition. For example, a girl may *think* she looks terrific in hot pants, even if onlookers actually are privately disapproving. She nevertheless buys and wears the hot pants for social approval as *she* perceives it.

18 "Conspicuous consumption" is the term used as early as 1899 by the economist Thorstein Veblen to explain product choices that departed from the "rational man" ideal of always buying the lowest-priced product, given comparable quality. Consumption of a known high-priced product leads to social approval from those members of the public concerned with status—and that's just about everyone! For a contemporary review of the social symbolism of products, see M.R. Solomon, The role of products as social stimuli: a symbolic interactionism perspective, *Journal of Consumer Research,* 1983, *10* (3), 319–329.

19 See note 15.

20 Benefit segmentation is a term coined by R.I. Haley, Benefit segmentation: a decision-oriented research tool, *Journal of Marketing,* 1968, *32* (3), 30–35; also see R.I. Haley, Beyond benefit segmentation, *Journal of Advertising Research,* 1971, *11* (4), 3–8.

21 R.I. Haley, first reference in note 20.

22 The concept of "determinance" of attributes (benefits) was proposed by J.H. Myers and M.I. Alpert, Determinant buying attitudes: meaning and measurement, *Journal of Marketing,* 1968, *32* (4), 13–20. For an update on the concept of determinance, see M.I. Alpert, Unresolved issues in the identification of determinant attributes, in J.C. Olson (Ed.), *Advances in Consumer Research,: Vol. 7,* Ann Arbor, MI: Association for Consumer Research, 1980, pp. 83–88.

23 In a scientifically bold article, the late and famous market researcher, Alfred Politz, suggested a formula for the three criteria of benefit selection which states that Importance is most influential in causing advertising to be effective, followed by Delivery (which he called believability), and last, Uniqueness:

$$E = I \times \sqrt[a]{D} \times \sqrt[a+b]{U}$$

Whereas there is no proof of the success of this formula, it does reflect the correct order of considerations in benefit selection. See A. Politz, Politz on copy: making the sales point stick out, *Printers' Ink,* 1955, *250* (April 1), 32–34. As *Printers' Ink* is now defunct and hard to obtain, a summary of Politz' theory is available in D.B. Lucas and S.H. Britt, *Measuring Advertising Effectiveness,* New York: McGraw-Hill, 1960, p. 123.

24 The simple matrix has appeared in many trade journals and also appears in J.A. Martilla and J.C. James, Importance-performance analysis, *Journal of Marketing,* 1977, *41* (1), 77–79.

25 See especially the article by C. Obermiller, Generating product ideas: a modification of the dual questioning technique, in J.C. Olson (Ed.), same reference as note 22, pp. 767–771.

26 P.L. Wright, Use of consumer judgment models in promotion planning, *Journal of Marketing,* 1973, *37* (4), 27–33. The major alternative choice rules are well summarized in P.L. Wright, Consumer choice strategies: simplifying vs. optimizing, *Journal of Marketing Research,* 1975, *12* (1), 60–67.

27 K.E. Miller and J.L. Ginter, An investigation of situational variation in brand choice behavior and attitude, *Journal of Marketing Research,* 1979, *16* (1), 111–123.

28 A sophisticated analysis of different types of benefits is provided by J.H. Myers and A.D. Shocker, The nature of product-related attributes, *Research in Marketing: Vol. 5,* Greenwich, CT: JAI Press, 1981, 211–236.

29 The more important the omitted benefits, the further below average the inferred level will be, so the brand normally couldn't omit *very* important benefits. For a thorough examination of this effect, see J. Huber and J. McCann, The impact of inferential beliefs on product evaluations, *Journal of Marketing Research,* 1982, *19* (3), 324–323. A very good discussion of inference is also found in J.B. Cohen, P.W. Miniard, and P.R. Dickson, Information integration: an information processing perspective, in J.C. Olson (Ed.), same reference as note 22, pp. 161–170.

DISCUSSION QUESTIONS

7.1 Find one example of each of the following types of product which, to the best of your knowledge, is:

a Low in both economic and psychosocial risk

b Low in economic risk but high in psychosocial risk

c High in economic risk but low in psychosocial risk

d High in both types of risk

Explain your answers and state whether the low involvement or high involvement designation (ignoring target audience) applies.

7.2 Level of involvement depends not just on the nature of the product but also on the target audience who is making the purchase decision. Discuss the contention in the text that "the 'habitual' buyer of Rolls-Royces probably is not making a high involvement decision in buying another one." Develop pro and con arguments for this conclusion.

7.3 In Figure 7.1, certain products were exemplified as informational and others as transformational. Think about the following product classifications and, to help, interview several acquaintances, probing for their reasons for *brand* choice. (You cannot necessarily tell from ads for these products, which may be following the wrong motivation.) Which motivation or motivations, in each case, do you think led to the classification?

a Light beer as informational

b Regular beer as transformational

     c Insurance as informational

     d Cars as transformational

7.4 You are the advertising manager for Chivas Regal scotch whiskey. You are trying to win customers from J&B's loyal drinkers. Advertising strategy research has produced the following results for the two brands as perceived by *J&B brand loyals* (all ratings on 0 to 10 scale where 10 = highest):

Benefit	Importance	Brand Delivery	
		Chivas Regal	J&B
Good tasting	10	9	10
Status image	7	10	5
Low price	6	2	7

Which benefit(s) would you emphasize, which would you mention, and which might you omit in advertising Chivas to J&B loyals, and why?

7.5 Suppose that research on service stations has revealed that drivers choose a station based on the following important benefits: convenience to home, gasoline price, reputation for repair work, and "attention" shown by gas attendants. Write a likely benefit composition rule for these benefits.

7.6 Name and discuss three product categories where you believe the importance of a benefit has been changed in a substantial way by *advertising*. Also note which brands seemed to have lost or gained by the change.

7.7 How does our definition of "positioning" differ from the concept of positioning as used in most marketing textbooks? In your answer, compare at least three other textbooks' definitions with ours. *Hint:* It may help to distinguish marketing positioning from advertising positioning.

FURTHER READING

Ehrenberg, A.S.C. Repetitive advertising and the consumer. *Journal of Advertising,* 1974, *14* (2), 25–34.

> Argues that for frequently purchased products, brand awareness is sufficient to cause trial. To brand awareness we would add that a tentatively favorable brand attitude is necessary as well. The article provides a strong argument for the view that low involvement brand choice applies to virtually all consumer packaged goods.

Hovland, C.I., Janis, I.L., and Kelley, H.H. *Communication and Persuasion.* New Haven, CT: Yale University Press, 1953.

> Classic presentation of high involvement attitude theory, which was described in textbooks until the late-1970s as the only type of brand attitude. Recent textbooks now describe low involvement attitude as well.

Nelson, P.E. Information and consumer behavior. *Journal of Political Economy,* 1970, *78* (2), 311–329.

> Nelson originated the distinction between experience or "try it and see" products and search or "conviction required" products—that is, between low and high involvement brand choice. Contains good arguments and good examples.

Wells, W.D. How advertising works. Working paper. Chicago, IL: Needham, Harper & Steers Advertising, 1981.

Introduced the terms "informational" and "transformational." However, it should be noted that Dr. Wells classifies advertisements in this way, whereas we propose that the distinction refers to the motivation for which the *brand* is purchased (the ad may be wrong).

Wright, P.L. Use of consumer judgment models in promotion planning. *Journal of Marketing,* 1973, *37* (4), 27–33.

Presents an easy-to-read explanation of why composition rules have to be understood when deciding on a benefit strategy. Later articles give more rules, but this is the best basic explanation.

CREATIVE STRATEGY

CHAPTER 8

PROCESSING

Advertisements work via the step in the buyer response sequence called *processing*—the step between exposure to the ad and the communication effects produced by it. A full understanding of the processing step and how processing relates to communication effects puts the manager in a much better position to commission and evaluate specific advertisements. Appraisal of creative executions (advertisements prepared in preliminary or finished form) depends on a clear understanding of *how the proposed advertisement is intended to work*.

After reading this chapter you should:

- Understand how processing fits into the buyer response sequence
- Become familiar with the four main processing responses: attention, learning, acceptance, and emotion
- Realize that the type of processing required for an advertisement depends on the particular communication effect under consideration

PROCESSING DEFINED

Processing can be defined as the potential buyer's immediate responses to elements of the ad.[1] By immediate responses, we mean reactions that occur while the buyer is looking at, listening to, or thinking about the ad.

Processing is the second step in the buyer response sequence (Figure 8.1). The first step, exposure, usually is defined as the *opportunity* for the decision maker to see or hear the advertisement (see Chapter 1). Processing is what goes on *during* exposure and sometimes *afterwards if* the decision maker still is thinking about the ad. Unsuccessful processing means that the buyer response

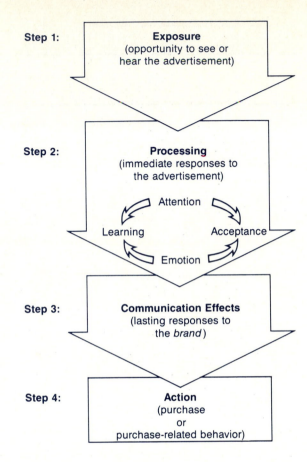

FIGURE 8.1   How the processing step fits into the buyer response sequence. Also shown are the four main types of processing responses.

sequence is "derailed" at step 2; whereas successful processing at step 2 leads to step 3, communication effects.

The immediate responses that constitute processing occur in what psychologists call active or "short-term" memory.[2] However, immediate responses to the ad are not always conscious responses that the buyer is actively aware of making.[3] Nor are all these immediate responses remembered later, as we shall see.

Four Processing Responses

As indicated in the figure, there are four main processing responses that can occur:

1 Attention
2 Learning
3 Acceptance
4 Emotion

Two Types of Processing

There are two different types of processing. This difference is shown in Figure 8.1 by the two arrows diverging from the attention response. For brand awareness, and when the brand attitude is low involvement, *rote learning* is required. For other communication effects, and when the brand attitude is high involvement, *acceptance* is required. The two different types of processing will be explained shortly.

Elements of an Ad

Processing responses are made to stimulus details (elements) contained in the advertisement. These elements, or stimuli, depending on the advertising medium, can be pictures (still or video), words (seen or heard), music, or other special effects, that comprise the various details of the ad.

Each *relevant element* in the ad must go *separately* through processing if the element is to produce a communication effect. For example, the picture of the package must be processed to produce brand recognition awareness; various copy points must each be processed to produce brand attitude; and so forth.

Let us now examine the four processing responses that are made to elements of an ad, while keeping in mind that two types of processing must be distinguished in relation to communication effects.

ATTENTION

An element in an ad must be attended to *before* other processing responses to it can be made. Attention is thus the first necessary processing response.

Attention is basically an "orienting" response to a stimulus. It signifies that the stimulus has made contact with a sense organ, such as the eyes or ears of the decision maker, and one or both of the nervous systems: the central nervous system or brain, or the autonomic nervous system, as in a purely "gut" reaction that may or may not be registered in the brain.

Reflexive and Selective Attention   Attention is a response that can be initiated in two ways: involuntarily, by a change in the external stimulus pattern (reflexive attention); or voluntarily, by prior responses occurring internally in the brain that lead a person to look for a particular external stimulus to attend to (selective attention). Reflexive attention is sometimes called "stimulus-driven" attention, whereas selective attention is sometimes called "goal-driven" attention.[4]

Gaining Initial Attention

Most ads automatically gain attention, reflexively, just by being in a medium that the buyer is watching, listening to, or reading. This is because an advertisement represents a change in external stimulation—as, for example, when a TV program fades out, or a song ends on the radio, or a page is turned in a magazine or newspaper.

However, reflexively induced initial attention lasts only about one-tenth of a second if the advertising stimulus is *visual,* as in the opening video in a TV commercial or an illustration in a print ad[5]; or about three-tenths of a second for *each word* looked at or heard, as in the opening audio in a TV or radio commercial or the headline of a print ad.[6]

Maintaining Continued Attention

The advertiser must use stimuli in the ad to maintain continued attention. The stimuli may be reflexive *or* selective, depending on the two main communication effects, brand awareness and brand attitude, that all advertisements seek to achieve.

Brand Awareness   Continued attention responses can be generated by using advertising elements that pose a change or contrast (Figure 8.2) and thereby elicit further *reflexive* attention responses to the ad. Reflexive attention is sufficient to begin processing for the *brand awareness* communication effect. Brand awareness can be achieved by gaining the buyer's attention reflexively—to elements that signify the brand and the category—without having anything "of interest" in the ad.

Brand Attitude   Brand attitude, the other universal communication objective, is a more complicated communication effect as far as attention is concerned. Because brand attitude requires associating the brand with a relevant buyer motivation, the buyer will tend to attend *selectively* (beyond initial reflexive attention) only to motivationally relevant stimuli. For example, the detailed copy elements in an ad aimed at hemorrhoid sufferers (Figure 8.3) probably will be read only by those consumers who have this particular problem removal motivation.

In terms of the eight buyer motivations, all the *informational* (negatively originated) motivations have a selective limitation. Unless the buyer "has" the problem—now, or from time to time—the attitudinal content isn't likely to be attended to. Only those people who have the particular problem that is the subject of the problem removal, problem avoidance, incomplete satisfaction, mixed approach-avoidance, or normal depletion motivation portrayed in the ads are likely to pay continued attention.

Attitudes based on the *transformational* (positively originated) motivations have an easier attentional passage in processing. Almost everyone, most of the time, likes to be "turned on" by positive stimuli—and transformational ads are loaded with them. Sensory gratification, intellectual stimulation, social approval—almost everyone wants these things. People actually will "tune in" ads that provide them.[7] That is, there is no (or very little) selective tuneout or inattention for ads aimed at transformational brand attitudes.

So, an ad can and should "hook a buyer in" via reflexive attention, but whether it can maintain the continued attention necessary to influence brand

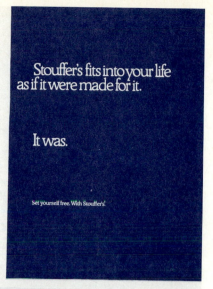

FIGURE 8.2   In this 3-page fold-out ad for Stouffer's, the right-hand page is seen first (using short copy on a large area of blank space to elicit reflexive attention) and then the two left-hand pages fold out (to engage selective attention). The original was in color, with the right-hand page using white type on "Stouffer's red" background. ("Stouffer's" is a registered trademark of Stouffer Foods Corp. Reprinted by permission of Stouffer Foods Corp.)

attitude largely depends on whether *other* stimuli in the ad are perceived by the buyer as motivationally relevant and therefore as being worth *selectively* attending to because they show promise of reducing (informational) or increasing (transformational) the buyer's motivational state.

Only rarely can an advertiser ignore advertising stimuli that produce reflexive

FIGURE 8.3   An advertisement illustrating how narrow *selective* attention (relating to the buyer's motivation) can be. Only hemorrhoid sufferers are likely to attend to the detailed copy. (Courtesy Whitehall Laboratories.)

attention as a forerunner to stimuli that produce selective attention. People, as TV program viewers, radio listeners, readers, commuters, and so on, rarely are thinking spontaneously about the motivation expressed in a particular advertisement, so most ads have to engage attention, at first, reflexively.

The rare exceptions occur with ads placed in the Yellow Pages, or in classified or "shopping special" sections of newspapers or magazines. Here, the potential buyer may be actively (selectively) looking for advertising information to meet a current motivation. But even in these selective attention instances, because of the simultaneous exposure of *competing* ads, reflexive attention-getting stimuli, such as an unusual layout or boldface classified entries, are often used to gain attention to your ad *before* the others are noticed, hoping that the decision maker will make a choice based on the first few ads attended to.

It follows that all ads should include reflexive attention-getting elements as well as selective attention-getting elements. As we shall see, the latter are *emotional* stimuli relevant to the brand's motivational (and thus attitudinal) foundation.

Attention, therefore, is the first processing response that an advertising element must generate if it is to produce or contribute to communication effects. However, attention alone is not a sufficient processing response. An advertising element also must be learned *or* accepted, depending on the particular communication effect to be achieved, as explained in the next two sections.

LEARNING

By "learning," we mean learning of the very simple or *rote* type, in which the potential buyer merely has to echo or mentally repeat the content of the stimulus identically, or virtually identically, as a response.

Rote learning requires very little mental activity by the decision maker. It is basically a "passive" or "mindless" process, even though the brain certainly is engaged during learning.[8] Rote learning is passive because it goes on automatically, regardless of whether we want it to or not, and often without our conscious awareness of it occurring. Because of the passive nature of learning, repetition of the to-be-learned stimulus-stimulus association (see below) usually is required.

Learning in advertising is a necessary and sufficient form of processing for two communication effects: brand awareness and *low involvement* brand attitude. Let us see how these two communication effects are learned.

Brand Awareness Learning

To become aware of a brand—so as to be able to recognize or recall the brand later—the decision maker has to learn the *association* between:

S_1:   The category need (for example, instant coffee)
and
S_2:   The brand (for example, Maxwell House)

Most of you have already learned that Maxwell House (S_2) is a brand of instant coffee (S_1). But consider a young person or an American visitor who has never heard of Maxwell House. When the person first sees an ad for Maxwell House, the first thought will be "What *is* it?"[9] To answer this question, the person has to learn the association between the brand and the category need. The learned association is not just that Maxwell House is a brand of instant coffee. Rather, Maxwell House must be associated with the *need* for instant coffee.

All new brands have to go through this category need–brand awareness learning process. So do all new category users for whom every brand is a new brand. And familiar brands must *maintain* the learned association.

What is the *response* to be learned? The response depends on whether the decision maker later has to choose the brand via brand recognition or via brand recall. We use the symbols S_1 and S_2 to emphasize that it is the stimulus-stimulus connection that has to be learned, with *either one* capable of emerging later as the response.[10]

Brand Recognition   In brand recognition learning, S_2 (the Maxwell House brand package or brand name) is the *stimulus* that will occur first in the decision situation, and S_1 (the instant coffee category need) is the *response*. The advertiser wants the decision maker to respond, "Ah, instant coffee—do I need some?" when he or she sees (for example, in a supermarket) or hears (for example, in a restaurant) the brand stimulus, Maxwell House.

Brand Recall   In brand recall learning, the same association is learned, but the functions of stimulus and response are reversed. In brand recall decision situations, S_1 (the instant coffee category need) occurs first, as the *stimulus,* and S_2 (the Maxwell House brand) is the advertiser-desired *response*.

Coffee purchase is mainly by brand recognition, so it's a bit artificial to think of a brand recall situation. However, brand recall might be the objective for a specialized brand of instant coffee that is seeking to have the buyer make a definite choice *before* going to the store.

Brand awareness learning—or "What *is* it?" processing—is conceptually simple. However, we shall see in Chapter 9 that the creative tactics for brand recall, which is the more difficult to learn of the two types of brand awareness, are quite complex. The creative tactics are simpler for brand recognition.

Low Involvement Brand Attitude Learning

In Chapter 7 we saw that the attitude upon which brand choice is based will be either low involvement (trial experience sufficient) or high involvement (search and conviction required prior to purchase) depending on the nature of the product and the target audience.

The brand benefits that comprise *low involvement* brand attitude require only rote learning during processing.

In learning what benefit or benefits a brand offers, the decision maker is thinking, simply, in connection with the brand: "What *of* it?"[11] The decision maker has already learned what the brand *is* (brand awareness, connected to category need) and now is about to learn what it *does* (brand benefits, which underlie brand attitude). The two to-be-learned associations or connections are compared in Figure 8.4.

For low involvement brand attitude learning, the stimulus and response roles are straightforward:

S_2:   The brand (for example, Maxwell House)
R_1, R_2, etc.:   The brand's benefits (for example, good tasting coffee, popular, reasonably priced)

The *stimulus* is always the brand. (This assumes *prior* brand awareness learning. As noted in Chapter 6, brand awareness must precede brand attitude, or the buyer cannot choose the brand.) The *responses* learned in connection with the brand are the benefits that the brand mentions in its advertising.[12]

FIGURE 8.4   Learning responses in processing of brand awareness and brand attitude.

1   "What *is* it?"   **Brand Awareness:**
                                  connection between category
                                  need and brand awareness of
                                  name or package

2   "What *of* it?"   **Brand Attitude:**
                                  connection(s) between brand
                                  awareness and brand attitude
                                  benefit(s)

With brand benefit learning, the decision maker simultaneously learns the *connection* and the *degree* of connection (brand benefit delivery). In the coffee example, the consumer may learn that:

- Maxwell House is *good* tasting coffee.
- Maxwell House is *great* tasting coffee.
- Maxwell House is *the best* tasting coffee.

The underscored mental adjectives (where we have tried to preserve consumer language rather than use the sterile good, very good, excellent type of adjective used in questionnaires) reflect the *degree* of brand benefit delivery learned.[13]

With low involvement brand attitude, the degree of brand benefit learning is temporary, until the buyer actually tries the brand. The learning that the advertiser is aiming for is an *extreme if tentatively held belief sufficient to generate trial*. In the example, the advertiser wants the decision maker to learn that Maxwell House is at least a "great" tasting coffee or even "the best" tasting coffee. Following trial, the brand has to *actually* deliver. The tentative belief has to be confirmed, to the degree promised by the brand benefit learning, for the brand to be purchased again.

This low involvement example brings us nicely into consideration of the processing response required for *high* involvement brand attitude, and for the remaining communication effects (when they are objectives) of category need, brand purchase intention, and purchase facilitation. The processing response for these communication effects is known as acceptance.

ACCEPTANCE

Acceptance can be defined as the decision maker's *personal agreement* with elements associated, in the advertisement, with the brand. The opposite response, rejection, reflects personal disagreement with an associated element.

Acceptance and the Other Communication Effects

Acceptance is necessary for successful processing of all communication effects except brand awareness and low involvement brand attitude:

- *Category Need* The decision maker has to *accept* that a category need exists, based on the ad's selling the category need or reminding the decision maker of a latent category need.
- *High Involvement Brand Attitude* The decision maker has to *accept* the ad-proposed brand benefits before he or she will try or buy the brand.
- *Brand Purchase Intention* The decision maker has to *accept* an ad's "hard sell" invitation to purchase (note that a hard sell invitation is made when a promotion offer is included). However, "soft sell" purchase intention inferred from *low involvement* brand attitude does *not* require an acceptance response.

- *Purchase Facilitation* The decision maker has to *accept* the ad's reassurance that the product, price, place, or other promotion problem has been facilitated.

Because the elements in advertisements that refer to category need, high involvement brand attitude, brand purchase intention, and purchase facilitation each link the brand to a motivation, they can all be thought of as advertising-induced high involvement *attitudes* toward, respectively, the category or brand. Unlike low involvement brand attitude, high involvement attitudes have to be *confidently held* before the decision maker will take action.

What takes place during processing that makes acceptance different from rote learning? The answer is *active* "cognitive responses" rather than passive rote-learned responses, as explained next.

Cognitive Responses

Acceptance responses were first identified in a classic series of studies of persuasion by Hovland, Janis, et al.[14] However, the full importance of acceptance as a processing response has only been realized relatively recently, with the emergence of *cognitive response theory*.[15] Cognitive response theory is revolutionizing our understanding of one major way in which ads work.

The phenomenon of cognitive response can be explained as follows. When people are exposed to an advertising message, they often attempt to relate the expected and actual information in the message to their existing knowledge about the product or brand (Figure 8.5). In seeking a relationship between new information and existing knowledge, people usually will generate a number

FIGURE 8.5   Examples of cognitive responses during processing by a consumer "in the market" for a new car.

"I *do* need a new car"	**Category Need**
"My best friend has a 300 ZX"	**Brand Attitude** (benefit belief)
"It looks terrific"	**Brand Attitude** (benefit belief)
"And it gets reasonable gas mileage, too"	**Brand Attitude** (benefit belief)
"I think I'll go visit a Nissan dealer on the weekend"	**Brand Purchase** (related) **Intention**
"Ah, there's a dealer just a couple of miles from here"	**Purchase Facilitation**

of message-relevant thoughts or images that may support or oppose the new information.

If these thoughts or images are primarily favorable, a positive shift in brand attitude will occur; if these thoughts or images are primarily unfavorable, a negative shift in brand attitude will occur.

The thoughts or images—cognitive responses—*originate from* a prior attitude toward the brand (familiar brand); a prior attitude toward the product category (new brand in a familiar product category); or from the advertisement itself when there is no prior attitude (a completely new product from the potential buyer's standpoint).

Cognitive response theory assumes that the potential buyer is *motivated to try to make sense* of incoming information from the advertisement in order to formulate or adjust his or her brand attitude. However, this is only likely to occur if the buyer is *highly involved* with the purchase decision. If the potential buyer is highly involved with the purchase decision, cognitive (acceptance) responses are *necessary* in processing if the advertisement is to have an effect on brand attitude.

Acceptance during processing is also necessary if the advertisement is to have an effect on category need, hard-sell induced brand purchase intention, and purchase facilitation. This is because, as previously explained, these communication effects function as (high involvement) attitudes when the decision maker is processing the ad.

Effect of Cognitive Responses on Low Involvement Brand Decisions

An advertisement, of course, is capable of promoting positive or negative reactions from the audience. This is especially true of TV commercials, because of the "captive" nature of the viewing audience, or what is often called the "intrusiveness" (reflexive attention-gaining capability) of TV.

For low involvement brand decisions, the decision maker *does not have* to make active cognitive responses during processing in order to learn brand awareness and brand benefits relevant to low involvement brand attitude. But what if the decision maker does make these responses? Their effect depends on the type of low involvement brand attitude.

If the brand attitude to be learned is low involvement/*informational,* cognitive responses made during processing are completely irrelevant. This is why "irritating" ads, which generate negative thoughts and comments, so often work—but only when the brand purchase decision is low involvement/informational.

If the brand attitude to be learned is low involvement/*transformational*—that is, based on a positive purchase motivation, such as sensory gratification, intellectual stimulation, or social approval—then negative cognitive responses *can* hurt. This is because, for low involvement/transformational brand decisions, the target audience must *like the ad.* The ad serves as a positive stimulus that heightens the positive motivation.

Consequently, whereas rote learning is necessary and sufficient for low involvement brand attitude acquisition, if cognitive responses do occur, their effect on brand attitude is zero in the informational case but contributory in the transformational case. Low involvement creative tactics (next chapter) reflect this difference in processing.

Rote-Learned Benefit Claims versus Accepted Benefit Claims

A final difference in the processing required for low involvement versus high involvement brand attitude is the nature of what is "learned" regarding the brand's benefits.

In rote learning, characteristic of low involvement brand attitude, the decision maker learns an *exact or close paraphrase* of the benefit claim(s) made in the ad. If the claim is made verbally, the decision maker must learn it either verbatim or in words that preserve the same meaning. If the claim is made visually (by implication), the "paraphrase" required is that the typical consumer would describe the visual content in very much the same way as the ad's *creator* would describe it.

By contrast, with the active cognitive responding that characterizes high involvement brand attitude, what is learned (retained after exposure) is a *stored personal interpretation* of the benefit claim(s). A verbatim or closely recalled paraphrase of the benefit claim is not likely and not relevant. What is "learned" is a favorable *impression* about the brand, in the decision maker's *own* or descriptive terms, with regard to the advertised benefit.

Quite evidently, the difference in low involvement and high involvement brand attitude processing—as reflected in rote learning of benefit claims versus active acceptance of them—has significant implications for the way ads are tested. These considerations we will meet in Part Eight on advertising research.

EMOTION

Look at the diagram of processing in Figure 8.6 (from Figure 8.1 earlier). As we have seen so far, each communication effect–relevant element in an ad has to be (1) attended to, then (2) *either* learned (to produce brand awareness and low involvement brand attitude), *or* (3) accepted (to produce all other communication effects and especially high involvement brand attitude). Now we turn to a further type of processing response: (4) emotional responses elicited by the ad.

As shown by the arrows, emotions elicited by elements in the advertisement "feed" learning and acceptance. In particular, emotional responses are necessary whenever an element relates to a *motivation* and thus to an *attitude*. As we saw previously, all communication effects *except* brand awareness have an attitudinal basis. By extension, it follows that emotional responses are critical to the attainment of category need, brand attitude, brand purchase intention, and purchase facilitation communication objectives.[16]

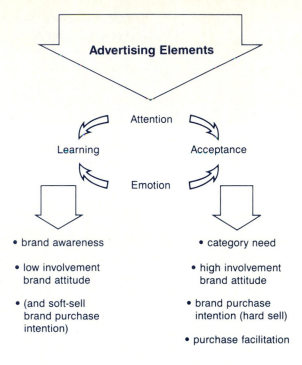

FIGURE 8.6   Detailed diagram of processing responses.

The Necessity of Emotional Responses

Perhaps the most vital contribution of creative input in advertising is in selecting advertising stimuli (pictures, words, music, special effects) that elicit appropriate emotional responses in the target audience. Brands competing in the same product category *partition* offer essentially the same benefits (for example, Coke and Pepsi in the cola beverage category; Cadillac and Lincoln Continental in the luxury car category). What differentiates the effectiveness of their advertising is the ability of the brand's agency to state or show these benefits in an emotionally more compelling (informational) or engaging (transformational) way than other agencies can.

Marketing managers and marketing researchers have very little contact with the emotional side of advertising. They work with objective lists of benefits (as in a manager's strategy document) or with questionnaires (as in a marketing or advertising research study) that ask people, objectively, how "important" a benefit is to them.

This is *not* how advertising works!

A benefit *claim,* whether stated verbally in an ad or implied visually, is a completely different stimulus from the benefit itself, objectively stated. A benefit lacks emotion; whereas a benefit claim *depends on* emotion.

To borrow psychologist George Mandler's words, an advertisement has to generate both "heat" and "light."[17] An effective advertisement, as it is being processed, stirs the prospective buyer's emotions and enlightens him or her about the brand.

Emotional elements are the surface means used in advertisements to contact and energize (stimulate) the decision maker's purchase motivations. How they do this we will see after first examining emotional stimuli and emotional responses in a little more detail.

Emotional Stimuli and Responses

Emotional responses are *elicited,* that is, they are automatically made to certain stimuli. They don't have to be learned by consumers because they are already learned.

Emotional stimulus-response connections are either (1) *genetically programmed,* such as an automatic feeling of fear to a loud noise, or an automatic feeling of joy, and even a covert smile in return, to a smiling face[18]; or else (2) they are *so well established by previous learning* that they are emitted automatically, such as the feeling of pride most adults experience when they see a red, white, and blue color scheme, or the feeling of contempt—or empathy, depending on what you have learned—when we see a clichéd "soap opera" scenario played out in a detergent commercial.

Emotional Stimuli   Creatives have a wide range of stimuli or elements that they can include in ads to elicit various emotions. They can be drawn from any of six stimulus types, depending on the advertising medium (Table 8.1)[19].

- *Heard words and sound effects* are available for creative use in broadcast media. (*Examples:* The convincing tone of Orson Welles' voice; the sound of "Schweppervescence" bubbling.)
- *Music,* likewise, is available in broadcast media. (*Examples:* The elating music of the "Coke is *it*" theme; the jangling music of "nervous headache tension".)
- *Seen words*—which "sound" in the mind, but in *your* voice, not theirs— are available in all media except radio. Creatives select emotionally laden words. (*Examples:* "Filth," "ground-in dirt," "wonderful," "free".)
- *Pictures,* which include drawings and photographs, are available in all media except radio. (*Examples:* The pitiable photographs of starving Third World children in UNESCO ads; the sophisticated sketches in Perrier ads.)
- *Color,* available in all media except radio and newspapers unless color inserts are bought. (*Examples:* The appetizing pictures of chocolate cakes in Betty Crocker cake mix ads; the powerful and sophisticated black backgrounds used in Johnny Walker Black Label scotch whiskey ads.)
- *Movement,* available in TV which, as Table 8.1 shows, is the most versatile medium for emotional stimuli. (*Examples:* The embarrassment of your workmates seeing "ring around the collar"; the excitement of a Mercedes-Benz whipping around a test track with consummate ease.)

Interestingly, and perhaps fortunately where media selection is restricted by other considerations such as target audience reach or cost, most emotions

TABLE 8-1   RANGE OF STIMULUS TYPES AVAILABLE FOR ELICITING EMOTIONAL RESPONSES (BY MEDIUM)

	Heard words and sound effects	Music	Seen words	Pictures	Color	Movement
Broadcast media						
TV	YES	YES	YES	YES	YES	YES
Radio	YES	YES	no	no	no	no
Print media						
Magazines	no	no	YES	YES	YES	no
Direct mail	no	no	YES	YES	YES	no
Outdoor	no	no	YES	YES	YES	no
Point-of-purchase displays	no	no	YES	YES	YES	no
Newspapers	no	no	YES	YES	?	no

Source: E. Crane, *Marketing Communications*, 2nd ed. New York: Wiley, 1972, Chap. 19. By permission.

can be elicited reasonably similarly by words or pictures or movement. A thoughtful study by Sweeney, Tinling, and Schmale[20] found that emotions such as fear, anger, pride, and bliss were similarly judged when presented via verbal descriptions (as in radio or print ads), sketched in color (also as in print but especially outdoor, when words are limited), or acted out on videotape (as in TV commercials). Creative experts, of course, have to be able to translate emotions into any medium.

Emotional Responses   So far, we haven't defined exactly what an emotional response *is*. This is difficult, because emotional responses are non-verbal and thus are hard to describe in words. Emotional responses are first of all *bodily* responses: commonly called "gut reactions" but more technically occurring in the autonomic (sympathetic and parasympathetic) nervous system.

There *may* be *concurrent cognitive responses* which occur in the brain or central nervous system: *verbal labeling* of the feeling (for example, "That's nice" or "Ooh! that's awful!") or *visual imagery* (as when you "see" yourself in a Pierre Cardin suit or imagine a nice cold Michelob on a hot day while watching TV). Many recent studies suggest that verbal labeling or visual imagery, or both, can *heighten* the emotional experience although they do not change its quality—it remains a bodily, physiological response.[21]

Not surprisingly, emotional responses during processing of an ad are extremely difficult to measure when testing advertising. First, the testing situation is often artificial and laboratory-like, rather than natural, like your own home or car where you are exposed to the ad in the real world. Second, people find it very difficult and often embarrassing to report on their emotions, as opposed to their "rational" thoughts (Table 8.2). And third, attempts to make physiological recordings of bodily changes suffer from the inability of *researchers* to interpret what the recordings mean. As we shall again note in Part Eight, accurate measurement of emotional responses is the most elusive

TABLE 8-2   THE DIFFICULTY OF REPORTING EMOTIONS IN RESEARCH, AND OF DETECTING THEM

One of the most innovative qualitative researchers in the business, Mike Brownlee of Creative Dialogue in Sydney, Australia, listens to consumers' *verbs* to detect thoughts (cognitive) versus emotions (affective). This takes a practiced ear and brain, because most consumers have difficulty separating and explaining their thoughts and feelings, as the following excerpt from a focus-group discussion indicates.

Consumer: When I bought my new Mazda, I felt, "What a bargain!"
Moderator: I hear what you *thought,* but what did you *feel*?
Consumer: Well, I felt that the price was fine.
Moderator: And what did you *feel*?
Consumer: You know, I felt a little cheap. . . .

Source: M. Elfverson and M.A. Brownlee, Group discussions, Pamphlet issued by Creative Dialogue Ltd., Sydney, Australia, no date. By permission.

aspect of advertising research, and perhaps the major reason that limits the predictive validity of ad tests in relation to the ad's real-world effectiveness or ineffectiveness.

Nevertheless, the student of advertising must try to understand the function of emotional responses in processing. With this aim, the next section attempts to identify these functions.

How Emotional Responses Relate to Motivation

Emotional stimuli are used in advertisements to elicit emotional responses that will "energize" a relevant motivation. Emotional stimuli and their associated emotional responses are *very* specific (Table 8.3) and no general scheme can do full justice to capturing the exact functioning of emotions.

Nevertheless, the "circumplex" theory of emotions developed by Russell and Pratt[22] shows how the *general* emotional categories can be organized (Figure 8.7). In the figure, we have indicated how informational and transformational motivations, also in general, depend on these emotions.

Informational Motivations   Informational motivations follow the general emotional path from "distressing" to "relaxing." A negative emotional state occurs first (the problem) followed by a positive emotional state (the brand as the solution). We will consider emotions for the respective informational motivations in more detail shortly.

Transformational Motivations   Transformational motivations follow the (completely uncorrelated) emotional path to "exciting." They may begin from a "dull" emotional state, or simply from a "neutral" state (the origin of the axes in the figure). Again, distinct emotions accompany the respective transformational motivations, as we shall see next.

Emotional Portrayal of the Eight Motivations   When we consider the five informational motivations and three transformational motivations separately,

TABLE 8-3   EXAMPLES OF THE SPECIFICITY OF EMOTIONAL STIMULI: SOME OF THE DESCRIPTIONS GIVEN TO ACTORS WHO ACTED OUT EMOTIONS ON VIDEOTAPE IN THE SWEENEY ET AL. EXPERIMENT. THESE ARE NOT UNLIKE INSTRUCTIONS GIVEN TO ACTORS IN TV COMMERCIALS TO GET THE RIGHT EMOTIONAL "TONE."

Negative emotions	
Anger	Organized attack on an object
Fear	Cornered by or defending against an attacking object
Anxiety	Unorganized, disconnected, diffuse activity
Shame	Shrinking and hiding from environment
Helplessness	Desolate, flaccid, finished, where environmental surroundings are of no consequence
Guilt	Set apart from environment by imposing object or group
Positive emotions	
Pride	Outstanding in relation to objects and environment
Helped	Receiving support from objects
Hope	Growing and reaching upward and beyond
Bliss	Floating, quiet solitude
Goodness	Objects close together in quiet harmony
Fascination	Attracted to organized but ill-defined patterns or themes

Source: D.R. Sweeney, D.C. Tinling, and A.H. Schmale, Dimensions of affective expression in 4 expressive modes, *Behavioral Science,* 1970, *15*(5), 393–407. By permission.

FIGURE 8.7   Relationship of general emotional categories to informational and transformational motivations.

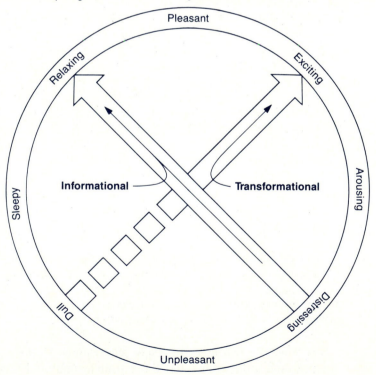

it is possible to give a *general* indication of typical emotions that *might* be used to portray them (and thus stimulate the motivation) in advertisements.

Table 8.4 attempts to do this. *Problem removal* generally is portrayed by anger or annoyance with the problem, followed by relief offered by the brand (*example:* detergents). *Problem avoidance* stimulates fear of an anticipated problem, followed by relaxation as you don't have to worry about the problem after using the brand (*example:* deodorants).

Incomplete satisfaction generally begins with disappointment at what's available, followed by optimism as the new brand is suggested as being closer to the satisfaction ideal (*example:* courier services). *Mixed approach-avoidance* often begins with guilt about indulging in a product with positive and negative features, followed by peace of mind when a brand that promises to solve the conflict is offered (*example:* low calorie desserts). *Normal depletion* relies on the mild annoyance of running out of a product, followed by the convenience of easy replacement (*example:* any regularly purchased product advertised by a local retailer).

The transformational motives *may* begin with the opposite of the positive end states shown in the table—or they may go straight to them. *Sensory gratification,* for instance, may focus solely on elation (*example:* soda beverages) or on the dull-to-elation transition (*example:* spices and herbs). *Intellectual stimulation* plays on the excitement of something new or challenging (*example:* personal computers).

Social approval ends with brand usage that flatters the user (*example:* fashion clothing, cars, vacation resorts). Mild apprehension in the social situation may precede the flattery to heighten the emotional effect, but when the apprehension plays on anxiety, the motivation is more properly classified as *problem avoidance*.

The Emotional Power of TV One of the great advantages of TV as an advertising medium is its capacity to portray a *sequence* of emotions. To some extent, radio and print ads can do this, too; it's possible, for example, to

TABLE 8-4 TYPICAL EMOTIONS THAT MIGHT BE USED TO PORTRAY EACH MOTIVATION

Informational motives	*Typical emotional states*
1 Problem removal	Anger → relief
2 Problem avoidance	Fear → relaxation
3 Incomplete satisfaction	Disappointment → optimism
4 Mixed approach-avoidance	Guilt → peace of mind
5 Normal depletion	Mild annoyance → convenience
Transformational motives	
6 Sensory gratification	Dull* → elated
7 Intellectual stimulation	Bored* → excited
8 Social approval	Apprehensive* → flattered

* Optional prior negative emotions for transformational motives. Positive emotions can arise from a *neutral* prior state and do not require negative emotions beforehand.

develop a sequence of emotions in a 60-second radio commercial, or in a long magazine ad that gains your selective attention. However, only TV advertising can portray sequences of emotion with ease.

Blonsky[23] uses the theory of cultural signs, or semiotics, to identify the themes or "tapes" used in TV commercials (Table 8.5). The relevance of these themes, from our standpoint, is that they elicit familiar patterns of emotions, allowing graphic, almost indelible emotional portrayals of a benefit (and thus a motivation) to which the brand can then be tied.

As we shall see in Chapters 9 to 11 where we examine creative tactics, authentic emotional portrayal of the motivation or motivations leading to brand purchase is one of the two key (and we mean "key" in its correct sense of "unlocking the door") factors in an advertisement's success.

SUMMARY

Processing refers to immediate responses to elements of an advertisement that occur during exposure to the *ad*. Appropriate processing responses have to occur in order to establish or maintain communication effects, which are enduring responses associated with the *brand*.

Four types of processing responses are relevant: attention, learning, acceptance, and emotion. Brand awareness requires attention and learning. Low involvement brand attitude requires attention, learning, and an elicited emotion in conjunction with each benefit. The other communication effects—category need, high involvement brand attitude, brand purchase intention (hard sell only), and purchase facilitation—require attention, acceptance, and elicited emotions.

TABLE 8-5 SOME FAMILIAR THEMES (OR "TAPES") USED IN TV COMMERCIALS TO EVOKE A FAMILIAR PATTERN OF EMOTIONS. LIKELY MOTIVATION IN PARENTHESES.

Sentimentality tape: You haven't talked to your childhood friends and old neighbors for years, so why not reach out and touch someone. Ma Bell will be glad you did. (Problem removal)

Family tape: The American family may be split apart by divorce, juvenile delinquency, etc., but in these commercials Mom, Dad, Tommy, Suzie, Grandma, and Grandpa sit around the table and share their daily experiences. Don't you wish your family was like this? (Problem removal)

Guilt tape: Ring around the collar . . . ring around the collar. You should be ashamed of yourself. Use Wisk. (Problem avoidance)

Nostalgia tape: Pepperidge Farm wants you to "remember" the wholesome, natural food from the turn-of-the-century corner store. The viewer nearly forgets that processed foods are mass-produced in a factory. (Sensory gratification)

The Me tape: The central character in the ad proclaims, "I deserve the best" or reminds viewers "You can never do enough for yourself." Vitamin ads often use this tape, and also Meredith Baxter Birney for L'Oreal hair coloring: "I'm worth it." (Sensory gratification)

The Snob tape: This is the "We're so great we can hardly stand ourselves" approach used by, for example, British Airways, Beck's and Heineken beer, American Express Gold Card, and E. F. Hutton. (Social approval)

Source: M. Blonsky, whose theory is summarized in B. Whalen, Semiotics: an art or powerful research tool? *Marketing News*, May 13, 1983, pp. 8–9. By permission.

Attention can be gained reflexively or selectively. Advertisements usually try to capitalize on both forms of attention: to gain attention reflexively initially and to maintain it selectively while motivating the decision maker.

Learning, in advertising, is strictly of the rote variety. What is learned are *associations*. The association between category need and a brand name or package must be learned to produce brand awareness. The association between the brand and a benefit (or several such associations) must be learned to produce low involvement brand attitude.

Acceptance reflects personal agreement with points expressed in the ad. Personal agreement during processing is necessary when the purchase decision is high involvement. Benefit claims for high involvement brand attitude must be accepted, as must claims designed to establish category need, brand purchase intention (as in promotion offers) and purchase facilitation.

Emotions are the responses through which advertisements engender motivations. All elements except those for brand awareness must elicit an appropriate emotional response. Emotional stimuli that automatically produce emotional responses are wide-ranging although they vary with the advertising medium. In processing, emotions must be elicited that correspond with the motivation or motivations upon which selection of the brand depends.

Creativity in advertising is largely a matter of selecting stimuli (elements) in advertisements that will have a high probability of being processed correctly by the decision maker so that they will produce the required communication effects. In Chapters 9 to 11 we will see how the selection can best be made.

NOTES

1 The definition and discussion of processing is given here in terms of advertising. It applies equally to *promotion offers* (see Part Six). It is convenient to refer to advertising alone in Part Five.

2 Short-term memory is a concept introduced by R.C. Atkinson and R.M. Shiffrin, Human memory: a proposed system and its control processes, in K.W. Spence and J.T. Spence (Eds.), *The Psychology of Learning and Motivation*, New York: Academic Press, 1968, pp. 89–195. Short-term memory also is called "active memory"; see D.J. Lewis, Psychobiology of active and inactive memory, *Psychological Bulletin*, 1979, *86* (3), 1054–1083.

3 R.T. Kellogg, Is conscious attention necessary for long-term storage? *Journal of Experimental Psychology: Human Learning and Memory*, 1980, *6* (4), 379–390. Also H. Shevrin and S. Dickman, The psychological unconscious: a necessary assumption for all psychological theory? *American Psychologist*, 1980, *35* (5), 421–434.

4 D.A. Norman, *Memory and Attention* (2nd ed.), New York: Wiley, 1976.

5 I. Biederman, J.C. Rabinowitz, A.L. Glass, and E.W. Stacy, On the information extracted from a glance at a scene, *Journal of Experimental Psychology*, 1974, *103* (3), 597–600.

6 K.A. Ericsson and H.A. Simon, Verbal reports as data, *Psychological Review*, 1980, *87* (3), 215–251; G.R. Loftus, Tachistoscopic simulations of eye fixations on pictures, *Journal of Experimental Psychology: Human Learning & Memory*, 1981, *7* (5), 369–376.

7 For example, in a study by Video Storyboard Tests Inc. of reasons why people pay attention to commercials, positive motivations (entertainment value) considerably exceeded negative motivations (information value). Reported in *Ad Forum*, 1984, *5* (1), 40.

8 E. Langer, A. Blank, and B. Chanowitz, The mindlessness of ostensibly thoughtful action: the role of "placebic" information in interpersonal interaction, *Journal of Personality and Social Psychology*, 1978, *36* (6), 635–642. For evidence that attitudinal (semantic) learning can occur from stimuli which the person cannot detect (subliminal perception), see J.A. Grueger, Evidence of unconscious semantic processing from a forced error situation, *British Journal of Psychology*, 1984, *75* (3), 305–314.

9 H.E. Krugman, Why three exposures may be enough, *Journal of Advertising Research*, 1972, *12* (6), 11–14.

10 The learning model described here is closest to that of B.R. Bugelski, Learning and imagery, *Journal of Mental Imagery*, 1982, *6* (2), 1–22.

11 H.E. Krugman, Same reference as note 9. More radically, Lastovicka and Bonfeld[24] have questioned whether buyers of brands of many supermarket products actually have attitudes toward them in the sense of rational personal reasons to support brand choice. When asked why they buy a given brand, consumers typically repeat rote-learned advertising points or rather empty platitudes such as "I just like it" or "It's the best brand." From our perspective, these buyers do have brand attitudes, but they are closely dependent on simple points or overall impressions learned from advertising. See J.L. Lastovicka and E.H. Bonfield, Do consumers have brand attitudes? *Journal of Economic Psychology*, 1982, *2* (1), 57–75.

12 Readers familiar with learning principles will realize that an *S-R* "chain" is involved, with response-produced stimuli. For example, in evaluating a *recognized* brand, the chain is: $S[1]$ (brand) $\rightarrow R_1$ (category need) $\rightarrow S_2$ (brand again) $\rightarrow R_2$ (benefits). In evaluating a *recalled* brand, the sequence is: S_1 (category need) $\rightarrow S_2$ (brand) $\rightarrow R_2$ (benefits). R_2 may also be a chain of learned benefits, simplified to one response here.

13 For "threshold" benefits, the degree of delivery is either 0 or 1. An example for instant coffee would be caffeine. The decision maker's mental adjectives describing delivery belief therefore become the adjectival phrases "does not have" or "has" the benefit.

14 C.I. Hovland, I.L. Janis, and H.H. Kelley, *Communication and Persuasion*, New Haven, CT: Yale University Press, 1953.

15 Good descriptions of the basic ideas in cognitive response theory can be found in R.M. Perloff, and J.T. Brock, And thinking makes it so: cognitive responses to persuasion, in M.E. Rolloff and G.R. Miller (Eds.), *Persuasion: New Directions in Theory and Research*, Beverly Hills, CA: Sage, pp. 67–99; R.B. Cialdini, R.E. Petty, and J.T. Cacioppo, Attitudes and attitude change, *Annual Review of Psychology*, 1981, *32*, 357–404; and P.L. Wright, Message-evoked thoughts: persuasion research using thought verbalizations, *Journal of Consumer Research*, 1980, *7* (2), 151–175.

16 Emotions also can affect brand recall, though not brand recognition, through a process called "state-dependent" retrieval. This effect is reliable although small. In our approach, state-dependent retrieval is better represented as a *brand attitude* effect in that a brand correctly connected in advertising (via emotions) to a motivation is more likely to be selected when that motivation recurs later. See H. Weingartner, H. Miller, and D.L. Murphy, Mood-state-dependent retrieval of verbal associations, *Journal of Abnormal Psychology*, 1977, *86* (3) 276–284; G.H. Bower, K.P. Monteiro,

and S.C. Gilligan, Emotional mood as a context of learning and recall, *Journal of Verbal Learning and Verbal Behavior,* 1978, *17* (5) 573–585; and M.P Gardner, Mood states and consumer behavior: a critical review, *Journal of Consumer Research,* 1985, *12* (3), 281–300.

17 G. Mandler, Emotion, in E. Hearst (Ed.), *The First Century of Experimental Psychology,* Hillsdale, NJ: Lawrence Erlbaum Associates, 1979, pp. 275–321.

18 For evidence of genetically programmed (or "unlearned") emotional stimuli and responses, see J. B. Watson, *Behaviorism,* New York: Norton, 1930, especially chap. 7; and P. Ekman, E.R. Sorenson, and W.V. Friesen, Pan-cultural elements in facial displays of emotion, *Science,* 1969, *164* (April 4), 86–88.

19 E. Crane, *Marketing Communications,* 2nd edition, New York: Wiley, 1972, chap. 19.

20 D.R. Sweeney, D. C. Tinling, and A.H. Schmale, Dimensions of affective expression in four expressive modes, *Behavioral Science,* 1970, *15* (5) 393–407.

21 For a review of how verbal labeling and visual imagery can amplify emotional responses, see J.R. Rossiter and L. Percy, Visual communication in advertising, in R.J. Harris (Ed.), *Information Processing Research in Advertising,* Hillsdale, NJ: Lawrence Erlbaum Associates, 1983, chap. 4. Emotion remains a bodily response, and in this connection, those interested in psychology may be interested to note that the famous experiments by Stanley Schacter and colleagues in which verbal labels were supposed to *alter* the emotional experience have never been replicated. The emerging evidence supports the original idea of Charles Darwin, that emotions are inborn, and not learned or amenable to cognitive change. (See G. Mandler, same reference as note 17.)

22 Russell and Pratt's (1980) circumplex model is recent conceptualization of a long history of emotional categorization theories beginning with Wundt (1891) and continuing through the landmark theorizing of Woodworth (1938), Schlosberg (1952), and Mowrer (1960). For a similar model to Russell and Pratt's, see also Plutchik (1980). The main references are W. Wundt, Zur Lehre von den Gemuthsbewegungen, *Philosophische Studien,* 1891, *6,* 335–393; R.S. Woodworth, *Experimental Psychology,* New York; Holt, 1938; H. Schlosberg, The description of facial expressions in terms of two dimensions, *Journal of Experimental Psychology,* 1952, *44* (4), 229–237; O.H. Mowrer, *Learning Theory and Behavior,* New York: Wiley, 1960; J.A. Russell and G. Pratt, A description of the quality attributed to environments, *Journal of Personality and Social Psychology,* 1980, *38* (2), 311–322; R. Plutchik, A general psychoevolutionary theory of emotion, in R. Plutchik and H. Kellerman (Eds.), *Emotion: Theory, Research, and Experience,* Vol. 1, New York; Academic, 1980, pp. 3–33.

23 M. Blonsky's analysis of semiotics in advertising is summarized in B. Whalen, Semiotics: an art or powerful marketing research tool? *Marketing News,* May 13, 1983, pp. 8–9. Blonsky's concept of "tapes" is similar to the concept of "scripts"; see R.P. Abelson, Script processing in attitude formation and decision making, in J.S. Carroll and J.W. Payne (Eds.), *Cognitive and Social Behavior,* Hillsdale, NJ: Lawrence Erlbaum Associates, 1976. Scripts are like a comic strip incorporating words, visual images, and affect. Tapes provide *ready-made* visual imagery and elicit well-learned emotions.

DISCUSSION QUESTIONS

8.1 Explain, in your own words, how processing differs from exposure, which precedes it, and communication effects, which follow it. At the conclusion of your explanation, see if you can also explain why this term is *not* called *information* processing as in consumer-behavior textbooks.

8.2 Processing typically consists of a series of immediate responses to elements of the ad. For brand awareness and low involvement brand attitude, these responses consist of attention responses, emotional responses, and learning responses. To appreciate just how many separate elements may be processed in an ad, make a photocopy of the Lava soap ad in Figure 9.6 and:

a Circle the separate elements that you think have to receive attention responses.

b Then mark in red those elements that you think would elicit reflexive attention.

c Then mark with an *"s"* those elements that you think would not be processed unless the ad received selective attention.

d Draw connecting lines between those elements that you think have to be associatively rote learned.

Write a brief explanation of your answers.

8.3 For all communication effects except brand awareness and low involvement brand attitude, acceptance responses are required during processing. Acceptance is defined as the potential buyer's personal agreement with elements in the advertising message. Next time you are watching TV with a friend, randomly pick three commercials, and "pop" the question: "What, if anything, went through your mind as you watched that last commercial?" Write down your friend's comments and, afterwards, analyze the comments by indicating which ones reflect acceptance (or alternatively rejection) responses. You may need more than three tries to obtain three commercials that were actually processed this far.

8.4 (Instructor to provide a videotape of a well-known informational TV commercial and a well-known transformational TV commercial.) Write a careful analysis of the emotions that each commercial is designed to elicit, then relate these to the probable motivation or motivations upon which purchase of each brand depends.

FURTHER READING

D.A. Norman. *Memory and Attention* (2nd ed.). New York; Wiley, 1976.

Interesting coverage of the historical study of attention, coupled with a clear explanation of reflexive (stimulus driven) and selective (goal driven) attention.

B.R. Bugelski. *Principles of Learning and Memory*. New York; Praeger, 1979.

The best contemporary account of association theory in learning. Also explains the role of imagery in learning, from a perspective that suits advertising.

Two volumes: R.J. Harris (Ed.). *Information Processing Research in Advertising*. Hillsdale, NJ: Lawrence Erlbaum Associates, 1983; and L. Percy and A.G. Woodside (Eds.) *Advertising and Consumer Psychology*. Lexington, MA: Heath, 1983.

These two books provide a comprehensive overview of processing as it applies to advertising. Each contains several chapters on cognitive response theory as well as chapters by us on visual processing of advertisements.

R. Plutchik and H. Kellerman (Eds.). *Emotion: Theory, Research, and Experience, Vol. 1: Theories of Emotion*. New York; Academic, 1980.

An advanced book selected to illustrate the breadth and seriousness with which emotion, a traditional concept in psychology, is now being regarded. The chapters contain no direct references to advertising but in many cases the applications are obvious. The chapters by R. Plutchik and J.R. Averill are particularly recommended.

BRAND AWARENESS AND LOW INVOLVEMENT BRAND ATTITUDE CREATIVE TACTICS

Brand awareness and a low involvement brand attitude are very often the only two communication objectives in a campaign (such as for many supermarket products). It makes sense, therefore, to present their creative tactics in a single chapter. After reading this chapter you should:

- Understand the general creative tactics recommended for brand awareness
- Know which specific tactics are best for brand recognition
- Know which specific tactics are best for brand recall
- Know the tactics that work best for low involvement/*informational* brand attitude strategy
- Know the tactics that work best for low involvement/*transformational* brand attitude strategy
- Realize that humor is not a separate strategy but rather a tactic that can be used with any of the brand attitude strategies

Brand awareness must be addressed in *all* advertisements prior to *either* low or high involvement brand attitudes being addressed. However, brand awareness shares with brand attitudes of the low involvement type a reliance on simple rote learning in processing. The rote learning emphasis is reflected in the creative tactics in this chapter. In Chapter 10 we will *presume* that brand awareness creative tactics have been decided and focus separately on high involvement brand attitudes.

BRAND AWARENESS: GENERAL TACTICS

Brand awareness is defined as the potential buyer's ability to identify (recognize or recall) the brand, within the category, in sufficient detail to make a purchase.

The type of processing required if the ad is to create or increase brand awareness is *rote learning:* specifically, rote learning of the *association* between the category need, on the one hand, and the brand identification response, on the other. The potential buyer must attend to those elements of the ad that describe the category need, attend to those elements of the ad that identify the brand, and learn the association between the two.

Table 9.1 lists the general tactical considerations for brand awareness in advertisements. We will explain these first; then we will present some more specific advertising execution tactics for the two forms of brand awareness: brand recognition and brand recall.

Determine the Predominant Type of Brand Awareness

In Chapter 6, we emphasized the importance of considering whether the target audience predominantly chooses the brand via recognition *at* the point of purchase or, alternatively via recall *prior* to purchase. Brand recognition is a comparatively easy task, although it is becoming more difficult in increasingly larger and more crowded supermarket or store displays; whereas brand recall is a comparatively difficult task, relying, as it does, completely on the buyer's memory with no aids present.

As we shall see following these general considerations, the advertising stimuli appropriate to the two types of brand awareness—brand recognition and brand recall—are quite different.

Intuitive Method   Determination of the predominant type of brand awareness required of the target audience can sometimes be made intuitively by managers—based on common knowledge of how the brand is purchased.

When using common knowledge or intuition, the manager must consider the alternative decision processes very carefully. For example, choice of airlines to call for travel decisions usually is based on brand-name recall.

TABLE 9-1   BRAND AWARENESS TACTICS (GENERAL) FOR ADVERTISEMENTS

1 *Determine the predominant type of brand awareness.* Decide on whether the predominant type of brand awareness response required by the target audience is brand *recognition* (at the point of purchase) or brand *recall* (prior to purchase) or, if required, *both.*

2 *Match the ad with the response.* Identify the precise response required in recognition or recall and make sure that the advertisement's brand awareness stimuli match that response exactly.

3 *Seek a unique advertising execution.* Make the in-ad association between the category need and the brand as unique and different as possible so as to minimize interference from other brands that are also trying to "attach" themselves to the same category need in the buyer's mind. In other words, strive for unique advertising within the category.

4 *Maximize brand awareness contact time.* The contiguous association between the category need and the brand should be maintained (for recognition) or repeated (for recall) as much as possible within the advertisement—subject, of course, to getting the rest of the advertising message across.

However, some people may look through the Yellow Pages for airline phone numbers and in this case the required response is brand recognition. Industrial brand (or vendor) choices pose similar complexities although brand recall probably is more prevalent.

Brand decisions for supermarket products are even more subtle and variable. For instance, a recent survey by Ogilvy & Mather[1] indicated that brand decisions for coffee, detergent, and headache remedies are predominantly made prior to going to the store, whereas brand decisions for margarine, cookies, and paper towels are predominantly made in the store at the point of purchase.

Moreover, product intuitions must be qualified by *target audience*. The indications above are too general. Brand loyals, brand switchers, other-brand loyals, and new category users would undoubtedly vary in the predominance of recall versus recognition decisions. For example, brand loyals and brand switchers should tend to rely on brand recognition of their favorite or acceptable brands, respectively; whereas other-brand loyals and new category users, who are making a more deliberate decision to try our brand, should tend to make this decision prior to purchase, thus using brand recall.

Selection of the right brand awareness objective is complicated further by (purchase-related) *shopping behavior*. Store loyalty or purchase facilitation through store convenience may win out over brand loyal tendencies and, conversely, store switching may lead a person to fall back on recognized brands in an unfamiliar store. Not only this, but *recalled* brands *may also have to be recognized* in the store, especially by other-brand loyals or new category users who have decided beforehand to try a new brand.

Behavioral Sequence Model: The Best Method   The best solution is to conduct research among the target audience concerning their predominant choice process for the brand. This is why we emphasized (in Chapter 5) the necessity for managers to construct a behavioral sequence model that describes decision stages, location, timing, and decision roles. It is only through this careful research and subsequent careful thought that an accurate advertising strategy can be developed.

Match the Ad with the Response

Once the manager has decided whether recognition or recall of the brand is the major awareness objective, then the precise brand identification response required of the target audience must be provided in the ad.

From the definition, identification consists of "sufficient detail" to enable purchase. But what is the detail? For instance, consumers may primarily have to respond by recognizing the package rather than the name (for example, the famous Stouffer's "red" packages of frozen foods). Or they may have to be able to recognize the name (for example, Arrow brand shirts). Or they may have to recall the name orally (for example, Yellow Cabs or USAir airline).

The tactical consideration here is that the brand awareness stimuli in the advertisement must match the desired brand awareness response exactly. In the above examples, Stouffer's would rely on color media ads on TV and in magazines to display the red packages; Arrow shirts would make the stylized Arrow name clearly readable in print and TV ads; Yellow Cabs and USAir would pronounce the name audibly in TV or radio commercials and try to make sure the name is read (mentally repeated orally) in print ads.

Remember, the processing for brand awareness is "mindless," requiring rather nondeliberate attention and learning, so the desired brand awareness response should be easily learnable by providing an exact match in the advertisement.

Seek a Unique Advertising Execution

What *actually* is to be learned in brand awareness is the association or *connection* between the category need (previously established or addressed in the ad according to the category need communication objective) and the brand identification response. Other brands are also trying to establish or strengthen their own connections to the same category need and even the first brand entering a new category must prepare for this eventuality.

The rote learning principle for establishing and maintaining the category need–brand awareness connection in the face of competing connections is to try to make the connection *unique,* or mentally "isolated" from similar connections.[2]

In plain terms, the advertiser should strive for a unique advertising execution for the brand. The execution should be unique within the category and it should tie the brand to the category need in a different way from competing brands. The ad should "stand out" from the competition.

The Difficulty of Being Unique   The difficulty of "standing out" from the competition can be demonstrated by comparing magazine advertisements for women's cosmetics (Figure 9.1). The cosmetics ads have a very high degree of similarity in their face-and-product executions. Another comparison is shown for "sporty" subcompact cars (Figure 9.2). The car ads are also disturbingly similar, although our friend from Chapter 6, the Datsun (Nissan) 280-ZX (now 300 ZX), seems to stand out well.

The necessity of standing out in the clutter of competing ads also holds for TV commercials. This was dramatically illustrated by Robert H. Levenson, vice-chairman of creative at Doyle Dane Bernbach, who switched the sound-track on a Coca-Cola TV commercial with one for 7-UP.[3] The switch was hardly noticeable, except for the brand name, even down to the precise choreography of the closing tag line, when the Coca-Cola actors opened their mouths to sing "America is turning 7-UP!"

Compare with Other Ads in the Category   When commissioning creative work, therefore, the manager should never ask for an ad that's "just like the

FIGURE 9.1   Ads for competing brands in the women's cosmetics category illustrating the difficulty of "standing out" from the competition (see also Figure 9.2). (Reprinted permission of *Adweek* November 1981.)

ad for that other brand." And when evaluating creative work once it is submitted, the manager should simultaneously review advertisements for competing brands within the category and check that the proposed creative execution is unique. Lack of uniqueness will seriously reduce the likelihood that the potential buyer will learn the brand awareness response.

Maximize Brand Awareness Contact Time

The other relevant rote learning principle for brand awareness is "contact time," or the total duration in which the category need elements and the brand identification elements are presented in contiguous association.[4]

Contact time is made up of time per exposure and number of repetitions of exposure—with exposure here referring not to the ad overall but to exposure

FIGURE 9.2   Ads for competing brands in the "sporty" sub-compact automobile category illustrating the difficulty of "standing out" from the competition. (Reprinted permission of *Adweek* May 1981.)

of the category need in conjunction with the brand. An advertisement may devote contact time to brand awareness by showing an attention-holding visual of the brand or repeating the brand in package shots, or by repeating the brand name in copy points made throughout the ad, along with the category need.

Of course, the ad itself could be repeated to increase contact time, provided the ad is attended to each time (see Part Seven on media scheduling). But here we are talking about contact time *within* a single advertisement.

Brand awareness contact time is of major importance in advertisements for both new brands and established brands. For new brands, brand awareness must be learned from zero, and contact time is the main influence on learning. For established brands, contact time must be continued because maintained brand awareness is a necessity for repeat purchase.

Brand awareness must never be neglected in advertising executions because it is the necessary "gatekeeper" to the other communication effects for the brand. Full executional emphasis on the category need–brand identification linkage can be lessened in only one circumstance. With a target audience that is fully aware and brand loyal, the ad can *deemphasize the category need* elements because, due to prior associative learning, this audience will automatically "plug in" the category need when they see or hear the brand. However, the *brand identification* elements still must be emphasized.

Brand recognition and brand recall tactics for increasing contact time are more easily discussed separately, since for brand recognition the contact usually will be visual (in video or in an illustration), whereas for brand recall it usually will be verbal (in audio or copy). We continue our review of brand awareness tactics by examining some specific considerations for brand recognition and brand recall.

BRAND RECOGNITION TACTICS

Brand recognition is the appropriate type of brand awareness objective for products that are chosen at the point of purchase. Brand recognition is the easiest communication effect to achieve—in stark contrast with brand recall. This is because, during recognition, at the point of purchase, the brand stimulus is *presented to* the decision maker, who then only has to associate it with (actually, recall) the category need, and the latter may be very obvious from the category placement of the brand in the point-of-purchase display.

Some brands have a natural (non-advertising) advantage in brand recognition because they are distinct from competing brands in the display and thereby elicit reflexive attention. Others must build brand recognition by making themselves familiar through advertising. To illustrate this, the Campbell Soup Company some years ago conducted an experiment in which they changed the distinctive red and white Campbell's Soup label to green and white.[5] Shoppers avoided the soup like the plague, even though the green and white package clearly said "Campbell's Soup." Imagine the advertising that a new green and white label soup would have to do to become as recognizable as Campbell's!

In advertising, there are three specific tactical factors that the manager should look for in commissioning or evaluating advertisements designed with brand recognition as an objective. These specific tactics are *in addition* to the four general tactics for brand awareness just discussed, and they apply only to brand recognition.

Ensure Sufficient Exposure of the Brand Package and Name in the Ad

TV commercials should show the package clearly on camera and it should appear for at least 2 seconds at a time.[6] Print ads should show a large picture of the package in an execution that gains and holds attention for at least 2 seconds (Figure 9.3). The brand name should be clearly visible *on the package* in the ad (International Soup Classics, by Lipton, in the ad shown) and the

FIGURE 9.3 A new product-launch by Lipton Soup, with a close-up of the package to generate brand recognition (original in color). (Courtesy Thomas J. Lipton, Inc., Charles Gold, photography.)

ad should be in color (as the original of this one was) to match the package as experienced at the point of purchase.

There is no advantage to showing a simulated display setting in the advertisement even though this is how the brand has to be recognized. Recognition theory in psychology would suggest that a display setting would be ideal in advertising because it enhances cue-target similarity (see Chapter 6). However, the obvious disadvantage of this to advertisers is that the display would show other brands also and thus facilitate competitors' brand awareness. An isolated focus on the advertiser's brand is sufficient.

The Category Need Should be Mentioned or Portrayed (Unless Immediately Obvious)

According to the brand recognition sequence, the prospective buyer first recognizes the brand and *then* checks the category need; for example, "Maxwell House . . . do I need instant coffee?" Now, whereas the category need may be obvious for many established brands, this may not be so for *new* or *newly "repositioned"* brands. Here it is best to spell out or clearly portray the category need in the ads, in close association with the package and brand name. This way, the particular category partition or competitive frame in which the brand is intended to compete is more likely to be correctly learned.

Consider, for instance, the launch a number of years ago of Cooking Ease, a non-stick cooking spray. Where should it best be positioned via category need—as being for "problem" foods that stick, such as chicken or eggs, or as being a "healthy" zero-cholesterol alternative to margarine or butter to use when cooking? This question also has implications for where the new brand should be placed in supermarkets to stimulate the most sales—next to the problem foods or next to margarine and butter? The marketer of Cooking Ease chose to portray the problem foods category need in its advertising, but one wonders with the subsequent health trend whether the health category need might have been better. Another example is Tab, which really had to work to communicate its category need, versus Diet Coke (like Diet Pepsi earlier) which conveniently included the category need in its brand name.

The tactical implication, especially for new or newly "repositioned" brands, is that the target audience should be unambiguously told or shown the category need so that the brand awareness–category need (S_2–S_1) association is learned. The same association works in reverse for brand recall, where S_1, the category need, occurs first and the brand, S_2, is thought of afterwards.

After the Initial Burst, Less Media Frequency Is Needed for Brand Recognition

Evidence from learning experiments on visual recognition and advertising media research using recognition indicates that brand recognition peaks after about two exposures to the ad.[7] Thereafter, brand recognition declines very slowly, so that a lighter media schedule (specifically, less frequency) is then sufficient to maintain the buyer's brand recognition response.

Advertisements for a new brand should therefore aim to attain two exposures (and here we mean *actual* exposures resulting in attention and learning) as early as possible with a heavy initial advertising "burst." Then, like established brands, the ad can be "placed" at less frequent intervals to maintain brand recognition.

Caution: Transformational Ads A strong caution here is that brand recognition awareness may not be the only communication objective of the campaign. In particular, if *transformational* brand attitude *also* is an objective, then frequent repetition of the advertisement in a heavy media schedule is necessary and would override the brand recognition consideration. This is discussed later in the chapter.

As we will see in Part Seven on media strategy, the manager has to jointly consider communication objectives in deciding on an appropriate media plan for the advertisement.

BRAND RECALL TACTICS

Brand recall is the appropriate type of brand awareness objective when brand alternatives are generated by the buyer *prior* to the point of purchase:

- A shopper thinking of which store to go to is engaging in brand recall, where the "brand" in this case is the store itself (retail advertising).
- The shopper then may engage in further recall of specific brands to buy at the store (consumer advertising).
- An executive thinking of which suppliers to telephone for quotations also is engaging in brand recall (industrial advertising).

The ability of the buyer to recall a brand depends entirely on the learned association between the category need (stimulus) and the brand name (response). Advertising elements that facilitate the learning of this association are therefore vital to successful brand recall.

Brand recall is typically a verbal response. This means that the *verbal copy* in the ad is the critical consideration—especially the *main copy line*. The main copy line is the theme line or tag line in broadcast commercials, and the headline in print ads and outdoor ads.

The manager can take advantage of several findings in advertising research when selecting or evaluating advertising tactics for brand recall.[8] A number of tactics have been shown to increase the chances that the buyer will recall the brand when he or she experiences the category need. Discussed next are six tactics that can be used to increase brand recall *in addition* to the four general brand awareness tactics covered earlier.

Include the Category Need and the Brand Name in the Main Copy Line

Because the main copy line is intended to be the focus of the verbal part of the ad, it should include the category need and the brand name so as to facilitate learning of the S_1-S_2 association. This is especially important for a new brand, or for a newly "repositioned" brand, where new learning of brand recall is the objective.

Remember, though, that the category need is often very specific. Simply naming the gross product category will rarely suffice. For example, the well-known campaign for Kraft cheese singles ad says "Every *single* time it's Kraft." The category need is for single slices of cheese, as in sandwiches or snacks, not cheese in general. Kraft is trying to position this product as the brand to recall when you need single slices of cheese.

Keep the Main Copy Line Short—Three to Eight Words

Headlines, theme or tag lines, and copy claims should be short when associating the brand name with the category need. This follows from the principle, in psychology, of "the magical number 7"[9] which indicates the approximate limit on short-term memory during processing. This principle applies to advertising copy[10] and is a sound rule to follow in statements that relate the brand to the category need to produce brand recall.

Use Repetition of the Main Copy Line for Brand Recall

Repetition of the category need–brand awareness association is far more important for brand recall than it is for brand recognition. Recall is a learned response that continues to increase in the buyer's mind with successive exposures and it takes many exposures to reach a peak or "asymptote." Several brands that have asymptoted in their categories for most buyers would be Budweiser, Coca-Cola, McDonald's, IBM, and Xerox. These brands virtually "own" their respective product categories[11] but only after having invested heavily in advertising repetition.

Repetition to enhance brand recall can be achieved both by media frequency (repeating the ad) and within the advertisement itself (repeating the main copy line). Repetition in media is discussed further in Part Seven and need not be elaborated here.

Repetition within the advertisement is, however, directly relevant to advertising execution and two points should be noted for the manager. One is to place the brand awareness elements early in the advertisement and then repeat them at the end (the well-known primacy and recency or "U" effect in recall).[12] The second is to make sure the category need–brand awareness association or *connection* is repeated. (This is *not* the same as merely repeating the brand name.) The brand must be connected to the category need.

Now we will consider several other advertising elements that facilitate brand-name recall. Note, however, that these apply *only* in the circumstances noted.

Include a Personal Reference (Unless It Is Already Strongly Implied)

Personal reference is achieved in copy by using personal pronouns such as "I," "me," or "you." These words increase the chance that in rote learning a main copy line, the prospective buyer will remember it. In psychology, this is known as "personal encoding" and it is stimulated by self-referent statements.

Sometimes a personal reference is already strongly implied, as in "[You should] Take Aim against cavities." Other well-known main copy lines are more explicit, such as "Give your cold to Contac" or "You deserve a break today . . . at McDonald's . . . we do it all for you."

U.S. advertisers seem to favor the word "you." However, two very successful overseas compaigns have used the even more personal words "I" and "me." The tag lines are "I feel like a Toohey's" (an Australian beer) and "Take me away, P & O" (an international cruise and holiday shipping line). Use of first-person personal words produces direct self-reference when the main copy line is learned and may well have stronger subsequent motivational capacity than the second-person "you" form.[13]

Use a Bizarre Execution (As Long as It Is Appropriate to the Brand's Image)

In the general recommendations on brand awareness advertising, uniqueness of the category need–brand awareness association was listed as a desirable factor. This is especially applicable to brand recall awareness, where bizarre executions have been shown to improve both immediate recall[14] and especially recall beyond 3 days after exposure.[15] Bizarre executions include visual gimmicks—humor, trick photography, and innovative print ad layouts—that reflexively gain attention and link the brand memorably to the category need.

However, the advertiser must *first ensure* that a really unusual or bizarre execution *does not reflect negatively* on the brand's "image" (brand attitude).[16] Bizarre executions designed to produce brand recall, as temptingly effective as they may be for *this* communication objective, must be carefully gauged against *other* communication objectives for the brand. Bizarre executions might be suitable for the Crazy Eddie brand (Figure 9.4) but not for a high-status electronics retailer.

(For Broadcast Ads) a Jingle May Increase Brand Recall

Jingles, obviously, can be employed only in television and radio commercials where jingle copy is possible through the audio track.

Effective jingles set the *main copy line* to music. Accordingly, jingles should adhere to the prior recommendations for brand recall. By way of review, these are: association of the brand with category need, brevity, repetition, personal reference, and a bizarre execution providing it has appropriate implications for the brand's image.

A well-planned and "catchy" jingle can be enormously successful in generating brand recall.[17] A good jingle "stays with you," thus providing rehearsal (extra exposures) of the main copy line. A jingle also can expand brand recall effects via word of mouth if it is frequently sung to others, as when children sing the jingles for McDonald's ("You deserve a break today . . . at McDonald's . . . we do it all for you") or Dr. Pepper ("Wouldn't you like to be a Pepper too?") to their parents and friends.

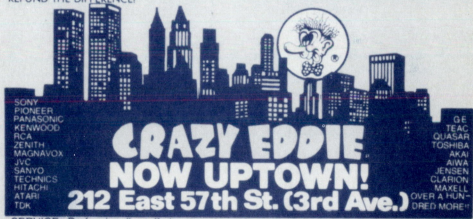

FIGURE 9.4 Appropriate use of a bizarre execution to stimulate brand recall. Note that a "quality" brand attitude is not an objective for this retailer (see text). (Courtesy Crazy Eddie, Inc..)

SUMMARY OF BRAND AWARENESS TACTICS AND A PREVIEW OF BRAND ATTITUDE TACTICS

Brand awareness creative tactics are summarized for convenience of reference in Table 9.2. As shown in the table and explained in the text, there are four tactics that apply to brand awareness in general, then three tactics that apply only to brand recognition, and six that apply only to brand recall.

We now move on to the creative tactics for low involvement brand attitudes. First, however, we need to set up the structure for creative tactics in *all* of the brand attitude quadrants.

Brand attitude tactics are the most complicated aspect of the creative task, both for creatives and managers. Because brand attitude is affective and cognitive, there are two central questions that the manager must ask about creative executions directed at brand attitude:

1 Affect Component Does the advertisement have *correct emotional portrayal* of the motivation?

2 Belief Component Does the advertisement have *adequate benefit claim support* for the brand's perceived delivery on the motivation?

Emotions, it will be remembered, are the surface means used in ads to contact the buyer's underlying motivation. Benefit claims similarly, are the surface means used in ads to connect the brand to the motivation. In this and the next chapter, covering the four brand attitude strategy quadrants, we examine the emotional portrayal and benefit-claim tactics for each type of brand attitude.

TABLE 9-2   SUMMARY OF BRAND AWARENESS TACTICS WITH SPECIFIC TACTICS FOR BRAND RECOGNITION AND BRAND RECALL

Brand awareness: general tactics
1 Determine the predominant type of brand awareness for the target audience.

2 Match the ad with the response.

3 Seek a unique advertising execution.

4 Maximize brand awareness contact time.

Brand recognition tactics	*Brand recall tactics*
a Ensure sufficient exposure of the brand package and the name in the ad.	a Include the category need and the brand in the main copy line.
b The category need should be mentioned or portrayed (unless immediately obvious).	b Keep the main copy line short.
c After the initial burst, less media frequency is needed for brand recognition (though check brand attitude strategy first).	c Use repetition of the main copy line for brand recall.
	d Include a personal reference (unless it is already strongly implied).
	e Use a bizarre execution (as long as it is appropriate to brand attitude).
	f (For broadcast ads) a jingle may increase brand recall.

LOW INVOLVEMENT/INFORMATIONAL TACTICS

Low involvement brand attitudes apply when the target audience decision maker regards purchase of the brand as low risk. Low involvement/*informational* brand attitude applies when the low risk purchase decision is based on a negatively originated purchase motivation.

The advertising tactics for low involvement/informational advertisements are listed in Table 9.3. For this type of advertising, correct emotional portrayal (consideration A) is not quite as important as adequate benefit-claim support (consideration B). Hence more of the tactics concern benefit-claim support and how it is achieved for low involvement/informational advertising.

A-1. Use a Simple Problem-Solution Format

The classical format for negatively originating motivations is to present the problem first (which could be any of the five negative motivations) and then the brand as the solution. This is the best format for low involvement/informational brand attitude.

The simple problem-solution format can be illustrated with two examples of Procter & Gamble's advertising. Many of P & G's brands are based on low involvement/informational brand attitude strategies:

- The leading detergent, Tide, has used the following theme: "You get a lot of dirt with children [problem]. . . . . You get a lot of clean with Tide [solution]."
- Another example is P & G's print ad for Lava soap (Figure 9.5). Again a simple problem-solution format is employed: "Do-it-yourselfers: Filthy, dirty hands? [problem]. . . . . We'll Lava ya clean! [solution]"

The simple problem-solution format also applies to TV commercials, where advertisers are sometimes tempted to employ more complex emotional sequences because of the extended time capacity of video relative to print. In a very instructive set of results from numerous commercial tests, Schwerin and Newell[18] report that a simple before (problem) then after (solution) sequence works best in inducing brand choice. Using an index score of 100 percent for

TABLE 9-3   ADVERTISING TACTICS FOR THE LOW INVOLVEMENT/INFORMATIONAL BRAND ATTITUDE STRATEGY

Consideration A (emotional portrayal of the motivation):

1 Use a simple problem-solution format.

2 It is not necessary for people to like the ad.

Consideration B (benefit-claim support for perceived brand delivery):

3 Include only one or two benefits or a single group of benefits.

4 Benefit claims should be stated extremely.

5 The benefits should be easily learned in one or two exposures (repetition serves mainly a reminder function).

FIGURE 9.5 Advertisement for Lava soap illustrating the simple problem-solution format. (Courtesy of the Procter & Gamble Company.)

the average of all problem-solution commercials tested, the brand choice scores for various sequences were: simultaneous before and after, -9 percent; before, then product in use, then after, -4 percent; after then before, $+12$ percent; and before then after, $+21$ percent. It seems that among the complex patterns that can emerge in TV commercials, the simple before-then-after format is best.

A-2. It Is Not Necessary for People to Like the Ad

Low involvement/informational advertisements are frequently annoying, especially on the "intrusive" medium of television, because they hammer away at the main selling point. Such ads do not have to be liked and indeed they usually address dislikable topics which must be portrayed with negative emotions such as anger (problem removal), fear or anxiety (problem avoidance), disappointment (incomplete satisfaction), or guilt (mixed approach-avoidance conflict). Positive emotions are introduced with the solution—relief, optimism, and so forth—but the ads have to portray a negative emotion first.

The main concern of the advertiser should not be whether people like the advertisement. Ad likability is irrelevant in the low involvement/informational brand attitude quadrant. The only thing that matters is that the emotional portrayal gets the point (the motivation) across to the target audience.

The "Mr. Whipple" commercials for P & G's Charmin toilet tissue are an example. The infamous "Please don't squeeze the Charmin" executions first appeared in 1968 and ran for 14 years. They consistently topped the list of TV commercials that viewers said they couldn't stand watching.[19] However, over 80 percent of adults learned the idea that Charmin is very soft.[20] Many tried the product and it rapidly became the leading brand in its category. In 1982 a new demonstration was introduced in the Charmin TV commercial series but the Mr. Whipple character comes in at the end to gloat, justifiably, that "The squeezing got you. The softness kept you." This is an excellent example of the low involvement/informational strategy for brands in which trial experience is sufficient.

Moving now to benefit-claim support tactics, we see that there are three main ones recommended for low involvement/informational advertising. These are described under the next three headings.[21]

B-3. Include Only One or Two Benefits or a Single Group of Benefits

The low involvement nature of brand decisions in the low involvement/informational quadrant means that the advertisement must be kept relatively simple in terms of the number of message points or benefits that the potential buyer will be willing to process (attend to and learn) in support of brand attitude.

Single Benefit   Advocates of the "USP" (unique selling proposition) or the "positioning" schools of advertising basically recommend that advertisements focus on a single point.[22] Examples would be: "7-UP—the uncola"; "Weekends are made for Michelob," which was later extended to "Put a little Michelob in your week;" as well as the competitive positioning strategy of "Avis—we try harder" (as opposed to "No. 1" Hertz); "Honeywell—the other computer company'' (than IBM); and Count Dracula's comment to a luckless victim, ''It is good. But it is not Perrier.''

Or Single Group of Benefits   A larger number of message points or benefits in support of brand attitude can be included in low involvement/informational advertisements provided they form a single and easily related *group* of benefits. The Johnson's Baby Lotion ad in Figure 9.6 illustrates how this can be done, with four benefits grouped to make the single brand attitude point that ''Johnson's Baby Lotion is good for adults to use.'' This is the brand attitude point to be rote-learned by the prospective buyer.

B-4. Benefit Claims Should be Stated Extremely

An interesting aspect of low involvement/informational advertising is that you can make extreme claims for the brand. Indeed, you *should* do so, provided that the claim is, in the words of famous copywriter Rosser Reeves, ''FTC-able'' and can be substantiated.

The main reason for making extreme benefit claims is again low involvement. When the brand is regarded by the target audience as a low risk decision, the decision maker rarely is motivated enough to dispute or counterargue with the brand's claims. Also, people have come to expect extreme or even exaggerated claims in such advertising, so a quiet statement in the low involvement arena won't get heard.

Curious Disbelief   The important consideration is that the prospective buyer *learns* the claim; *it does not have to be fully accepted* (see our discussion of low involvement brand attitude in Chapter 7 and of processing in Chapter 8). Whereas outright disbelief is a danger signal, there is a middle ground of ''curious disbelief'' that actually can increase the consumer's intention to try the brand to see if the claim is true.[23]

Ask More, Get More...and Retain More.   Reiterating what we said in Chapter 7 about the ''ask more, get more'' principle of persuasion[24], it should be noted that whereas extreme benefit claims (ask more) generate a highly favorable brand attitude (get more), this highly favorable attitude is only *tentatively held* pending the prospective buyer's trial of the brand. In low involvement/informational brand purchase, especially, the brand then has to deliver on the promised benefit to a reasonable extent if the buyer is to *firmly* hold the positive attitude after trial. Extreme claims are the best way to get trial in the first place. Thereafter, and especially with verifiable informational claims, actual satisfaction with the brand to a large extent governs repeat purchase.

However, now that the buyer is in the low involvement repeat purchase phase that follows a satisfactory low involvement or *high* involvement trial purchase, the informational benefit claims still should be kept extreme. (Remember that even high involvement target audiences move down to low

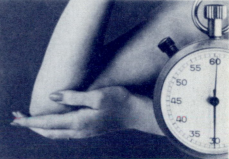

FIGURE 9.6   Advertising for Johnson's Baby Lotion illustrating multiple benefits grouped to support a low involvement/informational brand attitude. (Courtesy Johnson & Johnson Baby Products Co.)

involvement once they overcome the trial risk and are now repeat buyers, for all except infrequently purchased products).

As mentioned in Chapter 7, extreme claims for a *continuing* campaign are necessary because repeat buyers who now have a favorable brand attitude will require the same extreme claims that created the attitude initially to safely maintain it, and they certainly will require extreme claims if a further attitude increase is the objective, as when new executions of the strategy are tried in an attempt to make brand-switching repeaters switch more often or perhaps become brand loyals. Also, repeat buyers with favorable attitudes now are less likely to regard these claims as being quite as extreme as they previously might have seemed. Thus, continued extreme claims (continued ask more) for the repeat buyer are needed to reinforce the favorable brand attitude (retain more).

B-5. The Benefits Should be Easily Learned in One or Two Exposures (Repetition Serves Mainly as a Reminder Function)

Low involvement/informational ads achieve their "impact" in one or two exposures. With negative reinforcement, as in problem removal and the other negatively originated motivations, the *amount* of reinforcement plays a greater role in learning than the *number* of reinforcements.[25] The prospective buyer either "gets the point" (that is, learns the extreme benefit claim) quickly or not at all. Attitude toward the brand and intention to try it peak after the first or second processing by the prospective buyer.[26]

Thereafter, repetition of the advertisement primarily serves a reminder function to maintain the brand attitude at this peak level.

(Our reminder here is that repetition is also vitally important if brand choice depends on brand awareness by *brand recall,* as noted previously.)

But You Do Have to Remind   Because the brand attitude is low involvement–based and is therefore not personally accepted by the buyer,[27] the attitude must be maintained by periodically reinstating the advertising message which produced the attitude in the first place.[28] (This of course assumes that the action objective is repeat purchase. Reinstatement would not be necessary for a one-time purchase.) Repetition also guards against competitive brand attitude learning from other brands' advertisements in the same product category.

And finally, although acceptance is not necessary for low involvement brand attitude learning, Bacon[29] has shown that trivial claims tend to be believed more as they are repeated and when they are recognized as repeated. Hence the admonition to not depart from the brand's original "positioning" unless absolutely necessary for strategic reasons.

At Lower Frequency   The "quick hit" nature of low involvement/informational claims does, however, mean that the repetition frequency can be *relatively* lower than for transformational claims. We will return to this point later in the chapter and also in Part Seven, on media strategy.

LOW INVOLVEMENT/TRANSFORMATIONAL TACTICS

Low involvement/*transformational* brand attitude applies when the low risk purchase decision is based on a positively originated purchase motivation. Advertising tactics for low involvement/transformational advertisements are listed in Table 9.4. For this type of advertising, correct emotional portrayal (consideration A) takes precedence over benefit-claim support (consideration B). Thus more of the tactics are addressed to emotional portrayal in low involvement/transformational advertising.

A-1. Emotional Authenticity Is the Key Element and Is the Single Benefit

In transformational advertising, it is absolutely essential that the emotional portrayal be perceived by the target audience as authentic. As Wells[30] puts it, the advertisement must "ring true." The whole idea of transformational advertising is to get the target audience to put themselves emotionally into the role of using the advertised brand.

When coupled with the low involvement nature of the brand choice, the fact that the advertised brand elicits (through S_1-R_1 rote learning) the correct emotion *better* than other brands do is sufficient to favor that brand when the purchase decision is made.

An example of low involvement/transformational advertising is shown in Figure 9.7 for a magazine ad. Appealing to the social approval motivation, the original version of this Chanel No. 5 milk bath creme ad was in luxurious color.

The medium par excellence for low involvement/transformational advertising is television, because it can portray human emotions literally and dynamically.[31] Some well-known TV commercials with excellent emotional portrayal of the respective transformational (positive) motivations include:

- The "juicy" hamburgers in the early commercials for Wendy's (sensory gratification).
- The "frozen onlookers" scenes in the "When E. F. Hutton speaks, people listen" commercials (intellectual stimulation).

TABLE 9-4   ADVERTISING TACTICS FOR THE LOW INVOLVEMENT/TRANSFORMATIONAL BRAND ATTITUDE STRATEGY

Consideration A (emotional portrayal of the motivation):

1 Emotional authenticity is the key element and is the single benefit.

2 The execution of the emotion must be unique to the brand.

3 The target audience must like the ad.

Consideration B (benefit-claim support for perceived brand delivery):

4 Brand delivery is by association and is often implicit.

5 Repetition serves a build-up function and a reinforcement function.

FIGURE 9.7 Low involvement/transformational advertisement for Chanel No. 5 milk bath creme portraying social approval motivation (original in color). (Courtesy Chanel, Inc.)

- An unknown model gyrating in a low-budget but highly effective commercial for Jordache—the "Jordache look" that launched the designer jeans craze (social approval).

Visual Imagery from Visual and Verbal Elements   The foregoing examples illustrate the power of *visual stimuli* in advertising to achieve effective emotional portrayal of the motivation.[32] However, effective emotional portrayals also can be achieved with *verbal stimuli* in the copy that *also* generate visual imagery.[33] For example, compare the following pairs of literal claims with the actual wording selected:

Ultra Brite . . . "makes your breath fresh and your teeth white" versus "gives your mouth sex appeal" (social approval).

Volvo . . . "is preferred by better educated drivers" versus "the thinking man's car" (intellectual stimulation).

L'eggs . . . "sheer pantyhose to make your legs feel better" versus "sheer energy" (sensory gratification).

Single Benefit   Correct execution is crucial in transformational advertising. While the brand's benefit must be important to the target audience, this is not enough. The benefit in the ad must be perceived as *authentically portrayed*. Because of the difficulty and necessity of achieving this, it is most inadvisable to attempt to portray multiple benefits in a low involvement/transformational advertisement. Rather, the advertisement should concentrate on excellent portrayal of the single, main benefit to the would-be user.

A-2. The Execution of the Emotion Must Be Unique to the Brand

This recommendation is a direct corollary of the first. The most common error in low involvement/transformational advertisements is to fail to link an otherwise effective and authentic emotional portrayal to the specific brand. How many times have you heard people say in conversation, "That's a great ad" (usually a transformational one), but then they can't remember the brand?

There is far too much "me-too" advertising in transformational product categories (witness the anecdote earlier about being able to play a 7-UP sound track over a Coca-Cola commercial). Imitative advertisements run a real risk that they will cancel each other out in the consumer's mind. A unique execution guards against this. In William D. Wells' words again, the brand and the execution must be "tightly connected."

A "branding device" can be of great assistance here. Usually thought of as a creative technique to aid brand awareness, in the low involvement/transformational application the device should *extend* brand awareness to the transformational motivation. Perhaps the best example of such a branding device is "The Marlboro Cowboy," which extends to the "Marlboro Country" transformational executions. Jingles, too, can serve as branding devices in transformational advertising, but these are often less durable than visual stimuli. Coke and Pepsi, for instance, have tried to distinguish themselves with various transformational jingles over the years. Presenters (see Chapter 11) are another possibility, if one can be sure of a long-term presenter association.

A-3. The Target Audience Must Like the Ad

Low involvement/transformational advertising is the one quadrant of brand attitude strategy where it is essential that the target audience like the ad. There are two reasons for this:

1 The *low involvement* aspect dictates this because the advertisement carries relatively more weight than it does with high involvement, where the product is more important.[34]

2 The *transformational* aspect also dictates ad likability because the target audience, during the learning process, has to undergo positive conditioning by a positive emotional message.

Consistent with the foregoing two points, the several experiments demonstrating that "attitude toward the ad" contributes to "attitude toward the brand" have all been based on low involvement/transformational appeals. These included advertisements for beer[35]; for soft facial tissues[36]; and for brands of soda.[37]

Production Values   The manager commissioning or evaluating low involvement/transformational advertisements should make sure that the target audience *likes everything about the ad*—the visuals, the people, the settings, the words, the music, or whatever other elements are included in the ad. These "production values" all add to positive conditioning.

Benefit-claim support for brand delivery on the motivation is a much more subtle component in low involvement/transformational advertising and we only have to mention two tactical points regarding it.

B-4. Brand Delivery Is by Association and Is Often Implicit

There really is no formal selling proposition in low involvement/transformational advertising. The advertisement does not have to "argue" that the brand delivers on the sensory gratification, intellectual stimulation, or social approval motivation so much as to *show it or imply it by association*.

For example, there is no "logical argument" or "explicit claim" that Coke delivers on sensory gratification, nor that Fisher-Price toys deliver on intellectual stimulation, nor that Jordache jeans deliver on social appeal. The benefit claims are implied by association.

Not suprisingly, therefore, visual content, and visual imagery generated by pictures and words, play a major role in supporting brand attitude "claims" in low involvement/transformational advertisements. In fact, consumers often cannot recall or easily verbalize claims made in these advertisements.

Ask More, Nicely, and Get More   Because of the low involvement aspect of low involvement/transformational advertising, it is appropriate to apply the "ask more, get more" principle of persuasion—but with an important difference. In the low involvement/*informational* case, it doesn't matter how "nicely" the asking is done. But in the present case, the asking (or, more often, showing or implied asking) is modified by the requirement of the first tactic, which is that the portrayal be authentic and "ring true." (More technically, an extreme but unauthentic implied claim would be processed as a negative stimulus in rote learning the positive, transformational, brand attitude). The principle of persuasion for low involvement/*transformational* advertising therefore can be summarized as: "Ask more, nicely, and get more".

For example, "Coke adds life" is an extreme claim literally (a reference to the caffeine lift or that it adds years to your life?) but it "sounds" nice and "images" well. It seems authentic. In keeping with low involvement/transformational advertising, this campaign "illustrated" the claim with authentic visuals and music to emotionally portray the sensory gratification motivation to which the brand was connected. In a nice but extreme way, Coca-Cola was implying that Coke adds to *living* by making life more enjoyable.

B-5. Repetition Serves a Build-up Function and a Reinforcement Function

Repetition of low involvement/transformational advertisements serves dual functions instrumental to their effectiveness: build-up and reinforcement.

Build-up Function Prior to Trial   The first function can be described as "build-up." With positive reinforcement, as is characteristic of transformational appeals, the main factor in learning is the *number of exposures* rather than the amount of reinforcement per exposure.[38] A multitude of experiments on repetition, summarized by Zajonc,[39] has demonstrated the cumulative effect of repetition on liking in low involvement situations.

Reinforcement Function after Trial   Whereas repetition builds positive attitude gradually to a peak in the mind of the individual audience member who has not tried the brand, repetition *after* trial serves a crucial second function. It reinforces the brand-user's self-image.[40]

It is dangerous for a transformationally supported brand to stop advertising for any substantial period because a hiatus in advertising removes the "image" basis for brand loyalty.[41] This has been shown for Budweiser beer in the United States[42] and for the leading selling brand of liquor in the United States, Bacardi Rum, when in 1982 it stopped advertising for almost a year in the Australian market and lost sales rapidly until a new campaign was launched.

You have to have a large budget to effectively compete when using low involvement/transformational advertising. This is necessary to ensure a high frequency of advertising to the target audience (see Part Seven where we discuss media scheduling). In Wells' words, transformational advertising must have enough "presence" so that the brand becomes "part of the consumer's mental life."

THE USE OF HUMOR

A great deal of debate has focused on the use of humor in advertising. It is appropriate here to comment on humor because it most often is employed in *low involvement* advertising—of either the informational type (for example, humorous depictions of problem situations) *or* the transformational type (for example, humorous touches to increase ad likability). Occasionally, humor is used in high involvement advertising, such as the classic campaign for Volkswagen's Beetle, but its use is far more common for products that involve relatively low purchase risk.

Approximately 2 or 3 of every 20 television commercials employ humor, that is, 10 to 15 percent. So humor is a fairly prevalent tactic or stimulus element in advertising.[43]

Humor Is Not By Itself a Motivator

The first thing to observe regarding humor is that it is not a separate motivation. In people's reactions to TV commercials, humor never emerges as a separate factor.[44] Instead, humor is just one of several stimulus elements that can make an advertisement attention-getting and interesting.

The emotional portrayal of humor always occurs with some *other* emotion, and it is the latter emotion that relates to the motivation for brand purchase. Humorous executions can be used with any of the eight motivations. Here are some examples of humor used with different motivations, both negative and positive:

- Volkswagen's classic "ugly" campaign for the VW Beetle against larger and less efficient cars (problem removal)
- Federal Express' jibe against the mythical "Dingbats' Express" (problem avoidance)
- The "Where's the beef?" commercials for Wendy's hamburgers (incomplete satisfaction)
- Johnny Walker Black Label's magazine ads such as the one with the blueblood householder going next door to "borrow a cup of Black Label" (social approval).

Thus, humor is *not* a separate advertising appeal. It must be used in *conjunction* with some other appeal that relates to one of the eight basic motivations.

Does Humor Have To Be Product-Relevant?

Most advertising experts advocate that humor employed in advertising should be "product relevant." Doyle Dane Bernbach's creative director, Sam Levenson, creator of the VW Beetle campaign, applies the following test: If you take the product out of a humorous ad, the ad should no longer be funny. If it is still funny without the product then, in his view, the humor is misapplied and irrelevant.[45]

For Informational Advertising, Yes   However, the product-relevant humor principle only applies to *informational* advertising. In informational advertising, every detail in the ad should support the main selling point and must not distract from the processing of it.[46] This is what is meant by product-relevant humor.

Particularly to be avoided in informational advertising is the humorous punch line or "klinker" that many advertisers cannot seem to resist adding to an otherwise serious ad. Klinkers are irrelevant to the message and they detract from message processing in the critical recency effect zone at the conclusion of the advertisement.

It's okay, though, to use a "klitchik." This is Levenson's term for a *product-relevant* twist used only at the end of a *humorous* ad, such as, "Volkswagen—it doesn't go in one year and out the other." A good klitchik makes you pause and think about what the ad has just shown you or said. Klitchiks therefore make effective use of the recency effect in processing at the conclusion of a humorous advertisement.

For Transformational Advertising, No   For *transformational* advertising, unlike informational advertising, it is *not* essential that humor be product-relevant. "Irrelevant" humor in transformational advertising can contribute to one's liking the ad, creating a positive emotional response that can transfer to the advertised brand via classical conditioning.[47]

However, transformational advertisements cannot rely on humor alone since humor is not in itself a motivation. Transformational advertisements must inevitably have as their foundation one of the positive motivations such as sensory gratification, intellectual stimulation, or social approval.

Because humor is simply an adjunct to these positive emotions, the advertiser should carefully consider whether other positive stimuli in the form of likable characters, likable settings, or music may be more appropriate to the brand's motivation than humor:

- Sensory gratification can *often* be portrayed humorously (for example, Wendy's original "juicy hamburger" commercials)
- Intellectual stimulation *sometimes* can (for example, E. F. Hutton commercials)
- Social approval *rarely* can because social status is something the target audience takes seriously (for example, Johnny Walker Black Label does not rely on the previously mentioned humorous ad for its "image," and indeed mostly runs serious "status" ads under the "black" theme)

Humor in transformational advertising must not jeopardize the connection between the brand and the motivation. The humor itself does not have to be product-relevant. The positive context provided by even irrelevant humor can enhance the effect of a positive motivation.

Whimsical Use of Humor

A final comment on humor pertains to the use of "whimsy" (which is quaint, fanciful, or animated humor). Schwerin and Newell remind us that whimsical humor is useful in at least two advertising situations.[48] These are to:

- Illustrate a point that is difficult to convey literally, for example, "Put a tiger in your tank" to illustrate the power of Exxon, or at that time Esso, gasoline.
- Communicate a point that would be less believable if delivered factually or in a straightfaced manner, for example, Morris the Cat's "finickiness" compared with a human presenter stating this point.

Closely related to this purpose, but far removed from humor, is the use of animation to portray unpleasant stimuli related to negative motivations (informational). Pharmaceutical ads, for example, sometimes employ animation to show how drugs or medicines work on the human body.

Humor of the whimsical type is, like fantasy or animation, one of many techniques that the advertiser may choose to emotionally portray a motivation. Humor, whimsical or otherwise, is not a separate type of advertising.

SUMMARY

We should emphasize that the advertising recommendations for brand awareness and the other communication effects are just that: recommendations. They represent the factors that should improve the advertisement, on average. They are not intended to restrict creativity so much as to guide it in the right direction. No matter how creative an ad appears to be, it will not work unless its stimuli are aligned properly with the communication objectives for the brand.

Brand awareness is a relevant communication objective for all advertisements. Unless the prospective buyer recognizes or recalls the brand, the other communication effects may as well not exist. Brand awareness tactics therefore warrant careful study by the manager.

The key general tactic for brand awareness is to keep in mind clearly *which* type of brand awareness has to be addressed: brand recognition or brand recall, or in rare cases, both. A unique advertising *execution* within the brand's competing category should be sought and the package or brand name should be given substantial exposure in the ad.

Brand recognition basically employs visual exposure of the package and name, associated with the category need, and it can be achieved at lower media frequency than brand recall.

Brand recall can employ some more specialized tactics such as mentioning the brand name (with the category need) frequently in the ad; using a personal reference in the headline or main tag line; trying a bizarre execution (if appropriate to brand attitude); and, for broadcast commercials, considering the use of a jingle to increase brand name memorability.

Brand attitude creation, increase, maintenance, modification, or change requires a special set of creative tactics. Two creative tactics are applicable overall to *low involvement* brand attitudes:

- First, because the decision to purchase the brand is low risk, the advertiser cannot expect the target audience to learn more than one or two main benefits associated with the brand.
- Second, since there is considerable inertia in low involvement product categories, benefit claims must be stated (or shown) extremely in order to prompt buyers into action.

Thereafter, the creative tactics diverge for low involvement advertising depending on whether the brand's primary purchase motivation (and thus the brand attitude) is informational or transformational.

For low involvement/*informational* brand attitude, a simple problem-solution format works best. For low involvement/*transformational* brand attitude, on the other hand, there *is* no "problem," only a solution, in the form of a promised user self-image transformation if he or she will use this brand.

Ads aimed at low involvement/*informational* brand attitude do not have to be liked by the target audience. Many successful low involvement/informational campaigns employ distinctly dislikable advertisements that get the point across extremely well. But low involvement/*transformational* ads are quite different: they *do* have to be liked by the target audience, because the ad must contribute to the positive transformational motivation for the brand by being itself positively regarded.

A further difference is that low involvement/*informational* ads must state the benefit claim clearly and in words; whereas the benefit claims in low involvement/*transformational* ads may not be stated at all, but rather implied visually, and linked to the brand only by implicit association, for which uniqueness of execution (within the category) is at a premium.

Finally, the media strategies for low involvement brand attitude also differ between the informational and transformational quadrants. Low involvement/*informational* ads must work in one or two exposures, otherwise they'll never work; repetition, at reasonably spaced intervals, serves as a post-trial reminder. Low involvement/*transformational* ads, alternatively, require a large number of exposures to "build" the transformational brand attitude, and sustained repetition is needed to reinforce the attitude once it is built.

In addition to these low involvement brand attitude creative tactics, we examined briefly the use of *humor* in advertising. Humor is often thought of as a transformational motivation in its own right, because it makes us laugh. This view is wrong. Humor is no more than an adjunct to one of the basic informational or transformational motivations: it cannot by itself motivate purchase.

For *informational* brand attitude, humor, if used, must be product-relevant. For *transformational* brand attitude, the humor does not have to be product-relevant as long as it contributes positive stimulation.

In the next chapter we turn to *high involvement* brand attitude creative tactics. Again, we see that the recommended creative tactics depend on the type of brand attitude underlying purchase.

NOTES

1 Ogilvy & Mather (Australia) Pty. Ltd., *Listening Post,* April 1982, no. 48.

2 B. R. Bugelski, *Principles of Learning and Memory,* New York: Praeger, 1979.

3 *Advertising Age,* April 20, 1981. For evidence that consumers in Western European countries also see ads in most categories as being "generally about the same," see D. L. Kanter, It could be: ad trends flowing from Europe to U. S., *Advertising Age,* February 9, 1981, 49–51.

4 B. R. Bugelski, same reference as note 2.

5 L. Burnett, *Communications of an Advertising Man,* Chicago: Leo Burnett Company, Inc., 1961.

6 J. R. Rossiter, Visual imagery: applications to advertising, in A.A. Mitchell (Ed.), *Advances in Consumer Research: Vol. 9,* Provo, UT: Association for Consumer Research, 1982, pp. 396–401.

7 The evidence on visual recognition is reviewed in J.R. Rossiter and L. Percy, Visual communication in advertising, in R.J. Harris (Ed.), *Information Processing Research in Advertising,* Hillsdale, NJ: Lawrence Erlbaum Associates, 1983, chap. 4. Field evidence from Bruzzone Research Corporation (BRC) shows that TV commercial recognition (which is not the same as brand recognition but does relate to recognition of a visual stimulus, just like a package) also peaks at 2 to 3 exposures.

8 In applying syndicated test service findings to brand recall, care must be taken to select measures that reflect recall of the *brand,* not recall of the *ad* per se. For example, TV commercial day-after recall measures (cf. the testing services offered by Burke and also ARS) are not applicable because respondents are *given* the brand and asked to recall the advertisement. Similarly, for magazine ads, the Starch testing service has a measure called "Seen Associated" which measures whether consumers paid attention to brand elements in this ad, although it is not actually a measure of brand recall but rather brand recognition (see J.R. Rossiter, Predicting Starch scores, *Journal of Advertising Research,* 1981, *21* (5), 63–68). None of the syndicated services provides an entirely valid measure of either brand recognition or brand recall, and for this reason test service results must be interpreted with great caution.

9 G.A. Miller, The magical number seven, plus or minus two: some limits on our capacity to process information, *Psychological Review,* 1956, *63* (2), 81–97. The "plus or minus two" suggests the range is 5 to 9, but for advertising, 8 is a safer upper limit, with a minimum of 3 required to relate the brand to the category need.

10 L. Percy, Psycholinguistic guidelines for advertising copy, in A.A. Mitchell (Ed.), same references as note 6, pp. 402–406.

11 Case histories are given in A. Ries and J. Trout, *Positioning: the Battle for Your Mind,* New York: McGraw-Hill, 1981.

12 The primacy and recency effect (actually two separate effects) refers to the fact that, other things being equal, items placed toward the beginning and the end of a to-be-learned list will be best recalled, with a "dip" indicating lower recall for items in the middle of the list—hence the "U" effect when recall is graphed against the item's serial position.

Brand recall usually is *delayed* recall, because the decision maker has to recall the brand well after the advertising exposure; and for delayed recall, the *primacy* effect is far stronger than the recency effect. Thus we might conclude that for TV and radio ads, where a list of elements is presented *to* the audience, early presentation of the category need-brand name association is vital. In print ads, however, readers may glance at the bottom of the ad quickly, to see what the brand is, so for print we would advocate beginning-and-end presentation of the association. Perhaps the safest recommendation, however, is beginning-and-end presentation. These are the best two learning positions under any circumstances.

For a review of factors affecting primacy and recency effects in recall, see G.R. Loftus and E.F. Loftus, *Human Memory: The Processing of Information,* Hillsdale, NJ: Lawrence Erlbaum Associates, 1976, particularly chaps. 3 and 4.

13 Australian creative expert John Bevins is perhaps the world's most successful user of the personal approach. His campaigns are extremely memorable and, according to sales results, very motivating.

14 T.K. Srull, Person memory: some tests of associative storage and retrieval models, *Journal of Experimental Psychology: Human Learning and Memory,* 1981, *7* (6), 440–463.

15 E.J. O'Brien and C.R. Wolford, Effect of delay in testing on retention of plausible versus bizarre mental images, *Journal of Experimental Psychology: Learning, Memory, and Cognition,* 1982, *8* (2), 148–152.

16 For example, a rather unusual study found that commercials whose video track was swapped with another commercial's audio track elicited greater brand name recall (from both the video and the audio) than normal versions of the commercials. However, few advertisers would risk the brand's reputation with this gimmick. See S.W. Hollander and J. Jacoby, Recall of crazy, mixed-up TV commercials, *Journal of Advertising Research,* 1973, *13* (3), 39–42.

17 McCollum-Spielman & Company, Inc., Does music add to a commercial's effectiveness?, *Topline,* 1978, *1* (1), p. 4.

18 H.S. Schwerin and H.H. Newell, *Persuasion in Marketing,* New York: Wiley, 1981, pp. 165–167.

19 The Marschalk Company, Inc., *A Study to Evaluate Consumer Attitudes Toward Television Commercials,* New York: The Marschalk Company, Inc., 1981.

20 R.H. Bruskin Associates, *National AIM Study of 2,500 Adults,* New York: R.H. Bruskin Associates, 1977.

21 Note: In this chapter and the next, we will number the brand-attitude tactics 1, 2, 3, etc., for each quadrant, but precede each number with the letter A (for affect, i.e., emotional portrayal) or B (for belief, i.e., benefit claims). This way the emotional tactics and the benefit-claim tactics can be easily compared and contrasted across quadrants.

22 Rosser Reeves, then at Ted Bates advertising agency, originated the USP approach. David Ogilvy, founder of the Ogilvy & Mather advertising agency, is forever urging his proteges to be "single-minded" in advertising executions. Ogilvy, it is said, coined the term "positioning," which was later made more of a buzz word following publication of the book by A. Ries and T. Trout, *Positioning: The Battle for Your*

Mind, New York: McGraw-Hill, 1981, from which several of these examples are taken. See our Chapter 7 for a more thorough definition of positioning.

23 J.C. Maloney, Curiosity versus disbelief in advertising, *Journal of Advertising Research,* 1962, *2* (2), 2–8.

24 W.J. McGuire, The nature of attitudes and attitude change, in G. Lindzey and E. Aronson (Eds.), *The Handbook of Social Psychology,* Vol. 3, Reading, MA: Addison-Wesley, 1969, pp. 136–314.

25 See, for example, S.H. Hulse, J. Deese, and J. Egeth, *The Psychology of Learning* (4th ed.), New York: McGraw-Hill, 1975; and W.A. Wickelgren, *Learning and Memory,* Englewood Cliffs, NJ: Prentice-Hall, 1977.

26 Experimental evidence showing that low involvement/informational brand attitude and intention to try peak after one or two (actual) exposures comes from studies by A.G. Sawyer, A laboratory experimental investigation of the effects of repetition of advertising, Ph.D. dissertation, Graduate School of Business, Stanford University (see also M.L. Ray, A.G. Sawyer, M.L. Rothschild, R.M. Heeler, E.C. Strong, and J.B. Reed, Marketing communication and the hierarchy-of-effects, in P. Clarke (Ed.), *New Models for Mass Communication Research,* Beverly Hills, CA: Sage, 1973, pp. 147–176); A.J. Silk and T. Vavra, The influence of advertising's affective qualities on consumer response, in G.D. Hughes and M.L. Ray (Eds.), *Buyer/ Consumer Information Processing,* Chapel Hill, NC: University of North Carolina Press, 1974, pp. 157–186; and G.E. Belch, The effect of television commercial repetition on cognitive response and message acceptance, *Journal of Consumer Research,* 1982, *9* (1), 56–65.

27 T.S. Robertson, Low-commitment consumer behavior, *Journal of Advertising Research,* 1976, *16* (2), 19–24.

28 R.E. Petty, The role of cognitive responses in attitude change processes, in R.E. Petty, T.C. Brock, and T.M. Ostrom (Eds.), *Cognitive Responses in Persuasion,* Hillsdale, NJ: Lawrence Erlbaum Associates, 1981, pp. 135–139.

29 F.T. Bacon, Credibility of repeated statements: memory for trivia, *Journal of Experimental Psychology: Human Learning and Memory,* 1979, *5* (3), 241–252.

30 W.D. Wells, How advertising works, Mimeo, Chicago, IL: Needham, Harper & Steers Advertising, Inc., 1981.

31 The one exception to TV's generally superior capacity for transformational motivation portrayal might be ads for food (sensory gratification). Magazines, with their better color fidelity, are regarded as superior to TV for food ads that wish to show how "scrumptious" the product is (known as "beauty shots" in advertising production jargon). However, improvements in TV transmission, already available in many countries outside the United States, may eventually nullify this exception.

32 J.R. Rossiter, same reference as note 6.

33 L. Percy, same reference as note 10. Also J.R. Rossiter and L. Percy. Same reference as note 7.

34 R.E. Petty, same reference as note 28. The greater weight of the ad in influencing low involvement behavioral choice reflects what Petty calls the "peripheral route" to persuasion. In high involvement behavioral choice, the product carries greater weight, reflecting the "central route" to persuasion. See also R.E. Petty and J. T. Cacioppo, Central and peripheral routes to persuasion: application to advertising, in L. Percy and A.G. Woodside (Eds.), *Advertising and Consumer Psychology,* Lexington, MA: Heath, 1983, pp. 3–23.

35 J.R. Rossiter and L. Percy, Attitude change through visual imagery in advertising, *Journal of Advertising,* 1980, *9* (2), 10–16.

36 A.A. Mitchell and J.C. Olson, Are product attribute beliefs the only mediator of

advertising effects on brand attitude?, *Journal of Marketing Research,* 1981, *18* (3), 318–332.

37 T.A. Shimp and J.T. Yokum, Advertising inputs and psychophysical judgments in vending-machine retailing, *Journal of Retailing,* 1982, *58* (1), 95–113.

38 S.H. Hulse *et al.,* same reference as note 25.

39 R.B. Zajonc, Feeling and thinking: preferences need no inferences, *American Psychologist,* 1980, *35* (2), 151–175. Zajonc's theory asserts that the build-up of liking with repeated exposures does not depend on whether the person recognizes the stimulus as having been encountered before (which is contrary to our statement that brand awareness is a necessary precursor of brand attitude). However, for a reanalysis of the major experiments that concludes that familiarity or awareness *is* necessary and *does* mediate the exposure effect, see M.H. Birnbaum, letter in the *American Psychologist,* 1981, *36* (1), 99–101.

40 See especially A.S.C. Ehrenberg, Repetitive advertising and the consumer, *Journal of Advertising Research,* 1974, *14* (2), 25–34.

41 S.P. Raj, The effect of advertising on high and low loyalty consumer segments, *Journal of Consumer Research,* 1982, *9* (1), 77–89.

42 R.L. Ackoff and J.R. Emshoff, Advertising research at Anheuser-Busch, Inc. (1963–68), *Sloan Management Review,* 1975, *16* (4), 1–15.

43 Although no surveys of other media are available, one suspects that radio commercials employ humor at a higher incidence that that of TV, whereas print advertisements use humor much less often. The TV estimates come from an informal content analysis of prime-time commercials by A. Bellaire in *Advertising Age,* December 30, 1974, and a later survey reported in L.S. Unger and J.M. Stearns, The use of fear and guilt messages in television advertising, in P.E. Murphy, O.C. Ferrell, G.R. Laczniak, R.F. Lusch, P.F. Anderson, T.A. Shimp, R.W. Belk, and C.B. Weinberg (Eds.), *AMA Educators Conference Proceedings,* Chicago, IL: American Marketing Association, 1983, pp. 16–20. Cross-culturally, British TV advertising is known for its high incidence of humorous commercials.

44 That humor does not emerge as a separate emotional response during processing of advertisements has been demonstrated in factor-analytic studies of consumers' reactions to TV commercials. Humor never emerges as a separate factor. See M.J. Schlinger, A profile of responses to commercials, *Journal of Advertising Research,* 1979, *19* (2), 37–46; M.J. Schlinger and L. Green, Art-work storyboards versus finished commercials, *Journal of Advertising Research,* 1980, *20* (6), 19–23; and D.A. Aaker and D.E. Bruzzone, Viewer perceptions of prime-time television advertising. *Journal of Advertising Research,* 1981, *21* (5), 15–23.

45 Levenson's ideas are reported in D. Catterson, The unruly world of advertising humor, *ad forum,* 1981, June, 13–18.

46 B. Sternthal and C.S. Craig, Humor in advertising, *Journal of Marketing,* 1973, *37* (4), 12–18.

47 D. Zillman, B.R. Williams, J. Bryant, K.R. Boynton, and M.A. Wolf, Acquisition of information from educational television programs as a function of differently paced humorous inserts, *Journal of Educational Psychology,* 1980, *72* (2), 170–180.

48 H.S. Schwerin and H.H. Newell, same reference as note 18.

DISCUSSION QUESTIONS

9.1 One of the general tactics for brand awareness is to match the ad with the exact brand awareness response desired. Discuss how you might do this in an ad for:
 a Birdseye frozen beans

b The aperitif drink, Pernod

c PPG (Pittsburgh Plate and Glass) Company

9.2 Brand awareness is the learned *association* between the brand and the category need. Yet, at first glance, many ads seem to neglect mentioning the category need. Find two examples of magazine ads that do not mention the category need in the verbal copy and discuss why they may have done this.

9.3 To stimulate brand recall, what is right and what is wrong with the following main copy lines?

a "Only your dentist can give your teeth a better fluoride treatment than Colgate."

b "LaCoste." (As in signs at tennis tournaments.)

c "I dreamt I was Cleopatra in my Maidenform bra"

9.4 Write a short script for a radio commercial for Lifesavers designed to maximize brand recall. Type the script sentence by sentence, double-spaced, on the righthand half of the page. On the left, explain the brand recall tactics you have employed.

9.5 The general principle of persuasion for low involvement brand attitude is "ask more, get more." What does this principle mean in terms of creative tactics for the *two* low involvement brand attitude quadrants? Answer with examples.

9.6 Advertising testing services routinely include a measure of whether consumers like or dislike the ad. For a new TV commercial about to go on air, the testing service finds that 80% of *all* people tested dislike the ad. How would you interpret this finding?

9.7 In what circumstance might you include multiple benefit claims (say four to six) in an advertisement aimed at low involvement informational/brand attitude? If possible, find an example where this has been done, or make up an example to illustrate the circumstance.

9.8 Why is it so important that low involvement/transformational advertisements seek a unique advertising execution? Name one apparently transformational product category that you think suffers from too much similarity between the competing brands' advertising. Then name and describe another category where at least three brands have used distinctive ads for the *same* transformational brand attitude motivation.

9.9 Find three magazine ads that use humor. Then discuss their use of humor in the light of the chapter's comments about humor as a creative technique.

FURTHER READING

J.C. Maloney. Curiosity versus disbelief in advertising. *Journal of Advertising Research,* 1962, *2* (2), 2–8.

A classic article that nicely destroys the myth that all advertising has to be "believable." Fits the low involvement/informational brand attitude quadrant.

A. Ries and J. Trout. *Positioning: The Battle for Your Mind.* New York: McGrawHill, 1978.

Despite heavy reliance on anecdotal examples rather than objective survey evidence, this highly readable book makes two important points: first, the idea of a category "ladder" on which brands are ordered (vital for brand *recall*); and second, the importance of brand names (critical for *both* brand recognition and brand recall, and for relating the brand to its *category*). Note that "positioning" involves not just brand awareness but also brand attitude, because the brand has to be linked to a motivation and favorably evaluated, not just thought of first. However, Ries and Trout assume that brand recall is always desired and tend to overlook brand recognition as a path to purchase action.

Two adjacent references: J.R. Rossiter, Visual imagery: applications to advertising; and L. Percy, Psycholinguistic guidelines for advertising copy. In A.A. Mitchell (Ed.), *Advances in Consumer Research: Vol. 9,* Provo, UT: Association for Consumer Research, 1982, pp. 396–406.

These paired articles, one on visual elements in advertising and the other on verbal elements, discuss tactics that should increase brand awareness and other communication effects. Useful mainly for advanced readers interested in the psychological evidence underlying several of the recommendations in the chapter.

T.S. Robertson. Low-commitment consumer behavior. *Journal of Advertising Research,* 1976, *16* (2), 19–24.

Describes the disinterest and inertia that characterizes brand choice in so many consumer product categories. Also worthwhile because it equates involvement with the brand (the purchase decision) rather than with the advertising itself.

W.D. Wells. How advertising works. Working paper. Chicago: Needham, Harper & Steers Advertising, 1981.

Recommended earlier for Chapter 7, Wells' article on informational versus transformational creative tactics should make more detailed sense now having read our Chapter 9. This paper is not readily obtainable except from Dr. Wells but there are no other substitutes, as yet, in the literature.

CHAPTER 10

HIGH INVOLVEMENT BRAND ATTITUDE CREATIVE TACTICS

High involvement brand attitude applies when the target audience decision maker regards purchase of the brand as high risk. After reading this chapter you should:

- Know the tactics that work best for high involvement/*informational* brand attitude strategy
- Additionally know the tactics to try with very negative target audiences, namely, refutational and perhaps comparative advertising
- Know the tactics that work best for high involvement/*transformational* brand attitude strategy

At this point it is worthwhile to recapitulate the conditions under which high involvement brand attitude is operative. Both the product category *and* the target audience have to be taken into account.

If the product category itself is perceived as so low in purchase risk that even new triers of the brand would be making a low involvement purchase decision, then *low* involvement creative tactics apply. Moreover, for (otherwise) high risk product categories, advertising directed to a brand's brand loyal or routinized brand-switching customers is also *low* involvement, because the risk is no longer there for users of the brand.

For high risk product categories where a brand is trying to expand its franchise beyond its current users (to new category users, experimental brand switchers, or other-brand loyals), *high* involvement brand attitude applies and high involvement creative tactics should be used. *New brands,* in high risk product categories, should employ high involvement creative tactics. Established brands in high risk categories seeking *new users* likewise should employ these tactics.

Once again, there is also the motivational component of brand attitude to be considered, as reflected in the informational versus transformational distinction. Within the high involvement quadrants, creative tactics differ depending on whether the brand attitude is informationally or transformationally motivated.

HIGH INVOLVEMENT/INFORMATIONAL TACTICS

The recommended tactics for high involvement/informational advertising are listed in Table 10.1. This strategy quadrant, as might be expected from the label "high involvement, informational," is heavily weighted toward the benefit-claim support for perceived brand delivery component of brand attitude (consideration B). Correct emotional portrayal of the motivation (consideration A) is also important, but as we shall see in the first tactic, its importance in high involvement/informational advertising varies with stage in the product life cycle.

A-1. Correct Emotional Portrayal Is Very Important Early in the Product Life Cycle But Becomes Less Important as the Product Category Reaches Maturity

Correct emotional portrayal of the motivation is very important early in a product category's life cycle (see Chapter 6) because, during the introduction and growth stages, most prospective buyers have to be "sold" on the category need as well as on the brand. Advertisements for products when they are new, such as microwave ovens or more recently video disks, have to motivate people to want the category before they will seriously consider the particular brand advertised.

Later in the product life cycle, most prospective buyers will already know

TABLE 10-1   ADVERTISING TACTICS FOR THE HIGH INVOLVEMENT/INFORMATIONAL BRAND ATTITUDE STRATEGY

Consideration A (emotional portrayal of the motivation):

1. Correct emotional portrayal is very important early in the product life cycle but becomes less important as the product category reaches maturity.
2. The target audience has to accept the ad's main points but does not have to like the ad itself.

Consideration B (benefit-claim support for perceived brand delivery):

3. The target audience's "initial attitude" toward the brand is the overriding consideration that must be taken into account.
4. Benefit claims must be pitched at an acceptable upper level of brand attitude (don't over-claim).
5. Benefit claims must be convincing (don't inadvertently under-claim).
6. For target audiences who have objections to the brand, consider a *refutational* approach.
7. If there is a well-entrenched competitor and your brand has advantages on important benefits, consider a *comparative* approach.

about the category and be favorably disposed toward it, so correct portrayal of the motivation is less important as the product category reaches maturity.

However, advertisers would do well to note that product life cycles are really consumer life cycles[1]; that is, an established product for early adopters will still be a new product for later adopters. For example, to sell microwave ovens to the 70 percent or so of consumers who have never bought one, selling the category is still important, whereas advertising aimed at the 30 percent of current users to get them to trade up or buy another microwave would not have to sell the category. Thus, the status of the *category need* communication effect in the *target audience* is the determinant of whether correct portrayal of the motivation is required.

A-2. The Target Audience Has to Accept the Ad's Main Points But Does Not Have to Like the Ad Itself

This recommendation is similar to the one made earlier for low involvement/ informational advertising: when the basis of the brand attitude is information, whether people like the way the information is presented is a very minor consideration.[2]

Perhaps the best example of this would be the sort of ads that promise personal improvement, for example, weight reduction, body-building, or breast development. Such ads are often "schlocky" in overall appearance. They concentrate on loading the copy with convincing claims, often with a "money back if not satisfied" guarantee, to reduce the typically high perceived risk.

Not having to like the ad should not be interpreted as a recommendation to deliberately create dislikable ads. This sometimes is done in *low* involvement/ informational advertising as a tactic to increase attention to and *learning* of the message point, as in the Mr. Whipple commercials for Charmin. However, in attitudinal presentations in high involvement/informational ads, learning is only transient, and *acceptance,* the high involvement processing response, is what counts. In high involvement/informational advertising it doesn't matter whether the message points are presented in a likable or dislikable manner as long as the points are accepted by the target audience.

"Engineering" Acceptance The message points in high involvement/informational advertising must be very carefully engineered to gain target audience acceptance. This engineering requires the manager to understand the rationale behind a number of fairly complex tactics relating to high involvement brand attitude. These benefit-claim support tactics (consideration B) are presented next.

B-3. The Target Audience's "Initial Attitude" Toward the Brand Is the Overriding Factor That Must Be taken into Account

In Chapter 7, we emphasized the necessity of identifying benefits that are important, deliverable, and as unique as possible *with respect to* the particular attitudinally defined target audience to whom the advertising is directed.

For instance, if the target audience has a *negative* brand attitude, the manager (or researcher) must find benefits that will change this attitude to a sufficiently positive attitude to motivate purchase; likewise, a *moderately favorable* brand attitude must be increased (unless the brand is to be made additionally attractive to a moderately favorable target audience by sales promotion, which normally operates on brand purchase intention, not brand attitude); a *strongly favorable* brand attitude must be maintained; or a *new* brand attitude created—each with the particular set of benefits that have been found to be important, deliverable, and maximally unique to that attitudinal sub-group as a target audience.

The creative translation of the specificity of benefits idea is that the *claim* made for the benefit must also be tailored to the target audience. Benefit claims, like the benefits they represent, must take the target audience's initial attitude into account. In everyday terminology, this means that the claim should be worded in a way that reflects "where the audience is coming from."

The following examples show how this can be achieved by copywriters who know how to write "to" an audience (high involvement) rather than "at" an audience (low involvement).

1. In addressing a target audience with a *negative* attitude toward the brand, such as other-brand loyals who have rejected your brand, or new category users with negative attitudes toward all brands in the category, the benefit claim should acknowledge the negative attitude and try to "shake" the target audience out of this negative attitude with a new, convincing counter-claim (see also the refutational approach later in this chapter).

An example of "shaking" a would-be negative target audience is provided in the Frito-Lay ad in Figure 10.1. (We apologize for the larger and longer-copy ads in this section of the chapter, but remember, we are examining high involvement purchase decisions.) Copy lines in the ad such as "What about salt?" and "The facts about cholesterol and preservatives" indicate that the copywriter knows that the target audience is likely to be negative toward this or any other brand of potato chips as a "non-nutritional" food. The detailed copy is also sympathetic to this negative attitude. Of course, the sympathetic copy then attempts to convince negatively disposed decision makers to reconsider and make their final attitude more positive.

2. In addressing a target audience with a *moderately favorable* brand attitude, such as brand switchers early in the product life cycle who are still trying to settle on a favorite brand to use regularly, or such as "interested" positive new category users, the benefit claims should have more of a "reassuring" or reinforcing tone.

A good example of this is the umbrella campaign written by the famous copywriter, David Ogilvy, for Sears: "You can count on Sears." This umbrella has been the basis for a series of advertisements by Sears for high involvement/informational product and service decisions. Figure 10.2 shows how Sears advertises its automobile brake repair service. The copy is designed to bolster the moderately favorable initial attitude of prospective customers who may wonder what sort of job Sears would do in an area traditionally reserved for specialists in auto repair and servicing.

FIGURE 10.1   (Two pages.) An advertisement for Frito-Lay potato chips with benefit claims worded to take account of the largely *negative* target audience and "shake" them out of this negativity. (Skim the bold-faced copy if you're not involved enough to read the entire ad!) (Courtesy Frito-Lay, Inc.)

3. In addressing a target audience with *no firm prior* brand attitude, and perhaps a negative or "hesitant" initial attitude toward the category, such as negative new category users, the wording of the benefit claims should adjust to take account of the indecisiveness.

The marketers of complex technological products, such as computers or word processors, often adopt this approach, with claims that promise to take care of "all your computing needs," and so forth. Figure 10.3 shows how Nature's Way, Inc. has utilized this approach for a new yeast-control product called Cantrol. The headline copy invites the indecisive reader to "Take the Yeast Test" and asks "Do you have a yeast problem?" For the many adults who are concerned about health (or who are just plain curious about what a "yeast problem" is) the quiz format followed by benefit-claim support in the body copy is likely to be effective in gaining new users of the category via the brand.

Sears Tire & Auto Centers
WE INSTALL CONFIDENCE

THIS IS NO TIME FOR A BRAKE DOWN.

This is the time to check your brakes. Or, better yet, come to Sears and we'll check them for you.

We'll inspect your brakes and give you a written estimate for any work you need.

If you need a complete brake job, we'll install new brake shoes on your drum brakes (new pads on your disc brakes), new front oil seals, and new hold down and return springs.

to help make sure your brake job is complete. That's something some places charge extra for.

Then we'll give your brakes a road test.

Finally, we'll give you a Sears Limited Warranty. It says if your new Sears brake linings or disc pads wear out within 25,000 miles, we'll either furnish new ones, free, or refund the money you paid for parts.

Sears mechanics can usually fix your brakes the day you come in or the next Sears working day.

If Sears did the original installation, you pay only a prorated labor charge to install the replacements.

It takes a lot of confidence to offer a warranty like that. And we have it. Confidence in our mechanics' training. Confidence in our parts' quality.

Yet at Sears, a complete 2-wheel brake job for your car is just $69.99. (If

At Sears, a complete, 2-wheel brake job for your car, including rebuilding wheel cylinders and calipers (something many repair shops don't include), is just $69.99. Prices apply only to the continental United States.

We'll also turn and true the drums and/or rotors.

We'll clean, inspect and repack wheel bearings, adjust the emergency brake, flush and bleed the hydraulic system and replace the fluid. And if you care about getting your money's worth, this next point is very important.

We'll rebuild the wheel cylinders and disc brake calipers

you need to replace the drums or rotors, master cylinder, or other parts, the parts and labor are extra.) But there's never an extra charge for confidence.

You can count on Sears

© Sears, Roebuck and Co. 1982

FIGURE 10.2 Extension of the "You can count on Sears" umbrella campaign to encompass brake repair, where the target audience may have *only a moderately favorable* initial attitude toward Sears for this service. (Courtesy Sears, Roebuck & Co.)

Take the Yeast Test.

Do you have a yeast problem?
Here's what it is and how to fight it.

We call the type of yeast normally found in our bodies "Candida colonies." Normally they are harmless. However, they can sometimes grow rapidly due to a variety of conditions. When this happens they are no longer friendly microorganisms, but have developed into a "Candida albicans" problem. Worse, they have an adverse effect on our health.

Nature's Way, the makers of Cantrol™, a total nutritional plan designed to help control Candida albicans, has developed a simple test to help you determine if you have a yeast problem.*

Y N
- ☐ ☐ 1. Do you feel tired most of the time?
- ☐ ☐ 2. Do you suffer from intestinal gas, abdominal bloating or discomfort?
- ☐ ☐ 3. Do you crave sugar, bread, beer or other alcoholic beverages?
- ☐ ☐ 4. Are you bothered by constipation, diarrhea, or alternating constipation and diarrhea?
- ☐ ☐ 5. Do you suffer from mood swings or depression?
- ☐ ☐ 6. Are you often irritable, easily angered, anxious or nervous?
- ☐ ☐ 7. Do you have trouble thinking clearly, suffer occasional memory losses or have difficulty concentrating?
- ☐ ☐ 8. Are you ever dizzy or lightheaded?
- ☐ ☐ 9. Do you have muscle aches or stiffness with normal activity?
- ☐ ☐ 10. Have you had an unexpected weight gain without a change in diet?
- ☐ ☐ 11. Are you bothered by itching or burning of the vagina or prostate or a loss of sexual desire?
- ☐ ☐ 12. Have you ever taken antibiotics?
- ☐ ☐ 13. Are you currently or have you ever used birth control pills?
- ☐ ☐ 14. Have you ever taken steroid drugs, such as cortisone?

*This quiz is provided for general information only and is not intended to be used for self-diagnosis without the advice and examination of a qualified health professional. Some of the symptoms could indicate a more serious condition which could require the assistance of a health professional.

If you answered 6 or more questions with a "yes," you may have a yeast problem. Read about how Cantrol can help.

What causes a yeast problem?

A number of conditions can lead to Candida or yeast problems. Steroid drugs (such as cortisone), birth control pills and the long-term use of antibiotics (such as those used to control acne or various bacterial infections) can invite the problem. Poor nutrition or a sluggish or impaired immune system will often contribute to yeast populations. Stress and environmental pollutants also play a role.

Antibiotics can reduce the numbers of beneficial bacteria that normally keep the yeast under control. When this happens the yeast multiply in an unrestrained manner and a Candida problem may result.

How the Nature's Way Cantrol Program controls troublesome yeast.

Nature's Way Cantrol (Candida Control Pack) is a complete nutritional approach for the control of Candida albicans. Each Cantrol pack contains a combination of natural ingredients that helps to control Candida. These ingredients come in portion-controlled packages for added convenience and freshness.

Cantrol's high potency formula helps keep yeast colonies from overpopulating in the intestines where they grow. One major ingredient in Cantrol is Primadophilus® brand acidophilus, contained in unique enterosoluble capsules. This allows it to pass through the stomach and be released in the intestines for maximum benefit.

Additional ingredients such as Nature's Way anti-oxidant, linseed oil and vitamin E are included in the Cantrol portion-controlled pack for nutritional support. We have also included a free booklet, "Dietary Guidelines and Program Overview" which provides dietary suggestions along with complete information on the Cantrol program.

Properly following the Cantrol dietary and nutritional program gives you a fighting chance against yeast.

Proper diet and Cantrol: A sensible approach to good health.

Ask for Cantrol at fine health food stores everywhere.

If Cantrol is unavailable in your area, write Nature's Way, 10 Mountain Springs Parkway, Springville, Ut. 84663, or call toll-free 1-800-453-9000.

©1986 Nature's Way Products, Inc.

MAY 1986 • Let's LIVE **23**

FIGURE 10.3   An ad for a new product, Cantrol, with benefit-claim wording designed to attract new category users with *no firm prior attitude* toward first-aid products. (Courtesy Nature's Way Products, Inc.)

In all the foregoing examples, the benefit claims are stated in a way that "resonates" with the target audience's initial attitude while attempting to change, increase, or create a positive final (post-processing) attitude toward the advertised brand.

Theory of Initial Attitude   It is worthwhile at this point to emphasize once again the reason why initial attitude is so much more crucial in high involvement purchase decisions than in low involvement purchase decisions. The very notion of low risk in purchasing a brand means that the buyer'a initial attitude is likely to be weakly held. With high involvement decisions, in contrast, the prospective buyer's initial attitude reflects the higher risk and is likely to be strongly held.[3]

A strongly held initial attitude is almost sure to stimulate cognitive responses during processing.[4] These cognitive responses will be negative, moderately favorable, and so forth, depending on the target audience's initial attitude. High involvement/informational advertising has to provide benefit claims that sympathetically anticipate these reactions and either counter them or build on them accordingly. Unless cognitive responses are addressed effectively, the benefit claims will not be accepted and no change or improvement in *final* brand attitude will result.

B-4. Benefit Claims Must Be Pitched at an Acceptable Upper Level of Brand Attitude (Don't Over-claim)

Benefit claims in high involvement/informational advertising not only must take the target audience's initial attitude into account but also must be tempered by how far "up" they can go in proposing a new and more favorable attitude position. This is known in the classical attitude literature as the (upper limit of) "latitude of acceptance".[5]

Obviously, the manager would like as favorable a final attitude as possible for the brand. "As possible"—that's the operational concept for this tactic.

How Much of an Attitude Increase Is Feasible?   Early in the product life cycle—again actually the *consumer* life cycle—it should be possible to obtain large positive shifts in brand attitude among new category users who have neutral initial attitudes and among experimental brand switchers who are still sampling the category and also have neutral attitudes or weakly held positive attitudes. The yeast-control ad in Figure 10.3, earlier, has the potential for a large positive shift in creating brand attitude.

Later in the consumer life cycle, when the brand is better known and brand attitudes are more strongly held, smaller shifts of about one attitude "box" or "rung" are the most the advertiser can hope for—unless some hitherto unrealized benefits for the brand are discovered or unless there is a radical creative breakthrough in finding a more effective statement of current benefits.[6] For example, now that personal computers are well known, it's very difficult for any *brand*'s advertising to change the attitude of people who are dead-set against using one.

The likely upper limits or latitudes of acceptance are summarized in Figure 10.4. As indicated in the figure, *early* in the consumer life cycle it is often possible to attain positive attitude shifts of *up to two* "boxes" or "rungs" on our general-purpose brand attitude scale. New category users entering the category and brand switchers who are shopping around may be induced via advertising to rate the brand as one of the better brands or even the single best brand.

The figure indicates that, *later* in the life cycle, the most feasible positive shifts are reduced to *one* "box" or "rung." Hard-core brand switchers who are not currently including the brand may be induced to do so, but would

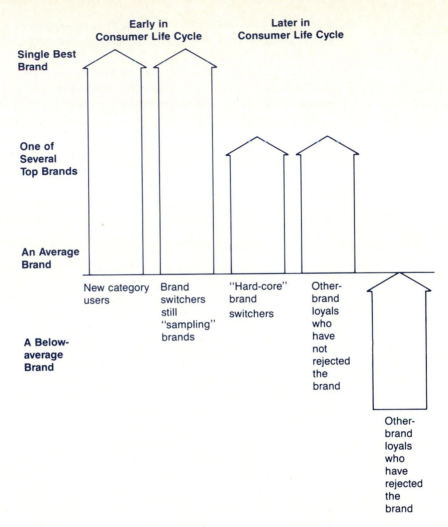

FIGURE 10.4   Likely upper limits (latitudes of acceptance) for brand attitude change in high involvement/ informational advertising.

hardly rate it single best. Similarly, other-brand loyals who have not rejected the brand may be induced to now include it as one of several top brands, but without a complete replacement of single best brand loyalty. For other-brand loyals who have tried and rejected the brand, the shift from below-average to average hardly seems worth aiming for unless the now average brand can be made additionally attractive to this target audience through promotional incentives.

How to Find and Address the Latitude of Acceptance   Latitudes of acceptance can be estimated for a given target audience through pre-testing of benefit claims (see Part Six). It is relatively easy to discover "how far you can go" before progressively more extreme claims are rejected. If the benefit claims stated in the pre-test versions of the ads do not move a significant proportion of the target audience "up" to the required favorable brand attitude position, then alternative statements must be sought and tested.

(If better statements of the brand's benefits sufficient to attain the required attitude increase *cannot* be found, the strategy for that target audience will have to be abandoned. The manager could, however, try a more radical strategy such as refutational advertising or comparative advertising—as explained in Sections B-6 and B-7 that follow—if these have not already been tried.)

In finding the upper limit of the latitude of acceptance for the target audience, the manager must be wary of trying to over-claim in the final version of the ad once a version acceptable to the target audience has been found. The manager must resist the temptation to subjectively "make a few improvements," unless he or she is willing to pay to have these tested as well.

For example, the main benefit claim for Stouffer's Lean Cuisine line of low-calorie entrees, "Good tasting entrees at less than 300 calories," was found to be eminently acceptable (believable) to the target audiences of new category users and other-brand loyal (Weight Watchers) users. To have said "*Great* tasting entrees at less than 300 calories" would have been over-claiming to these high involved target audiences. Over-claiming which produces a reversion to the initial pre-message attitude is called the "boomerang effect."

B-5. Benefit Claims Must Be Convincing (Don't Inadvertently Under-Claim)

After all we've said about the importance of benefit-claim acceptance in high involvement/informational advertising, it almost sounds redundant to say that benefit claims must be convincing and not inadvertently *under*-claim. However, this is not a trivially obvious recommendation. As Bauer and Cox have suggested, under-claiming is just as much an error as over-claiming.[7] Indeed, we may think of an underhand throw of the "boomerang" as well as the overhand throw with over-claiming.

The danger is in selecting the right benefits—that is, those that are important, deliverable, and as unique as possible—and then failing to execute the *statement* of them convincingly enough. An instructive experiment by Petty and Cacioppo[8] demonstrated that weak arguments (for important points know to be effective with strong arguments) can actually hurt the brand by making a negatively disposed audience's initial attitude even more negative or strongly held. This again is due to the cognitive response aspect of high involvement message processing. If the target audience's spontaneously occurring doubts about the brand's benefits aren't removed by sufficiently convincing statements of the benefits, then these doubts will undergo reinforcement from the ad, making the brand attitude more negative than before!

Thus it is not sufficient in high involvement advertising just to say the right thing. The right thing must be "said right" as well.

An example is the Coca-Cola claim of a few years ago, "Have a Coke and a smile." This claim apparently was not sufficiently convincing to Pepsi Cola brand loyals, a possibly high involvement target audience, whom Coca-Cola was trying to win over.[9] Coca-Cola then moved to stronger and presumably more convincing claims such as "The real thing" and, more recently, "Coca-Cola is *it*."

B-6. For Target Audiences Who Have Objections to the Brand, Consider a Refutational Approach

The advertiser whose brand is perceived as posing a high involvement/ informational decision often will be faced with negatively disposed audiences from whom sales must come if the brand is to succeed. If the typical "supportive" advertising approach hasn't worked, then a "refutational" approach is worth trying.

Refutational approaches acknowledge the negative reactions head-on and then try to refute or counter them. The refutational approach is like the selling tactic known as "Yes . . . but." Frequently used in personal selling, the refutational approach is under-utilized in advertising.

A test of the refutational approach by Sawyer[10] is very instructive because it is one of the few studies in the advertising research literature to examine the effects of advertising strategies on *different* target audiences.

Table 10.2 shows an example of conventional supportive ad copy used by Sawyer, together with the refutational version. Note that the refutational version mentions the likely objection, "Why pay $1.98 for a ballpoint pen?" and then attempts to refute it with, "You pay $1.98 for a Parker, but you never have to buy another." Five pairs of supportive and refutational ads for five brands were employed in the experiment, so the results do not depend on just this one ad.

The refutational approach was more successful than the supportive approach against a negative target audience (users of other brands). However, even the refutational approach, in this experiment, could not "move" negatively disposed consumers' attitudes "up" enough to get them to buy the brand. This overall failure represents an average across all negative consumers and

TABLE 10-2   AN EXAMPLE OF THE REFUTATIONAL APPROACH

Supportive version:
   Parker Pens
   Just one could be all you ever need. At $1.98 it's the best pen value in the world. . . .

Refutational version:
   Parker Pens
   Why pay $1.98 for a ballpoint pen? You can get them for 49¢, 69¢, or for free . . . The kind that skip, stutter, and run out of ink.
   You pay $1.98 for a Parker, but you never have to buy another.

Source: A.G. Sawyer, The effects of repetition of refutational and supportive advertising appeals, *Journal of Marketing Research*, 1973, *10* (1), 23–33. From Table 1, p. 25, by permission.

the results really should have been analyzed further to see how many *individuals* were favorably moved enough to purchase the brand; however, the average result suggests that the proportion of individuals moved to purchase would be disappointingly small. Remember, we said that negatively disposed audiences with strongly held attitudes may not be worth trying to win over.

Some real-world results nevertheless indicate that the refutational approach *can* be very successful. In the early 1970s, a large number of American adults had developed a negative attitude toward potatoes. The national farmers' cooperative, represented by the National Potato Promotion Board, commissioned the authors to conduct some research and recommend an advertising strategy designed to reverse the declining trend in U.S. per capita potato consumption.

Our research in 1973, prior to the campaign, indicated that although people still loved the taste of potatoes, this positive belief was being overtaken by a strong negative belief: that potatoes are fattening. This strong negative belief had to be countered if potato consumption was to increase again.

The advertiser had refutational ammunition to work with. Potatoes actually are lower in calories (per ounce) than other popular carbohydrate side dishes such as rice, bread, or noodles. And while it is true that people often add butter or sour cream to potatoes, these ingredients produce a relatively small addition to calories. Also, many people were already switching to margarine and low-calorie preparation and serving methods.

Hence the headline in Figure 10.5: "Don't blame potatoes." Notice the refutational approach in the ad's copy: ". . . automatically you assumed the culprit was that delicious baked potato. . . . . Not likely." Follow-up ads, as in Figure 10.6, continued the refutational message and added a positive message—that potatoes are an excellent source of vitamins.

The campaign was highly successful. Consumer surveys taken in 1973, before the campaign started, and again in 1975, after it had been running for 2 years, showed a substantial reduction in the number of people believing that potatoes are fattening and a dramatic increase in the belief that potatoes are nutritious. During the campaign, with no noticeable change in price or other market factors, consumption of potatoes by the average U.S. household not only stopped declining—it went up by over 17 percent. This major turnaround was attributable largely to successful refutational advertising.

B-7. If There is a Well-Entrenched Competitor and Your Brand Has Advantages on Important Benefits, Try a Comparative Approach

The final tactic for high involvement/*informational* advertising is the comparative approach. Like refutational advertising, comparative or comparison advertising is a rather radical tactic, to be used only if circumstances suggest it would be more effective than conventional supportive advertising.

Comparative advertising either names competitors openly or else clearly implies who the competitors are without actually mentioning them by name.

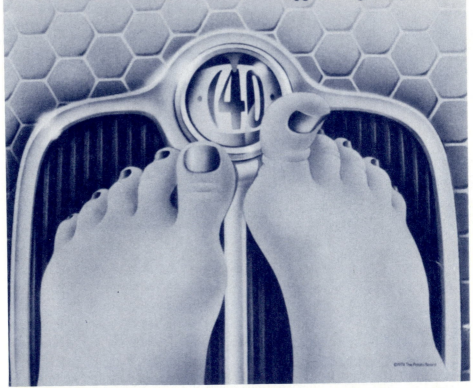

FIGURE 10.5   A National Potato Promotion Board ad demonstrating the refutational approach for a negative target audience. (Courtesy Potato Board.)

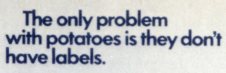

The only problem with potatoes is they don't have labels.

If they did, we wouldn't have to tell you that a medium-sized baked potato has fewer calories ounce for ounce, than rice, bread, or noodles.

Or that the potato contains significant amounts of Iron, Vitamin B₁, Niacin, and over half of the minimum daily requirement of Vitamin C.

There are a lot of good things you could say on a potato label. And one thing you wouldn't have to say.

They're delicious (we figure you already know that).

You and the potato should meet again. Look for it at your store. In a plain brown, white, or red wrapper.

INTRODUCING THE POTATO.

Something good that's good for you.

FIGURE 10.6 A second ad in the NPPB campaign illustrating continued refutation combined with a more supportive approach. (Courtesy Potato Board.)

It then claims superiority for the advertised brand on one or more benefits, to try to sway the target audience's attitude in the advertised brand's favor.

Because of the adversary and possibly disparaging nature of comparative advertising, it is not a tactic to be adopted without fully considering the likelihood of costs that may result. It can result in price wars (for example, when Datril was launched against Tylenol); complaints to self-regulatory commissions such as the NAD, and even lawsuits (for example, McDonald's against Burger King); and also counter-comparative advertising (for example, Coke's Bill Cosby commercials—"You know what *you* want to be when you grow up. . . . Number one!"—to defuse Pepsi's taste-test challenge commercials). Comparative advertising can be a very costly tactic indeed.

But it can also be enormously successful. For example, Tylenol itself became established by comparative advertising against pain reliever brands containing aspirin (although, due to the poisoning scare that unfortunately befell Tylenol, the brand was later withdrawn). Burger King's comparative campaign helped to gain market share and profit against McDonald's and Wendy's. Pepsi-Cola contends that its challenge campaign has worked in markets where it lagged behind Coke's sales. Campaigns for Avis against Hertz, Savin copiers against Xerox, Scope against Listerine, and more recently Intellivision against Atari in the TV games market also are regarded as successful applications of the comparative approach.

Consequently, almost one in every five TV commercials now employs a comparative approach. However, only about a quarter of these commercials name competing brands explicitly. The majority are implicit comparatives, and this technique is discussed shortly.

Factors in Successful Comparative Advertising

What are the main characteristics of successful comparative campaigns? There seem to be at least four:

1 The competitor or competitors advertised against should be well-entrenched in the target audience's mind, otherwise there's no sense in pursuing a comparative approach.

2 The advertised brand must be able to demonstrate equality or advantage on one or more important benefits sufficient to increase its overall attitude rating.

3 The advertised brand should dominate the presentation of the comparison both visually and verbally.

4 The execution of the comparison must be convincing (indeed all the foregoing tactics for high involvement/informational advertising apply).

Salient Competing Brand(s)   The first characteristic of comparative advertising is that it should be employed only when there are one or more competing brands more firmly entrenched in the target audience's mind than the advertised brand. The notion of "well-entrenched in the . . . mind" can mean simply brand awareness (see new category users, below) although more often it means brand awareness and brand attitude (as in the case of other-brand loyals and brand switchers). There is no sense in taking on competing brands that are not seriously considered by the target audience—unless you have good reason to believe that they will be considered in the very near future.

Not just smaller brands but even the market share leader may find it worthwhile to use comparative advertising. The leader would take on a lesser brand in order to increase sales among the leader's non-loyal buyers. When a recessionary economy causes category sales to flatten or decline, trying to grab share from smaller (or indeed any) competitors is a common strategy. Not surprisingly then, in the recessionary economy of 1981, almost one in four TV commercials was comparative, with many brands trying to take sales from other brands' customers.

Comparative advertising can be appropriate when addressing three of the four general target audiences:

- *Other-brand loyals. Example:* Pepsi against Coke.
- *Brand switchers. Example:* Avis against Hertz.
- *New category users* who have not yet decided which brand is superior but who are leaning toward a competitor's brand. *Example:* Intellivision against Atari.

Why not brand loyals? It is true that comparative advertising aimed at other target audiences is likely also to be effective with brand loyals, because it tends to reinforce their already favorable attitude when "their" brand wins the comparison.[11] However, comparative advertising should not be used when brand loyals are the *only* target, because a supportive approach would suffice at much lower risk.

Advantages on Important Benefit(s)   The second characteristic is that the advertised brand must be able to demonstrate equality or advantage on one or more *important* benefits—sufficient to generate a more positive overall attitude.

An interesting aspect of comparative advertising is that *equality* of benefits may be sufficient to improve the comparing brand's attitude—by making it appear similar to the compared-with brand.[12] This is the approach taken by "Why pay more?" advertisers.

Most brands, however, aim for superiority rather than equality, because only a superior brand attitude would convince the negative target audience to change from their preferred brand.

How many benefits does the advertised brand have to compare on? This depends on how many benefits are important in supporting the brand attitude or, more specifically, the purchase motivation underlying brand attitude.

Where the purchase motivation is singular and straightforward, superiority on a single benefit may suffice. For example, the ''Pepsi Challenge'' campaign is taking on Coca-Cola on a single benefit—taste—that supports the single purchase motivation (sensory gratification). More recently, Diet 7-UP has taken on Diet Coke, Tab, and Diet Pepsi on the comparative taste benefit (Table 10.3). The comparative taste strategy assumes, by the way, that the other motivation for buying *diet* soda, which is problem avoidance via the low-calorie benefit, is *equal* across the diet brands. Moreover, there is the reasonable assumption that brand loyalty in this category is very strong, thus justifying the use of a high involvement approach (comparative) to win other-brand loyals.[13]

Often, however, superiority on *several* important benefits will be necessary to achieve the required brand attitude increase. Burger King's comparative campaign against McDonald's is an example. Burger King has assessed that superiority on four benefits is necessary to support its sensory gratification motivation: better-tasting burgers, larger burgers, broiled rather than fried, and the continuity benefit from the previous campaign, ''Have it your way,'' instead of having the burger prepared one way as elsewhere.

Comparative advertising's attainment of a positive attitude shift also depends on what the *relevant motivation* (and thus the relevant attitude) is. For example, Burger King probably will win customers for whom the major motivation is sensory gratification (purportedly better-tasting burgers that also are larger). However, Burger King will not win against McDonald's for those customers for whom the major motivation is problem removal (namely, how to feed and entertain young children) because McDonald's, with Ronald McDonald and the in-store promotions and children's amenities, has this motivational segment virtually sewn up.

Visual and Verbal Dominance to Minimize the ''Free Ride'' Effect   The third characteristic relates to the fear that comparative executions may give the compared-with brand or brands a ''free ride,'' thereby boosting the competitors' brand awareness. Contrary to popular opinion that this doesn't matter if the challenged brands are leaders with maximum awareness anyway, it does

TABLE 10-3   CONSUMER TASTE-TEST EVIDENCE USED BY DIET 7-UP IN ITS COMPARATIVE ADVERTISING CAMPAIGN AGAINST DIET COLAS*

Diet 7-UP versus	Preferred Diet 7-UP (%)
Tab	72
Diet Coke	63
Diet Pepsi	62

* The taste tests were conducted blind (unlabeled) in 12 metropolitan areas by an independent testing service. See note 13.

matter, because of the repeat purchase nature of most products. You can never have over-awareness, at least not over time.

The executional way to minimize the free ride effect is for the sponsoring brand to dominate the visual and verbal comparison (in radio, of course, it is verbal only). This translates to video and audio *time* dominance for the sponsoring brand in TV commercials,[14] and visual and copy *space* dominance for print ads (Figure 10.7).

Another *apparent* way around the free ride problem is to employ an "implicit" comparison—that is, to avoid naming competitors' brands in ads. Bounty's comparative paper towel ads for example, refer only to "a top challenger" (obviously Viva). Why do we say "apparent"? Implicit comparisons are more complex than they appear (and it is vital that processing of these ads be carefully tested). First of all, let's consider brand awareness. An implicit comparison makes sense if the brands are competing for brand *recognition*. An explicit comparison that shows the competitor's pack plainly would indeed give the competitor a free ride; whereas an implicit comparison, where the compared brand's package is visually unclear, would not. If, however, the brand awareness objective is brand *recall,* then it all depends on whether the target audience seeing the ad *spontaneously* names the unnamed competitor[15]. If they do, then there's going to be free ride interference with the advertised brand's brand recall.

But, secondly, consider the effect of implicit comparisons on brand attitude. If the advertiser "hides" the competing brand so well that the audience doesn't spontaneously name it, then the only message the audience gets is that the advertised brand is better than "some other brand," and this may not be sufficient to cause a brand attitude increase and convince the audience to switch. Instead, an explicit execution, or an implicit one which is *effectively* explicit because the target audience spontaneously names the brand anyway, would be needed.

Thus we see again the vital importance of basing creative tactics on the communication objectives for the brand. Whether the advertiser should employ an explicit or an implicit comparison depends on how the creative execution is *in fact* processed, and on what the relevant brand awareness objective is.

Be Convincing But Within the Latitude of Acceptance   The final characteristic on our list for comparative advertising is that the execution of the comparison must be convincing but must be tailored to the target audience's latitude of acceptance. For instance, an interesting experiment by Belch[16] pitted an imaginary new brand of flouride toothpaste, called "Shield," against Crest. Subjects in the experiment, most of whom were probably market-leader Crest's loyals, simply could not believe that anything could "beat Crest for fighting cavities." The comparison over-claimed and failed.

In fact, all of the preceding recommendations for high involvement/informational advertising apply to comparative advertising. In summary form, the first four recommendations (of which comparative advertising is the fifth) were to:

FIGURE 10.7   A comparative advertisement for Trident showing space dominance by the sponsoring brand. (Courtesy Warner-Lambert Company.)

- Consider the initial attitude of the target audience.
- Don't over-claim.
- Don't under-claim.
- Consider a refutational approach if the target audience has objections to the brand.

Comparative advertising can also include the refutational approach if circumstances suggest it. The National Potato Promotion Board ads refuted the fattening claim by also comparing potatoes with other side dishes. *Refutational comparative* advertising should therefore be tried when *two* conditions apply: when the target audience has objections to your brand, *and* when the target audience prefers a well-entrenched competitor over whom you could demonstrate superiority.

HIGH INVOLVEMENT/TRANSFORMATIONAL TACTICS

The last of the four brand attitude strategy quadrants is high involvement/ transformational advertising. This is where the brand purchase decision is perceived as relatively high risk, requiring attitudinal conviction before purchase, and where the appeal is *primarily* to one of the positive motivations: sensory gratification, intellectual stimulation, or social approval. We say "primarily" with some emphasis in this case because, as we shall see, high involvement/transformational advertisements frequently have to provide *information as well*.

High involvement/transformational brand choices *often are dually motivated:* A secondary informational motivation must be met in order to attain the primary transformational motivation.

There are many high risk products and services that primarily meet positive motivations. These include vacations (sensory gratification), corporate "images" that influence investors' perceptions (intellectual stimulation), as well as new cars, fashion clothing, and other personal luxuries subject to reference group influence (social approval). The high involvement/transformational quadrant pertains to considered-purchase products where positive consumption experiences are the primary factor in brand choice.[17]

Recommended tactics for high involvement/transformational advertising are listed in Table 10.4. Correct emotional portrayal of the motivation (consideration A) assumes more importance, as we would expect, than with informational advertising. However, because of the high involvement aspect, there are also some important brand benefit-claim support delivery aspects (consideration B) though not, of course, as detailed as for the high involvement/informational strategy.

A-1. Emotional Authenticity Is Paramount and Should Be Tailored to Lifestyle Groups Within the Target Audience

Transformational advertising puts a premium on emotional authenticity in portraying the brand's usage motivation—emotional consequences of using the

TABLE 10-4   ADVERTISING TACTICS FOR THE HIGH INVOLVEMENT/TRANSFORMATIONAL BRAND ATTITUDE STRATEGY

Consideration A (emotional portrayal of the motivation):

1. Emotional authenticity is paramount and should be tailored to lifestyle groups within the target audience.
2. People must identify personally with the product as portrayed in the ad and not merely like the ad.

Consideration B (benefit-claim support for perceived brand delivery):

3. Many high involvement advertisements also have to provide information.
4. Over-claiming is recommended but don't under-claim.
5. Repetition serves a build-up function (often for subsequent informational ads) and a reinforcement function.

brand are the main causes of purchase. In the high involvement version of transformational advertising, the target audience's judgment of authenticity is likely to be very personal (varying across individuals) as well as very important to the person. This is because the higher risk "amplifies" the emotional consequences of a correct or incorrect brand choice.

Individual Differences   As Myers and Schocker[18] have observed, user-referent benefits are unlike other benefits, in that major individual differences in desirability are present. The high involvement, personal nature of the choice amplifies these differences. Examples in relation to our three positive motivations would be:

- *Sensory Gratification*   Some people want gourmet taste, some want delicious taste, and others just want a filling taste in a restaurant meal.
- *Intellectual Stimulation*   Some people want high-brow entertainment, some want middle-brow entertainment, and others want decidedly low-brow entertainment in a Broadway play.
- *Social Approval*   Most notably, people have different reference groups to whom they look as a guide for their purchases and consumption, particularly when psychosocial risk's contribution to involvement with the brand choice decision is high.[19]

Thus, with high involvement/transformational advertising, there are likely to be substantial individual variations *within* a given target audience (that is, within new category users, or within brand loyals, or within brand switchers, or within other-brand loyals) in precisely what constitutes emotional authenticity in a motivation's portrayal.

High involvement/transformational advertising is therefore the only brand-attitude strategy quadrant in which we would recommend segmentation *within* whichever of the prospect groups (NCU, OBL, BS or BL) constitutes the target audience. In all other quadrants, once the main benefits have been found for the target audience, it is rarely worth further segmentation because the benefits usually have relatively universal appeal to that audience. The highly individual nature of the brand-user image benefits in high involvement/ transformational advertising makes a justifiable exception.

Lifestyle Segmentation Within the Target Audience   The most relevant candidate for segmentation within the target audience for high involvement/ transformational advertising is *lifestyle*.

Portraying the brand user's lifestyle by showing people in the ad probably is the most effective tactic in high involvement/transformational advertising because the portrayed users serve as *presenters* with inherent source effects (as will be explained in Chapter 11). Lifestyle portrayals show a particular type of person experiencing positive reinforcement from using the brand.

Only larger advertisers can afford ads that appeal to different lifestyle groups in a single campaign (although the smaller advertiser can sometimes do this through the judicious use of different print media with slightly different visuals). An example is the Bell System's "Reach out and touch someone" campaign, which probably is high involvement because of the cost of long-distance phone calls, and probably transformational because of its apparent appeal to the "good feeling" (sensory gratification) that you get when calling friends and relatives (although the authors perceive a certain amount of "guilt reduction" and problem removal here). In two ads from the campaign, Figure 10.8 shows a white week-ending family as the lifestyle segment whereas Figure 10.9 shows a health-conscious black couple as the lifestyle segment. These are only two of the many lifestyle groups within Bell's large target audience to whom their ads have been directed in an effort to increase long-distance calling frequency.

If different lifestyle groups cannot be shown, for budgetary or other reasons, then the advertiser should use a "straight" focus on the brand's image benefits without showing people in the ad. Not showing people can allow possibly varying lifestyle groups to "project" themselves into the ad. This can be a good tactic if the brand happens to appeal to "discrepant" lifestyle groups (examples might be Cadillac automobiles and Chivas Regal scotch). Here it would seem that showing discrepant lifestyle users in ads could confuse the brand's image and perhaps alienate all lifestyle groups.

A-2. People Must Identify Personally with the Product as Portrayed in the Ad and Not Merely Like the Ad

Regardless of whether the multiple lifestyle approach is used, everyone to whom high involvement/transformational ads are directed should identify with the brand as portrayed in the ad. In the acceptance phase of processing, the target audience decision maker must experience a "That's for me" reaction. Processing for this type of advertising is highly dependent on personal "consumption imagery"—that is, people seeing themselves driving the new

FIGURE 10.8   A Bell System "Reach out and touch someone" advertisement aimed at one lifestyle group. . . .(Courtesy AT & T.)

"Do you believe it? Five whole miles! Yes, you really started something. Walter?
Oh, he didn't make it quite that far but he's coming along. What? Well I've lost 15
and Walter...I don't know, for some reason it seems to take him longer."
Share the feeling with someone who always knows just
how you feel. Reach out.   ⓐ Bell System

Reach out and touch someone.

FIGURE 10.9   . . . and another lifestyle group (see Figure 10.8). (Courtesy AT & T.)

car shown, or taking the vacation to the resort shown, or otherwise "putting themselves in the picture."[20]

More than Ad Likability   Identification with the brand portrayal goes well beyond mere liking of the ad, which was an essential feature of the low involvement/transformational advertising. In the high involvement version, the liking must be product (brand) focused because "peripheral" liking of the ad itself is not sufficient to influence brand attitude.[21] Of course, as with all transformational (positive motivation) advertising, the advertiser should strive to make the ad likable too. But with the high involvement nature of the brand

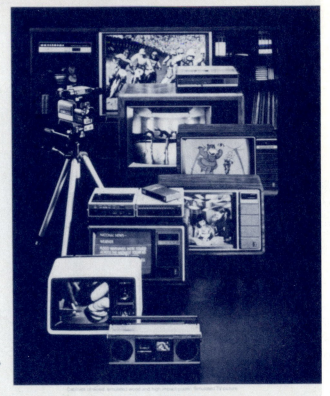

GE LETS YOU WATCH WHOEVER, WHATEVER, WHENEVER, WHEREVER, HOWEVER.

Nowadays, television is more than just a pretty picture.

There's everything from widescreens to portables.

And programming from cable to home movies.

But whatever kind of television intrigues you, General Electric gives you a seemingly endless variety of home video systems to choose from. And the information to help you make the right choice.

SMALL SCREENS, WIDESCREENS, IN-BETWEEN SCREENS.

Take your favorite programs on the road via the GE Road Show™ portable entertainment center. It includes a 3" (diag.) TV screen, AM-FM stereo radio and microcassette recorder.

For television on a movie-theater scale, the GE Widescreen features high-fidelity sound as beautiful as the 40" (diag.) picture.

And many GE sets offer the Emmy Award-winning* VIR Color System which automatically adjusts the picture 60 times a second.

GE LETS YOU WATCH MORE TELEVISION. OR LESS.

Most GE sets are designed to receive 112 channels.

If you don't want your children to watch them all, choose a GE television with Channel Block Out™ selective viewing control.

USE TELEVISION INSTEAD OF JUST WATCHING IT.

GE VHS Video Cassette Recorders play prerecorded tapes and let you record your favorite shows** to watch whenever you like.

Or, make your own shows with the lightweight VCR and color video camera. You can even use the camera to practice your golf game or send a video letter.

IF THE CHOICES CONFUSE YOU, GE OFFERS HELP.

There are over 5,000 video dealers to help you make the right choices.

You can also get help from the GE Answer Center™ information service. Just call toll-free 800-626-2000. Our experts will answer any questions you may have about any GE consumer product or service.

WE BRING GOOD THINGS TO LIFE.

GENERAL ELECTRIC

FIGURE 10.10   A high involvement/transformational advertisement for GE's video products that also provides information (see text). (Courtesy General Electric Company.)

decision, liking of, and further than this—identification with—the *brand portrayal* is the essential factor.

In addition to the tailored emotional authenticity and brand-portrayal identification tactics comprising the correct emotional content, there are several perceived brand-delivery factors to be considered. These are examined next.

B-3. Many High Involvement/Transformational Advertisements Also Have to Provide Information

When we analyzed brand delivery for low involvement/transformational advertising, we commented that brand delivery is by association and often is implicit. In the high involvement version of transformational advertising, the benefit claims for brand delivery usually are more explicit, in keeping with the necessary *acceptance* response in processing. The desired processing response is: "If I buy and use this brand, I will get these positive benefits."

The high involvement aspect of purchasing the brand often means that there are *some* obstacles to be overcome, in the audience's mind, on the way to getting the positive benefits. For instance, vacation resorts may have hidden costs; a new car costs money and you'd want to find out something about its technical features before you purchase; and so on. Figure 10.10 shows an example. The ad is for GE's video products where the primary motivation is almost certainly sensory gratification from more pleasurable TV viewing. However, the ad also provides plenty of information to answer the high involvement questions raised in the prospective buyer's mind regarding purchase of this expensive equipment.

Many high involvement/transformational advertisements are therefore obliged to provide information to allay the perceived risk in purchasing the brand. Although the provision of information may be seen as meeting a negative motivation, particularly problem removal or avoidance in the reduction of purchase obstacles, it is essential to realize that the ads are not thereby informational rather than transformational. Their primary appeal remains transformational: the primary energizer of purchase is the expectation of satisfying a positive motivation. That some negative motivations may have to be removed to get to the positive motivation is incidental though of course not unimportant. Such ads should be handled tactically from a high involvement/ transformational perspective although their informational *supporting* elements would do well to take note of the high involvement/informational tactics described previously.

B-4. Over-claiming Is Recommended but Don't Under-Claim

One departure from the over-claiming and under-claiming cautions that apply to high involvement/informational advertising is that, with high involvement/ *transformational* advertising, it is permissible—even recommended—to over-claim. The advertiser should try to "hypo" the brand's delivery on the positive motivation as much as possible. The upper limit for over-claiming will extend to all but the most outrageously exaggerated claim.

The reason for over-claiming (here we should say "peak-experience" claiming) is that the benefits from high involvement/transformational products are almost entirely subjective. Who can really say whether the advertiser is "really" over-claiming about, say, the fun of a vacation resort or the experience of driving a new car? "Proof" is subjective and is for the individual buyer or user to determine. And if you don't make strong positive claims, you may not get the purchase in the first place.

Credence Products and Public Inflation of the Brand User's Image   Many if not most of the benefits of high involvement/transformational products are difficult for the user to judge objectively, even after purchase. Darby and Karni[22] call these "credence goods," forming a third category from Nelson's earlier analysis of experience goods (where trial is sufficient) and search goods (where the prospective buyer must be convinced before trying).

For example, most people buy life insurance based on "faith" placed in friends or in the agent.[23] Similarly, the envy of your friends when you say you've taken a Club Med vacation or have just bought a new Mercedes SEL sports car is as much part of the product benefit as the product itself.

"Hypoed" advertising for these high involvement/transformational types of products is therefore effective in large part because it influences the public image of the product *among those who may never experience it* and thereby not have an opportunity to discount the hypoed claims. This inflated yet accepted public image then raises the buyer's own attitude to a level above its "reality" level.[24]

With high involvement/transformational advertising, then, the recommended tactic is to over-claim, even to quite an exaggerated extent. The advertiser who doesn't over-claim runs the risk of not inducing purchase. And quite obviously it follows that under-claiming is usually fatal in this type of advertising.

B-5. Repetition Serves a Build-up Function (Often for Subsequent Informational Ads) and a Reinforcement Function

Repetition is essential for transformational advertising. This final tactic duplicates the tactic for low involvement/transformational advertising with one difference. During the build-up phase, transformational advertising alone is sufficient to induce purchase of low involvement brands. However, for high involvement brands, transformational advertising (on the primary motivation) is often employed to pave the way for subsequent informational advertising (on the secondary motivation) or other informationally based selling methods that are necessary to ensure purchase.

One of the best examples of the transformational followed by informational sequence would be new car advertisements on television and also in relatively brief but highly visual print ads (as in the Nissan 300 ZX ad studied at length in Chapter 6). These ads are high involvement/transformational. For products where the purchase decision phase may be quite long, transformational advertising is often used to interest prospective buyers in a high involvement purchase that will be consummated only after the prospect has sought out more detailed information, either from more detailed ads (usually print ads) or from friends, auto sales staff, or auto rating publications.

More than Awareness Building The brief (but frequent) transformational advertising for these *high risk* products does not just "build awareness." It builds brand awareness, certainly, but also it builds the *transformational brand attitude*.

This largely informationless transformational "pre" advertising can be very effective in its own right. For many new car buyers, the subsequent search for "informational" advertising, or more objective information from other sources, frequently is just to consolidate a decision *already made* in favor of the brand from the transformational advertising.

Post-Purchase Reinforcement The second purpose for repetition of transformational advertising, including high involvement/transformational advertising, is to provide reinforcement to those who have already purchased the brand. Transformational advertising has a vital role to play *after* purchase, in reinforcing the buyer's attitude for having made the correct choice.

Some writers explain post-purchase advertising as working by reducing the buyer's "cognitive dissonance." However, there is no need for the buyer to have felt dissonant or uncertain for this post-purchase reinforcement to occur; it can be solely positive (reward) reinforcement, not negative (anxiety removal) reinforcement as the dissonance account implies.

High involvement/transformational purchases typically are infrequent, such as new cars, and vacations. Nevertheless advertising's post-purchase reinforcement contributes strongly to a favorable initial attitude for buying the same brand *next* time.

SUMMARY

Creative tactics for achieving high involvement brand attitude objectives (creation, increase, maintenance, modification, or change) are different and more detailed than those for low involvement brand attitude. High involvement with the brand purchase decision means that advertising claims—whether verbally stated or visually implied—are *carefully considered* and must be *accepted* by the target audience if purchase of the brand is to result.

The discovery of convincing ways to state benefits is of course the creative copywriter's forte. In fact, selection of (and switching between) agencies is motivated in many instances by precisely this: the search for a better way to state the same benefits. Most brands in a particular product category have a rather fixed set of benefits. The quest is for the most convincing way of stating them. Weak or unconvincing statements can actually make a high involvement brand attitude more negative!

High involvement/*informational* creative tactics are closest to the "textbook" tactics for attitude change, although textbooks usually ignore the emotional portrayal of the motivation. Correct emotional portrayal is important early in the product life cycle but not later. Further, it is not necessary for the target audience to like the advertisement, in this quadrant.

The perceived brand delivery component, achieved creatively through benefit claims, is the most vital factor. For high involvement/informational brand attitude, benefit claims must be engineered to the target audience's "latitude of acceptance." This means taking the target audience's initial (pre-exposure) attitude into account, then neither over-claiming nor under-claiming.

When the target audience's initial attitude toward the brand is highly involved and negative, *refutational* tactics should be considered. When the target audience's initial attitude toward a well-entrenched competitor's brand is more favorable than toward your brand, *comparative* advertising tactics should be considered.

High involvement/*transformational* creative tactics also are rendered more complex by the high involvement aspect. Emotional authenticity, vital to all transformational advertising, now relates to lifestyle groups within the target audience, not merely to the target audience as a whole. Moreover, the target audience must identify with the brand as portrayed in the advertisement, which is more than just liking the ad for its executional characteristics.

Many high involvement/transformational brand choices are primarily transformationally motivated and secondarily informationally motivated. This is because information often must be provided to the highly involved buyer to allow acceptance or "rationalization" of the primary transformational reason for buying and using the brand. Luxury cars and expensive vacation resorts would be two such examples.

For transformational brand delivery, benefit claims should *over*-claim. This is because transformational benefits are largely subjective and therefore are not as dependent on objective reality as are informational benefits; and because over-claiming tends to provide public image reinforcement of the user's attitude from those who don't use, and therefore don't reality-test, the brand but wish they did.

If informational motives must also be met in high involvement/transformational advertising, these benefit claims should adhere to the high involvement/informational creative tactics recommended for them. Quite often, the dual motivational task is achieved in two stages: by employing straight transformational advertising initially (as in new car commercials on TV) followed by additional informational advertising in other media (as in newspaper advertisements for the same new car). The brand choice is still high involvement in both stages and creative tactics should fit the high involvement quadrants.

NOTES

1 John A. Howard deserves full credit for emphasizing the essential dependence of product life cycles on consumer life cycles which entail different stages of decision making: from extended problem solving (introduction) to limited problem solving (growth) to routinized response behavior (maturity and decline). See J.A. Howard, *Consumer Behavior: Application of Theory,* New York: McGraw-Hill, 1977, especially chap. 1.

2 For an excellent explanation and demonstration of the irrelevance of ad likability in mediating high involvement/informational brand purchase decisions, see L. Percy and M.R. Lautman, Creative strategy, consumer decision goals, and attitudes toward the ad and advertised brand. Paper presented at the 3rd Annual Advertising and Consumer Psychology Conference, Ted Bates Advertising, New York, June 14–15, 1984.

3 It should be noted that brand loyals in high risk product categories *also* have a strongly held (loyal) attitude, even though the decision to repeat purchase is, for them, now low involvement.

4 See Chapter 8 for an explanation of cognitive responses during processing. The relationship of cognitive responses to *initial attitude* in *high* involvement choices is discussed in L. Percy and J.R. Rossiter, *Advertising Strategy: A Communication Theory Approach,* New York: Praeger, 1980.

5 See C.W. Sherif, M. Sherif, and R.E. Nebergall, *Attitude and Attitude Change,* Philadelphia: Saunders, 1965; also W.J. McGuire, The nature of attitudes and attitude change, in G. Lindzey and E. Aronson (Eds.), *The Handbook of Social Psychology,* Vol. 3, Reading, MA: Addison-Wesley, 1969, pp. 136–314; and L. Percy and J.R. Rossiter, same reference as note 4.

6 Although almost certainly in a low involvement product category unless aimed at cola-loyals, 7-UP would have to win a prize for the most original re-statement of an existing benefit: "7-UP . . . the *un*cola."

7 R.A. Bauer and D.F. Cox, Rational vs. emotional communications: a new approach, in D. F. Cox (Ed.), *Risk Taking and Information Handling in Consumer Behavior,* Cambridge, MA: Harvard University Press, 1967, pp. 469–486. This paper was first published in L. Arons and M. May (Eds.), *Television and Human Behavior,* New York: Appleton-Century-Crofts, 1963, but business school libraries are more likely to have the later reference.

8 R.E. Petty and J.T. Cacioppo, Issue involvement can increase or decrease persuasion by enhancing message-relevant cognitive responses, *Journal of Personality and Social Psychology,* 1979, *37*(10), 1915–1926.

9 According to an article in *Advertising Age,* January 18, 1982.

10 A.G. Sawyer, The effects of repetition of refutational and supportive advertising appeals, *Journal of Marketing Research,* 1973, *10*(1), 23–33.

11 L.L. Golden, Consumer reactions to comparative advertising, in B.B. Anderson (Ed.), *Advances in Consumer Research: Vol. 10,* Ann Arbor, MI: Association for Consumer Research, 1976, pp. 63–67.

12 G.J. Gorn and C.B. Weinberg, Comparative advertising: some positive results, in R.P. Bagozzi and A.M. Tybout (Eds.), *Advances in Consumer Research: Vol. 3,* Cincinnati: Association for Consumer Research, 1983, pp. 377–380.

13 L. Kesler, "Taste 'real issue' for Diet 7-UP," *Advertising Age,* May 28, 1984, p. 62. Note that Diet 7-UP is trying to break down cola *category* loyalty. The decision for cola-loyals to switch permanently to a non-cola is almost certainly a high involvement one.

14 The necessity for time dominance in comparative TV commercials has been demonstrated in commercial tests conducted by Gallup & Robinson, Inc.—see E.A. Rockey, Comparative advertising: fair or unfair? effective or ineffective?, paper presented at the Association of National Advertisers workshop, New York: February 1976; and McCollum-Spielman & Company, Inc., Success factors in comparative advertising, *Topline,* 1978, *1*(2), 1–2.

15 R.D. Wilson, Comparative advertising: some current considerations for managerial planning and strategy, in J. Leigh and C.R. Martin (Eds.), *Current Issues and Research in Advertising,* Ann Arbor, MI: University of Michigan Press, 1978, pp. 5–22.

16 G.E. Belch, An examination of comparative and noncomparative television commercials: the effect of claim variation and repetition on cognitive response and message acceptance, *Journal of Consumer Research,* 1981, *18*(2), 333–349.

17 For many years the esteemed Sidney J. Levy of Northwestern University has drawn attention to the fact that most products have positive symbolic value to their users. And, more recently, Holbrook and Hirschman have correctly criticized consumer researchers for not fully recognizing the obviously powerfully motivating "experiential" consequences of consumption. See S.J. Levy, Symbols for sale, *Harvard Business Review,* 1959, *37*(4), 117–124; M.B. Holbrook and E.C. Hirschman, The experiential aspects of consumption: consumer fantasies, feelings, and fun, *Journal of Consumer Research,* 1982, *9*(2), 132–140; and M.B. Holbrook and J. O'Shaughnessy, The role of emotion in advertising, *Psychology and Marketing,* 1984, *1*(2), 45–64, especially fig. 1.

18 J.H. Myers and A.D. Shocker, The nature of product-related attributes, in J.N. Sheth (Ed.), *Research in Marketing,* Vol. 5, Greenwich, CT: JAI Press, 1981, pp. 211–236.

19 W.O. Bearden and M.J. Etzel, Reference group influence on product and brand choice, *Journal of Consumer Research,* 1982, *9*(2), 183–194.

20 In Part Eight, where we discuss ad testing, the visual imagery version of the acceptance response is explained in more detail.

21 R.E. Petty and J.T. Cacioppo, Central and peripheral routes to persuasion, in L. Percy and A.G. Woodside (Eds.), *Advertising and Consumer Psychology,* Lexington, MA: Lexington Books, 1983, pp. 3–23.

22 M.R. Darby and E. Karni, Free competition and the optimal amount of fraud, *Journal of Law and Economics,* 1973, *16*(1), 67–88.

23 R.A. Formisano, R.W. Olshavsky, and S. Tapp, Choice strategy in a difficult task environment, *Journal of Consumer Research,* 1982, *8*(4), 474–479. In this survey, the authors found that 75% of people buying life insurance (median policy amount: $25,000) sought a quotation from, and purchased from, only *one* insurance company. Forty-eight percent bought from the first salesperson who contacted them (thus showing considerable "faith") and 27 percent bought from the first company recommended to them by an acquaintance.

24 Although described as public inflation of image, more technically the process is social reinforcement of the individual's brand attitude.

DISCUSSION QUESTIONS

10.1 In the high involvement/informational brand attitude quadrant, the target audience has to accept the ad's main points but does not have to like the ad itself. Find and discuss an example of a newspaper or magazine ad, clearly for a high involvement/informational brand, that is not particularly likable yet makes very convincing points about the brand.

10.2 For high involvement/informational advertising, the target audience's initial attitude is the overriding factor that must be taken into account. Interview a friend, who is a driver, about his or her overall attitudes and specific benefit beliefs about several makes of cars. Select a car toward which your friend appears to have a moderately favorable, but not a strongly favorable, brand attitude. Paying particular attention to wording, draft a set of benefit claims that you think would be effective in increasing this attitude to a strongly favorable one. Test the benefit claim statements with your friend. Then write a short report on this exercise.

10.3 The refutational approach and the comparative approach are two creative tactics that can be used when the target audience has a negative attitude toward your brand. Which of the two approaches do you think would be more appropriate, and why, for the following brands:

a IBM Personal Computer

b R-C (Royal Crown) Cola

c The Bell System's long-distance telephone service pre *and* post deregulation

10.4 Lifestyle segmentation would appear to be "backward segmentation," a practice we don't recommend. When is lifestyle segmentation appropriate and why? Illustrate your answer with a product example not given in the chapter.

10.5 a Find and discuss two examples of print ads that you think are providing information "just" to allow the target audience to achieve a primary transformational motivation.

b Find and describe a product category, other than automobiles, that uses high involvement/transformational advertising on TV, and high involvement/informational advertising in magazines. Why do you think this product category uses this dual advertising strategy?

10.6 "Over-claiming" refers to benefit claims that exceed (the upper limit of) the target audience's high involvement latitude of acceptance. Write a two-page memorandum on when you should over-claim in high involvement advertisements and when you should not.

FURTHER READING

L. Percy and J.R. Rossiter. *Advertising Strategy: A Communication Theory Approach.* New York: Praeger, 1980.

Our earlier book, prepared before low involvement theory was fully recognized in advertising, provides an excellent review of high involvement communication tactics in advertising. Much more detail appears there which has been condensed and adapted in tactics presented in the present book. As well, there are other topics not treated in depth in the present book, such as creative applications of visual imagery and psycholinguistics to produce more effective advertising.

Do *not* read books by famous advertising copywriters.

Books by Leo Burnett, Fairfax Cone, Claude Hopkins, David Ogilvy, and others, are interesting and entertaining reading. But they won't help you to be a better advertising manager. First, these books take no account of advertising communication models (particularly the two types of brand awareness and the four brand attitude strategy quadrants); rather they promote (their own) singular view of how advertising works, and no single view can cover all types of advertising. Second, because each writer tends to have had most of his experience with particular product categories—again, different communication models—the recommended creative tactics frequently are conflicting and contradictory. Third, while it can be contended that the views of these famous copywriters have been "tested by experience," in fact their views too often do not withstand more controlled testing by advertising testing services. Finally, apart from too rarely cited sales results, the criteria by which these authors judge "effective" advertising (e.g., advertising recall) are hopelessly mixed and off-base and serve to reinforce the confusion which our book, in systematizing advertising objectives in the six-step approach, has tried to prevent.

Whereas these are strongly worded criticisms, they seem necessary in light of the fact that the biggest problem in understanding how advertising works is to get managers (and students) to stop falling back on popular and often erroneous general conceptions and to think, instead, specifically about what the advertising is trying to do, and how, specifically, it might best be done.

CHAPTER 11

WHEN TO USE A PRESENTER

Now that we have reviewed the creative tactics for various types of advertisements, it is time to consider one further creative decision faced by managers—namely, when should you use a presenter?

More than one in every three TV commercials uses an on-camera spokesman or spokeswoman for the brand,[1] so the decision is a major one, creatively. After reading this chapter you should:

- Realize how the presenter effect is present in all advertisements
- Know when to use an in-ad presenter
- Understand how best to select an appropriate presenter in accordance with the communication objectives for the brand

The chapter begins with a broad consideration of the presenter (or "source") effect in advertising. We then consider the situations in which an in-ad presenter should be used, that is, as a deliberate and explicit component of the advertising message. Finally, using the VisCAP model of presenter characteristics, we show how an appropriate presenter can be selected to fit the communication objectives of the brand.

THE PRESENTER EFFECT: PRESENT TO SOME DEGREE IN ALL ADVERTISEMENTS

The Perceived Source of the Message

Advertisements are, by definition, sponsored messages. From a processing perspective, in watching or listening to an advertising message, the presenter can be thought of as the audience's answer to the question: "Who says so?"[2]

This is an important question for the manager to anticipate because the audience's attitude toward the perceived source or sponsor of the advertising message can contribute strongly to the audience's attitude toward the advertised brand.

As explained by Percy and Rossiter,[3] the entities that can be processed as the perceived presenter of the message are wide-ranging. They include:

- *The industry* For example, oil companies, and the ad industry per se
- *The product category* Feminine hygiene products, liquor, cigarettes, candy
- *The company* Dow Chemical, Sears
- *The brand name* Pierre Cardin, Ralph Lauren
- *The media vehicle* Violent TV programs, intellectual magazines
- *Any persons or characters or even settings shown in the ad* The Charlie perfume girls, the New York City (Manhattan) skyline

Any or all of these "sources" can produce predisposing attitudes that affect attitude toward the brand. Presenter effects are present, to a greater or lesser degree, in *all* advertising messages.

Most of these factors, however, are considered elsewhere in advertising planning. Industry and product category effects are best thought of as category attitudes (under the selling-the-category option of the category need communication effect). Brand name, used as such, is really a brand benefit claim (brand attitude). And media vehicle effects (if there *are* any) will be examined with media selection in Part Seven. Settings usually are not considered as presenters but rather as brand benefits (by association). This leaves persons and characters, and they will be our focus.

In-ad Presenters

In the context of creative tactics, our concern is with in-ad presenters, that is: *people or characters included in the ad to present the brand's benefit claims.* Accordingly, whereas presenter effects are always present to some degree, in-ad presenters are present to a "large" degree. That is, their characteristics are chosen purposefully and are intended to be processed along with the brand's advertising message.

People or characters in the ad may be:

1 Celebrities
2 Specially created product characters (human or animated)
3 People representing lifestyle groups
4 An anonymous presenter shown in the ad or employed as a "voice-over" in TV and radio commercials

The central concern is how these in-ad presenters' characteristics affect processing of the ad and thus influence the resulting communication effects (specifically the communication objectives) for the brand.

Hereafter, we will use the word *presenter* to refer to an in-ad presenter.

WHEN TO USE A PRESENTER

There are two advertising situations when a presenter should be considered (Table 11.1). Before examining these situations in detail, it should be emphasized that we are *not* just referring to the use of "celebrity" presenters. But more on this in the next section of the chapter.

When One or More Communication Effects Need "Boosting"

The principal way in which presenters work in advertising is by "boosting" (or amplifying, just like an amplifier in a stereo system does) particular communication effects. Personal characteristics of the presenter can serve as "amplifiers" of communication effects such as brand awareness (both types) and brand attitude (all four types) and indeed any of the five communication effects.

Any communication effect can be boosted by appropriate selection of presenter characteristics. The choice of a well-known celebrity presenter, for example, often is made with the purpose of increasing brand awareness. The boosting of brand attitude, however, has received most attention in the advertising research literature, and a couple of observations regarding presenters and brand attitude are worth making here.

Low and High Involvement Brand Attitude Strategies   Presenters are likely to achieve the most dramatic effect on brand attitude when the brand choice is low risk or low involvement. First, in advertising for low involvement brand choice, with a relatively unconcerned target audience, a presenter helps to draw *attention* to the main message point or points. And, second, the "boosting" capacity of the presenter helps to make the benefit claim(s) regarding the message point(s) *more extreme*. Extreme benefit claims, we have seen, are the recommended tactic for inducing low involvement brand choice.

Presenters also can assist in high risk or high involvement benefit claims—although the degree of boosting *required* is often considerably less than in low involvement advertising. A presenter can be used to boost an "almost-there" benefit claim up to the latitude of acceptance upper limit (high involvement/informational) or to deliberately over-claim above the upper limit (high involvement/transformational). The brand attitude difference with and without the presenter may not be as dramatic and large as in the low involvement

TABLE 11-1   WHEN TO USE A PRESENTER

1 When one or more communication effects need "boosting" above the level attainable by standard advertising. (Note that this applies to *any* communication effect and, in the case of brand attitude, to either low or high involvement brand attitudes.)

2 (High involvement brand attitude strategy). When the target audience is known to suffer "information overload" in making a brand choice.

situations,[4] but in high involvement situations, *fine-tuning* of claims is what is required, and presenters are one way of achieving this.[5]

Thus, in terms of the four brand attitude strategy quadrants, presenters can be chosen to effectively boost any type of brand attitude.

Celebrity Presenters as the Sole Benefit   In the extreme case where a brand has no other brand attitude benefits, a *celebrity* presenter can become the sole benefit (or at least the only benefit that is processed by the target audience). In this case, the "boosting" is complete: from no attitude to maximum favorable attitude.

Celebrity endorsement may be the only "attribute" that differentiates the brand from competing brands.

The celebrity-as-sole-benefit (or "because *X* uses it") phenomenon is obviously likely to be most effective when brand choice within the product category is low risk, that is, *low* involvement. The fact that Mr. Coffee coffee makers are endorsed by Joe DiMaggio, or that Fabergé products are recommended by Farah Fawcett (women's) or Joe Namath (Brut for men), or that Kellogg's Corn Flakes feature Tony the Tiger (a celebrity to children) may be sufficient reason for many people to try the brand.

However, there also is a special case where the celebrity-as-sole-benefit approach can be very effective for *high* involvement brand choice. This is the second presenter-use situation in Table 11.1, discussed next.

When "Information Overload" Affects High Involvement Brand Choice

Some high risk product categories are perceived (especially by new category users) as so complicated, either by virtue of having a very large number of important attributes, or attributes that are technically specialized and thus difficult to evaluate, that the decision maker trying to make a brand choice experiences "information overload."[6] Examples include: choice of life insurance (for almost 75 percent of consumers),[7] choosing major appliances (for about 40 percent of consumers)[8] and, we suspect, choice of many other complicated products or services.

One way to avoid information overload, which consumers typically do,[9] is to *rely on the recommendation of an expert*. Advertising can often provide the expert, by using an expert presenter. For example, Art Linkletter, a celebrity to older Americans, has been employed to sell life insurance in direct mail advertising. Similarly, a non-celebrity presenter who *looks like* an experienced insurance salesman urges people to put themselves "in the good hands" of Allstate for their car insurance needs.

Accordingly, if the manager knows that a large proportion of the target audience suffers from information overload in choosing a brand within the product category, then an expert presenter (usually a celebrity) is worth trying.

Although we have listed high involvement information overload as a separate presenter-use situation, it may be noted that the expert-fallback solution also depends on "boosting" of communication effects. The presenter, not always a celebrity but always central to the ad and drawing on perceived expertise, boosts brand awareness and, again completely from zero to maximum favorable, brand attitude. This double-boosting may cause the overloaded consumer to choose the brand as an easy but relatively safe resolution of a complex decision.

Summary of the Presenter-Use Decision

If the manager has tested a "standard" (non-presenter) advertising execution and finds that one or more communication effects fall below the level required as a communication objective, then a presenter should be considered as a potential solution. (The other two solutions—assuming the communication *strategy* is correct—are, of course, to adjust the copy or the visuals along the lines shown in Chapters 9 and 10.)

The procedure is to select a presenter, or several possible presenters, whose personal characteristics fit the communication effects to be boosted, then to devise presenter versions of the ad and test the ad or ads to see if the under-strength communication effects now meet their objectives. It is to the presenter selection process that we now turn.

THE COST AND RISKS OF CELEBRITY PRESENTERS

Celebrity presenters—famous people or characters whom the audience knows of prior to the advertising—are employed in approximately *one in three presenter* commercials on TV, that is, in about one in ten commercials overall. Whereas celebrities have some obvious advantages, there are two serious disadvantages that caution the rush to "use a celebrity." These are cost, first; and also various risks.

The Cost of Celebrity Presenters

The engagement of a celebrity presenter must be gauged against the resulting addition to production costs. The cost can be significant. Generally, the better-known the celebrity, the higher the cost. A top celebrity will cost the advertiser at least half a million dollars in contract fees. Correspondingly, lesser lights are less expensive. Examples based on reported fees in past years have included[10]:

- *$1,000,000 Category* Gregory Peck for Travelers Insurance Company; Henry Fonda for GAF film; Jack Benny for The Wool Bureau; and Steve McQueen for a motor cycle endorsement in Japan
- *$500,000 Category* John Wayne for Datril; James Coburn for Schlitz Light; Robert Blake ("Baretta") for STP
- *$250,000 Category* Shirley Jones ("The Partridge Family") for Sunbeam appliances
- *$25,000 Category* Howard Cosell for Canada Dry; Zero Mostel for Hamilton Beach irons
- *$5000 Category* Burgess Meredith and Eva Gabor for Ray-O-Vac; Don Adams and Steve Allen for local department store chains

The smaller figures, for smaller brands, and the larger figures, for larger brands, can cause a sizable reduction in the brand's available advertising budget. Non-celebrities, on the other hand, represent only a small cost. Thus, the manager must be sure that a celebrity is *needed* before committing funds to paying a presenter.

The Risks with Celebrity Presenters

As well, there are risks involved with celebrities' often-fluctuating fortunes. Examples include[11]:

- *Declining Celebrity Status* Joe Namath by 1978 had cut his endorsement fee to $50,000, half of the fee he commanded when quarterback of the New York Jets.
- *Political Activity* Anita Bryant lost her contract with the Florida Citrus Commission after taking a public stand against gay rights; Muhammed Ali, a popular presenter, was avoided during the Viet Nam war because of his pacifist views, outside the ring!
- *Sexual Indiscretion* Suzanne Sommers lost the Ace Hardware endorsement, among others, after an earlier Playboy nude sequence was discovered; Procter & Gamble dropped unknown model Marilyn Briggs' photograph from Ivory Snow ads when she later became porn-star Marilyn Chambers.

The most likely risk is declining celebrity status. When considering a celebrity presenter, the manager has to estimate the presenter's "celebrity life cycle." If possible, the celebrity should be signed during "growth" and terminated just prior to "decline." For example, how long will Michael Jackon (Pepsi-Cola) last? Some celebrities' status does seem to last forever, such as Bob Hope's. But this actually is not true, because the responsive audience ages as the celebrity does, which eventually makes the celebrity's effectiveness decline.

Semi-Celebrities Created Through Advertising

Given the cost of hiring celebrity presenters, and the risk involved with their often fragile status, many advertisers have instead sought non-celebrities with desirable personal characteristics (see VisCAP model following) and then compensated for their lack of pre-advertising visibility by the advertising exposure itself. Examples include[12]:

- Margaret Hamilton ("Cora") for Maxwell House coffee
- Jan Miner ("Madge") for Palmolive dishwashing detergent
- Jesse White ("Old Lonely") for Maytag washing machines
- Arthur O'Connell ("Mr. Goodwin") for Crest toothpaste
- Ronald McDonald for McDonald's restaurants
- Tony the Tiger for Kellogg's Corn Flakes

Generally speaking, then, it would seem advisable to try (test) a noncelebrity presenter first. If he or she is not effective enough in boosting the target communication effects, then a more expensive celebrity presenter could be considered.

HOW TO SELECT A PRESENTER USING THE VisCAP MODEL OF PRESENTER CHARACTERISTICS

Presenters should be selected in terms of personal characteristics that are aligned with the particular communication effects to be boosted in the campaign. The communication effects to be boosted will be one or more of the brand's communication *objectives* and will almost always include brand attitude and its accompanying brand attitude strategy as analyzed in the four quadrants.

A useful model for aligning presenter characteristics with communication objectives is the VisCAP model.[13] This model is based on the earlier work of Kelman[14] and McGuire[15] with the Visibility factor added along with specific adaptations for advertising.

The VisCAP model is shown in Table 11.2. It consists of four major presenter characteristics: *Vis*ibility, *C*redibility, *A*ttraction, and *P*ower. The second and third characteristics consist of two sub-factors, resulting in eight presenter characteristics in all. These are discussed shortly.

Use of the VisCAP Model   The VisCAP model can be used by managers in two ways:

1 As a "qualitative" checklist to evaluate potential presenters

TABLE 11-2   THE VisCAP MODEL OF PRESENTER CHARACTERISTICS ALIGNED WITH COMMUNICATION OBJECTIVES

Presenter characteristics	Communication objectives
1. *Visibility* (how well-known the presenter is)	Brand awareness
2. *Credibility*	
a. *Expertise* (knowledgeability regarding product category)	Informational brand attitude strategy: Low *and* high involvement
b. *Objectivity* (reputation for honesty and sincerity)	Informational brand attitude strategy: High involvement
3. *Attraction*	
a. *Likability* (attractive appearance and personality)	Transformational brand attitude strategy: Low involvement
b. *Similarity* (to target user)	Transformational brand attitude strategy: High involvement
4. *Power* (authoritative occupation or personality)	Brand purchase intention

2 In more precise quantitative rating format based on the target audience's perceptions of presenters

Qualitative[16] use of the VisCAP model by managers has considerable face validity in the sense that presenters, ideally, should have an obvious and quickly perceived "hook" to the product via the to-be-boosted communication effect. Target audience ratings of potential presenters can also be structured according to the VisCAP characteristics and can further improve presenter selection.

There are eight potential characteristics to be considered when selecting a presenter. These are now discussed, with examples.

Visibility

The presenter's visibility characteristic refers to how well-known or recognizable he or she is from previous public exposure.

Visibility is, of course, the *celebrity* presenter's immediate edge. However, non-celebrity presenters and also animated presenters (for example, The Jolly Green Giant, Charlie the Tuna, The Pillsbury Doughboy) can acquire visibility from previous advertising exposure.

The processing response linking visibility to brand awareness is, as we might expect, *attention*. The idea is that attention paid to a famous or well-known presenter will spill over to the brand. Despite the apparent logic of this process, field research evidence does not unequivocally support this idea.

Celebrity Presenters and Brand Awareness   Celebrity presenters in TV commercials should attract greater than normal attention to the brand because of their visibility advantage over lesser-known or unknown presenters. One study supports this but two don't.

The first two studies measure attention to the *advertisement*, that is, advertising recall. As such, they do not directly measure brand awareness. The research firm of Mapes & Ross, in a study of 800 commercials, found that celebrity presenters registered an average 22 percent premium in advertising recall.[17] However, Burke day-after recall norms[18] show no advantage for celebrity presenters.

The third study, actually norms published by McCollum-Spielman,[19] *does* measure brand awareness—but only brand recall, not brand recognition. McCollum-Spielman's results are equivocal: celebrity presenters are just as likely to produce below-average brand recall as above-average brand recall.

A common fear in using celebrity presenters is that *too much* attention will be paid to the celebrity. If this happens, in the extreme case the audience may not learn the brand name at all! Actresses Catherine Deneuve and Linda Day George, for example, reportedly were removed from Lincoln-Mercury ads and RCA Colortrak television ads, respectively, because eye-tracking research indicated that these beauties were drawing attention away from the brand name.[20]

The safest conclusion is that ad *testing* is required. We cannot assume that a celebrity presenter will automatically increase brand awareness.

Celebrity Presenters and Brand Attitude   Even if a celebrity presenter does not interfere with consumer learning of the brand name, he or she may interfere with processing of the remainder of the message, particularly benefit claims pertaining to brand attitude. (This doesn't matter if the presenter *is* the message, as in the aforementioned case of brands where celebrity endorsement is the sole selling point.) Most brands using a presenter do so to try to boost or amplify points made in the message. Here, a distracting presenter who causes interference with the processing of benefit claims would be a fatal problem. The solution, of course, is to pre-test the advertising to make sure the presenter doesn't "swamp" the advertising message.

Advertising research results on the persuasive (attitude increase) effectiveness of *celebrity* presenters is again mixed. The Mapes & Ross study found that *on average* celebrity presenter TV commercials were 21 percent *poorer* than all other types of commercials in producing an increase in attitude toward the advertised brand. This result seems to suggest the distraction effect. However, the McCollum-Spielman study found, again, up and down results with no average superiority for celebrity presenters.

There have been many campaigns where celebrity presenters have been tremendously successful, such as Robert Young for Sanka and James Garner for Polaroid; and others where celebrity presenters have not been able to help, such as Ricardo Montalban for Chrysler and James Coburn for Schlitz Light.

The answer to this dilemma would appear to be a thorough consideration of *how* the presenter is supposed to boost brand attitude. This we will see in the next four presenter characteristics. But first, a final word about visibility.

Visibility Hook   Going back to our recommendations on brand awareness tactics (Chapter 9), it helps to use a gimmick to link the brand to the category, and in the presenter situation, it helps if the presenter has a visibility "hook" to the brand.

An amusing example of this (for brand recall) is company president Mr. Frank Perdue as a presenter for Perdue chicken. In the words of one commentator, Mr. Perdue is "scrawny and baldish, with an egg-shaped head and a nose like a beak."[21] He looks like a chicken! Not too many advertisers have such luck.

Presenters can sometimes be *created* to have a visibility hook to the brand or the package. Examples are The Jolly Green Giant, and Tony the Tiger for Kellogg's children's cereals. In these examples, there is a visual tie-in between the characters in the ads and brand awareness (brand recognition) in the store.

Credibility: (a) Expertise

Presenter credibility consists of two characteristics, expertise and objectivity. A spokesperson can be perceived as expert but not objective, for example,

Richard Nixon; or vice versa, for example, the young George Washington when he chopped down his father's cherry tree—"Father, I cannot tell a lie."

The advertiser generally seeks both expertise and objectivity in a presenter, but the two characteristics can vary independently and have specialized relevance to communication objectives. Let's first consider expertise.

Expertise and Informational Brand Attitude   Expertise (the perceived knowledgeability of the presenter regarding the product category) is most relevant when the advertisement is based on an *informational* brand attitude strategy—either low or high involvement:

- In *low or high* involvement/informational advertisements, the presenter's perceived expertise may, as noted, be the solely effective benefit and the basis of the learned brand attitude. This occurs for high involvement specifically in the information overload decision situation.
- In *high* involvement/informational advertising in general, where acceptance of the brand attitude proposition is essential, the presenter's expertise helps to prevent counter-arguing and thereby to increase the likelihood of acceptance of claims supporting brand attitude.

Expertise Hook   An immediately evident expertise "hook" is what the advertiser seeks. The Robert Young campaign for Sanka, a presumably "healthier" form of coffee, provided an interesting example of the credibility hook. Sanka's advertising capitalized on Robert Young's then well-known TV program role as "Dr. Marcus Welby," and although real doctors cannot endorse products, make-believe doctors can.

Another example was actress Patricia Neal's endorsement of Anacin. Ms. Neal suffered and recovered from a stroke, so her perceived expertise about pain relievers probably rated very highly with the target audience.

The advertiser must *be sure that the presenter's expertise will indeed be perceived by the target audience* in processing the ad. Younger analgesic users, for example, may not have heard about or not remembered Ms. Neal's ordeal. Of course, younger users may not have been a major proportion of the brand's probably older target audience. Advertisers sometimes attempt to "patch up" the expertise hook by inserting extra copy telling people what the presenter is expert in. This is a poor solution. The presenter's expertise hook should be perceived immediately, otherwise you haven't got the right presenter.

Credibility: (b) Objectivity

The other component of credibility is objectivity (the presenter's reputation for honesty and sincerity). Some theorists refer to objectivity as trustworthiness. However, trustworthiness would seem to imply a degree of expertise (as in "trustworthy source") so objectivity is the preferred and more separable characteristic.

Objectivity and High Involvement/Informational Brand Attitude   Objectivity is most relevant for the *high* involvement/informational brand attitude strategy quadrant because the brand attitude benefits must be *convincingly* presented. It is much less relevant for the low involvement/informational quadrant because, here, the brand attitude merely has to be rote-learned, not fully accepted prior to trial of the brand. This does *not* mean that low involvement/informational presenters should look dishonest (although some do) but rather that they don't have to be highly positive on the objectivity characteristic.

Objectivity Hook: Natural or Stage-Managed   Some celebrity presenters have a "hook-like" reputation for honesty and sincerity. The signing of James Stewart for Firestone tires is regarded in advertising circles as a contract coup second only to the as yet unsigned Walter Cronkite.

However, objectivity is a personality characteristic that can easily be found in non-celebrity presenters and can fairly easily be *stage-managed* during commercial production. Objectivity is partly a function of eye movements and facial cues and very strongly a function of *voice* cues.[22]

Voice Cues   Voice cues are one reason why male voices are used as "voice-overs" in nearly 80 percent of TV commercials, even when the other characters are women.[23] Not only do male voices tend to attract greater attention than female voices, they are also, in general, perceived as less nervous, less emotional, and more logical—all traits that should increase perceived objectivity.[24] Clearly, for broadcast commercials, managers not only must evaluate the presenter visually but also must test the voice.

Legal Requirements and Objectivity   A question often occurring in the public's mind relating to objectivity is the issue of whether presenters must, in fact, be *users* of the products they endorse. Cohen[25] provides a good summary of the Federal Trade Commission's guidelines in this regard. The following two are of most frequent concern:

Generally, if a *special presenter* advertisement implies that the presenter uses the brand, then he or she must in fact use it. For example, in Ogilvy & Mather's "Do you know me" campaign for American Express, the agency would only sign personalities who had been cardholders for a year or more. Moreover, the advertiser may be required to check "at reasonable intervals" to ensure that the spokesperson continues to be a user if the campaign is continued.

Also, advertisers are required to disclose any financial connection that a presenter may have with the brand or company if this is not evident. For presenter Frank Borman, president of Eastern Airlines, for instance, the financial connection would be evident.

On the other hand, *consumers-as-presenters* represent an interesting case. Consumers who deliver testimonials implying that they are experienced users really must have a factual usage history. However, consumers interviewed as unwitting and random participants in "hidden camera" tests need not be bona fide users other than in the test. Advertisers can be selective about which interview test results to use in the advertising, although they must be able to substantiate that the average consumer can expect comparable performance from the brand.

There are many other legal issues surrounding the use of presenters, and these aren't always as rule-bound as the above cases. For example, the use of "look-alikes" for living celebrities is sometimes fought by suit and won (for example, Lady Diana, Barbra Streisand), yet is allowed in other circumstances (for example, the Joe Namath look-alike who appeared with Joe in Shaefer beer advertising). Deceased celebrity characters also are a legal quagmire. For example, the estate of Groucho Marx has successfully prevented unauthorized use of the "Groucho" character, whereas Bela Lugosi's estate lost entitlement to the "Dracula" character because Lugosi himself had not exploited this persona outside films.[26]

In general, it seems that consumers are reasonably well-protected against unobjective presenter testimonials in ads. In fact, the self-regulatory and FTC guidelines are probably stricter than most of the public realizes. And, even allowing for a normal degree of consumer skepticism about endorsements in ads, the critical factor is probably the perceived *emotional* sincerity of the presentation itself, underlining the importance of correct emotional portrayal in advertising.

Attraction: (a) Likability

Presenter attraction consists of two characteristics, likability and similarity. These can be independent characteristics. For instance, Charlie the Tuna is likable but not similar to the target audience; whereas "Mrs. Olson," for Folgers' coffee, may be similar but not necessarily likable. When presenters are chosen to be both likable *and* similar, the similarity is to the target audience's self-image, a consideration we will discuss in the section on similarity. Let's first consider likability.

Likability and Low Involvement/Transformational Brand Attitude   Likability (an attractive physical appearance and personality) is most relevant to *transformational* brand attitudes, particularly in the *low* involvement/transformational quadrant. This is because the presenter's likability serves as a positive stimulus that contributes to the positive motivation's portrayal, as explained in the tactics for low involvement/transformational advertising earlier.

Likability is a general personality trait, so it is not really appropriate to speak of a likability "hook" to a specific product or brand. However, the physical attractiveness aspect of likability can be a perceived *expertise* "hook" when used to advertise physical appearance products; for example, Farah Fawcett for Fabergé cosmetics. In the general case, however, likability refers in an uncomplicated way to the use of attractive and popular people as presenters in ads.

Several celebrities rate very highly on the likability factor. For TV personalities, Marketing Evaluations, Inc., of Port Washington, New York, conducts a "Performer Q" survey of performer popularity amongst viewers.[27] Among the high scorers in recent years are:

- Michael Landon for Kodak
- Bill Cosby for Jello-O and Coca-Cola
- James Garner for Polaroid
- Bob Hope for Texaco

As an illustration of the point that likability is not confined to celebrities, we may note that in the now-classic TV campaign for Polaroid One-Step instant cameras, Jim Garner's co-presenter, Mariette Hartley, also rated extremely high on likability. Her appearance in the Polaroid commercials reportedly saw her acting career soar.

A feature of Performer Q, although we don't mean to advocate any particular rating service, is that the likability score is based simultaneously on the visibility factor. The quotient, Q, reflects the performer's popularity among those viewers who *recognize* the performer. Accordingly, performers such as Gilda Radner and Helen Hayes achieve high Q scores because, although they are not very widely recognized, those viewers who do recognize them really like them. This knowledge can be very useful when appealing to particular target audiences and can save on the cost of a bigger name celebrity.

Attraction: (b) Similarity

The other component of attraction is similarity (of the presenter, to the target user). We couldn't resist the send-up of this, in Figure 11.1, but similarity is a very serious consideration.

Similarity and High Involvement/Transformational Brand Attitude Similarity to the target user is most relevant in *high* involvement/transformational advertising. The reason is again as stated in the creative tactics for this brand attitude strategy quadrant earlier: The target audience must *identify* with the emotional portrayal in the ad, and this is enhanced by showing people in the ad whose lifestyles are similar to those of target audience members.

Similarity Hook As applied to presenters, the similarity "hook" occurs when the target audience can not only identify with the lifestyle of the presenter but, more specifically, can empathize readily with the presenter's user status. User-status similarity often *modifies* the *expertise* factor (and thus applies to informational advertising as well). For example, Jim Garner probably is identified-with easily for Polaroid One-Step cameras precisely because he is *not* an expert on cameras but rather is similar to the amateur user seeking the problem avoidance that these cameras offer.

In another example, Brock[28] found that paint salesmen presenting themselves as typical painters sold more paint than salesmen who presented themselves as experienced painters, an apparent case of similarity modifying expertise.

"I'm just an ordinary person."

FIGURE 11.1   The similarity characteristic in presenter attraction: an ideal selection! (Drawing by Richter; copyright 1981, The New Yorker Magazine, Inc.)

Similarity and the Target User's Self-image   For a time in the 1970s there was a creative trend toward "real-life" portrayals in advertising. We saw real beer drinkers with pot-bellies and T-shirts and real housewives with their hair in curlers. Lately we have seen a return to somewhat more trim-looking and better-dressed beer drinkers as well as the more "Hollywood" type of homemaker of the 1950s.

Which presenter approach is correct: similarity to the target user's *real* self-image or similarity to the target audience's *ideal* self-image? This would seem to depend on which transformational quadrant the presenter is selected for—low involvement or high involvement.

In *low* involvement/transformational advertising, likability, not similarity, is paramount. Similarity, in this case, can be thought of as an extension of likability. You should choose a presenter who is similar to the target user's *ideal* self-image. Cosmetics advertising would be a good example.

In *high* involvement/transformational advertising, the reverse is true: Similarity is more important than likability because the target user must *identify* with the brand user as portrayed in the advertising. However, the purpose is still to *transform* the target user's self-image. Thus, some "aspirational" increase toward a more ideal self-image must be shown. The recommendation for high involvement/transformational presenters would therefore be a *little bit above the real* self-image: "Similar, but a little better." Luxury car advertising would be an example.

Power

The power characteristic of presenters (an authoritative occupation or personality) is the eighth and final characteristic in VisCAP. Power can increase brand purchase intention, though not attitude, by appearing to command the audience to act. It is only occasionally relevant in advertising.

Power and Problem Avoidance Motivation   Power is relevant for products or services sold via an element of "fear appeal" (a type of problem avoidance motivation). These *may* include pharmaceutical or medicinal products, insurance, some financial services, and, of course, public safety campaigns.

The occupational "hook" to power in a presenter may be seen in Robert Young's campaign for Sanka (doctor) and Karl Malden's campaign for American Express Traveller's Checks (policeman-detective from "The Streets of San Francisco").

The personality "hook" to power may also be present with Karl Malden, as well as in the late David Janssen's campaign for Excedrin. Both actors have an authoritative appearance and voice. Public safety campaigns, too, typically select authoritative personalities as presenters or voice-overs.

If the motivation for action has some basis in fear, then a powerful presenter is appropriate.

VisCAP Profile Evaluation

The VisCAP model of presenter characteristics therefore provides a *profile* of eight characteristics—in terms of which a potential presenter may be negative, neutral, or positive.

The presenter's characteristics should be aligned with the particular communication effects that need "boosting." When the communication objective is brand attitude (which it nearly always is, following brand awareness), the alignment must further fit the brand attitude strategy quadrant.

In terms of the overall profile, the presenter must be *positive* on those characteristics relevant to the to-be-boosted communication effects and *not negative* on the other communication effects. By "not negative," we mean that neutral is satisfactory, and that positive is fine too, even though these other effects don't need boosting. It is fatal, of course, for a presenter to be neutral or negative on a target communication objective that needs boosting, or to be negative on a communication objective that attained its objective satisfactorily prior to insertion of the presenter.

SUMMARY

A presenter with special characteristics should be considered in advertising only when particular communication effects require a "boost," depending on the communication objectives of the campaign. If any of the brand's communication effects—brand awareness, brand attitude, and brand purchase intention—are suspected to be below the maximum attainable for the target audience using a "straight" ad, then the manager should try a presenter with the aim of amplifying these effects.

A presenter is one creative technique for making low involvement brand attitude benefit claims more extreme. Sometimes, the presenter's endorsement is the *sole* benefit. This approach can be used in low involvement brand choice, and also in high involvement brand choice in product categories where a majority of decision makers suffer "information overload."

Presenters must be chosen very carefully so that their characteristics are aligned with the particular communication effects to be boosted. A useful model to help managers in making this selection is our VisCAP model. Although we discussed the eight presenter characteristics in this model as separate presenter dimensions, the manager should seek a presenter who offers a *profile* of characteristics that has positive "hooks" to the targeted (to-be-boosted) communication objectives and is not negative on the others.

The VisCAP model provides a useful "desk-top" procedure for evaluating potential presenters. More elaborately, it can be used to make presenter evaluations with greater reliability by conducting a survey in which a sample of the target audience rates presenters—in conjunction with the brand—on the VisCAP factors.

Finally, we saw that celebrity presenters are not necessarily the best choice. They may add significantly to production costs and also may have fragile viability due to career downturns. The main advantage of celebrity presenters is their immediate visibility, which is relevant to brand awareness; however, the manager must be sure that attention paid to the celebrity does not inadvertently detract from brand awareness nor from other relevant communication objectives.

The manager should test a non-presenter version of the advertisement first. Then, if boosting is required, a non-celebrity presenter (with the correct characteristics) should be tested next. If the regular presenter is insufficient to attain the communication objectives, then a celebrity presenter may be considered. Alternatively, boosting can be pursued by strengthening the advertisement's brand awareness stimuli or brand attitude benefit claims visually or verbally, without using a presenter.

NOTES

1 An incidence of 36 percent of TV commercials using an on-camera spokesperson in a major role was reported in a 1974 survey by A. Bellaire, *Advertising Age,* December 30, 1974, 17–18. Everyday observation suggests that a figure of more

than one in three is still currently correct. This makes presenters the most common "creative technique" in TV advertising. Although no figures are readily available, radio advertising would appear to use special presenters in a major role with a similar incidence to TV advertising. Print ads seem to use presenters less often; although in magazine advertisements, special models would appear in about one in four ads, by rough estimate.

2 R.G. Haas, Effects of source characteristics on cognitive responses and persuasion, in R.E. Petty, T.C. Brock, and T.M. Ostrom (Eds.), *Cognitive Responses in Persuasion,* Hillsdale, NJ: Lawrence Erlbaum Associates, 1981, pp. 141–172.

3 L. Percy and J.R. Rossiter, *Advertising Strategy: A Communication Theory Approach,* New York: Praeger, 1980, chap. 3.

4 Most recently, see the discussion and experiment by R.E. Petty, J. T. Cacioppo, and D. Schumann, Central and peripheral routes to persuasion: the moderating role of involvement, *Journal of Consumer Research,* 1983, *10*(2), 135–146.

5 Presenters are one way of boosting a benefit claim. Two other major ways are: *psycholinguistics*—especially for *informational* benefit claims; and *visual imagery*—especially for *transformational* benefit claims. See Chapter 8's references to our recent research for more detail on these advanced creative techniques.

6 The concept of "information overload" was introduced in marketing by Professor Jacob Jacoby who, with colleagues, conducted a long series of investigations of the phenomenon. See the article in note 9 for references.

7 R.A. Formisano, R.W. Olshavsky, and S. Tapp, Choice strategy in a difficult task environment, *Journal of Consumer Research,* 1982, *8*(4), 474–479.

8 Relevant studies are summarized in a provocative article by R.W. Olshavsky and D.H. Granbois, Consumer decision making—fact or fiction?, *Journal of Consumer Research,* 1979, *6*(2), 93–100.

9 J. Jacoby, Perspectives on information overload, *Journal of Consumer Research,* 1984, *10*(4), 432–435.

10 Compiled from J. Emmerling, Want a celebrity in your ad? O.k., but watch your step, *Advertising Age,* September 1, 1976, pp. 63–64; and E. Cohn, Take a million dollars—please!, *TV Guide,* June 24, 1978, pp. 30–32.

11 Described in J. Cooney, Celebrities brighten more ad campaigns—and darken a few, *The Wall Street Journal,* August 15, 1978, no. 1, p. 41; and B. Abrams, When ads feature celebrities, advertisers cross their fingers, *The Wall Street Journal,* December 4, 1980, p. 33.

12 The actual names, which few people know, of these semi-celebrities created through advertising were given in an article by L. Raddatz, Buy!, *TV Guide,* July 9, 1977, pp. 9–12.

13 The VisCAP model was first presented in L. Percy and J.R. Rossiter, *Advertising Strategy: A Communication Theory Approach,* New York: Praeger, 1980, chap. 3.

14 H.C. Kelman, Compliance, identification, and internalization: three processes of opinion change, *Journal of Conflict Resolution,* 1958, *2*, 51–60.

15 W.J. McGuire, The nature of attitudes and attitude change, in G. Lindzey and E. Aronson (Eds.), *The Handbook of Social Psychology,* Vol. 3, Reading, MA: Addison-Wesley, 1969, pp. 136–314.

16 "Qualitative" here refers to "yes-no" checklist use of the model (which is really zero-one quantitative use) or simply to identifying the relevant presenter dimensions as bases for discussion.

17 Mapes & Ross' results are cited in D. Ogilvy and J. Raphaelson, Research on advertising techniques that work—and don't work, *Harvard Business Review,* 1982,

60, 14–15, 18. The first author, David Ogilvy, is the famous author and agency head. It is rather interesting that he cites this research because, as he notes, it counts against the use of celebrities: they tend to increase advertising recall but decrease (or not increase) brand attitude—thus damning them because of a distraction effect. Ogilvy & Mather is noted for its frequent use of celebrities.

18 Burke Marketing Research, Inc., *The Effect of Environmental and Executional Variables on Overall Memorability Using the Television Day-After Recall Technique,* Cincinnati, OH: Burke Marketing Research, Inc., 1979.

19 McCollum-Spielman & Company, Inc., Starpower: will the force be with you?, *Topline,* 1980, *2*(3), 1–8.

20 Results from Telcom's eye-tracking technique. Reported in B. Whalen, Eye-tracking technology to replace day-after-recall by '84, *Marketing News,* November 27, 1981, pp. 18, 20.

21 D. Kowet, It helps if you look like a chicken, *TV Guide,* February 21, 1981, 20–23. Quote is from p. 20.

22 M. Zuckerman, M.D. Amidon, S.E. Bishop, and S.D. Pomerantz, Face and tone of voice in the communication of deception, *Journal of Personality and Social Psychology,* 1982, *43*(2), 347–357.

23 *TV Guide,* June 20, 1981, p. A-21, citing statistics provided by the American Federation of Television and Radio Artists and Screen Actors Guild.

24 J. Robinson and L.Z. McArthur, Impact of salient vocal qualities on causal attribution for a speaker's behavior, *Journal of Personality and Social Psychology,* 1982, *43*(2) 236–247.

25 D. Cohen, In re final guides concerning endorsements and testimonials in advertising, *Journal of Marketing* (Legal Developments in Marketing section), 1980, *44*(4), 95.

26 S.A. Diamond, A matter of survival, *Advertising Age,* December 28, 1981, p. 20.

27 See K. Stabiner, Willie Stargell, you're hot; Shelley Hack, you're not, *TV Guide,* March 1, 1980, pp. 14–18; and *TV Guide,* July 15, 1978, p. A-14.

28 T.C. Brock, Communicator-recipient similarity and decision change, *Journal of Personality and Social Psychology,* 1965, *1*(10), 650–654.

DISCUSSION QUESTIONS

11.1 What *is* a presenter, as defined in this chapter? When should an advertiser consider using a presenter? What alternatives are there to using a presenter?

11.2 Discuss the pros and cons of using celebrity presenters.

11.3 After first listing the likely communication objectives (including the brand attitude strategy or quadrant) for each of the brands below, conduct your own VisCAP profile ratings of the respective presenters, discussing their appropriateness in each case:

   a Robert Morley for British Airways

   b Ali McGraw for Lux beauty soap

   c Michael Jackson for Pepsi-Cola

   d The Pillsbury Doughboy

   e The typical on-camera presenter and setting in the "charts and facts" type of pain reliever commercial

   f The voice-over presenter in Kraft mayonnaise commercials

FURTHER READING

Percy, L., and Rossiter, J.R. *Advertising Strategy: A Communication Theory Approach.* New York: Praeger, 1980, chap. 3.

Whereas in the present book we focus on in-ad presenters, this earlier book discusses presenter characteristics from the broader perspective of the perceived sender of the advertising communication. Provides more detail on the processes underlying credibility, attraction, and power. Also shows an application of the VisCAP model.

We wish there were more outside readings on presenter effects with direct application to advertising. However, most previous research on presenters has a narrow focus (usually on credibility, sometimes on attraction) and fails to consider the particular communication objectives for which the presenter is sought.

PART **SIX**

PROMOTION STRATEGY

CHAPTER **12**

PROMOTION'S ACTION AND COMMUNICATION OBJECTIVES

Promotion (sales promotion) consists of a repertoire of techniques designed to "move sales forward" more rapidly than would otherwise occur. In this introductory chapter to Part Six, we examine the three major ways in which promotion is used to move the brand more rapidly through the marketing channel and thus speed sales: trade promotion, retail promotion, and consumer promotion.

Throughout, we emphasize promotion's target audience action objectives (step 4) and the communication objectives (step 3) through which promotion causes sales to be accelerated.

After reading this chapter you should:

• Understand how trade promotion, retail promotion, and consumer promotion are used in the marketing channel
• Distinguish the target audiences and action objectives for promotions initiated by manufacturers (trade promotion, consumer promotion) and by retailers (retail promotion)
• See how promotions (like advertisements) work through the five communication effects

TARGET AUDIENCES AND ACTION OBJECTIVES FOR PROMOTIONS

Initiators and Audiences for Promotions

As was mentioned in Chapter 1, there are two main initiators of promotions: manufacturers and retailers (Figure 12.1). And altogether, there are three general audiences for promotion: (1) the salesforce, (2) distributors, and (3)

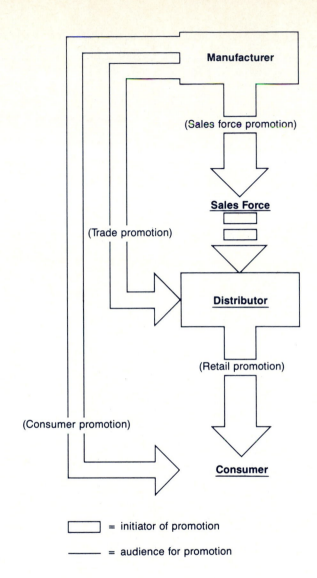

FIGURE 12.1   Initiators and audiences
for promotion.

consumers. Manufacturers promote to all three audiences. Retailers promote
mainly to consumers.

Salesforce Promotion   Promotions by manufacturers to the salesforce include techniques such as motivational meetings, training programs, selling
aids, and monetary and non-monetary incentive plans to spur sales. Salesforce
promotions usually are planned and administered by the company's sales
manager rather than the advertising manager and, therefore, will not be
considered in this book. Salesforce promotions are more fittingly covered in
sales management texts.

Trade Promotion Promotions by manufacturers to their distributors are known as *trade* promotions. Manufacturers spend more on promotions to the trade than they spend on promotions to consumers. The largest U.S. manufacturers spend their overall advertising and promotion budget in approximately the following way[1]:

Advertising (to consumers)	40%
Trade promotion	35
Consumer promotion	25
	100%

Trade promotion takes precedence over consumer promotion because the brand first must gain and hold distribution before consumers can buy it. For most manufacturers, trade promotion has become one of the necessary costs of doing business. They must offer distributors inducements to carry the brand because competitors are doing likewise.

Trade promotions mostly consist of *trade discounts* offered to carry and display products (which includes the provision of point-of-purchase displays and other selling aids) and cash payments or contributions for retail *cooperative advertising*. Trade discounts are similar in principle to consumer discounts and are managed by the manufacturer. Cooperative advertising, however, is primarily a retailer-managed form of promotion. We will examine this in our more detailed section on retail promotion later in the chapter.

Retail Promotion Promotions initiated by distributors (usually retailers) to consumers are known as retail promotions. Most often these take the form of price-offs and special displays—again initiated and offered by the retailer. In most product categories, retail promotions are quite independent of promotions that the manufacturer, also, is aiming at consumers. As we shall see, this can lead to a conflict of promotional objectives between manufacturers and retailers.[2]

Consumer Promotions Promotions initiated by manufacturers direct to consumers (managerially bypassing the retailer even though the consumer may receive the offer in retail outlets) are known as consumer promotions. Again, we use the term "consumers" broadly, to include all *end-customers for both industrial and consumer products*. Consumer promotions are incentives aimed, by the manufacturer, at the final customer to encourage trial or usage of the product.

Manufacturers use 10 basic types of consumer promotions: sampling, coupons, trade coupons, refunds and rebates, price-offs, bonus packs, in/on packs, premiums, contests and sweepstakes, and continuity programs. There are many executional variations of these 10 basic consumer promotions for specialized purposes as explained in Chapters 13 and 14.

Trial and Usage Action Objectives

All promotions are aimed at gaining either trial or usage. Trial and usage are the behavioral action objectives of promotion. As shown in Table 12.1, the target audiences for trial and usage differ for the three types of promotion.

For *trade* promotion, the target audience for trial is new stores or outlets, and the target audience for usage is present stores or outlets. Trial in this context means to induce the store to carry the brand. Usage means to induce the distributor to re-order the brand and also to give it favorable display via shelf space and position.

For *retail* promotion, the target audience for trial is new customers to be attracted to the store, and the target audience for usage is present customers to be induced to visit the store more often. As we shall see in this chapter's section on retail promotion, retailers also have a special overriding objective, which is to transfer inventory holding costs as much as possible to consumers.

For *consumer* promotion, the several potential target audiences for trial are new category users, other-brand switchers (who are not buying our brand), and other-brand loyals; and the potential target audiences for usage are brand loyals and favorable brand switchers (who buy our brand among others).

We should emphasize here that advertising and promotion often have different target audiences. For instance, a brand's advertising may be aimed at new category users, whereas its promotion may be aimed at consumers who are already loyal to the brand. Target audience selection reflects various prospect groups' leverage to advertising and to promotion, respectively, and the target audiences for advertising and promotion may differ.

In the next two sections of the chapter, we will consider trade promotion and retail promotion in more detail, drawing managerial conclusions from the marketer's perspective. In the final section of the chapter, we turn our attention

TABLE 12-1　ACTION OBJECTIVES AND TARGET AUDIENCES FOR PROMOTION

	Trial	Usage
Trade promotion	New stores: • Carry brand	Present stores: • Re-order • Display
Retail promotion	New customers: • Try store	Present customers: • Visit store more often
Consumer promotion	New buyers: • New category users • Other-brand switchers • Other-brand loyals	Present buyers: • Brand loyals • Favorable brand switchers

to consumer promotion. The manager has to plan the communication objectives and promotion strategy for consumer promotion with much more precision than with the two prior types of promotion, so our analysis of consumer promotion will continue in the succeeding chapters.

TRADE PROMOTION

Trade Promotion Action Objectives

Trade promotion is designed to get distribution for new products (which for distributors is the equivalent of *trial*) and, for all products, to obtain favorable shelf position and special display (which are equivalent to *usage*, although here it is the distributor who is "using" the product, rather than the consumer). As discussed in Chapter 4, and shown in Table 4.2, usage encompasses the more specific buyer behavior objectives of repeat purchase, where the action objective for manufacturers is to keep the distributor re-ordering the product; and brand switching, which is repeat purchase viewed from a competitive standpoint, in that the action objective is to have distributors carry the manufacturer's products while reducing or dropping distribution of competitive products.

Target Audiences for Trade Promotion

Trial Promotions   Target audience considerations in trade promotions emerge most strongly in the distribution of new products, where the distributor is deciding on trial of the product. In this case the potential target audiences are different wholesale or retail outlets—more precisely the buying groups[3] or individual managers responsible for new product acquisition decisions for these outlets.

Distributors can be arrayed—just as in the consumer analogy—in terms of their "brand loyalty" toward the manufacturer. As discussed in Chapters 4 and 5, brand loyalty involves not just behavior but an *initial attitude* toward the manufacturer. Montgomery[4] has shown that trade promotion strategy is linked vitally to the distributor's initial attitude toward the manufacturer. Montgomery's study focused on new product distribution (distributor trial) in supermarkets.

If the manufacturer is regarded by the supermarket decision maker as *one of the top four or five companies* (strongly positive attitude), then the path for new product acceptance is relatively easy (Figure 12.2). A significant new product from a leading manufacturer is accepted without any promotional support. A "me-too" new product or a line extension product from the same manufacturer would require promotional support to consumers in the form of sampling or couponing.

Contrast the position of a manufacturer regarded by the supermarket decision maker as *just an average or somewhat above-average company,* but not one of the top four or five. These average companies (slightly positive attitude)

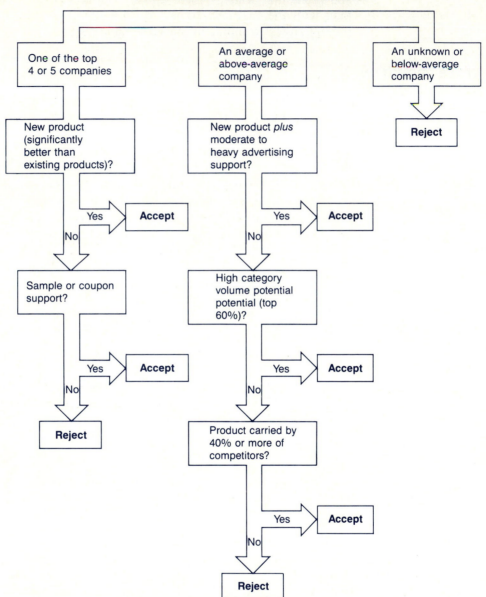

FIGURE 12.2 Trade promotion effectiveness depends on the distributor target audience. (*Source:* Adapted from D.B. Montgomery, New product distribution: an analysis of supermarket buyer decisions, *Journal of Marketing Research,* 1978, *12*(3), 255–264, by permission.)

have to guarantee advertising support, even for a decidedly new product, and to pass one and possibly two more barriers if the product is not relatively new for its category.

A manufacturer regarded by the supermarket decision maker as an *unknown or below-average company* (neutral or negative attitude) faces a complete barrier. Lack of a positive attitude toward the supplier brings immediate rejection. Trade promotion, within normal limits, cannot ''buy'' distribution for manufacturers whose retail target audience holds a negative attitude.

The specific findings of the Montgomery study which, by the way, exhibited a 93 percent success rate in explaining the adoption or rejection of new products in supermarkets, should not be generalized to other types of products or other types of distributors. Nevertheless, two principles are clear:

1 Attitudinal target audiences for trade promotions exist just as they do in the consumer market.
2 Distinctly different promotional strategies are required to successfully appeal to the different target audiences.

Trade Advertising   Trade trial promotions usually are packaged with trade advertising to inform distributors about the new product. A concerted effort must be made to determine what information will best help the distributor to accept the product and to sell the product. There are two extremes here, representing a continuum on which trade advertising should vary.

One extreme is represented by *self-service retailers* such as supermarkets and mass merchandisers. They do not want the sort of information about product benefits that appears in consumer advertising (although samples of consumer ads should be appended in the package). Trade ads to self-service retailers should emphasize *acceptance* details such as margin, expected turnover, shelf space required, and manufacturer support services.

The other extreme is represented by *personal-service retailers,* such as gourmet stores, boutiques, the better department stores, and appliance and hardware stores. They want lots of product information in trade ads to help their sales staff to *sell* the product. Trade ads to these stores should contain more than the average consumer would want to know, arranged in a sales-education-kit format to make the store manager's training task easier.

Trade advertising should be based on careful research among distributors just as consumer advertising is based on careful consumer research. The trade are customers, too: They're the first and vital customers in the distribution channel, without whom the product can never reach the second level of customers—consumers. Good trade advertising is an essential component of trade trial promotions.

Usage Promotions   Following trade trial of the new product by distributors, if the product does not sell as well or as profitably as the distributor expects, then additional trade promotion incentives will be required to keep the product in distribution. These incentives are trade usage promotions.

Little research exists on trade usage promotions in relation to distributor target audiences. But it is safe to say that manufacturer or supplier loyalty is again a major strategic factor. If a manufacturer has gained loyalty with a distributor, either through other products that the manufacturer also places with that distributor or through the many aspects of service and interpersonal relationships that characterize the channel network, then the manufacturer has more leverage for obtaining continued stocking (trade usage) of a less than successful product.

If, on the other hand, the relationship is typified as one of distributor disloyalty (seen especially in the powerful retailer control exhibited in European countries and in some industries in the United States) or distributor "other-brand" loyalty (as for the many smaller manufacturers trying to compete with the P & G's or Lever Brothers of this world), then trade usage promotion may have to approach outright bribery to keep a less than successful product on the shelf.

Nor is it usually sufficient just to keep a product on the shelf. Manufacturers employ trade usage promotions to obtain favorable *shelf space*. Shelf space, in most retail outlets, means as many facings of the brand as possible (horizontally) and the best shelf height to catch the shopper's eye (vertically).

The advantage of broad horizontal facings is the increased attention gained as the shopper walks past the display. The advantage of eye-level positioning is shown in an extensive experiment by *Progressive Grocer* magazine in

FIGURE 12.3 Sales effects of shelf height in supermarkets. (*Source:* Adapted from a privately conducted study by *Progressive Grocer* and A & P Supermarkets, ca. 1982, by permission.)

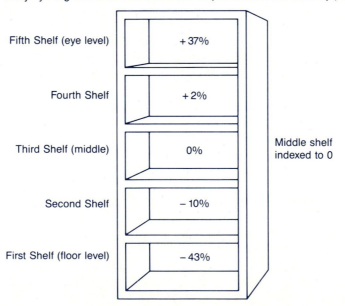

conjunction with A & P supermarkets (Figure 12.3).[5] In the extreme case, shifting a brand from the top (eye-level) shelf to the bottom shelf results, on average, in approximately an 80 percent decrease in sales. It should be noted that these results apply to adult shoppers. Children's eye-level position (for example, for children's cereals and snacks) would be on lower shelves.

Trade usage promotions, quite naturally, are most effective when timed to accompany promotions to consumers.[6] If the distributor knows that consumer demand for the promoted item is likely to increase, *special display* is more likely to be given. Special displays can take the form of end-of-aisle bins, in-store signs, and so forth. Also, the manufacturer may be able to effectively offer less discount to the trade if distributors know that consumers will want the item.

Summary of Trade Promotion   Trade promotions have to be planned with the target audience distributor in mind. The main techniques of trade promotion are trade allowances (discounts) and cooperative advertising allowances (the percentage that the manufacturer contributes toward the distributor's advertising).

However, as Montgomery's study has shown, the manufacturer additionally may have to convince the trade that there is a sufficient program of *consumer* promotion supporting the brand. There are no firm generalities about the types of trade or consumer promotions that best satisfy distributors, except to say that the less the loyalty, the larger the financial guarantee will have to be. The mix of these techniques is something to be negotiated with particular distributors.

RETAIL PROMOTION

Retail promotion refers to promotions that are largely *controlled by the distributor* rather than by the manufacturer. The distributor may be actually passing on a manufacturer's requested promotion, or the promotion may be entirely initiated and paid for by the distributor. Most often, the channel members involved in these promotions are retailers, such as large grocery chains or department stores, rather than wholesalers (although the trend toward "warehouse outlets" selling direct to consumers is changing this picture somewhat), and hence the term *retail promotion* is usually given to this form of promotional activity.

Retailers' Action Objectives

Manufacturers and retailers both promote directly to consumers. However, whereas manufacturers' action objectives for the consumer are centered on the *brand,* retailers' action objectives for the consumer are centered on the *store.* The retailer pursues the *purchase-related* objective of getting people into the store rather than the purchase objective of buying a particular brand.

Retailers' action objectives therefore do not coincide with those of manufacturers. The potential conflict in action objectives is as follows:[7]

Retailer: My store . . . . to buy anything
Manufacturer: Any store . . . . to buy my brand

Retail Target Audiences

The retailer generates a sales base from *store-loyal* customers. For retailers, the store *is* the "brand."

Indeed, the target audience concepts of brand loyals, brand switchers, and other-brand loyals translate, for the retailer, into store loyals, store switchers, and other-store loyals; the fourth target audience concept, new category users, is appropriately named already, where the new category consists not of a product category but a store category that is new to the potential buyer, such as, for example, warehouse outlets for clothing, health food stores, or retail computer stores. The more specific prospect sub-group target audience framework of Chapter 4, too, is easily recast from the retailer's perspective into store target audiences instead of brand target audiences.

Evidence that retail promotions work on store audiences differentiated by loyalty in the target audience sense comes from a large-scale study by the Nielsen organization.[8] Although the study is confined to supermarkets, which are only one type of retail outlet, it illustrates the idea of promotional target audiences nicely. Nielsen tracked the purchase patterns of households known to conduct nearly all (average 90 percent), just over half (average 60 percent), or a relatively small proportion (average 25 percent) of their supermarket shopping at a particular store. Purchases at the store by each type of household were measured before and during 15 retail promotions. The promotions averaged about one-fifth off the usual price across a range of product types. The results are shown in Table 12.2.

Retail promotions have their largest effect on low-loyalty customers (prob-

TABLE 12-2   EFFECT OF RETAIL PROMOTION ON TARGET AUDIENCES FOR SUPERMARKETS

Target audience	Draw index[†] (base = 100)
High loyalty: 90% of purchases at this store	1320
Moderate loyalty: 60% of purchases at this store	1360
Low loyalty: 25% of purchases at this store	2700

Source: Adapted from P. M. Schmitt, Store loyalty: does it affect buying patterns? *The Nielsen Researcher,* 1980, No. 2, 18–23, by permission.

[†]Draw index $= \dfrac{\text{households buying during promotion}}{\text{households buying before promotion}} \times 100$

ably experimental store switchers and other-store loyals). While the heavy promotions caused more than a 10-fold increase in sales overall, the increase among low-loyals was over 20-fold. There was much less *relative* effect of the promotion among moderate-loyals (probably routinized favorable store switchers and multi-store loyals between this and one or two other stores) and among high-loyals (mainly single-store loyals) who shop most often at that store.

An interesting aspect of these results that can easily be overlooked by concentrating on the relative effects is the massive *absolute* effect (at least a 10-fold increase in repeat purchase rate) that occurs among customers who would have bought the brand at that store anyway and who simply stepped up their purchase *timing* during the promotion. Purchase timing is very important to retailers. Through promotion, retailers manipulate purchase timing to suit their own ends rather than those of the manufacturer, as explained next.

Inventory Transfer: The Overriding Objective for Retailers

Blattberg, Eppen and Lieberman[9] have shown, through a detailed analysis of consumer panel purchases in relation to retail promotions, that the overriding promotional action objective for retailers is not so much to attract customers from other stores (which can lead to price wars to the detriment of all retailers) nor even to satisfy manufacturers' plans for promotion through retail outlets (about which more later). Rather, the action objective that accounts for over half of retail promotions is to *transfer inventory holding costs to the consumer*. When consumers are induced to stockpile products, this keeps shelf space available for new products, increases turnover relative to other stores, and maximizes the retailer's profit. To move stock from their inventory to the consumer's home inventory, retailers will tend to select any brand for promotion, at times which suit their stock-clearing needs.

Blattberg et al.'s panel data give strong support to this "inventory adjustment" explanation of retailer promotions. The actual effects of retail price deals (the primary and quickest form of retailer-initiated promotion) differ from the "textbook" effects of retail promotion as planned by manufacturers. For example:

- Deals are supposed to be a main avenue for launching new brands; yet, in fact, existing brands are bought on deal just as often as new ones, through deals offered by the retailer and not necessarily by the manufacturer.
- Deals are also supposed to be a prime technique for inducing trial that will lead to repeat purchase; yet the majority of deal purchases cut into future purchases—an inventory effect rather than an increased purchase rate effect.
- Similarly, it is commonly supposed that small sizes are dealt more often because they are more likely to gain trial; yet the actual findings show that retailers deal large sizes just as often as small sizes.

Faced with retailers who so often deviate from a brand's promotional plan, what can managers (manufacturers) do?

Counter-Strategies Open to Manufacturers It should be noted that there are many ways in which manufacturers can promote directly to consumers without retailer intervention (for example, through coupons, refunds, samples, and so forth). However, the point emphasized by the foregoing study is: For the many promotions that *have* to go through retailers—notably price reduction and cooperative advertising promotions—the retailer's objective can be quite different from the manufacturer's objective and can lead to quite a different outcome than the manufacturer intended.[10]

Manufacturers seeking greater control over attainment of promotional action objectives (trial, or usage, as the case may be) with particular target audiences (new category users, brand loyals, and so forth) for the brand consequently have two options:

1 Divert promotion to consumer-direct media (including on-pack and in-pack but also promotions in "mass" media rather than in "store" media).

2 Develop better retail cooperation by improving trading terms or increasing trade allowances.

Both these options will increase promotional costs. However, the sales return should be worth the increased cost for the manufacturer faced with retailers who deviate from the manufacturer's promotion plan for the brand.

Retail Promotion Techniques

Table 12.3 lists the promotion offers most frequently used by supermarket retailers as measured in a Nielsen study[11] in a fairly typical year for the U.S. economy (1977). Because of the Nielsen Audit service, we know more about supermarkets and to some extent drugstores than other types of retailers, so the findings should not be overgeneralized. This Nielsen survey included for

TABLE 12.3   RETAIL PROMOTION TECHNIQUES (FOOD STORES)

Type of promotion offer	Retailers using (%)	
	Large supermarkets	Convenience stores
Displays *	100	100
Price-offs	100	100
Newspaper ads (mostly co-op)	90	15
In-ad coupons	73	4
Shoppers continuity promotions †	44	6
Handbills, fliers	28	4
Stamps	14	0

Source: A look at sales promotion, *The Nielsen Researcher,* 1977, No. 4, 2–14. By permission.
* Displays not in original survey but used by virtually all retailers.
† Mainly used by chain supermarkets rather than large independents.

comparison promotion offers used by small convenience stores like 7-Eleven. Also, we have inserted the promotional category of displays, which were omitted from the Nielsen survey but which are used by virtually all retailers.

Three forms of promotion come to the fore for retailers: displays, price-offs, and newspaper advertising (though the latter is used mainly by larger retailers). A brief look at each of these types of retail promotion is in order before we return to the general promotional approach from an overall managerial perspective.

Displays   Displays are a very common retailing device for drawing consumer *attention* to a promotion (see discussion of the processing step in Chapter 8). As such, displays are considered by marketers to be a form of "merchandising" rather than a form of sales promotion per se. Meyer[12] states the distinction as follows: promotions (such as price-offs, coupons, premiums) move the product, whereas merchandising *sells the idea* that moves the product (such as displays, package flags, sales brochures). Thus, one way in which displays work is by eliciting *reflexive* attention, since displays are a contrasting stimulus, to the promotional message and thus to the brand.

But do displays only work in this way? Consumer behavior theory suggests that displays also may gain *selective* attention.[13] Specifically, consumers in the past have been rewarded or reinforced by purchasing promoted brands from displays, so that the mere fact of a display causes them to believe that the brand on display is also "on special," when in reality it may not be, or when in reality the "deal" may be very minor. If so, displays also help the promotion offer (or in unscrupulous instances, the perceived promotion offer) to be *accepted* during processing and therefore constitute a *promotion offer in themselves* rather than being solely "merchandising."

Of course, either or both processes—the "exposure" effect and the "on special" effect—may operate in particular circumstances. The realization that we are not sure how displays work points up the need to pre-test promotion offers just as ads are pre-tested. A display that is processed by consumers as a promotion offer, via the "on special" attribution, will need to offer less of a real incentive than a display that is processed as mere attention-getting merchandising.

Displays are often cited in marketing textbooks as producing spectacular increases in sales; examples of sales increases of 200 to over 1000 percent are not uncommon. However, these spectacular results must be assessed against the production and labor costs to establish the display: Most displays are *not* very profitable either to the manufacturer or to the retailer and thus they are not an exceptional promotional technique.

But the main reason for not including displays as one of the principal promotion techniques available to manufacturers (in the following section on consumer promotions) is that displays are so narrowly retailer-controlled. The proprietary study conducted by *Progressive Grocer*[14] for the A & P supermarket chain, for example, estimates that only about 15 percent of p-o-p promotions offered to retailers actually get used. Displays are mainly at the retailer's discretion and are not usually a promotion technique available to manufacturers for a particular brand at a desired time, as are other promotion techniques.

Far more basic and, in the long run, more important for manufacturers is the overall battle for *shelf space*. Shelf space means more facings (horizontally) and better shelf position (vertically). Shelf space is not a special display and thus does not involve extra production and labor costs. As noted previously, shelf space is a major usage objective of trade promotion.

Price-offs   Price-offs are the other technique which, along with displays, is used by virtually all retailers. Conceptually, price-offs offered by retailers are very similar to price-offs offered by manufacturers, except that if they are clearly perceived by consumers as being retailer-initiated rather than manufacturer-initiated, they may avoid the general franchise-reducing effect of price-offs. We will examine this aspect of price-offs when discussing price-offs as a consumer promotion technique.

Cooperative ("Co-op") Advertising   "Co-op" is a third, widely used, retail promotion technique. Cooperative advertising takes the form of a cash contribution (cooperative advertising allowance) from the manufacturer to the *retailer's* advertising budget. According to an industry estimate by Middendorf,[15] retailers advertise primarily in newspapers (about 70 percent of co-op money), and to a lesser extent in catalogs, brochures, and fliers (about 12 percent), radio (about 10 percent), with other media such as TV, magazines, outdoor, or Yellow Pages together making up the remaining 8 percent.

Depending on the degree to which the manufacturer "cooperates"—that is, on the percentage contribution that the manufacturer makes to the retailer's advertising budget—manufacturers can buy greater control over how their brands are portrayed in retail advertisements. Cooperative advertising allowances can range from about 5 percent (low control) up to nearly 100 percent (high control) depending on how important it is for the manufacturer to oversee the communication presentation of the brand in retail advertising.

Manufacturer control of advertising and promotion channeled through retailers often proves to be a very real problem. Many retailers tend to regard co-op money as cash: They don't necessarily place all the money in advertising as the manufacturer intended, nor in the form of advertising that the manufacturer intended. Manufacturers have to some extent become resigned to this slippage as an inevitable "cost of doing business."

Fortunately, with the major retail advertising medium, newspapers, control can be exerted by monitoring this relatively visible and easy-to-sample form of advertising. But for broadcast media, the problem of monitoring is substantial. To help monitor retail advertising on television, the TV Bureau of Advertising recently instituted a program called "Proof of Performance," whereby a sworn affidavit is obtained from TV stations attesting that the advertising has been placed. The manufacturer receives the affidavit before actually paying the TV co-op money to the retailer.

CONSUMER PROMOTION

Consumer promotion is promotion by the manufacturer to the consumer. Consumer promotion offers can be consumer-direct or they can be offered through retailers. The figures cited earlier indicate that consumer advertising outweighs consumer promotion by about 2 to 1. However, when it is realized that retailers also are (independently) promoting to consumers through retail promotion, it is easy to see why advertising and promotion are of equal prevalence in reaching the consumer.

The target audiences and action objectives of consumer promotions are exactly the same as those for advertising. These can be conveniently organized by the general action objective sought:

1 *Trial*   Early in the product life cycle, the emphasis is on gaining trial of the brand. Target audience possibilities include:
- *New category users* (who have not yet tried any brands)
- *Other-brand switchers* (who have not tried the brand)
- *Other-brand loyals* (also who have not tried the brand)

2 *Usage*   Later in the product life cycle, the emphasis is on increasing the repeat purchase rate. Target audience possibilities include:
- *Brand loyals* (to encourage them to use more of the brand than they are using now)
- *Favorable brand switchers* (who use the brand occasionally, to get them to switch-in and use it more often)

As with advertising, a more refined identification of alternative target audiences is provided by the prospect sub-groups identified in Chapter 4. The associated action objectives for these sub-groups are reproduced in Table 12.4, where we see that "trial" may include category trial as well as brand trial for certain sub-groups, and brand re-trial rather than brand trial for others; similarly, "usage" may be straight repeat purchase for certain sub-groups, but repeat purchase based on brand-switching behavior for others. The manager should refer to the specific prospect sub-groups and action objectives when planning an actual promotion campaign.

Consumer Promotion Techniques

An estimate of the types of promotions consumers are likely to encounter from *manufacturers* is provided in Table 12.5. (Unfortunately, the promotion offer categories from this survey do not exactly match the categories we will use in Chapters 13 and 14. However, they're indicative, and this is the only survey available of the extent of usage by managers of each type of consumer promotion.) Couponing, money back offers or cash refunds, and premiums head the list.

Noticeable is that direct price-off offers are fairly far down the list, despite their obvious prevalence in ads and in stores. The reason for this is that price-

TABLE 12-4   ACTION OBJECTIVES FOR SPECIFIC TARGET AUDIENCES

Target audience	Action objectives
1 Negative new category users (NNCU)	Trial (including category trial) or retrial (including category re-trial)
2 Unaware new category users (UNCU)	Trial (including category trial)
3 Positive new category users (PNCU)	Trial (including category trial)
4 Single-brand loyals (SBL)	Repeat
5 Mutli-brand loyals (MBL)	Switching-in
6 Experimental other-brand switchers (EOBS)	Trial
7 Experimental favorable brand switchers (EFBS)	Repeat
8 Routinized other-brand switchers (ROBS)	Trial (or re-trial)
9 Routinized favorable brand switchers (RFBS)	Switching-in
10 Favorable other-brand loyals (FOBL)	Trial (or re-trial)
11 Neutral other-brand loyals (NOBL)	Trial (or re-trial)
12 Unfavorable other-brand loyals (UOBL)	Trial (or re-trial)

offs are the most frequent form of promotion used by *retailers,* rather than by manufacturers. Retailers use price-offs, as noted, because this is the quickest way to move inventory to the consumer.

COMMUNICATION EFFECTS OF ADVERTISING AND PROMOTION: PROMOTION'S STRENGTHS

Promotions work on the same five communication effects as advertising. The manager should think of the prospective buyer in the target audience as having the five basic communication effects to be inserted in his or her head, and then decide whether (1) advertising, (2) promotion, or (3) a combination of advertising and promotion would be the best means of achieving these effects.

In general, the relative communication strengths of advertising and promotion are as depicted in Figure 12.4. Advertising generally makes its strongest contributions to brand awareness and brand attitude (as emphasized in Part Five). Promotion generally makes its strongest contributions to brand awareness and brand purchase intention.

But, a point we wish to make early and then continually emphasize is that the best promotion offers are those which *also* work on brand attitude. In the words of Prentice (see Chapter 1), these are consumer franchise building (CFB) promotion offers.

Also, it must be realized that promotion *alone* can create all five necessary

TABLE 12-5   CONSUMER PROMOTION TECHNIQUES USED BY LEADING MANUFACTURERS*

Type of promotion offer	Companies using (%)
Couponing	
Consumer-direct	94
In retailers' ads	49
Money back offers or cash refunds	85
Premiums	82
Sweepstakes	74
Price-offs	64
Sampling	
New products	60
Established products	50
Pre-priced shippers	45
Contests	42

*The percentages in this table are 3-year averages calculated from surveys of leading from manufacturers' consumer promotion usage in 1981, 1982, and 1983. See Donnelley Marketing, *Sixth Annual Survey of Promotional Practices,* New York: Dun & Bradstreet, 1983. Adapted and used by permission.

communication effects. Some brands, especially so-called "price brands," are marketed successfully without advertising, by using point-of-purchase promotion. Promotion, just like advertising, works through communication, and either one can perform all the communication tasks. It's a matter of which avenue to communicating with the target audience will work best at least cost.

FIGURE 12.4   Relative communication strengths of advertising and promotion.

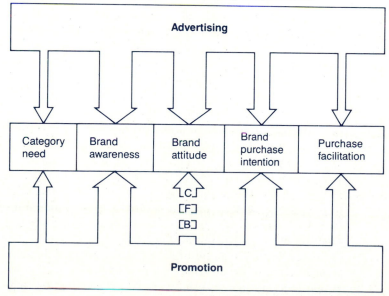

Category Need

Category need, in most product categories, originates mainly from cultural changes (for new categories) and arises from the individual's overall or temporary circumstances (for new and existing categories). Advertising can have some effect on category need by "selling the category" (see Chapter 6's category need options). However, selling the category is more a matter of suggesting the category, for example, aerobics as a solution to an already reasonably strong buyer motivation, such as problem avoidance of being overweight. Only rarely can advertising create a motivation as such. Rather, it positions the category as a better way of meeting an existing motivation.

Promotion can accelerate category need—make it occur earlier—although usually to a fairly minor degree. For example, note the relatively minor effect of the massive rebates offered by U.S. car manufacturers in trying to pull U.S. auto sales out of the slump of the late 1970s. Accelerate is the operative term here. Promotion doesn't really "sell" the category need so much as attempt to speed it up somewhat.

In the figure, advertising and promotion are shown as having—in general— a relatively minor influence on category need. Again, this is their general effect although many specific instances of successfully selling or accelerating category need do occur.

Brand Awareness

Brand awareness is a traditional strength of advertising. However, promotion is an equally strong contributor to brand awareness. From Chapter 1, it may be remembered that new product introductions, where brand awareness is a major objective, typically are launched with equally heavy expenditures on advertising and promotion.

Promotion offers help prospective buyers to "cognize," or consider, new brands and to "*re*cognize," or reconsider, existing brands. Promotion offers achieve this by drawing reflexive attention to the brand (for example, a display or a sample pack) and also by producing selective attention (for example, a price-off or a coupon promising extra value). An excellent example of a coupon offer designed to increase brand recognition is shown in Figure 12.5 for Right Guard deodorant. The coupon includes a picture of the package to facilitate brand recognition.

Promotion offers are mainly useful for increasing brand *recognition* (or initial cognition for previously unfamiliar brands) at the point of purchase. Because most promotion offers are made at the point of purchase or at least at the point of decision, as in promotion offers in the mail, rather than prior to purchase, brand *recall* is less often a communication option for promotion. Nevertheless, a clever promotion offer can contribute to brand recall—if brand recall is the relevant brand awareness objective—by emphasizing, repeating, or otherwise drawing attention to the brand name. In assessing the presentation of promotion offers in Chapters 13 and 14, we will show how promotions can be variously designed to increase brand recognition or brand recall.

FIGURE 12.5 Coupon promotion for Right Guard that contributes to brand recognition. (Courtesy The Gillette Company.)

Accordingly, advertising and promotion are shown as being equally strong contributors to brand awareness as a communication effect.

Brand Attitude

Brand attitude communication traditionally is the province of advertising. However, the best promotion offers *also* work on brand attitude. These are what Prentice[16] has called consumer franchise building promotions. While many promotions are aimed simply at causing a short-term increase in sales, for competitive or inventory-moving reasons, the ideal promotion should also create longer-term communication effects and thereby *maximize full-value purchases when the promotion is withdrawn.*

Consumer franchise building (CFB) promotions contribute to inducing full price purchases by working, like advertising, on brand attitude (*example:* free samples). Short-term (non-CFB) promotions, in contrast, do not affect brand attitude but operate instead on temporary brand purchase intention (*example:* price-off offers).

In our analysis of the 10 major consumer promotion techniques, we will give considerable attention to how the manager can *tactically* implement promotion offers to work on brand attitude. Whereas some promotion techniques, as identified by Prentice, are naturally more amenable to franchise building, we will show that most promotion techniques, if thoughtfully implemented, can produce more permanent brand attitude effects and thus continue to positively influence sales after the promotion period has ended.

Brand Purchase Intention

Brand purchase intention is a second communication strength of promotion, after brand awareness. All promotions are aimed at "moving sales forward" immediately (regardless of their longer-term consequences) and they achieve this by stimulating immediate brand purchase intentions. More particularly, promotions engender *purchase* intentions to:

- Buy/not buy
- Buy now/buy later
- Buy multiple units/buy normal amount

as well as the many *purchase-related* intentions for consumer durables and industrial products—such as to visit showrooms, call for a sales demonstration, and so forth.

Dramatic evidence of the opportunity for promotions to influence brand purchase intentions for consumer products comes from the on-going Point-of-Purchase Advertising Institute (POPAI) studies conducted in conjunction with the DuPont Company. A recent study consisted of pre- and post-shopping interviews with 2000 consumers buying supermarket products.[17]

On average, 65 percent of the final brand choices for supermarket items are made at the point of purchase (Table 12.6). Although the incidence varies by

TABLE 12.6 INCIDENCE OF POINT-OF-PURCHASE BRAND CHOICES FOR SUPERMARKET PRODUCTS.

Type of choice	%
Overall results	
Specifically planned brand choice	35
Point-of-purchase brand choice	65
	100
Types of point-of-purchase brand choices	
Generally planned (category but not brand)	15
Substitute (switched from intended brand)	3
Impulse (neither category nor brand intended)	47
	65
Specific products: point-of-purchase brand choice	
Snack foods	78
Cosmetics	69
Soft drinks	67
Drugs/medicines (non-prescription)	49
Cigarettes	33
Alcoholic beverages	20
Prescription drugs	0

Source: POPAI/DuPont studies (see notes 17 and 18). By permission.

product category as shown, this indicates that in about two out of every three decisions that consumers make for supermarket items, there is an opportunity for brand purchase intention to be influenced by promotion.[18]

Of further interest is that 47 percent of choices, overall, are so-called "impulse" purchases, where the category itself was not planned before entering the store. Most of these choices, we believe, are not purely "impulse" but rather reflect the sequence of brand recognition reminding shoppers of a category need. Nevertheless, for the probable 10 percent or so of "pure impulse" choices, point-of-purchase presentation can be credited with generating all prior communication effects up to and including brand purchase intention.

Purchase Facilitation

Purchase facilitation is shown in Figure 12.4 as being subject to moderate influence by promotion. In Chapter 6 we saw that advertising, unless it is particularly innovative, generally has a limited influence on purchase facilitation, especially if there is a severe problem with the rest of the marketing mix that through poor planning has been left for the advertising to try to solve.

Purchase facilitation problems with the 4 P's of product, price, place, and personal selling *can* more often be overcome with promotion, though at considerable *cost*. A promotion, with of course a severe price reduction, can sometimes sell a poor product. A promotion along price lines can also—

temporarily—solve an overpricing problem. A promotion can also help poor distribution, by inducing customers to visit distant stores. And lastly, a promotion, such as free demonstrations or trial offers, can aid personal selling problems. All these are costly corrections, however, to marketing mix problems that should not have been left to promotion.

We must conclude that promotion, in general, has moderate influence on the purchase facilitation communication effect.

INTERDEPENDENCE OF ADVERTISING AND PROMOTION

Advertising and promotion can be employed together to produce a "synergistic," or interactive, effect. This of course presumes that there is overlap in the target audiences for advertising and promotion, and the overlap aspect will be discussed first.

Target Audience Overlap in Exposure to Advertising and Promotion

Earlier in the chapter, we saw that typically there are three forms of promotion in the brand's marketing channel: trade promotion, retail promotion, and consumer promotion. To what extent do promotion target audiences for each form of promotion overlap with target audiences for the brand's advertising? This question must be considered separately for each form of promotion.

Trade Promotion   In trade promotion, which is employed to get the brand accepted by distributors and then re-ordered and displayed, promotion is the major marketing tool, not advertising. Any advertising—trade advertising—that accompanies the trade promotion thereby will go directly to the *same* target audience as part of the trade promotion package.

Accordingly, for trade promotion, there is effectively 100 percent overlap in the target audience for advertising and promotion. Although it could be reasoned, following Montgomery's analysis earlier in this chapter, that neutral or negative-attitude distributors should receive more advertising (and also personal selling) to improve the manufacturer's awareness and reputation, any such advertising material that is prepared undoubtedly would be included in trade promotions to all distributors, as the production costs of this special advertising would hardly justify limited usage.

The opportunity for advertising and promotion "synergy" therefore is excellent with trade promotion when and if trade advertising is used.

Retail Promotion   Retailers generally utilize two types of advertising: store image advertising and specific product advertising (see Part Seven). Retail promotion usually accompanies product advertising but may be played down or omitted from store image advertising. Retail promotion also occurs separately, in the store. Target audience overlap, nevertheless, is often quite high.

The overlap occurs in a three-step manner, beginning with store image advertising. Store image ads may be placed on TV or in magazines or newspapers without any accompanying promotion. "High end" retailers, such as Saks or I. Magnin, run pure image advertisements quite frequently. However, customers who see this advertising will be exposed quite probably to any product advertising the store does, because stores tend to use the same media for both forms of advertising.

Similarly, most "walk-in" customers exposed to in-store retail promotion are highly likely to have previously been exposed to store image or product advertising in local media. Only the very few who don't watch much TV or read magazines or newspapers would be unexposed to the advertising.

Thus, whereas store image advertising may be directed to more "remote" prospect groups such as new category users, other-store loyals, or other-store switchers, and at the other extreme, in-store promotions may reach mainly favorable store switchers and store loyals, the likelihood of overlapping exposure is quite high. In the middle link of the chain, product advertising by retail stores rarely occurs without product promotion, so target audience overlap here is assured.

Altogether, then, we may conclude that there is often a good, though not perfect, opportunity for "synergy" between retail advertising and promotion because of considerable target audience overlap.

Consumer Promotion   The extent of overlap in target audiences for consumer advertising and consumer promotion very much depends on the brand's "media" selection for *promotion*. As we shall see in Chapters 13 and 14, use of on-pack, in-pack, or point-of-purchase "media" can restrict promotions quite effectively to the brand's already loyal or favorable switcher target audiences. By contrast, use of out-of-store promotion "media," such as sampling or in-ad coupons, will reach the brand's more distant prospect groups, including other-brand loyals, other-brand switchers, and new category users.

However, whereas it is fairly easy to target promotions by selective use of promotion "media," it is considerably more difficult to direct the brand's advertising so specifically. By selecting advertising media vehicles against prospect groups (see Part Seven), the manager can increase the *frequency* with which a particular advertising target audience is exposed to the brand's advertising—but the frequency with which non-target prospect groups are reached will nearly always be above zero.[19]

Accordingly, some degree of communication effect generation almost always will have taken place from advertising (assuming advertising is used) before any of the prospect groups are exposed to the promotion.

The manager's decision then becomes—for each prospect group—whether to continue communication effect establishment with more advertising (additional frequency) or to complement partially established communication effects with a promotion campaign (with the added but usually short additional frequency now coming from *promotion*). This depends on the respective prospect groups' *leverage* to advertising versus promotion, as explained earlier in conjunction with target audience selection.

The Advantages of Using Advertising and Promotion Together

If promotion to a particular prospect group is decided upon, what are the relative advantages of also reaching the prospect group with advertising, rather than using promotion alone? Whereas advertising can contribute to all five communication effects, the critical communication effect with regard to the joint effectiveness of advertising and promotion is advertising's establishment of brand attitude.

Prior advertising that has been effective in producing a strongly held favorable brand attitude makes subsequent promotion of the brand more effective. There are two reasons for this:

- First, with a favorable brand attitude established, consumers now perceive better value from the *brand's own* promotion offers.
- Second, with a favorable brand attitude established, the brand is more resistant to *competing brands'* promotions.

Consultant William T. Moran provides plenty of case histories to support the principle that good advertising leads to more effective promotion. As Moran puts it, an increase in the advertising budget is the best argument for a subsequent increase in the promotion budget.[20]

Consumer-product brands increasingly are finding that advertising alone is not sufficient to maintain the brand's sales. Advertising's brand attitude emphasis may hold brand-loyal customers for the brand's core sales, but over the last decade or so there appears to be an increasing proportion of brand switchers switching in and out of the fringe of the brand's sales who must be held with promotion.

As evidence of declining loyalty, Johnson,[21] in an 8-year analysis of 50 supermarket brands in 20 product categories, showed that from 1975 to 1983: the average brand's share of category purchases per household fell by 6 percent; corresponding with this lowered loyalty, the number of brands bought in the average category per household per 6-month period increased by 9 percent; and, reflecting the increased need to hold brands with promotion, the average brand's percent of purchases on deal (with a promotion) increased from only 23 percent in 1975 to 40 percent in 1983.

Increasingly, therefore, most brands are reliant on a combination of advertising and promotion. Let us now examine, at a more tactical level, how the strategy of combined advertising and promotion should be implemented. Timing is all-important, giving rise to the phenomenon that Moran calls the "ratchet" effect.[22]

The "Ratchet" Effect of Advertising Followed by Promotion

Effective advertising *prior* to promotion produces a "ratchet" effect that generates sales at a higher level than promotion in the absence of effective prior advertising (Figure 12.6). Average sales level is higher with advertising followed by promotion than with promotion alone. Of course, the sales revenue would have to outweigh the increased cost of the dual approach, unless the

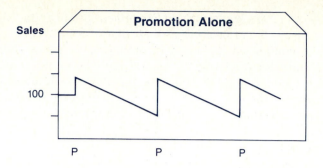

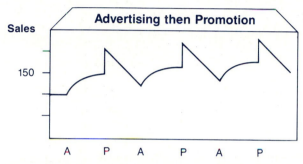

FIGURE 12.6   The "ratchet" effect of effective advertising prior to promotion. (*Source:* W.T. Moran, Insights from pricing research, in E.B. Bailey (Ed.), *Pricing Practices and Strategies,* New York: The Conference Board, 1978, pp. 7–13. By permission.)

marketing objective is to gain market share without concern for short-run profit.

More specifically, Moran emphasizes the importance, in planning advertising and promotion, of understanding the brand's "upside" demand elasticity and "downside" demand elasticity, relative to the corresponding elasticities of competing brands:

- *"Upside" elasticity* refers to the amount of *sales increase* that results from a given price cut (promotion). The more effective the brand's prior *advertising,* the greater the sales increase will be from a given promotional price reduction. Effective advertising produces high upside elasticity relative to other brands.
- *"Downside" elasticity* refers to the amount of *sales fall-off* that results from a given price increase (or a psuedo price increase caused by the relative effects of *other* brand's promotions). Once again, the more effective the brand's *advertising,* the less the fall-off will be. Effective advertising produces low downside elasticity and makes the brand more resistant to other brand's promotions.

The interdependence of advertising and promotion can also operate in reverse, with negative consequences. A heavily price-promoted brand, in the *absence* of prior advertising that strengthens brand attitude, risks being regarded as a "cheap" brand or a brand that "must be in trouble." Heavy or frequent price promotion on its own can produce a negative shift in brand attitude. Then, subsequent advertising cannot save the brand's sales.

(The one exception would be if the subsequent advertising deliberately is also "price brand"-oriented, with the manager having resolved to pursue a low price positioning. In this case, since the selling price and profit margin will be lower, it may pay to stop advertising altogether and put the funds into volume-generating promotions.)

We hasten to add that Moran's excellent analysis, and also the effects shown in Figure 12.6, refer to short-term, *price-oriented promotions*—that is, to promotion offers that are not franchise building. By contrast, consumer franchise building (CFB) promotions contribute to brand attitude and thus could substitute fully or partially (depending on other communication effects) for the prior advertising. CFB promotions, like advertising, increase upside demand elasticity and reduce downside demand elasticity.

SUMMARY

The action objectives and target audiences for promotion vary according to who is initiating the promotion (the manufacturer or the retailer) and to whom it is directed (distributors in the case of trade promotion and consumers in the cases of retail promotion and consumer promotion). The action objectives for all promotions are trial and usage—differentially considered:

- For trade promotion, trial involves distributors carrying the brand, and usage involves re-ordering and giving the brand increased display.
- For retail promotion to consumers, trial and usage are centered on the retail *store* rather than on particular brands; brands are promoted to any customers who will help remove the retailer's inventory, and thus retail promotion may conflict with manufacturers' promotional plans for brands.
- For manufacturer promotion to consumers, trial and usage are identical to the action objectives for advertising.

The concept of target audience applies to all three forms of promotion. The target audience represents a selection of those distributors or consumers who will be most responsive to promotion, gauged in relation to the cost of the promotion, to produce a leverage estimate.

Trade promotion, retail promotion, and consumer promotion rely on different promotion techniques to accomplish their respective target audience action objectives. Trade promotion relies on trade discounts offered to carry and display products, and provision of funds for cooperative advertising. Retail promotion relies on price-offs and special displays, which often are supported by cooperative advertising. Consumer promotion employs a much wider variety of techniques discussed in the following chapters.

All promotions attain their behavioral action objectives through communication effects.

Communication effects for a brand can be produced by advertising, by promotion, or by a combination of advertising and promotion. The manager's task is to decide which techniques will meet particular communication objectives best. Whereas promotion traditionally is specialized for generating brand awareness and stimulating immediate brand purchase intention, the manager should try to select and tactically design promotions that *also* increase *brand attitude*. These are called consumer franchise building (CFB) promotions and they produce a longer-term sales pay-off than the typical non-CFB promotion.

Prior effective advertising (and CFB promotions) enhance the sales effects of a subsequent price promotion and render the brand more resistant to competitive promotions. This is known as the ''ratchet'' effect.

NOTES

1 These figures are extrapolated and rounded from annual surveys conducted since 1976 among the 60 or so largest U.S. marketing companies by Donnelley Marketing. For the latest survey at the time of writing, see Donnelley Marketing, *6th Annual Survey of Promotional Practices,* New York: Dun & Bradstreet, 1983.

2 This book is written from the perspective of marketing managers rather than retail managers. Therefore, we have described retail promotion from the marketer's perspective. For a more specialized view of retail advertising and promotion from the retailer's perspective, see J.B. Mason and M.L. Mayer, *Modern Retailing: Theory and Practice* (3rd ed.), Plano, TX: Business Publications Inc., 1984.

3 For an explanation of the concept of buying groups or buying centers, see F.E. Webster and Y. Wind, *Organizational Buying Behavior,* Englewood Cliffs, NJ: Prentice-Hall, 1972. Members of buying groups occupy decision roles just as occurs in consumer buying behavior—initiator, influencer, decider, purchaser, user— although the roles usually are more formalized in distributor buying behavior, especially with larger distributors.

4 D.B. Montgomery, New product distribution: an analysis of supermarket buyer decisions, *Journal of Marketing Research,* 1975, *12*(3), 255–264.

5 Adapted from a privately conducted study by *Progressive Grocer* magazine and A & P Supermarkets, ca. 1982.

6 J.A. Quelch, It's time to make trade promotion more productive, *Harvard Business Review,* 1983, *61*(3), 130–136.

7 E.C. Crimmins, Co-op advertising: a history of problems and promise. *Advertising Age,* September 1, 1980, pp. S–1, S–10.

8 Schmitt, P.M., Store loyalty: does it affect buying patterns? *Nielsen Researcher,* 1980, No. 2, 18–23.

9 R.C. Blattberg, G.D. Eppen, and J. Lieberman, A theoretical and empirical evaluation of price deals for consumer nondurables, *Journal of Marketing,* 1981, *45*(1), 116–129.

10 Other retailer deviations from manufacturers' promotional plans are common. One is failure to provide merchandising support. Even when trade allowances require this, one survey found that in 67 percent of instances merchandising was not provided. Another is failure to pass deal allowances through to the consumer as intended by the manufacturer. For supermarket items, only about 45 percent of products on allowance result in a price reduction to consumers. In new car sales, only about a quarter of the dealer's allowance (a rebate to the dealer) gets passed

on as a reduction in the negotiated selling price. For the supermarket survey, see M. Chevalier and R.C. Curhan, Retail promotion as a function of trade promotion: a descriptive analysis, *Sloan Management Review,* 1976, *17*(1), 19–32. For the car dealer survey, see S.M. Crafton and G.E. Hoffer, Do consumers benefit from auto manufacturer rebates to dealers? *Journal of Consumer Research,* 1980, *7*(2), 211–214.

11 A look at sales promotion, *The Nielsen Researcher,* 1977, No. 4, 2–14.

12 E. Meyer, Promotion: 29 things to remember about it, *Advertising Age,* December 21, 1981, p. 35.

13 The "exposure" effect and the "on special" effect hypothesized for special displays are described in J.F. Engel and R.D. Blackwell, *Consumer Behavior,* (4th ed.), Hinsdale, IL: Dryden, 1982, pp. 554–556. For evidence that sales from displays increase even with a price cut of *zero,* see P.M. Guadagni and J.D.C. Little, A logit model of brand choice calibrated on scanner data, *Marketing Science,* 1983, *2*(3), 203–238.

14 Same reference as note 5; unfortunately, this reference is not generally available.

15 B. Middendorff, How to put the media to work for you, *Advertising Age,* September 1, 1980, p. S–2.

16 Robert M. Prentice is a marketing and advertising consultant who spent 30 years with General Foods and Lever Brothers. His concepts of consumer franchise building (CFB) and non-consumer franchise building (non-CFB) forms of promotion have been published in two articles in *Advertising Age* as well as presented at many seminars. See R.M. Prentice, How to split your marketing funds between advertising and promotion dollars, *Advertising Age,* January 10, 1977, pp. 41–42, 44; How to reduce tension, improve ad productivity, *Advertising Age,* November 13, 1980, pp. 71, 72, 76. The term "consumer franchise building" actually was introduced into the marketing literature earlier, by Nielsen researcher J.O. Peckham, *The Wheel of Marketing,* Chicago, IL: The A.C. Nielsen Company, 1973. However, it is now more closely associated with Prentice, who developed and published the CFB and non-CFB concepts.

It should be noted that whereas the Prentice system divides promotions into CFB and non-CFB techniques, our approach is to select the best promotion technique and then try to make its presentation as CFB-inducing as possible. That is, he treats CFB as a dichotomous, "all-or-none" variable, whereas we treat it as a continuous, "more-or-less" variable. Also, consistent with our approach in Part Five, we add brand awareness as a precursor of brand attitude to produce a successful CFB promotion.

17 The POPAI/DuPont supermarket study from which the data in the top half of Table 12.6 are drawn was conducted in 1977. See L.J. Haugh, Buying-habits study update: average purchases up 121%, *Advertising Age,* June 27, 1977, pp. 56, 58.

18 The product category-specific data in the lower half of Table 12.6 are taken from a further POPAI/DuPont study conducted in 1982. As this later study was conducted in mass merchandiser chains and drugstores, rather than supermarkets, the figures should not be precisely translated to supermarkets. It is of interest to note in conjunction with findings on brand loyalty that the more physiological types of products seem less open to point-of-purchase changes of brand choice. The 1982 study was reported in *Marketing News,* August 6, 1982, p. 5.

19 The main but occasional exception would be new category users when print advertising is used exclusively. Print media vehicles are specific enough to virtually exclude non-users of the category if desired—for example, ads placed in personal computer magazines would not reach non-users of personal computers; ads placed in serious "runner" magazines would not reach non-runners; and so forth.

20 W.T. Moran, paper presented at the Association of National Advertisers' research workshop, New York, December 9, 1981. Summarized in "Use sales promotion yardstick, ANA told," *Advertising Age,* December 14, 1981, p. 12. See also D.R. Wittink, Advertising increases sensitivity to price, *Journal of Advertising Research,* 1977, *17*(2), 39–42; and A. Ghosh, S.A. Neslin, and R.W. Shoemaker, Are there associations between price elasticity and brand characteristics? in P.E. Murphy, G.R. Laczniak, P.F. Anderson, R.W. Belk, O.C. Ferrell, R.F. Lusch, T.A. Shimp, and C.B. Weinberg, (Eds.), *AMA Educators Conference Proceedings,* Chicago: American Marketing Association, 1983, pp. 226–230.

21 Mr. Johnson's article is, in our view, misleadingly titled, as his data, summarized here, provide clear evidence of a decline in brand loyalty. In our opinion, if a brand's share of household purchases declined (for example) from 33 to 31 percent (with 33 percent indexed at 100, 31 percent translates to an index of 94, that is, a 6 percent decline as reported in our text) then this would seem to be a large enough change to cause the manager to review the brand's advertising and promotion strategies.

The figures are 20-category, 50-brand *averages*. More specifically, food and beverage brands experienced a relatively large decline in loyalty (10 percent on the brand's-share-of-household-category-purchases measure), whereas household products/health and beauty aids, which perhaps represent somewhat higher personal risk, showed only a marginal decline (1 percent). This emphasizes the need to monitor loyalty by product category, as most managers would do.

The introduction of generic products during the survey period appeared to affect mostly the major, advertising-based brands, which were thereby forced to use more promotion. Market share trends (in percentage of units) for the *average* product category are as follows:

Market Share	1975	1983
Major brand's share	20.8	18.0
Store brand's share	6.7	6.8
Generic share	—	3.5
(Other brands)	(72.5)	(71.7)
Total	100.0	100.0

Source: T. Johnson, The myth of declining brand loyalty, *Journal of Advertising Research,* 1984, *24* (1), 9–17, by permission.

22 The "ratchet" effect, and the dependent concepts of "upside" and "downside" demand elasticities, are explained in W.T. Moran, Insights from pricing research, in E.B. Bailey (Ed.), *Pricing Practices and Strategies,* New York; The Conference Board, 1978, pp. 7–13.

DISCUSSION QUESTIONS

12.1 Arrange and conduct interviews with manufacturers from two different industries regarding their planning and use of trade promotion. In the interview, try to test Montgomery's hypothesis about target audiences for trade promotion. Write a short report comparing your two case histories with the text.

12.2 How do retailers plan and evaluate retail promotion, overall, for their stores? Interview two retailers in two different lines of business based on the retail promotion concepts in this chapter. Write a short report comparing your two case histories with the text.

12.3 How do special (in-store) displays work? To answer this question, interview a sample of 20 customers at displays in stores.

12.4 Discuss methods whereby manufacturer marketing managers might be able to lessen retailers' "independent" influence on consumer promotion plans for the brand.

12.5 The traditional communication effects view of promotion is that its strengths lie in generating brand awareness and brand purchase intention. How might promotion operate on the other three communication effects of category need, brand attitude, and purchase facilitation? Answer with actual or hypothetical examples other than those provided in the chapter.

12.6 What are the advantages and disadvantages of using (a) advertising alone, (b) promotion alone, and (c) advertising and promotion together to produce communication effects for a brand?

FURTHER READING

American Association of Advertising Agencies (Sales Promotion Committee). *Sales Promotion Techniques*. New York: A.A.A.A., 1978.

The best brief overview of promotion. Much of the groundwork for this publication was compiled in a privately circulated manuscript by Hank J. Aniero. The one weakness of this booklet is the description of communication and behavioral "effects" in broad terms that are too imprecise for the advanced manager.

R.M. Prentice. How to split your marketing funds between advertising and promotion dollars. *Advertising Age,* January 10, 1977, pp. 41–42, 44.

Advertising managers cannot afford to miss this article (it should be available on microfiche in college or public libraries). Note that Mr. Prentice classifies advertising as CFB (consumer franchise building) as well as certain types of promotions—both of which are to be distinguished from non-CFB promotions.

W.T. Moran, Insights from pricing research. In Bailey, E.B. (Ed.) *Pricing Practices and Strategies*. New York: The Conference Board, 1978, pp. 7–13.

A very important article on advertising's role (and, we would add, CFB promotion's role) in affecting "upside" and "downside" price (and price-promotion offer) elasticity of brands. Like the Prentice article, this is non-technical and clearly explained.

CHAPTER 13

CONSUMER TRIAL PROMOTIONS

In this and the next chapter we focus on consumer promotions. This chapter examines the promotion techniques that are most effective in generating trial of the brand. After reading this chapter you should:

- Realize the importance of trial promotions
- Know which four promotion techniques work best in generating trial
- Understand how to present trial promotion offers (promotion's "creative" tactics) to maximize their consumer franchise building effects

THE FOUR BASIC TRIAL PROMOTIONS

Four types of promotion offers are especially effective in generating trial of the brand.[1] The four best trial promotions are:

1 Sampling
2 Coupons
3 Trade coupons
4 Price-off techniques

Whereas these types of promotion offers can also be used to generate usage, they are relatively more effective than other techniques for stimulating trial. Similarly, whereas the other six types of promotion offers (Chapter 14) *can* stimulate trial, their main role is to generate usage. Thus, we will classify promotions by specialization as trial promotions or usage promotions, respectively.

Trial Revisited

As explained in Chapter 4, where we discussed action objectives for advertising and promotion, *trial* applies not only to new brands but also to established brands. Trial is an action objective for:

1 *New Brands* Trial is the initial action objective for all target audiences.
2 *Established Brands* Trial by *new buyers* can be an action objective.

New buyers can come from new category users, other-brand loyals, or other-brand switchers. For the latter two groups (depending on the specific prospect sub-group), trial may in fact be *re-trial*. Short of a complete change in advertising strategy for the brand (often requiring a product improvement), promotion may be the only hope of gaining re-trial.

The Importance of Trial

Relatively speaking, trial promotions are more important than usage promotions. The British marketer, Ehrenberg,[2] and his colleagues, have provided voluminous evidence demonstrating that a brand's *penetration* is the major determinant of sales levels and thus market share. Sales, of course, are the product of:

$$\text{penetration (the number of people who buy the brand)} \times \text{buying rate (the number of times they buy it in a given period)}$$

Penetration varies widely across brands, and is highly dependent on marketing inputs—notably distribution, price, and initial advertising and promotion efforts. And although penetration represents the *final* number of people who *buy* the brand, unless the brand is really inferior, penetration obviously is a close correlate of the *initial* number of people who *try* the brand.

The other component of sales level, buying rate, as reflected in repeat purchase or *usage,* varies surprisingly little across brands in a given product category and is much less responsive to marketing inputs except via the short-term "inventorying" effect of promotion described earlier.

While influencing the usage rate is often of considerable tactical importance, the ultimate success of the brand depends mostly on brand penetration, based on *trial*. With this in mind, let us now consider the four main trial-generating promotion techniques.

SAMPLING

Sampling includes a variety of procedures for inducing the prospective buyer to try the brand on a zero-cost or low-cost basis. Free samples, trial-size samples that are paid for, trial offers, demonstrations, trade exhibits, and even feasibility studies—all are examples of trial promotion by sampling.

Sampling: The Most Effective but Initially Most Expensive Trial Technique

Sampling is generally considered to be the strongest known trial-generating technique. It is also the most expensive way of gaining trial. However, if the brand is superior to whatever the trier was using before (and for new product categories the comparison is with previous product categories), then this initial high cost can be "amortized" over repeat usage, making sampling a very profitable technique indeed. Profitability is further assisted by the fact that sampling, as we will see, is a fully CFB technique, thus maximizing full-value purchases as soon as it is withdrawn.

For consumer products, on average, about 75 percent of sampled households will try the sample, and about 15 to 20 percent of all sampled households will proceed to make a subsequent full-priced purchase.[3] These very high figures must be tempered by the realization that sampling is often done selectively rather than randomly, by using particular sampling media, so that potential triers are somewhat predisposed toward the type of product they receive. Nevertheless, these trial rates are well above those produced on average by other promotion techniques.

When to Use Sampling

There are five main marketing situations in which the manager should use sampling. (If none of these situations applies, then the manager should use another, less expensive, trial-generating promotion, or simply rely on advertising alone to create trial.) The situations are as follows:

1 *New Product Category Introduction* When a new product *category* is being introduced to the market, *speed* of trial is usually of the essence for the initial brands launched in the category. This is because of the Hendry "polarization" process described in Chapters 2 and 4: consumers will often settle on the first "good" brand tried. Note that this situation goes against the usual admonition that only demonstrably superior brands should use sampling. A parity brand, if tried first, could get the advantage (see also our earlier discussion on the importance of the initial number of triers).

2 *Superior Brand Introduction in an Established Category* The second situation is the traditional one for sampling. When a new or improved brand enters an established product category, sampling is an excellent way to gain trial. With an established product category, the new or improved brand has to be perceived as superior, otherwise the sampled triers will revert to their previous brand or brands. With the routinization or "inertia" of buyers in established product categories, sampling is perhaps the *only* technique that will successfully produce trial among *routinized other-brand switchers* and *other-brand loyals* whom, as we have seen, are two of the hardest target audiences for advertising alone to convert.

3 *Where Advertising is Inadequate to Demonstrate the Brand's Benefit or Benefits* Advertising is most successful for the many brands whose benefits can be shown visually or described verbally (tantalizingly, for low involvement decisions, or convincingly, for high involvement decisions—see Chapters 9 and 10). However, some brands are in product categories where the benefits are best *experienced directly or by continued usage*. Direct experience products may include the various sensory modes of consumption: taste (for example, foods, beverages); smell (perfumes, aftershaves); touch (hand lotions, fabrics); and hearing (records, stereo sets). Continued usage products include those whose performance is difficult to gauge immediately, such as shampoo or cosmetics in the consumer realm, or machines or components in the industrial realm, and also *service* products, such as couriers or consultants. Sampling, through free or low-priced trial offers, is an excellent means of demonstrating that the product or service will in fact deliver the often subtle benefits promised. If the benefits are not subtle, or are easy to gauge immediately, then sampling is not warranted, because of the high cost (unless situation 1 or 2 holds).

4 *To Precede Seasonal Purchasing* A lesser-known use of sampling applies in seasonal product categories. This is the use of pre-season sampling to induce brand switching that may carry over into seasonal purchases.[4] The reason sampling is more effective than other trial-inducing techniques in this application is that it places the brand with the prospective buyer when the pre-season "zero" category need would not otherwise be strong enough to lead to purchase. The early-placed brand therefore has an edge in having initial trial when seasonal purchasing begins.

5 *To Force Retail Distribution* Distributors like sampling because it generates fast action at the retail level at little or no cost to the retailer. Sampling therefore is used to "force" distribution, either for new brands or for older brands in areas where their distribution is weak. However, this is a dangerous game. The retailer has to agree to carry the brand *before* the sampling takes place; sampling in the absence of the brand being available in stores is not only a waste of money, it may also engender a negative brand attitude among resentful consumers whose expectations were raised by the sample. As we have seen, manufacturers must do their homework on distributors as *target audiences* before undertaking this or any other type of promotion designed to gain trial by distributors.

The Media of Sampling

Our tactical examination of sampling would not be complete without a brief review of the "media" or methods of sampling. These are important for the manager because the method chosen is affected by: (a) directness and therefore cost, (b) size of product to be sampled, and (c) perishability.

There are eight basic sampling "media." The pros and cons of each are summarized in Table 13.1, compiled from various sources including: Aniero; the American Association of Advertising Agencies; and Schultz and Robinson.[5] The methods range from the extremely fast and direct (but also more costly) media of door-to-door, direct mail, and central location, to the less expensive but slower methods via distributors. Appropriate selection is easily made from the table.

TABLE 13.1   EIGHT BASIC SAMPLING MEDIA

	Uses	Limitations
1. *Door to door*	• Virtually any product can be delivered in this way	• Most expensive means of sampling • Problem with leaving perishables if occupant absent • Illegal in some areas
2. *Direct mail*	• Best for small, light products that are non-perishable	• Rising postal costs
3. *Central location*	• Best for perishables such as food, or when personal demonstration is required	• If in-store, same offer must be made to all retailers (Robinson-Patman Act) • Usually involves cost of sales training • If in public place, may be illegal in some areas
4. *Sample pack in stores*	• Best method for attracting retail support, because retailers sell the packs at a premium unit price	• Requires retail acceptance like any other new product • May necessitate special production for trial sizes
5. *Cross-product sampling in or on pack*	• Good for low-cost sampling of a manufacturer's other products	• Trial limited to users of "carrier" product • Restricted for large products
6. *Co-op package distribution*	• Good for narrow audiences such as college students, military personnel, brides	• Little appeal to trade
7. *Newspaper or magazine distribution*	• Relatively low-cost method of sample distribution for flat or pouchable products	• Seem to be regarded by media vehicle recipients as "cheap" and are often disregarded, resulting in less trial than with other sampling methods • Obviously limited to certain product types
8. *Any of above with coupon*	• Increases post-sample trial rate by using purchase incentive	• Additional cost of coupon handling

CFB Presentation of Samples

Sampling is the one promotion technique that is automatically consumer franchise building. Receipt of the sample generates immediate brand awareness, and trial of the sample establishes brand attitude (the key communication effect in the CFB approach) and brand purchase intention. A further CFB bonus is that favorable trial of a sample seems more likely, than other trial offers, to generate favorable word-of-mouth communication to other prospective triers. Of course, unfavorable trial experience can generate negative word-of-mouth communication, though fortunately at a lower level than the positive effect.[6]

A conceptual note is appropriate here. Sampling is described by many marketing writers as an example of behavior change leading to attitude change, which apparently reverses the normal sequence—in advertising—of attitude change leading to behavior change. However, this description is not correct. Before a person would try a sample, he or she must at least have a tentatively favorable attitude toward it. Would you, for example, try a new shampoo or a new aspirin that you did not at least tentatively trust? Some degree of attitude change (actually positive attitude creation—see Chapter 6) therefore *precedes* the trial behavior. It is true that a *confirmed* attitude follows the trial behavior but this happens, too, in low involvement brand trial induced by advertising (see Chapters 7 and 9).

Thus, the contention in many textbooks that promotion, and especially sampling, somehow works differently than advertising is not true. Both work through *communication effects*. Furthermore, the behavioral step in the six-step sequence still occurs after the communication effects, in that the behavior of interest is *purchase* behavior, not sample trial behavior.

While we are still speaking of concepts, another frequent textbook practice is to describe post-trial attitude increases as being due to "cognitive dissonance" or, more recently, as an example of "self-perception" phenomena. But in most cases, post-trial attitude confirmation—or disconfirmation if the trial experience is poor—is more simply explained by satisfaction-dissatisfaction following expectations.[7] Only in a high involvement situation where the "choice" has been "forced" on the person (forced compliance, as when a secretary is obliged to use a new word processor) would cognitive dissonance or self-perception phenomena be likely to occur. There is no forced choice with sampling or indeed with any other form of promotion.

Example of Sampling: Agree Conditioner Launch

A good example of sampling is the launch in 1977 of Agree conditioner. Details of the program are from Robinson.[8]

The S.C. Johnson Company decided to launch Agree, a new brand, into a fast growing category in which there were already five strong brands of conditioner by unit market share: Tame, 17 percent; Revlon's Flex, 10 percent; Wella Balsam, 10 percent; Breck, 10 percent; and Alberto Balsam, 6 percent. In home testing, Agree was found to be preferred to the category leader, Tame, by 68:32, and to the premium-priced brand, Breck, by 64:36, so sampling of Agree was likely to be successful in gaining repeat purchase following trial.

Agree spent $17.8 million on the launch promotion: $4.5 million on trade promotion, $6.0 million on consumer advertising ("Helps stop 'the greasies' "), the same amount, $6.0 million, on sampling, and a further $1.3 million on sample tags and miscellaneous items. The trade promotion consisted of a total of 30 percent off the wholesale purchase price: an introductory allowance of 16.7 percent off, a re-order allowance of 8.3 percent, and 5.0 percent toward co-op advertising.

The sampling was done by the direct mail method (recommended in Table 13.1, earlier, for small, light products that are non-perishable). Over 30 million 2-oz trial-sized free samples were mailed, reaching about 50 percent of the nation's households. With this mass sampling, an impressive 38 percent of conditioner (category) users tried Agree. Aided by a coupon with the sample (to increase the post-sample trial rate; see Table 13.1 again), 78 percent of triers, representing 30 percent of all category users, made a first purchase. Data on full-value repeat purchases are not available.

The campaign, centering on sampling, was successful. Within 5 months—illustrating the superior speed of sampling in gaining trial—Agree had become co-leader in the conditioner market with Flex, which surpassed Tame, with 20 percent unit share and 18 percent dollar share.

COUPONS

A second major trial-generating technique is manufacturer's coupons. Coupons may be defined as vouchers or certificates that entitle the buyer to a price reduction on the couponed item. Coupons—especially manufacturer's coupons—are somewhat more than a simple price reduction or price-off offer. A coupon is a tangible object that typically is regarded with appreciation by consumers as a small gift from the manufacturer.

In this section "coupons," using common terminology, refer to *manufacturer's* coupons—not trade coupons, which are discussed separately as a third trial technique. Manufacturer's coupons are designed and distributed by the manufacturer (marketer). Consumers can redeem them by sending them directly to the manufacturer or, more commonly, they can be redeemed indirectly by turning them in for a discount on the brand at *any* retail outlet that sells the brand. Trade coupons, in contrast, are designed and distributed by the distributor (retailer), although they are usually paid for by the manufacturer and the retailer jointly, out of co-op funds; they are redeemable only at the outlet or outlets of the *particular* retailer who offers them (one store or chain of stores). As we shall see, the two types of coupons differ in their ability to generate trial.

Coupons: The Second-Best Trial Generator

Couponing is generally acknowledged to be second-best to sampling as a promotion technique for generating trial. Fewer prospective buyers will redeem a coupon than will try a sample. This is because there are various "response costs" associated with redeeming a coupon.[9] Responses may include most or all of the following 10 events, depending on the type of coupon and where it is redeemed: (1) cutting, (2) trimming, (3) saving, (4) filing, (5) storing, (6) remembering to take it to the store, (7) finding product, (8) checking product size, (9) juggling coupon among others at checkout counter, and (10) possibly receiving intolerant treatment by the checkout clerk.

Nevertheless, about 80 percent of the nation's households use coupons at least occasionally (this estimate is for 1977, a typical year for the U.S. economy).[10] There are only minor differences in usage across socio-economic groups. The large observational study by POPAI/DuPont indicates that on any given day, 24 percent of customers entering supermarkets are carrying coupons, with about 19 percent able to use them in the store that day.[11]

Recent studies—conducted in years in which the recession caused coupon usage to peak—suggest there is a heavy user phenomenon in coupons, in that one-third of all shoppers who redeem coupons carry five or more coupons per store visit and account for two-thirds of total redemptions.[12] Heavy coupon users may be skewed toward homemakers, who presumably have more time than working women to clip coupons and redeem them, even though both types of women are equally price sensitive.[13] The implication of the homemaker skew will be considered shortly.

Managers can expect about 3 to 5 percent of couponed households to buy the brand, as compared with about 15 to 20 percent of households who will make a purchase following sampling. It should be noted that *direct mail* distribution often produces up to 10 percent response for couponing, and up to 40 percent response for sampling, but these are higher-than-average figures caused by the selective targeting of direct mailing to higher-buying-potential households.

Because couponing is considerably less expensive than sampling—on an immediate basis, although the long run profit comparison might be quite different—it is the most prevalent promotional technique used by manufacturers.

When to Use Couponing

There are four main marketing situations in which the manager should use couponing as a brand *trial* technique:

1 *New Brand or New Users in Established Category* In an established product category, speed of trial of a new brand, or speed of extending an existing brand to new users, is generally *not* a critical factor. This suits couponing because the average (median) time taken for consumers to redeem coupons is, depending on the medium of delivery, about 2 to 6 *months*. Consumers typically wait until they are low in product supply before they use a coupon.

2 *For Trial: Never Without Prior Advertising (or Sampling)* Coupons work best in prompting trial when the would-be trier has a favorable (if tentative) prior attitude toward the brand. The "recognized" brand with a coupon represents good value, whereas an unknown brand does not. Establishing a favorable attitude requires advertising prior to the couponing, or sampling prior to the couponing (if justified by the situations for sampling discussed earlier) or both.

3 *When Usage is an Acceptable Secondary Target Behavior* Sampling, for completely new brands, is the only situation in which response to the promotion offer consists entirely of new triers. With couponing, the response usually consists of a mix of triers and users. For a *new* brand, users get "in" because, with the delay in redeeming coupons, they already may have tried the brand, or with coupon distribution through magazines and newspapers, they may receive and redeem more than one coupon and thus go beyond trial into usage. For an *existing* brand that is trying to attract new triers with coupons, it is virtually impossible to prevent the coupons from being received and redeemed by current users.

On a gross basis, and this includes the use of coupons to load users as well as to generate trial, only about one in three coupon redemptions represents brand trial; two in three redemptions are by users.[14] As an obvious qualification to these figures, the newer the brand in the market, the higher the ratio of triers to users.

The manager can raise the proportion of triers by using the more expensive consumer-direct methods of coupon distribution rather than "mass" media distribution which tends to repeat coverage to the same household. The media of coupon distribution will be considered shortly.

4 *When the Target Audience is Skewed Toward Full-time Homemakers* Triers, of course, will come from the potential target audiences of new category users, other-brand switchers, or other-brand loyals who have not (recently) tried the brand. If the demographic *profile* of the target audience (see Chapter 5) shows that a majority are homemakers, then coupons would seem to have a higher probability of being redeemed. As indicated earlier, full-time homemakers are presumed to have somewhat more time available to collect and use coupons.

On the other hand, if the target audience's demographic profile is skewed toward working women, then a price-off promotion, which involves no response cost, would generate higher trial.

The manager must indeed have the research data on the *brand's* target audience and not *assume* that certain "demographic segments" will be better targets. For example, despite the alleged greater time pressures facing working women, they are not more likely than full-time homemakers to use "convenience" foods or appliances. However, for various "family life cycle" products, such as baby food, there is naturally a skew toward homemakers, and coupons should be differentially effective for these products.

The Media of Couponing

The "media" available for the distribution of coupons have particular applications regarding trial (Table 13.2). The variations are in: the proportion of triers versus users, redemption rate, cost, and reproduction quality, with the latter relevant to the CFB effectiveness of coupons. Included for completeness as the sixth medium of distribution are in-pack or on-pack coupons. This

Table 13.2   SIX BASIC COUPONING MEDIA FOR GENERATING TRIAL

	Uses	Limitations
1. *Consumer-direct* (direct mail, door-to-door, central location, in-store take-one's)	• Best method for maximizing proportion of triers over users since each household gets only one coupon • High quality reproduction (CFB) • High redemption rate (average: 11%)	• Expensive unless co-oped with other coupons—which doesn't affect redemption rate • Slow redemption (median: 5 months)
2. *Free-standing card inserts in newspapers*	• Second best method of maximizing proportion of triers • Less expensive than consumer-direct if not misredeemed • High quality reproduction (CFB) • Moderate redemption rate (average: 5%)	• Very open to theft and misredemption—perhaps 20% of redemptions • Moderately slow redemption (median: 3 months)
3. *In-ad in Sunday newspaper magazines* (supplements)	• Probably third best method overall • Fair to high quality reproduction (CFB) • Low redemption rate (average: 3%)	• Somewhat open to theft and misredemption through gang-cutting • Moderately slow redemption (median: 3 months)
4. *In-ad in magazines*	• Best for special interest products that appeal to the magazine's readers • High quality reproduction (CFB) • Low redemption rate (average: 3%, though more expensive "pop-ups" redeem at 5%)	• Broad target would mean multiple magazines are needed to reach enough triers • High competition for attention unless pop-ups • Very slow redemption rate (median: 6 months)
5. *In-ad in newspapers* (but in manufacturer's ad, not retailer's ad)	• Cheapest method • Low duplication if offer not repeated too often • Low redemption rate (average: 3%)	• Low quality reproduction so not advisable for new brands • Moderately slow redemption (median: 3 months)
6. *In/on packs* (see usage promotions)	• Mainly for stimulating usage	• In/on pack coupon is good for next purchase, not trial purchase

* The right-hand column consists of four *price-off* techniques (see text), hence our reference to only four main trial techniques in total, where price-offs are the fourth.

medium is not discussed here because in/on packs are primarily a *usage* medium: they are good only for the *next* purchase and thus reward mainly current users who have previously tried the brand, rather than new triers. In/on packs will be examined in the next chapter, on usage promotions.

The recommendations are our estimates from various sources including Aniero; Aycrigg; Haugh; and Schultz and Robinson.[15] The applications should be self-explanatory to the manager concerned with these finer tactical aspects of coupon implementation.

CFB Presentation of Coupons

Coupons can be an excellent technique for instilling communication effects that are consumer franchise building for the brand. Coupons can increase brand awareness as well as brand attitude.

The processes of paying attention to a coupon, clipping it, saving it, taking it to the store, and so forth—the very limitations that were mentioned earlier—are assets in that the prospective trier is getting extra exposure to the brand name on the coupon, which increases *brand awareness*. If the brand typically is chosen by brand recognition, then the coupon should include a picture of the brand—preferably a color picture, hence the limitation of newspaper on-page coupons. If the brand typically is chosen by brand recall, a salient brand name on the coupon is sufficient.

The other necessary communication effect for CFB creation is *brand attitude*. To increase brand attitude, the brand benefits or the main selling message should be reproduced on the coupon. This reinforces the prior advertising by serving as an extra exposure to the message. Several extra exposures may be attained if the prospective buyer reads the coupon not only when clipping it but also when filing it and retrieving it to take to the store.

Independently contributing to brand attitude is the "good feeling" that occurs because a coupon is seen as a gift. Evidence that coupons are perceived as a gift beyond their (price-off) face value (currently about 30 cents) comes from Nielsen data indicating that the average face value of coupons over the years has risen far more slowly than have prices themselves. Moreover, a 30-cent coupon will not produce twice the response of a 15-cent coupon, indicating that the coupon itself has extra value.[16]

A further advantage with coupons is that the CFB effects on brand awareness and brand attitude can occur even if the coupon is not ultimately redeemed. Many consumers clip coupons, save them, but forget to take them to the store—yet still buy the brand.[17] Thus, communication effects can be established without the manufacturer bearing the cost of redemption.

Example of Couponing Failure for Trial of an Established Brand: Maxwell House

Coupon presentation was well exemplified earlier for Right Guard, in Chapter 12, Figure 12.5.

Let us instead provide a negative example that illustrates the problem of ensuring that coupons intended to generate trial indeed do so. In early 1981, General Foods decided to cut back on the use of coupons in promoting Maxwell House coffee.[18] General Foods had been couponing the brand every five weeks, using attractive 40-cent coupons, and achieving an 8 percent redemption rate in comparison with the coffee industry average of 5 percent.

But consumer research for Maxwell House revealed that the coupons were mostly being redeemed by current Maxwell House users. Maxwell House, with the expensive couponing program, was mainly "buying its own customers"! A review of the situations in which couponing is appropriate for generating trial, and selection of the couponing medium that maximizes the proportion of triers (consumer-direct), might have indicated to General Foods that this promotion would not work well.

TRADE COUPONS

Trade coupons are coupons offered in the *retailer's* ads or fliers, redeemable at the retailer's store or chain of stores. Since trade coupons require the manufacturer's prior agreement (unlike many retail price-off offers), they constitute a promotion technique which is largely under the manufacturer's or marketer's control. However, trade coupons are quite different in their strategic implications for trial than are manufacturer's coupons.

Trade Coupons: Fast and Localized Trial Generator

The main advantages of trade coupons versus manufacturer's coupons are that trade coupons are fast—there is usually a several days' redemption limit on the offer—and, because of the retailer tie-in, they can be used to stimulate trial in local areas where the brand's penetration is differentially low.

The fast trial aspect might at first suggest that mass advertising followed by trade coupons would be an effective strategy for new brands in a new category, where speed of trial is crucial. However, this is not true, for several reasons. For one, a trade coupon program on a multi-retailer basis (needed for wide distribution of the new entry) is complicated and time-consuming to set up, because trade allowance details have to be negotiated with every individual retailer or retail chain. For another, there is no guarantee that consumers who see the mass introductory advertising will also see the trade ads in which the coupons—along with many competing coupons—will appear. Finally, trade coupons are weak on CFB aspects. As we will see later, this doesn't help a new brand.

When to Use Trade Coupons

There is really only one situation in which trade coupons are recommended as a trial-generating technique: *when trade trial is a problem in particular areas*. Retailers love trade coupons. They're an inexpensive way of promoting their own stores. The retailer gets the allowance up front—often covering the full 100 percent upper limit of redemption. And sometimes trade coupons don't even require retailer redemption—they can be destroyed at the cash register after they've done their selling job, which is an increasingly common arrangement.

The manufacturer who is having problems getting shelf space in certain areas may therefore find trade coupons an effective strategy. Trade coupon arrangements are one way of ensuring that a trade allowance indeed gets used. The manufacturer achieves trial from retailers and trial from consumers (note that if distribution in the area is non-existent or low, then most redeemers must be triers).

Trade couponing is not, however, a broadly usable trial technique for the reasons mentioned earlier, namely, the program is complex to set up with different retailers, the coupons may not be seen by all triers, and trade coupons usually are not consumer franchise building.

The Media of Trade Couponing

The vast majority of trade coupons appear in retailers' ads in newspapers or in retail store "shoppers" or fliers distributed in mailboxes. These are fine because they reach people at home when people are inquisitively looking for local store specials and are thus attentive to new brands. The least frequent method, whereby trade coupons are attached to the package in the store, is much less desirable for trial because package coupons are most likely to be seen by people already looking for the brand—that is, current users.

CFB Presentation of Trade Coupons

Trade coupons are relatively weak, in relation to manufacturer's coupons, in generating brand awareness and brand attitude.

Brand awareness is restricted overall via an attention limitation, in that trade coupons typically appear on pages crowded with the retailer's other in-ad trade coupons. Brand recall is good thereafter *if* the consumer clips the coupon. But brand recognition—the relevant brand awareness objective for so many supermarket products—is hampered severely by the fact that the visual of the package is a *black and white line drawing* of the package rather than an actual full-color photograph. For a new (unfamiliar) brand, this is far from ideal.

Brand attitude is not built, either, by trade coupons—unless the manufacturer can persuade the retailer to include brand benefits or the main selling message on the coupon. The manager should insist on this inclusion—although usually there is only room for a very short message.

A final important aspect for the manager with regard to the use of trade coupons for stimulating consumer trial of the brand is that the retailer functions as an *endorser*. A new brand intending to generate a high-status "image" may therefore find some retailers inappropriate because the store image doesn't complement the brand image. A properly thought out distribution plan would include only brand attitude-compatible retailers.

Case histories of trade coupon programs directed at triers, specifically, are hardly ever reported, so it's hard to give an example. You may be able to find an example, yourself, by looking through your newspaper on "shopping days" for retailers' ads. A coupon for an unfamiliar brand is quite likely a trade coupon being used to generate trial, the brand being unfamiliar because it's new. However, as we noted, a new brand would probably only be in a trade coupon if it had a distribution objective in the local area.

PRICE-OFF TECHNIQUES

Price-offs are the fourth and sometimes most narrowly applicable means of inducing trial; they are much more widely applicable for increasing usage. In this chapter, we will concentrate on the utilization of price-off offers for generating trial. In Chapter 14, on usage promotions, we will further examine price-offs in their wider role of increasing usage.

Four Different Price-off Techniques

Price-offs can be implemented tactically in four different ways:

- Refunds or rebates
- Bonus packs
- Direct price-offs
- Warranties

The four variations are ordered on the basis of general to narrow applicability as trial techniques.

Refunds or Rebate Offers

Refunds or rebates are *partial* money-back offers. They are not used in the old sense of a refund, which implied all your money back if not fully satisfied (this is a money-back guarantee, discussed later under warranties). Rather, modern refunds—or the equivalent name, rebates—function much like a coupon. To induce trial, a refund or rebate offer, like a coupon, must be processed by the would-be trier as if representing *immediate* value, even though the trier does not in fact receive the money back until after the product is purchased and the refund offer redeemed.

In support of the idea that refunds represent immediate value, it is estimated that as many as half of all purchasers never claim the refund. Redemption is typically about 1 or 2 percent, but purchase is estimated at about 3 to 4 percent.[19] The purchase rate is similar to that achieved by coupons.

Indeed, although most refunds are paid in cash or, for larger amounts, by check, it has become increasingly common to offer coupons back ("bounce-back" coupons) in place of money, thus emphasizing the similarity between the two techniques. Bounce-back coupons, offered as the refund, can stimulate repeat purchases of the brand.

When to Use Refunds for Trial   For trial, refund offers should require only *one proof of purchase*. With only a single purchase required, the prospective buyer will be less hesitant to buy than when multiple purchases are required.

Refunds rarely seem to be appealing in amounts less than $1.00. This means *trial* refunds should only be considered *for new products that are priced at $5.00 or more at retail*. A discount of $1.00 on products selling for less than $5.00 would be too expensive for most manufacturers to bear, and would be overdoing the consumer incentive needed to induce trial. For discounts smaller than $1.00, and thus for low-priced product categories, a coupon is more appropriate.

Refunds can be used for *very* expensive products to induce trial. In 1981, Chrysler's president, Lee Iacocca, offered a $500 rebate on the purchase of any Chrysler model, and $1000 on some models, to boost sinking sales. This was a pioneering use of refunds or rebates for such expensive products. In the recession-racked economy of the early 1980s, these massive offers seemed to work, although many other factors, not the least of which was Iacocca himself, contributed to Chrysler's successful turnaround.

CFB Presentation of Refund Offers   Refund offers are clipped from ads like coupons and thus represent message delivery opportunities. They are perhaps not quite as good as coupons in getting extra exposure, as refund offers typically are mailed immediately rather than being saved and then taken to the store.

Managers, however, often miss the opportunity to include brand awareness and especially brand attitude elements with the refund offer. Depending on the brand awareness objective, the refund offer should reproduce a picture of the package to increase the likelihood of brand recognition at the point of purchase, or include the brand name prominently to increase brand recall for subsequent purchases. To assist brand attitude, the main message—the main benefit claim or claims—should be featured on the refund certificate.

A further CFB tactic with refund offers prevents them from being perceived as "just" price-offs which, for a new brand, can undermine brand attitude. The accompanying copy in the refund offer's advertisement—such as "We're so confident that you'll like this product . . . ." or "We'll send you $1.00 to prove it to yourself"—should be worded in a way that minimizes the idea that it is just another discount and emphasizes the manufacturer's faith in the product.

Bonus Packs

Bonus packs offer more product in (a) a larger container or (b) multiple units, for the same or a reduced price. Thus, there is effectively a price-off per unit for bonus packs, and the buyer ends up with more product than he or she would normally buy. Bonus packs have obvious implications for increased usage (as discussed in the next chapter) because of the extra product received. But they can also be used to induce trial.

When to Use Bonus Packs for Trial   The conditions in which bonus packs can be utilized as a trial offer are somewhat restricted. First of all, the product has to be one that is *"divisible" into units* for packaging into bonus packs. Coffee, for example, would qualify, but computers would not. For food products to be bonus packed in a larger container, the product must be able to retain its freshness after the larger container is opened. Again, coffee would qualify, but milk wouldn't.

Second, bonus packs seem most appropriate as a trial device when the brand choice is *low involvement*. Contrast the trier of a high involvement product, who would not want more, but rather less of the product (a sample) to try. This is relaxed for low involvement products. The low involvement trier has not lost much if the bonus pack brand is less satisfactory than expected. The buyer lost no extra money, and is simply stuck with a little extra of a low-risk item. The initial "immediate value" of the bonus pack may have sufficient appeal for low involvement brand trial.

Third, bonus packs can only be used when the manufacturer's *relationships with retailers are good*. Bonus packs require more shelf space than normal packs and are therefore not as easily accepted by retailers. When used to increase retail distribution, bonus packs will not penetrate unless the manufacturer is regarded as a favored client by the retailer.

Bonus packs therefore are a limited-application trial technique. If the product is divisible, if it is also relatively low risk, and if retail relationships are strong, then bonus packs are worth considering.

CFB Presentation of Bonus Packs Bonus packs part ways on consumer franchise-building potential in the difference between larger containers and multiple units. Bonus packs do not increase brand awareness prior to the trial purchase (unlike a sample, coupon, or refund offer) because they are not encountered until the consumer is in the store. However, larger containers provide an opportunity to catch and recapture attention when they are purchased and used, thus facilitating brand recognition and brand recall for *subsequent* purchases. Furthermore, the increase in size of the package and label provides an opportunity to portray the brand's advertising message, thus increasing brand attitude—although again, not prior to the point of purchase for trial but rather for subsequent purchases.

Multiple unit bonus packs are a different matter. The wrappers in which they are presented work only at the point of purchase, where they may facilitate brand recognition. But then, the wrappers, even if carrying a message, usually are discarded immediately and lose the ability to communicate further about the brand. Multiple unit bonus packs therefore have no CFB advantage beyond the point of purchase and do not make a long-term contribution to brand awareness and brand attitude.

Direct Price-offs

Direct price-offs are a reduction in the "normal" price of the brand. The discount is offered directly, rather than indirectly through a coupon or refund. The word "normal" is in quotes because, as we will see, the normal price against which the discount is compared is often subject to managerial influence when designing the offer.

Here we are talking about manufacturers' introductory price-offs offered directly to the consumer (not retailers' price-offs which were discussed earlier in the section on retailer promotion). The discount comes out of the manufacturer's margin, not the retailer's margin. The retailer's margin must be maintained to keep the brand attractive to retailers.

Two Forms of Price-offs: Both Limited   Price-offs can be offered either (a) in advertisements or (b) through the use of specially labelled "price packs" sent by manufacturers for display by retailers (price-offs marked on signs in stores are almost invariably retailer price-offs, not manufacturer price-offs). Both methods have their limitations.

In-ad price-offs instituted by manufacturers for a new brand are problematic in that the advertised price may not coincide with the price individual retailers would like to charge; thus, strict control over retailers is required, which is increasingly difficult to implement.

Price packs also have limitations. Many retailers—about half of all retailers on average—won't accept price packs.[20] The reason is the same: price packs circumvent the retailer's desire to set prices.

When to Use Introductory Price-offs   The use of introductory price-offs to induce trial is appropriate in only one circumstance: for attracting trial among *new users for a familiar brand in an established category*. Why? Because price-offs only work when the prospective buyer knows beforehand what the "normal" price of the brand would be and can equate this price with the brand's perceived quality or "value." In Monroe's terms, there must be a *reference price* in the prospective buyer's mind against which the discounted price can be compared.[21] An Apple computer offered with a price-off, for example, will only attract new triers if they have a firm idea of the quality of an Apple computer and know its normal price.

Accordingly, price-offs cannot be used to introduce a new brand that represents an entirely new product category—such as Apple computers when they *first* appeared on the market and introduced the personal computer *category*. A new product category has no reference price and so there is nothing to compare a discount against. Hence the first-in brand in a new product category usually sets the highest price that the manufacturer believes prospective buyers will be willing to pay, because a high price in the absence of other information will imply high quality. For new product *category* introductions, as we saw earlier, *sampling* is the appropriate trial promotion technique. Note that small computers can be "sampled" in retail stores and larger computers sampled via trial offers.

Additionally, price-offs cannot be used to introduce a new (unfamiliar) brand into an established category—unless the price-off is preceded or accompanied by advertising that makes the brand familiar and establishes its value. In the latter respect, price-offs are *an alternative to coupons*. Generally, a price-off will be used rather than a coupon:

- If fast trial is desired (because price-offs are immediate, whereas coupons take a while to be redeemed), or
- For higher priced products and industrial products where a coupon, even for a large face value, would seem out of place.

CFB Presentation of Introductory Price-offs   Introductory price-offs can be consumer franchise building if they are presented correctly. The first CFB communication effect, brand awareness, can be heightened by flagging the price-off offer in ads or on price packs. This can be done through color contrast and with words, e.g., "Regular price . . . Sale Price . . . .." Note the advantage of using in-ad price-offs to generate brand awareness: ads reach more prospective triers in the mass audience than price packs can reach at the point of purchase.

Brand attitude also can be increased via thoughtful price-off presentation. Four presentation tactics appear to increase purchase by operating on brand attitude and thence brand purchase intention: (1) showing the savings clearly; (2) describing the "value" of the offer effectively in words; (3) including the brand's main benefit in price-off signs or ads; and, (4) if appropriate, using the retailer's store image as an endorsement.

First and most important, the price-off presentation should show the value of the savings clearly. The Federal Trade Commission has enforced this in a way that aids the marketer by aiding communication. Price-off offers must show (1) the regular price, (2) the cash savings, and then (3) the new price. The regular or "normal" price is subject sometimes to collusive and possibly misleading manipulation by marketers, and especially by retailers.[22] This, however, is an ethical issue separate from the undoubted effectiveness of the format.

Interestingly, consumers tend to attribute a 10 percent savings to *any* advertised price, even if it is not a price-off offer.[23] For a new brand, even the seemingly innocuous wording of "reasonably priced" implies to consumers a price that is lower than average for the category.[24]

This raises the important question of *how much* of a discount to offer. Blair and Landon[25] tested price-off amounts for a Texas Instruments calculator, which at that time was retailing for about $50. (This fits our recommendation of being a familiar brand in an established product category.) They found that while prospective buyers were skeptical of very large discounts, that nevertheless, the larger the discount, the stronger the intention to buy. However, a 40 percent discount was needed before purchase intention increased significantly over a 10 percent discount (which would be attributed to a non-discounted price mentioned in an ad anyway). We suspect that if the study had been confined to people who were "in the market" for a calculator (that is, who had the category need) then a much smaller discount would have been effective.

Many textbooks recommend that at least 15 to 20 percent off the "normal" price must be offered in order to stimulate trial. The exact amount can be pre-tested by measuring purchase intentions, among category prospects, at increasing amounts of price-off (see the promotion testing section of Chapter 14).

The second price-off presentation tactic relies on the fact that the words (semantic cues) chosen to accompany price-offs can have powerful effects on perceptions of value and thus, we presume, purchase intention. Table 13.3 shows ratings of four commonly used semantic cues in terms of perceived value for money.[26] The words "Sale Price" appear to be most effective, and considerably more effective in suggesting value than the words "Now Only." Presentation of price-offs in words, and not just numerically, is well worth the manager's consideration.

A third tactic is to include the brand's main *benefits* in a price-off ad or p-o-p sign. This can significantly increase sales of the item. McKinnon, Kelly and Robinson[27] conducted an experiment in a major national department store chain in which six products' sales were tracked for 54 observation days under three rotated conditions: normal price-off ticket (regular price, sale price); price-off standing sign; and the same-sized price-off standing sign with two or three benefits included (e.g., a women's slacks product included the benefits "dressy or causal," "elastic waist," and "see our coordinated top"). Compared with the normal price-off ticket, whereas the price-off standing sign increased average sales of the products by 24 percent, the price-off standing sign *with benefits mentioned* increased sales by 50 percent. Clearly, there is much to be gained by this direct CFB presentation of price-off promotions.

Last, the store image of the retailer through which the brand is offered also can affect brand attitude. A price-off offered for the brand in a discount retailer's ad or in a discount store might be very effective because of a "double

TABLE 13.3   FOUR COMMONLY USED PRICE-OFF SEMANTIC CUES IN TERMS OF PERCEIVED VALUE FOR MONEY

Semantic Cue	Rating:* "Usually means a good buy for the money"
"Total Value _____; Sale Price_____"	5.04
"Regular Price _____; Sale Price _____"	4.96
"Compare at _____; Our Price _____"	4.54
"_____ Percent Off; Now Only _____"	3.82

* Seven-point scale where 7 = strongly agree; 4 = neither agree nor disagree; 1 = strongly disagree.

Source: J.R. Walton and E. Berkowitz, Information needs for comparative pricing decisions, in P.E. Murphy et al. (Eds.), *Proceedings: AMA Educators Conference,* Chicago: American Marketing Association, 1983, pp. 241–245. By permission.

discount'' attribution. However, a price-off offered through a higher price-image store that doesn't discount regularly may imply good value and also may be effective. The retailer endorsement effect is by no means clear-cut and should be tested for the brand.[28] Also, given that price-offs to attract new buyers should be used only with *familiar* brands, the brand's already established attitude in the prospective trier's mind may tend to minimize the retailer effect.

Warranties

A warranty is a contract offered by a manufacturer to a customer to provide restitution in some form (such as money back, replacement, or free service or repairs) should the product prove deficient within a given time period. Warranties are actually a form of price-off offer, although not usually thought of as such.

Although it is really a future conditional price-off, to the extent that the warranty serves as an immediate incentive to buy—by reducing perceived risk—it is functioning subjectively like an immediate price-off promotion. For example, American Motors some years ago spurred car sales by offering a 2-year/24,000 mile service warranty when the standard for the industry was 1-year or 12,000 miles.

Warranties have the most limited application of all price-off techniques. They are suitable mainly for *high involvement* products. This usually means high-priced products such as cars, appliances, or industrial equipment. Although several stores such as Sears have made 100 percent money-back or credit guarantees a purchase incentive for almost any item, such guarantees (warranties) should be most effective on high risk products offered by the store.

CFB Presentation of Warranties   Warranties have only a minor effect on brand awareness; they don't really need to if offered on high involvement products for which prospective buyers engage in deliberate search.

Warranties have a much larger effect on brand attitude. In fact, an attractive warranty can completely create a favorable brand attitude leading to purchase. Shimp and Bearden[29] examined the effect of warranties on the trial purchase of three high risk, innovative products: a multi-screen TV set, a plastic auto tire, and a computerized indoor jogging device. The investigators found that high quality warranties reduced perceived purchase risk significantly. High quality warranties covered every component, for full repair, for a substantially long usage period.

The significant aspect from the brand attitude standpoint is that high quality warranties worked regardless of the introductory price and regardless of the manufacturer's reputation. If they functioned *simply* as a price-off, high quality warranties would work best with better-reputation brands, via a brand purchase intention effect. However, they seem just as likely to reduce risk for unknown brands, which means that warranties are capable of creating brand attitude, a true CFB effect.

This discussion of warranties completes our assessment of trial promotion techniques.

TABLE 13-4   PRINCIPAL CONDITIONS FAVORING TRIAL PROMOTION TECHNIQUES*

Sampling
- New product category introduction
- Superior brand introduced in established category

Coupons
- New brand in established category
- Especially if target audience is skewed toward homemakers

Trade coupons
- When trade trial is a problem in particular areas

Refunds or rebates
- Alternative to coupons for products priced at $5.00 or more at retail

Bonus packs
- Low involvement products only (and must be quantity-divisible, with good shelf life)

Direct price-offs
- New users for familiar brand in established category
- Especially for consumer durables and other expensive products where coupons would seem inappropriate

Warranties
- High involvement (high perceived risk) products

* The right-hand column consists of four *price-off* techniques (see text), hence our reference to only four main trial techniques in total, where price-offs are the fourth.

SUMMARY

Trial is the most important action objective for virtually every brand because of the importance, to sales, of penetration. Penetration is the main factor in sales because usage rates tend to be quite constant across brands once trial (presuming satisfaction) is achieved. Trial promotions can be used with new brands and also to attract new buyers to established brands.

It may be useful now to provide a summary (Table 13.4) of the *principal* situations in which the various trial techniques are most appropriate. This should not substitute for a careful review of the specific conditions and media implementation of each technique. The table provides a general overview only.

The two best trial-generating promotion techniques are sampling and coupons. The distribution "media" of these two techniques are complicated and require separate study by the manager. We provided tables of the advantages and disadvantages of alternative sampling and couponing media to aid this decision.

Trade coupons are best used to generate trial in local areas rather than as a broad-based trial technique.

Price-offs in four main forms also require careful consideration when utilized to generate trial. More than any other trial technique, price-off techniques (except warranties) tend to attract current users rather than triers. But by thoughtful implementation, such as limiting refunds or rebate purchase requirements to one unit of the brand, these techniques can be steered more effectively toward triers.

With all four types of trial promotions, the manager must plan the promotion offer's presentation so that it stimulates brand awareness and brand attitude (consumer franchise building or CFB presentation) and thereby operates beyond short-term purchase intentions to maximize full-price purchases when the promotion offer is withdrawn. Whereas sampling does this automatically, the other trial promotion techniques have to be designed specifically to generate CFB effects along the respective tactical lines suggested in this chapter.

NOTES

1 Most promotion experts would agree with these four choices as the best trial-inducing promotions. The expert who has been most responsible for these selections in the published literature is William A. Robinson, who writes a regular column, "Robinson on Promotions," for *Advertising Age* and compiles the annual *Best Sales Promotions of the Year* publications (Crain Books). For an excellent summary of Mr. Robinson's selections, see W.A. Robinson, "What are promos' weak, strong points?", *Advertising Age,* April 7, 1980, pp. 53–54. Readers of this article should note that in this book we focus on consumer promotion as a *trial* technique and have split Robinson's usage promotions slightly differently.

2 For a brief description of Professor Ehrenberg's empirically-based theory of the importance of penetration, see A.S.C. Ehrenberg, Predicting the performance of new brands, *Journal of Advertising Research,* 1971, *11*(6), 3–10. For more detail, see A.S.C. Ehrenberg, *Repeat-Buying: Theory and Applications,* Amsterdam: North-Holland Press, 1972.

3 Hank Aniero, another expert advisor on promotion, provided these estimates, which are based on wide experience, in a privately circulated document in 1977.

4 This strategy is described in D.E. Schultz and W.A. Robinson, *Sales Promotion Essentials,* Chicago: Crain Books, 1982, chapter 13.

5 The Aniero and Schultz and Robinson references are given in the previous two footnotes; see also The American Association of Advertising Agencies, *Sales Promotion Techniques: A Basic Guidebook,* New York: American Association of Advertising Agencies, 1978.

6 J.H. Holmes and J.D. Lett, Jr., Product sampling and word of mouth, *Journal of Advertising Research,* 1977, *17*(5), 35–40.

7 R.L. Oliver, Predicting sales promotion effects: assimilation, attribution, or risk reduction?, in J.C. Olson (Ed.), *Advances in Consumer Research: Vol. 7,* Provo, UT: Association for Consumer Research, 1980, pp. 314–317.

8 W.A. Robinson, *Best Sales Promotions of 1977/78,* Chicago: Crain Books, 1979, pp. 22–23.

9 L.J. Haugh, "Women cool to promotions, 'LHJ' tells premium executives," *Advertising Age,* October 10, 1977, pp. 10, 102.

10 R.H. Aycrigg, *Current Couponing Trends,* Northbrook, IL: A.C. Nielsen Company, 1977.

11 To be able to use a store-redeemable coupon, the brand has to be in stock, and the coupon must still be valid (not expired). The 1977 POPAI/DuPont study is summarized in L.J. Haugh, "Buying-habits study update," *Advertising Age,* June 27, 1977, pp. 56–58.

12 John Blair Marketing and Donnelley Marketing, *Cents-off Couponing and Consumer Purchasing Behavior,* Stamford, CT: Donnelley Marketing, 1982.

13 Opinion Research Corporation study, 1981, summarized in: Cost effectiveness of sales promotion efforts, *Marketing Review,* New York Chapter, American Marketing Association, 1981, *37*(3), p. 12.

14 Same reference as 13.

15 References cited previously (see notes 3, 4 and 10), plus L.J. Haugh, "How coupons measure up," *Advertising Age,* June 8, 1981, pp. 58, 63.

16 Schindler and Rothaus have coined the term "the coupon effect" to refer to the widely observed ability of cents-off coupons to cause a greater short-run sales increase than the equivalent reduction in price. (Of course, coupons also *cost* more to implement as a promotion program than simple price-off offers or straight price reductions, and cost must be considered against increased sales in calculating profitability.) In a laboratory experiment in which leading brands from 12 frequently purchased supermarket product categories were offered at either a low price or at the equivalent low price via a coupon, the coupon form of the price reduction caused almost double the brand choice incidence than the straight price reduction (45 percent versus 26 percent, in relation to the chance level of 20 percent for the five brands in each category). These figures are indicative but are not generalizable and hence not emphasized in the main text because this was a laboratory experiment with student subjects. See R.M. Schindler and S.E. Rothaus, An experimental technique for exploring the psychological mechanisms of the effects of price promotions, in E.C. Hirschman and M.B. Holbrook (Eds.), *Advances in Consumer Research: Vol. 12,* Provo, UT: Association for Consumer Research, 1985, pp. 133–137.

17 John Blair Marketing study, cited in *The Wall Street Journal,* September 25, 1980, p. 1.

18 Case history described in N. Giges, "GF trims its use of coupons," *Advertising Age,* December 7, 1981, p. 22.

19 D.E. Schultz and W.A. Robinson, same as note 4.

20 H. Aniero, same as note 3.

21 K.B. Monroe, *Pricing: Making Profitable Decisions,* New York: McGraw-Hill, 1979; also K.B. Monroe, The influence of price differences and brand familiarity on brand preferences, *Journal of Consumer Research,* 1976, *3,*(1), 42–49.

22 For evidence of deceptive reference prices used as a sales tactic, see: M.A. Sewall and M.H. Goldstein, The comparative price advertising controversy: consumer perceptions of catalog showroom reference prices, *Journal of Marketing,* 1979, *43*(3), 85–92; E.A. Blair and E.L. Landon, Jr., The effects of reference prices in retail advertisements, *Journal of Marketing,* 1981, *45*(2), 61–69; and S.A. Ahmed and G.M. Gulas, Consumers' perceptions of manufacturers' suggested list price, *Psychological Reports,* 1982, *50*(1), 507–518.

23 E.H. Blair and E. L. Landon, Jr., The effects of reference prices in retail advertisements, working paper, College of Business Administration, University of Houston, 1979. Despite the same title this is a different study than the 1981 study cited in the previous footnote.

24 J. Faberman and A. Tarlow, Point-of-view: price—the forgotten marketing variable, *Journal of Advertising Research,* 1981, *22*(5), 49–51.

25 The 1979 study, same reference as note 23.

26 J.R. Walton and E. Berkowitz, Information needs for comparative pricing decisions, in P.E. Murphy, G.R. Laczniak, P.F. Anderson, R.W. Belk, O.C. Ferrell, R.F. Lusch, T.A. Shimp, and C.B. Weinberg (Eds.), *Proceedings: AMA Educators Conference,* Chicago: American Marketing Association, 1983, pp. 241–245. The sample in this study consisted of 562 consumers with a broad range of demographics; value-for-money ratings did not differ across respondent demographic characteristics.

27 G.F. McKinnon, J.P. Kelly, and E.D. Robinson, Sales effects of point-of-purchase in-store signing, *Journal of Retailing,* 1981, *57*(2), 49–63.

28 E.N. Berkowitz, Contextual influences on consumer price responses: an experimental analysis, *Journal of Marketing Research,* 1980, *17*(3), 349–358.

29 T.A. Shimp, and W.O. Bearden, Warranties and other extrinsic cue effects on consumers' risk perceptions, *Journal of Consumer Research,* 1982, *9*(1), 38–46.

DISCUSSION QUESTIONS

13.1 You are the advertising manager of a new brand of mini-pizzas (like Jeno's) about to be introduced. Write an evaluative review of the alternative trial promotion techniques you could use.

13.2 Dr Pepper does not sell as well in the Northern half of the United States as it does in the South. Which promotion techniques to gain new triers in the North might be worth considering, and why?

13.3 International Harvester is about to introduce a radically new type of tractor. Explain how the following trial promotion techniques might be used, and justify which one(s) you think would be best:

a Sampling
b Rebate
c Direct price-off
d Warranty

13.4 Suppose the manager of the Polo line of men's clothing (by Ralph Lauren) wanted to offer a substantial price-off for a limited time early in the summer on its expensive summer suits to attract new buyers to try the line. How might the offer best be implemented?

13.5 Prepare a summary table of the CFB potential (covering brand awareness as well as brand attitude) of each of the trial promotion techniques described in the chapter.

FURTHER READING

Schultz, D.E. and Robinson, W.A. *Sales Promotion Essentials*. Chicago: Crain Books, 1982.

This is the most comprehensive review of promotion techniques available. Academician Schultz draws on the extensive practical experience of second author Robinson who reviews promotion programs for *Advertising Age*. It includes many examples that can easily be updated by reading *Advertising Age* using the framework developed by these authors.

When reading the Schultz and Robinson text in conjunction with our Chapter 13, you have to be very careful to focus on the *trial* objective, as the book is organized overall by techniques, not by trial promotions versus usage promotions. The same would apply, of course, when searching their text for *usage* techniques in conjunction with our Chapter 14. Also, some mental translation has to be done in comprehending the descriptions of how the promotion techniques work in terms of our five communication effects. Nonetheless, this remains the most detailed and practical text on promotion techniques.

CONSUMER USAGE PROMOTIONS AND PROMOTION TESTING

This chapter examines promotion techniques that are specialized for increasing *usage* of the brand. It is a relatively short chapter, so, for proximity to promotion concepts, we have included an Appendix at the end of the chapter on promotion *testing,* which applies to *both* trial and usage promotions. After reading this chapter you should:

- Appreciate the objectives of usage promotions
- Know which six techniques work best to increase usage, and the circumstances in which to use them
- Understand how to present usage promotions tactically to maximize consumer franchise building effects
- Realize the need to pre-test and post-test promotion offers and understand how to calculate the financial return on promotion

THE SIX USAGE PROMOTIONS

Six promotion techniques are especially suitable for increasing usage by *previous* triers of the brand. The initial three of these techniques include particular tactical implementations of techniques we have already discussed for trial; the last three are additional for usage. The six techniques are:

1 Price-offs (direct)
2 Bonus packs
3 In/on packs
4 Premiums
5 Contests and sweepstakes
6 Continuity programs

Remember, in this section we concentrate on utilizing promotion to build usage, assuming that trial has previously been achieved.

The Nature of Usage

Usage is the action objective that follows trial. The manager now wants to ensure that those who've tried the brand will continue to buy it regularly. Usage promotions, however, usually are employed to *increase* the buyer's usage of the brand, either through an increased buying *rate* over the long term or through an increased *amount* purchased in the short term. We will assume that the primary purpose of usage promotions is to increase the buying rate of the brand, although some exceptions where amount and timing are important will also be discussed.

The potential target audiences for usage promotions are:

- Brand loyals (to use more)
- Favorable brand switchers (to switch-in more often *or* to use more)

The "use more" objective is difficult to attain, and invariably it requires *advertising* of the new uses rather than promotion alone. New uses can include completely new uses (e.g., Arm & Hammer baking soda's use as a refrigerator deodorizer) or new usage situations (e.g., the Florida Citrus Commission's campaign: "Orange Juice . . . it isn't just for breakfast any more"). Because new uses amount to finding and establishing a new *category need,* most brands are not amenable to increased usage from this category expansion source.

The main strength of *promotion* is to get favorable brand switchers (brand users) to "switch-in" more often—that is, to devote more of their *current* category need purchases to the brand, relative to other brands that also meet the category need.

Usage promotions work primarily on *brand purchase intention,* a communication effect which, in brand switchers, typically is responsive to the (attitudinally acceptable) brand that offers the best deal on a particular purchase occasion. Despite the focus on brand purchase intention, some usage promotions have the potential to increase brand attitude (CFB) and thus may, in certain circumstances, be able to further entrench the brand in the buyer's acceptable set and perhaps make the switcher brand loyal. However, the reality of most usage promotions is that they mainly alter the *timing* of purchases through manipulating brand purchase intentions. Usage promotions "buy" customers when the promotion is on, then lose them when it's off.

Usage promotions are therefore effective in meeting short-term competitive threats. The long-term success of the brand depends much more on good advertising and wide penetration (trial) promotions than on usage promotions.

Inventory Clearing by Manufacturers

A second purpose of usage promotions is a less frequent one: to clear the manufacturer's inventory. (This is a short-term analogy to the continuous inventory transfer objective that motivates retailers to use retail promotion). The manufacturer, from time to time, may have excess production to sell off, or may have a new product or new seasonal or perishable stock that should replace current product in distribution as soon as possible.

Usage promotions to consumers help to clear the manufacturer's inventory faster. Because of the need for speed, the usual inventory-clearing promotion is a direct price-off. Retailers will accept direct price-offs readily, provided *their* profit margin is maintained. However, the manufacturer is restricted in frequency of using consumer price-offs, so the usual method is to heavily discount the product to the retailer (trade promotion) and insist that the *retailer* offer a price-off (retail promotion). Only rarely is some other—slower—form of consumer promotion used by the manufacturer to clear inventory.

Now let us consider the six usage promotion techniques in detail. Again, we identify when to use each technique, and (where possible) how to maximize consumer franchise building communication effects through the offer's presentation.

PRICE-OFFS (DIRECT)

Nearly every manufacturer, at some time or another, uses a price reduction to try to increase sales. Whereas retailers are free (within manufacturers' varying degrees of control) to use price-offs as often as they like, the *manufacturer's* use of price-offs, as opposed to permanent price reductions, is limited. The Federal Trade Commission dictates that no more than three price-off promotions may be offered in a year on a given size of the brand, and no more than 50 percent of the brand's total distributed volume can be price-offed *by the manufacturer* within a year.

For middle and high quality brands, the limitation on manufacturer price-offs probably is in their own interest. Otherwise, a brand could be discounted so frequently that buyers come to view the discount as a permanent benefit of the brand so that it in fact becomes a "cheaper" brand (negative CFB). But for the manufacturer of the lower quality (or, we should say, lower-price positioned) brand, the FTC's rules must seem quite restrictive. The reason for the FTC's rules, of course, is that if the list price or "normal" price is so little used, then discounts from this rarely used higher price are deceptive to consumers.

When to Use Price-offs   The principal application of price-offs is in *short-term competitive situations in localized areas*. Price-offs are the fastest sales promotion technique to implement, hence their frequent use as a short-term tactical device. Moreover, they can be confined to local areas where competition is strongest, although the price-off must be offered to all retailers in that area.

Price-offs can maintain usage rates against competitive inroads. Because heavy users of the category tend to be most deal-prone, as they have the most to gain from the savings,[1] a price-off on an existing brand can keep the largest-quantity prospective triers of the new competing brand or brands out of the market—at least temporarily. The manufacturer hopes that trial of the new brand or brands will be somewhat reduced as a result.

Price-off promotions have only a short-term effect on usage of the brand. Purchasers readily go back to other brands when the deal is off. This is demonstrated, for consumer packaged goods, in a diary panel study by Shoemaker and Shoaf covering five typical supermarket product categories.[2] Of those who bought the brand at the regular price—mostly loyals—67 percent will buy it at the regular price next time. But of those who bought the brand on deal—loyals *plus* switchers—only 45 percent will buy it at the regular price next time.

Of general interest is the volume increase that must result from a price-off (or for that matter a price reduction or any other promotion that cuts into profit) in order to maintain the same gross profit. Table 14.1 gives an indication of the increase in volume needed for different levels of discount to maintain various levels of gross profit.[3] For a 10 percent price-off, for example, a brand operating at anything less than 10 percent unit profit would be selling at a loss. If the unit profit were 15 percent, the price cut of 10 percent would have to generate 3 times the present volume (+200 percent) to maintain the same gross profit. Obviously, the manufacturer or marketer has to be very sure of the brand's upside demand elasticity—the sales increase resulting from a given price cut—before using a price-off promotion.[4]

CFB Presentation of Price-offs Price-offs *other than* clearly-marked and clearly-believed *introductory* price-offs are not in themselves consumer franchise building. Users respond to the price-off as simply short-term value that stimulates temporary purchase intention without altering their attitude toward the brand.

However, there is one very important aspect of price-off presentation that is tactically related to *competing* brand attitudes. A carefully chosen price-off amount can bring the brand down, temporarily, into a lower-priced product

TABLE 14.1 VOLUME INCREASE NEEDED TO MAINTAIN GROSS PROFIT FROM VARIOUS LEVELS OF PRICE-OFF

	Gross profit* to be maintained						
Price-off (%)	5%	10%	15%	20%	25%	30%	40%
1	+25†	+ 12	+ 8	+ 6	+ 5	+ 4	+ 3
5	(loss)	+100	+ 50	+ 34	+ 25	+ 20	+ 15
10	(loss)	(loss)	+200	+100	+ 67	+ 50	+ 34
15	(loss)	(loss)	(loss)	+300	+150	+100	+ 60
20	(loss)	(loss)	(loss)	(loss)	+400	+200	+100
25	(loss)	(loss)	(loss)	(loss)	(loss)	+500	+167

* Gross profit = unit profit × volume. This assumes that unit costs remain the same.
† The entries in the table show the *volume increase* required (rounded).
Source: Courtesy Miller Publishing Company by permission.

category (if one exists). A premium-priced instant coffee such as Moccona, for example, might price-off close to the regular price for Maxwell House, hoping to get Maxwell House buyers to trade up. Or, a middle-priced brand might price-off close to store brands and generics. This tactic can't be used too often, though, or the brand will be re-perceived as a lower-priced brand, with an attendant loss in brand attitude and probably sales.

Price-offs, therefore, are best used as a short-term competitive technique for protecting usage. As Schultz and Robinson observe, price-offs can put blips in the sales curve, but they cannot stem a long-term sale decline caused by other problems with the brand.[5] The same could be said for the remaining usage promotions.

BONUS PACKS

Bonus packs, which can be employed to induce trial in low involvement product categories, are very good for increasing usage when the manager wishes to do so. The very nature of bonus packs—more product for a reduced per-unit price—means that, if the buyer responds to the offer, it will take him or her out of the market for longer than the normal purchase cycle. Thus, bonus packs are ideal for "loading" consumers and reducing their usage of competing brands.

When to Use Bonus Packs

The most obvious situation for a brand to be packaged in bonus packs is *when a new competing brand is about to enter the category*. By loading consumers, this prevents them, at least temporarily, from trying the new brand. As with price-offs, bonus packs cannot be used as a continuous promotion, unless the manufacturer is willing to accept the permanent per-unit revenue decrease that would result.

Bonus packs can be used to load users of any product as long as the product itself is divisible for larger size packaging and has a reasonable in-use shelf life. Bonus packs—for usage—are *not* confined to "low involvement" products, as they are for trial promotion. This is because they attract the brand's current users (loyals and switchers) and, for them, the brand choice is always low involvement even if the "product" is normally considered to be high involvement.

CFB presentation of bonus packs was discussed in conjunction with their role as a trial device. The same recommendations apply to their role in usage: in particular, the manager should be sure to reinforce the advertising message on the larger container or on the multiple-unit wrapper.

IN/ON PACKS

Incentives placed in, on, or near the product package, or even the packaging itself (decorative or reusable containers) are a medium that can be used to deliver several types of promotions:

- Premiums
- Coupons
- Refunds

Although each promotion has a slightly different role to play (especially premiums), they are united in that the use of the *package as the medium* is most likely to limit consideration of the promotion offer to *current users* of the brand. Observational studies in stores have shown that prospective buyers are most likely to notice only a few familiar brands in the typical 12 seconds it takes to shop the average category.[6] Thus, brands that are new to would-be triers are unlikely to get a look-in with this point-of-purchase method.

In/On Pack Premiums

Of the three types of promotions that can be used in or on packs, premiums are the only ones likely to stimulate trial as well as usage. Closely related premiums, such as a Trac II razor blister-packed onto Trac II shaving cream,[7] or decorative containers that virtually become the product, such as Kleenex designer boxes, can induce trial in low involvement brand choice situations.

The reason in/on pack premiums were not included as a trial technique in Chapter 13 is that such premiums do little to focus the trier's attitude on the original product. The types of in or on pack premiums that work are those that are so attractive they create a separate attitude toward the premium. In extreme cases (for example, many premiums in children's cereals) the premium "carries" the original product, which is rejected as soon as the premium offer is discontinued.

Despite isolated success of in/on pack premiums as trial generators, we believe that the other techniques of sampling, couponing, refunds, and various forms of price-offs—which focus the trier's attitude on the product itself—are generally more suitable alternatives as trial promotions.

As a usage promotion, in/on pack premiums are but one way of differentiating a brand's temporary appeal to brand switchers. Their best role is in *generating usage of related products that the manufacturer also makes*. In the Trac II example, for instance, the razor helps sales of the shaving cream, but the shaving cream also helps sales of the razor, since both products are offered at a discount in the total package. Non-related premiums in or on packs have narrow appeal. Instead, a general-currency incentive (either of the two below) is preferable.

CFB aspects of premiums will be examined later in conjunction with premiums as a separate usage technique.

In/On Pack Coupons

In or on pack coupons are redeemable for the *next* purchase of the brand, not the trial purchase. Accordingly, they are a usage technique, not a trial technique.

In or on pack coupons can of course be used to *follow through on a trial coupon*. They are also often used to *follow through on a sample*, by including in the sample pack a coupon good for the next (the first paid post-trial) purchase.

Redemption rates for package coupons typically are high[8]: about 23 percent for in pack coupons; 15 percent for on pack coupons; and 7 percent for "cross-ruff" coupons—coupons good for purchase of a *different* product, usually by the same manufacturer but sometimes for tie-ins with another manufacturer's product. These in/on pack redemption rates must be tempered by the realization that the more "hidden" the coupon, the more likely that the buyers are current users, thus accounting for the more favorable redemption rates.

CFB aspects of package coupons are exactly the same as for trial coupons. Coupon design should include a picture, or feature the name prominently, depending on whether brand choice is by brand recognition or brand recall, and should reinforce the main selling message.

In/On Pack Refunds

Refund or rebate offers placed in or on packs can be used to encourage repeat purchase usage by incorporating a *multiple purchase requirement*. The number of purchases to qualify for the refund can be stretched, in theory, to any number, although consumers seem to resist making more than three purchases to qualify for a refund.[9] Still, three repeat purchases can stall switching to a competing brand for quite a long time. Many multi-purchase refund offers are designed on a sliding scale such that a greater number of purchases brings a larger refund but at a lower per unit saving, for example, 1 for 50 cents, 3 for $1.00, 6 for $1.50.

Because the usual refund will be $1.00 or more, usage refunds can be used with *any* product (unlike refund offers for trial purposes, which are limited to products retailing for $5.00 or more). For inexpensive products, a $1.00 refund can be spread over multiple units. A relatively large refund can then be offered without crippling the revenue per unit.

Package refunds typically redeem at a lower rate (about 4 percent) than package coupons. This is probably because people must send in for refunds whereas coupons usually are store-redeemable. However, the redemption rate understates the actual incidence of purchase effectiveness because of the "slippage" factor when people buy because of the refund then fail to claim it.

CFB presentation of multi-purpose refund offers has one important new aspect. To maximize the brand awareness and brand attitude impact of the technique, the *proof-of-purchase* that the buyer saves should be used as a communication vehicle. With multiple proofs to be saved, there is also the opportunity to include different benefits on each proof.

PREMIUMS

Premiums are articles of merchandise offered free or at a price less than their retail value as an incentive to buy one or more units of the brand. There are two types of premium offers:

- *Free premiums* are simply a giveaway just like a free sample, coupon, or refund offer. They are usually inexpensive merchandise.
- *"Self-liquidating" premiums,* on the other hand, can include very expensive merchandise (e.g., Kool's sailboats) because the customer sends money with the proof-of-purchase—enough money to cover the marketer's purchase and delivery costs (hence the self-liquidating aspect) while still representing a price to the customer that is well below the normal retail price of the item.

Premiums are not broad trial generators because of the almost inevitable selective appeal of the merchandise offered. The well-cited figure is that less than 10 percent of households have *ever* sent in for a free or self-liquidating premium. The average send-for premium redemption rate is about 1 percent.[10]

Perhaps one exception should be noted here. Banks and S&L's, which incidentally are the largest users of premiums, do seem to be successful in gaining triers. One bank's premium offers, studied by Preston, Dwyer and Rodelius,[11] increased new account openings by 43 percent. Although these new customers tended to keep lower deposit balances and to terminate sooner, the promotions were still profitable. Premiums may be effective for trial when the brands are at parity in a "commodity" category.

Premiums, however, are mostly effective in holding present users through a *multiple purchase requirement*. The selective appeal of a premium can even be used to tactical advantage by *helping to skew purchase toward a particular sub-group of users*. For instance, a women's premium could be used to increase purchase by women of a unisex brand, such as Head & Shoulders shampoo. Or a "classy" self-liquidator, such as a Perrier umbrella, could be employed to try to increase "upmarket" usage.

CFB Choice of Premiums

Herein lies the potential disadvantage of premiums. An ill-chosen premium can hurt the brand image (brand attitude) of the product and actually lose sales. Premiums should be chosen not just to be attractive in their own right but also as a communication vehicle that is consumer franchise building for the brand.

Several excellent examples of premiums that reinforce the brand-user's image for *transformationally* motivated brand purchase include:

- Western gear for Marlboro
- Racing decals for Cam-2 high performance motor oil
- Perrier umbrellas for Perrier mineral water

Appropriately selected premiums can reinforce *informationally* motivated brand choices as well. For example:

- Summer t-shirts (with the brand logo) offered by Chesebrough-Ponds in trying to extend usage of Vaseline Intensive Care Lotion as an after-sun remedy

- Potato recipe cookbook offered by the National Potato Promotion Board in trying to alleviate the "menu boredom" problem hindering potato usage

Premiums therefore are a potentially powerful CFB technique—not because they encourage repeat purchase (which other non-CFB usage promotions can do) but because a premium chosen to appeal to the *same motivation* as the product itself can influence the user's attitude toward the brand to the point where the previous switcher becomes brand loyal. If you are wearing a Western jacket with a Marlboro logo, you'd look silly smoking Camels. Likewise, a potato recipe cookbook is likely to improve your attitude toward potatoes versus rice, noodles, or other starch side dish competitors.

CONTESTS AND SWEEPSTAKES

Contests are supposed to require a degree of *skill* (often not very much) to enter and are judged on the basis of the best entry or the first winning entry drawn; they can (and should) *require* proof-of-purchase to enter.

Sweepstakes are based purely on *chance,* with the first series of randomly drawn entries winning prizes. Sweepstakes naturally attract more entries than contests; however, sweepstakes cannot require proof-of-purchase (which would contravene lottery laws—only the state government can legally operate a lottery). Sweepstakes can *suggest* a proof-of-purchase be sent with the entry, but they must accept a handwritten facsimile. About 75 to 90 percent of entries are facsimile entries,[12] so the higher participation rate for sweepstakes over contests is largely offset by the widespread avoidance of purchase.

Contests and sweepstakes are supposed to be useful for generating "excitement" about the brand. Just what this excitement is or does is never spelled out. We suspect it mainly consists of *increasing brand awareness or re-awareness,* through attention to the advertising announcing the offer, and in the gathering of purchase proofs (or writing or sketching of them) among those who enter. Re-awareness—putting the brand back into the buyer's evoked set or recognition set—can be effective *if* the buyer has a favorable attitude toward the brand.

How many people enter contests or sweepstakes? The oft-cited figure indicates that fewer than 20 percent of households have *ever* entered a contest or sweepstakes (though, with the growth of instant "rub-off" sweepstakes, the figure for the latter may be an underestimate). A small but informative survey of 200 women by the Ladies' Home Journal[13] suggests that the reasons for low participation are the perceived high odds against winning and the belief, correct or otherwise, that many such promotions are not entirely honest, in that not all entries are opened. State and local laws are also a limitation. The complex variations in these laws inhibit many marketers from utilizing contests or sweepstakes.

Contests and sweepstakes, like premiums, are perhaps best used to *skew a brand's usage toward a younger or older sub-group,* if so desired for tactical reasons. Schoolchildren aged between seven and thirteen seem particularly partial to contests. And if you want to appeal to the growing retirement market, contests and sweepstakes have differentially strong appeal to this group because retirees have more time to prepare entries. Lastly, if there happens to be a psychographic skew in the target audience toward intellectuals (contests) or risk-takers (sweepstakes) then these techniques might be appropriate.

CFB Presentation of Contests and Sweepstakes

A thoughtfully designed contest can present a CFB opportunity. To increase learning of brand attitude benefits, a contest might involve asking consumers questions whose answers are obtainable only on the package, or requiring purchasers to state reasons they like the brand. A contest aimed at extending use may ask consumers to think up new uses for the brand—for example, the Arm & Hammer baking soda promotion discussed in Chapter 1. For sweepstakes, entry tokens in ads (which do not require purchase) can be used to carry a brand message. Benson & Hedges 100's, for example, prints "100" on in-ad tokens.

The manager should remember to keep the promotion relevant to the brand, thus helping to build or reinforce brand attitude. Contests should be designed around the brand's benefits. Sweepstakes should offer prizes that relate to usage of the brand; although there is no doubt that large cash prizes are the most attractive, cash does little for brand attitude and, with the absence of a purchase requirement for sweepstakes, may do little for sales either.

In general, contests and sweepstakes must be regarded as the most limited of all usage promotion techniques. Expensive since contests and sweepstakes must be advertised, they are an expensive and unusual choice compared with other promotion alternatives unless a good target audience rationale can be found for them.

CONTINUITY PROGRAMS

Continuity programs should be distinguished from other multiple purchase requirement offers in that continuity programs are intended for *really long-term holding* of brand users.[14] Stamps (such as S & H Green Stamps) are a common example. A lot of purchases—often 100 or more—must be made to get enough stamps for a reasonably attractive redemption purchase (a premium of your choice). The airlines' "frequent flier" programs are a similar example. Often thousands of miles must be flown, or numerous trips taken, before you qualify for a free flight.

When brands are at parity, so that the buyer may just as well use one as another, continuity programs can be an effective differentiating device. Industrial suppliers may be involved in another situation that does not necessarily involve parity: faced with a new and threatening competitor about to enter the market, they would do well to give their long-standing customers a large reward for continuity, in order to obligate loyalty. This would tend to make current customers resistant to trying the new competitor.

TABLE 14.2   PRINCIPAL CONDITIONS FAVORING USAGE PROMOTION TECHNIQUES

Price-offs
- Short-term competitive situations in local areas
- Used temporarily to bring brand into competition with lower-priced brands

Premiums
- To skew usage, by choice of premium, toward a particular sub-group, if desired
- Conspicuous premiums can move switchers to loyalty to the product associated with the premium

Bonus packs
- Used when a new brand is about to enter the category, thus loading consumers and preventing or delaying competitive trial (any divisible product with reasonable shelf-life)

Contests and sweepstakes
- Creating re-awareness (to get the brand back into evoked or recognition set) for those with favorable attitudes
- To skew usage to younger or older sub-groups

In/on packs
- Premiums: to generate usage of related products made by the same manufacturer
- Coupons: to follow through on a trial coupon or sample
- Multi-purchase refunds: best for continuous multiple repeats (especially if bonus packs inapplicable)
- Stamps: for purchase of premiums chosen by brand loyals

Continuity programs
- To differentiate parity brands for long-term purchase
- Industrial products: to reward long-term customer loyalty when new supplier is about to enter the category

SUMMARY OF USAGE PROMOTIONS

Usage promotions, like trial promotions discussed earlier, have their specialized applications; these are summarized in Table 14.2. The applications are varied, but perhaps the summary table will help the manager with a particular brand usage problem find a suitable short-term solution, or perhaps even increase long-term consumer franchise with one of the last three techniques. Again, we stress that promotion offers are such individualized, empirical tools that summary applications are of necessity too restrictive.

APPENDIX: TESTING PROMOTION OFFERS

Promotion offers can be just as complex as advertisements. There is every reason to test (pre-test) promotion offers just as the intelligent manager would always test an advertisement. The objective is the same: to determine whether the promotion offer is being *processed* in a way that will meet its *communication objectives*.

Most often the two main communication objectives for a promotion are brand awareness and brand purchase intention. However, brand attitude should always be a complementary objective (for the CFB aspect of offer implementation). Also, there are often two target audiences for whom communication effects are relevant: distributors, and the prospective customers themselves. We will concentrate on customer pre-testing here.

Processing of Promotion Offers

To produce communication effects, the promotion offer has to be *processed* correctly by the prospective buyer. Elements of the promotion offer pertaining to the respective communication effects have to be attended to and learned (for brand awareness and low involvement brand attitude) or attended to and accepted (for promotion offers that attempt to stimulate category need, high involvement brand attitude, brand purchase intention, or purchase facilitation).

As Russo[15] has reminded us, promotion offers are not automatically processed. The first processing response, attention, is far from a guaranteed response in point-of-purchase offers amid the profusion of other stimuli, although it is more probable in media or direct offers. And, following initial attention, the prospective buyer must decide whether to further process the offer based on the expected benefit it entails in relation to the time and effort costs that responding to the offer involves.

Attribution as a Processing Response for Promotion Offers   Of most interest to the manager is the processing of promotion offers such that they result in acceptance of an immediate purchase intention and—via the CFB concept—an increase in brand attitude. With regard to purchase intention, it is meaningful to speak of the *attribution* the prospective buyer makes regarding the promotion offer. The attribution response can occur during or after acceptance, and in either case represents an additional processing response that is unique to promotion and does not occur for advertising.

As Raju and Hastak[16] have observed, there are many diverse attributions that prospective buyers may make in response to promotion offers. However, it is possible to organize these attributions into four main categories (Table 14.3). Our approach postulates that promotions cause attributions that reinforce purchase intention in one of four ways. Two of the attributional mechanisms are negatively reinforcing and therefore represent *informational* motivations for brand choice. Two are positively reinforcing and therefore represent *transformational* motivations for brand choice. Thus, promotion offers operate via the motivational foundations of brand attitude introduced in Chapter 6.

Immediate Value   Four types of promotion offers—price-offs, bonus packs, rebates and refunds, and trade coupons—prompt an attribution of immediate value which reinforces the purchase intention "negatively" by *removing the problem* of paying a high normal price. These four types of promotion are perceived as immediate rewards that represent "good value" to the buyer.

Future Value (Risk Reduction)   Two types of promotion offers—free or discounted samples (or their more common industrial counterparts, trial offers or free demonstrations) and warranties—prompt an attribution of future value. By trying the brand on a sample basis before committing to a full-price purchase, or by committing to full price but with recompense or replacement if something goes wrong, these promotions operate on *problem avoidance*

TABLE 14-3   ATTRIBUTIONS MADE IN PROCESSING PROMOTION OFFERS

Informational attributions
1. *Immediate value*   (Problem removal)
   - Price-offs
   - Bonus packs
   - Rebates, refunds
   - Trade coupons

2. *Future value: risk reduction*   (Problem avoidance)
   - Samples, trial offers, free demonstrations
   - Warranties

Transformational attributions
3. *Gifts*   (Sensory gratification)
   - Coupons
   - Premiums
   - Stamps, continuity plans

4. *Chance: Risk-taking*   (Intellectual stimulation)
   - Contests, sweepstakes

motivation. As such, they are "negatively" reinforcing. It is important to note that they work on current purchasing behavior but via the expectation of "future value" rather than by providing the buyer with immediate value.

Gifts   Three types of promotion offers—coupons, premiums, and stamps or other continuity plans—prompt an attribution of gift reception.[17] In numerous interviews with shoppers, it is clear that (manufacturers') coupons are regarded as something more than the equivalent price-off. A 20-cent coupon will usually be more effective than an equivalent 20-cents price-off.[18] Coupons, premiums, and continuity offers such as stamps, leave the buyer with something tangible, which consumers tend to regard as a gift. The gift aspect invokes the psychology of exchange whereby the buyer often feels a reciprocal obligation to continue to patronize the brand. The "good feeling" generated by these types of offers is a form of *sensory gratification* and the attribution is "positively" reinforcing.

Chance (Risk-Taking)   The tenth type of promotion—contests and the related variant of sweepstakes—appeals to mild risk-taking motivation in the prospective buyer by offering participation in a game of chance. The motivation here is *intellectual stimulation* and the attribution is "positively" reinforcing.

Understanding How Promotion Offers Work   All of the above categories of attribution in the processing of promotion offers suggest that there is a lot to be understood about the "psychology" of promotions. Promotion offers are not simply mechanistic economic incentives. Rather, they involve processes of adaptation level in perception[19]; response costs and reinforcement schedules[20]; social exchange[21]; and subjective probability[22] and skill versus luck or internal versus external control.[23] Academic researchers are beginning to examine the implications of these theories for promotion.[24] Managers, while not expected to be psychologists, should at least be thinking more about how promotion offers actually work.

Pre-testing Promotion Offers Based on Processing

It is important for the manager to understand the basic differences in the way promotions are processed attributionally to produce brand purchase intentions. The managerial questions to be answered (via pre-testing of promotions) correspond with the way the promotion is processed:

- Does the offer represent enough immediate value (price-offs, bonus packs, rebates or refunds, trade coupons)?
- Does the offer sufficiently reduce perceived risk and thereby promise future value (sampling, warranties)?
- Does the offer constitute an appreciated gift (coupons, premiums, continuity programs)?
- Does the offer excite through a reward for skill or chance (contests, sweepstakes, lotteries)?

Promotion offer pre-tests must be conducted with a properly screened target audience sample. For trial promotions, you want people who have not yet tried the brand, or at least not recently. For usage promotions, you want *only* triers of the brand. Further pre-test sample divisions will allow precise analysis of how each prospective target audience sub-group processes the promotion offer in its alternative (pre-test) executions.

Immediate Value Promotions   Price-offs, bonus packs, refunds, and trade coupons must suggest immediate value to prospective buyers. The most straightforward way to pre-test the *amount of price-off* (in all of the above) that will be effective is to present the brand, in a survey interview format with several other closely competing brands—all at their normal prices—then progressively introduce better and better offers on the to-be-promoted brand until an acceptable percentage of the target audience sample indicates that they would switch to the promoted brand.[25]

Future Value (Risk Reduction) Promotions   Samples, trial offers, demonstrations, and warranties function by reducing the perceived risk of trial of the brand.

The major method of testing *samples* is by home placements. The sample is placed with several hundred target audience prospects and a count is made of how many try the sample, prefer it to whatever prior product or brand they are currently using, and indicate an intention to switch to the sampled brand. An introductory price or price-plus-coupon test (as above) can then be conducted with the intentional triers.

Trial offers and demonstrations (usually for consumer durables and industrial products) can be tested by trying them on a limited basis—usually with those prospects, or in geographic areas, that the manager regards as relatively expendable should the offer not work. During testing, trial offers can be sweetened by varying the time or the terms of the offer. But if a free demonstration doesn't convert prospects in the test, then the product may be in trouble!

Warranties contain three attributes that can be varied, which makes pre-testing very important: the parts of the product covered by the warranty, the extent of replacement or repair, and the time period of the offer. The manager should offer a good enough warranty to induce an acceptable percentage of prospects to buy, but not so good as to lose money on post-trial servicing and repairs. A multi-factor experimental design is necessary, covering combinations of the feasible range for each attribute.

Gift Promotions   Coupons, premiums, and continuity plans are attributed primarily as gifts, overlaid on their price-off characteristics. With *coupons*, the testing procedure is the same as for price-offs. A coupon should stimulate trial usage, depending on its purpose, at a lower face value than a direct price-off (it has to cover the additional cost of couponing). For the CFB aspects of the coupon, immediate recognition of the package portrayed on the coupon and immediate recall of the brand and main message (following brief exposure to the coupon) also should be tested.

Premiums need to be tested first and foremost for their *product* appeal to the target audience, quite aside from their value appeal. The most efficient method is to test several alternative premiums side-by-side as gifts—without price—one of which, if possible, is a previous premium with known performance among the target audience, to be used as a "control." Second, the one or two most widely appealing premiums then should be shown with the (carrier) brand and questions should be asked about each premium's compatibility with the brand's "image." Finally, unless free, the price of the premium should be tested for intention to buy, on a downward progressive price scale. Obviously, for self-liquidators, the lowest price tested would be the break-even price, allowing for distribution and handling costs.

Continuity plans can be tested by varying the purchase ratio (number or dollar amount of purchases required) against various types of gift merchandise. Magnitude estimation is a good procedure for this. Start with a standard gift at an agreeable redemption number, then ask consumers to provide numbers (like "bidding") for other items. Human nature being what it is, the marketer could probably add slightly to the consumers' bids without reducing the offer's appeal.

Chance (Risk-Taking) Promotions   *Contests* and *sweepstakes* basically appeal to mild risk-taking motivation. Prizes should be tested for target audience appeal first. For cash prizes, this is straightforward. For merchandise prizes, the first two steps in premium testing are applicable here: audience appeal and compatibility with the to-be-promoted brand.

Contest *versus* sweepstakes entry requirements should then be examined. Sweepstakes entry is easy but is less preferable because it doesn't require purchase. (If recreating brand awareness among as many "lapsed" users as possible is the communication objective, then sweepstakes would probably be the choice.) Contests should not be so difficult as to discourage entry and thus reduce entry-qualifying purchases, but they should not be so easy as to lose their "intellectual" appeal and degenerate into a sweepstakes. Test consumers, notified of the prize, should be asked to state their likelihood of entry under contest *then* sweepstakes conditions.

Post-testing Promotion Offers

Whenever possible the final promotion offer should be "post-tested" on a limited geographic basis (this isn't always possible with fast reaction promotions). This is important for obtaining a good estimate of the promotion offer's redemption rate. Field testing provides a more reliable estimate than pre-testing under "lab" conditions. Fractions of a percentage point can mean the difference between profit and loss on a promotion.

Two other types of post-testing are extremely informative for the manager who really wants to understand how promotions work. These are in-store observation and interviews, and follow-up survey interviews with responders and non-responders to the promotion.[26]

In-store observation and intercept interviews with shoppers at the point of purchase are relevant for store-distributed promotions. Bettman[27] even had shoppers "think aloud" into a tape recorder, to see how promotion offers fit in with other brand benefits in influencing brand choice. Much can be learned from this type of investigation to improve the effectiveness of p-o-p promotions.

Follow-up survey interviews with samples of consumers (or industrial prospects) who did or did not respond to the company's promotion offer is a useful research exercise for all forms of promotion. By follow-up surveys (equivalent in advertising research to Campaign Evaluation, see Chapter 20), the manager can measure the communication effects that did or did not occur during the promotion and thus gain diagnostic insight into the promotion's causal influence on buyer behavior. In particular, follow-up surveys can determine which target audiences the promotion actually reached; whether the promotion was consumer franchise building; and whether it resulted in trial, usage, or both, in producing sales.

Calculating the Return on Promotions

The return on promotions is relatively straightforward to calculate after the fact, but obviously the return must be estimated beforehand in deciding whether to launch a promotion offer in the first place. Holbert, Golden, and Chudnoff[28] provide a general summary of the steps involved. Hypothetical figures are shown with the steps as follows:

A.	Number of offers distributed	500,000
B.	Cost of promotion	$600,000
C.	% Response rate	15%
D.	Number responding ($A \times C$)	75,000
E.	% Conversion to full-price purchasers	13%
F.	Number of converters ($D \times E$)	9,750
G.	Net profit per converter per year	$40
H.	Total profit from converters per year ($F \times G$)	$390,000
I.	Loss of sales due to buyers who would have bought anyway	$50,000
J.	Net profit per year ($H - I$)	$340,000
K.	Payback period ($B \div J$)	1.76 years

As you can see, there are a number of steps to be estimated if the financial results of the promotion are to be gauged in advance.

The *cost* of mounting promotion offers is particular to the promotion technique. For some techniques, the cost varies with the redemption rate, such as for coupons or refunds. For others, it is relatively constant, such as for self-liquidating premiums. The components of cost—advertising, production, distribution, handling, and so forth—are far too specific and complicated to summarize here. Schultz and Robinson[29] provide an excellent review of the main cost components of each technique and its main "media" implementation methods.

The *return* on promotions can be estimated with either and, if possible, both pre-testing and field testing procedures. The only substitute for testing is to rely on internal company experience with similar promotions, or to consult an experienced promotion house.

Conversion to full-price purchasers (after the promotion is withdrawn) can also be estimated by pre-testing, or field-testing, or on the basis of previous or expert experience. The related step of estimating the *number of people who would have bought anyway* (without the offer) can be made in the same way.

(Note that if no-one is converted by the offer—that is, if it has only a temporary "inventorying" effect—then steps E through I are replaced by an estimate of the total number of buyers, at the reduced price, and the calculation becomes equivalent to a price-reduction calculation.)

We cannot go further into the detailed financial aspects, such as discounted rate of return, that an accountant would apply to promotion offers. However, the summary steps provide a general outline of the financial evaluation procedure.

NOTES

1 For evidence that heavy users of the category are the most deal-prone, see: J.M. Carman, Correlates of brand loyalty—some positive results, *Journal of Marketing Research*, 1970, 7(1), 67–76.

2 R.W. Shoemaker and F.R. Shoaf, Repeat rates of deal purchases, *Journal of Advertising Research*, 1977, 17(2), 47–53.

3 This table is adapted from a more detailed table published originally in *Farm Store Merchandising* (courtesy Miller Publishing Company, U.S.) and found by us republished in an Australian publication, *Rydge's in Marketing*, August 1983, p.8.

4 Although remember that profit, or at least short-run profit, may not be the objective. As noted, reducing competitive trial, or simply clearing inventory, are alternative objectives of consumer promotion deals.

5 D.E. Schultz and W.A. Robinson, *Sales Promotion Essentials,* Chicago: Crain Books, 1982, chapter 6.

6 Study by P.R. Dickson and A. Sawyer reported in M.J. Shields, ''Who cares about price?'' *ADWEEK,* January 13, 1986, pp. 1, 10.

7 The Trac II example, a promotion by the Gillette Company, is from D.E. Schultz and W.A. Robinson, same reference as note 5, chapter 7.

8 Expert estimates made by H. Aniero, privately circulated document, 1977.

9 L.J. Haugh, ''Cash refunds multiply,'' *Advertising Age,* May 5, 1980, p. 48.

10 D.E. Schultz and W.A. Robinson, same reference as note 5, chapters 8 and 9.

11 Two separate premium offers were studied: cookware (a free premium) and a discount on purchase of a calculator (the calculator thus being a self-liquidating premium). Both premiums were quite similarly effective. See R.H. Preston, F.R. Dwyer, and W. Rudelius, The effectiveness of bank premiums, *Journal of Marketing,* 1978, *42*(3), 96–101.

12 D.E. Schultz and W.A. Robinson, same reference as note 5, chapter 3.

13 L.J. Haugh, ''Women cool to promotions, 'LHJ' tells promotion executives,'' *Advertising Age,* October 10, 1977, pp. 10, 102.

14 Continuity programs involve large rewards similar to contests and sweepstakes: cash or a premium of some sort, which includes prizes and free trips. However, unlike the *single* purchase usually necessary to enter a contest and perhaps helpful when entering a sweepstakes, the reward in continuity programs is contingent only on making *many* purchase responses (high fixed-ratio reinforcement in learning theory terminology).

   Proof of having made the purchases can take many forms. Most often the proofs are: trading stamps, such as S&H Green Stamps, issued with every dollar's worth of purchases (used almost exclusively by *retailers* as a retail promotion); or in- or on-pack coupons, a large collection of which is redeemable for premiums as prizes (e.g., Raleigh cigarette coupons, Betty Crocker coupons, box tops functioning as coupons in children's cereals).

   No proof of purchase is needed with ''collectibles''—individual self-liquidating premiums, such as cookware, that make up a set *and* that are perceived largely as only worth having if you acquire the complete set. Multiple purchases do not have to be required because the only way you can acquire the set is to make multiple purchases, or multiple visits when collectibles are used as a retail promotion.

15 J.E. Russo, The decision to use product information at the point of purchase, working paper no. 57, Chicago: Graduate School of Business, University of Chicago, 1980.

16 P.S. Raju and M. Hastak, Consumer response to deals: a discussion of theoretical perspectives, in J.C. Olsen (Ed.), *Advances in Consumer Research: Vol. 7,* Provo, UT: Association for Consumer Research, 1980, pp. 296–301. Also see R.L. Oliver, Predicting sales promotion effects: assimilation, attribution, or risk reduction?, in the same volume, pp. 314–317.

17 C.M. Siepel, Premiums—forgotten by theory, *Journal of Marketing,* 1971, *35*(2), 26–34.

18 B.C. Cotton and E.M. Babb, Consumer response to promotional deals, *Journal of Marketing,* 1978, *42*(3), 109–113; R.M. Schindler and S.E. Rothaus, An experimental

technique for exploring the psychological mechanisms of the effects of price promotions, in E.C. Hirschman and M.B. Holbrook (Eds.), *Advances in Consumer Research,* Vol. 12, Provo, UT: Association for Consumer Research, 1985, pp. 133–137.

19 H. Helson, *Adaptation-level Theory: An Experimental and Systematic Approach to Behavior,* New York: Harper, 1964.

20 B.F. Skinner, *The Behavior of Organisms,* New York: Appleton-Century, 1938; and C.B. Ferster and B.F. Skinner, *Schedules of Reinforcement,* New York: Appleton-Century-Crofts, 1957. For marketing applications of Skinner's concepts, see W.R. Nord and J.P. Peter, A behavior modification perspective on marketing, *Journal of Marketing,* 1980, *44*(2), 36–47; M.L. Rothschild and W.C. Gaidis, Behavioral learning theory: its relevance to marketing and promotions, *Journal of Marketing,* 1981, *45*(2), 70–78; and J.P. Peter and W.R. Nord, A clarification and extension of operant conditioning principles in marketing, *Journal of Marketing,* 1982, *46*(3), 102–107.

21 G.C. Homans, *Social Behavior: Its Elementary Forms,* New York: Harcourt, Brace & World, 1961: R.P. Bagozzi, Marketing as exchange, *Journal of Marketing,* 1975, *39*(4), 32–39; R.W. Belk, Gift-giving behavior, in J.N. Sheth (Ed.), *Research in Marketing,* Vol. 2, Greenwich, CT: JAI Press, 1979, pp. 95–126; J.F. Sherry, Jr., Gift giving in anthropological perspective, *Journal of Consumer Research,* 1983, *10*(2), 157–168.

22 F.W. Irwin, *Intentional Behavior and Motivation,* Philadelphia: Lippincott, 1971.

23 J.B. Rotter, Generalized expectancies for internal versus external control of reinforcement, *Psychological Monographs,* 1966, (see all of no. 80).

24 For a recent summary of these efforts, see A.G. Sawyer and P.R. Dickson, Psychological perspectives on consumer response to sales promotion, working paper, Cambridge, MA: Marketing Science Institute, 1985.

25 Some researchers, such as Chris Blamires, recommend randomized presentation of price-off amounts to prevent respondents from "rationally" waiting for progressively larger price-offs in the ordered series. This probably is a more valid procedure because price-offs are encountered randomly in actual shopping trips. However, it is more cumbersome to administer in a test and may, to the contrary, tend to confuse respondents. See C. Blamires, Pricing research: a review and a new approach, *Journal of the Market Research Society,* 1981, *23*(3), 103–126.

26 N.B. Holbert, R.J. Golden, and M.M. Chudnoff, *Marketing Research for the Marketing and Advertising Executive,* New York: American Marketing Association, 1981.

27 J.R. Bettman, The structure of consumer choice processes, *Journal of Marketing Research,* 1971, *8*(4), 465–471.

28 N.B. Holbert et al., same reference as note 26, p. 202.

29 D.E. Schultz and W.A. Robinson, same reference as note 3.

DISCUSSION QUESTIONS

14.1 You are the advertising manager for Lipton's Tea in the United States. The product line you are responsible for is tea bags. Your consumer research indicates that most adults have tried Lipton's Tea Bags but use them at a fairly low rate which you believe indicates considerable potential for increased usage. Write an evaluative review of the alternative usage promotions you could use.

14.2 Contrast the strategies and the tactical implementation of the following types of promotion offers for trial objectives *versus* usage objectives:

a Coupons

b Price-offs (direct)

c Refunds or rebate offers

14.3 Joy perfume, by Jean Patou of Paris, is advertised as "the most expensive perfume in the world." Management has decided that some form of premium offer would help to maintain brand loyalty in the highly competitive upper end of the perfume category. As a promotion consultant, outline the main considerations in selecting a suitable premium offer. Then describe how you would test alternative premium offers for Joy perfume.

14.4 Soft drinks are a product category that quite frequently uses contests and sweepstakes to boost sales. But when should a soft drink brand use a contest and when should it use a sweepstakes promotion?

14.5 Project: Form a team and collect examples of the following consumer promotion offers: price-offs, bonus packs, rebates or refunds, sampling, coupons, premiums, stamps (if available), contests and sweepstakes. Note: advertised promotion offers will suffice; you don't have to buy a lot of promoted products. Then convene a focus group of other students (or interview parents and neighbors) about what they think about when they encounter (process) the respective types of offers. Write up a group report about the attributions that promotion offers appear to generate during processing.

14.6 How should a (manufacturer's) coupon offer be tested? How can the manager calculate the financial return on a coupon promotion program? Exemplify your answers with reference to a coupon promotion for Sanka Freeze-Dried Decaffeinated Coffee for which $500,000 has been budgeted.

FURTHER READING

Schultz, D.E. and Robinson, W.A. *Sales Promotion Essentials*. Chicago: Crain Books, 1982.

Recommended for Chapter 13 on trial promotions, this text is equally relevant for Chapter 14's coverage of usage promotions. Discusses types of promotion offers and their implementation in much more depth than we could afford in our chapters.

Holbert, N.B., Golden, R.J., and Chudnoff, M.M. *Marketing Research for the Marketing and Advertising Executive*. New York: American Marketing Association, 1981.

One of the few books which, when describing advertising research, includes also the recommendation to conduct research on promotion offers. Makes some very good general observations about promotion testing. Unfortunately lacks detail, as does every other marketing research text, on how to test different types of promotions.

Blamires, C. Pricing research: a review and a new approach. *Journal of the Marketing Research Society*, 1981, 23(4), 103–126.

This article, from a British market research journal that should be available in most libraries, provides an overview of pricing research that is entirely consistent with our target audience approach. The author's methodological points for pricing research can easily be extended to the testing of all forms of price-off promotions.

PART **SEVEN**

MEDIA STRATEGY

CHAPTER 15

MEDIA SELECTION

The chapters in Part Seven examine media planning for advertising (media planning for promotion was covered in Part Six). On average, over 90 percent of the advertising budget is spent in media, with the minor part going to advertising research and production of the ads themselves. So, monetarily at least, media planning is the most important part of advertising.

Media *strategy* comprises two main decisions: "where," or in which media, to advertise (media selection); and "how often" to expose the advertising to the target audience (media scheduling). Following an overview of media strategy, we address the media selection decision. After reading this chapter you should:

- Know new definitions of the three major parameters of media strategy—reach, frequency, and continuity—and appreciate how these three parameters must be traded off against each other in formulating a plan to fit a given media budget
- See how media selection is based on the communication objectives of the campaign
- Understand the concepts of primary and secondary media for a campaign
- Know which primary and secondary media are most suitable for different types of advertising

A word about what we do *not* cover is appropriate before we begin. The emphasis in this book is on media *strategy*—that is, on decisions about media as a means to attain the brand's communication objectives and hence target audience action and sales. We take the manager's perspective, glossing over the technical details of implementation which can be found in more specialized books on media planning. A topic we omit is media *buying*.[1] Our reason for what many may see as a major omission is again the principle that correct strategy is more important than correct execution.[2] We have also omitted some mathematical details of media scheduling that can be comprehended only by the most advanced media planners.

Appendix B (at the back of this book) provides a review of basic media selection options for those interested in these details (helpful when doing a media planning project). Here, we will concentrate on the strategy aspects of media selection.

THE IMPORTANCE OF MEDIA STRATEGY

Media strategy is at least as important as creative strategy. Too often, great creative managers minimize the importance of media strategy. For instance, the late Bill Bernbach, of Doyle Dane Bernbach, once stated that "ninety percent of the battle is what you say and 10 percent is what medium you say it in." The countering quotation to this is attributed to another famous manager of the past, John Wanamaker: "Half of all advertising money is wasted, but I wish I knew which half." With 90 percent or more of the money being spent in media, media strategy is where most of the "half" must be wasted.[3]

Contemporary advertising managers accord media strategy a place of importance that is close to creative strategy but secondary to communication objectives. A survey of 162 leading advertiser and agency executives[4] (Table 15.1) shows that whereas the overall message strategy (*what* to say or show—communication objectives) was rated as the most important factor in campaign success, message execution (*how* best to say or show it) and media execution (*where and how often* to say or show it) were seen as similarly important thereafter.

This fits our view introduced in Chapter 3 in conjunction with budgeting, that the sales response to advertising expenditure is affected at least equally by the accuracy of the media plan as by the execution of the message—because

TABLE 15-1   RELATIVE IMPORTANCE OF MESSAGE AND MEDIA FACTORS AS RATED BY MANAGERS

Message Factors	Importance Rating*
• Overall message strategy	100
• Execution—copy	85
• Execution—visual	77
Media Factors	
• Media selection	77
• Media repetition	72

* Ratings reflect importance weighed on the basis of 1 point for "very important" and a half-point for "somewhat important." Virtually all managers (99 percent) rated the first factor very important and this is shown as 100.

both are answerable to communication objectives. We will have ample cause to support this conclusion as the complexities of the media plan are examined.

PARAMETERS OF THE MEDIA PLAN

There are three main ways in which a media plan can vary: reach, frequency, and continuity. Because all media plans contain these three factors, they can be called the *parameters* of the media plan. A parameter is a quantity that is constant in a particular case, such as in a particular media plan, but which varies in different cases, such as in alternative media plans that are being considered.

1 *Reach* we define as the number of target audience individuals exposed to the advertising, in a purchase cycle. (The purchase cycle is the time interval, between purchases in the product category, for the average target audience member. The purchase cycle is examined in detail in the next chapter.) Reach needs to be refined into the concept of effective reach, which takes effective frequency (see below) into account.

2 *Frequency* is the number of exposures, per individual target audience member, in a purchase cycle. Individuals may be exposed to the advertising once, twice, three times, or many times between purchases. The most difficult decision in media strategy is how many times the target audience needs to be exposed to the advertising, per purchase cycle, to maximize the chance that they will purchase the brand. The minimum number of exposures that will maximize the likelihood of the average target audience member purchasing the brand is known as the *minimum effective frequency* (MEF). The number of target audience individuals exposed at this frequency (or higher) gives us the *effective reach* of the plan, per purchase cycle.

3 *Continuity* is the distribution of exposures, over successive purchase cycles, for the average target audience member for the entire planning period (usually one year). The planning period usually contains multiple purchase cycles. People may be exposed to the advertising in every purchase cycle (high continuity) or in only one or a few of these cycles (low continuity). Continuity patterns can take many forms and so this is the third parameter of the media plan.

Reach, frequency, and continuity are not unlimited or open-ended quantities in most media plans. Rather, their amounts have to be "traded-off" against one another, by the manager, in order to conform to the allocated media budget. These trade-offs are most easily illustrated with the visual metaphor of the "media balloon."

The "Media Balloon"

In essence, the manager faced with the overall decision about how best to spend the media budget has to grapple with a three-sphere "balloon" (Figure 15.1). Any manager who has had to allocate a media budget will appreciate

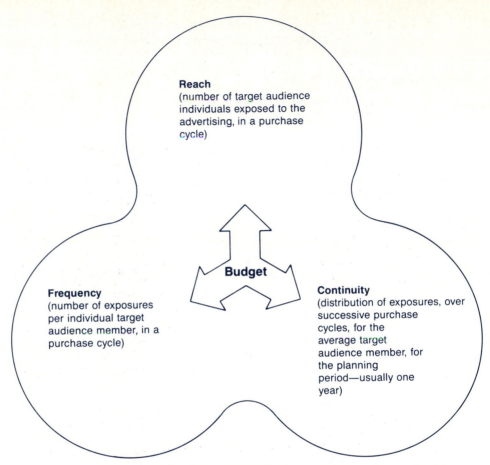

FIGURE 15-1   The "media balloon" metaphor for the main parameters of the media plan.

the reality of this metaphor. If the balloon is "tied off" (representing a fixed media budget), the manager cannot make one sphere larger without squeezing at least one of the other two.

However, if the manager is allowed to "inflate" the balloon to any necessary size (representing an open media budget) then all three spheres will enlarge and a more comprehensive media plan will result. Inflating from a flat balloon, so to speak, represents the *task method* of media budget estimation, and this is the method we describe in the remaining chapters.

We should emphasize that in most management situations, the media balloon will have a maximum size. The balloon's size will be constrained by the media budget, set either by the marginal method (see Chapter 3) or by some higher level corporate decision. The budget constraint forces *trade-offs* between the spheres—that is, between reach within a purchase cycle; frequency within a purchase cycle; and continuity over the entire planning period. These trade-offs are outlined next.

The principle that governs these trade-offs is a simple but vital one: *It is better to sell some people completely than many people not at all.* As we shall see, this principle is based on effective frequency as the governing factor of the media plan.

Reach versus Frequency

A media plan with a fixed budget can either be designed to reach a lot of people a few times, or a few people a lot of times. This is the trade-off between reach and frequency. For example, by scattering the budget, and hence the advertising exposures, across a lot of different media types (such as TV, radio, magazines, newspapers, and outdoor media) and across many different media vehicles (such as different TV programs, radio stations, and times of day), a large number of different people will be exposed to the advertising, but they won't be exposed very often.

In contrast, by spending the same budget in only one media type, such as magazines, and in very few vehicles, such as Time and Newsweek magazines, a much smaller number of people will be exposed to the advertising, but they will be exposed very frequently.

Geographic Reach versus Frequency   A similar trade-off operates geographically. The advertiser can either try to reach every prospect in the nation, at low frequency, or every prospect in a more limited geographic region, at high frequency.

Even if the brand is nationally distributed, it would be better to spend, for example, just in Philadelphia, provided the return on that expenditure is larger than alternative uses of the money, than to spend across the United States at too low a frequency and realize a smaller return or no return.

Reach versus frequency represents the most common trade-off in the media plan. As we will see in the next chapter, frequency, properly conceptualized as effective frequency within the purchase cycle, should always govern this trade-off. Reach at too low a frequency is wasted advertising.

Frequency versus Continuity

There is no sense in trying to stretch a limited budget over an entire year just because it is supposed to be an annual budget and the planning period is one year. This is the trade-off between frequency and continuity. It follows from the same axiom of selling some people completely rather than many not at all.

Effective advertising requires a certain minimum frequency of exposures to the prospect within the product's purchase cycle. For example, for instant coffee, at least two exposures within the average purchase cycle of 21 days seems to be an effective frequency when brand switchers are the target audience (see Chapter 16). If the effective frequency level (actually a *rate* level, since it is frequency per unit time) means that the assigned budget would be used up in three months, so be it. If good results are demonstrated in the first three months, then the budget should be increased for the next three months, and likewise, to the end of the planning period.

If the budget cannot be increased to cover a more continuous time period (and, by the way, not increasing the budget would be a poor investment decision), then the manager should retain the effective frequency concept and consider "flighting" the budget over the period (discussed briefly in the next paragraph and in Chapter 20). The best *general* solution, however, given that the advertising is known to be working, is to increase the budget.

In the trade-off between frequency and continuity, we should distinguish severe discontinuity from deliberate short-term discontinuity. Severe discontinuity occurs when the entire budget is expended early and a long delay or hiatus occurs until the next advertising period. The delay can result in a damaging loss of communication effects (such as brand awareness) that can be very expensive to restore. Deliberate short-term discontinuity is different; it occurs in the media strategy known as "flighting," whereby effective frequency is packed into alternating purchase cycles. In *certain circumstances,* described in Chapter 20, flighting may be the best way of allocating a limited budget.

In any case, with a fixed media budget, there will be a trade-off between frequency or concentrated advertising and continuity over the advertising period.

Reach versus Continuity

To complete the balloon metaphor, we see that a trade-off also occurs between the number of people reached by the advertising and continuity over the advertising period—again unless the budget is increased. At first, this trade-off would seem to be subsumed in the reach versus frequency trade-off, because continuity is nothing more than frequency over a longer period. However, there is a very good reason that this is not so, whenever multiple purchase cycles occur within an advertising period.

Purchase cycles are also consumption or usage cycles: at the end of each cycle, the person *becomes a new prospect again* and is functionally a new individual to be reached even though he or she may have been reached before. (Thus, the potential reach is 100 percent of prospects on *each* purchase cycle. If there are, for example, 12 purchase cycles on average during the year, the yearly potential reach is 1200 percent!) Reach per purchase cycle, therefore, trades off with continuity over purchase cycles.

Effective frequency based on the purchase cycle governs the reach and continuity trade-off just as it did the previous two trade-offs. Extreme examples may help to illustrate the reach and continuity trade-off. For a short purchase cycle (fast "use-up") product, such as instant coffee, the advertiser would want to continuously go back to the same person, especially if he or she likes our brand, because the required frequency, and thus the advertising expenditure per purchase cycle, would reduce if and as the person becomes more loyal to the brand (see Chapter 1's discussion of repetition in the buyer response sequence and Chapter 16). This plan would produce low reach, in the conventional sense of *different people* reached, with high continuity. At the other extreme, for a long purchase cycle (slow "use-up") product, such as a refrigerator, the advertiser would not want to go back to the same person continuously, especially if he or she has just purchased a refrigerator. Rather, the advertiser would seek high reach with very low personal continuity, hoping to catch different individuals who are just about to enter the refrigerator purchase cycle.

So, unless the budget can be increased, the manager can either choose limited reach of the same people with high continuity, or broad reach of many people with low continuity. Again this decision is governed by the consideration of effective frequency within the purchase cycle.

MEDIA SELECTION BASED ON COMMUNICATION OBJECTIVES

Media are the means of delivering the creative message (to the target audience) to thereby achieve the communication objectives of the campaign. The basic requirement of media selection is that the medium or media selected must be able to convey the creative content of the campaign in a way that meets the communication objectives.

As we have seen in Part Four, there are two universal communication objectives: brand awareness and brand attitude. We will see that the creative content and also the frequency tactics for these two communication objectives (given in Part Five on creative strategy) largely dictate media selection. Like creative strategy, media strategy must fit the brand's communication objectives.

Media Selection Table Based on Brand Awareness and Brand Attitude

Table 15.2 is a media selection table based on the creative content and frequency tactics for the two types of brand awareness (brand recognition and brand recall) and the four types of brand attitude (low involvement/informational, low involvement/transformational, high involvement/informational, and high involvement/transformational). These factors are discussed next.

Brand Recognition If the campaign's brand awareness communication objective is brand recognition, the creative content and frequency tactics usually are as follows:

1 *Visual* content to show the brand's package, store logo, or name for subsequent recognition.[5]
2 *Color* content to further aid recognition of the brand.
3 Relatively *brief processing time* is sufficient.
4 Relatively *low frequency* is sufficient.

Working down the column for brand recognition on the media selection table we see that: television is a suitable medium; radio is eliminated (cannot

TABLE 15-2   MEDIA SELECTION BASED ON BRAND AWARENESS AND BRAND ATTITUDE

	Brand Awareness	
	Brand recognition	**Brand recall**
Television	YES	YES
Radio	*Eliminated*	YES
Magazines	YES	(Limited)**
Newspapers	(Limited)*	YES
Outdoor	YES	(Limited)**
Direct mail	YES	(Limited)**
P-o-p	YES	*Eliminated*

	Brand Attitude			
	Low involvement/ informational	**Low involvement/ transformational**	**High involvement/ informational**	**High involvement/ transformational**
Television	YES	YES	*Eliminated*	YES
Radio	YES	(Limited)*	*Eliminated*	(Limited)*
Magazines	YES	(Limited)**	YES	YES
Newspapers	YES	(Limited)*	YES	(Limited)*
Outdoor	YES	(Limited)**	(Limited)***	YES
Direct mail	YES	(Limited)**	YES	YES
P-o-p	YES	(Limited)**	(Limited)***	YES

* = color limitation
** = frequency limitation
*** = processing time limitation

show visual content[6]); magazines are suitable; newspapers are limited (cannot provide good color, except with expensive color inserts); outdoor is suitable; direct mail is suitable; and point-of-purchase vehicles are suitable.

Brand recognition requires visual, color media. Therefore, radio (definitely) and newspapers (usually) are "knocked out" of consideration when brand recognition is the objective.

Brand Recall   When the campaign's brand awareness communication objective is brand recall, the creative content and frequency tactics usually are as follows:

1 *Verbal* content (written or spoken words) to convey the brand name.
2 There is *no color* requirement.
3 Relatively *brief processing time* is sufficient.
4 *High Frequency* within the purchase cycle usually is necessary to allow frequent repetition of the brand name–category need association.

Working down the second column of the media selection table, for brand recall, we see that: television is suitable; radio is suitable; magazines are limited (cannot provide high frequency for short purchase cycles[7]); newspapers are suitable; outdoor is limited (cannot provide high frequency for short purchase cycles); direct mail is limited (cannot provide high frequency for short purchase cycles); and p-o-p is eliminated (cannot provide high frequency *prior* to the point of purchase as required for brand recall).

Brand recall requires verbal, high frequency media that permit frequent repetition. Repetition for brand recall is necessary for new products, where a new brand name is being learned, and for established products, to protect against competitive brand recall. Unless the purchase cycle is very long, thus allowing the lower frequency media of magazines and outdoor advertising to provide sufficient repetition, the main media for brand recall are television, radio, and (daily) newspapers.

Both Types of Brand Awareness   In the occasional event that both brand recognition and brand recall are required—such as for a new, planned- or considered-purchase brand that will be sold in a crowded, multi-brand retail display—the media selection table provides a "double knockout" function.

Because the campaign has to meet *both* brand recognition and brand recall media requirements, from both of the brand awareness columns, it can be seen that the only suitable medium under normal circumstances will be *television*.

Brand awareness therefore constitutes the first universal communication objective upon which media selection is based. Brand attitude is the second universal communication objective; its four options further govern media selection as indicated by the lower four columns of the media selection table.

Low Involvement/Informational   When the campaign's brand attitude objective is to be attained via a low involvement/informational brand attitude strategy, the creative content and frequency tactics usually are as follows:

1 *Verbal* content to convey the informational benefit claim or claims.
2 There is *no color* requirement.
3 Relatively *brief processing time* is sufficient because with low involvement the focus is on just one or two benefit claims.
4 Relatively *low frequency* is sufficient because informational benefits must be learned in one or two exposures.

Entering the media selection table for brand attitude and working down the low involvement/informational column, we see that *all media* are suitable. The brief, verbal claims characterizing most low involvement/informational campaigns can be conveyed in any medium.

The one exception here would be when the informational benefit claim requires *demonstration*. Television is the only medium that allows moving visual content, and would be the sole selection.

Low Involvement/Transformational   When the campaign's brand attitude objective is to be attained via a low involvement/transformational brand attitude strategy, the creative content and frequency tactics usually are as follows:

1 *Visual* content if the transformational motive is sensory gratification or social approval (only with the intellectual stimulation motive is visual content not an advantage).

2 *Color* likewise enhances sensory gratification and social approval.

3 Relatively *brief processing time* is sufficient.

4 *High frequency* within the purchase cycle usually is necessary because of the slower build-up of transformational brand attitude and the typically short purchase cycle for low involvement/transformational products.

Working down the low involvement/transformational brand attitude column of the media selection table, we see that: television really is the only suitable medium; radio is limited (except for the intellectual stimulation motive); magazines are limited (cannot provide high frequency for short purchase cycles); newspapers are limited (cannot provide good color, except with expensive color inserts, but are suitable if the motive is intellectual stimulation); outdoor is limited (cannot provide high frequency for short purchase cycles); direct mail is limited (cannot provide high frequency for short purchase cycles); and p-o-p is limited (cannot provide high frequency between purchases, that is, within the purchase cycle).

For low involvement/transformational brand attitude, television is the only medium that meets all requirements. If, however, intellectual stimulation is the transformational motive, rather than sensory gratification or social approval, then the high frequency media of radio and (daily) newspapers also are suitable.

High Involvement/Informational   When the campaign's brand attitude objective is to be attained via a high involvement/informational brand attitude strategy, the creative content and frequency tactics usually are as follows:

1 *Verbal* content to convey the informational benefit claims.

2 There is *no color* requirement.

3 *Long processing time* usually is required so that the target audience can process multiple benefits and longer, more carefully reasoned benefit claims.

4 Relatively *low frequency* is sufficient because informational benefits must be accepted in one or two exposures.

Print media are favored for high involvement/informational advertising. Working down this column in the media selection table, we see that television is eliminated (insufficient processing time); radio is eliminated (insufficient processing time); magazines are suitable; newspapers are suitable; outdoor is limited (unless *stationary* outdoor media are used, with the display and the audience stationary); direct mail is suitable; and p-o-p is limited (it is unreasonable to expect shoppers to process long copy in the usual pressure of the shopping situation).

Print media come to the fore for high involvement/informational advertising unless the brand happens to be a high risk purchase that depends on one major benefit that can be conveyed convincingly with short copy. It is noteworthy, reading across the table, that high involvement/informational brand attitude is the only communication objective for which television is unsuitable.

High Involvement/Transformational   When the campaign's brand attitude objective is to be attained via a high involvement/transformational brand attitude strategy, the creative content and frequency tactics usually are as follows:

1 *Visual* content if the transformational motive is sensory gratification or social approval (only with the intellectual stimulation motive is visual content not an advantage).

2 *Color* likewise enhances sensory gratification and social approval.

3 Relatively *brief processing time* is sufficient *unless* the high involvement/transformational strategy also has to provide *information*.

4 Relatively *low frequency* usually is sufficient because, although transformational attitude builds slowly, the purchase cycle for high involvement/transformational products is generally quite long, thus allowing a relatively low *rate* of frequency to be sufficient.

Working down the final column of the media selection table, and for high involvement/transformational advertising, we see that: television is suitable (see next paragraph); radio is limited (except for the intellectual stimulation motive); magazines are suitable; newspapers are limited (cannot provide good color, except for expensive color inserts, but are suitable if the motive is intellectual stimulation); outdoor is suitable (see next paragraph); direct mail is suitable; and p-o-p is suitable.

There are, however, limits to the foregoing selections when the high involvement/transformational strategy also has to provide *information*. When the primary purchase motivation is transformational but a secondary informational purchase motivation *also* must be addressed (for example, new cars, luxury vacations), television and outdoor become limited.

Television's transformational capacity really cannot be ignored; but now an *additional* medium will be needed to handle the informational component. This may be a print medium or, in many cases, the information function may be left for the "non-advertising" medium of personal selling. New car sales and vacation sales are typical examples where personal selling is often utilized to "close" a high involvement/transformational sale.

Outdoor media are a different case when information has to be provided. As we saw earlier, if the outdoor media vehicle offers a stationary display to a stationary consumer, thus allowing a relatively long processing time, then *stationary* outdoor media vehicles are suitable for high involvement/transformational advertising with information. In this capacity, stationary outdoor ads function similarly to magazine ads.

Other Communication Objectives

So far, we have concentrated on the two universal communication objectives of brand awareness and brand attitude. Many campaigns have other communication objectives as well; for example, all campaigns except low involvement/transformational have immediate brand purchase intention as an objective.

As discussed in Chapter 8, certain options within these other communication objectives require acceptance by the target audience. They operate essentially like high involvement attitudes and therefore may require *print media* to allow the target audience sufficient time to process their content and accept their claims. In particular, print media should be considered for the following communication objectives:

- *Category Need* When the objective is to *sell* category need, more space usually is required to present category benefits, so print media usually are required.
- *Brand Purchase Intention* When the tactics suggest *hard sell*—especially in the form of a promotion offer—again, print media usually are required.[8]
- *Purchase Facilitation* When there is a *major* problem with one of the 4 P's that advertising is attempting to solve, more reassurance will be needed and thus print media usually are required.

THE CONCEPT OF PRIMARY AND SECONDARY MEDIA

Almost every advertising campaign makes use of a primary medium, in which half or more of the media budget will be spent, and one or more secondary media. In this section of the chapter, we will examine which medium should be designated as primary and which media should be used as secondary or "backup" media.

The Primary Medium

The *primary* medium is selected because it is the single most *effective* medium for achieving all of the brand's communication objectives and causing buyer behavior. Although cost is a factor, effectiveness is more important. The advertiser should continue to allocate the budget to the primary medium as long as the known or estimated profit derived from sales exceeds the cost of the primary medium's advertising.

Combined Brand Awareness and Brand Attitude Objectives The primary medium must be capable of achieving all of the brand's communication objectives. The most important communication objectives are brand awareness and brand attitude; also, one or more of the other three communication objectives may have to be addressed. In selecting a primary medium from the general media selection table (see Table 15.2, earlier), brand awareness requirements now must be *combined* with brand attitude requirements.

Beginning from the left in the table, and going across to the right, a medium that is "knocked out" by brand awareness requirements "stays out" when brand attitude is considered. This is seen more easily by constructing a "positive" version of the table (Table 15.3) showing the media left for consideration after brand awareness and brand attitude constraints have been jointly applied.

TABLE 15-3   PRIMARY MEDIA FOR MEETING COMBINED BRAND AWARENESS AND BRAND ATTITUDE COMMUNICATION OBJECTIVES

Brand Recognition and:			
Low involvement/ informational	**Low involvement/ transformational**	**High involvement/ informational**	**High involvement/ transformational**
• television • magazines • outdoor • direct mail • p-o-p	• television	• magazines • direct mail	• television* • magazines • outdoor* • direct mail • p-o-p
Brand Recall and:			
Low involvement/ informational	**Low involvement/ transformational**	**High involvement/ informational**	**High involvement/ transformational**
• television • radio • newspapers	• television • radio** • newspapers**	• newspapers	• television*

* See text if information *also* has to be provided.
** Suitable only if the transformational motivation is intellectual stimulation.

We see that in most "cells" of this table, the options for *primary* media are very limited; in three cells, the choice is limited to a single medium. Again, this should be seen as an advantage for the manager. It makes the choice easier as to which medium or media are capable of conveying the main message of the campaign and therefore should be given the primary role.

If more than one medium survives the primary medium selection process, a single primary medium can be selected on the basis of superior target audience reach by using direct matching (described in Chapter 17). The "losing" primary medium or media would then be very strong candidates for secondary media, whose functions are explained next.

Secondary Media

Secondary media are used for three reasons:

1 There may be some *significant proportion of the target audience* whom the primary medium does not reach or cannot reach at an effective frequency level; for example, very light television viewers, or non-readers of newspapers. Thus, a secondary medium is "imperative" in the plan if these people are to be reached.

2 There may be *one or two communication objectives* that can be attained equally effectively, but at lower cost, with a medium other than the primary medium. Secondary media may be used in the role of attaining *particular*

communication objectives (such as increased brand awareness, maintained brand attitude, or reminder purchase intentions) either: (a) *simultaneously* with the primary medium during the early phases of the media plan, to contribute to overall communication objectives[9]; or (b) *later* in the media plan after the main shifts in communication effects have been attained and the communication objectives become maintenance or "reinforcement" objectives,[10] which may be attainable with lower-cost media.

3 There may be a *timing advantage near or at the point of purchase,* that is, close to the target audience's decision, offered by a secondary medium.

Recommended primary and secondary media selections are examined next for five main categories of advertising: national consumer advertising, retail advertising, industrial advertising, corporate image advertising, and direct response advertising. (Respective sections can be skipped if you are not interested in all these types of advertising.)

NATIONAL CONSUMER ADVERTISING

National consumer advertising refers to advertising for consumer products or services that are available nationwide. Advertising campaigns for national brands usually are standard across the nation, although sometimes the media strategy and occasionally the creative strategy (more likely its creative execution) may vary regionally or locally. Note that most media provide geographic options (see Appendix B) if the advertising plan requires them.

Primary Medium Is Almost Always Television

For national advertisers of consumer products and services, the best primary medium is almost always *television*. We say "almost always" because the exception is high involvement/informational products that require long copy. Even here, for the national advertiser, television may be used as a secondary medium for the brand awareness communication objective.

It has been estimated[11] that the typical national advertiser uses about 60 percent television and 40 percent secondary media. Emphasis on television in the media mix is highly related to purchase frequency (the purchase cycle). For example, the three major national airlines—TWA, United, and American—which have a fairly long purchase cycle for the general public, average about 48 percent television; the three largest auto manufacturers—GM, Ford, and Chrysler—which similarly have quite a long purchase cycle, average about 56 percent television; whereas the two largest soft drink manufacturers—the Coca-Cola Company and PepsiCo Inc.—which have a short purchase cycle, both use about 90 percent television.[12]

Why is television the primary advertising medium of choice for most national consumer advertisers? The explanation lies in the fact that television is undeniably the single most effective medium for achieving overall communication objectives and producing sales.[13]

The reasons for television advertising's persuasive superiority are fairly easy to discern in terms of the first two steps of our six-step approach. No other medium can match television for exposure and processing:

1 *Exposure* TV offers very high reach in a relatively short period and also can deliver high effective frequency levels, if needed, to most target audiences.

2 *Processing* Whereas most media provide initial attention to the ad at the same level as TV, none can equal the "intrusive" nature of television for sustaining attention to the entire message. (When a commercial comes on TV, it is easier to watch and listen than to do anything else unless TV is being used for background sound, like radio, as happens for some daytime programs). The attention-sustaining characteristic, as well as TV's unique ability to carry multiple advertising stimuli (pictures, color, movement, seen words, and heard words) also make it the superior medium for rote learning, needed for brand awareness of either the brand recognition or brand recall type, and low involvement brand attitude registration. With multiple exposures, TV *may* also provide the opportunity for acceptance responses, needed for high involvement brand attitude shifts. (However, TV can do this only for a limited number of benefits. It is not suitable for processing multiple or detailed logical support benefit claims where the target audience has to consider each claim carefully.)

Our recommendation is that the media planner for nationally advertised consumer products should consider television as the first choice against which all other choices should be compared. The national consumer advertiser should only move to another medium as primary if the brand choice is high involvement and television advertising cannot handle the informational message requirements.[14]

Secondary Media and Substitutes for Television

Many national consumer advertisers have little need for a secondary medium beyond television advertising. You may remember, for example, that Coke and Pepsi spend only 10 percent of their (consumer) advertising budget outside TV. These non-TV expenditures are most likely to be for the third use of secondary media listed earlier: *point-of-purchase reminders.*

Point-of-purchase (really point-of-decision) reminder ads are relatively easy to experiment with to see if they contribute to sales because p-o-p ads can be easily installed or removed to observe the effect on sales. P-o-p reminder ads can be powerful communication devices. Think of a Coke ad in a restaurant: It can remind you of category need, cause brand recognition, and, given a favorable prior attitude, create an immediate intention to buy.

Other national consumer advertisers seek secondary media to *back up TV* as the primary medium because particular secondary media may be very effective in contributing to *one* of the brand's communication objectives of either brand awareness or brand attitude. Here, we can go back to Table 15.2 for suitable choices and construct a new table (Table 15.4) for *secondary* media based on the communication effect to be "boosted."

TABLE 15-4   SECONDARY MEDIA* TO "BOOST" SINGLE COMMUNICATION EFFECTS FOR NATIONAL CONSUMER ADVERTISERS

Communication effect to be boosted	Recommended secondary media
BRAND AWARENESS: Brand recognition	• outdoor • p-o-p
Brand recall	• radio • newspapers
BRAND ATTITUDE: Low involvement/informational	• radio • newspapers • outdoor • p-o-p
Low involvement/transformational	• radio with imagery transfer (see later)
High involvement/informational (when TV is primary)	• magazines • newspapers
High involvement/transformational	• magazines • outdoor • p-o-p

* Primary medium is television.

The remaining use of secondary media is to reach those *hard-to-reach target audience members* for whom the primary medium, TV, cannot deliver enough frequency to achieve the effective frequency level for the brand. Note, however, that even light viewers of TV—as long as they have a fairly regular pattern of light viewing, such as one or two favorite programs or the late news on most weeknights—can be reached at high frequency by using impact scheduling, that is, by running the commercial several times during the one program. The advantages and disadvantages of impact scheduling are discussed in Chapter 17.

The media planner must ensure that these "extra reach" secondary media, selected on their ability to provide target audience reach at additional frequency, are capable of delivering the required communication effects. As we saw in Table 15.2 and 15.3 earlier, most media have limitations or are eliminated when joint communication objectives are required. There *are* creative ways of getting around most of the negatives and limitations listed in the table, but most of these creative alternatives are expensive and are not practical unless that medium represents the only way of reaching the target audience, or unless that medium has some other distinct advantage that makes it worth using. These alternatives are discussed next as *substitutes* for television for hard-to-reach target audiences.

Radio   Radio normally is eliminated if brand *recognition* is a communication objective. Radio, of course, is unable to show packages. Brands that later have to be recognized at the point of purchase cannot be advertised effectively on radio.

The creative way around the brand recognition problem on radio involves describing the package in the radio commercial. This was often done in the old days of radio before TV emerged as a major advertising medium (for example, Pepsodent's "Look for the yellow tube at your grocer's"). However, package descriptions are rather imprecise, especially in relation to today's typically crowded shelf displays, and descriptions take away time from the copy needed for the commercial.

Radio has limited effectiveness if the brand attitude strategy is *transformational,* in either the low involvement or high involvement quadrants. Of the three positive motivations, radio is most handicapped for sensory gratification (for example, it cannot show appetizing "beauty shots," as they are called, for food products) and for social approval (for example, it cannot show people as brand-users). Radio is less handicapped for intellectual stimulation as a motivation (although the handicap applies if the brand requires a demonstration).

The creative way around transformational brand attitude limitations on radio is for the radio copywriter to select words and sentences that stimulate imagery in the listener's mind. For example, gustatory (taste) imagery can be stimulated by kitchen sounds, drinks pouring over cracking ice, and so forth. Similarly, visual imagery of brand-user types often can be generated through voice cues, particularly for social class perceptions. However, these imagery effects can be difficult to generate reliably and consistently across all listeners.

A second creative solution to the transformational brand attitude limitation of radio is to attempt to generate *imagery transfer* from TV advertising to radio advertising. Coffin and Tuchman[15] conducted an imagery transfer experiment in which the audio tracks from 12 previously aired TV commercials were used as radio commercials. Respondents were played the radio commercials and asked to describe "what was happening on the TV screen." On average, 72 percent of respondents were able to give an acceptable description of the visuals of the TV commercial upon subsequently hearing the radio commercial.

Aside from radio, other *visual* media also could be used for imagery transfer, where the illustration duplicates a key scene from a previously viewed TV commercial.[16] John Hancock has used a magazine advertisement that duplicates a key scene from a John Hancock TV commercial as the illustration and audio from the commercial as copy (Figure 15.2). Levi's Jeans has used outdoor billboards and posters that show a video frame from their TV campaign.

Imagery transfer may be worth trying as a means of getting "additional mileage" from secondary media that support TV as the primary medium.

Magazines   The main limitation of magazines is in terms of relatively poor ability to deliver the *high frequency* needed for the many nationally advertised consumer products which have brand recall or low involvement/transforma-

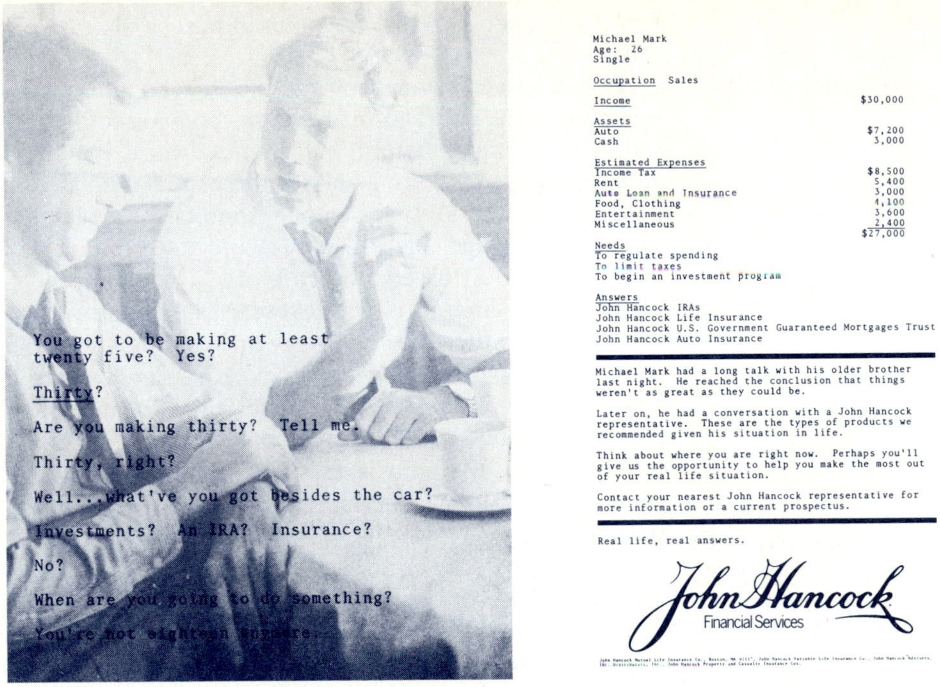

FIGURE 15-2 An example of attempted imagery transfer from TV to print, for John Hancock Financial Services. A video scene from the TV commercial forms the illustration for this magazine ad, and the commercial's audio forms the copy. (Courtesy of John Hancock Mutual Life Insurance Company.)

tional brand attitude communication objectives. Weekly magazines, of course, have an advantage over monthly magazines in this respect.

Magazines also have relatively narrow audiences. To achieve high frequency for most target audiences, the advertiser would have to buy a variety of magazines because each target audience member may read only one or two, and these one or two magazines may differ widely from individual to individual.

A reasonably good creative solution to the high frequency problem with magazines is *impact scheduling,* which we mentioned previously for television. In the magazine application of impact scheduling, multiple ads (which should be executionally a little different to renew attention) for the one brand are placed in the same issue of the magazine. The main weakness of impact scheduling, as discussed in Chapter 17, is that the piling up of frequency into one reading timeslot leaves a delay period during which competitive brand advertising can interfere. However, this may average out if competing brands also are confined to magazines.

More generally, for new brands, where the brand awareness and brand attitude communication effects have a long way up to go from zero, the frequency limitation of magazines can be a substantial problem. Later in the brand's life cycle, when targeting brand loyals or brand switchers who have well-established communication effects, magazines are a more attractive secondary medium, and may become the primary medium if they can now achieve the brand's communication objectives at a lower cost than TV.

Newspapers Practically considered, newspapers lack color as a creative content element. Although color ads can be purchased at a 20 to 30 percent price premium, normal or run-of-paper (R-O-P) color is notoriously unreliable from market to market and from paper to paper within press runs.

The color limitation poses a problem when *brand recognition* is an objective. (Note that later, when we assess retail advertising, lack of color in newspaper ads is less a problem for those retail *re-advertisers* who show brands whose color recognition has been achieved in the manufacturer's advertising in other media. Ability to recognize a black and white version of a colored package could be regarded as an instance of imagery transfer.) Furthermore, many *transformational* campaigns rely on color to provide full positive reinforcing stimulation.

The creative alternative to the color limitation of newspapers is to buy high quality color inserts or supplements[17] However, since many newspapers will take these on weekends only, the color insert or supplement route can negate the high frequency advantage of newspapers. It may be noted that daily availability of high quality color would give newspapers a very considerable high frequency advantage over magazines.

Outdoor One limitation of outdoor ads occurs when *high frequency* is required. Nevertheless, careful examination of target audience exposure to outdoor (or indoor transit) sites can often provide opportunities to deliver high frequency. The extra cost is in conducting detailed audience research to detect commuting or shopping patterns that allow frequent outdoor exposure.

The other limitation of outdoor ads is for *high involvement brand attitude* strategies, because the multiple benefit or detailed benefit claim capacity of outdoor ads typically is limited. However, there are two very important qualifications to this. First, *stationary* outdoor vehicles, such as subway or train posters, often allow substantial processing time, so these are *not* limited for high involvement messages. Second, not all high involvement brand decisions require multiple message points or detailed benefit claims. If a high involvement campaign requires a strong but relatively short message, then outdoor advertising can be an effective medium.

Direct Mail The main limitation of direct mail for the national consumer advertiser is its inability to deliver *high frequency*. In fact, most direct mail campaigns are designed to effectively close the sale in a single exposure, not repeated exposures. Hence, direct mail is hardly ever used purely as an advertising medium for frequently purchased consumer products. However, it can be used to deliver *promotion offers* (which attempt to close the sale) when consumers are aware of the brand from other media and when a good target audience mailing list is available. Stouffer's, for instance, periodically uses direct mail coupons which are sent to a list of prime Stouffer's brand loyals.

On its own, or even as a secondary medium, direct mail is not an effective medium for the national consumer advertiser because is would be too expensive to mail at high frequency.

Point-of-Purchase (p-o-p)   The main limitation of point-of-purchase advertising is that the exposure comes too late to affect brand *recall:* Brand recall must occur *prior* to the point of purchase. There is no creative solution to this brand recall problem, because of the timing of p-o-p in the purchase decision sequence.

Point-of-purchase is, in contrast, an excellent secondary medium in *brand recognition* situations, when the decision is made *at* the point of purchase. A good p-o-p display can serve as a near-perfect recognition cue if it duplicates visual and verbal elements shown previously in the brand's advertising, such as on TV.

Point-of-purchase has a second limitation: it is of limited effectiveness for *high involvement* brand attitude objectives. The prospective buyer of *frequently purchased* consumer products, trying a new high-risk brand, cannot be expected to process detailed information at the last minute.

However, for *consumer durables,* p-o-p advertising can be an effective *secondary* medium for the national advertiser because the customer is likely to deliberate carefully before making a final decision. Examples include brand purchase decisions for expensive calculators and cameras, or complex home appliances. Manufacturers' brochures or detailed display cards at the point of purchase are often consulted to find out more about risk-laden brands that are only superficially familiar from mass-medium advertising.

A final limitation of p-o-p advertising is that it cannot provide *high frequency,* if needed, *between* purchases, that is, during the purchase cycle. The prospective purchaser is only likely to attend to p-o-p advertising at the beginning of each purchase cycle when "in the market" for the product.

Thus, although p-o-p can be a very effective secondary medium for products purchased via brand recognition, it is rarely sufficient *alone* as a *primary* medium for national consumer products.

Summary   The national consumer advertiser should use TV as the primary medium unless the brand attitude strategy requires long copy, where a print medium will be primary. Secondary media for the national consumer advertiser depend on the purpose for which they are needed—most often, the need is for a secondary medium to boost a particular communication objective at relatively low cost. A wide range of choices for secondary media is available, but these are quickly narrowed according to communication objectives. An "unsuitable" medium that otherwise has excellent target audience reach can be used in some instances by creatively getting around the communication limitation, but such substitutions usually are expensive and less effective than using suitable media with lower reach.

RETAIL ADVERTISING

Retail advertising fundamentally is *local* advertising because each retail store draws customers from only a limited geographic area (most of the target audience lives or works within several miles of the store). Furthermore, nearly all retailers have two "brands" to advertise:

1 The products sold by the store (product advertising)
2 The store itself (store image advertising)

These two types of retail advertising have different communication objectives. Accordingly, the best selection of media for retail product advertising and store image advertising usually differ, as we will see next.

Retail Product Advertising

Many local advertisers, such as supermarkets or department stores, have a wide range of products that they wish to expose to prospective buyers. There are too many products to be shown on TV—although there is no doubt that local advertisers would use (local) TV if they could afford detailed and lengthy commercials, as TV is the most effective selling medium. (With the emergence of shop-at-home cable TV, or "electronic newspapers" available on TV screens connected to home computers, there will in the future be a large movement of retail advertisers to TV.) For the local, multi-product retailer, the product advertising options depend on whether they are a "re-advertiser" of national brands or an "original advertiser" of local brands.

Retail Re-advertisers: Newspapers   Many retailers—notably supermarkets—sell products that already have been advertised by the manufacturer. These retailers are therefore *re-advertisers*. Retail ads in this case are functionally "point-of-purchase" media that work primarily on brand purchase intention (that is, by telling the prospective buyer that a known brand is available, at an intention-inducing price, at that store). For this purpose, *newspapers* are the best medium.

Because brand awareness and brand attitude already have been established and are addressed only in a reminder role in the newspaper ad, newspapers for the retail re-advertiser are not subject to any of the limitations that newspapers pose for the national advertiser. In particular, lack of color, which normally would hinder brands seeking brand recognition, or using a transformational brand attitude strategy, or both, is not a problem for the retail re-advertiser.

The choice of newspapers as the primary medium for local advertisers is further encouraged by newspapers' practice of giving local advertisers very attractive low rates. Local advertisers provide the main financial support for newspapers. Thus local newspapers (both city and suburban) are vitally concerned with maintaining for local advertisers an attractive price compared with other local media alternatives, notably local TV and local radio. But only retail *re-advertisers* should automatically use newspapers.

Original Retail Advertisers: TV, Sunday Newspaper Supplements, Catalogs, or Handbills   Other retail stores are *original advertisers;* that is, they sell their own products rather than national brands advertised by national manufacturers. These retailers include banks, department stores which sell mainly their own brand name merchandise, and various specialty and smaller stores.

Original advertisers at the local level have the same product advertising communication objectives as the national consumer advertiser does at the national level. However, media choices for the original retail advertiser are contingent on three additional factors: (a) product versus service retailing, (b) breadth of product mix, and (c) number and geographic dispersion of customers.

Television is the best choice for the original retail advertiser who sells products or services but with a limited product mix that can be typified by a small number of leading items, and draws a large number of customers to one store or a chain of stores. Examples include furniture stores, banks, and local chain restaurants.

Sunday newspaper supplements (color brochure inserts[18] or ads in the color ''magazine'' section) are the best choice when the original retail advertiser has a wide product mix and draws a large number of customers to one store or a chain of stores. Examples may include discount department stores and chain hardware stores.

Direct mail is the best choice for the original advertiser who sells products with a narrow or wide mix, and also has geographically dispersed customers in large enough numbers to make the printing of direct mail (which can range from fairly inexpensive color brochures to multi-page color catalogs) worthwhile. Some examples are the more ''exclusive'' department stores, specialty clothing stores, and sports stores.

Handbills (in mail boxes or centrally distributed at high traffic locations) are the best choice for original retail advertisers who sell services and have a small number of very localized customers. Examples include dry cleaners, plumbers, and lawn and garden services. These types of advertisers don't need to use color and can't afford expensive advertising media. Alternatives are small-space ads in *suburban* newspapers, or *miscellaneous* media such as calendars.

Small stores which sell products but also have very localized customers also should use handbills. Although color would be an advantage, it's too expensive. Some examples are corner grocery stores, local hardware stores, and local independent restaurants whose special menu items change regularly.

Store Image Advertising

Retailers not only sell the products in their stores but first must get people attracted to the store itself. This is the purpose of store image advertising. While we might think of retailers' product advertising media as primary and store image advertising media as secondary, for many retailers store traffic is vital for success and the primary and secondary roles for the two types of retail advertising may be reversed.

Store image advertising typically has the following communication objectives (with the *store* now serving as the *brand*):

1 *Brand Recall*—so that prospective customers will include the store in their evoked set (the exception is stores in high traffic areas that rely on "walk-in" traffic, but many of these stores would do better to predispose customers through brand recall).

2 *Brand Attitude*—but *only if* the store's "image" is not well known to the target audience.

3 *Brand Purchase Intention*—that is, *intention to visit* the store when the category need arises, which usually is hard-sell.

The focus on brand *recall* and short-term brand purchase intention means that all high frequency media (see Table 15.2 earlier) are possibilities: TV, radio, and newspapers. We have re-included TV here because for shorter, store-reminder ads, TV may now become cost effective for the local advertiser. If not, radio or newspaper advertising certainly would be cost effective. Radio or newspaper can be used just prior to, or on, major shopping days.

If the retailer is trying to create or increase a brand attitude (store image) that is largely transformational, the two media that drop out of the above are radio and newspapers, unless a creative solution can be found, leaving only local TV.

Some retailers do not require high frequency, even for brand recall, because the purchase cycle is very long. A furniture store, for example, does not require high effective frequency because the purchase cycle is probably up to a decade long. A Kentucky Fried Chicken outlet, on the other hand, has a short purchase cycle and requires high frequency. If low frequency is adequate, several more possibilities for store image advertising open up: outdoor; radio; city magazines, when available; and direct mail. Indeed, these media are preferred for the low frequency store image advertiser because they allow a high quality store image to be maintained through good color-reproduction graphics.

These complex considerations for retail advertisers' media selection are summarized in Table 15.5.

INDUSTRIAL ADVERTISING

Media selection for the industrial or business-to-business advertiser depends mainly on two factors: (a) the size of the target audience and (b) the decision makers (in their respective) roles to whom the advertising is directed. In the following, we assume the target audience *already* has been identified as either new category users, brand loyals, brand switchers, or other-brand loyals. Target audience size and roles therefore apply *within* these groups. The possible

TABLE 15-5   MEDIA SELECTION FOR RETAIL ADVERTISERS

Retail product advertising	
Retail re-advertisers (e.g., supermarkets)	• newspapers
Original retail advertisers (e.g., furniture stores)	• local TV (narrow product mix)
	• direct mail (smaller or dispersed audience)
	• handbills, suburban newspapers, calendars (local service retailers)
Store image	
Store recall and store purchase intention (store image known)	• local TV
	• radio
	• newspapers
Above, plus transformational store attitude (store image to be created, increased, modified, or changed)	• local TV
	• outdoor (long purchase cycle)
	• city magazines (long purchase cycle)
	• direct mail (long purchase cycle)

decision roles, discussed in Chapter 5, are initiator, influencer, decider, purchaser, and user.

Small Target Audience

Some businesses have a relatively small target audience—say, less than 100 individual decision makers, in total—to reach. Many small local businesses have small target audiences but so, too, do many large businesses selling to several large customers.

When the target audience is small, *no advertising* is recommended, at least in major media. Personal sales calls can achieve the communication objectives more effectively and produce orders and sales at much lower cost. The media used, if any, would consist of pamphlets or brochures as *sales aids* carried by the sales force.

Moderate-sized Target Audience

If the target audience size is moderate, then *trade publications* and *direct mail* are the best choices. Moderate-sized target audiences of, say, 100 to 1000 decision makers are too small to justify use of a mass medium but are large enough to justify advertising in narower-reach media as a cost-effective means of paving the way for sales calls.

Target audience size includes multiple decision makers (across all five decision-making roles) in the same prospect- or customer-firm. The industrial or business-to-business advertiser should always conduct a careful analysis of decision roles within the typical buying center. The major division in nearly all cases is between important but lower-level decision makers (especially initiators and users) and top management upper-level decision makers (deciders). Most lower-level decision makers read *trade publications,* but upper-level decision makers don't. Hence, another medium, *direct mail,* is needed to reach top management when the target audience size is moderate.

Large Target Audience

The same principle of the division in decision roles by organizational levels, of course, applies to the large industrial or business-to-business advertiser. For lower-level decision makers, *trade publications* are again the obvious choice because they reach initiators and product or service users, by industry, with very little target audience waste.

For the now numerous upper-level decision makers, top management deciders, the use of *business magazines* is recommended. The target audience size justifies the use of a more "mass" medium than direct mail. And possibly, the perceived prestige of advertising in business magazines ("they must be a large and successful company," the management thinks) gives this medium an effectiveness advantage over direct mail.

Because of the technical nature of most industrial products or services, print media are required that reach specialized target audiences (users or top managers) with low waste. The cost factor of too broad a vehicle audience rules out mass print media such as newspapers or general magazines.

Only occasionally, with a *simple* product or service and a *very* large target audience, should a mass medium be considered—for example, Federal Express' use of television.

Most firms' industrial or business-to-business *product or service* advertising therefore will be placed in the specialized print media of trade publications or business magazines (Table 15.6). For *corporate* advertising, however, they may make a wider choice, as discussed next.

CORPORATE IMAGE ADVERTISING

Just as the retail advertiser has a store image to project and remind people about, industrial *and* consumer advertisers have a corporate image—an "um-

TABLE 15-6   MEDIA SELECTION FOR INDUSTRIAL (BUSINESS-TO-BUSINESS) ADVERTISERS

Size of target audience (number of individual decision makers)	Recommended media
Small	• none (use personal selling, perhaps with pamphlets or brochures as sales aids)
Moderate	• trade publications (lower-level decision makers) • direct mail (upper-level decision makers)
Large	• trade publications (lower-level decision makers) • business magazines (upper-level decision makers)

brella'' for specific product and brand messages—to project and remind people about. Who are the target audiences for corporate image advertising and what exactly *is* a corporate image?

Corporate Image Target Audiences and Action Objectives

The target audiences for corporate image advertising (which should be subdivided into new category users, brand loyals, brand switchers, and other-brand loyals) consist of the following groups, each with its respective action objective:

1 *Customers*—prospective and current, to buy the company's products or patronize its services.
2 *Stockholders*—if a publicly held company, to invest in its stock.
3 *Employees*—prospective and current, to work for the company.
4 *Government*—to regulate in favor of the company's operations.
5 *Special Interest Groups*—not to hinder the company's operations.

Note in each case that there is a specific, measurable, behavioral action objective as the desired outcome of corporate image advertising. Corporate image advertising is not just undertaken to create "goodwill" or "warm feelings" (although these may be relevant attitudes) but rather, like all other forms of advertising, it must have an ultimate payoff in profits.

Corporate Image Communication Objectives

Corporate image advertising consists of three main communication objectives. (Here, the company is the "brand.")

1 *Brand Recognition* For the business customer, although some ordering will be done by recall, the main purpose of corporate image advertising is to get the company's name recognized when the salesforce calls on prospects; likewise, other target audiences must recognize the company name when considering it for stock purchase investments, employment, regulation, or special interest action.

2 *Transformational Brand Attitude* For customers and investors, the primary motivation for accepting the corporation as a "brand" is intellectual stimulation (making a "wise" choice). This is of course transformational, and usually high involvement, because of the ego risk and also the financial risk in giving time to a salesperson or in buying a company's stock. For the other target audiences, employees, government, and special interest groups, the transformational motive of social approval is usually primary, although, as with many high involvement/transformational brand attitudes, information about the company's benefits also may have to be provided.

3 *Delayed (Soft-Sell) Brand Purchase Intention* The prospective target audience decision maker should deduce, from the well-known company (brand recognition) and well-regarded company (brand attitude), that, when the need arises, he or she should see the salesperson, invest, join the company, or otherwise support it governmentally or socially. Corporate image advertising is therefore soft-sell, with delayed purchase-related behavior as the intention objective.

Corporations are sold just like brands. Corporate "image" is therefore the equivalent of brand attitude. But, as we have seen, the preceding communication objectives of brand recognition (number 1) and the ensuing communication objective of brand purchase intention (number 3) *also* are necessary as corporate image communication objectives.

Small Companies

For the small company with a small or very localized target audience, corporate image advertising, in the conventional sense, is too costly to be used *in addition* to product or service advertising. However, small companies advertising products or services in handbills, suburban newspapers, calendars, or sales aids should plan to include a corporate image component—such as a tested company slogan or logo.

As well, small companies have much to gain from *local sponsorships*. Financial assistance to community organizations, local athletic programs, and for concerts and social events, for example, is almost always worthwhile; the company's name (brand recognition) will reach all local target audiences through the use of programs or other printed materials.

Medium to Large Companies

Looking back at Table 15.3 for joint communication objectives, we see that television, magazines, outdoor, direct mail, and point-of-purchase are the media that best allow brand recognition and high involvement/transformational brand attitude to be delivered. These communication objectives, you may remember, along with a soft-sell action intention, are the ones required for corporate image advertising.

Television, used nationally or locally, is the most persuasive corporate image medium and can be used for corporate image advertising even when the company's product or service advertising is placed primarily in other media. The intrusive nature of TV, especially for catching executives off-the-job in a relaxed mood, and its ability to dynamically depict company achievements, make television the most effective corporate image medium.

If the cost of television is prohibitive in relation to known or estimated sales effectiveness, because of a small or extremely low TV-watching target audience, then business or consumer *magazines, direct mail,* or *point-of-purchase,* in this order based on diminishing target audience size, would be the alternative choices.

Outdoor advertising is the remaining medium from the five identified as suitable for corporate image communication objectives. This is an appropriate choice when the corporate image message is *short*. Outdoor corporate image advertising is a good choice when the target audience has a reasonably consistent commuting or shopping pattern, especially in relation to the company's products or services. Billboards on main roads to office areas or airports (industrial) or shopping centers (consumer) provide excellent target audience reach for short corporate image messages.

Medium to large companies also should consider sponsorships as a "medium" for impressing government, employee, and special interest-group target audiences. However, whereas small companies are well known in local areas, medium to large companies may not be, unless they have a local plant or office. Accordingly, medium to large companies should seek *advertised sponsorships* for events that are advertised in broader media such as television or magazines.

Corporate image media selection is summarized for convenient reference in Table 15.7.

DIRECT RESPONSE ADVERTISING

Direct response advertising is at the opposite end of the spectrum from corporate image advertising; it calls for behavioral action immediately rather than later and usually is directed at a relatively narrow target audience rather than broad or multiple target audiences. Direct response advertising is used primarily to:

1 Sell merchandise outright, or to
2 Produce sales inquiries (to "qualify leads") for personal selling

Direct response advertising is the fastest growing form of advertising: direct mail alone (just one medium for direct response) is the third largest medium in terms of expenditures, preceded by newspapers and television. As consumers, 85 percent of us have ordered something by direct mail, 45 percent of us within the last 12 months.[19] When we add to this the use of direct response to qualify sales leads, direct response is indeed seen as a very large form of advertising. Sales-lead advertising is used most often by industrial

TABLE 15-7   MEDIA SELECTION FOR CORPORATE IMAGE ADVERTISING

Small Companies	
	• corporate slogan or logo in handbills, suburban newspaper, calendars, or sales aids
	• local sponsorships
Medium to Large Companies	
a. large target audience b. smaller target audience	• television
	• business or consumer magazines
	• direct mail
	• outdoor (short message only)
	• point-of-purchase (short message only)
	• advertised sponsorships

companies to get new business customers, but also by nearly all companies to canvass for new employees, and by private citizens placing classified ads.

Numerous causes have contributed to the growth of direct response: From the consumer's perspective, the contributory causes are less time to shop (for working women in particular), fear of downtown areas, and the convenience of credit card ordering. From the business customer's perspective, the efficiency of having sales literature sent or a salesperson visit on an "as needed" basis rather than a haphazard or "cold call" basis has helped direct response advertising. From the marketer's perspective, increasingly good computer-accessible information on prospective customers, and the exact measurement of profitability in comparison with less direct forms of advertising, are the main attractions.

Communication Objectives for Direct Response

The communication objectives for direct response advertising in most cases cover the full five communication effects:

1 *Category Need* Selling category need is an objective for new products that are sold outright (for example, encyclopedias, magic knives). However, for other products, only a reminder is needed for customers already in the market (for example, travel baggage, established industrial products).

2 *Brand Recognition* With direct response, the customer does not have to recall the brand; there is no delay between exposure and purchase because an order or an inquiry should result immediately. The brand awareness process is *closest to brand recognition* but not identical: while it may help to have a "recognizable" brand name, an unknown brand must create "recognition," or more precisely, "cognition," right there in the ad.

3 *High Involvement/Informational Brand Attitude* Direct response is high involvement advertising at its peak (all of the tactics in Chapter 10—initial attitude, believability and latitude of acceptance, and, if necessary, refutational or comparative tactics—apply and this growing form of advertising is seeing the resurgence of great copywriters as in the pre-TV era). It is informational, or else transformational with such a high component of informational support that the informational tactics predominate.

4 *Immediate (Hard-Sell) Brand Purchase Intention* Direct response is by nature "hard-sell." There is almost always an inducement, in the form of a price-off, bonus offer, or premium, to "act now."

5 *Purchase Facilitation* Finally, in direct response advertising, the ordering or inquiry action must be facilitated in the ad—by providing a telephone number or postal address and, for large ticket items sold outright, check or credit card payment options.

It is instructive now to go back to our joint media selection table (Table 15.3, earlier) and see which media types are best suited to direct response. For this unique form of advertising, we shall have to make some qualifications.

Direct Response Media Selection

Table 15.3 indicated that magazines and direct mail are the best media for delivering brand recognition and high involvement/informational communication objectives. But, in fact, expenditures for direct response advertising by media are quite different, except for direct mail (Table 15.8).[20] Why is this so? For the answers, we will briefly review each medium's potential for direct response.

Telephone   The leading position of the telephone as an "advertising medium," accounting for 47 percent of direct response advertising, is misleading. The large majority of telephone expenditures is for *order-taking,* on toll-free WATS numbers, rather than for advertising (or selling) in the conventional sense. The telephone has now overtaken return mail as the preferred response mechanism for *direct mail* advertising.[21] Although a large amount of business is conducted by telephone, very little of this is direct response advertising or even direct response selling, despite the notoriety of the latter practice. Telephone *is* a direct response advertising medium, but it is not the largest.

As an advertising medium, the telephone would be closest in creative content characteristics to radio, with the big advantage that, as in personal selling, the message can be tailored to the individual target audience prospect.

The non-visual nature of the telephone makes it suitable only for selling services (for example, insurance) or for selling products that are so well known to the prospect that the product doesn't have to be seen (for example, subscriptions to well-known magazines). Visual brand recognition is impossible by telephone although verbal brand recognition, including company name recognition, can be used.

The limitation that applies to radio for high involvement/informational messages does not apply to telephone. Telephone as a medium provides the capacity to personally tailor the message (thus taking into account initial attitude and allowing the use of refutation and comparative tactics for this quadrant) and to extend the message as long as necessary (long copy format).

TABLE 15-8   DIRECT RESPONSE ADVERTISING EXPENDITURES BY MEDIA (1982)

	$ (millions)	Percent
Telephone (see text)	12,936	47
Direct mail	11,359	41
Newspapers	2,571	9
Television	339	1
Magazines	233	1
Coupons	127	*
Radio	33	*
Totals	$ 27,597	100

* Less than 1 percent.
Source: B. Stone, *Successful Direct Marketing Methods* (3rd ed.), Chicago: Crain Books, 1984, p. 6, by permission.

Telephone is a good high involvement/informational medium as long as visual information is not required.

Accordingly, we amend our original table and acknowledge telephone as a medium for *direct response* advertising when a visual medium is not required.

Direct Mail   Direct mail is the best direct response medium for accomplishing all five communication objectives. Direct mail can carry advertising as brief as postcards or as extensive as catalogs and can even deliver products for sampling or trial offers. Over the years, postal charges have risen less than costs of other media and this helps to retain direct mail's attractiveness to advertisers.

The growing appeal of direct mail to marketers has been aided by the increasing sophistication of mailing lists, computerized addressing and letter-writing, 800-number telephone ordering, and credit card payment. There is now no product or service that cannot be advertised by direct mail.

Newspapers   Over 95 percent of the direct response advertising in newspapers is in the form of free-standing, pre-printed color inserts. Newspapers, then, mainly are a medium for carrying what would otherwise be more direct mail. The advantage of newspaper distribution, of course, is that the advertiser doesn't have to address the mailing pieces. The corresponding disadvantage is that the advertising reaches everyone who subscribes to the newspaper, without the targeting provided when mailing or telephoning from a list. Accordingly, for products with demographically broad appeal, newspapers are a suitable direct response medium.

Magazines   Magazines, although listed in Table 15.3 as theoretically suitable for direct response advertising, have some practical problems. First, magazine *on-page* direct response ads are more restricted in format than pre-printed newspaper inserts (in effect, newspapers are distributing "unique little magazines"). Second, long copy advertisements in magazines usually require a full page ad plus, often, a special insert for the reply form, which is expensive compared with the cost of simply mailing the material or distributing it in newspapers.

Magazines, however, have a place in direct response advertising because they fall between the broad coverage of newspapers and the specific coverage of addressed direct mail. Magazines, business or consumer, reach fairly well-defined occupational groups (business) and demographic groups by sex, age, and, income; or psychological groups by interests or lifestyles (consumer). Magazines should be considered by advertisers whose target audience corresponds well with one of these defined groups.

Television   The limitation of television for high involvement/informational advertising is circumvented, in direct response advertising, by employing 60-second, 90-second, or 2-minute commercials to allow long copy. Often these appear in off-peak timeslots when advertising is cheaper.

Television—at present—is not a large direct response medium. It accounts for only 1 percent of direct response expenditures. It doesn't offer precise targeting. And, even with longer commercials, television doesn't really give the target audience decision maker as much time to pause and consider multiple benefit claims as does a print medium. In fact, a common technique in direct response TV creative is "momentum spiel"—a fast-talking sales pitch, loaded with benefit claims one after another, that, often placed in late-night timeslots, tries to catch the audience off-guard with an "irresistible" offer.[22]

Television is an obvious choice for direct response when the benefit claim or claims depend on *demonstration*. Kitchen and workshop appliances, and also record collections with audio sequences, are among the most frequently appearing direct response products on TV.

Television direct response, however, is beginning to offer an exciting new alternative medium with the advent of two-way *interactive* television (videotex). Subscribers to videotex systems can "shop" by dialing, via telephone or computer, on-screen video catalogs from various stores; they then order and pay for items by telephone or computer. Videotex is the ultimate in shopping convenience.

The problem with videotex at present, however, is that its penetration is very low. One estimate is that only a selective 10 to 15 percent of homes will have videotex by 1990; the adopters are mainly upper-income professional households.[23] For now, videotex is best thought of as similar to an upper-income *magazine,* suitable only if the direct response advertiser's target audience fits this demographic profile.

Coupons   Coupons are the shortest form of direct response advertising but obviously are rarely sufficient on their own to sell a product. Nevertheless, it is interesting that our reference for Table 15.8 includes coupons as direct response *advertising* in light of our analysis, in Chapter 13, that coupons should contribute to communication objectives and not just brand purchase intention. Coupons, however, cannot carry a high involvement/informational message, which severely limits their use for direct response. Moreover, coupons are not in themselves a medium. Most are distributed by newspapers, magazines, in or on packs, and occasionally by direct mail.

Radio   The least used conventional medium for direct response is radio; its usage is much less than 1 percent. There are communication limitations in using radio for direct response. Brand recognition, obviously, is limited to verbal description on radio, as it is for telephone. High involvement/informational brand attitude messages also are limited, although this limitation can be overcome, as in television, by buying longer radio commercials.

However, the main problem with radio as a direct response medium is with the communication objective of *purchase facilitation* together with radio's typical use as a "background" medium. It would be ridiculous to expect a radio listener in the shower or driving to work to be able to write down an address or telephone number for direct response! Radio direct response advertising may be suitable only in the somewhat rare instances of daytime or evening radio programs that reach a high proportion of a particular demographically defined or psychographic-interest defined target audience *known* to be listening in a setting that permits the response to be made, and then only if the advertiser's target audience fits such a group.

Direct response advertising media selection is summarized in Table 15.9. We have assumed that one primary medium will be used for direct response. However, we should note the occasional use of television or radio as "support media" whereby commercials are run telling viewers or listeners to look for a particular direct response offer in newspapers, magazines, or in the mail. Also, when direct response advertising is employed to produce sales leads rather than sell merchandise outright, it is itself serving as a secondary medium for the primary "medium" of personal selling.

SUMMARY

Media strategy is a very important component of advertising planning because, no matter how effective the advertising message may be, if it isn't exposed to potential buyers often enough, then the message is wasted.

In translating media strategy into a specific media plan, the manager faces three major trade-offs. These trade-offs are inevitable unless the media budget can be increased to avoid them. The trade-offs involve reach (the number of target audience individuals exposed to the advertising, in a purchase cycle); frequency (the number of exposures, per individual target audience member, in a purchase cycle): and continuity (the distribution of exposures, over successive purchase cycles, for the average target audience member, for the entire planning period). The principle governing these trade-offs is effective frequency within the purchase cycle, reflected in the axiom that it is better to sell some people completely than many people not at all.

A corollary of this axiom is the importance of thinking about the media

TABLE 15-9   MEDIA SELECTION FOR DIRECT RESPONSE ADVERTISING

Nature of product and target audience	Recommended direct response medium
Any product or service sold to a broad or narrow target audience	• direct mail
Product or service that is well known and doesn't have to be seen	• telephone
Products or services with broad target audience (no mailing list available)	• newspaper • television (demonstration products)
Products or services whose target audience is well defined by an occupational or other demographic or psychographic readership or listenership group	• magazines • radio (daytime or evening) • videotex (upper income)

plan at the level of the individual advertising recipient. Advertising works on individuals, not on averages or aggregates of people, and it is very important to consider the effect of the plan from the perspective of *each individual reached*. It is personal frequency in the purchase cycle and, in the longer term, personal continuity over the advertising period, that causes purchase behavior—not the total number of exposures, or overall reach, or average frequency of exposure, which are all too general to tell whether the media plan is a good one and how effective it will be.

Media selection (selection of general media types) is based on the brand's communication objectives. More specifically, the medium or media selected must be capable of transmitting the creative content required of a given communication objective, with sufficient frequency to achieve the objective.

Most advertisers will employ a primary medium, in which the majority of the advertising budget is spent, and one or more secondary media. The primary medium must be capable of conveying all the brand's communication objectives, and it is selected by jointly considering whether the brand requires brand recognition versus brand recall (the brand awareness objective) *and* whether the brand choice is low versus high involvement and informational vs. transformational (the brand attitude strategy). From this joint consideration, one primary medium usually will emerge or easily can be selected, from the few options remaining, based on target audience reach.

Secondary media are employed to reach target audience members who are not reached sufficiently frequently by the primary medium, or to boost (raise the frequency delivery of) *particular* communication objectives, or because of a special timing advantage near or at the point of purchase.

National consumer advertising generally will use television as the primary medium unless the brand attitude is high involvement/informational with a long copy format that requires print. Secondary media for national consumer advertisers, depending on the brand's communication objectives, include: outdoor and p-o-p, to boost brand recognition; radio and newspapers, to boost brand recall; radio, newspapers, outdoor, or p-o-p to boost low involvement/ informational brand attitude; radio with imagery transfer to boost low involvement/transformational brand attitude; magazines or newspapers (if these aren't primary) to boost high involvement/informational brand attitude; and magazines, outdoor, or p-o-p to boost high involvement/transformational brand attitude, with the latter two eliminated if there is a large informational support requirement.

Retail advertising consists of retail product advertising and store image advertising. Retail re-advertisers of nationally advertised products (such as supermarkets) generally will use newspapers for their product advertising. Original retail advertisers, on the other hand, will use: local TV, if the product mix is narrow; Sunday newspaper supplements, if the mix is wide and the retail drawing area large; direct mail, for a dispersed target audience; or locally distributed print media if they are a local service retailer or a very small retailer.

Retail store image advertising is different from retail product advertising. If the store image is well known, the retail store's brand recall and immediate intentions to visit can be stimulated by store image advertising in local TV, radio, or newspapers. Alternatively, retailers with a store image to promote (visually) will use local TV or, if the visit cycle is longer, outdoor advertising, city magazines, or direct mail.

Industrial or business-to-business advertising largely occurs in print media because of, first, the technical nature of most industrial products and services (high involvement/informational) and, second, because particular print media can be channeled to business audience decision makers with little target audience waste. Industrial advertisers with a small target audience will use personal selling rather than advertising, although pamphlets or brochures may be prepared for the sales force as sales aids. Industrial advertisers with a moderate-sized target audience will use trade publications to reach lower-level decision makers (initiators and users) and direct mail to reach top management decision makers (deciders), who rarely read trade publications in detail. Industrial advertisers with a large target audience will also use trade publications to reach lower-level decision makers, but to reach top management deciders, business magazines now become cost-effective and possibly more effective due to prestige.

Corporate image advertising sells the company to customers, investors, prospective and current employees, government regulators, and special interest groups, whose actions, positive or negative, affect the company's profits. Corporate image can be projected by small local companies through in-ad attention to the company slogan or logo and by local sponsorships. Companies with a large target audience should use television, the most persuasive medium. Companies with a target audience too small or narrow for television should use magazines (business or consumer, respectively), direct mail, point-of-purchase sales literature, or, for short corporate messages, thoughtfully placed outdoor ads.

Direct response advertising is the fastest growing form of advertising. With credit card ordering, any product or service can be sold direct. Direct mail is the largest direct response medium and is now the third largest advertising medium in the United States. Telephone direct response is suitable for advertising well-known products or services that don't have to be seen. Television is the best choice for demonstration products and will compete strongly with direct mail when two-way interactive (cable) TV shopping facilities become widely available. For direct response advertisers with a demographically broad audience, newspaper inserts are worthwhile, whereas advertisers with a demographically or psychographically narrow target audience should use magazines, or possibly radio, steering clear of times when listeners cannot write down a direct response address or phone number.

Having explained and reviewed media *type* selection, we now move on to the second decision in media strategy—that of *media scheduling*. We begin the next chapter with the concept of effective frequency and conclude in the following chapter with media vehicle and advertising unit selection for implementation of the media schedule.

NOTES

1 The complexities of media buying vary with each medium. For an example of the methods of media buying for TV, see R.S. Kaplan and A.D. Shocker, Discount effects on media plans, *Journal of Advertising Research,* 1971, *11* (3), 37–43. Some reference is made to media buying options in our Appendix B, although discount buying is not covered.

2 Again this is Peter Drucker's dictum that effectiveness (doing the right things) is more important than efficiency (doing things right). Len Lodish's similar principle applies very well to media strategy: it is better to be vaguely right than precisely wrong. As we shall see, a great many media plans are precisely wrong because of a lack of understanding of media strategy based on the advertising communication process. Too many media plans rely on "traditional" media truisms that most clients accept without ever bothering to test them except by witnessing falling sales—for which the *creative* work, not the media plan, usually is blamed.

3 William Bernbach's comment was quoted in R. Townsend, *Up the Organization,* Greenwich, CT: Fawcett Publications, 1970, p. 124. John Wanamaker's comment has been widely cited but we couldn't trace it to a specific source; it also has been attributed, equally unspecifically, to Lord Leverhulme in the U.K.

4 The survey was conducted by the editors of *Advertising Age.* See H. Zeltner, "Ads work harder but accomplish less," *Advertising Age,* July 3, 1978, pp. 3, 30–33.

5 As discussed in Chapter 6, the exception is when the brand recognition objective is *auditory recognition*—for example, recognizing a brand name when a salesperson tells you what brands are in stock.

Auditory recognition is only occasionally an objective so it is not incorporated in the media selection table.

For auditory recognition, media which convey *spoken words,* allowing consumers to hear and learn to pronounce the brand name, are superior. TV and radio convey spoken words and are best for auditory recognition. Note the eligibility of radio here, although it is eliminated for visual recognition.

6 In the section on primary and secondary media selection for consumer advertising, we will make use of this table again, this time from the perspective of individual media. We will see that there are creative ways around most of the eliminations and limitations. However, the creative solutions usually are expensive, requiring extra time or space, and are rarely as effective as selecting another medium that can meet the communication objectives directly.

7 A possible creative solution for overcoming low frequency in magazines is "impact scheduling," discussed in the next section of the chapter and in Chapter 17.

8 For completeness, we should remember (from Part Six) that promotion offers may have their own specialized media. In the case of sampling, which can meet all five communication objectives, for new products the sampling program often constitutes the primary medium—with advertising, from the standpoint of communication objectives, as a secondary medium. Sampling is most akin to a print medium. At the other end of the promotion scale, in- or on-packs, aimed mainly at current users, seem most akin to a print medium also. Thus, hard-sell promotion offers indicate the use of print media, with the latter term broadly considered.

9 The most common simultaneous use of secondary media is to increase brand recall. High frequency media such as TV (here in a secondary role), radio, or newspapers can be used for this purpose. The second most common reason is timely brand purchase intention reminders. Television, radio, newspapers, outdoor, and p-o-p can be used for this purpose.

10 If the advertising campaign has been successful, initial high involvement target audiences (new category users, other-brand switchers, or other-brand loyals) would now have become repeat buyers (brand loyals or favorable brand switchers) who are now making *low* involvement (re-)purchase decisions. Therefore, not only in secondary media (Table 15.4) but also in primary media (Table 15.3) the options widen for continuing campaigns as opposed to new campaigns directed toward high involvement target audiences.

11 These estimates are from W.E. Barlow and E. Papazian, (Eds.), *The Media Book 1980,* New York: The Media Book, Inc., 1980, p.10. The estimates cover the four major "measured" media only; that is, they exclude outdoor, direct mail, and miscellaneous media such as point of purchase.

12 "100 leaders' media expenditures compared in 1979," *Advertising Age,* February 16, 1981, pp. S-2, S-4.

13 In sales or sales-related tests with a broad variety of nationally advertised super-market brands, for *every* brand tested, TV has been shown to generate more sales than radio, and more sales than magazine ads.

These studies employed only a single exposure to TV commercials, radio commercials, or magazine ads, respectively, and it is sometimes argued that the results are misleading because one could buy several radio commercials or several magazine ads for the price of one TV commercial. However, this "lower cost" argument is not convincing. First of all, the sales results for TV are two or three times as high as for other media, and there is little likelihood that these sales levels could be achieved just by repeating ads in non-TV media. Secondly, for most consumer products, the advertising has to work quickly. There is no doubt that for short-term sales effectiveness, sought by most nationally advertised consumer products, TV is the most effective medium.

The media experiments are from privately published studies by CBS 1960–61, and 1970–71; and Teleresearch 1968–69, 1970–71, and 1980. The first four experiments are abstracted in W.E. Barlow and E. Papazian, (Eds.), *The Media Book 1979,* pp. 566–568, and *The Media Book 1980,* p.41, New York: The Media Book, Inc., 1979, 1980. The fifth experiment is abstracted in the Radio Advertising Bureau, Inc., *Radio Facts,* New York: Radio Advertising Bureau, Inc., 1980, p.37.

14 Legal restrictions also may prevent the use of television; for example, for cigarette advertising or liquor advertising.

15 T. Coffin and S. Tuchman, TV without pix, *Media/Scope, 12* (February), 46–53.

However, there are several problems with this otherwise promising technique. First, consumers in the experiment were prompted; the experiment did not estimate the proportion of radio listeners who would *spontaneously* experience visual imagery transfer. Second, the extent to which the "second-hand," radio-stimulated image is sufficiently detailed and vivid to provide an effective substitute for a TV commercial exposure is not known. Last, the audio tracks of most TV commercials would not be suitable or complete enough to serve as radio commercials; TV commercials whose audio tracks can double as radio commercials would have to be specially produced.

16 R.C. Grass and W.H. Wallace, Advertising communication: print vs. TV, *Journal of Advertising Research,* 1974, *14* (5), 19–23.

17 The color-printed newspaper, *USA Today,* is an exception. However, this newspaper at present has very limited circulation (less than 2 million) and would not suit the *national* consumer advertiser who instead would use a "national" package of all major local newspapers.

18 Color brochures can be alternatively distributed by hand, in mailboxes. This method of distribution should be used when the retailer's circumstances meet the criteria for handbills (see paragraph after next).

19 R.A. Sawyer, "Direct marketing: the shape of things to come," *Advertising Age,* January 18, 1982, section 2, S-1, S-48, S-49.

20 B. Stone, *Successful Direct Marketing Methods* (3rd ed.), Chicago: Crain Books, 1984, p.6. Data are national figures for 1982.

21 Industry wisdom has it that the response rate with toll-free telephone is three times greater than with return mail, and that telephone orders tend to be larger in dollar amounts.

22 J. Witek, *Response Television,* Chicago: Crain Books, 1981, chapter 1.

23 This forecast is provided by Jay James, senior vice-president of video technology/ programming at Doyle Dane Bernbach, Inc., and chairman of the Advertising Research Foundation's Video Electronic Media Council. Videotex and related systems are reviewed in W.S. James, The new electronic media: an overview, *Journal of Advertising Research,* 1983, *23* (4), 33–37.

DISCUSSION QUESTIONS

15.1 Generally considered, do you think media strategy is less important, equally important, or more important than creative strategy? Argue for each of the three positions, then state your conclusion.

15.2 (Advanced question that will require looking up media chapters in other advertising texts or a media text.) Below is an example of a media plan for a target audience of 10 people (this could as well be 10 million people, but smaller numbers are easier to work with). It is based on a 3-week purchase cycle. An exposure is indicated by an x.

Individual	Purchase cycle 1 (Week no.)			Purchase cycle 2 (Week no.)			Purchase cycle 3 (Week no.)		
	1	2	3	1	2	3	1	2	3
1			x	x	x				x
2									
3	x						x	x	x
4				x	x			x	
5									
6	x	x	x	x					
7					x	x	x	x	x
8			x	x	x	x			
9	x	x							
10		x	x				x		x

a According to the definition in the chapter, what is the reach of this plan?

b According to the conventional definition of reach in any advertising textbook, what is the "cumulative reach" of this plan for the 9-week period?

c In a sentence or two, describe why the "cumulative reach" figure is misleading.

d Suppose the minimum effective frequency is estimated or known to be two exposures per purchase cycle. Calculate the *effective* reach figures for each of the three purchase cycles.

    e Calculate, as per the conventional textbook definition, the *average* frequency for each purchase cycle. Then, in a sentence or two, explain why this is a virtually useless statistic; specifically, are purchase cycles 2 and 3 equally effective for the advertiser?

    f If the advertiser could afford just three insertions of the ad over the 9-week period, would you advise "continuity," or some other distribution of exposures, and why? Note: assume that this is a frequently purchased product.

15.3 Answer the following questions in a paragraph or two: (You may need to read Appendix B at the end of the book first.)

    a Are high involvement/informational campaigns impossible in outdoor media vehicles?

    b If you were targeting brand loyal buyers of Uncle Ben's rice, attempting to get loyals to use more of the product, which miscellaneous or specialty media would you choose, and why?

    c Is commercial cable TV most likely to compete, from a media planner's standpoint, with network TV, local TV, magazines, or newspapers? Briefly evaluate the competitive threat of commercial cable TV with regard to each of these four media.

15.4 Select and explain the most likely primary media type and one likely secondary media type for each of these situations:

    a A corporate image campaign for Du Pont

    b A retail "store specials" advertisement for the Safeway supermarket in White Plains, New York

    c The national introduction of Silkience shampoo

15.5 You are the advertising manager for unrecorded blank cassette tapes made under license for Capitol Records. Your advertising claims that Capitol cassettes are the best technical recording tapes to buy, and you want prospective buyers to recognize Capitol tapes at the point of purchase. Radio is your primary media choice because of its high reach against the target audience. Are there any problems with employing radio in this situation, and if so, how would you solve the problems?

15.6 You are an advertising consultant to the manager of a new chain of luxury decorating stores. At present you have outlets in only 10 states, scattered throughout the United States. You wish to run a store image campaign. Which medium would you recommend for this campaign and why? Discuss alternatives before making your recommendation.

15.7 You are the advertising manager for Hewlett-Packard's consumer products division, which sells computers, calculators, and other equipment for personal home or office use. Discuss the media that you would most likely be using throughout the year.

FURTHER READING

Longman, K.A. *Advertising*. New York: Harcourt Brace Jovanich, 1971.

    Although published some time ago, in our opinion, this is the only book that comes close to explaining media strategy from a correct perspective. Particularly to be studied is Longman's excellent discussion of how advertising media strategy must take into account purchase cycles.

Sissors, J.Z., and Petray, E.R. *Advertising Media Planning,* (2nd ed.) Chicago: Crain Books, 1982.

> Detailed coverage of basic options is provided in this book. However, the strategic approach is limited, and follows conventional media wisdom. The topic of media buying, omitted in our text, is covered here.

The references above are good for identifying the strengths and weaknesses of various media, but there are no references that discuss the concepts of primary and secondary media selection in any detail. Instead, the further reading is devoted to the two forms of advertising that have not received much attention elsewhere in the book: corporate image advertising and direct response advertising.

Garbett, T.F. *Corporate Image Advertising.* New York: McGraw-Hill, 1981.

> This book provides comprehensive, practical coverage of corporate image target audiences, action objectives, communication objectives, and media selection.

Stone, B. *Successful Direct Marketing Methods.* (3rd ed.) Chicago: Crain Books, 1984.

> Bob Stone's text is a classic in the field of direct response advertising (and marketing). Packed with how-to-do-it details, the text is nicely updated with current research findings. Direct response media choices are well discussed together with creative guidelines for each direct response medium, including videotex.

CHAPTER 16

MEDIA SCHEDULING BY EFFECTIVE FREQUENCY

We are now ready to address media scheduling—*how often* the advertising needs to be exposed to the target audience to attain its communication objectives. Central to media scheduling is the conceptualization and estimation of effective frequency. After reading this chapter you should:

- Appreciate the importance of effective frequency in the media plan
- Understand the idea of the purchase cycle and know how to estimate the purchase cycle in exceptional cases
- Learn the factors that determine effective frequency and know how to measure or estimate the minimum effective frequency level for any advertising campaign
- By incorporating effective frequency with continuity to the target audience, begin to see what the media schedule should look like for the length of the media plan

THE CONCEPT OF EFFECTIVE FREQUENCY

The concept of *effective frequency* is based on the idea that an individual prospective customer has to be exposed to a brand's advertising a certain minimum number of times, within a purchase cycle, in order for the advertising to influence purchase.[1] Effective frequency actually consists of a range of exposures between the minimum effective frequency level and a possible maximum effective frequency level. Exposures within this range raise the individual's disposition to purchase the brand, or to engage in other appropriate purchase-related behavior, to an actionable "threshold" level.

In this section of the chapter, we examine the effective frequency concept in more detail, along with its component concepts of exposure, disposition to purchase, and the derivative concepts of minimum effective frequency, maximum effective frequency, and effective reach.

Exposure

What is exposure? By "exposure" we mean *placement of the advertisement in a media vehicle* that the target audience is known or expected to see, hear, or read (see Chapter 1). Advertisers expose ads; thus we use the term synonymously with the action of *insertion* of the advertisement in the media vehicle. The British term for exposures, *OTS*, or *opportunities to see* (hear or read) the advertisement, nicely expresses what we mean by exposure.

Whether target audience individuals do in fact see, hear, or read the advertisement—that is, in our terminology, whether they begin to *process* the advertisement by at least paying initial attention—is jointly a function of: (1) the attention-getting characteristics of the media vehicle itself; (2) the size (time or space) of the advertising unit; and (3) the creative content of the advertisement.

There is, you will realize, a "gray area" between *exposure,* in the sense of "opportunity to see" based on insertion, and exposure in the everyday sense of "being exposed to the ad," which implies attention to the ad and is where *processing* begins. Here's how we handle this from a media standpoint. In estimating effective frequency, we begin with exposures (insertions or OTS) and then adjust for *media-caused* attention, that is, for attention elicited by the media vehicle *and* attention elicited by the size of the advertising unit. Whereas the creative director undoubtedly will advise on the latter, we will treat the advertising units used in the plan as a factor that the media planner must consider. This takes the audience right to the point at which the creative content takes over. A reasonably clear division thereby is drawn between where media strategy ends and creative strategy takes over—both, of course, being necessary to attain communication objectives.

Exposure, then, as we use the term here, refers to an insertion of the ad in the media schedule, an OTS. In translating exposures into effective frequency, however, we allow for attention generated by media factors as well. This means that effective frequency allows for the *real* exposure opportunity offered by the media plan.

Disposition to Purchase

The other component of the effective frequency concept that requires clarification is the notion of "influencing" the next purchase. Whereas any degree of processing that occurs on any of the five communication effects can be said to influence purchase to some extent, we focus here on *disposition to purchase* and the idea of effective frequency raising this disposition to actionable threshold.

As we shall see in Part Eight in conjunction with advertising research, disposition to purchase (or for the target audience to take other, purchase-related action) is reflected best by:

- *Brand awareness* (a necessary prerequisite to purchase) *plus*
- *Brand attitude* for low involvement/transformational advertising, *or*
- *Brand purchase intention* for the other three types of advertising, namely, low involvement/informational, high involvement/informational and high involvement/transformational advertising.

Effective frequency is the frequency of exposure to the individual that raises to threshold disposition to purchase as reflected in the criterion measures of brand awareness plus, depending on the advertising communication model, brand attitude or brand purchase intention.[2]

The Meaning of ''Threshold''   Threshold is the level of stimulation (in this case communication effects caused by advertising exposure) below which there is no reaction (in this case purchase or purchase-related action). It is the minimum level of stimulation for action to occur.

The idea of effective frequency is to bring the *individual* target audience prospect up to threshold—to cause him or her to enter the brand choice situation predisposed to buy the advertised brand (which also may be a promoted brand if promotion exposure has taken place) and no other brand. Now, whereas this threshold disposition obviously is dependent on the communication effectiveness of the creative content of the advertising, in media scheduling we are concerned with giving the creative content sufficient exposure(s) to work. An illustration of this, using the singular concept of disposition to purchase to represent the multiple communication effects that in fact must occur, is shown in Figure 16.1.

FIGURE 16.1   Individual threshold of disposition to purchase as a function of frequency of exposures.

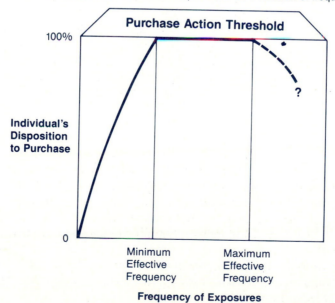

For example, we may know that the creative content can produce brand recall, if that is the brand awareness objective, but it may take multiple exposures or repetitions to bring the individual's recall of the brand up to a level where the brand will be in the individual's "evoked set" of two or three brands next time he or she makes a purchase decision in that category.

Similarly, with brand attitude or brand purchase intention, we may know that the advertisement—given a sufficient number of exposures as in the forced or "hypoed" exposure of an ad test—is capable of, for example, converting an other-brand loyal to try the advertised brand. The media planner's responsibility is to give the advertisement this "sufficient" threshold number of exposures.

We may note here the creative director's responsibility: if the ad doesn't work, no amount of repetition is going to save it. But an ad that is known to work must not be limited by the media schedule through a repetition rate too low to allow it to work.

Minimum Effective Frequency

In estimating the effective frequency level for a campaign, we are interested primarily in the *minimum* effective frequency level necessary to raise disposition to purchase to action threshold (again see Figure 16.1). This is because we want to reach threshold disposition to purchase with the fewest insertions, that is, at lowest cost.

In the easiest-to-grasp case, the minimum effective frequency to cause disposition to purchase would be one exposure in the purchase cycle. This may occur, for example, with direct response advertising, such as a direct mail offer, where the target audience only has a chance to go through the buyer response sequence of exposure-to-action once (see Chapter 1's discussion of repetition and the buyer response sequence). However, as we shall see, a minimum effective frequency of 1 may also be sufficient in some situations when advertising to a brand loyal target audience.

With an extremely brand loyal target audience (single-brand loyals) the minimum effective frequency may even fall below 1, that is to 0 or no advertising, at least for one or two purchase cycles. That is, the communication effects comprising disposition to purchase may be strong enough from previous purchase cycle's advertising to "carry over" for one or more subsequent cycles without continued advertising exposure (see the same section of Chapter 1 on independence from advertising). Word-of-mouth or personal influence is another factor that could reduce the required minimum effective frequency of advertising to 0, at least temporarily.

In most cases when targeting less loyal audiences—for example, brand switchers—the minimum effective frequency per purchase cycle will be greater than 1. The nature of the brand's communication objectives or the presence of competing brands' communication effects also will increase the required minimum effective frequency to a number above 1 exposure per purchase cycle.

Shortly, we will examine the factors that determine minimum effective frequency, and also show how to estimate minimum effective frequency for any advertising situation.

Maximum Effective Frequency

In Figure 16.1, we showed a horizontal line for when exposure frequency goes above the minimum effective frequency needed for purchase. Although it may be hard to imagine "too much" effective frequency, this can happen when the individual has been "oversold," after 100 percent disposition to purchase has already been attained. For example, you may be on your way to an IBM computer retailer's fully resolved to buy an IBM PC when you hear another advertisement for the IBM PC on your car radio or see a window poster for the IBM PC as you are entering the store. If you were indeed fully resolved to buy, these extra exposures would be "overkill"—unnecessary, because they wouldn't affect your decision.

At the same point, further exposures *might* turn your disposition in a negative direction, that is, downward below threshold. As we shall see in Chapter 20 concerning "wearout," this downturn fortunately is a rare event (hence the question mark in Figure 16.1). If wearout does occur, the frequency of exposure at which disposition to purchase would decline below threshold if there were one more exposure is called *maximum* effective frequency.

Exposures above minimum effective frequency (which we will now abbreviate to MEF) *up to* maximum effective frequency are wasted exposures from a cost standpoint even though they do *not* affect sales. The less than perfect accuracy of media plans is such that the key is to advertise at *at least MEF* when in fact you may be above that.

Effective Reach

Effective *frequency* is inherently an individual phenomenon: during a purchase cycle, an individual target audience member is either exposed at MEF level or not. Effective *reach,* in a purchase cycle, is simply the *number of individuals reached at at least MEF*. For example, if the MEF is 2 exposures in a purchase cycle, then the effective reach of the media schedule is given by the number of individuals who receive *2 or more* exposures in that purchase cycle. (For now, we will assume no maximum effective frequency upper limit.) This often is known as "2+ Reach," or "k+ Reach" for an MEF of k exposures in the general case.

At this point we may comment that the conventional definition of reach is virtually useless to the media planner. The conventional definition of "reach" is the number or, more often, percent of a particular audience reached at least once in some standard period. Similarly useless is "cumulative reach," the number or percent reached at least once over the entire planning period. Neither of these traditional concepts bears any relationship to a media plan's effectiveness. "Reach" would coincide with effective reach only in the rare event that the MEF equalled 1 and the purchase cycle equalled the arbitrary period used in conventional reach measurement, and "cumulative reach" would coincide with effective reach only if the MEF equalled 1 and the purchase cycle equalled the *planning* period. Not only media planners but managers, too, should forget the conventional approach and concentrate on effective reach.

To look ahead, the idea of media planning is to maximize effective reach per purchase cycle at the lowest cost. Effective reach depends on what the minimum effective frequency (MEF) is within the purchase cycle; it is to purchase cycle measurement that we now turn.

THE PURCHASE CYCLE

A purchase cycle is the average number of days between purchases of a product category for the average target audience member. For example, the average buyer of instant coffee buys in the category every 21 days or 3 weeks (this is a general figure and the purchase cycle for particular target audiences for a given brand may vary from this, though probably not very widely).[3] A 3-week purchase cycle means that a coffee brand's advertising would have to reach the individual coffee buyer once every 3 weeks, and perhaps more often, depending on the communication objectives and the competition, as explained later.

Note that although the purchase cycle duration is based on the average target audience member, the advertising is not. The advertiser must *not* try to maximize *average* frequency (a very misleading statistic) but rather the *number* of coffee buyers *reached at least k times,* or at whatever the minimum effective frequency level is, within the purchase cycle.

The problem with average frequency—another conventional term best forgotten—is that it ignores effective frequency. This can be illustrated easily with several diagrams (Figure 16.2) showing hypothetical *frequency distributions* for alternative media plans. All have an average frequency of exactly 2 (total exposures divided by reach equals average frequency). But in terms of effective reach, if the MEF is 1, then plans A and B are best; if MEF equals 2, then Plan A is best; if MEF equals 3, Plan B is best; if MEF equals 4, Plan C is best; and if MEF equals 5, Plan D is best. Obviously, average frequency tells us nothing about a media plan's effectiveness.

Also note that the target audience "renews" itself, on average, every 3 weeks in the coffee example and at other intervals for other products. This means that the use of a *standard* period (usually 4 weeks) for reach and frequency is meaningless (for any product whose purchase cycle is not exactly 4 weeks). The manager must measure the actual purchase cycle if reach and frequency, the two basic parameters of any media plan along with continuity, are to have any meaning.

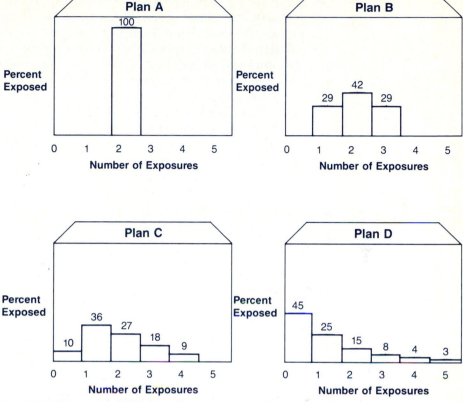

FIGURE 16.2   Hypothetical frequency distributions of exposures, all with average frequency = 2. Now compare them for increasing levels of MEF.

Purchase Cycles for Established Consumer Products

Purchase cycles for established consumer products with fast turnover can be easily measured from survey or, preferably, panel data (see Chapter 4 for a description of these techniques). In a survey, you simply take a random sample of the target audience and ask them how often they buy, for example, instant coffee. Better still, because it doesn't rely on memory, purchase frequency can be measured from a target audience sample that participates in a continuous panel study.

Normal Purchase Patterns

In the general case, advertising exposures in a purchase cycle should be evenly spaced, and in the simple general case of 1 exposure per purchase cycle, exposures should occur at the spacing of the purchase cycle interval. For instance, for the instant coffee example, exposures should occur once every

3 weeks, if only 1 exposure is needed. Correspondingly, if 2 exposures are needed, then these should occur every one-and-a-half weeks.

In the general case, even spacing of exposures will minimize the average personal delay between exposure and purchase opportunity. For instance, in the 1 exposure instant coffee example, it can be shown mathematically that the average delay is 21 days divided by 2, or 10½ days, which is a shorter delay than is provided by any other exposure pattern.

Minimizing the delay between exposure and purchase is important because it minimizes the opportunity for competitive advertising interference prior to purchase. Of course, if competitors detect a precisely constant advertising schedule, they could counter-schedule just after each exposure. Hence, a wiser pattern is probably *a slight random deviation* around the even-spacing pattern. This is fairly easy to achieve when the primary medium is TV, or radio, or newspapers, because these media are available daily. With, say, an 8-week purchase cycle and weekly magazines, the extension of this idea is to avoid predictably regular insertions and vary, for instance, insertions between the first and second weekly issues.

There are five special situations, however, that deserve separate mention because the purchase cycle is either more difficult to measure or has to be estimated rather than measured. These are: (1) long purchase cycles; (2) retail store purchase cycles; (3) "fad" purchase cycles; (4) purchase cycles for new products; and (5) seasonal or concentrated purchase patterns.

Long Purchase Cycles

Whereas consumer packaged goods have relatively short purchase cycles, and industrial products durables often have purchase cycles that are 6 months to several years in duration. New cars, for example, are purchased, on average, about every 4 years. Clearly, for a car manufacturer or dealer to advertise once or twice every 4 years would be far too low a frequency to be effective.

With long purchase cycles, the best procedure is to monitor *relative* brand awareness in the category—assuming that brand awareness is the "carrier" of brand attitude. As long as the advertiser's brand remains in the top few recalled or recognized (depending on how consumers choose brands), then the advertising frequency can remain low. However, since the advertiser and competitors will undoubtedly be introducing new "brands," such as annual auto models, this will force the "noise" level in the category up, and along with it the frequency needed to retain a leading brand awareness position. Continual monitoring is the best way to determine effective frequency for products with long purchase cycles.[4]

Retail Store Purchase Cycles

As noted in Chapter 15, in which we examined retail advertising, the retailer is selling not only specific products and brands, but also the store-as-a-brand. The purchase cycle for retail store advertising should be based on the average customer's interval between store visits to stores of that type. That is, store categories are regarded as product categories, with individual stores as the brands. For supermarkets, for example, the store category purchase interval usually will be weekly. Thus, supermarket *store* ads should appear at least weekly—although the products featured in these ads should be governed by the respective *product* purchase cycles.

The procedures when estimating effective frequency in retail advertising are the following: for store visit advertising, use the store category purchase cycle; for advertising products within the store, for multi-product stores, use the respective product category purchase cycles.

"Fad" Purchase Cycles

Well-discussed in the marketing and consumer behavior literature is the fact that some products are strictly "fad" products with a short product life cycle. Some of these products, such as inexpensive fashion wear or Star Wars toys, may be purchased more than once while the fad lasts. If so, these products have a purchase cycle just like any other new product (see below).

However, *single-purchase* fads obviously do not have a purchase cycle. Examples over the years would be hula hoops, pet rocks, U.S. Bicentennial memorabilia, and many direct mail novelty items. The effective frequency level for single-purchase fad products, then, can be estimated at 1 or 2 exposures per target audience member, period. If the product concept doesn't appeal to the individual immediately, it probably never will, so further advertising is unnecessary.

The complication with fad purchase cycle advertising is *when* to inject the 1 or 2 exposures. Unlike "normal" new product categories, where it pays to be first into the market with advertising, for fads, the best time is during the growth phase of the product life cycle. Broad reach to the middle majority is better than narrow reach to innovators or early adopters unless there is a large personal influence effect, in which case you still want low frequency and broad reach, but spread out over the entire first half of the fad product life cycle.

New Product Purchase Cycles

For really new product categories, there are no historical data from which to measure the purchase cycle. In such instances, the manager has to look to similar product categories and try to estimate the purchase cycle as accurately as possible. For example, the videodisc marketer may look to videocassette purchase or rental intervals or even to record album purchase intervals. A product is rarely so radically new that a reasonable estimate of the purchase cycle cannot be made.

Alternatively, for new consumer durables or larger industrial products, the manager can assume a short purchase cycle and *eventually* use competitive brand awareness monitoring to set the advertising frequency level.

For the *initial launch* advertising of a new product, the manager should act as though the purchase cycle were very, very short and pile on as much high frequency reach as the launch budget can afford. (It is almost impossible to over-advertise a new product. Instances of apparent over-advertising cited in the literature apply exclusively to *established* products.[5]) For a really new product—because of the difficulty of defining a precise target audience with virtually everyone being a potential new category user—broad reach and *also* high frequency are needed. Not surprisingly, it has been estimated that the typical advertising cost for a national launch of a new consumer product with a new brand name is about $30 million, whereas for a line extension of a national brand the cost is about $15 million.[6]

The way to explain the high initial intensity of initial advertising for a new product while still retaining the purchase cycle concept is to think of the *first* purchase cycle as beginning with availability of the product and ending with the first trial purchase. Obviously, unless there is no threat of competition, the marketer wants this initial cycle to be as short as possible. And, because the communication effects (category need, brand awareness, and so forth) will start at 0, the required effective frequency will be very high in a very short period.

Seasonal or Concentrated Purchase Patterns

With some product categories, there are

- Category demand effects (for example, ski equipment), or
- Purchase facilitation effects (for example, paydays)

that tend to homogenize or cluster the purchase patterns of many individuals within the purchase cycle. Thus, most ski equipment is purchased just prior to or early into the winter ski season. Similarly, grocery purchases are concentrated on Thursday or Friday paydays.

When these seasonal or time-variant purchase patterns cause large concentrations within the purchase cycle, it is naturally advantageous to expose the advertising near (just prior to or early into) the purchase concentration, because it will reach more people whose category need is strong or for whom purchase facilitation is optimal, as the case may be.

However, most other competitors usually will be following the same media strategy, so that there is a lot of competitive advertising around the peak. An effective alternative is to advertise somewhat earlier: Category need or purchase facilitation for the category may be lower in terms of number of individuals in the market at that time but there is also less competitive interference from other brands within the category. Real estate advertising, which peaks on Fridays and weekends, is an example. A careful experiment by Draper, Hansen and Scott[7] found that an individual realtor's advertising placed on Mondays and Tuesdays produced double the inquiry rate on the properties listed, compared with Friday and Saturday placements used by the majority of realtors.

For seasonal products that have long purchase cycles, such as ski equipment, simulations conducted by Strong[8] suggest that pre-seasonal advertising can "prime" seasonal advertising, probably because early exposures move consumers toward MEF without competitive interference. Pre-season priming is worth trying for the seasonal advertiser.

Summary and Preview

Overall, then, we see that the purchase cycle is readily measurable for all products. Unless the purchase cycle falls into one of the five special cases, advertising exposures should be spaced evenly within the purchase cycle. Also what is relevant is effective reach based on effective frequency within the purchase cycle, not reach or frequency measured on any other basis. The advertiser's objective in the media plan is to *maximize the number of target audience individuals reached,* during the purchase cycle, at *at least the minimum effective frequency level,* within the budget constraint.

Determining the *minimum* effective frequency will be our concern in the remainder of this chapter. The question of whether there is a *maximum* effective frequency level, beyond which exposures are negatively effective, will be left to Chapter 20 concerning campaign evaluation.

ESTIMATING MINIMUM EFFECTIVE FREQUENCY

Strictly speaking, the only exact way to determine the minimum effective frequency level in a particular advertising situation is by trial and error—that is, by experimentation. However, precise experiments are prohibitively expensive for most advertisers. For a new product, such experimentation would require multiple test markets to cover the frequency levels, an expensive undertaking. For an established product, there is legitimate managerial concern about "playing around with the brand," especially at advertising frequencies that are feared to be destructively low.

Hence an approach based on logic rather than experimentation must generally be used.[9] This is true even if an experiment is subsequently conducted, because the experimental frequency levels would still have to be chosen on some reasonable basis.

Our approach to effective frequency *estimation* makes use of the theory and concepts in the previous chapters relating to target audiences and communication objectives. We assume that 1 exposure in the purchase cycle is the beginning or "building block" level. We then add or subtract exposures according to four strategic factors:

1 Vehicle attention
2 Target audience
3 Communication objectives
4 Interpersonal influence

These four factors for estimating effective frequency are explained next.

Factor 1: Vehicle Attention

Media vehicles differ in the level of attention given them by the typical audience member. Vehicle attention constrains exposure, that is, it places limits on the opportunity for advertising attention. There have been many studies of attention to various media types and media vehicles using observational methods or, more often, self-report measures. However, detailed perusal of these studies suggests that the media planner can achieve a reasonably accurate frequency weighting factor by dividing media vehicles into just two classes: high attention vehicles and low attention vehicles (Table 16.1).

For *high* attention vehicles—prime-time TV and daytime serials, primary-reader magazines, primary-reader newspapers, direct mail, outdoor, miscellaneous, and point-of-purchase—the effective frequency stays at 1 exposure (prior to the other three correction factors being applied).

For *low* attention vehicles—all other TV dayparts, radio, passalong-reader magazines, and passalong-reader newspapers—the effective frequency should be *doubled*. This means doubling the effective frequency calculated from the remaining three correction factors. The reason for the doubled frequency is that the individual's probability of attention to these three media vehicles is about half that of high attention vehicles, so that double the frequency is needed to give the ad an equal chance of being attended to.[10]

Factor 2: Target Audience

The rationale for a target audience correction factor is that some target audiences have more to learn about the brand than other target audiences (Table 16.2).

Brand loyals have little or nothing extra to learn, so that no adjustment is needed when advertising to this audience (however, see Factor 3 which may modify this judgment). Brand switchers seem to need at least 2 exposures in the purchase cycle before switching is induced,[11] so we have added 1 more exposure to the building block level of 1 exposure. Other-brand loyals, assuming that a message strategy has been found that promises to be effective with this

TABLE 16-1   VEHICLE ATTENTION AND EFFECTIVE FREQUENCY

Vehicle	High attention vehicles (no correction)	Low attention vehicles (double frequency)
TV	prime time; serials	all other dayparts
Radio	—	all dayparts
Newspapers	primary readers	passalong readers
Magazines	primary readers	passalong readers
Direct Mail	all	—
Outdoor	all	—
Miscellaneous*	all	—

* Including point-of-purchase advertising.

TABLE 16-2   TARGET AUDIENCE AND EFFECTIVE FREQUENCY

Target Audience	Correction Factor
Brand loyals	no correction
Brand switchers	+1 exposure
Other-brand loyals	+2 exposures
New category users	+2 exposures if market share leader; if not leader, set equal to largest competitor's overall frequency *plus* one exposure (called LC + 1)

target audience, such as refutational advertising or comparative advertising (see Chapter 10), have substantial new learning to undergo, so we have added 2 exposures (3 total) when advertising to this group.

New category users, on the other hand, are a more variable target audience for whom to estimate effective frequency. Essentially we recommend a competitive approach. Most new category user target audience situations will occur with new brands early in the product category life cycle in a growing market, hence market share is the major objective. Following the argument developed in Chapter 2, the only way to increase market share (assuming equivalent message effectiveness) is to advertise more than the leading competitor. Viewed now from the perspective of this chapter, this means trying to reach more new potential category users than competitors are reaching (greater penetration) and reaching each new user with higher frequency than the leading competitor. Actually this would produce several possible levels of effective frequency since individual new category users would be exposed to varying levels of competitors' advertising. However, a practical criterion would be to estimate the frequency level of the largest competitor (for example, from Broadcast Advertisers' Reports or Leading National Advertisers syndicated report services) and then exceed this frequency by at least 1 exposure per purchase cycle (called LC + 1 in the table). Exceeding the largest competitor's overall frequency by more than 1 would be even better, remembering that it is almost impossible to over-advertise a new brand. However, a margin of 1 exposure, if carefully checked at the individual level by thorough vehicle reach and frequency analysis, should be sufficient frequency to wage an effective market share battle if the advertising message is comparably good.

A special situation occurs when advertising to new category users when the brand *already is* the largest competitor. For the first-in brand, or for the leading brand when others are also in the market, the advertiser has to set effective frequency according to the other factors, since there is no larger competitor to overtake. However, we would recommend a minimum level of at least +2 exposures above the building block level (equal to that for other-brand loyals) because the amount of new learning, even for a monopolizing brand, is substantial. A fast-gaining competitor using heavy advertising would, however, indicate a competitive posture and use of LC + 1 *as if* the fast-gaining brand were the largest competitor.

Factor 3: Communication Objectives

To a considerable extent, the foregoing target audience correction factor already has allowed for the initial level of communication effects within target audience individuals by using a higher frequency when the effects are at or near zero (new category users) down to no adjustment when the effects are at or near a maximum (brand loyals). However, further adjustments are necessary depending on particular communication objectives.

The two communication effects whose objectives require the most variation in effective frequency are brand awareness and brand attitude (Table 16.3). The reasoning underlying the brand awareness and brand attitude adjustments is presented in detail in Chapters 9 and 10 and will be recapped here.

The first decision concerns the type of brand awareness. If brand *recognition* is the objective, then the effective frequency needed will be relatively low, and no correction is necessary (subject, of course, to the other correction factors and notably introductory advertising to new category users). In contrast, if brand *recall* is the communication objective, then the effective frequency needed will be relatively high. It is virtually impossible to make the frequency for brand recall too high.[12] The maximum level for brand recall would be everyone in the target audience recalling the brand first, which happens for only a very few heavily advertised brands. More realistic would be to use the LC + 1 guideline for brand recall; that is, to set the effective frequency level at least 1 exposure higher than the frequency used by the largest competitor, with at least +2 if the brand already is the largest competitor in the category.

Brand attitude strategy also has implications for effective frequency in the media plan, as discussed in Chapters 9 and 10. The involvement component of brand attitude strategy already is allowed for in the target audience correction factor, whereby involvement increases as we move from brand loyals to new category users; to correct again would be redundant. However, we do apply a correction for the purchase motivation component. An *informational* brand attitude strategy should be effective within the first one or two exposures— the brand is either perceived immediately as solving a problem or as irrelevant to the consumer's current motivation or need. Hence no adjustment is recommended for informational advertising. A *transformational* brand attitude

TABLE 16-3   COMMUNICATION OBJECTIVES AND EFFECTIVE FREQUENCY

Communication effect and objective	Correction factor*
Brand awareness	
• recognition	no correction
• recall	+2 if leader; LC + 1 otherwise
Brand attitude	
• informational	no correction
• transformational	+2 if leader; LC + 1 otherwise

* Brand awareness and brand attitude corrections are additive on the numerals only.

strategy, by contrast, requires heavy repetition—for build-up *and* for reinforcement of the brand image or attitude.

Brand awareness and brand attitude correction factors for effective frequency are additive. Look again at Table 16.3 to see how the addition of the two factors works. A brand recognition/informational attitude campaign would require no additional frequency (subject again to the other correction factors). A brand recognition/transformational attitude campaign, or a brand recall/ informational attitude campaign, would require +2 or LC + 1 exposures. And, highest of all, a brand recall/transformational attitude campaign would require +4 or LC + 2 exposures (note that only the +1's are added when adding LC + 1's). Examples of brand recall/transformational attitude campaigns would be the main campaigns for Coca-Cola and McDonald's, who are among the most frequent of the nation's advertisers.

Factor 4: Interpersonal Influence

The final correction factor for estimating effective frequency is interpersonal influence. This refers to social diffusion of the advertising message, usually via word-of-mouth but also by visual influence, as when brands are seen by others in a reference group or reference individual context.[13]

Every advertiser would like his or her campaign talked about or displayed visually on T-shirts, etc., because this publicity serves as free advertising. At the very least, interpersonal communication provides brand awareness, and if favorable comments are made about the features of the advertised brand (for informational advertising) or about the ad campaign itself (for transformational advertising) then brand attitude can be influenced as well.

Some years ago, Ozga[14] proposed that social diffusion serves as a substitute for part of the total amount of advertising that would otherwise be required. He introduced the notion of a *contact coefficient,* indicating the average number of other people told about the advertising by the average individual exposed to it (this could of course be extended to include visual contact). More recently the word-of-mouth contact coefficient has been included with advertising in models of new product diffusion.[15]

For example, there is no doubt that the Miller Lite "ex-jock" ads benefited considerably from frequent favorable comments among beer drinkers; beer is one product where peer-group influence stemming from the advertising has now been recognized as a major factor in advertising's success.[16] Some TV commercials over the years, such as Life Cereal's Mikey commercial, the infamous Brooke Shield's commercials for Calvin Klein jeans, as well as the equally infamous "Mr. Whipple" commercials for Charmin, and Wendy's comparative "Where's the beef?" commercials, and Aussie comedian Paul Hogan's commercials promoting Australia and Foster's lager, would seem to have generated plenty of opportunities for interpersonal influence as an augmenter of advertising frequency.

Interpersonal influence, providing it is favorable (which the advertiser should check during the advertising strategy and ad testing stages of research and then double-check during campaign evaluation once the campaign is launched), has a number of advantages over advertising per se. First, it is free, which means that the advertiser saves on advertising costs. Second, one word-of-mouth contact appears to be about twice as effective as one advertising exposure, probably because a favorable brand or advertising *attitude* is nearly always conveyed rather than just awareness.[17] Third, interpersonal influence can operate at any stage of the life cycle for any type of product, not just new, high risk products as was commonly believed.[18] In particular, a new *advertising* campaign, even for an old brand, can trigger word-of-mouth.

Based on a synthesis of the available studies of interpersonal influence, we would estimate that a contact coefficient of at least .25 is necessary to justify reducing the effective frequency estimate by 1 exposure (Table 16.4). This means that for every four people reached by the advertising, at least one person contacts at least one other person during the purchase cycle. Because this contact should be doubly effective, and because it may spread, it in effect replaces an exposure. Thus, a contact coefficient of at least .25 seems a reasonable figure to justify a reduction of −1 exposure in the minimum effective frequency calculation. For an interpersonal contact coefficient of less than .25, no adjustment is made.

With the −1 exposure reduction in effective frequency under conditions of frequent interpersonal influence, it should be noted that there is no recommended reduction in the *reach* of the media plan. This is because the interpersonal influence phenomenon works best when the "other" person contacted has also seen the campaign (discussing an ad with someone who has not seen it is somewhat frustrating, whereas discussing it with someone who has seen it is usually mutually reinforcing). Thus, the idea is to maintain the reach while reducing the required number of exposures because of the bonus exposure created by interpersonal influence.

MEF Calculation Summary Formula

A summary of minimum effective frequency estimation using the four correction factors is given in Table 16.5. A summary formula can now be stated to allow combined application of the correction factors and produce a minimum effective frequency estimate for any advertising situation. The formula is:

$$MEF = 1 + VA(1,2) (TA + BA + BATT - PI)$$

TABLE 16-4   INTERPERSONAL INFLUENCE AND EFFECTIVE FREQUENCY

Contact Coefficient	Correction Factor
≥ .25 (i.e., every fourth person tells or shows another person during the purchase cycle)	− 1 exposure
< .25	no correction

TABLE 16-5   SUMMARY OF EFFECTIVE FREQUENCY ESTIMATION

Factor	Correction (starting from 1 exposure in purchase cycle)					
	− 1	0	+1	+2	LC + 1*	Double
1. Vehicle attention		high attention				low attention
2. Target audience		brand loyals	brand switchers	other-brand loyals	new category users	
3. Communica-tion objectives (two factors)		brand recognition			brand recall	
		informational brand attitude			transforma-tional brand attitude	
4. Personal influence	high (average contact ≥ .25)	low (average contact < .25)				

* If market share leader, use +2 exposures; if not leader, set equal to largest competitor's average frequency +1 (called LC + 1). LC + 1 is additive on the 1 only; e.g., a campaign aimed at new category users, with brand recall and transformational brand attitude objectives, would use LC + 3 exposures.

where

$$MEF = \text{miniumum effective frequency}$$

$$1 = \text{the building block or starting level of 1 exposure}$$

$$VA(1,2) = \text{media vehicle attention correction factor: a multiplier which is 1 for high attention vehicles, and 2 (doubled) for low attention vehicles}$$

$$TA = \text{target audience correction factor}$$

$$BA = \text{brand awareness correction factor}$$

$$BATT = \text{brand attitude correction factor}$$

$$PI = \text{interpersonal influence correction factor}$$

Several examples will illustrate how the formula can be applied.

The very lowest effective frequency would be no advertising (0 exposures) in the purchase cycle. However, this would only occur in one particular circumstance, and not indefinitely but rather between bursts or flights. This circumstance would be following a high-attention vehicle campaign (for ex-ample, prime-time TV) aimed at brand loyals, for a brand purchased via recognition, and sold via an informational brand attitude strategy—that also generated strong interpersonal influence. It would be quite rare for a campaign to meet all these criteria simultaneously. In particular, campaigns likely to generate strong word-of-mouth would be new campaigns rather than directed with low frequency at brand loyals (for example, the Brooke Shields campaign for Calvin Klein jeans). Also, with the apparent trend toward "safe" ad testing in recent years, it is fair to say that American campaigns in general have become more conservative and therefore less likely to spark the strong public reaction that is needed to meet the high personal influence criterion.

Most estimates of minimum effective frequency will be between 1 and 13 exposures per purchase cycle. Some hypothetical examples calculated from the formula include:

- Hellmann's mayonnaise (1), advertising in primary-reader magazines (1×), to brand switchers (+1), via a brand recognition (0), and a taste-based transformational brand attitude strategy (assume Kraft, the largest competitor, is using + 2 and then add 1) = 5 exposures per purchase cycle, which is probably about two weeks for mayonnaise.
- Bold detergent (1), advertising on daytime TV serials (1×), to other-brand loyals (+2), via a brand recognition (0) and informational brand attitude strategy (0) = 3 exposures per purchase cycle, which is probably about three weeks for detergent.
- Blue Nun Wine (1), advertising on radio (double the following, i.e., 2×), to new category users as the market leader (+2), via a brand recall (+2) and informational brand attitude strategy (0) = 9 exposures per purchase cycle, which is probably about monthly for dinner wines.

We may note that the highest minimum effective frequency would occur with a late entry trying to break into a new category, with communication objectives that require brand recall and a transformational brand attitude, by using a low-attention medium, such as radio, passalong-reader newspapers or magazines, or daytime TV other than serials. Such media normally would not be chosen for a new product campaign, but if they were, we can see that a minimum effective frequency of at least 13 exposures per purchase cycle would be needed. For frequently purchased consumer products, this could be a very expensive campaign; however, for consumer durables or industrial products it may be feasible because of the longer purchase cycle.

GEOGRAPHIC SCHEDULING

The media plan's geographic reach must be considered in terms of MEF. It is not satisfactory to spread the advertising geographically (for example, to all American states) with some vague aim of obtaining "complete coverage." As should be eminently clear by now, extended coverage is wasted unless that coverage is at MEF, with one possible exception, retailer support.

Geographic Scheduling and MEF

Let's return for a moment to the "media balloon" and look at the trade-offs necessary in the media plan. Once the media planner has calculated the minimum effective frequency (MEF) for the brand per purchase cycle, the next step is to decide how many of the available purchase cycles in the planning period, considering the budget, can be "filled with MEF." The media balloon tells us, now that the frequency parameter has been fixed at MEF, that the two remaining parameters are *reach* and *continuity*. That is, purchase cycles can be filled horizontally (geographic reach) or longitudinally (continuity over time) or, as is usual, with a combination of both parameters.

Complete geographic coverage at MEF rarely can be afforded for all purchase cycles (this introduces the continuity parameter). It rarely is possible to advertise in all markets all year long. And it is pointless to advertise at below the MEF level in any market; however, there is one possible exception.

Retailer Support

It could make sense to advertise at below MEF in a particular geographic market when the *retailer also is advertising the brand there*. In this case, the manufacturer's extra advertising, even at low frequency, may help to achieve total MEF.

More practically, too, some continued advertising, even in a weak area, can help to convince retailers that the brand is being supported in the area and thus is still deserving of shelf space and perhaps special display. Because of the undeniable importance of display to the sales of products sold through retailers, this continued advertising can be vital.

Note, however, that "retailer conviction" advertising differs from the previous situation of "MEF top-up" advertising. Because retailer conviction advertising will be below MEF for consumers, it is advisable to place it in media (or media vehicles) to which *the retailer will be exposed* while occupying his or her out-of-store role as a private consumer. Retail attention to the brand could then maintain sales even though the advertising is not, except by its influence on retailers.

SCHEDULING OVER TIME: CONTINUITY AND EFFECTIVE FREQUENCY

The final media scheduling decision concerns *continuity*. Essentially, this is a decision about how many of the available purchase cycles in the planning period should be filled with MEF—for the maximum number of individual target audience members. That is, over the usual medium-run planning period of 52 weeks, how often and in what pattern should the typical target audience member be exposed to our advertising?

Generally, the media planner should work out an overall pattern for the period, then make already-known short-term adjustments for special events (discussed shortly) and, still further, hold some of the budget (and thus frequency) for very short-term contingencies such as actions or reactions to competitors' plans. We will examine the overall pattern of continuity first.

Continuity and "Outer" Target Audience Change

Clearly, the usual purpose of advertising to a particular target audience is to have that target audience *change*—in awareness, attitude, and behavior status—to an audience that is more favorable toward the brand.

There are only two *exceptions* to this: *routinized favorable brand switchers* and *brand loyals*. These two groups, which already comprise most of the fringe and the core, respectively, of the brand's sales, would, if targeted, not be expected to change their status over the course of the campaign. Routinized favorable brand switchers, for example, are not expected to become brand loyals (but rather just to switch-in a little more often) because their purchasing patterns are routinized. Brand loyals are expected to stay loyal and to use the brand a little more often, but again not to change.

All other target audiences are expected to *change* as the campaign works on them—and to change to groups requiring *less frequency*. The target audience requiring the highest MEF, new category users, in most campaigns is expected to become brand loyals, with a dramatic reduction in MEF from LC + 1 to 0 (on the target audience correction factor). Similarly, other-brand loyals in most campaigns are expected to convert to loyalty to our brand, with a consequent reduction (on the target audience factor) of 2 exposures. And although we did not differentiate types of brand switchers in the target audience correction factor, we might judge that experimental brand switchers or other-brand switchers could be reduced by about 1 exposure should they become routinized favorable brand switchers and definitely if they become brand loyals.

In fact, when you think about it, it is not very likely that you would want to continue to advertise to these "outer" target audiences—new category users, other-brand loyals, non-favorable brand switchers—for more than a few purchase cycles (the exception here being a continuous target audience of new category users, such as for wedding dresses, or any other product with a *very* long purchase cycle). If the campaign hasn't worked after several purchase cycles in which the target audience has been reached at MEF each time and now has had several purchase opportunities, chances are the campaign will not work and it is time to reconsider the advertising strategy and perhaps even the marketing objectives.

If, on the other hand, the campaign aimed at one or more of these "outer" target audiences *has* been successful, they then will have moved to a more favorable, lower MEF group.

Accordingly, the media planner's task regarding continuity over multiple purchase cycles in the advertising period is to estimate when the shift to lower required MEF will occur. (It is noteworthy that one of the best new product tracking models for supermarket products, BBDO's NEWS, based on experience, allows only two purchase cycles' worth of advertising for trial purchase to occur[19].)

"Outer" targeting tends to produce a "sliding scale" of frequency whereby a high MEF burst is used in the first few purchase cycles to try to persuade the outer target audience to try or re-try the brand; a moderate MEF burst then follows for several more purchase cycles as the outer audience goes through the brand trial or re-trial phase and functionally becomes brand switchers; and finally a reduced MEF continuation is aimed at the now-favorable buyers captured by the campaign.

Thus, only with "inner" targeting, to routinized favorable brand switchers or brand loyals, would an even pattern of continuity be used, and then only if there are no seasonal fluctuations in sales.

"Inner" Target Audiences and Continuity

Ideally, with continuing advertising to the "inner" target audiences of routinized favorable brand switchers and brand loyals, you should advertise to them at (their) MEF in *every* purchase cycle in the planning period. To contend that "the budget can't afford this" is to admit that the advertising is not profitable! In other words, you should keep spending against these inner groups as long as the profit from advertising exceeds alternative ways of spending the money.

Some media researchers have promoted the idea that it is better to schedule advertisements in alternating cycles (either in on-again, off-again "flights" or in heavy-light-heavy-etc. "pulses") than to spread the *same* number of exposures evenly across purchase cycles.[20] However, an alternating schedule can only be superior because the evenly spaced schedule is falling below MEF in *each* purchase cycle whereas the flights or pulses attain MEF in *some*—the "on" or "heavy"—purchase cycles. Obviously, though, the uneven schedule falls below MEF in the "off" or "light" purchase cycles and it would be best to attain MEF on all purchase cycles by increasing the total number of exposures and the advertising budget.[21]

Short-Term Adjustments in Frequency

"Short-term" here is used to mean less than a year. The overall pattern of continuity for the year may need to be adjusted to accommodate *known* events throughout the budgeting year. (We exclude seasonality here, which already has been discussed under purchase cycles, in terms of balancing low competitive interference before the seasonal peak or peaks against increased category need during the peak or peaks.) Most often these known events consist of:

1 Promotion dates to consumers, or
2 Special promotions to the trade

In the case of promotion dates to consumers, the important strategy is to shift the *timing* of advertising exposures so that they precede the promotion date and create the "ratchet effect" discussed in Chapter 12. Note that the MEF requirement remains the same, so more frequency is not needed, but rather frequency that *precedes* the promotion date *within* the purchase cycle.

Because the promotion itself—if consumer franchise building (CFB)—contributes to MEF, advertising can accordingly be *reduced* by at least 1 exposure during the purchase cycle in which the promotion occurs, and by more than 1 exposure if the promotion incorporates multiple exposures.

With special promotions to the trade, advertising to consumers is used in many cases to impress distributors that the brand is being given strong consumer support at the same time as the trade drive. As in the foregoing case, some concentration of exposures within the consumer purchase cycle leading up to the trade promotion can add to this impression. Where possible, use of media that the retailer also is exposed to is desirable because of the dual (trade and consumer) target audience.

Very Short-Term Scheduling

On top of the overall scheduling pattern and the short-term adjustments for known events, the media planner will want to keep some reserve frequency, and thus part of the budget, for very short-term actions and reactions.

The most obvious of these very short-term contingencies is *response to a leading competitor*. Unanticipated competitive actions, such as the surprise launch date of a new campaign or even a new brand, have the effect of raising our brand's MEF under three circumstances (see Table 16.5 earlier): (1) when the target audience is new category users (for example, for personal computers); (2) when brand recall is the brand awareness objective (for example, for airlines, especially with "outer" target audiences); or (3) when the brand attitude strategy is transformational (for example, soft drinks, liquor). All these use the LC + 1 adjustment, so if the "LC" increases advertising, you should too.

Conversely, notice that for target audiences, other than new category users, who are being reached with brand recognition/informational communication objectives, the "LC" term doesn't enter the calculation and *no reaction* would be the appropriate reaction.

A second frequent very short-term circumstance is caused by *variation in supply*. Just as a factory breakdown or distributor problem could cause advertising to be withdrawn that otherwise would be wasted, a factory over-run or large purchase of stock could require extra advertising to stimulate demand. For the brand that already is advertising at MEF, this extra advertising would be used to increase the number reached at MEF, or perhaps to attract an outer, higher MEF target audience. For example, a fire-damage sale at Saks Fifth Avenue probably would attract many first-time Saks visitors.

A last very short-term variable that affects a surprising number of products is *variation in demand caused by the weather*. We are not talking here about well-known seasonal patterns but rather unexpected daily or weekly variations. Unseasonable rain can cause the demand for umbrellas and raincoats to skyrocket. Unseasonable fine weather can boost sales of house-and-garden products. But among the products most affected by daily variations in weather are food and beverages. Advertiming, a new service in New York that monitors product demand in relation to weather, reports that soda consumption increases in gusty weather, and hot cereal and soup consumption increase in stormy weather. Increases of 50 to 100 percent have been demonstrated for some products. Campbell's Soup now apparently sets aside $750,000 of its media budget for very short-term radio commercials on days when storms threaten.[22]

What MEF should be assumed if advertisers wish to take advantage of weather variations? It depends on the target audience. The increase in category need doesn't change the frequency required to direct choice toward a particular brand. Rather, it temporarily shortens the purchase cycle, thus pushing the frequency *rate* up. Because there is usually a corresponding decrease during opposite weather patterns, the overall effect is to keep total advertising frequency constant while simply varying its timing.

SUMMARY

In this chapter we have seen that correct media scheduling (the "how often" decision) depends primarily on the manager's capacity to estimate the minimum frequency of exposures, to the average target audience member, in the purchase cycle, that will effectively achieve the communication objectives. The best estimation method would be by experimentation, but this is expensive and is not without problems even when it is affordable.

We propose instead a logical approach to minimum effective frequency (MEF) estimation based on media vehicle attention, target audience, communication objectives, and the extent of interpersonal influence. First, the manager must measure, or in certain cases estimate, the purchase cycle, that is, the target audience's average interval between purchases in the product category. The minimum effective frequency per purchase cycle is then calculated by starting with 1 exposure and adjusting upward for low attention media vehicles, target audiences with more to learn about the brand, brand recall, and transformational brand attitude communication objectives, and then making a downward adjustment for interpersonal influence if the brand is fortunate enough to have this operating.

Although this logical approach to MEF calculation is far from finalized, it at least helps the manager think about the right sorts of issues in determining how frequently the advertising should be scheduled.

Geographic scheduling is the next decision, an extension of the reach parameter. It is indefensible to advertise at below MEF in any market. That is, effective reach should govern the media plan, not "geographic coverage" per se. The one exception to below-MEF advertising in an area is for retailer support. If the retailer also is advertising the brand, consumer advertising combined with the retailer's may reach MEF; or it may nevertheless encourage the retailer to push the brand.

The final scheduling decision is scheduling over purchase cycles in the planning period: the continuity parameter. For "outer" target audiences—new category users, other-brand loyals, and non-favorable brand switchers—the MEF requirement will reduce if the campaign is successful and these audiences change to become more favorable or "inner" customers. For "inner" target audiences of routinized favorable brand switchers and brand loyals, advertising in every purchase cycle at MEF was shown to be the best strategy.

Short-term adjustments to the schedule then need to be made for known events occurring in the planning period. Last, some of the budget has to be saved for concentrating frequency to meet unanticipated very short-term contingencies.

Effective frequency is the soundest basis for deciding advertising "weight," the objective being to maximize the number of target audience individuals reached, in each purchase cycle, at at least the minimum effective frequency level—effective reach. In the next chapter we turn to the reach aspect of this objective in considering media vehicle selection.

NOTES

1 Historical appreciation of the concept of effective frequency and its importance can be gained from the following references: Longman, K.E. *Advertising,* New York: Harcourt Brace Jovanovich, 1971, chapter 7; A.A. Achenbaum, Effective exposure: a new way of evaluating media, paper presented at the Association of National Advertisers' Media Workshop, New York: Association of National Advertisers, Inc., February 1977; and M.J. Naples, *Effective Frequency: The Relationship Between Frequency and Advertising Effectiveness,* New York: Association of National Advertisers, Inc., 1979.

2 The concepts of advertising communication models and the criterion measures for each are discussed in Part Eight, Chapter 19, on ad testing.

3 For supermarket products, most brands attract the same *proportion* of heavy, medium, and light buyers as other brands. Thus the average purchase cycle remains similar no matter what brand or brands the target audience favors. Interestingly, the same holds for supermarkets considered as "brands"; each tends to attract the same proportion of frequent and less frequent customers, so that overall patronage is determined by penetration, not repeat buying rate. See A.S.C. Ehrenberg, *Repeat-Buying,* Amsterdam and New York: North-Holland, 1972; and A.K. Kau and A.S.C. Ehrenberg, Patterns of store choice, *Journal of Marketing Research,* 1984, *21* (4), 399–309.

4 See the discussion, in Chapter 20, of "how often to track," that is, how frequently you need to survey the market.

5 D.A. Aaker and J.C. Carman, Are you overadvertising?, *Journal of Advertising Research,* 1982, *22* (4), 57–70. Their conclusions, as they note, apply only to established products, not new products.

6 "Packaging strengthens brand franchises," *ad forum,* May 1981, p. 37–39. The figures are from p. 37.

7 J.E. Draper, R.W. Hansen, and R.A. Scott, Timing of real estate advertising, *Journal of Advertising Research,* 1970, *10* (6), 21–24.

8 E.C. Strong, The spacing and timing of advertising, *Journal of Advertising Research,* 1977, *17* (6), 25–31.

9 Experiments on effective frequency are becoming feasible for *television* advertising with the advent of split-cable technology such as that offered by AdTel, IRI, or Nielsen. Different frequency levels can be programmed into randomly selected

cable houses, whose purchases are then recorded on UPC scanners at stores. Reported cost is about $50,000 per experimental level or, say, $200,000 to test four estimates of MEF.

10 As noted earlier, our approach to effective frequency is based on frequency of *insertions;* we define exposures as opportunities to see/hear/read the ad, or OTS, regardless of whether the ad is in fact attended to and processed.

In developing the estimates for the correction factors and the summary formula for calculating minimum effective frequency, we have, for this "exposure versus attention" or "opportunity for exposure versus actual exposure" reason, erred on the liberal side to allow for this slippage. The more technically inclined reader may be interested in the support for this, and also for the doubling of insertion frequency with low attention vehicles.

Simon Broadbent, a very experienced media researcher, in his book *Spending Advertising Money* (3rd ed., London: Business Books Ltd., 1979) estimates that 85 to 88 percent of the average prime time program's TV audience is watching or within hearing range during a commercial break (p. 90). The estimate for primary reader newspapers and, we may infer, primary reader magazines is similarly impressive: 90 percent of the average vehicle's readers look at the page on which an advertisement appears (p. 120). He also claims a high figure of page openings by secondary "skim readers" of magazines and newspapers, but we have chosen to assume that relative to primary readers, secondary readers pay low attention to the vehicle.

If we take a conservative estimate of probability of initial attention to the ad of .8 for high attention vehicles, and a conservative estimate of .4 for low attention vehicles, some simple simulations with the binomial theorem (exposed versus unexposed over successive insertions) indicate that you need about double the number of insertions in low attention vehicles. For example, if the MEF is 2 exposures, you need four insertions to get 90 percent 2+ "attention reach" in a high attention vehicle, and double that, eight insertions to get 90 percent 2+ "attention reach" in a low attention vehicle.

Our formula, then, can be regarded as a formula for *insertions,* which is what the media planner wants. The *outcome* of the formula, MEF, already allows for media vehicle attention. MEF can be adjusted further for ad unit differences as explained in the next chapter and shown in Appendix C.

11 We rely primarily here on a very carefully performed field experiment: C. McDonald, What is the short-term effect of advertising?, Special Report No. 71–142, Cambridge, MA: Marketing Science Institute, 1971. A summary of his study is given in M.J. Naples, same reference as in note 1, pp. 83–103. This study appeared to have brand switchers as the target audience.

12 The most direct evidence on the extent of repetition needed for the two types of brand awareness comes from a laboratory experiment by S.N. Singh and M.L. Rothschild, Recognition as a measure of learning from television commercials, *Journal of Marketing Research*, 1983, *20* (3), 235–248. In their experiment, different groups of respondents saw a commercial 1, 2, or 4 times within a half-hour program. Brand recognition (package) and brand recall (name) measures were administered two weeks later. Three new commercials were used, representing three new brands from different product classes of supermarket products, so the results are quite generalizable.

Supporting our conclusion about the relative ease of brand recognition learning, pack recognition was very high two weeks later after only 1 exposure (71 percent) and peaked at 2 exposures (81 percent): an increase to 4 exposures added only an insignificant 2 percent to the 2-exposure peak.

In contrast, brand recall was at a much lower absolute level, and showed direct increases with repetition with no indication of peaking. Brand recall for 1 exposure was 0 percent, for 2 exposures 5 percent, and after 4 exposures still only 21 percent. That is, after 4 concentrated exposures in a half-hour program, only one in five consumers could recall the new brand's name two weeks later.

Obviously, brand recall depends not only on the number of exposures but also on the number, and degree of learning of, competing brand names in the category, especially during the exposure-to-purchase opportunity interval (two weeks in the above experiment). For comparison, the McCollum-Spielman ad testing norms for brand recall after 1 exposure, just half an hour later, with seven commercials (so chance level $= \frac{1}{7}$ or 14 percent) shown in the program, is 39 percent for new brands and 56 percent for established brands.

Thus, we can see that brand recall not only increases with exposure, but also drops off very rapidly (mostly within 24 hours) the longer the delay between exposure and the purchase opportunity. This is quite unlike brand recognition, which peaks quickly and stays high for long delay periods (of at least one month) until purchase.

13 T.S. Robertson, *Innovative Behavior and Communication,* New York: Holt, Rinehart and Winston, 1971, pp. 174–175.

14 S.A. Ozga, Imperfect markets through lack of knowledge, *Quarterly Journal of Economics,* 1960, *74* (1), 29–52.

15 See especially J.A. Dodson and E. Muller, Models of new product diffusion through advertising and word-of-mouth, *Management Science,* 1978, *24* (15), 1568–1578. Some theorists have pointed out that word-of-mouth about a new *product* should decline as knowledge about the product spreads; see, for example, V. Mahajan, J. Wind, and S. Sharma, An approach to repeat-purchase diffusion analysis, in P.E. Murphy, G.R. Laczniak, P.F. Anderson, R.W. Belk, O.C. Ferrell, R.F. Lusch, T.A. Shimp, and C.B. Weinberg (Eds.), *1983 Educators' Conference Proceedings,* Chicago: American Marketing Association, 1983, pp. 442–446. However, a new *advertising* campaign or a new advertisement in a pool-out campaign can re-generate word-of-mouth even for an established product.

16 J.M. McCann and E.S. Ojdana, On the form of the lagged effect of advertising, in R.P. Bagozzi, K.L. Bernhardt, P.S. Busch, D.W. Cravens, J.F. Hair, Jr., and C.A. Scott (Eds.), *1980 Educators' Conference Proceedings,* Chicago: American Marketing Association, 1980, pp. 298–301.

17 In two field experiments on word-of-mouth effects, positive information was conveyed more often than negative information. See J.N. Sheth, Word-of-mouth in low risk innovations, *Journal of Advertising Research,* 1971, *11* (3), 15–18; and G.S. Day, Attitude change, media and word-of-mouth, *Journal of Advertising Research,* 1971, *11* (6), 31–40.

18 See notes 15 and 17 and also J.H. Holmes and J.D. Lett, Product sampling and word-of-mouth, *Journal of Advertising Research,* 1977, *17* (5), 35–40.

19 L.G. Pringle, R.D. Wilson, and E.I. Brody, NEWS: a decision-oriented model for new product analysis and forecasting, *Marketing Science,* 1982, *1* (1), 1–29.

20 See, for example, E.C. Strong, same reference as note 8; H. Simon, ADPULS: an advertising model with wearout and pulsation, *Journal of Marketing Research,* 1982, *19* (3), 352–363.

21 We will return to flighting as a defensive move to prevent one type of wearout in Chapter 20.

22 The information about the Advertiming Company, which advises clients when to run advertisements in short-term media such as television, radio, or newspapers, as well as the examples, were reported in the journal of the Association of Canadian Advertisers and reproduced in the Australian Association of National Advertisers' newsletter, *National Advertiser*, 1985, *231*, 55, 57.

DISCUSSION QUESTIONS

16.1 Why is exposure a difficult concept to define? Comment on how well we resolve this difficulty in the chapter, with particular reference to where the media planner's responsibility ends and the creative director's responsibility takes over.

16.2 What is a purchase cycle? Why does the purchase cycle override any "standard" intervals (such as four weeks) used in conventional media planning to calculate reach and frequency?

16.3 In a sentence or two each, explain how the purchase cycle concept needs to be modified when advertising:
  a A new but imitatable brand in a new product category
  b A fad product
  c Sunburn lotion
  d Home renovation service
  e A variety store

16.4 Estimate (calculate) the minimum effective frequency for each of the following examples:
  a Digital mini-computers, advertising in industry management magazines, to brand switchers, via a brand recall, informational brand attitude strategy.
  b Kraft cheese, advertising in daytime non-serials TV, to brand loyals, via a brand recognition, transformational brand attitude strategy.
  c Southern Comfort bourbon, advertising on billboards, to other-brand loyals, via a brand recall, transformational brand attitude strategy, using a campaign that is known to generate favorable word-of-mouth from one in every three people exposed.
  d Radio Shack, advertising Sony Walkmans, on radio, to new category users, via a brand recall, informational brand attitude strategy.

16.5 For each of the examples in Question 16.4, discuss the likely continuity patterns over the course of one year. Be sure to spell out the reasons for your distribution of exposures by purchase cycle.

FURTHER READING

M.J. Naples. *Effective Frequency: The Relationship Between Frequency and Advertising Effectiveness*. New York: Association of National Advertisers, Inc., 1979.

Makes a good case for the centrality of effective frequency in media strategy. Unfortunately, the varying criteria of "effectiveness" limit the conclusions to be drawn from the studies reported in the book (it takes an empirical rather than a logical or theoretical perspective on identifying MEF).

S. Broadbent. *Spending Advertising Money* (3rd ed.). London: Business Books Ltd., 1979.

This is perhaps the most sensible book ever written for the practicing media planner. Broadbent's book is both theoretical and practical, but compromises through the use of phrases such as "it depends" or "this is how it's usually done" when it comes to the most difficult theoretical issues in media strategy. There is excellent coverage of media buying which, although written in the British context, is easily applied to the U.S. media market in terms of the principles involved.

CHAPTER 17

VEHICLE SELECTION IN THE MEDIA PLAN

Having calculated minimum effective frequency for the advertising for each purchase cycle, the media planner's next task is to *select specific media vehicles* (particular TV dayparts or programs, particular magazines, and so forth, depending on the primary and secondary media types previously selected) that, in combination, will deliver the required level of MEF to as many target audience individuals as possible within the media budget for the advertising.

After reading this chapter you should:

- Understand how to make a first-stage selection of vehicles by direct matching, and appreciate the advantages of this method over the traditional method of demographic matching
- Know which "qualitative" media vehicle factors to use, if any, to adjust the initial list, thereby achieving the second stage of vehicle selection
- Learn how to accomplish the final stage of vehicle selection by profit potential, not simply by cost

FIRST-STAGE SELECTION OF MEDIA VEHICLES BY DIRECT MATCHING

The initial or first-stage selection of media vehicles is best made by a method known as direct matching, although it can also be made by demographic matching. In this section we explain direct matching, but first we have to introduce a concept fundamental to media vehicle selection: duplication of exposures.

Duplication of Exposures to Attain MEF

The basic concept to be grasped in media vehicle selection is the idea of duplication of exposures. To appreciate this concept, let's begin with a simple case where the minimum effective frequency is 2 and the purchase cycle is one week. If our advertising were a TV commercial, we could, for example, "roadblock" the TV audience by putting the commercial on all three networks on the 6 P.M. evening news on Monday night. This would mean that those members of the target audience who were watching the evening news on Monday night would get 1 exposure.

But how would they get their second exposure? Should we, for example, insert the commercial again in the three respective programs on each network that immediately follow the news, hoping the same people are watching (duplication *across* vehicles, or "audience overlap") or would we be able to deliver the second exposure to more of the Monday night news target audience viewers by inserting it again in the evening news on *Tuesday* night (duplication *within* vehicles, or "repeat audience")? A third possibility, mentioned in Chapter 15, would be to put two insertions in the Monday night evening news—if there is time available and the networks allow it—which is called "impact scheduling."

All this says nothing about those members of the target audience who were not watching the evening news on Monday night and thus missed out on the first exposure. How do we get two exposures to them? We would have to select other vehicles that reach these other members of the target audience and repeat the entire process.

This was a simple example. Consider a more complex case where the MEF is 8 exposures in the first month and the advertiser is restricted to magazines (say, for the launch of a new brand of rum, targeted to win brand loyals from Bacardi, with brand recall/high involvement/transformational communication objectives). Let's further assume that the effective reach goal in the first month is 80 percent of adults loyal to Bacardi (whatever that *number* is). What combination of magazines could guarantee 80 percent 8+ reach in a month to Bacardi brand loyals?

The usual solution to this type of problem is to try to find demographic correlates of Bacardi loyals, or more likely, heavy users of rum (Is there a sex skew? Does any age group stand out?); then try to find magazines whose readership profiles show a similar demographic pattern; then pump into those magazines as much advertising as the launch budget can afford—hoping to reach the "right" people "enough" times.

This primitive, but common, "demographic matching" method is the way in which a good deal of advertising money is wasted. (Only an industrial advertiser with a particularly narrow occupationally-related product could hope to get by with demographic matching: the occupational demographic limits the choice to one or two trade journals. But even this would overlook how to reach top managers if they also are a decision-role target for the advertising.)

Demographic matching not only is a crude way of hoping to catch the target audience, it also ignores the issue of duplication of exposures (between and within vehicles). Duplication of exposures is necessary knowledge if the media planner is to have any idea how many exposures the target audience actually *is* getting. Duplication of exposures allows the media plan to deliver effective frequency and thus also determines effective reach.

The media vehicle selection problem is therefore really two problems: that of how exactly to reach the target audience; and that of knowing, through duplication, how many exposures the individual target audience member actually received.

Direct Matching as the Reach and Duplication Solution

The best method for selecting media vehicles is direct measurement of the target audience's media exposure. This is known as *direct matching*. Direct matching, as forewarned in Chapter 5 in conjunction with target audience profile variables, is to be distinguished from the traditional but inferior method of vehicle selection using demographic matching. (Figure 17.1 summarizes the two methods.) Direct matching provides two major advantages:

1 *More Accurate Target Audience Reach*   As we will demonstrate, direct matching provides the greatest degree of accuracy in reaching individuals in the target audience, and thus the least amount of wasted coverage of non-target audience individuals.

2 *Solves the Duplication Problem and Thus Measures Effective Frequency Delivery*   Direct matching measures each individual's overlap (across vehicles)

FIGURE 17.1   Direct matching and demographic matching in media vehicle selection.

Direct Matching

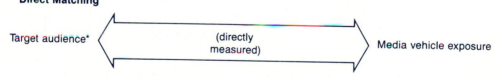

Target audience*   (directly measured)   Media vehicle exposure

*Target audience defined by awareness-attitude-behavior as one of the 12 prospect sub-groups or, at minimum, as one of the 4 groups from which sales must come: brand loyals, brand switchers, other-brand loyals, or new category users.

Demographic Matching

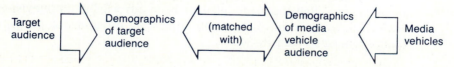

Target audience → Demographics of target audience ← (matched with) → Demographics of media vehicle audience ← Media vehicles

and repeat patterns (within the same vehicle on successive occasions) exactly, whereas other methods provide only an estimate of duplication on a gross audience basis.

We will describe the procedure for direct matching shortly. Before doing so, we need to demonstrate what is wrong with the most widely used media vehicle selection procedure, demographic matching.

The Inaccuracy of Demographic Matching   Demographic matching relates target audiences to media vehicles through demographics. As Figure 17.1 shows, this requires three intervening steps:

- First, the advertiser has to profile the target audience in terms of its demographics.
- Second, the media planner has to profile the media vehicle's audience in terms of *its* demographics. (As most media owners sell their vehicles on the basis of head counts by demographic categories, demographic profiles of vehicle audiences are readily available, which accounts for the widespread use of demographic matching in media selection.)
- Third, in the final step, the demographic profile of the target audience must be compared, in some way, with alternative prospective vehicles, to find vehicles whose demographics most closely match the demographics of the target audience.

Most often, and most crudely, the demographic match-up is achieved by picking just one or two demographic variables that differentiate the target audience from all other consumers, for example, sex and age. The media planner then searches through the alternative vehicles' profiles to find one or more vehicles that also are differentiated by, or are "skewed" towards, the sex and age groups desired.[1]

For instance, an advertiser might know from research that the target audience, in this case brand loyals, has the following sex and age composition:

- *60* percent females; 40 percent males
- *50* percent are aged 18–34; with 25 percent each from the under-18 and 35-plus age groups, respectively

These are single demographics. Even better, though not always done, would be a cross-tabulation of sex by age among brand loyals. The cross-tabulation may show the largest proportion of brand loyals, say 40 percent, to be in the female 18–34 cell, which would be one of six cells or categories in the cross-tab table. These sorts of figures are typical.

Given this "female 18–34 skew" in the target audience, the media planner now searches for media vehicles whose vehicle audiences also have a "female 18–34 skew." Had the media planner been advertising on television in 1982, Nielsen data would have shown the following programs to have the highest ratings among women 18–34:

- *AfterMASH* (CBS)
- *Dynasty* (ABC)
- *NBC Monday Night Movie*

At an average showing, 20 percent of women in the nation aged 18–34 will be watching, respectively, the above programs.

Now, can you see what's happening? Refer again to Figure 17.1 and the demographic matching diagram. First, there's serious slippage on the left-hand (target audience demographics) side: 40 percent of brand loyals may be females aged 18–34, but what about the other 60 percent of brand loyals who are either males or younger or older females? Second, there is serious slippage on the right-hand (media vehicle demographics) side: 20 percent of females aged 18–34 may be watching AfterMASH, but so too are 16 percent of men aged 18–34, not to mention the other age groups. You're paying for audiences that you "don't want" who actually outnumber the so-called demographic target group!

Any degree of misfit between the target audience and its demographics, on the one hand, and any degree of misfit between the vehicle audience and its demographics, on the other, will be *compounded* when the two demographic profiles are put together. This can be seen in correlational terms. Let us optimistically suppose that there is a good fit between the target audience and its demographics, a correlation of .7. Let us further suppose that there is a good fit between the vehicle audience and its demographics, also a correlation of .7. When the two demographic profiles are put together, the resulting correlation, that is, the demographic match, will be .7 × .7 = .49, or if you like, only about 50 percent correspondence between the target audience and the vehicle audience. This is an optimistic example. The demographic fit on both sides of the match-up usually is far worse than this, and the resulting match-up accuracy far lower.

Furthermore, what if there are no distinctive demographic characteristics of the target audience? Consumer behavior findings have long demonstrated that there *rarely are* marked demographic differences between buyers of different brands in well-defined product categories.[2] How then can demographics be used, for instance, to single out brand loyals or brand switchers? The usual solution—to buy media vehicles on the basis of category rather than brand demographics—is a financially wasteful method of reaching brand groups. The second most common solution—to buy media vehicles that reach a broad demographic audience if the brand users' demographics are not distinctive—is even more wasteful and also ignores precise target audience reach.

In summary, regarding demographic matching, there is no good reason to try to infer a link between a target audience and a media vehicle audience through some third set of variables such as demographics. This conclusion also applies to "psychographic matching." As pointed out by Wells and Tigert,[3] indirect match-ups through *any* third set of variables, be they demographics or psychographics, are bound to produce lower accuracy than if a direct linkage is sought.

The Accuracy of Direct Matching   Direct matching of target audiences with the media vehicles to which they are exposed, without going through the intervening and inefficient step of demographic matching, was first proposed by Garfinkle[4] and given further publicity in the article by Wells and Tigert. The greater accuracy of direct matching has been demonstrated in two subsequent empirical studies by Assael and Cannon[5] and Winter[6] and in proprietary projects conducted by the authors.

The Assael and Cannon study is the broader of the two published studies and will be summarized here to illustrate the greater accuracy of direct matching. The study covered five consumer product categories: furniture, color TV, garden tools, plays, and movies. The media vehicles used were 22 magazines and newspapers (this is a very fair test of the two procedures because magazines are regarded as the most demographically segmented medium, so that the comparison favors demographic matching). Also, an unusually comprehensive set of 17 demographic measures was employed, far more than would be used by most media planners. The target audience was defined as product users, for the first two products above, and high interest consumers, for the last three products.

Averaged across the five product categories, demographic matching produced only 22 percent accuracy in reaching the target audience (Table 17.1). Direct matching, by contrast, was 58 percent accurate. While this is not perfect, because to match near the 100 percent level would require a very fragmented and expensive media buy, note that direct matching was more than twice as accurate as demographic matching. Looked at another way, with demographic matching the waste or mis-hit rate was 78 percent, whereas with direct matching it was a comparatively low 42 percent.

Assael and Cannon's finding of a 36 percent net increase in media selection accuracy is fairly typical of the sorts of results we have observed in proprietary studies. Haley[7] notes that net improvements of 20 to 30 percent are commonly found with direct matching. With most of the advertising budget being spent

TABLE 17-1   THE COMPARATIVE ACCURACY OF DIRECT MATCHING VERSUS DEMOGRAPHIC MATCHING

	Media selection accuracy (r^2)	
Product	Direct matching (%)	Demographic matching (%)
Furniture	13	12
Color TV	37	1
Garden tools	87	24
Plays	71	13
Movies	82	59
Average	58%	22%

Source: H. Assael and H. Cannon, Do demographics help in media selection? *Journal of Advertising Research,* 1979, *19* (6), 7–11, by permission.

in media, this improvement obviously can make the difference between an unprofitable and a profitable campaign.

The absolute level of accuracy in media selection—even with direct matching, which suggests that "half the exposures are wasted"—reinforces our earlier point that media strategy is as important as creative strategy in determining the success of advertising. Certainly there is little reason to waste so many expensive exposures by using the traditional demographic matching method.

Exceptions to the Need for Direct Matching   Occasional exceptions to the need to measure target audience media exposure directly might occur with local retail re-advertisers and with industrial advertisers. These two types of advertising were discussed in Chapter 15. Demographic matching is suitable in part:

- For local retail re-advertisers. The *product* advertising medium usually will be the local newspaper—a choice of only one vehicle, that is, no choice at all and no difference between demographic and direct matching, or in some larger cities, two vehicles, where the demographic match may be obvious and sufficient. However, if the local retailer is also seeking a *store image* advertising medium, then direct matching would indeed help to decide between, for example, local TV stations, local radio stations, city magazines, or direct mail.
- For industrial advertisers. The *product* advertising target audience in many cases is so tightly contained within a particular industry or occupational "demographic" that a more direct measurement becomes unnecessary. However, larger industrial advertisers—and especially those using *corporate image* advertising aimed at upper-level decision makers as an umbrella for specific product advertising—have a considerably broader set of vehicle options, and here, direct matching would be an advantage.

The national consumer products advertiser, on the other hand, almost always can develop a more accurate media plan by employing direct matching rather than demographic matching.

How to Gather Direct Matching Data

Direct matching data on media exposure can be gathered during the quantitative advertising strategy phase of research, simultaneously with the awareness, attitude, and behavior data used to define the target audience, by including a section on media exposure in the questionnaire (see Part Eight).

Alternatively, *a separate media exposure study* can be conducted. It is worth conducting a separate media exposure study if media exposure data were not collected during the quantitative advertising strategy research. In fact, it is more efficient to conduct a separate study on media exposure after one or more target audiences have been identified from the strategy research because, now, awareness-attitude-behavior "marker" variables can be used to briefly screen target audience groups, leaving more time for detailed media exposure recording. This type of study can be conducted for the equivalent price of about two national TV commercial insertions—say about $100,000. The resulting direct matching data almost surely will save many times that amount in increased media plan accuracy.

Panel Method (Diary) is Best   The best method for data collection is through the use of a consumer panel (see Chapter 4) where consumers maintain diary records of their media exposure. Continuous diary measures are more reliable than one-shot questionnaires or interview measures, because memory for media exposure, like memory for brand purchases, is not highly accurate. Also, the advertiser may wish to investigate a very large number of media vehicle options. It is easy for respondents using a diary to indicate these options, because the vehicles are arranged by day and daypart.

Further, the media planner wishes to know *how often* each vehicle is watched, listened to, or read, so that vehicle exposure frequency can be related to effective advertising exposure. Vehicle exposure frequency is more accurately recorded in the diary panel methodology than by a one-shot estimate of recalled or estimated frequency of exposure. One-shot estimates overstate diary records for TV program viewing frequency by about 20 percent (for example, 5 rather than 4 exposures) and for "educational" programs like news or documentaries by at least double (for example, 2 rather than 1 exposure).[8] The diary record of media vehicle exposure should be kept for at least one and preferably two or three purchase cycles (for reliability).

One-shot Questionnaires: Media Types Are Satisfactory for Broadcast Media but Specific Vehicles Should Be Listed for Print Media   On a questionnaire or personal interview, specific media vehicle options can be very time-consuming to go through. In an attempt to short-cut this problem, some researchers have advocated the use of broad vehicle *types,* to which similar vehicles can then be related. For TV, for example, vehicle types might be movies, westerns, sit-coms, and so forth.[9]

The use of vehicle types may be fairly satisfactory for broadcast media, because these media are "free" to the audience and there is virtually no limit, for instance, on the number of TV movies an individual viewer may choose to watch.

A more accurate alternative for one-shot TV exposure, we have found, is to photocopy the previous week's TV guide listings and have respondents check off the programs they watched and state how often they've watched them in the last 4 weeks. For movies and specials, which are one-time showings, the question has to be modified to refer to "this type of program." This method seems more accurate than complete reliance on TV program types.

Radio stations can be quickly narrowed down from a list to those stations the respondent listens to—usually no more than six. These can then be asked by daypart to gauge frequency of station exposure. Again, this seems more accurate than "station types."

The use of vehicle types is not appropriate for print media because these vehicles are not free and there is a substitution effect. For instance, among the newsweeklies type of magazine, most individuals are unlikely to subscribe to both *Time* and *Newsweek*. With print media, all the individual vehicles must be listed.

"Single-Source" Syndicated Services Are Too General   Syndicated services that supply media and product data on the same sample of respondents— hence the name "single-source" data—are not, in most cases, a satisfactory substitute for a customized media exposure study. Services such as SMRB in the United States, or TGI in the United Kingdom, for example, provide cross-tabulations between brand usage (heavy, medium, light, non-users) and media vehicle audiences.

However, as we have seen in our discussion of target audience definition in Part Three, neither category usage nor single-brand usage can provide sufficient definition of a target audience for advertising. For advertising, an awareness, attitude, and usage (behavior) definition must be used to identify the prospective target audience groups as in Chapter 4. Syndicated services cannot provide this degree of target audience definition.

It would be possible, from category usage data, to identify non-category users, if the target audience for the campaign happens to be NCUs. But without the accompanying awareness and attitude data, which are not provided by these services, we could not identify positive, neutral, or negatively disposed (potential) new category users for more precise targeting.

Similarly, in a very stable and established category, it may be tempting to infer that users of a particular brand are the brand's brand loyals. However, users of a brand consist of brand loyals and brand switchers. To identify the proportion of brand switchers in the brand user group would require special analysis of the syndicated data to see which other brands are used by the brand's users. This special analysis is hardly ever done because it is expensive. Also, if it is done, it assumes that usage subsumes attitude, which doesn't give a good indication of the attitudinal vulnerability of a particular user group.

The other problem with syndicated single-source data is on the media side. While cross-tabulations of category or brand usage are provided against single media vehicles, it again requires a special, expensive analysis to extract exposure to multiple vehicles (for example, to a combination of three magazines). Moreover, broadcast media exposure are provided in extremely general categories—heavy to light TV viewing and radio listening—not by TV programs or radio stations.

In conclusion, single-source syndicated service data such as SMRB or TGI are too general for anything other than a rough idea of which media grossly defined target audiences are exposed to. The only alternative for the specificity of media planning advocated in this book is a customized media exposure study using either a panel, preferably, or a one-shot questionnaire survey.

Data Analysis for Direct Matching

The basic data analysis for direct matching consists of cross-tabulations.[10] First, you cross-tabulate target audience membership with the frequency of exposures to each vehicle. An example is shown in Table 17.2. If there is only one target audience, a frequency count can replace the cross-tabulation.[11] Vehicles with zero or very low frequencies of exposure to the chosen target audience can then be eliminated immediately.

This leaves you, usually, with several medium- to high-frequency vehicles for each suitable medium (unsuitable *media,* of course, would have been knocked out earlier in the primary and secondary media selection process as explained in Chapter 15). With luck, you might find one vehicle that delivers MEF on its own. However, typically you will need more than one vehicle to deliver MEF. Also, to extend reach at MEF (effective reach), you will need more than one vehicle.

The next step, therefore, is to compute what might be called *multiple cross-tabs*. This is easiest to see by beginning with a simple, two-vehicle case. From Table 17.2, let's say we're considering *Monday Night Football* and *Time* magazine for reaching brand loyals. If we cross-tabulate the brand loyals' exposure frequencies to these two vehicles, we get a joint frequency table as in Table 17.3. If the MEF in the purchase cycle (3 weeks) is 2 exposures, there are several ways a brand loyal could get these (2+) exposures: either all in one vehicle or some in one and some in the other. Only those brand loyals in the (1,0), (0,1), and (0,0) cells could not get 2+ exposures.

TABLE 17-2   SINGLE-VEHICLE EXPOSURE CROSS-TABULATION FOR TWO TARGET AUDIENCES

Number of exposures to ABC's *Monday Night Football* in purchase cycle (3 weeks)	Target audiences	
	Brand loyals (%)	Brand switchers (%)
3	20	5
2	20	10
1	30	15
0	30	70
	100%	100%

Number of exposures to *Time* magazine in purchase cycle (3 weeks)	Target audiences	
	Brand loyals (%)	Brand switchers (%)
3	10	15
2	5	5
1	10	5
0	75	75
	100%	100%

In Table 17.3, it can be seen that if we placed the advertisement 3 times in *Monday Night Football* during 3 consecutive weeks and 3 times in *Time* magazine in the same 3 weeks, the effective reach of this two-vehicle plan for this purchase cycle would be 50 percent of brand loyals. (It is convenient in these examples to work with percentages. But we urge the use of raw numbers— it's too easy in media planning for the base to be forgotten when working with "percent reach." So, for example, if we project from our advertising strategy research sample that there are 10 million brand loyals in the United States, the effective reach for this purchase cycle would be 5 million.)

Now let's assume that we want 60 percent effective reach. Thus, we have to add a third vehicle. We go back to our initial cross-tabulation or frequency distribution for brand loyals and pick another vehicle with high single-vehicle exposure frequency. Let's say it's *Sports Illustrated,* another magazine. To find the three-way exposure frequency, we now have a three-way cross-tabulation.

The quick way to calculate the efective reach of three (or more) vehicles is not actually to compute these multi-way cross-tabulations but rather to directly compute the *joint frequency distribution*—that is, of *Monday Night Football* plus *Time* plus *Sports Illustrated.*[12] The frequency count of 2 exposures and above then gives you the effective reach of the multi-vehicle plan. The example is carried through for completeness in Table 17.4.

On the computer, much more elaborate variations of the multi-vehicle plan can be tried. For example, the effective reach of putting only 2 insertions in each vehicle (rather than the 3 assumed above) can be estimated. A computer program for this purpose, using direct matching data, has recently been developed by Craig and Ghosh.[13]

Also, the cost of the advertising placements can be figured in. As we shall see in the next section, this is where the ubiquitous "cost-per-thousand" (CPM) statistic breaks down. For instance, the CPM total audience figure for *Monday Night Football* might be considerably higher than the CPM total audience figure for *Time* magazine, so conventional CPM analysis would favor *Time.* But *Monday Night Football* reaches more of the *target* audience than does *Time,* so it isn't this simple. As we shall see, profitability should govern the final vehicle selection process.

TABLE 17-3   CROSS-TABULATION OF BRAND LOYALS' JOINT EXPOSURES TO TWO MEDIA VEHICLES

Number of exposures to *Monday Night Football* (3 weeks)	Number of exposures to *Time* magazine (3 weeks)				
	3	2	1	0	
3	0	5	1	14	(20)
2	2	0	4	14	(20)
1	3	0	2	25*	(30)
0	5	0	3	22	(30)
	(10)	(5)	(10)	(75)	(100)

* Italicized cells receive less than 2 MEF exposures.

TABLE 17-4   JOINT FREQUENCY DISTRIBUTION OF EXPOSURES FOR THREE
MEDIA VEHICLES (BRAND LOYALS)

Number of exposures to *Monday Night Football*, *Time*, and *Sports Illustrated* (3 weeks)	Percent of brand loyals exposed	
9	0	
8	1	
7	2	
6	3	60%
5	8	2+ reach
4	13	
3	15	
2	18	
1	20	
0	20	
	100%	

The Duplication Problem Revisited   As we explained at the beginning of the chapter, duplication of the individual's exposures to the same vehicle on a repeated basis within the purchase cycle or to other vehicles considered in the media plan is essential for calculating effective reach (number of different individuals reached in the purchase cycle at at least the minimum effective frequency level). Direct matching *solves* the duplication problem by measuring duplication directly. Direct matching directly records frequency of exposure to each vehicle, and thus to combinations of vehicles, at the individual level. As described above, the media planner then tries several combinations of high target audience reach vehicles to determine which combination delivers the minimum effective frequency level to the largest number of individuals— thereby maximizing effective reach.

For the media planner *not* using direct matching, duplication has to be indirectly estimated. This poses a substantial problem for TV stations and programs, radio stations and dayparts, and magazines, when there are many vehicle options for the target audience. Within media types, advanced media planners employ duplication formulae such as the beta-binomial formula or the multinomial Dirichlet formula,[14] whereas others merely guess at duplication or do not allow for it at all.

Moreover, duplication formulae only estimate the *media* audience duplication within and across vehicles. They do not give you *target* audience duplication, which is what is needed. A far easier procedure, quite obviously, is to employ direct matching and thereby obtain target audience duplication directly in the resulting media plan.

Strategic Use of Direct Matching

NPD Research Company has shown how direct matching data on target audiences can be used strategically by a brand.[15] In a hypothetical example, let's assume our brand is Procter & Gamble's Tide detergent, and that we are advertising in magazines (although this can be done for any media) with a brand recognition/low involvement/informational communication model.

With direct matching data we can set up quadrants (Figure 17.2) where the dimensions are: (1) high effective reach to users of Tide; and (2) high effective reach to users of other brands of detergent, with all brands lumped together as "Other." The opposite ends of the dimensions are zero or very low effective reach to Tide users and Other users, respectively.

Strategically, now, we could deliver one creative message to Tide brand loyals (such as brief reminder ads) via *Glamour* or *Star* magazines; another creative message (such as an ad with a multi-pack rebate) to favorable brand switchers via *Woman's Day, People,* or *Enquirer;* another to other-brand loyals and unfavorable switchers (say a hard-sell comparative ad) via *Family Circle, Good Housekeeping,* or *Ladies' Home Journal;* and still another to potential new category users (perhaps with a coupon reply for a sample in the mail) via *Redbook, McCall's, Ebony,* or *Seventeen.*

FIGURE 17.2   Example (hypothetical) of strategic use of direct matching for magazine vehicles. (Adapted from *Insights,* Port Washington, NY: NPD Research Inc., 1983, p. 19, by permission.)

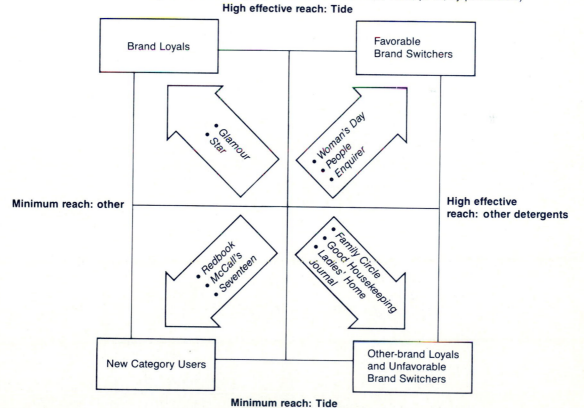

NPD's direct matching example is for magazines, which many media planners would contend are the most "audience-specific" media vehicles. However, media vehicle differences in target audience reach by direct matching occur also for television, which is often thought to be the most general or "mass" medium. Eskin[16] reports examples of TV programs that have very high reach to instant coffee category users (brand switchers and other-brand loyals) yet very low reach to regular users of a particular brand (brand loyals) and vice versa. Some of these programs are shown in Figure 17.3. Thus, it is possible to use direct matching for strategic purposes even in a mass medium like television.

Not all examples may turn out this clearly in terms of the divisions between media vehicles by target audience. However, such analyses are worth doing with direct matching data. They cost little, and if vehicle differences emerge, the potential payoff for advertising strategy against competitors is large. We may note that such precise strategic selection of media vehicles would be impossible with the demographic matching method of media vehicle selection.

FIGURE 17.3   Example (actual) of strategic use of direct marketing for television vehicles. (Adapted from the article by G.J. Eskin, Tracking advertising and promotion performance with single-source data, *Journal of Advertising Research*, 1985, 25(1), 31, 33–39, by permission.)

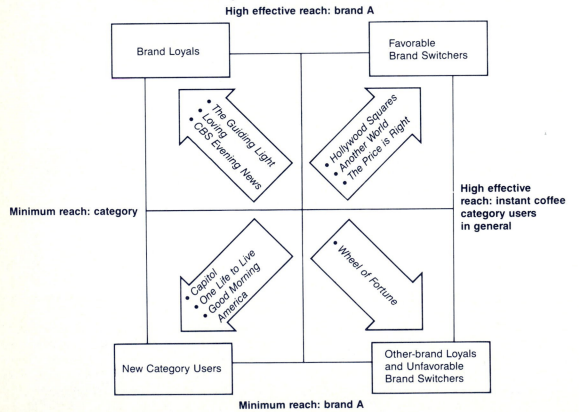

ADJUSTMENT FACTORS FOR SECOND-STAGE MEDIA VEHICLE SELECTION

Effective reach is the most important criterion in media vehicle selection but it is not the only one. From the first-stage list of vehicles selected by direct matching or alternatively by demographic or psychographic matching, we can make further adjustments based on "qualitative" considerations concerning each vehicle. There are five main factors for which adjustments can be made:

1 *Vehicle Environment Effects on Ads* Certain vehicles may be more, or less, compatible with the brand's advertising and thus make it more, or less, effective even with target audience reach held constant.

2 *Competing Ads in the Vehicle* The presence of competitors' ads in the same vehicle may inhibit our ad's effectiveness.

3 *Timing of Vehicle* The time at which the vehicle reaches the typical target audience member may be either inopportune or opportune from the standpoint of the ad's effectiveness.

4 *Impact Scheduling* We may be able to increase effective reach (reach at MEF) by placing more than one ad in a single vehicle.

5 *Advertisement Unit Effects* The length (broadcast) and size (print) of the advertisements to be used in the media plan may produce differing attention levels *regardless* of creative content and are therefore a media consideration that can affect MEF delivery.

But before we review these adjustment factors and recommend which ones to adjust for and when, what do we mean by "adjustment"? How can "qualitative" factors be allowed for in media vehicle selection?

Qualitative Adjustments Become Quantitative

Qualitative factors become quantitative when applied to the media plan. Although the causes of hypothesized media vehicle superiority or inferiority may be qualitative, the effect on the media plan is quantitative.

In the extreme case, which is not uncommon, media vehicles such as TV programs or magazines are added to, or more often deleted from, a plan purely on the basis of a manager's judgment about the vehicle's compatibility or incompatibility with the brand's advertising. For example, when the nuclear disaster TV movie, *"The Day After,"* was first televised in late 1983, family advertisers such as McDonald's refused to advertise in it even though the program was watched by an estimated 46 percent of the nation's homes and would have had very high target audience reach.

Deletion or addition of vehicles on a purely qualitative judgment is equivalent, quantitatively, to applying *zero-one weights* to vehicle selection. Zero-one weights are radically quantitative, and managers had best be sure that such vehicles do have the hypothesized radically negative or positive effect on their advertising, because, in the deletion situation, they are overriding vehicles that have appeared in the plan because of their high reach to the target audience, and in the addition situation, they are adding vehicles that otherwise would not have been used because of low target audience reach.

The alternative method of allowing for qualitative factors also is quantitative. This is to apply *indexed weights* to each vehicle based on its expected compatibility or incompatibility with the brand's advertising. Average vehicles are given a weight or index of 1.0, then compatible vehicles may be weighted up to a maximum of, say, 2.0, with incompatible vehicles weighted down from 1.0 to as low as 0.0.

Operationally, the effect of indexed weights is *to adjust the vehicle's contribution to effective frequency*. A moderately positive vehicle with a weight of 1.5, for example, may be regarded as contributing "1.5 exposures" to MEF, whereas a moderately negative vehicle may be regarded as contributing "0.5 of an exposure." If both vehicles are used, they together would contribute 2 exposures to the MEF level. Because of the difficulty of thinking in terms of fractional exposures, and the specialized computer program required to apply the weights, such weighting schemes are not used in practice as widely as they should be. Theoretically, they are the correct way to incorporate qualitative judgments in media vehicle selection.

Under what circumstances should qualitative adjustments be made? Let us now assess the evidence for the five adjustment factors.

Vehicle Environment Effects on Ads

Vehicle environment effects fall into three common classes as well as an interesting and extreme fourth class. The research evidence for each of these effects, while not as extensive as we would like, is nevertheless too detailed to summarize here.[17] Instead, we present our suggestions from this evidence.

1 *Likable Vehicles*   No adjustment; likability is already reflected in vehicle exposure frequency obtained in direct matching.[18]

2 *Dislikable Vehicles*   Delete extreme negative (depressing or distressing) vehicles from the plan *if* the advertising is high involvement/transformational or if immediate action is required, such as usage. For all other types of advertising, retain such vehicles.

3 *Prestigious Vehicles*   No adjustment; there is no good evidence that any types of ads work better in more prestigious or high quality vehicles.

4 *Design or Adapt Ads to Suit Vehicles*   No; the evidence favors the hypothesis that an ad already designed for the *target* audience will work virtually anywhere. There is no payoff in redesigning ads for the respective *vehicle* audiences.

Qualitative vehicle effects imply that the vehicle's *contribution to effective frequency for those reached* should be up-weighted or down-weighted accordingly or, in the extreme zero-one application of weights, that the vehicle should be deleted from or added to the plan. This is necessary in only one case above.

Competing Ads in the Vehicle

Is the presence of competing ads a serious problem in media vehicle selection in the vehicle? On an average day, the average TV viewer watches 4½ hours of TV, and even college-educated viewers watch about 3 hours daily![19] At the current prime-time rate of about 18 commercials per hour, this amounts to about 80 potential commercial exposures per night for the average viewer, and about 54 for the college-educated viewer. Many of these commercials will be for competing brands.

Similarly, leafing through a copy of *House Beautiful,* or *Redbook,* the magazine reader is likely to be exposed to 100 or so ads, many for competing brands.

Whereas all ads in a media vehicle to some extent compete with each other for the viewer's, listener's, or reader's attention, producing what is commonly known as "clutter," we have concluded (in Chapter 8) that competition for *attention* is *not* in most cases a serious problem.[20] This is because an ad demands only micro-seconds of an audience member's time to pay the ad reflexive attention, and only a second or two more to pay selective attention. Only in retail advertising or Yellow Pages advertising, where there are *simultaneous demands* on the person's attention due to multiple ads on the same page, should competition for attention pose any problem—and here, the ad that best elicits reflexive attention, through its mechanical elements, usually wins the attention battle.

Rather, the main problem caused by competing ads occurs in the *learning* phase of processing. The problem is known as *interference.*[21] Interference occurs for:

1 *Brand Recall*[22]   when the consumer is faced with learning two or more different responses (brand names or packages) to the same stimulus or originating cue (the category need).

2 *Low Involvement Brand Attitude*   where again the consumer is faced with learning which (different) brand names or packages possess which (similar) benefits.

As this learning-based explanation reveals, the real problem is one of *brand competition* in ads in the vehicle, not competition between ads in general in the vehicle.

Learning experiments indicate an increase in brand recall interference, the more often two or more to-be-learned responses (Coke, Pepsi, R-C) one presented in conjunction with the same stimulus (cola beverages) are presented together. The interference extends backwards and forwards and affects each brand.

Low involvement/*informational* brand attitude is mainly subject to interference during the first few exposures in which it is being learned; once learned, it becomes quite resistant to competitive interference, provided that there are at least occasional learning reminders in the form of continuing ads to maintain the attitude. Low involvement/*transformational* brand attitude, in contrast, is continually subject to interference because of the larger frequency of exposures necessary prior to acquisition and the somewhat tentative positive-affect conditioning process which maintains the attitude. Indeed, all transformational brand attitudes are sensitive to competition (hence the LC + 1 correction factor for transformational brand attitude when estimating media frequency) but the low involvement type is interfered with by learning whereas the high involvement type is more sensitive to the acceptance strength of competing ads rather than just their number.

The cause of interference with brand recall and low involvement brand attitude is *not the proximity* of competing brands' ads (since time is not a causal factor in verbal interference[22]) but rather their *competitive frequency,* relative to our brand, in the *overall purchase cycle,* That is, it is the number of competitors' ads that matters, not how close they are to ours.

The foregoing analysis leads to the conclusion that the only situations in which advertisers should worry about competing ads in the vehicle are:

- In retail advertising and Yellow Pages advertising when there is simultaneous competition for attention on the same page (here the solution is to use a reflexive attention-getting creative execution, not to avoid the vehicle)
- When only one or two vehicles are available to deliver MEF in the purchase cycle, and competitors face the same vehicle selection constraint (this happens mainly with newspapers and specialized consumer or trade magazines).

The latter case is a problem. The advertiser cannot really avoid such vehicles, because they are likely to have the largest reach to the target audience, which is why they attract so many competitors. We would estimate that the interference effect when there is at least one other competitor in the vehicle is sufficient to halve an ad's contribution to MEF; that is, each exposure contibutes only 0.5 to MEF. Thus, the recommended procedure is to double the number of our ads in these unavoidable but competitive vehicles.

Under more normal circumstances, characteristic of most TV, radio and other consumer media plans, the delivery of MEF in the purchase cycle is not highly dependent on any one or two media vehicles. Neither the number of competing ads in any one vehicle nor, as we have seen, the proximity of these ads to ours in the vehicle, should matter. The only thing that matters is relative frequency over the *entire* purchase cycle, for brand recall and for low involvement brand attitude. Consequently, the advertiser should make no allowance for competing ads when selecting media vehicles for normal media plans.

Timing of Vehicle

Another potential factor in making second-stage adjustments to the initial list of media vehicles is the timing of the vehicle. Certain vehicles in various media tend to be avoided because they reach the target audience at a particularly unsuitable time; whereas, certain other vehicles are widely believed to have a timing *advantage* in terms of when exposure occurs in relation to purchase or purchase-related action opportunities.

All media types have timing options to some extent, as described in Appendix B at the end of this book:

- *TV*   dayparts and specific programs within dayparts.
- *Radio*   dayparts including, notably, drive-time versus in-home listening.
- *Newspapers*   morning versus evening newspapers.
- *Magazines*   much less patterned in timing although a division might be made between office or "work" reading versus home or "leisure" reading in terms of types of magazines.
- *Outdoor*   time of day the outdoor (or indoor) display is usually passed or encountered; also timing in the sense of mobile versus stationary time of exposure duration.
- *Miscellaneous Media*   time of day the medium is encountered; also, perhaps, non-pressured versus pressured situations, such as p-o-p ads encountered in stores or supermarkets during peak periods.

Vehicles to Avoid for High Involvement Brand Choice   Considering, first, vehicles to avoid because they tend to reach the target audience at an unsuitable time, we see that this depends almost entirely on the type of brand attitude the advertising is trying to achieve. (Brand awareness, a rote-learned response, should not be affected by the time at which exposure occurs.) As we saw in Chapter 8, on processing, *high involvement* brand attitude formation or change is facilitated by positive thoughts or cognitive responses and is inhibited by negative thoughts or cognitive responses during processing. This was one of the main reasons, in Chapter 5 (profiling the target audience decision maker), that we advised assessing the decision maker's likely personality state during exposure. In particular:

1 For *complex* (high involvement/informational) products, vehicles should be deleted that reach the target audience when a majority of such individuals are in one or more of the following moods:
   a Tired
   b Anxious
   c "Low I.Q." state, for example, hangover

2 For *expensive luxury* (high involvement/transformational) products, vehicles that reach the target audience decision maker in a "leisure" state for weekends or just before or during typical vacation periods) probably should be up-weighted (say, to the equivalent of 2.0 exposures).

An interesting situation arises with the advertising of *food* products that include the motive of sensory gratification. These could be high involvement for a target audience that would be trying a new food product for the first time. Television, of course, is a major medium for new food products. However, should you avoid advertising during prime-time after the target audience has just eaten?

It so happens that, although normal-weight consumers may be turned off by food ads after they've recently eaten, overweight consumers—who may be heavy users in more ways than one—tend to be more excited by food stimuli the more recently they've eaten, a sort of "can't-stop-eating" phenomenon.[24] Thus, food commercials should work well right through prime-time preceding and following the dinner hour and, for daytime TV, the breakfast or lunch hour.

Vehicles to Seek for Immediate-action Advertising   An important minority of advertising campaigns are those intended to stimulate immediate action, with either a purchase-related or direct purchase action objective. For immediate-action advertising, it makes obvious sense to seek vehicles whose timing (1) capitalizes on category need and (2) allows the best opportunity for brand purchase intentions to be carried out in the form of purchase or purchase-related action.

The three most common immediate-action advertising situations are:

1 *Retail Shopping Opportunity Ads*   Vehicles that reach the target audience just prior to shopping trips or on the way to shopping (outdoor, or drive-time radio) should be favored by retailers.

2 *Usage Reminder Ads*   Ads timed to coincide with usage opportunities include, for example, serving suggestion ads before meal-times, beer ads at ball games or during sports programs, or credit card ads in stores.

3 *Direct Response Ads*   Vehicles that reach the target audience when they are near to a phone or a pen and are likely to have the time to make the response should be most advantageous for direct response advertisers.

Such vehicles, which can be elicited easily with the use of a behavioral sequence model (Chapter 5), should, in our opinion, be up-weighted to an MEF contribution of 2.0. This will have the effect of causing ideal-timing vehicles to dominate the media plan, which they should for immediate-action campaigns. Whereas communication effects can be transmitted at other times, the likelihood of maximizing all five communication effects is greatest when using the category need and brand purchase intention-maximizing vehicles.

Overall, then, we see that vehicle timing is a relevant media vehicle selection-list adjustment factor if brand choice entails a high involvement purchase decision, or if immediate action is called for, or both.

Impact Scheduling in a Single Vehicle

For brands whose minimum effective frequency requirement in the purchase cycle is high—for instance, a new brand facing an "outer" target audience of new category users or other-brand loyals, or any brand with brand recall and transformational brand attitude communication objectives—impact scheduling should be considered. As defined previously, impact scheduling is the practice of repeating the ad several times in the one vehicle on a single occasion, such as a commercial repeated three times in the TV program *60 Minutes* on a given Sunday, or the same ad (or better still, with a slight variation) run twice in the one issue of *Newsweek*.

When Lacoste entered the Australian market in late 1982, for example, they impact-scheduled three "teaser" ads in the one issue of Australia's national newspaper (Figure 17.4). The "record" number of insertions that we have observed in a single vehicle is 13. In the October 31, 1983, issue of *The New*

FIGURE 17.4   An example of impact scheduling. These teaser ads for Lacoste appeared on separate pages in a single issue of *The Australian* newspaper when Lacoste entered the Australian market in October 1982. Note the slight variation in copy, as recommended in Chapter 8, to maintain attention. (Courtesy Sportscraft Consolidated Pty, Ltd.)

The most sought after crocodile in the world.

Crocodilus Lacoste. *Origin of species:* Genus originated in France but first official sighting recorded at Singles Tennis Finals in Forest Hills. USA in 1926. Since sighted in rapidly increasing numbers at major sporting and social events around the world. Now surfacing at select locations throughout Australia.

The most sought after crocodile in the world.

Crocodilus Lacoste. *Identifying marks:* Only ½" in length. Vibrant green in colour with large red mouth. Hence also known as "Laughing Crocodile". A prized trophy in the sporting world. Now surfacing at select locations throughout Australia.

The most sought after crocodile in the world.

Crocodilus Lacoste. *Habitats:* Known to frequent major sporting and social events throughout the world. Always certain to be spotted at International Tennis tournaments, usually in the company of famous personalities. Now surfacing at select locations throughout Australia.

Yorker, London Fog placed 13 consecutive quarter-page ads, each featuring a different London Fog clothing item, with a common corporate theme.

Most media will accept multiple insertions in the one vehicle, although there may be a practical upper limit, especially for broadcast media where time cannot be added, unlike space in a magazine or newspaper.

Impact scheduling is basically in keeping with the media strategy principle that it is better to sell some people completely than many people not at all. However, as briefly discussed next, its advantages have to be weighed against its disadvantages.

Advantages of Impact Scheduling   Impact scheduling sacrifices overall reach, but for the same number of insertions, it tends to maximize effective reach (reach at effective frequency). Let us suppose, for instance, that the minimum effective frequency for a brand is estimated to be 3 exposures over a two-week purchase cycle. Three commercials placed in one program of *60 Minutes* would deliver more people at the effective frequency level than placing one commercial a week for three weeks in *60 Minutes* (Figure 17.5). The average

FIGURE 17.5   Example of how impact scheduling tends to maximize effective reach (see also limitations in text). Two-week purchase cycle with MEF = 3.

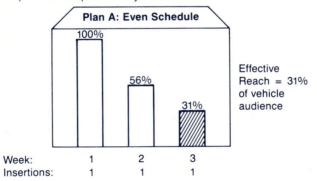

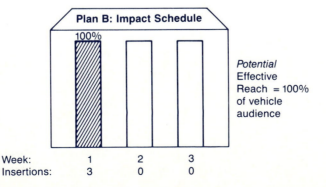

repeat viewing figure for weekly programs is about 56 percent[25], so immediately the second week's insertion has lost 44 percent of the first week's individuals. The three-week repeat viewing incidence is 56 percent of 56 percent, or only 31 percent. This compares very poorly with the close to 100 percent, allowing for some partial viewing of the program, who attained the effective frequency level of 3 exposures under the impact schedule.

For a low-frequency vehicle in which the vehicle frequency is longer than or equal to the purchase cycle (for example, a monthly magazine with a monthly or shorter purchase cycle), impact scheduling is the *only* way for that vehicle to achieve an MEF requirement that is 2 or more exposures per purchase cycle.

Limitations of Impact Scheduling As is true for most media strategy decisions, there are trade-offs to be considered with impact scheduling. One limitation is the increase in average delay between exposure and the individual's purchase opportunity. In the *60 Minutes* even schedule, the average delay would be $3\frac{1}{2}$ days, whereas for the impact schedule it is $1\frac{1}{2}$ weeks—over twice as long as for the separate weekly ads.[26]

The effect of this delay depends on the amount of competitive activity in the delay period (again for the average individual). It is impossible to pin an exact number on this but, generally speaking, the greater the frequency of competitors' ads, the less effective impact scheduling will be.[27] However, compared with the drastic loss of reach at effective frequency for *high frequency brands,* as in the *60 Minutes* example, the net outcome is very likely to favor impact scheduling.

Another limitation is the probable loss of attention when an ad is repeated at short intervals, either in broadcast or print vehicles. The loss is somewhat less for TV because of its intrusive or captivating nature, but attentional wearout through the tedium factor (see Chapter 20) is likely to be increased in any medium. Although somewhat more expensive, the creative solution to this is to use slightly different ads (variations on a theme). The Lacoste ads in Figure 17.4, earlier, illustrate this creative technique. By varying the content slightly, attention loss with an impact schedule should be lessened.

The *smaller* the budget, the more impact scheduling is favored. A really large budget advertiser, with a very expandable "balloon," can afford to buy effective frequency, very high reach, *and* continuity without resorting to impact scheduling (at the upper limit the advertiser approaches a continuous impact schedule in all vehicles). However, for advertisers with a more typically limited budget who in vain try to stretch reach and thereby fall below MEF, impact scheduling is an effective strategy.

MEF Adjustment for Impact Scheduling What should the MEF adjustment for impact scheduling be? Obviously it is conditional on the factors mentioned above, notably competitive interference, but the following general guideline seems appropriate. The first exposure in an impact sequence should contribute the normal 1.0 to MEF. If varied executions are used, the second and subsequent exposures should also come close to 1.0—perhaps even a bit above, as the audience remembers the previous exposure, somewhat like imagery transfer—*but* the delay to purchase opportunity is longer. Overall, an average estimate is 0.5 for second and subsequent exposures. Safely, the advertiser should assume *3* insertions for every 2.0 exposures contributed to MEF.

Advertisement Unit Effects

The "unit" or "units" of advertising—different ad lengths or sizes, color, and several other physical characteristics apart from the creative content of the ad itself—are a fourth possible adjustment factor. For instance, if a 30-second TV commercial contributes 1 exposure to the MEF level required, does a 60-second commercial contribute the equivalent of 2 exposures? Similarly, does a half-page magazine ad contribute 0.5 of an exposure compared with the normal one-page size? The answer to both questions is "not exactly." But the particular ad units used in the media plan do have an effect on effective frequency. In this section we will see which ad unit dimensions matter and how to adjust for them. *Whether* to adjust is a question we'll consider shortly.

Notice that we adjust only for *initial attention* attributable to differing ad units—*not* for the subsequent performance of different ad units in producing *communication effects.* Different lengths or sizes of ads do differ in communication effectiveness. The differences are not surprising, because larger (longer) or smaller (shorter) ads are completely different in terms of:

- The sorts of target audiences they are aimed at (for example, new category users versus brand loyals)
- The products they are used for (for example, new versus established brands)
- Communication objectives (for example, all five communication effects versus the basic two of brand awareness and brand attitude)
- The length of copy or audio permitted (and thus brand awareness and brand attitude benefit mentions), and
- In print, the picture-word ratio varies with ad size

Therefore, it is spurious to try to compare advertising units in terms of communication effectiveness because different units are used for quite different communication purposes.

The advertising unit or units should be selected by the creative director, based on target audience type and communication objectives. The media planner then adjusts only for the *ad unit's or units' physical ability to gain initial attention,* as this factor (just like media vehicle attention earlier) will alter the attained MEF level.

Initial Attention Adjustment Measures   In Appendix C at the end of the book, we have presented our "best estimate" adjustments for advertising units in six major media: television, radio, newspapers, consumer magazines, business and industrial magazines, and outdoor.

In Appendix C, we have assumed that advertising units have to make at least a *20 percent* (plus or minus 0.2) difference to initial attention before they are worth adjusting for. A 20-percent increase in attention, for instance, means that five units of that type are equivalent in MEF to six standard advertising units, in terms of initial attention-gaining capability.

Should you adjust MEF for advertising units? The main reason we have placed ad unit adjustments in an appendix is that, in most cases, such adjustments to MEF may be beyond what is needed for an effective media schedule. Advertisers thinking of placing just a few ads may use them (such as an industrial advertiser wondering whether a double-page spread to announce a new product is worthwhile). So also should advertisers using sustained *non-standard unit* campaigns (such as many short commercials aimed at brand loyals). But for most advertisers, the general MEF calculation itself is a sufficient control on media vehicle selection and to adjust further for advertising units would probably be "overkill."

PROFIT AND FINAL-STAGE MEDIA VEHICLE SELECTION

So far we have ignored the cost of placing an ad in the respective media vehicles as a consideration in vehicle selection. Cost (in relation to the budget) and expected profit constitute the final stage of media vehicle selection. As mentioned earlier, the advertiser essentially pays for the total *vehicle* audience when placing an ad in that vehicle, whereas the advertiser is interested in reaching only the *target* audience, within the total vehicle audience.

Furthermore, we assume that only individuals in the target audience are likely to buy the product. We will show how to easily adapt this assumption below.

Profitability of an Insertion or Multiple Insertions

The profitability of an advertisement placed in a vehicle can be calculated as follows:

1 Number of target audience individuals reached by the vehicle, *multiplied by*

2 The probability that the average target audience individual will buy the product, once reached, *multiplied by*

3 The profit contribution of one unit of the product, which is the unit selling price minus the unit cost of goods sold, other than the unit advertising cost (see Chapter 2), *minus*

4 The cost of the advertising insertion

For example, suppose an ad in *Reader's Digest* reaches one million target audience individuals; and their probability of buying, once reached, is 0.7; and the profit contribution per unit sold is $1.00; and the cost of the *Reader's Digest* ad is $200,000. The profit expected from this ad placement is then $1,000,000 \times 0.7 \times \$1.00 - \$200,000 = \$500,000$.

The tricky figure in this formula is "the probability of buying" from a single insertion. The idea of minimum effective frequency, of course, is to bring the target audience individual up to a *maximum predisposition* to buy. The maximum predisposition, represented here by a probability of 0.7, may require several insertions, perhaps in several vehicles, before the individual receives effective frequency. This is handled in the above formula by subtracting the total advertising cost of the *multiple* insertions.[28]

A vehicle may reach several target audiences of varying response potential. For instance, the ad may be directed at brand loyals, yet the vehicle may reach not only brand loyals, but also brand switchers and other-brand loyals. The ad may influence some of these latter individuals as well, but presumably not to the extent that brand loyals are influenced. This is handled in the above formula by repeating steps **1** and **2** for each target audience. For example, brand loyals may be assigned a purchase probability of 1.0; brand switchers, 0.5; and other-brand loyals, 0.1. The products of steps **1** and **2** are summed, and steps **3** and **4** are then carried through to calculate profitability.

Don't Use the CPM Method

Notice that the profitability criterion of media vehicle selection makes no reference to "cost-per-thousand," or CPM. The advertising cost per thousand *people* is a virtually useless statistic. Criticisms of the CPM method of media vehicle selection are:

- First, it is not just "people" who will buy the product but rather *target audience* people. Two vehicles could have an identical cost-per-thousand total audience but reach very different numbers or percentages of the target audience. This is the usual case with the possible exception only of very large mass audience vehicles such as the most popular family TV programs.
- Second, cost-per-thousand, or even cost-per-anything, is meaningless without considering revenue and profit.
- Third, ads are purchased for lump sum amounts, not for rates such as CPM, which are too abstract to be meaningful. The advertiser doesn't pay a "cost-per-thousand" but rather a lump sum amount for each insertion.

The vital statistics are: the number of target audience individuals reached, the profit contribution that comes from them if they buy the product (with the "if" quantified by a probability estimate), minus the cost of the advertising. For effective reach profitability, subtract the cost of multiple (MEF) insertions of the ad.

SUMMARY

Media vehicle selection—the selection of specific programs, publications, and so forth, in which the ads in the campaign actually will be placed—should proceed in three stages.

In *first-stage* media vehicle selection, we need to find a set of vehicles that not only *reach* the target audience but which in *combination,* achieving duplication of exposures either across vehicles or by repeating the ad in the same vehicle, provide as much reach as is affordable at the *effective frequency* level—that is, a set of vehicles that maximizes effective reach.

Direct matching is the best method of first-stage media vehicle selection. Direct matching measures which vehicles (a representative sample of) the target audience is exposed to and how often. It is worth a separate survey to gather direct matching data, as the increased accuracy in attaining effective reach will increase the profitability of the plan well above the survey cost.

By contrast, the usual method of demographic matching, except for industrial advertising, and the occasionally employed method of psychographic matching, both have low accuracy in reaching the target audience and do not provide duplication-of-exposure information for calculating whether effective frequency has been attained. These "indirect but easy" methods of media selection often are the source of where "half the money is wasted" in advertising.

Direct matching, the preferred method, also can be used strategically to select vehicles that allow different campaigns to be aimed at alternative target audiences. Of course, multiple target audience campaigns presume that each target audience has sufficient leverage to make multiple campaigns worthwhile and, in practice, no more than two simultaneous campaigns usually are run except by the very largest advertisers.

In *second-stage* media vehicle selection, the original list of vehicles from the first stage may be subjected to a series of adjustment factors for processing of advertising in the vehicle. These adjustments up-weight or down-weight the contribution of an advertising insertion in the vehicle to the required minimum effective frequency (MEF) level. An extreme down-weighting, a contribution of 0 to MEF, means deleting the vehicle. The adjustments are for: vehicle environment effects; competing ads in the vehicle; timing of the vehicle; multiple insertions in a single vehicle, known as impact scheduling; and advertising units to be used.

Vehicle environment effects are less important than most advertisers believe. In general, a good ad will work anywhere. However, there is one exception to this. Advertisers whose brand depends on normal depletion (immediate usage reminder) or positive (transformational) motivation should delete extremely negative-mood-inducing vehicles from the plan. On the other hand, the widespread practice of up-weighting vehicles whose program or editorial content appears to be "compatible" with the ad's content (or even including vehicles solely on this qualitative basis) receives virtually no support in the research literature and should not be followed.

Competing ads in the vehicle are a problem in only two circumstances. First, simultaneous demands on the consumer's attention can occur when *multiple ads appear on the same page,* as often happens in retail advertising and in Yellow Pages advertising. These vehicles cannot be avoided, and the solution is not a media one but a creative one, namely, make sure you use an attention-getting creative execution when using these vehicles. Second, interference occurs for *brand recall* and *low involvement brand attitude* learning when competing ads occur in the same purchase cycle. This is negligible for any one vehicle when the vehicle is one of many in the plan, but if the vehicle is one that you and the competitors must rely on to deliver a *high proportion of MEF* for the purchase cycle, because of its high target audience reach, then your ad's contribution to MEF will be approximately halved, to 0.5. So, if possible, double the number of your ads in such vehicles for brand recall or low involvement brand attitude. In all other media plans, make no allowance for competing ads when selecting media vehicles.

Timing of the vehicle with respect to the target audience's purchase or purchase-related action opportunity is a further potential adjustment factor. It should be used in the following circumstances. If the brand attitude strategy is high involvement/informational (a "complex" multi-attribute brand choice), delete vehicles that reach the target audience when most of these individuals are tired, anxious, or otherwise "non compos mentis." If the brand attitude strategy is high involvement/transformational (such as for a vacation or a new car), up-weight vehicles that reach a majority of the target audience in a "leisure state" to 2.0 (contributions to MEF) exposures.

Additionally, for ads in which immediate action is required, up-weighting (to 2.0 exposures, that is, a contribution of 2 to the required MEF) is appropriate in three circumstances: for retail shopping opportunity ads, up-weight vehicles that reach the target audience just prior to shopping trips or on the way to shopping; for usage reminder ads, up-weight vehicles timed to coincide with the usage opportunity; and for direct response ads, up-weight vehicles where the target audience has the time and opportunity (telephone or pen and paper) to respond immediately.

The fourth adjustment factor, when applicable, is for impact scheduling. The placement of an ad twice or more in a single vehicle on a single occasion (but done with slight executional variations) is an excellent way of increasing effective reach for a brand with a high MEF requirement. Because impact scheduling has the disadvantage of increasing the average delay between exposure and purchase opportunity, which allows competitive interference, we estimate close repetitions of the first exposure to be worth only about 0.5 of an exposure; that is, you need 3 impact-scheduled ads to get 2 MEF.

Advertising units—physical characteristics of the ad or ads to be used apart from the creative content *per se*—constitute a fifth possible adjustment factor. The advertising unit(s) should be selected by the creative director, in line with the brand's target audience and communication objectives, then adjusted for, if non-standard, by the media planner. The adjustments for advertising units are rather detailed and are summarized in Appendix C. Only with short or really unusual-unit campaigns is it actually worth making an adjustment for advertising units.

The *final stage* of media vehicle selection consists of comparing the effective reach of the plan with the budget. Per purchase cycle, the revenue expected from the insertions (*number* reached at effective frequency × probability of purchase or purchase-related action × profit contribution from that action) must exceed the cost of the insertions (totalled for the purchase cycle) and the overall cost over purchase cycles must be within the budget. Typically, ideal plans exceed the total budget, so calculations of the profitability of compromised plans with lower levels of effective reach are necessary.

NOTES

1 A somewhat better demographic match-up can be obtained by using *multiple demographics,* such as age, sex, income, education, occupation, and so forth, to profile both the target audience and prospective vehicle audiences. This can be done by using *index numbers* for each classification catgeory within each demographic variable, and then computing the sum of the absolute differences, or the squared differences (d^2), between the target audience index and the vehicle audience index across all the demographic categories or simply by computing a correlation coefficient between the two sets of index numbers.

Either d^2 or the conventional correlation coefficient is an improvement over the use of just one or two demographic variables, because these correlational approaches use more information and thus provide a better match.

Details of the multiple demographic index numbers approach can be found in J.Z. Sissors, Matching media with markets, *Journal of Advertising Research,* 1971, *11*(5), 39–43.

The biggest problem with the multiple demographic index numbers approach is that, whereas detailed demographic information may be available on the target audience side, it is rarely available for media vehicle audiences other than, perhaps, for magazine audiences. Simmons Market Research Bureau, for example, does not provide demographic data on TV programs but only on heavy-to-light viewing "quintiles" regardless of network or program.

A second problem is the computation. Only in the occasional instance outside academic studies are d^2 or correlations ever computed. And the computations are tedious to set up.

Finally, why go through this tedium when you can use direct matching?

2 See, for example, the many studies of correlates of brand loyalty cited in J.F. Engel and R.D. Blackwell, *Consumer Behavior* (4th ed.), New York: Dryden, 1983; and the work of A.S.C. Ehrenberg, *Repeat-Buying,* New York and Amsterdam: North-Holland, 1972. A recent example of lack of demographic discrimination in people's preferences for family restaurants can be seen in A.S. Boote, Market segmentation by personal values and salient product attributes, *Journal of Advertising Research,* 1981, *21*(1), 29–35.

3 W.D. Wells and D.J. Tigert, Activities, interests, and opinions, *Journal of Advertising Research,* 1971, *11*(4), 27–35.

4 N. Garfinkle, A marketing approach to media selection, *Journal of Advertising Research,* 1963, *3*(4), 7–15.

5 H. Assael and H.M. Cannon, Do demographics help in media selection? *Journal of Advertising Research,* 1979, *19*(6), 7–11.

6 F.W. Winter, Match target markets to media audiences, *Journal of Advertising Research,* 1980, *20*(1), 61–66.

7 R.I. Haley, Beyond benefit segmentation, *Journal of Advertising Research,* 1971, *11*(4), 3–8.

In a recent but relatively small-scale study, again with magazines, which should favor demographic matching, one of the authors of the Assael and Cannon study found an average correlation, across five products, of 0.59 between the rank order of magazines selected by direct matching and the rank order of magazines selected by demographic matching. This result was regarded as quite encouraging for the simple demographic approach. However, a 0.59 correlation represents only 35 percent shared relationship between the two methods—or 65 percent discrepancy. And direct matching has to be the correct method. This study, if anything, is therefore further evidence of the loss of accuracy with demographic matching. See H.M. Cannon, The "naive" approach to demographic media selection, *Journal of Advertising Research,* 1984, *24*(3), 21–25.

8 A.S.C. Ehrenberg and G.J. Goodhardt, Attitudes to episodes and programs, *Journal of the Market Research Society,* 1981, *23*(4), 189–208.

9 D.H. Gensch and B. Ranganathan, Evaluation of television program content for the purpose of promotional segmentation, *Journal of Marketing Research,* 1974, *11*,(4), 390–398.

10 For reasons cross-tabulations, not correlations, should be used, see F.W. Winter (same reference as note 6).

11 The SPSS computer programs, FREQUENCIES and CROSSTABS, are widely available and eminently suitable for analyzing direct matching data.

12 With the COMPUTE command in SPSS, this is easy. For any vehicles A, B, C, the instructions are:

COMPUTE ABC = A + B + C; FREQUENCIES ABC

13 The calculations become complex even for this seemingly simple case. From the tables given, we know how many brand loyals see 0,1,2,3 out of *3* insertions, but we don't know the exposure distribution for *2* insertions over the 3 weeks. The probability of the three times in 3 weeks readers of *Time,* for example, seeing 2 *insertions* is 1.0; that of two times in 3 weeks readers seeing 2 insertions is 0.33 (only) because only one-third of these readers will have seen any two particular issues; and for less frequent readers, it's zero. The probabilities of seeing 1 of the 2 insertions are: for 3 in 3 readers, 1.0; for 2 in 3 readers, .67; for 1 in 3 readers, 0.33; and for non-readers, 0. You need a computer to estimate the new distribution, and especially the *joint* frequency distributions of multiple vehicles, when you don't buy insertions in every issue of the vehicles. Fortunately, a suitable computer algorithm is available in C.S. Craig and A. Ghosh, Maximizing effective reach in media planning, in R.F. Lusch, G.T. Ford, G.L. Frazier, R.D. Howell, C.A. Ingene, M. Reilly, and R.W. Stampfl (Eds.), *1985 AMA Educator's Proceedings,* Chicago: American Marketing Association, 1985, pp. 178–182.

14 See, for example, R.S. Headen, J.E. Klompmaker, and R.T. Rust, The duplication of viewing law and television media schedule evaluation, *Journal of Marketing Research,* 1979, *16*(4), 333–340; R.T. Rust and R.P. Leone, The mixed-media Dirichlet Multinominal Distribution: a model for evaluating television-magazine advertising schedules, *Journal of Marketing Research,* 1984, *21*(1), 89–99.

15 NPD Research, Inc., *Insights,* Port Washington, NY: NPD Research, Inc., 1983, pp. 17–19. In their example, NPD used brand *usage* data, from a single-source service survey, in which magazines are listed individually. The procedure can, however, be applied to target audiences defined by variables other than usage, such as Chapter 4's awareness-attitude-behavior sub-groups, and to other media or combinations of media besides magazines—if you have customized direct matching data.

16 Eskin, G.J., Tracking advertising and promotion performance with single-source data, *Journal of Advertising Research,* 1985, *25*(1), 31, 33–39.

17 The authors are preparing a research review of vehicle environmental effects. Our research so far indicates fewer and much smaller effects than have commonly been supposed. For example, see studies by: D.A. Aaker and P.K. Brown, Evaluating source effects, *Journal of Advertising Research,* 1972, *12*(4), 11–16 (this study has been widely cited—incorrectly—as supporting the advertisement-vehicle compatibility hypothesis when in fact results show otherwise); J.N. Axelrod, Induced moods and attitudes toward products, *Journal of Advertising Research,* 1963, *3*(2), 19–24; K.J. Clancy and D.K. Kweskin, TV commercial recall correlates, *Journal of Advertising Research,* 1971, *11*(2), 18–20; A.S.C. Ehrenberg and G.J. Goodhart, Attitudes to episodes and programmes, *Journal of the Market Research Society,* 1981, *23*(4), 189–208 (note especially their Table 2: although a British study, these authors report virtually identical findings with U.S. TV programs; stated liking of programs closely reflects frequency of viewing, so likability data add practically nothing to exposure frequency data); M.P. Gardner, Mood states and consumer behavior: a critical review. *Journal of Consumer Research,* 1985, *12*(3) 281–300; J.R. Kennedy, How program environment affects TV commercials, *Journal of Advertising Research,* 1971, *11*(1), 33–38; G.F. Soldow and V. Principe, Response to commercials as a function of program context, *Journal of Advertising Research,* 1981, *21*(2), 59–65; and C. Winick, Three measures of the advertising value of media context, *Journal of Advertising Research, 1962, 2*(2), 28–33.

18 If the inferior method of demographic matching is used instead of direct matching to select first-stage vehicles, frequency of exposure will not be available. In this case, you could adjust by obtaining vehicle likability ratings from SMRB. We would suggest giving favorite vehicles an MEF value maximum of 1.5, down to least-favored vehicles at minimum 0.5. For example, if 10 million demographic target audience women aged 18–34 watch an episode of *Dynasty* in which the ad is placed, and *Dynasty* receives a likability weight of 1.2, then these 10 million women have received the equivalent of 1.2 exposures. A duplication formula such as beta-binomial would show roughly how many of them would "complete" the second exposure by watching a second program whose likability rating was at least 0.8

19 Nielsen diary data reported in *TV Guide,* May 24, 1980, *28*(1), p. A-4.

20 Our conclusion is supported by extensive data on day-after advertising recall (a measure of attention to the ad) for TV and magazine advertisements. Attention loss for competing-brand TV commercials within 10 minutes of one another averages only 6 percent. No comparable figure is given for proximity of competing-brand ads in magazines but the overall relationship (R^2) between magazine ad recall and competing ads in the magazine averages only 2 percent. On average, then, *attention* to ads is *not* affected by competing ads in the vehicle. We thank William F. Greene of Gallup & Robinson, Inc., for providing these data.

21 B.R. Bugelski, *Principles of Learning and Memory,* New York, Praeger, 1979; W.A. Wickelgren, *Learning and Memory,* Englewood Cliffs, NJ: Prentice-Hall, 1977.

22 Brand *recognition,* where the package is the stimulus to be recognized, should not be subject to interference because it is a visual response affected only by eventual time decay (see Chapter 20). The category need, as the in-store response when the package is seen, is usually evident from the shelf placement of the brand as well as from the package itself.

23 B.R. Bugelski and W.A. Wickelgren, same references as in note 21.

24 The experiments on normal-weight versus overweight shoppers' responsiveness to food stimuli were conducted by: R.E. Nisbett and D.E. Kanouse, Obesity, hunger, and supermarket shopping behavior, *Proceedings,* Seventh Annual Meeting, American Psychological Association, 1969, pp. 683–684; and S.A. Steinberg and R.F. Yalch, When eating begets buying: the effects of food samples on obese and non-obese shoppers, *Journal of Consumer Research,* 1978, *4*(4), 243–246.

25 T.P. Barwise, A.S.C. Ehrenberg, and G.J. Goodhardt, Watching TV at the same time on different weekdays, working paper, London Business School, London, 1978. Their analysis is based on U.S. data from Arbitron's television rating service.

26 Assuming that purchase of the brand is going on continuously, so that any 2-week purchase cycle has an arbitrary starting point, for the even schedule, the average consumer is "topped up" to MEF every week, leaving an average of $3\frac{1}{2}$ days to purchase before the next exposure occurs; for the impact schedule, the average consumer and indeed all consumers reach MEF every 3 weeks only, producing an average delay of $1\frac{1}{2}$ weeks to purchase before MEF can be attained again.

27 Note that time, per se, is not a relevant variable if the brand is chosen by brand recall because the "forgetting" process is due to interference, not trace decay (see Chapter 20). Nor is time relevant for brand recognition except over very long periods, say, a couple of months or more. Interference is the critical factor, too, for brand attitude. As brand awareness is the "carrier" of brand attitude, an interesting divergence occurs. For brand recall, a competitive campaign only has to be effective in interfering with brand recall (even if it is ineffective attitudinally); whereas for brand recognition, as this is not subject to interference, a competitive campaign has to interfere with brand attitude to be effective. A good example of this latter theory in practice (assuming soda purchase in supermarkets is by brand recognition) is the perennial battle of Coke versus Pepsi advertising on the "image" (transformational brand attitude) factor.

28 When using non-standard advertising units, such as broadcast ads shorter or longer than 30 seconds, or print ads smaller or bigger than one page, the computation is a little more complicated. First, the adjusted MEF contribution to exposure has to be compared against the required MEF level, so that effective reach will change. Then, since non-standard units cost less or more, the cost component of the profit calculation also will change. In practice, this is not very difficult because most variations from standard units are of one type—for instance, occasional 10-second amid 30-second spots in a broadcast campaign, or a lead-off of a double-page spread in a print campaign.

DISCUSSION QUESTIONS

17.1 In this chapter, demographic matching was criticized as being inferior to direct matching as a method of media vehicle selection. Is psychographic matching better than demographic matching—in general? Under what conditions would psychographic matching be (a) inferior to and (b) superior to demographic matching? Give a likely example for (a) and (b).

17.2 Write a memo to your manager, a national consumer products advertiser, arguing why the company should spend $100,000 on a media exposure study after the company has recently spent a lot of money on advertising strategy research.

17.3 Suppose that it costs $100,000 to place a full-page, four-color advertisement in *Time* magazine. The purchase cycle for your product is 5 weeks (for example, liquor) and you estimate that the effective frequency is 2. Moreover, you know that there is virtually a perfect likelihood that *Time's* primary readers read every issue. There are 500,000 target audience individuals among the primary readers of *Time*. Assume that the probability of purchase, at effective frequency, is 0.3

and that the profit contribution per unit purchased is $2.00. What profit would you expect, per purchase cycle, for advertising in *Time*?

17.4 You are the media director of an advertising agency and one of your clients habitually adds and deletes vehicles from your proposed media plans for "qualitative" reasons. Write a memo of no longer than two double-spaced pages, in your own words, that explains to the client how qualitative factors (those in second-stage vehicle selection) *should* be handled.

17.5 Calculate the contributions to MEF of the following advertising units and plans (use Appendix C and show detailed calculations). Assume the target audience is exposed to every insertion.

a Three 10-second radio commercials on successive days.

b A double-page black-and-white ad, followed by three single-page, right-hand page, black-and-white ads, all four with bleed, in successive weeks in a consumer magazine.

c A left-hand page, first inside cover, four-color ad, with an in-ad coupon, in an engineering magazine.

d A one-eighth page, below the fold, two-color newspaper ad for toothpaste, in the sports section.

e Two 60-second television commercials, with slight executional variations, impact-scheduled in the NBC *Sunday Night Movie*.

17.6 You are addressing a conference of soft-drink marketers, from different companies, about the problem of TV advertising "clutter." What would you advise them to do? What would you advise regarding retail store cooperative newspaper advertising, where their brands are featured with other brands?

17.7 Using Birdseye frozen vegetables and *McCall's* magazine (a monthly with a high proportion of passalong readers) as an example, outline the advantages and disadvantages of impact scheduling.

FURTHER READING

N. Garfinkle. A marketing approach to media selection. *Journal of Advertising Research,* 1963, *3*(4), 7–15.

This was the first publication, to our knowledge, to advocate direct matching of media vehicles with target audiences. Garfinkle, then president of a syndicated service called Brand Rating Index (since superseded by SMRB), shows examples of the inadequacies of demographics for media selection.

G.J. Eskin. Tracking advertising and promotion performance with single-source data. *Journal of Advertising Research,* 1985, *25*(1), 31, 33–39.

Eskin's article, written 20 years after Garfinkle's, reinforces the value of direct matching in media vehicle selection by using the modern technology of consumer panels linked to store purchase scanners.

Most of the literature on media vehicle selection is dangerously out of date, for example, by ignoring duplication (the exceptions are several recent *Journal of Marketing Research* articles on media models), advocating demographic matching, overemphasizing qualitative factors, and using the old definitions of reach and average frequency.

PART EIGHT

ADVERTISING RESEARCH
AND EVALUATION

CHAPTER 18

ADVERTISING STRATEGY RESEARCH

The first and most important stage of advertising research is *advertising strategy research*. In this first stage of research, the marketing objectives and budget are established, the target audience is defined, and the general advertising (or promotion) approach is identified, leading to the development of a detailed advertising strategy statement for the brand.

After reading this chapter you should:

- Realize the importance of a thorough situation audit
- Understand the contributions of both qualitative and quantitative research to advertising strategy development
- Know how advertising content research can help to generate and evaluate creative executions of the advertising strategy
- Be able to conduct a management judgment ad test
- Be able to write a summary advertising strategy

Advertising strategy research is the single most important stage of advertising research. If the strategy is wrong, then everything that follows—the creative, promotion offers, the media plan—will be wrong too. In marketing, the correct strategy is more important than correct execution: with an excellent strategy, you can succeed with even an average execution, but an excellent execution will not save a poor strategy. As Professor Len Lodish of The University of Pennsylvania's Wharton School puts it: "It is better to be vaguely right than precisely wrong." Of course, one should aim for correct strategy *and* correct execution, but the correct strategy is more vital.

Advertising strategy research ideally consists of five types of research, in this order:

1 Situation audit
2 Qualitative research
3 Quantitative research
4 Advertising content research
5 Management judgment ad test

These five types of research are the focal points of this chapter. The chapter shows how to prepare a one-page summary of the advertising strategy, which most managers find useful, although operationally the advertising manager must work with the detailed strategy statement as exemplified by the advertising plan described in Appendix A.

SITUATION AUDIT

Purpose of the Situation Audit

A situation audit consists of background (or "secondary") research into all factors that do, or could, affect the profit, sales, or market share performance of the brand. Advertising is just *one* of these factors, as is promotion.

It is surprising to note, from our experience, how frequently the situation audit is neglected. Most advertising managers are keen to get ahead with the new campaign and are unwilling to do their "homework" first. Yet most of these managers cannot tell you with any precision what factors *do* affect sales and profit and therefore whether it is worth advertising or promoting the brand in the first place. Advertising *agency* managers particularly are guilty of neglecting situation audits; understandably, they want to go ahead and advertise, with as much money as the client will allow.

A very experienced and respected advertising researcher, Dr. Russell Haley, recommends that at least one-quarter of the manager's advertising strategy research budget (and time) should be spent on the situation audit.[1] We agree. Skipping the situation audit is like not studying for a major exam.

Table 18.1 lists the research methods that should go into the situation audit. These areas can be divided into external sources of information and internal sources of information. As will become evident, the information applies to several sections of the advertising plan, but mainly to the first section: marketing objectives.

External Sources of Information

Commission a Library Search of Competing Companies, Category, and Brands A wealth of data on virtually every product category exists in the nation's libraries. With computer-aided retrieval, these searches can be conducted relatively quickly, although there is still the task of obtaining or photocopying the original articles.

In our experience, most managers are too time-pressured to do a thorough library search themselves. A sensible alternative is to call the marketing department of a nearby university and arrange to commission a senior marketing

TABLE 18-1   SITUATION AUDIT RESEARCH METHODS*

External sources
- Commission library search of competing companies, categories, and brands (student)
- Check U.S. Government publications and legal restrictions relevant to category (student)
- Subscribe to syndicated services covering category, e.g., Nielsen, SMRB (manager)
- Compile clipping file of competing advertisements and promotion offers (student)

Internal sources
- Analyze previous company data and research reports on the category (manager)
- Interview those who produce or provide the product or service (manager)
- Interview the company's distributors through the channel of distribution (independent research service)
- Interview financial managers to obtain the cost, pricing, and profit basis of the product or service (manager)
- Conduct statistical analysis if data are available and poll managers to set overall advertising and promotion budget (manager)

* Those best suited to carry out each type of research are noted in parentheses.

student (undergraduates are keener and have more time than MBA students and *also* have more time than the manager's own research assistants) to conduct the search and obtain the major articles. This invariably turns out to be money well spent.

The manager should use this information to prepare a thorough analysis of competing companies' financial and marketing mix strengths and weaknesses (see Chapter 1). As well, the search will often produce category if not brand-by-brand sales data that can be incorporated into a (category) product life cycle plot (see Chapter 1) to further assist in strategy determination.

Check U.S. Government Publications and Legal Restrictions Relevant to the Category   The U.S. Government conducts a surprising amount of research on various products and services. Lists of publications are available through the U.S. Government Printing Office.

Frequently, as well, there are legal restrictions on how products or services can be sold and advertised. The *Journal of Marketing*'s section on legal developments in marketing is worth a ''back-search'' of recent to previous abstracts to check on legal restrictions. Again, a responsible marketing student can conduct this search for the manager.

If there are any legal restrictions on the way the product is sold or advertised, these should be summarized in the manager's brief to creative, so that creative personnel know what they can *not* write about or show regarding the brand.

Subscribe to Syndicated Services   If the company is not already doing so, the manager should subscribe to syndicated audit services for the product category, when available (such as Nielsen or SMRB—see Chapter 3). First-time subscribers should contact the service directly and arrange to buy past reports, as necessary, to trace back the product life cycle and brands' sales histories.

Armed with data on competing brands' actual (for example, Nielsen) or estimated (for example, SMRB) sales, the manager can then begin to sketch the overall category partitioning structure and compute size ratios for market shares (see Chapter 4). Usually, however, proper determination of categories and sub-categories—true markets—will require primary research (qualitative and usually quantitative) with customers, so this should be planned for the next phase of advertising strategy research.

Compile a Clipping File of Competing Advertisements and Promotions in the Category   If the category has been advertised on TV, one-page "photoboards" of competing brands' commercials can be obtained through Radio TV Reports, Inc. or ADBANK in New York. For print campaigns, either in newspapers or magazines, copies of print ads for most product categories can be obtained through Vance Coughlan & Woodward, Inc.

If the product is sold at retail, store visits are an essential step in compiling a point-of-purchase advertising and promotion file. The manager should make store visits personally. Then the student researcher can re-visit and record and photograph details.

The manager should then conduct (or commission the student or a research assistant to perform) a content analysis of the clipping file. A summary of creative approaches, benefits emphasized, and promotion offers used by the major competing brands should be the outcome. The content analysis can assist in identifying benefits to be discussed in qualitative research, as well as being of direct use to the creative team—to borrow from *or* to avoid duplication, as decided by the strategy, in developing creative executions.

Internal Sources of Information

Analyze Previous Company Data and Research Reports on the Category   Unless the category is completely new, the manager's own company generally will have sales records and previous research reports in the company's files. Sometimes the problem is that the *manager* is completely new, and doesn't know what the company already has, or is reluctant to re-trace "old" work. This is always a mistake; the historical pattern must always be traced.

The manager should *analyze,* not just read, previous data and research reports. The manager should arrange the information to suit the advertising plan's checklist sections. Company data can be used to plot trends in brand sales and, if competing brands' sales data are available, market shares. From research reports, information can be extracted to supplement other sections of the plan, such as target audience profile characteristics, and benefits for brand attitude strategy.

Interview Those Who Produce or Provide the Product or Service   The manager should personally compile a "fact book" of technical details of the product or service. This entails interviews with (as appropriate) the company's physicists, engineers, chemists, nutritionists, or service managers.

Many excellent campaigns are derived from technical characteristics of the product. (For *informational* buying motives, less so transformational where the usage consequences are more subjective, advertising's task basically is to turn product *attributes* into consumer *benefits,* and more specifically into benefit claims—see Chapters 7, 9, and 10.) Claude Hopkins' early campaign for Budweiser—"It's beechwood aged"—is a good example. More recently, Federal Express has technically described its "hub system" of package routing, whereby all packages go to Memphis and then out on the next plane going to the "spoke" destination city, as an advertising explanation of faster service.

Of course, primary research with potential or actual customers will be required to see which technical attributes can indeed be turned into *benefits.* This comes at the next stage of advertising strategy research.

Interview the Company's Distributors   Many advertising and promotion campaigns either are directed to, or depend largely for their success upon, the trade. It is *always* worth conducting interviews with each link in the channel of distribution to obtain distributors' opinions on what's been done in the past by way of product, price, distribution, and promotion efforts, and what distributors believe will work in the future.

While the manager should become familiar with the product's present and potential distribution, it is better to commission an independent research firm to conduct distributor interviews. This is because the company's own distributors (especially the immediate sales force) are likely to provide somewhat biased or guarded answers if they know they are talking to a senior representative of one of the companies for which they distribute.[2]

Distributor information fits various sections of the advertising plan. At a brand level, it might indicate a major strategy of advertising and promoting to the trade whereas this is too often an afterthought in many advertising plans. At a more specific level, it may indicate the incorporation of purchase facilitation (see Chapter 6) as a communication objective.

Interview Financial Managers to Obtain the Cost, Pricing, and Profit Basis of the Product or Service   In Chapter 2, we discussed how advertising and promotion contribute to profit through price margin, cost reduction, or increased volume. The manager cannot complete the marketing objectives section of the advertising plan unless he or she understands the financial basis of the product or service. Obviously, interviews with financial officers should be conducted personally by the manager.

Conduct Statistical Analysis if Data are Available and Poll Managers to Set the Overall Advertising and Promotion Budget   The final application of the situation audit is to obtain the information necessary to set the overall advertising and promotion budget. As explained in Chapter 3, if the campaign is for a continuing brand, statistical analysis—including a graphic plot—should be conducted on trend relationships between respective marketing expenditures and the decided-upon market performance criterion of market share, sales, or profit.[3]

For continuing brands (usually) and for a new brand (of necessity) management judgment will then be used to establish the overall advertising and promotion budget. This involves a poll of 6 to 10 managers, as explained in Chapter 3. In sophisticated applications, a computer-interactive marketing model such as BRANDAID can be utilized to set the budget.[4]

In summary, we see that the situation audit is an extremely important, if arduous, part of advertising strategy research. A situation audit is necessary to set sound marketing objectives. It is, basically, secondary research because we have not yet interviewed customers. Primary advertising strategy research, with customers, is described next.

QUALITATIVE RESEARCH

To help select the target audience and set appropriate action objectives and communication objectives, interviews with potential and actual customers are nearly always necessary: it is particularly risky to attempt these steps in the plan through management judgment alone, although this often has to be done for very small budget campaigns.

Qualitative research is absolutely crucial in customer interviews to develop advertising strategy. (Shortly, we will see how quantitative research can add some very useful refinements to the qualitative results. But one could, in practice, simply extend the number of qualitative research interviews until they *become* quantitatively reliable.) Qualitative research is the only research method capable of—and we stress capable of, not assured of—discovering the causes of buyer behavior.[5]

What is Qualitative Research?

Qualitative research consists of either focus groups or individual depth interviews. Focus groups are the usual method, although individual interviews are often used in industrial, medical, or personal product fields where purchase decisions are too sensitive to disclose in front of others. With either the group or individual procedure, the interviews consist of open-ended questions focusing on a range of topics that help the advertiser to arrive at an advertising strategy.

A skeleton discussion outline (from which the qualitative researcher would write actual, askable questions and probes) is provided in Table 18.2. The qualitative research interviewer elicits and probes buyers' or potential buyers' opinions about the product category, various brands, the people who use those brands, and different advertising approaches.[6]

Even the smallest advertiser usually can afford qualitative research; the cost is generally about $2000 to $2500 per group, depending on the product category usage incidence and hence the availability of respondents (participants) as well as the experience and skill of the moderator-analyst (see below). Several group discussions with potential and actual customers can be sufficient

TABLE 18-2   SKELETON DISCUSSION OUTLINE FOR QUALITATIVE RESEARCH

Introduction and purpose
- Moderator's preamble: purpose is to ask your opinions on (category); interaction encouraged; no majority rule; recorded, to get all valuable comments

Decision maker roles
- Which members of household initiate, influence, decide, buy, use the general product category

Decision sequence
- Trace through each person's decision process from beginning to end: what, when, where, how, and why they buy in this general product category

Category partitions
- Awareness (recalled then recognized) of types and brands
- Which types and brands are similar, dissimilar—and why
- Probe extensively for all motivations for purchase and benefits sought in category

Brand behaviors and attitudes
- Which brands not tried, tried and rejected, tried and purchased again, purchased most often—and why
- Each brand in turn: strengths and weaknesses
- User images associated with each brand

Advertising
- (Show samples of each brand's advertising); which advertisements are most appealing, least appealing—and why
- Suggestions for new brand benefits to be advertised
- Suggestions for new media to be employed

Promotion
- (Show samples of each brand's promotions); awareness and opinion of media promotions for each brand
- Awareness and opinion of p-o-p promotions
- Preferred types of promotion

Summary
- Identify client's brand and review by asking people what the brand would have to do to get them to buy it, or buy it and use it more often
- Thank, pay, and dismiss group

to supplement the smaller advertiser's own ideas and lead to a reasonably good advertising strategy.

For larger advertisers in very competitive product categories, however, the qualitative research should be more extensive and more precise. It should sample across all potential target audience groups and replicate with at least three groups on each to provide more reliable findings.

The *validity* of qualitative research findings is largely dependent on the psychological and marketing ability of the interviewer—the moderator-analyst. The person who is going to analyze the results by listening to the tapes of the sessions and writing the report should *also* be the moderator, or discussion leader, of the groups. Only the same person can know *why* certain questions or probes were asked and why particular avenues of thought were pursued. A skilled and experienced *moderator-analyst* is the most important ingredient in qualitative research because the research results are so heavily based on his or her interpretation of what the participants do and say.

Applying Qualitative Research Results to the Advertising Plan

Like all forms of advertising research, qualitative research is undertaken to provide information to aid the manager in preparing the advertising plan (see Appendix A for a detailed description of the advertising plan). Table 18.3 summarizes the main purposes for which qualitative research is used to contribute to the advertising plan.

1 *Identify the Most Leverageable Target Audience(s) for Advertising and Promotion* Qualitative research can *broadly* identify the best (most persuasible at least cost) target audience for advertising and for promotion. This broad identification is sufficient for many advertisers.

Note, however, that qualitative research usually cannot make a good estimate of the *size* and thus detailed sales potential of alternative prospect groups, especially if the manager wants to go beyond the basic four prospect groups and into the sub-groups identified in Chapter 4. Large advertisers generally will want to do this, and therefore will need quantitative research, or a very large number of qualitative interviews, *unless* they are fortunate enough to have prospect group sizes available from secondary research (situation audit).

2 *Identify Decision Roles and Action Objectives* A second purpose of qualitative research is to identify the participants in the purchase decision. The *roles* to which advertising and promotion can most effectively be directed, and therefore the associated action objectives, can be most validly isolated through qualitative research. This is because the qualitative research can probe beyond the typically surface answers given by respondents in surveys which ask respondents directly about their relative decision influence.[7]

3 *Construct a Behavioral Sequence Model* One of the topics in the qualitative research outline has the researcher asking buyers to trace back their decision sequence. The researcher then, from a number of such "protocols" as they are known, pieces together a typical behavioral sequence model for the product category or, if different, for the particular brand. The procedure for this was explained in Chapter 5.

4 *Determine Communication Objectives* A further (essential) purpose of qualitative research is to determine the communication objectives for the advertising or promotion campaign—for the particular target audience:

a The *category need* objective will be fairly obvious from the nature of

TABLE 18-3 PURPOSES OF QUALITATIVE RESEARCH IN RELATION TO THE ADVERTISING PLAN

1. Identify the most leverageable target audience(s) for advertising and promotion.
2. Identify decision roles and action objectives.
3. Construct a behavioral sequence model.
4. Determine communication objectives (including brand awareness type, brand attitude quadrant, and benefits to support brand attitude).
5. Suggest advertising or promotion stimuli that might be suited to the communication objectives.

the target audience; qualitative research also has the prior task of deciding precisely what the category *is*, from the consumer's standpoint.

b The *brand awareness* objective should be evident from the behavioral sequence model, which indicates whether most buyers decide (or should be induced to decide) on the brand prior to purchase via brand recall, or at the point of purchase via brand recognition.

c The *brand attitude* objective likewise should be fairly evident from the target audience selected, but the brand attitude *strategy* requires careful analysis: qualitative research is the *best* way to determine the level of involvement with brand choice and the real underlying motive or motives to which purchase of the brand is connected or could potentially be connected—hence quadrant placement must be done from qualitative research.

d The *brand purchase* (or purchase-related) *intention* objective follows from the behavioral sequence model and from the brand attitude quadrant.

e The *purchase facilitation* objective may arise in the qualitative interviews, or it may be something that customers don't yet know about (from the situation audit).

Accordingly, we can see that qualitative research is vital for deciding the campaign's communication objectives. Of particular importance is the qualitative analyst's skill in identifying the best brand attitude strategy for the brand. As explained in Chapter 7, the qualitative researcher also has to identify the important, deliverable, and unique *benefits*, and the benefit composition rule, to support the brand attitude strategy.

5 *Suggest Advertising or Promotion Stimuli That Might Be Suited to the Communication Objectives* This final purpose of qualitative research is stated cautiously: it is seen by some people as encroaching on the creative function. Nevertheless, there is no reason other than creative's elitism or defensiveness that should prevent a qualitative report from *suggesting* effective types of stimuli (visual, verbal, musical) and also tactics (see Chapters 9, 10, 11, 13, and 14) for creative executions of advertisements and promotion offers.

Special Techniques for Uncovering Motivations

Qualitative research is often aptly called "motivation research." Although we have just seen that qualitative research has additional purposes besides detecting motivations, an essential purpose is to uncover the *real* motivations, and the associated benefits, that are used to influence brand attitude. If the motivational "triggers" to purchase of the brand are not found, then qualitative research has not fulfilled its most valuable function.

The understanding of motivations requires a skilled moderator-analyst using either the focus group method or, for complex or socially sensitive products, the individual depth interview method. The flexible questioning and deep probing of qualitative research are required because:

1 Respondents may not easily understand what the interviewer is looking for
2 They may not know what their motivations are
3 They may be unable to remember them even if they do know
4 They may not be able to articulate them even if they do remember
5 They may not want to tell the interviewer even if they could
6 The interviewer must probe deeply enough to enable correct classification of the answers in terms of basic motivations

Only the skilled qualitative researcher with psychological training can reasonably circumvent these ever-present barriers to identifying motivations.

In qualitative investigations, the interviewer asks consumers why they do or do not buy or use the product. Specific brands also are asked about because answers at the product category level, alone, are often too general or abstract. The interviewer is seeking two main types of information: (a) the nature of the *motivation or motivations* operating in the product category—negative or positive, from the eight identified in Chapter 7 earlier; and (b) elicitation of *benefits*, described in "consumer language," that appear to be *important* in removing or satisfying these needs.

Special Techniques Written-answer techniques are sometimes used to supplement the usual oral questions and answers in qualitative research. For negatively originated motivations, and associated removal-type benefits, *problem detection analysis* can be useful. Developed by the BBDO advertising agency from the Hotpoint Company's technique of "reverse brainstorming," problem detection analysis employs the following types of questions.[8] They can be asked for the product category in general but usually are asked for each brand.

1 Does this product (brand) *solve* a problem or need? If so, please describe.
2 Does this product (brand) *produce* any problems? If so, please describe.
3 (For each problem or need mentioned): How *important,* to you, is this problem or need?

        very important   _____
        moderately important   _____
        slightly important   _____
        not important   _____

For positively originated motivations, and associated satisfaction or enhancement-type benefits, *benefit chaining* can be useful, a technique popularized by Grey Advertising from a procedure copyrighted by Hal Lee in 1970.[9] Benefit chaining is a system of sequential probing. In the written version, the consumer begins by writing down two benefits (an arbitrary number) derived from using the product. For each of the two benefits, the consumer next writes down two more, and so forth. The resulting chain for one of the benefits may be as follows (for a hairspray product):

holds without sticking	→	leaves hair easy to manage	→	get compliments on natural-looking hair

Of course, it still remains for the analyst to infer from these types of responses the actual motivation and how "surface" benefits relate to it. Also, it should be noted that despite the names of the two techniques and the classification above, each can identify negative as well as positive motivations, although they seem likely to favor one or the other type. Both techniques can of course be used in the same qualitative study.

Another useful technique, actually a set of techniques, is *projective techniques*. These are able to detect all types of motivations but are especially effective for products where deep personal motives or unadmitted social influence may be operating. Projective techniques include procedures such as "What do your friends buy and why?" which is perhaps the most widely used type of projective question; similarly, they include the presentation of incomplete or ambiguous stimuli such as cartoons of characters in brand purchase or usage situations in which respondents are asked to fill in the words in the cartoon characters' word balloons; they also include "be-a-brand" role-playing, in which respondents try to personalize various brands, thereby revealing personal and social likes and dislikes about each. Projective techniques are described in most market research texts and they often produce valuable insights in qualitative research.

QUANTITATIVE RESEARCH

Adding quantitative research to the prior qualitative research in advertising strategy research serves a number of additional information needs in preparing the advertising plan. We emphasize that this is *additional* information. Quantitative research can in no way replace—and is *not* "better than"—qualitative research.[10] Rather, quantitative research supplements the advertising plan in ways to be described shortly.

What is Quantitative Research?

In the context of advertising strategy research, quantitative research consists of a questionnaire survey with a large number of target audience consumers (200 to 1000, depending on the number of *prospective* target audience groups and the degree of precision or reliability required) followed by appropriate statistical analysis of the results.[11]

The quantitative research interviews are *not* administered by psychologically trained interviewers as in qualitative research, so their suitability is in gathering objective "numbers" data rather than in obtaining the subjective psychological inferences that come from qualitative research.

Questionnaire content areas covered in quantitative advertising strategy research are listed in Table 18.4. Again, of course, these content areas have to be converted to actual questions for survey administration. Because of the interview length and the large sample sizes, it is not unusual for quantitative research to cost between $50,000 and $150,000. Considered in relation to a large advertising budget, which may be over a thousand times the lower amount (that is, $50 million), this money is considered well spent.

As might be inferred from the table, there are two main purposes of quantitative research:

1 To align benefits more precisely with target audiences
2 To fully profile the target audience decision maker (including media exposure)

These functions are explained next.

Aligning Benefits with Target Audiences

For the large advertiser who may be developing advertising and promotion campaigns for several target audiences and is trying to decide which *precise* prospect sub-groups (see Chapter 4) are the most feasible targets, quantitative research can be of great assistance. This is because, in qualitative research, it can be difficult to keep track of which benefits, from numerous candidates, are preferred by which potential target audiences.

(For smaller advertisers, or for larger advertisers where the target audience and benefits are eminently clear from qualitative research, the benefit rating part of quantitative research can be omitted.)

TABLE 18-4   QUANTITATIVE RESEARCH: QUESTIONNAIRE CONTENT AREAS

Target audience classification
Category and brand awareness, attitude, and behavior measures to classify respondents into the 12 prospective target audience sub-groups

Brand benefit ratings
Ratings of each brand in terms of benefits (stated in consumer language) relating to *situations* (motives)

Demographics
Geographic: region, state, urban-suburban-rural
Individual: age, sex, race, income, education, occupation

Psychographics
General: various A-I-O inventories, including social class values
Category-specific: A-I-O for category attitudes and behaviors

Personality traits
Reliable measures of intelligence, anxiety, introversion-extraversion, imaging ability, etc., that relate functionally to persuasion

Media exposure
Frequency of exposure to media vehicles in each medium
Locations and personality states during exposure

The purpose of obtaining benefit ratings is to perform an I-D-U analysis (see Chapter 7) for selecting benefits to employ in advertising to each target audience. Several methodological considerations can now be noted that were passed over in Chapter 7.

Situational Benefit Ratings   As explained in Chapter 7, benefits are relevant only in relation to particular purchase or usage motivations for the brand.

Motivations are psychological inferences (in the analyst's mind) whereas the specific benefits are in consumer language (in the consumer's mind). To repeat an example used earlier, the "fresh taste" benefit in a toothpaste may be desired because of underlying problem removal motivation (bad taste in mouth) or sensory gratification motivation (nice taste without any "problem") or social approval motivation (for example, Ultra-Brite's "sex appeal"). The questionnaire cannot, in most cases, state the benefit in relation to the motivation by referring directly to the psychological motive, such as "Do you want fresh taste in a toothpaste so as to enhance social approval?"

Instead, the motivational basis of the benefit usually must be stated indirectly, without reference to the psychological mechanism. This can be achieved by stating the motivation, for the consumer, in terms of a *situation*. The situation avoids direct reference to the psychological mechanism. Examples covering several possible motives in the toothpaste category might be "a toothpaste for problem tastes" versus "a refreshing toothpaste" versus "a toothpaste for social occasions." Situations then form the motivations against which brand benefit delivery is rated. Thus, for example, a person might have three separate brand *attitudes* for Crest, depending on three different motivations, disguised as "situations." Fortunately, most target audiences have a single overriding motivation, in which case only one brand attitude is operating.

Preserving Benefit Statements in Consumer Language   When placing benefits in questionnaires for brand ratings, the quantitative researcher must stay as close to the exact consumer wording (from qualitative research interviews) as possible. This is where many crucial errors are made. Often, in the attempt to simplify benefit statements to suit questionnaires, the original consumer wording is lost. The sterile wording of rating scales in most questionnaires loses the meaning or the emotionality of the actual benefit claims and produces misleading if not useless results. Ironically, sterilized ratings from questionnaires then typically are taken to the creative department with a request to "put these into consumer language." The copywriter, in effect, is being asked to recreate the original qualitative research that contained the consumer language in the first place! The researcher must preserve this language in questionnaire rating scales.

For instance, if consumers say they avoid "el cheapo" brands, this benefit belief *cannot* be represented on a questionnaire by the item "low price." The benefit statements must preserve the original meaning; indeed, three items may be required, such as "cheap quality," "low status," and "inexpensive."

Allied to this is the need to be very careful, in wording benefits, to preserve the *nature* of the benefit—for example, more-the-better, or just-right, benefits (see Chapter 7). In other words, the correct benefit statement may be "just the right sweetness," not "high sweetness."

A safeguard: Let the qualitative researcher screen the benefit statements before they are finalized on the questionnaire.

How Should the Benefits Be Rated? Whereas different types of benefit (brand benefit delivery) rating scales may seem to produce similar results, in fact the communication relevance and thus managerial interpretation of the rating scale results is a vital methodological consideration. Because benefits are again rated in the subsequent ad testing stage of advertising research (as a diagnostic measure), we will defer discussion of rating scales until Chapter 19, where measures for all communication effects are provided.

Deciding Benefit Importance In the I-D-U analysis, selecting important (I) benefits is the first step. Quantitative benefit ratings yield brand delivery ratings (D) which can then be compared across brands for uniqueness of delivery (U). But importance should *not* be rated directly.

Importance of benefits can be selected in two ways. One way is to have the *qualitative researcher infer* importance. The qualitative researcher's classification of low importance and high importance benefits—again, for the particular motivation—can then be used to set up the I-D-U matrices.

Alternatively, many researchers prefer to *derive* importance statistically.[12] This is achieved by correlating *specific* brand benefit (delivery) ratings with *overall* ratings of the brand's suitability for various situations (that is, each overall brand attitude). If a large number of benefits are rated, many of which will not be used in the final advertising strategy, the simple correlation coefficients should be used initially to screen benefits for importance.[13] Then, when a smaller set of final benefits is selected, a regression of benefit ratings on overall brand attitude should be computed and, because the benefits may interact, standardized regression weights should be used to decide benefit importance.[14]

Both ways of deciding benefit importance can be used and compared, and this is probably the best procedure.

Profiling the Target Audience Decision Maker

The advertising plan also calls for the manager to develop a personal profile of the target audience decision maker—that is, of the initiator, influencer, decider, purchaser, or user, to whom the advertising or promotion campaign is directed (see Chapter 5). A fairly good profile of the decision maker in terms of obvious demographics and obvious psychographic characteristics may be evident from the qualitative research. However, a detailed profile that also includes personality traits and, most importantly, media exposure, requires quantitative research.

Table 18.4 indicated the types of profile measures under each personal characteristics category that are useful to advertisers. Detailed measures and their applications are beyond the scope of this book.[15] However, some general methodological observations about profile measures are offered below.

Demographics Demographic variables covering geographic, individual, and group-membership personal characteristics of the decision maker are useful for copywriters in developing a better idea of whom they are addressing. Traditionally and still commonly, demographics are also used in media vehicle selection although, as shown in Chapter 17, this is a waste of money because it produces much less accurate target audience reach than direct media measurement.

Statistically, to develop a demographic profile of target audiences, you simply cross-tabulate each demographic variable's categories (for example, age groups) by prospect group membership (for example, single-brand loyals, multi-brand loyals, and so forth). The manager then considers the percentage of individuals in each demographic category (not the mean level, which is too ambiguous and in any case means nothing for nominal demographic variables such as sex or race).

Psychographics Psychographic measures come in two varieties, and both can be useful in gaining a more detailed picture of the target audience decision maker, as well as in deciding what background stimuli to put in advertisements.

General psychographic inventories cover a broad range of activities, interests, and opinions (A-I-O measures) that apply universally to all consumers. Two cautions: First, as explained in Chapter 5, you should never try to develop target audiences using psychographics as the primary basis.[16] This is backward segmentation. Segmentation by awareness-behavior-attitude groups comes first, as in our four prospect groups (or their respective sub-groups) then psychographics can be used to describe *these* groups. Second, you should not use shortened inventories of psychographic typologies—either syndicated ones such as VALS *or* custom designed inventories.[17] In quantitative research, use the *full* set of psychographic items.

Category-specific psychographic inventories can be constructed from the prior qualitative research. In the discussion outline provided earlier, consumers are asked to give their opinions on what types of people do or do not use the product category and particular brands. From their opinions, and from any previous research discovered in the situation audit, category-specific items can be compiled.

Statistical analysis of psychographic profile data generally will consist of an initial factor analysis (there may be over 200 individual measures or items) followed by cross-tabulation against target audience prospect groups. What, on the psychographic side, should be cross-tabulated? Some researchers favor using factor scores from the factor analysis, dividing these into categories such as high negative, moderate negative, neutral, moderate positive, and high positive. This is probably the most reliable method, but the practical validity to copywriters can be obscured when summary factors are used instead of individual psychographic items. Alternatively, but less reliably, high-loading items on each factor can be cross-tabulated.[18]

Personality Traits   For most personality traits of interest to advertising researchers, highly reliable measures are available in the psychological literature. The essential step in using personality traits to profile target audience decision makers is not measurement, which is relatively straightforward, but, rather specifying how each trait, or constellation of traits, relates functionally to persuasion.[19]

Statistically, each multi-item trait measure can be summed to a total trait score that is then divided into categories, such as low versus high, and cross-tabulated against target audience prospect groups.

Media Exposure   Direct measurement of target audience media exposure was discussed extensively in Chapter 17. Briefly, this section of the questionnaire contains a long list of media vehicles for each major medium (except outdoor, p-o-p, and specialty media, which have to be inferred from the behavioral sequence model). Consumers then record (in a panel study) or estimate (in a survey) their frequency of exposure to each. Because of the length of the media exposure inventory, it may be necessary and more efficient to obtain the media measures from a separate sample of consumers. The separate sample has only to be screened for target audience classification and does not have to complete the other sections of the questionnaire.

Statistically, a frequency count for each media vehicle can be applied first (within target audience) to eliminate very low-exposure vehicles, followed by multiple cross-tabulation (see Chapter 17) of frequency of exposure by target audience groups. *Within* each target audience or prospect group, the multiple cross-tabulations *between* high exposure-frequency media vehicles reveal duplication patterns at the minimum effective frequency level and indicate the effective reach of various combinations of vehicles.

In summary, it can be seen that quantitative research *adds to* qualitative research in preparing the advertising strategy. It buys refinements that qualitative research alone can't provide (including, most importantly, direct media measurement) and it is therefore of immense value to the large advertiser.

ADVERTISING STRATEGY SUMMARY

The output from advertising strategy research—be it intuitive, or qualitative only, or qualitative plus quantitative—should not only be fitted into the advertising plan but should also be prepared in the form of an *advertising strategy summary*. This is what managers refer to as being able to summarize the advertising strategy (for each target audience) in "one page."

The summary should briefly describe the main characteristics of the target audience at the top of the page, then summarize the essential content, only, of the four steps in the buyer response sequence, that is, exposure → processing → communication objectives → action, in "flowchart" form.

An example of an advertising strategy summary is shown in Table 18.5 for a campaign for American Express (Personal) Green Card. The strategy is addressed to a high involvement target audience, new category users, to attempt to persuade them to apply for the card. Note the emphasis on acceptance in processing and the fact that all five communication effects are objectives for this campaign.

To illustrate the point that a separate advertising strategy must be prepared for each target audience, a second summary strategy is shown in Table 18.6. This describes a campaign for a low involvement target audience—current loyal American Express cardholders—to stimulate increased usage. The emphasis here is on learning, for increased brand awareness and for maintaining (their low involvement) brand attitude, with the other communication effects being already at full strength.

Note that the advertising strategy summary, while a very useful document for quick reference by managers, cannot replace the detailed advertising strategy spelled out in the advertising plan. The advertising plan's first three sections (in Appendix A) are needed *in detail* for advertising content research and management judgment ad testing (see below), and for ad testing with the target audience (next chapter).

TABLE 18-5   AN ADVERTISING STRATEGY SUMMARY FOR AMERICAN EXPRESS GREEN CARD (ACQUISITION)

Target audience: Non-cardholders who qualify on income requirement (new category users). Current attitude to AE Green neutral; target attitude top box positive. Primarily men, wide range of occupations, lifestyles, and personalities.

1. *Exposure*
- See and hear AE Green "Acquisition" commercial on TV
- Attentive programs, e.g., *60 Minutes*

2. *Processing*
- Accept category need for credit cards to avoid emergency payment problems
- Learn to recognize card and "blue box" and typical "blue box" locations
- Accept attitudinal message that AE Green is "for me," based on benefits of having card for unexpected business lunch, extended business trip, and emergency purchases when on business trip
- Accept intention to look for and fill out application

3. *Communication objectives*
- Category need: sell (problem avoidance)
- Brand awareness: recognition
- Brand attitude: create (high involvement, problem avoidance)
- Brand purchase intention: soft sell
- Purchase facilitation: distribution

4. *Action*
- Find application box and fill out AE Green application form and mail

---

TABLE 18-6   AN ADVERTISING STRATEGY SUMMARY FOR AMERICAN EXPRESS CARD (USAGE)

Target audience: AE Green cardholders who use the card less than once a month. Mostly non-executives and wives of cardholders. Meet income requirement but wide range of other socio-demographics.

1. *Exposure* • Hear AE Green "Usage" commercial on radio • Moderately attentive programs in morning timeslots	2. *Processing* • Learn AE Green Card as response to situational category stimulus of leaving house (recall "leaving house . . . take AE Card" from tag line "Don't leave home without it") • Learn (re-learn) how versatile the AE Card is
3. *Communication objectives* • Brand awareness: recall • Brand attitude: maintain (low involvement, problem avoidance)	4. *Action* • Increased frequency of carrying AE Green (assumed to increase chances of usage when usage situations naturally occur)

ADVERTISING CONTENT RESEARCH

Many advertisers skip advertising content research and proceed directly to the preparation and testing of rough ads. However, there are several frequently occurring circumstances in which research on creative content can be useful:

- For advertisers developing a *new* campaign, even though the overall strategy has been determined, the creative team may get "blocked" in generating specific ideas for the execution of the campaign. Advertising *idea generation* research can often break the block.
- For advertisers seeking "fresh ideas" to spruce up a *continuing* campaign (see Chapter 20 regarding "wearout"), advertising *idea generation* research, similarly, can help to provide new executions.
- Finally, for the fortunate advertiser for whom *too many ideas* have been forthcoming from advertising strategy research, advertising *content screening* research can help the creative team to reduce these ideas to a reasonable number for incorporating into rough ads for ad testing.

Therefore, let us proceed with describing, first, advertising idea generation research, then advertising content screening research. Then, in the concluding section of the chapter, we will show how content screening can be adapted for use by managers in conducting a management judgment ad test.

Advertising Idea Generation

As one of America's foremost creative directors, Stephen Baker, as well as many geniuses and some psychologists have observed, creativity can rarely rely on intuition alone. Creative idea generation can almost always benefit from various aids which serve as stimulus inputs to the "intuitive" breakthrough. Three such aids are described here.

Thought-Starter Lists   A virtually costless research method is to acquire previously published thought-starter lists. Many experienced creative personnel have their own lists tacked on the wall. Baker[20] provides many useful lists covering a variety of advertising situations. To give just one example, he lists 30 possible benefits to use when advertising a service. Services don't have physical attributes like products, of course, and it can be difficult to find service benefits to advertise. If more creatives used these lists we might have fewer "me too" campaigns where the thought starter was nothing but a competitor's campaign.

Brainstorming Groups   Brainstorming groups are a special variation of focus groups using participants especially selected for their creativity rather than using typical consumers. Agencies can convene these groups in-house, using creative people from the agency. Alternatively, research firms can utilize creativity tests to screen potential participants from, for example, industry groups.[21] Brainstorming groups should employ a professional moderator whose task is to elicit ideas but to discourage evaluation, which might inhibit the birth of a great idea, until after the session.[22]

The cost of a professionally conducted brainstorming group is higher than for a conventional focus group. An externally screened group of about four or five innovative thinkers, with a professional moderator, may cost $3000 to $5000. Again, the manager has to assess the extent of the creative blockage in relation to the likelihood of a breakthrough in spending this money.

Benefit Chaining   Benefit chaining, which was described earlier in the chapter as a technique that can be incorporated in qualitative research to develop advertising strategy, can also be used in advertising idea generation research. Benefit chaining is very useful for the small advertiser who has done no strategy research and has to begin with the brand's obvious attributes. For example, Jolt, the new high-caffeine cola, could use benefit chaining to generate situations in which high caffeine is most likely to be seen as beneficial. Benefit chaining also is particularly useful for all advertisers seeking to generate new ideas for a continuing campaign; that is, one that continues the same basic strategy but seeks new executions to "spruce up" or revive the campaign. Airlines, for example, probably have this problem when advertising to the same target audience with the same basic benefits year after year.

Individual interviews (not focus groups) should be employed for the benefit chaining procedure. This is to ensure that logical chains of ideas can be traced at the individual consumer level. The most frequent or typical individual thought patterns are then selected for final (or to-be-tested) advertising executions.

Computer Dictionary   One of these authors is experimenting with a computer program, called Copytester, that will output words in various semantic categories for copywriters' consideration. For example, the program can generate power words for describing, say, a new automobile, or negative words for describing, say, the drudgeries of waxing a floor. Preliminary applications of this program have been regarded as successful by the agencies using it.

If the creative team is blocking on ideas for a campaign, one of these advertising idea generation research methods usually can help, and at no cost or fairly low cost depending on the method chosen.

Advertising Content Screening

The other circumstance in which creative guidance is sometimes needed is when the creative team has *too many* ideas. The creative team, particularly when the strategy research has been extensive, may have developed numerous specific elements or "stimuli" that may or may not work in an ad. Examples of such content include:

- Headlines (print), tag lines (broadcast), or slogans
- Illustrations (print) or story-board video illustrations (TV)
- Benefits stated in alternative wordings (benefit *claims*)
- Presenters
- People representing lifestyle groups
- Settings
- Situations

These elements are often too numerous and too specific to be tested in just a few overall advertising executions, so content screening research is indicated *before* the advertising executions are prepared.

Three methods can be used for advertising content screening. The first is (again) qualitative research but with a quantitative refinement; this is the most widely used method and also a little more expensive. The second is the Q-sort procedure, which employs individual interviews at moderate cost. The third is to analyze creative elements by means of "execution guidelines." This latter method is not yet widely used in any systematic form, but it is very inexpensive and holds considerable promise.

Qualitative Research (Modified) Qualitative research can be used as a relatively convenient way of screening a large number of advertising ideas. The sample for this research should be selected from the target audience or audiences, which will of course be known from the prior advertising strategy research.

The main modification is the introduction of quantitative measures coupled with an emphasis on individual reactions to the ideas. In a group setting, each participant should be asked to write down his or her private opinion or rating of each idea presented before any group discussion of the idea is allowed. In the individual depth interview setting, the same procedure is followed except that the discussion would be between the individual and the moderator rather than a group discussion.

The group influence problem is substantial—and ads themselves should *never* be tested in focus groups (see Chapter 19). The main reason for resorting to groups in content screening research is the saving on interviewer time, since 6 to 12 respondents can be interviewed at once. A really expert group moderator is not needed as in strategic qualitative research; competent interviewers who probe well are sufficient.

However, the best content screening research uses *individual* interviews to avoid group influence altogether, and 50 of these can be obtained for the equivalent price of two or three focus groups totalling only about 30 respondents. Because of the quantitative nature of this research, a sample size of at least 50 respondents *per* target audience is recommended, to produce reasonably reliable ratings of the advertising stimuli or ideas.

Q-Sort Procedure   A very useful method of screening a large number of advertising stimuli is the Q-sort procedure. Again, a representative sample of the *target audience,* or target audiences if there is more than one, must be taken, but a sample of 50 consumers per target audience is sufficient.[23]

Q-sort is a method that allows a large number of stimuli of a particular type —advertisement headlines, benefit claims, illustrations, and so on—to be rated by consumers without inducing the fatigue and errors that would result if they rated or ranked them all at once. Up to about 60 stimuli can be rated.[24]

Any desired rating criterion can be employed. Some *examples* might be:

- *Strong* to *weak* for benefit claims to be used in a low involvement/informational brand attitude strategy
- *Like* to *dislike* for settings to be used in a low involvement/transformational brand attitude strategy
- *Convincing* to *unconvincing* for benefit claims to be used in a high involvement/informational brand attitude strategy
- *Similar to me* to *not similar to me* for presenters to be used in a high involvement/transformational brand attitude strategy

The Q-sort procedure itself is straightforward. Beforehand, the items are typed (verbal stimuli), or photographed or pasted (visual stimuli) onto 3×5 cards for ease of sorting. The respondent is first asked to read or look through all the cards. Secondly, the respondent is instructed to place the cards into three general piles: $+$, 0, and $-$ (for example, strong claims, moderate claims, weak claims; or like, neutral, dislike). Then, working from each pile in turn, the respondent performs a finer sort into a fixed frequency distribution, usually of 11 categories along the criterion scale, with a specified number of cards in each category. An example for 50 stimuli might be:

Dislike most										Like most	
-5	-4	-3	-2	-1	0	$+1$	$+2$	$+3$	$+4$	$+5$	(categories)
1	2	4	6	7	10	7	6	4	2	1	(frequencies)

Each item's score is then averaged across (target audience) respondents. The highest scoring stimuli are selected for incorporating in advertisements.

Execution Guidelines   Execution guidelines provide a means of screening visual content (prospective illustrations or video scenes) and verbal content (prospective headlines and written or audio copy) based on recommendations developed from visual imagery research and psycholinguistic research, respectively. Whereas guidelines have been offered in the past by famous copywriters such as Leo Burnett, David Ogilvy, and Rosser Reeves, their guidelines often conflict. Our guidelines are based on theoretical considerations as well as research evidence.[25]

An important thing to note about these guidelines is that they are *only* guidelines, not rigid rules. However, we would estimate that they will be right about 75 percent of the time; so while an advertising idea can deviate from a particular guideline, the manager should be convinced, in talking to the artist or copywriter, that the departure has a good rationale.

The execution guidelines are predicated on *processing*. That is, they isolate elements in ads that should increase either the attention → learning sequence (for brand awareness and low involvement brand attitude) or the attention → acceptance sequence (for high involvement brand attitude and the other communication effects, category need, hard-sell brand purchase intention, and purchase facilitation).[26] Execution guidelines can be used by themselves to screen elements being considered for use in ads or, as explained below, they can be employed as part of a management judgment ad test.

The visual element guidelines are summarized in Table 18.7 and the verbal element guidelines in Table 18.8. We will demonstrate their application next, as part of a management judgment ad test.

MANAGEMENT JUDGMENT AD TEST

By employing management judgment in a systematic and disciplined manner, it is possible to conduct a reasonably valid ad test *without* formal consumer testing. In fact, a leading marketing consultant, William T. Moran, foresees management judgment ad testing replacing much of consumer ad testing.[27] Our viewpoint is that management judgment ad testing is a very useful initial step for all ads, but that the additional step of testing ads with consumers is essential when introducing a new product or a new campaign.

Overview of the Method

The Checklist   Management judgment ad testing employs a checklist approach to evaluate the ad's content. It is an "expert system" approach, drawing on the knowledge provided in this book. Basically, the purposes of management judgment ad testing are to check that the ad is "on strategy" and that the "execution seems right." To check whether the ad is "on strategy," we need input from the two areas of target audience action objectives and

TABLE 18-7   VISUAL EXECUTION GUIDELINES

General

G-1 *Visual content is on average more influential than verbal content.* There is a general superiority for:
   learning
   acceptance

G-2 *Use high imagery (more concrete) visuals rather than abstract visuals.* Concrete visuals depict objects, persons, places, or things that can be seen, heard, felt, smelled, or tasted—they arouse images in the audience's mind more readily than abstract scenes or sketches, although animated real objects or characters are all right. Superior for:
   learning
   acceptance

G-3 *Interact the product with the usage context or user in visuals.* Superior for:
   learning

G-4 *Use color in visuals for emotional motivation but black and white is sufficient for information provision.* Relative superiority for:
   acceptance (transformational—color; informational—black and white)

Print ads

P-1 *Use as large an illustration as possible.* Superior for:
   learning
   acceptance

P-2 *Use multi-element illustrations (interesting details) to hold rather than just get attention.* Superior for:
   learning

P-3 *Place the illustration where it will be seen before the headline and copy are read.* This does not mean that the headline should necessarily be below the picture, just that the picture should catch the eye earlier than the headline. Superior for:
   learning

P-4 *Vary the illustration on the same theme across ads in the campaign.* This prevents attentional wearout. Superior for:
   learning
   acceptance

Television commercials

T-1 *Make sure that key scenes are "held" for at least 2 seconds.* Key scenes either show the brand, or depict the main message points. Superior for:
   learning

T-2 *The audio relating to key scenes should follow the key scene, in a redundant scene.* Key scenes as defined above; redundant scenes are fillers or continuation scenes that give the viewer time to pause and attend to the audio copy describing the preceding video point. Superior for:
   learning
   acceptance

T-3 *For visual-word "supers" use high imagery words in positive sentences and the reverse for disclaimers.* Relative superiority or inferiority, as desired, for:
   learning
   acceptance

T-4 *Vary the video on the same theme across commercials in the campaign.* This reduces all forms of wearout. Superior for:
   learning
   acceptance

TABLE 18-8   VERBAL EXECUTION GUIDELINES

Headlines/tag lines

H-1   *Limit to between 3 and 8 words.* Superior for:
    learning

H-2   *Emphasize nouns and adjectives, and personal words.* Superior for:
    learning

H-3   *Place brand name last.* Superior for:
    learning

H-4   *Don't use dangling questions.* Inferior for:
    learning

H-5   *Don't command or demand.* Inferior for:
    acceptance

All copy/audio

C-1   *Use simple and familiar words.* Superior for:
    learning
    acceptance

C-2   *Use high imagery (concrete) words.* Superior for:
    learning
    acceptance

C-3   *Use active rather than passive sentences.* Superior for:
    learning
    acceptance

C-4   *Use positive words rather than negatives.* Superior for:
    learning
    acceptance

C-5   *Do not use ambiguous words or puns.* Inferior for:
    learning
    acceptance

communication objectives, which can be taken from either the advertising strategy summary (earlier) or the advertising plan (Appendix A). To check whether the "execution seems right," note first that we include brand awareness and brand attitude creative tactics with their respective communication objectives (from Chapters 9 and 10). Then, finally, we apply the execution guidelines from the present chapter. Table 18.9 shows the factors we use in our checklist. The checklist is detailed to compile, but it's worth the trouble for the fairly low cost in management time and the insights gained.

The Judges   In management judgment ad testing, *multiple* judges should be used, and they must make their judgments *individually,* that is, independently and without any sort of meeting or discussion until after the results have been collected and summarized.[28] Ideally, six to ten (and at the very minimum three) judges should be selected. Ideally, too, the client and the agency should be represented among the judges.

The judges need not be experts, and, indeed, diligence rather than experience (which actually could get in the way of careful analysis) is required. Although it is illuminating for senior managers to make the judgments, we have had excellent results by employing research assistants or management trainees as

TABLE 18-9   MANAGEMENT JUDGMENT AD TEST CHECKLIST

1. *Target Audience Action Objectives*
   a. Target audience
   b. Decision role targetted
   c. Specific action objective

2. *Communication Objectives (and Tactics)*
   a. Category need objective
   b. Brand awareness objective (and tactics)
   c. Brand attitude objective, strategy (and tactics)
   d. Brand purchase intention objective
   e. Purchase facilitation objective

3. *Execution Guidelines (as Applicable)*
   a. Visual general
   b. Visual print
   c. Visual TV
   d. Headlines/tag lines
   e. All copy/audio

judges. When the number of such judges is six or more, they almost always will find one or more major improvements for the proposed ad.

An Application

Let us take an advertisement for which the advertising strategy is known: the (second) National Potato Promotion Board ad from Chapter 10 earlier. We have reproduced it as Figure 18.1 for convenient reference when presenting the findings.

Table 18.10 shows findings from the management judgment ad test applied to the NPPB ad. The findings are very detailed and in this case represent the composite opinions of eight judges. A number of improvements are suggested for this ad. If certain deficiencies are generally agreed, these should be discussed with the creative team.

Managers have long sought a systematic procedure for evaluating creative submissions of ads. Management judgment ad testing, using a strategy and execution checklist such as suggested here, offers such a procedure.

Management judgment ad testing is painstaking work, but every ad should receive this analysis if the manager is serious about improving it.

Thus, the management judgment method provides an overall "meaning" assessment followed by a detailed "structural" assessment of the advertisement's content (the same can be done for promotion offers). The assessment covers all except the exposure step in the buyer response sequence, namely: processing → communication objectives → target audience action objectives.

When to Use a Management Judgment Ad Test

Quite frankly, the typical "formal" ad test is so badly designed that we would advocate universal use of the management judgment "substitute" ad test. The

The only problem with potatoes is they don't have labels.

If they did, we wouldn't have to tell you that a medium sized baked potato has fewer calories ounce for ounce, than rice, bread, or noodles.

Or that the potato contains significant amounts of Iron, Vitamin B₁, Niacin, and over half of the minimum daily requirement of Vitamin C.

There are a lot of good things you could say on a potato label. And one thing you wouldn't have to say.

They're delicious (we figure you already know that).

You and the potato should meet again. Look for it at your store. In a plain brown, white, or red wrapper.

INTRODUCING THE POTATO.
Something good that's good for you.

FIGURE 18.1   National Potato Promotion Board ad (one of the two ads from Chapter 10) used here to exemplify management judgment ad testing. (Courtesy of Potato Board.)

TABLE 18-10   MANAGEMENT JUDGMENT ASSESSMENT OF THE NPPB AD*

Checklist Factor	Assessment: Correct (✔); Incorrect (x)
1. *Target Audience Action Objectives* a. Target audience: potato ("brand") switchers in the side dish category	The reference to what to choose for a side dish could be more explicit. The comparison with other "starch" side dishes is buried in the body copy (**x**).
b. Decision role: meal planning (decider role)	There could be more emphasis on the meal planning decision, which has to be inferred from the ad (**x**). Adult women, especially married women and mothers, are likely to occupy the decider role and the ad doesn't address them specifically (**x**). The ad is suitable, however, as one ad in the campaign for a general audience of users (✔).
c. Action objective: serve potatoes more often (use more)	The body copy says "Look for it in your store;" the direction seems to be toward purchase rather than serving potatoes more often (**x**).
2. *Communication Objectives (and Tactics).* a. Category need: omit	Although the side dish or "starch" side dish category is not mentioned directly, most people should make the connection automatically (✔).
b. Brand awareness: recall potatoes top-of-mind in response to side dish or starch side dish category need (brand recall)	Execution, featuring the labeled potatoes, is unique within the side dish category (✔).
	Brand awareness contact time seems good: people are likely to say "potatoes" from the picture; the word "potato" is in the large headline; and there are five other mentions of "potatoes" in the copy (✔).
	The most apparent main copy line, the headline, "Introducing the Potato," does not include the category need (side dishes) along with the brand (**x**). Although somewhat obvious, we want to force specific recall of potatoes when people think of side dishes.
	The main copy line is not repeated (**x**), which it should be for brand recall.
	There is no personal reference except in the lower, smaller print tag line, "Something good that's good for you." Personal reference should be in the headline (**x**).
	The somewhat bizarre execution, showing labels on potatoes, seems appropriate for generating brand recall (✔).

TABLE 18-10   MANAGEMENT JUDGMENT ASSESSMENT OF THE NPPB AD* (*Continued*)

Checklist Factor	Assessment: Correct (✓); Incorrect (x)
	Main copy line would not adapt to a jingle if we used broadcast ads in the campaign (**x**) although the bottom tag line would (✓).
c. Brand attitude: objective is to change or increase attitude from negative or low positive to high positive; strategy is high involvement (to serve potatoes more often is seen by the target audience as high risk) and informational (mixed approach-avoidance) via taste appeal versus avoiding nutrition and weight problems.	The emphasis is clearly on increasing people's attitude toward potatoes (✓). Long copy format is suitable for high involvement brand attitude (✓). Approach factor (good tasting) is weakened by not showing appetizing potato (**x**), although the copy says "They're delicious" (✓). Problem-avoidance factor is good regarding nutrition (✓) but less so on weight-watching (**x**). These two negative motivations may require separate ads. Emotional portrayal could better emphasize the problem of concern about nutrition (**x**), assuming another ad in the campaign emphasized the weight problem dramatically (✓). Although the ad does not strictly have to be likable, the approach aspect of potatoes (delicious) should be kept in mind. In color, the ad should be reasonably likable (✓). Initial negative (or low positive) attitude held by target audience is well addressed in the copy (✓) but not in the headline or top and bottom tag lines (**x**). The benefit claims appear to be logically stated and within the target audience's upper limit of the latitude of acceptance (✓). However, the cautious wording "we wouldn't have to tell you . . ." could be bordering on under-claiming (**x**). Overall, the benefit claims use the refutational approach quite effectively (✓). However, the potato's comparative advantages against other starch side dishes should be highlighted more (**x**).
d. Brand purchase intention: hard-sell immediate	The action intention is addressed by an exhortation, "Look for it in your store . . ." (✓). However, the intention to serve more often could be more explicit (**x**).

TABLE 18-10   MANAGEMENT JUDGMENT ASSESSMENT OF THE NPPB AD* (*Continued*)

Checklist Factor	Assessment: Correct (✔); Incorrect (✗)
e. Purchase facilitation: point of purchase	The labels make the potatoes more attractive than "raw potatoes" in the typical display (✔). We should perhaps initiate a trade drive to tidy up potato displays.
3. *Execution Guidelines*	
a. Visual general	G-1. The picture of the potatoes dominates and very cleverly communicates the main benefits (in the words in the visual labels). This will help acceptance of benefits (✔).
	G-2. Imagery value of concrete illustrations is reduced by having the potatoes in wrappers with labels; they look a bit like Easter eggs (✗). Perhaps cut-in of appetizing baked potato should also be used.
	G-3. Product is not shown in usage context or with typical user, which might affect learning, for side-dish brand recall (✗). Subsequent ads should show this.
	G-4. Finished ad will have potatoes in color to aid acceptance via the approach factor (✔). Black and white is sufficient for the rest of the ad addressing the avoidance factor (✔).
b. Visual print	P-1. Illustration is large yet allows room for high involvement/informational copy (✔).
	P-2. Labels provide multiple elements for holding attention (✔).
	P-3. Illustration catches attention before headline and body copy (✔) and thus fits the recommended picture-then-word sequence.
	P-4. Varied illustrations (e.g., baked potato, pictures of users) can be utilized in other ads in the campaign (✔).
c. Headlines/tag lines	H-1. The main headline is 3 words, which is okay except that it doesn't associate category need with the brand for learning (✗). The bottom tag line is 6 words (✔) but if read with headline is too long (✗). Must combine and shorten the two. Top tag line, 10 words, is too long (✗).
	H-2. The top tag line has 3 nouns, no adjectives, and no personal words (✗). The bold headline has 1 noun, only (✗). The bottom tag line has 1 noun, 2 adjectives, and 1 personal word (✔). Resolution needed!

TABLE 18-10   MANAGEMENT JUDGMENT ASSESSMENT OF THE NPPB AD* *(Continued)*

Checklist Factor	Assessment: Correct (✔); Incorrect (x)
	H-3. The brand name "potato" is placed last in the bold headline (✔) but not in the tag lines (**x**). We need a resolution for the headline, such as "The best side dish is potatoes."
	H-4. The top tag line, "The only problem with potatoes is they don't have labels," might possibly be seen as inviting an answer and thus being an implied question (**x**).
	H-5. There are no commands or demands in the headline or tag lines (✔).
d. All copy	C-1. The copy contains simple and familiar words with the possible exceptions of "Vitamin B1, Niacin." However, these "sound" nutritious (✔).
	C-2. Overall, the body copy and labels use many concrete words such as "potatoes," "calories," "vitamins" and "delicious" (✔). However, the headline and tag lines contain too many abstract words: "problem," "introducing," "something good" (**x**). These should be changed to higher-imagery words to improve acceptance of the potato benefit claims.
	C-3. Most of the sentences are active although the third paragraph of the copy contains two passive sentences: "There are a lot of good things (object) you (subject) could say . . ." and "And one thing (object) you (subject) wouldn't have to say" (**x**). The first sentence could be reconstructed to "You could say a lot of good things . . ." so the reader will better accept what we do have to say. The second sentence could be changed to, "Also, you already know they're delicious," by joining it with the next paragraph.
	C-4. There are several negatives, namely, "don't," "wouldn't," (twice), and perhaps the word "problem" itself in the opening tag line (**x**). The latter is risky because it may make the reader think of problems with potatoes and not read further. Perhaps, "If potatoes had labels . . ." would remove the first and last negatives in the top tag line. Likewise, "they would tell you" instead of "we wouldn't have to tell you." The other "wouldn't" is removed

TABLE 18-10 MANAGEMENT JUDGMENT ASSESSMENT OF THE NPPB AD* *(Continued)*

Checklist Factor	Assessment: Correct (✔); Incorrect (x)
	in C-3. However, we should discuss this because the negatives seem appropriate for the refutational approach (✔).
	C-5. The pun about the "brown, white, or red wrapper" might lead people to think that the "newly introduced" potatoes *are* wrapped as in the illustration, instead of being a humorous reference to different skin colors (**x**). It's not worth the risk to be cute in this necessarily high-acceptance copy.

Source: Compiled from the following parts of this book: the Advertising Plan in Appendix A, sections B.1 (decision roles) and B.4 (brand behavior only) and all of section C (communication objectives): Chapter 9 (for general brand awareness and specific brand recall creative tactics) and Chapter 10 (for high involvement/informational brand attitude creative tactics); and this chapter (for general and print ad execution guidelines).

management judgment ad test *forces* managers (and creatives) to consider exactly how the ad is intended to work, which too often is not considered thoroughly until after the ad has "bombed" in the marketplace.

However, as we shall see in the next chapter, ad testing with target audience customers—if the test is properly designed—is a very strong additional assurance of good advertising. Ad testing with potential customers is vital for a new brand, or for a new strategy for an existing brand. This leaves two situations in which a substitute management judgment ad test is *alone* sufficient:

- For a very low budget advertiser
- For continuation campaigns: new executions of the *same* advertising strategy, where target audience action objectives and communication objectives remain constant

Quite clearly, management judgment ad testing can contribute substantially towards ensuring that creative executions will meet their communication objectives. The judges in this method are nonetheless managers who, apart from creative managers, may not be able to intuit the target audience's responses to ads or promotion offers to the degree of accuracy required to forecast success. Testing with the target audience is therefore the next advisable stage of advertising research.

NOTES

1 R. Haley, Benefit segments: backwards and forwards, *Journal of Advertising Research,* 1984, *24* (1), 19–25.

2 J. M. Fouss and E. Solomon, Salespeople as researchers: help or hazard? *Journal of Marketing,* 1980, *44* (3), 36–39.

3 In plotting trends in the relationship between advertising and sales, the manager has to be alert for the possibility of advertising "carryover" to future sales. The

presence of substantial carryover or, alternatively, customer "holdover" with print advertising that may not be read or acted upon immediately, can make a *current* plot look as if there is no relationship between advertising and sales when really there is a relationship. Trial-and-error plotting with some simple carryover or "lag" functions, such as $S_t = \text{base sales} + .57A_t + .29A_{t-1} + .14A_{t-2}$, such that the coefficients of current and prior advertising add up to 1.0, with advertising having in this case about 40-percent carryover, can often reveal carryover effects.

4 See P. Kotler and G. Lilien, *Marketing Decision Models,* Englewood Cliffs, NJ: Prentice-Hall, 1983, for an overview of BRANDAID and similar models.

5 Quantitative (survey) methods are purely descriptive, not causal. The experimental or hypothetico-deductive method of hypothesis generation and painstaking testing *is* capable of yielding causal explanations, but in its usual form, it takes far too much effort and time. Qualitative researchers essentially engage in a fast (and sometimes unreliable) form of the hypothetico-deductive method. For an excellent analysis of this point, see B. J. Calder, Focus groups and the nature of qualitative research, *Journal of Marketing Research,* 1977, *14* (3), 353–364.

6 Qualitative researchers often use a variety of supplementary techniques to stimulate ideas. Some of these are described in the "special techniques" section following shortly. Also see, for example, D. N. Bellenger, K. L. Bernhardt, and J. L. Goldstucker, *Qualitative Research in Marketing,* Chicago: American Marketing Association, 1976.

7 Witness, for instance, the confused state of the family decision-making literature in consumer behavior—largely due to superficial surveys rather than a more valid investigatory method such as evaluative participation.

8 Adapted from E. Tauber, Reduce new product failures: measure needs as well as purchase interest, *Journal of Marketing,* 1973, *37* (3), 61–70.

9 S. Young and B. Feigin, Using the benefit chain for improved strategy formulation, *Journal of Marketing,* 1975, *39* (3), 70–74.

10 Again, see the article by B. J. Calder, note 5.

11 Many quantitative researchers use two phases of research: a first phase, consisting of "exploratory quantitative" interviews with a sample of about 200 consumers to develop reliable target audience profile measures and also benefit or motivation segments (see Chapter 7); followed by a second phase of "quantitative probability" research interviews using the reliable measures with a national probability sample of about 1000 consumers, plus a media exposure inventory. See L. Percy, How market segmentation guides advertising strategy, *Journal of Advertising Research,* 1976, *16* (5), 11–22, for a description of this two-phase quantitative research.

12 A third method, which asks consumers to *rate* importance, tends to produce non-valid results because consumers often do not have good insight into how they actually make their brand choices (note that the qualitative researcher *infers* this and doesn't take what consumers say at face value). For damaging evidence on direct consumer measures of importance, see J. Jacard and D. Sheng, A comparison of six methods for assessing the perceived consequences of behavioral intentions, *Journal of Experimental Social Psychology,* 1984, *20* (1), 1–28.

13 See, for example, P. E. Green and C. M. Shaffer, Ad copy testing, *Journal of Advertising Research,* 1983, *23* (5), 73–80.

14 A division into unimportant, low importance, and high importance benefits usually is sufficient. The predictive validity of importance weights tends to be insensitive to small numerical differences in regression coefficients. See, for example, J. M. Blin and J. A. Dodson, The relationship between attributes, brand preference, and

choice, *Management Science,* 1980, *26* (6), 606–619. However, *qualitative* research inference might suggest a finer division of importance levels, and this should be examined.

15 The article by L. Percy (see note 10), indicates how these profile measures can be applied. The details are too numerous and complex to summarize here.

16 Psychographic segmentation rarely works in practice as a primary basis for selecting target audiences and when it does, it is generally because of relationships with, or direct inclusion of (for example, the VALS system), *demographic* measures. For a negative appraisal by a researcher who has tried psychographic segmentation many times, see S. Yuspeh, "Slamming syndicated data," *Advertising Age,* May 17, 1984, magazine section.

17 A common advertising industry practice is to use "marker items" from a previous psychographic study to classify respondents into psychographic types in later studies. Shortened measures are so unreliable as to be useless if not dangerously misleading. For an example using a carefully constructed customized inventory rather than a syndicated one, yet still failing, see S. Yuspeh and G. Fein, Can segments be born again?, *Journal of Advertising Research,* 1982, *22* (3), 13–22.

18 In either case, the factor analysis should be internally "cross-validated" (checked for reliability) by conducting separate analyses on split-halves of the sample.

19 The functional relationship of selected personality traits to persuasion (brand attitude and brand purchase intention) is exemplified in L. Percy and J. R. Rossiter *Advertising Strategy: A Communication Theory Approach,* New York: Praeger, 1980, pp. 31–48.

20 S. Baker, *Systematic Approach to Advertising Creativity,* New York: McGraw-Hill, 1979.

21 Innovators can be screened by co-workers' reports or by administering a creative thinking test. The psychology section of most libraries has books on creativity; authors to look for include J. P. Guilford and F. X. Barron. Creative thinking tests require high scores on all three of the following abilities: fluency (production of many ideas); flexibility (many different categories of ideas); and originality (uncommon, unique ideas) among the ideas generated.

22 Two good books on professional brainstorming techniques are: A. F. Osborn, *Applied Imagination: Principles and Procedures of Creative Problem Solving* (3rd ed.), New York: Charles Scribner's & Sons, 1963; and W. J. J. Gordon, *Synectics, The Development of Creative Capacity,* New York: Harper, 1961.

23 The sample of 50 presumes a homogeneous target audience: other-brand loyals, for example, might differ considerably in being loyal to various other brands, in which case it would be advisable to take a reasonable sample, say 30, of those loyal to each of the major brands. Note that this consideration refers to Q-sort as a rating technique, *not* Q-factor analysis which requires a small heterogeneous sample of respondents and a large but reasonably homogeneous or factorially balanced set of stimuli. See J. C. Nunnally, *Psychometric Methods* (2nd ed.), New York: McGraw-Hill, 1978, chap. 15; and also W. C. Stephenson, *The Study of Behavior,* Chicago: University of Chicago Press, 1953.

24 The best practical description of Q-sort methodology is in M. J. Schlinger, Cues on Q-technique, *Journal of Advertising Research,* 1969, *9* (3), 53–60. For researchers interested in performing a quick "benefit segmentation," this article shows how to do it with a Q-sort followed by Q-factor analysis. Because this is backward segmentation, we won't promote this use of Q-sort here.

25 For further explanation of the guidelines, see the paired articles by J. R. Rossiter,

23 B.R. Bugelski and W.A. Wickelgren, same references as in note 21.

24 The experiments on normal-weight versus overweight shoppers' responsiveness to food stimuli were conducted by: R.E. Nisbett and D.E. Kanouse, Obesity, hunger, and supermarket shopping behavior, *Proceedings,* Seventh Annual Meeting, American Psychological Association, 1969, pp. 683–684; and S.A. Steinberg and R.F. Visual imagery: applications to advertising, and L. Percy, Psycholinguistic guidelines for advertising copy, in A. A. Mitchell (Ed.), *Advances in Consumer Research*: Vol. 9, Provo, UT: Association for Consumer Research, 1982, *9,* pp. 396–406.

26 See Chapter 8 of this book. We have omitted emotional responses because they are content-specific. Emotional responses are assumed to occur for processing of all communication effects except brand awareness.

27 W. T. Moran, Advertising research: What is it all coming to? *Journal of Advertising Research,* 1986, *26* (1), 107–111.

28 Management judgment methodology was described in Chapter 3 as a method for setting the advertising budget. It is worth re-reading that section.

FURTHER READING

Lucas, D. B. and Britt, S. H., *Measuring Advertising Effectiveness*. New York: McGraw-Hill, 1963.

This text, now out of print but available in libraries, is the *only* good book ever published on advertising research. Even for the modern manager, it remains a gold mine of information about what types of research to do and when, lacking only some of the newer statistical techniques.

Calder, B. J. Focus groups and the nature of qualitative research, *Journal of Marketing Research,* 1977, *14* (3), 353–364.

Enlightening reading (for academics) on the validity of qualitative research. Readers will note that the type of qualitative research required for developing advertising strategy is, in his terminology, "analytic" qualitative research. We will take this opportunity to emphasize that qualitative research, while virtually essential for the *development* of advertising (this chapter), should never be used to *test* advertisements (next chapter) once they have been prepared.

Percy, L. How market segmentation guides advertising strategy. *Journal of Advertising Research,* 1976, *16* (5), 11–22.

This is further reading for advanced practitioners with statistical training. Although this article favors benefit segmentation rather than the awareness-behavior-attitude segmentation we now advocate, it illustrates the sophisticated use of target audience profile research in detail unavailable from other sources.

CHAPTER 19

AD TESTING

Ad testing provides additional assurance from the *target audience* that creative executions of advertisements are "on strategy"—that is, that they are capable of producing the communication effects that together comprise the communication objectives for the brand. Ad testing can also be called "pre-testing" because it is done *before* the ads are placed in media.

After reading this chapter you should:

- Know how to choose the overall design and methodology for an ad test
- Understand the necessity of selecting a particular set of measures that fit the advertising strategy (and in particular the *advertising communication model*) for the brand
- Know how to analyze the results and how to decide what action should be taken as a result of the test

We begin the chapter with a consideration of what ad testing actually is, what it can and cannot do, and how much it costs. Once it is decided that testing is worthwhile, the manager then has to select a design (overall) and measures (specifically) to fit the communication objectives; most of the chapter is devoted to how to do this. Finally, we explain how to analyze the results so as to select advertisements for the campaign.

THE PURPOSE OF AD TESTING AND THE DECISION TO TEST

General Purpose of Ad Testing

The general purpose of ad testing[1] is to improve the chances that *finished* ads will work as planned when placed in media. Whether the ads *will* work as planned depends on three factors (assuming no changes in marketing mixes or in the market):

1 *Creative content* being able to meet the brand's communication objectives
2 *Correct Media* placement and scheduling
3 *Competitive Advertising* activity

Ad testing evaluates only the *first* of these factors. Campaign evaluation (or tracking)—the fourth stage of advertising research—is needed to assess all three factors.

In terms of our six-step approach, ad testing is concerned with evaluating the link between step 2, processing (of creative content), and step 3, communication effects (specifically, the brand's communication objectives). Ad testing sometimes proceeds to step 4 (target audience action). However, the advertising strategy research should have specified communication objectives that are *fully expected* to produce the desired actions. Hence, ads are usually tested only against communication objectives.

Specific Purposes of Ad Testing

There are two forms of ad testing and three specific purposes for testing. The first purpose pertains to the testing of preliminary or "rough" executions of ads and the second and third purposes pertain to the testing of finished ads.

Rough Ad Testing to Select Finished Ads   The general purpose of ad testing is to assess how well finished ads will work when they are placed in media. However, because it is expensive to produce finished ads, testing is usually conducted first with *rough* executions of the ads to decide whether each ad is indeed worth producing. (Just how "rough" these executions can or should be we will consider in the design section of the chapter.) A comparatively large number of inexpensive rough ads can be tested to select the best executions for production. (A careful analysis of ad testing by Gross[2] suggests a guideline of producing and testing three rough ads for every intended finished ad.) For example, an advertiser might test 10 rough executions with the aim of producing three finished ads.

To provide an idea of the economics behind the decision to test rough ads, let's consider television commercials, which are generally the most expensive type of advertisement. It costs about $6000 to prepare and test a rough "storyboard" version of a TV commercial. This is about one-tenth of the $60,000 cost of producing the average finished commercial.[3] Our hypothetical advertiser could therefore test the 10 rough executions for $60,000—whereas it would cost over $600,000 to test 10 finished versions. The outlay for testing 10 rough versions and then producing three finished commercials would be about $240,000.

Testing Finished Ads Before Media Placement   Many advertisers proceed directly to media from finished ads based on the rough-tested versions, without testing the finished ads. At first this seems understandable. The media expenditure on a typical TV commercial is about $1,200,000.[4] Thus, there is $3,600,000 to be spent on the three commercials in media. Our hypothetical advertiser already has spent $240,000, for a total of $3,840,000.

The cost of additionally testing the three *finished* commercials (about $12,000) would only increase the *total* cost ($3,840,000) by less than half of 1 percent, which seems very reasonable considering that more than a 1 percent increase in sales effectiveness should result.

And this is why large advertisers, and many not-so-large advertisers, test *finished* ads before accepting or rejecting them for the campaign: *It costs just as much to run an ineffective ad as it does to run an effective one but the profit difference can be enormous.*[5] You have to look at the expected *profit* and not just the costs. Let's switch to magazine advertising to illustrate this.

A single insertion of a full-page color ad in *Playboy* costs about $60,000. Its potential exposure is about 5 million readers. Let's suppose only 10 percent of readers actually pay attention to, and process, the ad: that's 500,000 readers. By ad testing several good rough versions for about $10,000 (which *seems* exorbitant relative to the media cost of one insertion) we could probably find a final version that is processed by 20 percent of readers—1 million readers. Suppose further that (a constant) 1 percent of those who process the ad buy the brand (a travel bag, for example) and that the profit contribution per unit of product sold is $10. The comparison is then as follows:

	Without testing	With testing
Exposed	5,000,000	5,000,000
Processed ad	500,000	1,000,000
Bought item	5,000	10,000
Contribution	$50,000	$100,000
Cost of ad	$60,000	$60,000
Cost of testing	$ 0	$10,000
Net profit (loss)	($10,000)	$30,000

In this example, the untested ad has resulted in a $10,000 loss whereas the tested ad produced a $30,000 profit.

Large advertisers will therefore "shelve" a finished advertisement, even after paying a lot to produce it, if it fails to meet the communication objectives in its finished form. It's actually profitable for them to do so, provided they have other advertisements to use instead. This brings us to the third use of ad testing.

Assigning Initial Relative Exposure Frequencies in a Pool of Ads   All but the smallest of advertisers do, or should, run multiple advertisements (a "pool") in a campaign. Multiple executions of the strategy help to prevent particular types of wearout (see Chapter 20). Ad testing with finished versions of the ads prior to the campaign can be used to establish the initial relative exposure frequencies across the ads. It is naive to use an equal "rotation" unless all the ads performed virtually identically in the ad test, which is a rare occurrence. Rather, the best ad should receive the largest early exposure frequency, the second best the next largest, and so on.

The ratio of percents of individuals converted on the brand attitude or brand purchase intention criterion measure (explained later in the chapter) is the best way of assigning *initial* weights. The weights—exposure frequencies—for the pool of ads can *later* be more validly adjusted as campaign evaluation (tracking) results come in.

Don't Test Ads in Focus Groups

Focus groups are highly appropriate for *advertising strategy research* but totally inappropriate for *ad testing*. There are four principal reasons for not testing ads in focus groups:[6]

1 *Non-Valid Exposure Conditions*   The first validity problem is that focus groups vastly over-expose ads in comparison with media exposure conditions in which ads must actually operate. In focus groups, an ad typically is shown and discussed for 10 minutes or more. Over-exposure leads the research participants to exaggerate positive and negative aspects as well as to focus on elements that would never get processed in the minute or less in which a TV commercial has to communicate or the few seconds available to most print ads.

2 *Non-Valid Processing Reactions*   The second validity problem is that group settings produce group interactions that largely prevent individual reactions to the ad from occurring as they would normally. Consumers process ads as individuals, even when they are watching TV together. In real-life advertising exposure, group reactions are an extreme rarity, yet in focus groups they are inevitable unless all discussion is suppressed.

3 *Lack of Reliable Projection of Results*   Even if focus group test results were valid, there remains a serious reliability problem. Most ad tests with focus groups use three groups, for a "two-out-of-three" decision if necessary, totalling about 30 consumers. The statistical projection error from a sample of 30 people can be as high as plus-or-minus 20 percent (see Table 4.3, in Chapter 4). In other words, a factual 50 percent approval rating could be observed in the focus group sample as 70 percent (a success) or 30 percent (a bomb). In any event, the interactive observations from group results prevent proper statistical analysis.

4 *The Lower Cost Is Misleading*   For the price of three focus groups, about $6000 to $7500, the advertiser could conduct 100 to 200 individual interviews—for a much larger, more reliable, and more valid test.

Ad testing, therefore, should always be conducted by using individual interviews. Furthermore, the test ad presentation should be controlled, and the interviewing procedure should be quantitative (generating measurable responses from individual consumers) not qualitative.

HOW TO DESIGN THE AD TEST

Valid ad testing depends on designing the ad test to fit the advertising strategy for the brand. The fact that so many ad tests (especially by syndicated single-method services) do *not* fit the advertising strategy is what makes so many creative people justifiably angry with ad testing and also produces results that mislead managers. This problem is so serious that, in the previous chapter, we recommended first conducting a substitute ad test via management judgment of the executions *in relation to the strategy*. Going through the management judgment exercise is a convincing way of demonstrating why it is necessary, if an ad is tested, to base the ad test on the strategy.

Whereas the advertising strategy covers all four steps in the buyer response sequence, from exposure to processing to communication effects to target audience action (see the advertising strategy summary format in the previous chapter), the critical consideration that identifies the *type* of ad testing to be conducted can be called the *advertising communication model* for the brand.[7]

The advertising communication model focuses on the:

1 *Brand Awareness Objective*   Brand recognition versus brand recall (or both when applicable) *and* the

2 *Brand Attitude Strategy*   Low involvement versus high involvement brand choice coupled with informational versus transformational purchase motivation—that is, the particular brand attitude strategy quadrant upon which brand choice is based.

The two types of brand awareness and the four types of brand attitude result in eight basic advertising communication models (Figure 19.1) of which *one* will fit the brand's advertising strategy. As we will see, the differences in these models determine the *design* and the *measures* for the ad test.

Let us proceed with the actual decisions to be made in constructing the ad test and analyzing the results, and we will see how most of them depend on the advertising communication model. There are seven decisions to be made:

1 Interview method
2 Design
3 Sample (cell) sizes
4 Test ads' degree of finish
5 Number of exposures
6 Order and selection of measures
7 Analysis and action standards

1. Interview Method

Because test advertisements have to be shown to respondents, ad testing has to be conducted via personal (face-to-face) interviews.[8] The one exception is

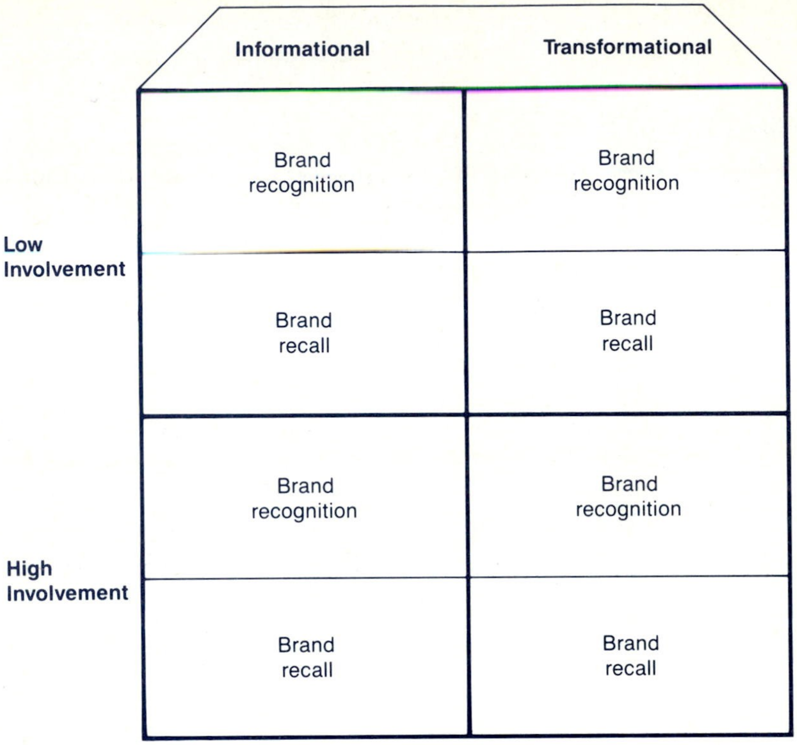

	Informational	Transformational
Low Involvement	Brand recognition	Brand recognition
	Brand recall	Brand recall
High Involvement	Brand recognition	Brand recognition
	Brand recall	Brand recall

FIGURE 19.1 The eight basic advertising communication models based on brand awareness (rectangles) and brand attitude (quadrants).

radio commercials, which can be played over the phone and tested via telephone interviews.[9] As we shall see in the next chapter, campaign evaluation (tracking) studies can be conducted by telephone or even by mail, but ad testing, with the exception of radio ads, has to be done by personal interviews.

Central Location   For ease of administration, most ad tests are conducted in a central location—most often in shopping malls where the research company has an office, or occasionally using caravan testing facilities as a mobile office that can be placed in "high-traffic" locations such as shopping center parking lots or downtown areas. It is *possible* to test print ads, radio commercials, and even TV commercials by door-to-door interviews at respondents' homes, by carrying a print ad portfolio, audiocassette recorder, or lightweight video-cassette recorder, respectively, but most testing of all types of advertisements nowadays is central location testing.

How the Test Ads are Shown   Test ads should be shown *singly* to respondents, not in a competitive context with other ads (for the actual number of exposures, see decision number 5).

Some research methods make the mistake of showing ads in a competitive or "clutter" context—for example, in a portfolio or simulated magazine for print ads, or in a commercial break embedded in a TV program or radio segment for broadcast ads. The competitive exposure context confounds testing of the ad's capability of producing communication effects with its probability of gaining *attention* in the *media* (compare our extensive discussion of this in Chapter 8 on processing, specifically reflexive attention, and in Chapter 16, on effective frequency estimation, specifically low and high attention media). In an attempt to get around this confounding of the two assessments, other research methods, such as the procedure employed by McCollum-Spielman testing service, use clutter-exposure first, then single-exposure to test communication effects. This is not worth the effort. The so-called "clutter awareness" performance of the ad in the test has absolutely no relationship to its effectiveness in the real world.[10] Not only is it impossible, practically speaking, to sample the "real media environments" in which the ad will be exposed, but also to attempt to do so interferes with a proper communication effect assessment of the ad. Clutter-awareness testing is not a valid procedure.

As we will explain shortly, attention-testing only needs to be undertaken in an *ad test* as a diagnostic measure (at the end) in case the ad doesn't meet its communication objectives. Attention in media, on the other hand, can only be assessed *in* the media, during campaign evaluation (or tracking) research.

2. Design

The design of the ad test refers to the nature and number of test "cells" (groups or sub-divisions of respondents) that will be required.

One Ad per Respondent The first rule is that each respondent should be shown only one test ad. It is an error to try to economize by showing two or more test ads to each respondent, in rotated order across respondents. Instead of "counter-balancing" and equating each ad's results, you in fact only obtain valid results for the *first* ad shown to each respondent, and then only if the test measures are administered immediately following the first ad. Accordingly, you will need at least as many cells as the number of test ads.

Pre-post versus Experimental-control Design The advertising communication model dictates the ad test design (the first of many such considerations in designing the test to fit the model)[11]:

1 If the brand attitude strategy is *informational,* then the *pre-post* design can be used. In this design, each cell is given *disguised* pre-measures (for several brands including the test brand), then exposed to the test ad, then given post measures. The total number of cells is equal to the number of test ads.

2 If the brand attitude strategy is *transformational,* the "ego-involving" nature of the attitude as well as, almost paradoxically, the resulting "softer" nature of the image-like benefit beliefs, together mean that even a disguised

pre-measure would sensitize respondents. More plainly, to bring the almost subconscious image of a brand such as Coke to the surface by rating it on a pre-measure, then showing a Coke ad, then rating the brand image again, would be too "obvious."[12] Accordingly, an *experimental-control* design is recommended in which test ad (experimental) cells receive the ad then the post-measures, and an additional (control) cell receives only the *pre*-measure. The pre-measure for the control cell in this design need not be disguised. This adds one cell—serving as a comparison or control for all other cells—to the number of test ad cells.

In the pre-post design for informational communication models, the communication effects produced by the test ad are assessed by measuring, for each respondent, the change from pre-scores to post-scores. In the experimental-control design for transformational communication models, the communication effects produced by the test ad are assessed by measuring the change from the proportion of individuals reaching the criterion on the pre-score in the control cell to the proportions of individuals reaching the criterion on the post-scores in the various experimental cells.

In both designs, respondents must be randomly assigned to cells to ensure that the cells do not differ in any way other than exposure to the test ads. In practice, this is achieved by having recruiters assign respondents to cells in rotation, that is, first respondent to cell 1, second to cell 2, and so on, which is near enough to random assignment.

3. Sample (Cell) Sizes

Ad testing needs reliable numbers of respondents *in each cell* in order to:

1 Project reasonably accurately the *absolute* effects produced by a single ad
2 Compare *differences* in effects pre-to-post or control-to-experimental, or between different ads, in order to conclude that differences in scores are real.

The reader can refer to Chapter 4, Table 4-3, for sample size calculation based on reliability. A normal minimum would be 100 respondents per cell, which will produce a projection error of no more than plus-or-minus 10 percent, and a required difference score of no more than 14 percent.

4. Test Ads' Degree of Finish

"Degree of finish" is the advertising term for how close the test ads are to the final quality of ads that appear in media. Black and white sketches for a TV storyboard or a magazine storyboard, for example, would be the lowest (visual) degree of finish.

Test ads are presented to respondents in ad testing as follows:

- TV: storyboard, slide series (animatic or photomatic), or videotape
- Radio: audiotape

- Magazines, newspapers, outdoor, direct mail: storyboard or slide
- Promotion offer: storyboard (in-ad promotion) or actual (for example, p-o-p or premium)

Degree of finish of test ads is not a trivial question from a cost standpoint. For TV commercials, a storyboard costs about $2000; an animatic or photomatic on slides about $15,000; and a finished commercial costs about $60,000. Evidently, it would save time and money if quite rough black and white sketches could be used in the initial ad test, even if finished ads will be tested later. But the decision is not this straightforward, as we shall now explain.

Informational Models: Rough Ads are Sufficient   For ads based on *informational* communication models, black and white executions of the test ads are sufficient. (Of course, if you can get color versions done cheaply, do so, because better finish will increase predictive validity to the finished version— but for informational ads, not by that much.) Rough ads are sufficient because the informational ("reason why") message should be apparent regardless of the executional quality of the test ad presented to consumers.[13]

Transformational Models: Close-to-finished Ads Required   As explained in Chapters 9 and 10 in conjunction with creative tactics, advertisements based on the positive motivations inherent in *transformational* brand attitude strategy depend greatly on "production values." Emotional authenticity is crucial for the extreme, unique, usually single, and often implied benefit claim in low involvement/transformational ads. Emotional authenticity is very important, too, in high involvement/transformational ads, where you should emotionally over-claim on the transformational benefits. Transformational communication models require authentic production of the test ads.

Accordingly, for transformational test ads, more money should be allocated to produce color-photograph quality visuals, and for TV and radio ads, professionally recorded audio. For TV visuals, it seems to make little difference whether the visuals are on a storyboard, or on slides, or shot dynamically on video tape—as long as the color and finish of the storyboards is very good.

Rough transformational TV commercials are the hardest to get close-to-finished. We have been able to simulate the results of finished transformational commercials quite closely by: (a) paying for near magazine-quality photographs of the video sequence; (b) asking respondents to glance through the video frames in sequence while a (tape recorded) *professional announcer describes what is happening* in the video sequence; then (c) asking respondents to look through the video sequence again while the actual soundtrack is played.[14] This costs only about $3000 to $4000 per test ad, including the announcer's fee, and seems an ideal alternative to more elaborate test ad preparation.

As a safeguard, it makes sense for managers using transformational advertising (especially TV commercials, which depend so much on movement) to proceed and test the *finished* commercials before committing them to media. But to select which ads to produce in the first place, close-to-finished test ads are required, as described.

Equivalent Degree of Finish   It should almost go without saying that to make valid comparisons *between* test ads, they should all be tested in an equivalent degree of finish. This applies to informational as well as transformational communication models.

Although equivalent degree of finish is easy to accomplish when all the ads are new, the problem arises in testing new (test) ads against *previous* (finished) ads. Such a comparison is relevant, for example, to estimate whether the new campaign will be an improvement on the previous campaign, or to see whether a new "pool-out" ad performs similarly to ads in the existing, currently running, pool.

If the previous ads have not been used in media for a considerable time (a year or more), the best solution is to "break them down" to the same degree of finish as the new test ads. This can be done by retrieving *their* storyboards or by preparing new storyboards based on the finished ads.

If, however, the finished ads are currently in the media, then it's pointless to break them down, because the target audience already is seeing the finished ads outside the test setting. To then see a stripped down version would strike respondents as strange, in addition to not representing the real-world test the new ads have to pass. Again, the communication model dictates the decision:

- For informational ads, it shouldn't matter too much if rough ads are tested against current finished ads, although a better finish than normal for test ads would be advisable.
- For transformational ads, the test ads have to be "taken up" to near-finished quality and, ideally, finished versions of the winning test ads should further be tested.

5. Number of Exposures

The next decision the manager or researcher has to make is how often—in the test setting—to expose the test ads to respondents.

The number-of-exposures decision is governed by three factors:

1 Broadcast and mobile exposure outdoor[15] versus print ads
2 Informational versus transformational advertising communication models
3 Test situation-produced wearout

Let's go straight to the recommendations, justifying them in terms of these three factors.

Print Ads: One Ad-lib Exposure   With print ads (magazine, newspaper, direct mail, and "stationary" outdoor) the target audience decision maker, in the real world, can control the exposure duration, spending as little or as much time with the ad according to interest. This should be simulated in the ad test with a single ad-lib (untimed) exposure. The usual instruction is: "Just look at this ad as you would normally."

Although transformational print ads should reach their peak effectiveness after multiple exposures (but note the recommended variations-on-a-theme to maintain attention, especially to print campaigns), there is no realistic way of simulating this in the test situation.[16] Thus, whether the communication model is informational or transformational, one ad-lib exposure is the best solution for print ad testing.

Informational TV and Radio Commercials: Two Exposures   The recommendation to show or play informational commercials twice comes from a compromise. The message in informational TV and radio commercials should be apparent quickly, thus suggesting one exposure. However, because broadcast commercial exposure duration is fleeting, the respondents should be allowed a first exposure to begin to comprehend the commercial ("What is it?"), then a *second* exposure for the ad to work ("What of it?").[17]

"Mobile" informational outdoor ads (see Chapter 15) also should be given two exposures. Exposure is on slides, each exposure approximating the time that a driver (mobile audience) or pedestrian (mobile ad) will see the ad for in real conditions.

Transformational TV and Radio Commercials: Three Exposures   The recommendation to show or play transformational TV and radio commercials and, as should be evident, "mobile" transformational outdoor ads three times, is based on all three factors outlined earlier. First, broadcast means at least two exposures will be necessary for respondents to process the commercial. Second, transformational commercials should continue to increase brand attitude beyond two exposures. However, third, more than three successive exposures in a single-ad test setting might begin to induce either attentional wearout (unlikely for broadcast) or attitudinal wearout (likely, and counter-arguing is fatal for transformational ads[18]).

A transformational commercial should, though, still be peaking at three successive test exposures; three exposures is our recommendation.

6. Order and Selection of Measures

There actually are two order-of-measures decisions to be made. The first is the overall order of measures according to the design of the study. This order is summarized in Table 19.1; we will discuss it now. The second is the order of measures within the ad test questionnaire itself, discussed later in this section.

Order for the Pre-post Design   In the pre-post design, the *same* respondents go through the entire procedure. After screening for target audience membership, the (disguised) pre-measures are administered, then the test ad, then the post-measures. Shortly, we will explain why there is a delayed post-test for brand awareness, and why attention is measured later if required.

TABLE 19-1   OVERALL ORDER OF MEASURES FOR THE TWO AD TEST DESIGNS

Pre-post design (same respondents)
1. Target audience screening (disguised)
2. Brand awareness: pre-test (disguised)
3. Other communication objectives: pre-test (disguised)

Exposure(s) of test ad
4. Processing measures
5. Other communication objectives: post-test
6. Brand awareness: delayed post-test (immediate if direct response broadcast ad; omit if direct mail ad)
7. Attention diagnostics (later if required)

Experimental-control design (different respondents)

Control cell	Experimental cells
1. Target audience screening	1. Target audience screening
2. Brand awareness	**Exposure(s) of test ad**
3. Other communication objectives	2. Processing measures
	3. Other communication objectives
	4. Brand awareness: delayed
	5. Attention diagnostics (later if required)

Order for the Experimental-control Design   In the experimental-control design, *different* respondents undergo the control procedure and the test procedure. The control cell, in effect, takes the (undisguised) "pre" measures and the experimental cell takes the "post" measures. In other words, apart from leaving out the false brands disguise on the pre-measures, the same measures are used as for the pre-post design except that different respondents take them and both cells have to be given the screening questions.

Why Is the Post-measure of Brand Awareness Delayed?   Brand awareness is the "kingpin" communication effect that has to result from advertising. It forms a "gate" to the other communication effects (and thus purchase of the brand) because if the prospective buyer does not recognize or recall the brand, it can't be purchased—regardless of how well established or how favorable the other communication effects for the brand are in the prospective buyer's mind.

Only in the special case of *direct response broadcast* advertising—such as the "call or write now" type of ad that appears on TV or radio—should the brand awareness post-measure in the ad test be immediate. (Direct response ads are designed to produce immediate and obvious effects so the pre-post design applies.) For broadcast direct response ads, there is often a short delay while the viewer or listener grabs a pencil or goes to the phone, so in this instance, a very short-term measure of brand recall (about one minute after exposure) is the appropriate post-test measure.

For *direct response print* ads—including *direct mail* ads—brand awareness should pose little problem because the brand name is right there in front of the reader. There is no need for a post-test of brand awareness for direct response print ads: they have to work *now*.

In all other types of advertising, there will be a *delay* between advertising exposure and the next purchase decision opportunity. This may range from an hour or so for "same day" retail advertising, to a week or more for other products. The advertiser should estimate the average exposure-to-decision interval for the target audience and then measure brand awareness after that interval from the time of the ad test. For seasonal advertisers or advertisers who use pulsing or flighting, this requires looking ahead to the media plan. It is not an easy task, but it is essential if a reliable brand awareness effect is to be assessed.

Brand awareness administered at short delay intervals within the ad testing session itself (for example, about 30 minutes for ad testing services that use "theater" tests of TV commercials) do not provide a reliable measure of the advertisement's ability to create or increase brand awareness.[19] Short interval measures should never be interpreted as absolute measures of the ad's ability to create or increase brand awareness, particularly for *brand recall*, which declines drastically. For instance, recall of a single item, such as a new brand name, after a single exposure, will drop after 24 hours to about 18 percent, and after 48 hours to about 11 percent; recognition, however, stays considerably higher, at about 75 percent and 70 percent, respectively.[20]

The only reliable way to estimate brand awareness is to administer a delayed test:

- For *brand recall*, this can be achieved by phone: an interviewer calls the test respondents back at the appropriate interval and asks them what brands in product category X (actually *category need* X) they recall.
- For *brand recognition*, the measure is more difficult because it requires a personal re-interview in which the test respondents are shown a brand display photograph and asked which brands they recognize at a glance (see brand recognition measures at the end of this chapter). Two-way TV methodologies will greatly help for brand recognition measurement, but at present, a personal follow-up interview is essential.

We cannot say enough about the necessity of measuring brand awareness correctly in ad testing. Remember that an ad test "forces" brand awareness to an artificially inflated level; on an immediate post-test, brand awareness will be close to 100 percent! Brand attitude or brand purchase intention ad test results have to be *discounted* by the brand awareness level that occurs under actual exposure and purchase interval conditions.[21]

As we shall see in conjunction with action standards, only those respondents who meet the delayed brand awareness criterion should be eligible for "passing" the ad test.

Why Measure Attention Separately, and Only as a Diagnostic Procedure if Required?   Attention (actually a series of attention responses) is necessary if an ad or promotion offer is to be processed by the target audience. So why isn't attention measured as the first post-measure (in the processing measures) during the ad test?

The reasons for not measuring attention during ad testing are practical. Crude measures of attention, such as asking respondents what they noticed in the ad, would disrupt the assessment of communication effects. Refined measures of attention (see later) are very expensive, requiring separate testing equipment and detailed recording and analysis.

It is therefore advisable to go to the expense of measuring attention to the ad only if the ad fails, in the test, to meet one or more of the communication objectives. Attention is measured in a *diagnostic* capacity as the final step in ad testing if this should be necessary due to communication failure.

The second order-of-measures decision is the order *within* processing (measured, of course, only on the post-test or for the experimental group, after exposure to the ad) and the order *within* communication effects (measured pre- *and* post-, or for the control *and* experimental groups). This "within measures" decision must be made so as to prevent responses to earlier measures biasing responses to later ones.

Table 19.2 shows the order of measures to use. For convenience of discussion in the measurement section (later), we have numbered the measures 1 through 9. There are two things to note from this table:

- Measures 1 and 2 (processing) would not appear in the pre-measures or for the control group.
- Measures 3 to 8 (communication effects) may not all be necessary, depending on the communication *objectives* that you are testing against.

Finally, selection of *particular* measures to employ depends on the advertising communication model. This is more easily explained in conjunction with the measures themselves, which follow shortly.

TABLE 19-2   THE ORDER OF RESPONSE MEASURES IN AD TESTING

A. *Processing responses* (post- only or experimental group only)
Measure 1: Acceptance . . . . .if *high* involvement brand attitude is an objective
Measure 2: Learning . . . . .if *low* involvement brand attitude is an objective

B. *Communication Effects* (pre- and post- or control *and* experimental)
Measure 3: Category need . . . if an objective
Measure 4: Brand purchase intention . . . except if low involvement/transformational brand attitude is an objective
Measure 5: Brand attitude (overall) . . . except if low involvement/transformational brand attitude is an objective
Measure 6: Brand attitude benefit beliefs
Measure 7: Purchase facilitation . . . if an objective
Measure 8: Brand awareness (delayed)

C. *Communication failure*
Measure 9: Attention (diagnostic)

7. Analysis and Action Standards

Percent of Individuals Attaining the Criterion   In ad testing, the analysis of results must be conducted in terms of the percent of *individual respondents* attaining the criterion. (What the criterion is we will explain below.) Ads, or promotion offers, work by persuading individuals, so it is in terms of individuals that the manager must assess the results.

Group results averaged *across* individuals are misleading and should not be used. Let us illustrate this point. Suppose the criterion measure is a four-point brand purchase intention scale, conventionally scored as follows:

Definitely will buy	=	3
Probably will buy	=	2
Might buy	=	1
Will not buy	=	0

Suppose that the mean score on the pre-measure (or control group measure) is 1.5, indicating that the "average" respondent "might or probably will" buy. Well, it doesn't mean this at all. Perhaps 50 percent of the individuals said 2 and 50 percent said 1; or perhaps 50 percent said 3 and 50 percent said 0; these two vastly different distributions of *individual* responses will give a *mean* of 1.5. Do you see the problem?

Let's go further. Suppose that the mean on the pre-measure (or control group measure) is 1.5 and the mean on the post-measure (or experimental group measure) is also 1.5. Does this mean that the ad was ineffective? Not necessarily. In fact, using the two distributions above as examples, the ad could have moved all the 2 respondents up to 3, and all the 1 respondents down to 0, which would hardly be the "no effect," as 50 percent now definitely intend to buy the brand whereas 0 percent did previously. (In the experimental-control design, this would be equivalent to 0 percent saying 3 in the control group, and 50 percent saying 3 in the experimental group.) The fallacy of using group-averaged results should be evident.

In ad testing, you must analyze the results in terms of the *percent of individuals* who attain the criterion.

What Is the Criterion?   The criterion is a designated *position* on the *brand attitude or brand purchase intention measure* (depending on the communication model) *given* that the individual has also attained a designated *position* on the *brand awareness measure* (which again depends on the communication model). The designated positions are known or estimated by the manager to be sufficient to lead to purchase (or purchase-related) action. For example:

- A brand recognition/high involvement/informational model might designate as the criterion top-box brand purchase intention (definitely will buy) *given* that the respondent recognized the brand within 5 seconds (on the delayed brand recognition measure).

- A brand recall/low involvement/transformational model might designate the top two boxes on two main brand attitude (semantic differential) benefit measures *given* that the respondent recalled the brand within the first two brands recalled (on the delayed brand recall measure).

This approach to defining the criterion (actually joint criteria incorporating brand awareness and brand attitude or its resultant intention) is consistent with the principle previously emphasized: The would-be buyer has to *first* be aware of the brand before he or she can buy, and *also* have a favorable attitude toward the brand.

More guidance on how to pick the criterion *position* on the brand awareness and brand attitude measures will be provided in conjunction with the measures themselves in the following sections.

Action Standards   The very last but very important decision that the manager has to make before actually conducting the ad test concerns "action standards." Action standards are the manager's *prior* considerations of what should be done with the ad depending on alternative outcomes of the results.

Action standards are worthwhile because they force consideration of what percentage of the target audience in the ad test sample, projected to the population and then translated to the *number* of people, needs to be persuaded in order to achieve enough people taking action and thus meeting the sales goal[22] for the campaign.

For example, the manager might calculate that an increase of 20 percent of the target audience (other-brand loyals, for instance) who meet the criterion (brand awareness *and* brand purchase intention) is the minimum required to meet the sales goal. Here it is helpful to look ahead in this chapter to the brand purchase intention measure, where the manager can estimate the *probability that the individual will buy* given that he or she said "definitely will buy" (or some lesser intention level) in the ad test. Unfortunately, softer brand attitude measures, when used as the criterion, do not have this relatively straightforward translation to probability of purchase, so the manager must estimate instead. Action standards might then be as follows. We emphasize that this is an *example:*

Increase in the percent of individuals meeting the criterion (example only)	Action
20+	Approve ad
15–19	Revise ad
14 or fewer	Drop ad

As an experienced advertising manager and researcher, Dr. Neil Holbert, has pointed out, there is no need to be completely rigid about the action standards.[23] They can never be that precise, because of the error in the chain-of-effects estimates required to lead to sales. In the example, for instance, the observed increase might be 19 percent, which is right on the borderline, and the manager may decide to go with the ad anyway.

Nevertheless, action standard specification, if only to within an approximate range, *is* necessary. The manager is deciding, essentially, whether to go with, revise, or reject an advertisement upon which perhaps millions of media dollars will be spent. This decision requires careful forethought, and the requirement of having to set action standards before the ad is tested is a good way of ensuring that the decision will not be made in haste.

In total, then, there are seven overall decisions that the manager has to make in designing an ad test: (1) interview method, (2) design, (3) sample (cell) sizes, (4) test ads' degree of finish, (5) number of exposures, (6) order and selection of measures, and (7) analysis and action standards. There is yet another set of decisions to be made. These decisions concern the selection of *actual* measures (questions and response categories) to put in the ad test questionnaire.

SCREENING QUESTIONS AND PRE-MEASURES

Screening Questions

We will assume that target audience screening questions are fairly easy for the researcher to work out. Ad testing should always be conducted with a sample that is randomly or at least representatively chosen from the target audience for the advertising.

Employing a target audience sample means that potential participants in the ad test will have to be asked screening questions about the product category and brand. These questions are disguised in a set of dummy screening questions for other product categories and brands so respondents will not be alerted to the purpose of the test. The questions ask potential respondents:

1 Whether they are aware of the category (if new) and whether they are aware of (can recognize from a set of photographs, preferably, or a list of names) the relevant set of brands including the test brand

2 Whether they've tried each of the brands and, if so, how often

3 How each brand rates in terms of overall attitude (including *expected* attitude for those brands that are new or that the respondent is not aware of): single best brand, one of several top brands, an average brand, a below-average brand

With a little thought, screening questions to identify any of the target prospect sub-groups can easily be constructed.

Pre-measure Questions

This is where ad test questionnaire design becomes difficult. For the pre-measures (*pre-post* design only), depending on the advertising communication model, questions measuring brand recall, brand purchase intention, and (if deemed necessary) brand benefit beliefs have to be "woven in" with the screening questions, also disguised for the test brand. For example, brand recall should be measured *between* category awareness and brand recognition in the first question set. Then, brand purchase intention precedes the second question set, and brand benefit beliefs (if measured) follow the third question set. These placements are to avoid bias. It's tricky, but with clear thinking and pre-testing of the questionnaire itself, the pre-measures can be properly designed and inserted. Note, of course, that each pre-measure must correspond exactly with its associated post-measure.

There are, of course, no pre-measures in the *experimental-control* design. After screening, the control group goes straight to the communication effects measures. The main measurement selection decisions pertain to the processing measures and the communication effect measures. These are discussed in the next two sections of the chapter, using the measure order (1 to 9) from Table 19.2, which appeared earlier.

PROCESSING MEASURES

At this point, the test ad is exposed to the respondents (in the pre-post design or to the experimental group in the experimental-control design). The number of exposures was covered earlier. Following exposure, the processing measures are administered.

Measure 1: Acceptance

If the advertising communication model is based on *high* involvement brand-attitude strategy (or requires selling category need, inducing a hard-sell brand purchase intention, or achieving a major purchase facilitation objective—any of which are clearly high involvement), then acceptance responses should be measured first. The astute reader may notice, following the above argument regarding measurement of attention only in a diagnostic capacity, that the next two (alternative) processing responses, learning and acceptance, also are diagnostics for communication failure and could therefore be omitted pending the latter event. This is true. However, unlike attention, the responses of learning and acceptance are relatively easy to measure, so it is convenient to obtain these diagnostic measures here, in case they are needed to interpret communication failure on the brand attitude communication effect measure. Moreover, these processing measures do not affect the subsequent measurement of communication effects.[24]

The acceptance measure must reflect *spontaneous* responses during processing. These responses are immediate and transient, so they have to be measured immediately following exposure to the test ad; to measure them during processing, when they actually occur, would of course disrupt processing.

There are two basic types of measures of acceptance: open-ended cognitive response measures and closed-ended adjective checklist measures. The most valid measure of processing is *cognitive response measurement*, where respondents are asked a question like:

1 While you were watching and listening to the commercial (or reading the ad), what *thoughts, feelings,* or mental *images* did you have? What did you think about it? How did you feel? What did you see in your mind?

2 Now, I'll read your comments back to you and I'd like you to tell me whether you regard each comment as positive, neutral, or negative.

More about cognitive response measures can be found in a comprehensive review of the technique by Petty, Ostrom, and Brock.[25]

The alternative *adjective checklist measure,* while it has yet to have its validity fully established, offers a practical administrative advantage, as well as a possible theoretical and interpretive advantage.[26] An adjective checklist is very easy to administer and score because it only asks the respondent to check off adjectives (or short descriptions) that reflect their reactions to the advertising.

The important point in considering an adjective checklist is the selection of appropriate adjectives to match the appropriate advertising communication model. For example:

- *Attention* interesting, held my attention, distracting $(-)$, and so on.
- *Low Involvement/Informational* made me more interested in the brand, a bit too good to be true, but I would like to try it to see, not informative $(-)$, and so on.
- *Low Involvement/Transformational* likable ad, leaves you with a good feeling, unappealing ad $(-)$, and so on.
- *High Involvement/Informational* convincing, no better than similar brands $(-)$, and so on.
- *High Involvement/Transformational* I could really relate to this ad, this brand is not for me $(-)$, and so on.

With the cognitive response measure or the alternative adjective checklist measure, it is essential to check that the respondents are acquiring an attitude to the right brand. This can be checked by scoring the cognitive response answers for references to the brand, or by following the adjective checklist with a question that asks the respondent to name the brand that was advertised.

Measure 2: Learning

Learning responses of the ''rote'' type are relevant to *low* involvement brand attitude strategies. (Learning is also necessary for brand awareness, but this is measured later.) In the low involvement brand attitude strategy, what counts is the *perceived* message regarding the brand. It doesn't matter whether the target audience fully accepts, or is convinced by, the message during processing, as long as it is perceived correctly: a successfully registered low involvement attitude shift will show up on the communication effect measures of intention to *try* the brand (low involvement/informational advertising) or brand attitude ''image'' benefit increases (low involvement/transformational advertising) as will be explained shortly in conjunction with measures 4 and 6 respectively.

The processing measure for low involvement attitudinal learning is straight-forward. It consists of the following type of question: "In this ad, what do you think the advertiser is trying to tell you about the brand?" The respondent's answer is recorded and then compared with the actual benefit claim itself. Answers, for example, might be: "The advertiser is trying to tell me that Visine is the best product for getting the 'red' out of your eyes" or "The ad shows you that kids who drink Dr Pepper have a lot of fun." Verbatim playback or accurate paraphrases of the ad-proposed brand benefit are scored as successful learning during processing.

Once again, the interviewer should ask: "What was the brand advertised?" (if not already mentioned in the answer). This is because the association to be learned is between the brand (awareness) and the benefit (attitude) and not the benefit in isolation.[27]

COMMUNICATION EFFECTS MEASURES

The order of communication effects measures is different from the order in which they typically occur in the buyer's mind (see again Table 19.2). The reasons for the differing order of measurement from the buyer's more typical sequence of category need, brand awareness, brand attitude, brand purchase intention, and purchase facilitation are twofold.

First, as previously explained, the brand awareness measure has to be delayed because, except in the case of a direct response ad, it is pointless to measure brand awareness after the respondent has just seen or heard the ad. Not only would nearly everyone have perfect awareness with this virtually immediate measure, but also it would not validly reflect the usual post-advertising retention interval for which a brand has to be remembered in the real world.

The second reason for the altered order of measurement pertains to brand attitude and brand purchase intention. The order of these two measures is reversed so as to prevent respondents from forming or modifying their purchase intentions from the attitude measure rather than from the ad. These points are elaborated in relation to the respective measures.

Measure 3: Category Need (If an Objective)

The first communication measure taken is category need—if *reminding or selling* of the category need is a communication objective of the campaign. Let us first consider measurement when the objective is to remind the target audience of category need, then we will consider measurement for the more complicated objective of selling category need.

Reminding of Category Need When the category need communication objective is to remind the prospective buyer of a previously existing or latent category need, the measure to be used is *category purchase intention*. For example, if the objective is to remind current owners of personal computers of the category need in order to influence them to buy a new one, ask: "How likely is it that you will buy a *new* personal computer for home use in the next 6 months?"

Selling Category Need   To measure the communication objective of selling the category need requires three measures at the category level: *category purchase intention, category benefit beliefs,* and *category awareness* (delayed). Category benefit beliefs are required to assess whether, indeed, the advertisement has "sold" the prospect on the need to buy this product category. Category awareness is required to ensure that the prospect "remains sold" by remembering the product category. Category awareness occurs within the context of competing purchase *categories* (for example, "What new items are you thinking of buying for your use at home within the next 6 months?"). The brand measures then follow.

The multiple measures at the category level are required by the consideration, when selling category need, to "treat the category as if it were a brand." The potential buyer must first be aware of the category, accept its (category attitude) benefits, and intend to buy within the category—before the particular brand's communication effects can come into play. Brand communication effects are then measured at this "second level."

Category communication effects, from a measurement standpoint, are conceptually identical to brand communication effects, although the respondent is rating the category in the first instance and the brand in the second. The measures themselves are therefore discussed only at the brand level in the sections to follow. All one has to do for constructing category measures is to treat the category as a brand and revise measures 4 through 8 to reflect the category as the measurement level.

Measure 4: Brand Purchase Intention (Except Low Involvement/ Transformational Models)

There is one situation (applying *only* to ad testing) in which brand purchase intention should not be used as a measure. This is for *low involvement/ transformational* communication models. The reason is that the low involvement "image" type of attitude that this advertising addresses takes "time to build." In the ad test situation, it is not reasonable to expect an immediate effect on brand purchase intention. Indeed, the effect may be largely subconscious.

Instead, the effect of low involvement/transformational ads should be inferred from increases on the *brand attitude benefit beliefs* (measure 6) because this is the only reasonable effect that can be expected during the ad test. In campaign evaluation after the ad has been running for a while, on the other hand, both brand purchase intention (measure 4) and overall brand attitude (measure 5) would be used because the transformational advertising has now had time, that is, a sufficient number of exposures, to work.

For all other communication models, a brand purchase intention measure is included. And it should be the first communication effect measured (other than category need when that is an objective) so that this desired result of the advertising is not "contaminated" by the brand attitude measure.

Constructing the Purchase Intention Measure   Measures of purchase intention involve four considerations: (1) the wording of the intention question in terms of "try," "buy," or "use"; (2) a time frame for intention; (3) the type of rating scale; and (4) how to interpret the ratings.

The first consideration, wording, should be elementary but it's not. In the authors' experience, for new product categories (and brands), consumers are more willing to state intentions to "try" a brand, which implies less commitment, than they are to state intentions to "buy" it. Similarly, purchase versus usage may be relevant, depending on the specific action objective of the advertising. For example, many consumers own power tools, or dangerous chemical fertilizers, or drugs, but for a number of reasons are not really classifiable as "users," since they own them but rarely or never use them. The wording of the intention measure should *reflect precisely the purchase or purchase-related action objective*.

The second consideration, time frame, must be included for the *category* purchase intention measure. For example, many consumers "intend" to buy a microwave oven, but most of them have somewhat vague ideas as to when. The new car purchase intentions (7 percent) cited in Chapter 6 and in the sample question above about personal computers specified a time frame of six months. For a consumer packaged good, a more relevant time frame might be "next time you visit the supermarket." The point is that open-ended intention measures can be misleading. The manager needs a time frame in order to make an unambiguous assessment of category purchase intention results.

Time frame for the *brand* purchase intention measure is incorporated by making the intention *conditional* on category need.[28] For example:

- *If* you were going to buy a personal computer for home use, how likely is it that you would buy an IBM "PC"?
- *Next time* you buy yogurt, how likely is it that you will buy Dannon?

The third consideration concerns the type of rating scale to employ. We favor "unipolar" scales ranging from 0 to positive; in our view, an intention cannot be negative, since you cannot "unbuy" a product—you either don't buy (0) or you do (positive). The exception is when *amount* of purchase is also a consideration, for example, "Do you intend to buy more, the same, or less frozen food in the coming year?" Apart from this, unipolar scales should be used.

The type of scale has to be combined with the fourth consideration, interpretation. At the *individual* buyer level, with which communicaiton objectives are concerned, we believe the fractional or "box" measure is the most interpretable and meaningful to the manager.[29]

For *low involvement* products where *trial* or a *single purchase over a long purchase cycle* is the action objective, a four-point brand purchase intention scale can be used and interpreted (parentheses) as follows: "definitely will buy" (90 percent of these individuals will actually buy); "probably will buy" (40 percent); "might buy" (10 percent); and "will not buy" (0 percent). For low involvement products where *usage* of the brand *among several acceptable brands bought reasonably often* is the action objective, we need to allow for more than one brand. A good measure is: "If you were shopping for (product category), which brand would you be most likely to buy? What would be your second choice?" Indications are that, on the next purchase occasion, 75 percent of consumers who nominated the brand as first choice will buy it; 15 percent who nominated it as second choice will buy it; and 7 percent, also, who did not name it will buy it. The heavy weighting toward the "top box" in both the foregoing measures reflects consumers' tendencies to develop clear cut and simplified brand purchase intentions for low involvement products.

For *high involvement* brand purchase intention, such as for industrial products and major consumer durables, when more discriminating judgments by consumers seem feasible, Juster's 11-point probability or percentage scale can be used:

Certain or practically certain (99 percent chance)
Almost sure (90 percent)
Very probable (80 percent)
Probable (70 percent)
Good possibility (60 percent)
Fairly good possibility (50 percent)
Fair possibility (40 percent)
Some possibility (30 percent)
Slight possibility (20 percent)
Very slight possibility (10 percent)
No chance or almost no chance (0 percent)

When measuring brand purchase intention for brand *recognition* communication models, the validity of the measure will be increased if a *picture of the brand* is used. We will discuss this further in conjunction with brand awareness (measure 8).

Measure 5: Brand Attitude (Except Low Involvement/Transformational Models)

Next comes the overall measure of brand attitude. This measure is omitted only when testing low involvement/transformational advertisements, as explained above.

Brand attitude measurement helps to interpret the ultimate ad test criterion measure: brand purchase intention (given brand awareness). Whereas in brand purchase intention we measure how likely the respondent is to *buy* the brand, in overall brand attitude we measure how favorably the brand is *evaluated relative to other brands,* regardless of whether the respondent would buy it at the next purchase opportunity.

Constructing the Brand Attitude Measure   The main thing to remember in preparing the brand attitude measure is to specify the "situation" (motivation) for which the brand is to be evaluated. Note that, if there's any doubt, the situation *also* should be specified in the *purchase intention* measure (for example, a personal computer for *home use*). As we have seen in Chapter 6, global evaluations, without the motivation, are meaningless.

The set of brands against which the test brand is to be rated has to be chosen. Generally, the relevant set will be apparent from advertising strategy research—for the target audience. If the relevant set is not known, which is almost inexcusable, McCollum-Spielman testing service recommends that leading competing brands accounting in total for at least 70 percent of market share be included. Unless the category is a product such as shampoos, where the market is atomized by an incredible number of small-share brands, this usually will provide a list of manageable length! For brand *recognition* communication models, again, *pictures* of the brands will increase the validity of the brand attitude measure.

Many researchers favor the "constant sum" measure for overall attitude rating.[30] However, we favor a four-level measure in which respondents are asked if they would rate the advertised brand, along with competitor brands, as "the single best brand," "one of several top brands," "an average brand," or a "below-average brand," for a specific situation. It is conceptually equivalent to constant sum, and much easier for the manager to interpret. Notice too that the focus is on *evaluation*, not purchase.

Measure 6: Brand Attitude Benefit Beliefs

Having respondents rate the brand's perceived delivery on the specific benefit or benefits employed in the advertisement to influence brand attitude serves as a *diagnostic* measure for the overall brand attitude result as well as serving as the *sole* measure of brand attitude when low involvement/transformational brand attitude is an objective. This measure (a set of measures) follows the overall brand attitude rating (measure 5) so as again to avoid contamination. The advertiser does not want the respondent forming a spurious attitude based on benefits suggested in the measures rather than on benefits spontaneously processed in the ad. Hence, the diagnostic benefit measures follow the overall attitude measure.

The *form* of brand benefit belief scales should be adapted to the type of brand attitude (advertising communication model), as explained next.

Low Involvement/Informational Model   In the low involvement/informational brand attitude strategy, the brand is perceived as either having the benefit or not having it. Consumers are *not* involved enough to discriminate *degrees* of benefit delivery, and even if they do, the brand choice probably is made on a "pass-fail" basis of benefit possession anyway. Thus we recommend a *yes–no* (1, 0) set of benefit belief measures for the low involvement/informational model.

High Involvement/Informational Model   When consumers are highly involved with brand choice, degrees of benefit delivery *do* make a difference. Often researchers employ what are called Likert scales to reflect gradations of perceived delivery. For example: "How strongly do you agree that the IBM PC is expensive: Do you agree strongly, agree slightly, neither agree nor disagree, disagree slightly, or disagree strongly?" However, the gradation really should not be a part of the agreement. Rather, the gradation should be in *amount of benefit possession*. For example: "Do you believe the IBM PC is: Very expensive, moderately expensive, somewhat expensive, or not at all expensive?" The latter type of scale is much easier for the manager to interpret.

A refinement in measuring benefit beliefs for high involvement/informational advertising communication models is to add a *confidence measure*. After each benefit delivery rating, a second scale asks respondents how sure they are of the rating scale *point* they chose on the benefit delivery scale, for example, "not at all sure," "somewhat sure," "moderately sure," "very sure."

Moran[31] contends that advertising can work by making consumers more *sure* of a brand's benefit delivery without necessarily making them believe that the brand delivers an increased amount of the benefit than previously. This increased confidence fits high involvement theory whereby consumers have to be convinced by advertising (be very sure or confident) before trial. What the advertisement is doing in this case is producing a more *strongly held* benefit belief.

Low Involvement/Transformational Model   When testing low involvement/transformational advertisements, measure 6 is the sole attitude measure and it also substitutes for the purchase intention measure. The theoretical rationale for this was explained at length in Chapter 6.

Recommended is a "softer" measure of perceived benefits popularly known as semantic differential scales.[32] For *each* benefit, and there may be only one (for example, that a brand of Scotch is socially sophisticated), several scales are employed to improve the reliability of this softer measure. The scales consist of bipolar adjectives separated by seven-point intensity ratings. For example, to measure the brand's perceived "sophisticated" image, the advertiser may use the following three scales:

An upscale drink	⊔⊔⊔⊔⊔⊔⊔	A downscale drink
My friends would not approve	⊔⊔⊔⊔⊔⊔⊔	My friends would approve
A discriminating choice	⊔⊔⊔⊔⊔⊔⊔	A choice of the masses

The manager unfamiliar with semantic differential scales should consult a good marketing research text for details of labeling, rotation of order and scale direction, and calculation of significant "image" shifts when using these measures.

High Involvement/Transformational Model   Brand benefit delivery ratings for *high* involvement/transformational brand attitudes require some thought on the part of the manager or researcher. Because of the high involvement aspect, gradations of benefit delivery are appropriate, suggesting the same type of scales as for a high involvement/*informational* model. However, if the product type is such that the brand attitude is "soft"—such as, for example, choice of expensive designer jeans for a first-time buyer (NCU) target audience—then semantic differential scales, which also are graduated, would be a better selection.

Common Sense in Benefit-delivery Measure Selection   Throughout this section, we have tried to demonstrate that rating scales should be selected according to two common-sense considerations:

1 The advertising communication model, which is *how the consumer decides*
2 Ease of interpretation of what the ratings *mean* in terms of diagnostic or corrective action

With these two principles in mind, it shouldn't be too difficult to select appropriate measures, for brand benefits or, indeed, for any other communication objective to be measured.

Measure 7: Purchase Facilitation (if an Objective)

The last immediate communication effect measure is purchase facilitation, if this is an objective of the advertising. Usually, the measure will simply consist of a direct open-ended question (for example, for a distribution problem: "Do you think this brand will be easy to obtain in your area?"). Alternatively, purchase facilitation items can be *added to the benefit belief ratings* of measure 6 (for example, easy to obtain . . . difficult to obtain). Either measure should be capable of rating whether purchase facilitation has been successfully addressed in the advertisement.

Measure 8: Brand Awareness (Delayed)

Because of its importance in valid ad testing, we gave considerable discussion previously to the delayed brand awareness measure. Here we will focus on the physical measures themselves—one for brand recognition and the other for brand recall.

Constructing the Brand Recognition Measure   The main consideration in constructing the measure of brand recognition is to *simulate the real-world recognition situation as closely as possible*.

Usually this will be visual recognition,[33] so a personal re-interview is required, at the average exposure-to-decision interval. However, when using the *experimental-control* design so that there is no pre-measure sensitization, it could be argued (see Chapter 9 and Chapter 20) that because visual recognition declines relatively little over time, an *in-test* rather than a delayed measure would be satisfactory. Tomlin[34] has used the in-test (experimental versus control) brand recognition measure with, he reports, realistic results.

When visual recognition in the real world occurs singly—as in, say, choosing a motel or a fast-food restaurant when traveling on a freeway or turnpike—then the visual stimuli in the test should be administered singly. Actual logos or, better still, photographs of storefronts, should be used. The recognition response to each is yes-no.

When visual recognition in the real world occurs in a multiple brand, competitive display—as is the case with most supermarket products—a simulation of the display must be used. Color photographs are best for this. And if the number of competing brands, shelf space, or shelf position vary widely, then several photographs, randomized across respondents, should be used.

What should the *cutoff* for brand recognition be, in the competitive context? There is no *general* answer to this question. (And it is a vital question, because the criterion measure for ad tests is brand purchase intention or brand attitude *given* brand awareness.) The best answer is empirical: in the advertising *strategy* research, find out how many brands a buyer typically looks at before deciding. The next best answer is theoretical: for low involvement purchases, the maximum would be about three brands, whereas for high involvement decisions, there probably should be no cutoff, as long as the buyer *does* recognize the test brand.

Constructing the Brand Recall Measure Brand recall measures, because they are completely verbal (aural), can be conveniently administered on a delayed basis by telephone interview. The delay *is* important for accurate brand recall communication effect measurement, because brand recall declines quickly from the test situation, and is far more subject to competitive interference than brand recognition.

An example of a typical brand recall measure would be: "When you think of personal computers for home use by people like yourself, what brands come to mind?" The main thing to remember is to specify the *category need cue* or stimulus, to which recalled brands are the responses, in the brand recall question itself; for example, personal computers for *home* use, rather than personal computers for *office* use at the person's place of work, which normally would not be a personal purchase.

The brand recall *cutoff* criterion must be set to provide valid interpretation of brand recall results. Again, empirical determination of the number of brands the typical buyer usually recalls before making the purchase decision provides the best answer to the cutoff measure. For low involvement decisions, this very often will be the first or "top-of-mind" brand recalled, but for high involvement decisions, up to five or six brands may be recalled for purchase consideration. Specification of a realistic cutoff becomes vitally important when ad test results are analyzed because, as explained, the criterion is brand purchase intention or brand attitude *given* that the brand was recalled within the real-world cutoff number.

COMMUNICATION FAILURE

Measure 9: Attention (Diagnostic)

If an advertisement fails to meet its "action standard" on the criterion measure, and if the other diagnostic measures (1, 2, or 6) have not revealed the problem, then this is the time to employ a diagnostic *attention* measure.

The "Show-and-tell" Measure of Attention   A basic but sometimes adequate diagnostic measure of attention is the "show-and-tell" method. The researcher takes a sample of about 30 target audience respondents and re-presents the ad to them individually. To measure *visual* attention, you hand them a print ad, or show them a TV commercial by "freezing" on key scenes, and ask them to describe what they noticed during the ad test's earlier exposure. To measure *auditory* attention, TV audio tracks or radio commercials can be re-presented sentence by sentence, and respondents are asked what they remembered hearing during the ad test's earlier exposure.

The weakness of this method is that it does not represent normal processing (natural attention). Nevertheless, because of its relatively low cost, it should be tried as a first resort to see whether the attentional problem or problems in the ad can be easily pinpointed.

Physiological Measures of Attention   More valid but considerably more expensive diagnostic attention measures require the use of physiological (for example, eye movement, pupillometric, or EEG) apparatus, or semi-physiological (for example, CONPAAD) apparatus.[35]

Visual attention problems—which include TV video and print visuals, *and* copy, since it is visually read—are most accurately traced through eye-tracking analysis. Burke's Telcom division in Teaneck, NJ, can analyze TV commercials in dynamic presentation. Print ads or still video frames can be analyzed by commercial firms such as Perception Research Services, Englewood Cliffs, NJ, The Pretesting Co., Inc., Fairlawn, NJ, or E.Y.E., Inc., New York.

Auditory attention problems—which include TV audio and radio commercials—require a device like ARBOR, Inc.'s CONPAAD, in which respondents depress a foot or hand switch to maintain audio intensity. Because you can't "see" the ear responding, auditory attention is particularly difficult to measure. However, CONPAAD can detect which parts of a TV or radio commercial soundtrack respondents appear to tune out and which parts they find useful (informational) or attractive (transformational) to listen to.

The general conclusion is that detailed diagnostic attention measures are affordable only by the very largest advertisers. The diagnostic capacity of these measures seems good but their "prognostic" or predictive capacity for developing more effective advertising has yet to be established. We must conclude that such measures should only be employed as a last resort in ad testing, when communication failure cannot be diagnosed by simpler and less expensive analysis.

BUYER BEHAVIOR MEASURES

Some ad testing methods incorporate buyer behavior (target audience action) measures. These include: follow-up self-report interviews of brand purchases; providing test respondents with coupons for an entire product category or all major brands within a category including the test ad brand, redeemable only at a nearby store; and the split cable method for testing TV commercials, used by Burke's AdTel and IRI's BehaviorScan, which is very much like split-run testing for print or direct mail ads.[36] All such measures are reasonably straightforward for the manager to interpret. These measures, step 4 in the buyer response sequence (target audience action), provide a useful but expensive *addition* to the measures of step 2 (processing) and step 3 (communication effects) in our six-step sequence.

However, buyer behavior measures such as AdTel or split-run tests cannot *alone* substitute for testing on the two prior steps unless the advertiser is willing experimentally to vary the elements in an ad across a number of possible combinations in a large-scale and costly experiment. Even then, diagnosis of why various elements in the ads did or did not work is indirect. So most managers prefer to test processing and communication effects directly in the manner described in this chapter. A buyer behavior test can then be added if the testing budget is large and the manager wants a *really* high level of assurance before approving the ad's use in the campaign.

NOTES

1 It is convenient to confine this chapter to ad testing. Promotion offer testing was covered in Chapter 14. However, it should be noted that the conceptual issues discussed in conjunction with testing advertisements apply *also* to the testing of promotion offers.

2 I. Gross, The creative aspects of advertising, *Sloan Management Review,* 1972, *14* (1), 83–109. Professor Gross's analysis further suggests that it's worth spending at least 15 percent of the advertising budget on creating and testing ads—a figure that is high by actual standards yet not unrealistic if advertisers truly believe creative execution to be important (for transformational advertising, we could endorse this figure, but probably not for informational advertising, where execution is comparatively less important). As one observer put it: ad testing constitutes only 5 percent of the expenditure but creates 80 percent of the controversy in advertising research. We will see why, perhaps, in this chapter.

3 Obviously, the costs can vary widely above or below these averages. The $6000 figure is based on a fairly generous estimate of $4000 for the ad test, a cost that remains quite constant no matter what form the ad is tested in, rough or finished. Only $2000 has been allowed for "storyboard" preparation, and this is where the dilemma comes in. For $2000, the advertiser gets a series of color sketches (like a big comic strip pasted across a board) for the video, and an unprofessionally recorded sound track for the audio. A better rough version, known as an "animatic" (color sketches) or a "photomatic" (color photographs) on *slides,* with a professionally recorded audio, costs about $15,000—or about one-fourth the cost of a finished commercial. A rough *videotape* (that is, dynamic, not stills) version of the commercial can cost about $30,000—or half the cost of the finished version—which clearly begins to become uneconomical. This puts enormous pressure on the

predictive validity of testing inexpensive storyboards, about which we will have more to say in the design section. See also E. Tauber, Editorial: can we test storyboards?, *Journal of Advertising Research,* 1983, *23* (5), 1.

4 Updated estimate from B. J. Coe and J. MacLachlan, How major TV advertisers evaluate commercials, *Journal of Advertising Research,* 1980, *20* (6), 51–54.

5 See E. Young, Use eye tracking technology to create clutter-breaking ads, *Marketing News,* November 27, 1981, p. 19. For the large advertiser, the additional reassurance, in other words, the stronger expectation of profit, from testing finished TV commercials easily outweighs the additional cost. For example, in 1984, Burger King spent $40 million in its comparative TV campaign against McDonald's and Wendy's. Obviously, the profit implications of the success or failure of the comparative commercials are enormous. At, say, $400,000 to produce and test the commercials in both rough and finished form, the testing costs would only be 1 percent of the media budget.

6 For more detail on these criticisms, see J. R. Rossiter and R. J. Donovan, Why you shouldn't test ads in focus groups, *Australian Marketing Researcher,* 1983, *7* (2), 43–48.

7 Because of the vital way in which brand awareness and brand attitude affect the choice of creative content, the media strategy, and the means of testing and evaluating advertising, we have begun to promote use of the term *advertising communication models* to encompass primarily these two communication effects and their strategic and tactical considerations. See J. R. Rossiter and L. Percy, Advertising communication models and their implications for advertising research, in E. C. Hirschman and M. B. Holbrook (Eds), *Advances in Consumer Research: Vol. 12,* Provo, UT: Association for Consumer Research, 1985, pp. 510–524. An adapted version of this article was also published by J. R. Rossiter, L. Percy, and R. J. Donovan, The advertising plan and advertising communication models, *Australian Marketing Researcher,* 1984, *8* (2), 7–44.

8 The future possibilities of two-way interactive cable TV may allow testing of TV commercials, radio commercials (blank screen), print ads, direct mail, and outdoor—as well as promotion offers—very conveniently by a combination of TV presentation of ads and questionnaires with TV response via the phone line.

9 The testing of radio commercials by phone interviews presumes that the brand awareness objective is *brand recall,* which it usually is when radio is the primary medium (see Chapter 15). If *brand recognition* is the objective for radio commercials, then personal interviews have to be used, at least for the delayed brand recognition test (see later in the present chapter), because visual brand recognition stimuli have to be administered in person.

10 Evidence on the predictive validity failure of McCollum-Spielman's clutter-awareness measure is presented in P. R. Klein and M. Tainiter, Copy research validation: the advertiser's perspective, *Journal of Advertising Research,* 1983, *23* (5), 9–17. See also note 19 and Chapter 20, note 1.

11 The best design for either informational or transformational ad testing is the Solomon four-group design. Although rarely used in practice, it should be understood by managers for use in high-risk decisions. Four cells are needed:

1.	Pre	AD	Post
2.		AD	Post
3.	Pre		Post
4.			Post

This design enables statistical assessment of the pre-measure's sensitizing effect (3 versus 4) as well as the advertising exposure effect (1 versus 3) as well as a possible interaction between the pre-measure and the advertising exposure (1 versus 2 versus 3 versus 4). See D. T. Campbell and J. C. Stanley, *Experimental and Quasi-Experimental Designs for Research,* Chicago: Rand McNally, 1966. However, it is rarely used because the Solomon four-group design adds *at least three* cells to the test for informational ads (cells 3 and 4, plus another cell 2 for every cell 1 depending on the number of test ads) and *at least two* cells to the test for transformational ads (cell 3, plus another cell 1 for every cell 2 depending on the number of test ads). For academic theory-testing research, or in applied advertising research when the manager wants a highly accurate calculation of each ad's effects (accuracy depending also on the size of the sample), this is the design that should be used. It is hardly ever used in practice.

12 If the manager levels the same charge against pre-post ratings for an informational test (where, we argue, the benefit and thus attitude shift *should* be obvious), then the Solomon four-group design should be used to resolve the issue.

13 Detailed comparison of test results for rough (artwork storyboard) TV commercials versus finished TV commercials indicates that the rough versus finished correspondence is noticeably higher for informational processing measures than for transformational processing measures. For transformational communication models, you need to test close-to-finished ads. Test results are reported in M. J. Schlinger and L. Green, Art-work storyboards versus finished commercials, *Journal of Advertising Research,* 1980, *20* (6), 19–23.

14 As explained in decision number 5, multiple exposures are recommended for testing transformational broadcast commercials, so the re-exposure helps rather than damages the test.

15 Also "mobile exposure" outdoor media—where either the *audience* is mobile or the *ad* is (see Chapter 15). Mobile exposure outdoor media, such as drive-by billboards and exterior bus or taxi signs, function like TV: the audience cannot control exposure duration.

16 By using a simulated magazine (usually called portfolio presentation but it can also be presented on slides, where the respondent "turns the pages" with the remote control switch on the slide projector), the same print ad could be inserted more than once to produce multiple exposures for transformational ads. However, as stated earlier, the interference caused by the particular selection of competing ads and editorial material would not be generalizable to real exposure environments, so attempted multiple exposure of print ads is not worth the effort.

17 H. E. Krugman, Why three exposures may be enough, *Journal of Advertising Research,* 1972, *12* (6), 11–14. In this article, Dr. Krugman theorizes that processing is essentially complete in *two* exposures, with the third and subsequent exposures serving as reminders to maintain the communication effects already established. We believe this to be correct for *informational* commercials. However, *transformational* commercials should continue to *increase* brand attitude *beyond* two exposures. (Note that by "exposure," Krugman means *attention*. This depends, actually, on media vehicle attention, as explained in Chapter 16.)

18 McCollum-Spielman's TV commercial testing service uses two exposures to measure brand attitude effects. (They use one "clutter" exposure first, then measure brand recall, then a "solus" single-commercial exposure before measuring brand attitude.) The service hypothesizes that these two exposures are equivalent to six natural "on air" exposures (again, attentions). We doubt this. Given that the first exposure

is cluttered, and the second delayed somewhat, we suspect that their procedure probably brings a commercial up to sufficient exposure for informational commercials but *not* enough for transformational commercials. See McCollum-Spielman & Company, Inc., Choosing the right attitude measure, *Topline,* 1980, *2* (2), whole issue but especially page 1.

19 For example, the brand *recall* measure used by the McCollum-Spielman testing service lacks reliability *and* validity. (The ARS testing service measures *advertising* recall, not brand recall.) McCollum-Spielman measures only brand recall, *not* brand *recognition,* so this service will not suit brand recognition communication models. Moreover, brand recall is not measured in relation to other brands in the *category,* but against other non-competing brands advertised at the testing session. As a measure of brand recall, the way it occurs competitively in the real world, the results are meaningless. At best, attention to brand stimuli in the commercial is being measured, and in a non-generalizable context.

20 C. W. Luh, The conditions of retention, *Psychological Monographs,* 1922, *31,* whole of no. 3.

21 As an example of this, let's suppose that the advertising communication model is a brand recall model, and that McCollum-Spielman's measure *is* valid and reliable. According to *ad forum,* May 1981, p. 13, the service's norm for brand recall is 39 percent (of individuals) and the norm for attitude or purchase intention change is 20 percent (of individuals). Roughly calculated, this means that only 39 percent of 20 percent, or *8 percent,* of individuals would buy the brand.

In fact, the entire brand awareness measurement issue is immensely complicated, and we have been forced to make some heroic assumptions. Brand *recognition* should be okay, because the one (print) or two or three (broadcast) test ad exposures should be enough to bring brand recognition to a peak. But for brand *recall,* it could be argued that the ad in the actual media plan will get many more exposures to build brand recall (assuming continued attention) and thus is disadvantaged by the few test exposures when recall of the test brand is assessed against the recall of competing brands that have had many more exposures in media. However, the competitive isolation of the test ad, as well as the inherent personal memorability of attending the test, plus the one to three exposures, should, we believe, reasonably simulate the number of in-media exposures necessary to put the test brand's recall on a fair basis to measure against competing brands. The relationship between number of exposures (per individual) and brand recognition or brand recall can be measured more accurately in tracking studies, but until someone suggests a better solution for measuring brand awareness on the basis of *ad tests,* we'll stay with our recommended delayed measure.

22 Strictly speaking, sales *goals* can be set only for a total campaign, not for individual ads or promotion offers where directional objectives, only, are appropriate (see Chapter 2). However, the manager will have a fair idea of how any single ad is expected to contribute to the campaign (for the small advertiser, the single ad or promotion offer may *be* the campaign). Thus, this estimate is a reasonable one to require.

23 N. B. Holbert, Before we start any research, let's look at it from ends to end, *Marketing Review* (American Marketing Association, New York Chapter), 1984, *39* (9), 11–14.

24 J. T. Cacioppo, S. G. Harkins, and R. E. Petty, The nature of attitudes and cognitive responses and their relationship to behavior, in R. E. Petty, T. M. Ostrom, and T. C. Brock (Eds.), *Cognitive Responses in Persuasion,* Hillsdale, NJ: Lawrence Erlbaum Associates, 1981, pp. 31–54.

25 R. E. Petty, T. M. Ostrom, and T. C. Brock (Eds.), *Cognitive Responses in Persuasion,* Hillsdale, NJ: Lawrence Erlbaum Associates, 1981.

26 The origin of adjective checklists to measure reactions to advertisements seems to be attributable to, independently, researchers at the Leo Burnett advertising agency in Chicago, and the research firm of ARBOR, Inc. in Philadelphia. For examples of the Burnett lists over the years, see W. D. Wells, C. Leavitt, and M. McConville, A reaction profile for TV commercials, *Journal of Advertising Research,* 1971, *11* (6), 11–17; M. J. Schlinger, A profile of responses to commercials, *Journal of Advertising Research,* 1979, *19* (2), 37–46; M. J. Schlinger and L. Green, Art-work storyboards versus finished commercials, *Journal of Advertising Research,* 1981, *20* (6), 19–23; and D. A. Aaker and D. E. Bruzzone, Viewer perceptions of prime time television advertising, *Journal of Advertising Research,* 1981, *21* (5), 15–23. The ARBOR list is not publicly available.

27 Acquisition of an attitude to an unspecified or wrong brand would, of course, signal a serious problem with the ad. Again, we emphasize the necessity of brand awareness preceding brand attitude.

28 P. R. Warshaw, A new model for predicting behavioral intentions: an alternative to Fishbein, *Journal of Marketing Research,* 1980, *17* (2), 153–172.

29 The sources for the interpretation of the measures are as follows. For the four-point intention measure, see G. L. Urban and J. R. Hauser, *Design and Marketing of New Products,* Englewood Cliffs, NJ: Prentice Hall, 1980. For the three-point intention measure, see J. MacLachlan, *Response Latency: A New Measure of Advertising,* New York: Advertising Research Federation, 1976. For the eleven-point intention measure, see T. F. Juster, Consumer buying intentions and purchase probability: an experiment in survey design, *Journal of the American Statistical Association,* 1966, *61* (3), 658–696, and also D. G. Morrison, Purchase intentions and purchase behavior, *Journal of Marketing,* 1979, *43* (2), 65–74. For evidence that low involvement intentions basically are dichotomous and high involvement intentions graduated, see M. U. Kalwani and A. J. Silk, On the reliability and predictive validity of purchase intention measures, *Marketing Science,* 1983, *1* (3), 243–286.

30 In the constant sum measure, the respondent is asked to allocate a total of 11 points across the brands to reflect evaluation, allocating as many or as few as appropriate to each brand. This amounts to the same thing as arranging *brands* along a scale, which is what the four-level measure does. For interpretation of point allocations in constant sum, see J. MacLachlan, same reference as in note 29, Table 4.8.

31 W. T. Moran, The circuit of effects in tracking advertising profitability, *Journal of Advertising Research,* 1985, *25* (1) 25–29. Related theory is in R. S. Wyer, *Cognitive Organization and Change,* Potomac, MD: Lawrence Erlbaum Associates, 1974, chap. 2.

   The concept of increased confidence (reduced variance) also fits Moran's contention that good advertising will reduce the price-increase elasticity of the brand and make it more resistant to competitive promotions (as explained earlier in Chapter 15 on the interdependence of advertising and promotion). Reduced variance at the *individual* level is also a good way to explain the post-purchase *reinforcement* effect of *transformational* advertising. However, the transformational brand attitude measure is too fragile, in most cases, to withstand the addition of confidence scales.

32 C. E. Osgood, who invented the semantic differential, used the term to refer to the factorial structure obtained from ratings on these scales, not to refer to the scale format itself. However, the latter usage has become popular. See C. E. Osgood, P.

H. Tannenbaum, and G. Suci, *The Measurement of Meaning,* Champaign: University of Illinois Press, 1957. This book is of more than historical interest. It indicates how brand attitudes, or "brand images," are learned, and also has several sections on applications of the semantic differential technique to marketing and advertising, as well as discussing measurement considerations in more detail than we can provide here.

33 The occasional occurrence of *verbal* or, more precisely, *auditory* recognition was discussed in Chapter 6 (for example, when a waiter tells you what kind of drinks the restaurant has). Auditory brand recognition could be measured in a telephone interview by reading a list of brands.

34 E. R. Tomlin, Pot pourri: a miscellany of practical market research techniques, Paper presented at the Annual Conference, Market Research Society of Australia, Wrest Point, Tasmania, September 1982.

35 Eye movement apparatus, known as eye-tracking, traces a dot of light reflected off the cornea as the eye scans the ad, or more recently uses a tiny video-camera that clips on to an eyeglasses frame to record the direction and duration of gaze. Pupillometric apparatus measures dilation of the eye's pupil, which can measure attention over time (for a TV commercial) but not *where* attention is directed within the visual field (for example, within a TV commercial video scene or within a print ad). Electro-encephalographic, or EEG, apparatus provides a gross measure of attention in the form of decline in alpha-waves from the brain, but is notoriously unreliable and expensive. For a review of these measures, see D. W. Stewart and D. H. Furse, Applying psychophysiological measures to marketing and advertising research problems, in J. H. Leigh and C. R. Martin (Eds.), *Current Issues and Research in Advertising,* Ann Arbor: Graduate School of Business Administration, University of Michigan, 1982, pp. 1–38. CONPAAD is a foot-pedal or button-pressing "operant response" apparatus. For TV commercials, one foot pedal or hand button controls the brightness of the TV screen, which fades if you don't press it, thus providing a rough measure of visual attention; the other foot pedal or hand button controls the loudness of the audio track, which also fades if you don't press it, thus providing *the only known measure* of auditory attention. CONPAAD is offered by ARBOR, Inc, Philadelphia. For a description, see: P. E. Nathan and W. H. Wallace, An operant behavioral measure of TV commercial effectiveness, *Journal of Advertising Research,* 1965, *5* (4), 13–20; and R. L. Grass, L. C. Winters, and W. H. Wallace, A behavioral pretest of print advertising, *Journal of Advertising Research,* 1971, *11* (5), 11–14.

36 AdTel or BehaviorScan (for TV) and split-run (any medium, but usually print) are methods in which different test ads are delivered to randomly selected "cells" of households, using cable TV, or "tip-ins" in print media. Purchases in each household are then recorded in a diary, or electronically at stores. Direct response ads in any medium can be split-run tested by "keying" the reply to a particular ad. Results for alternative test ads are thus compared in terms of buyer behavior.

FURTHER READING

The best preparation that a manager can have for designing an ad test is to call or write the major ad testing services (listed in the American Marketing Association's *Green Book* or in the advertising section of the *Journal of Advertising Research*) and ask to be sent *descriptions* of their ad testing methodologies. Then, the manager should re-read this chapter, make up a table of all the processing and communication effects, and try to align each service's measures appropriately. You'll see that no one syndicated service is adequate. None of the services takes into account advertising communication models. Of the major syndicated services, McCollum-Spielman probably offers the greatest flexibility in choice of measures, but the manager would still have to know the advertising communication model for the brand in order to choose the measures appropriately. There should, however, be sufficient information in this chapter to enable the manager to custom-design an ad test.

CHAPTER 20

CAMPAIGN EVALUATION

The final stage of advertising research is campaign evaluation. In this chapter we will concentrate on *tracking research* (which includes the post-testing of advertisements) and on the managerial action to be taken when an advertising campaign seems to be "wearing out."

After reading this chapter you should:

- Understand the purpose of tracking studies and know which measures to use
- Know when to use partial (aggregate) tracking methodology and when to use complete (market survey) methodology
- Within the advertising plan, know which problems cause various types of wearout, and how to correct these problems

As with all the stages of advertising research, campaign evaluation, in the formal sense, is optional. The majority of campaigns are not tracked formally; instead, the manager observes the brand's sales trend before and during the campaign and then *infers* that the advertising (or promotion) is working or is not working.[1]

Sophisticated (and large budget) advertisers conduct campaign evaluation or tracking research even when all signs in the marketplace imply that the advertising is meeting—or not meeting—its sales goals. The sophisticated manager wants to be sure that the advertising is *causally responsible* for sales, rather than other factors in the marketing mix, or in competitors' marketing mixes, or in the market itself, such as economic conditions, being the sole causes. Further, the manager also wishes to estimate the *extent* of advertising's contribution, for the next budgeting period.

Tracking research is expensive. First of all, the manager will need to conduct a *pre-campaign* or "benchmark" survey, if this has not already been done as part of advertising strategy research. Then, one or more "waves" of surveys will be needed *during the campaign,* to compare with the benchmark and "track" the campaign's progress. Each survey wave will cost $20,000 at minimum, depending on sample size, purchase incidence, and the length of the survey questionnaire.

MEASURES USED IN TRACKING

A complete tracking study will use measures of all six steps of the advertising effects sequence: (1) exposure, (2) processing, (3) communication effects, (4) target audience action, (5) sales or market share, and (6) profit. In this section, we recommend and describe which measures to use.

Exposure Measures

In this book, we have defined exposure as the *opportunity* for exposure. That is, exposure occurs when the advertisement is *placed* so that the prospective buyer can see, read, or hear it. Whether or not the prospect *does* see, read, or hear it is a matter of attention, which is part of the second effect, processing.

Exposure, then, is essentially a *media measure*—specifically, a *rate of media input*[2] that can then be related to sales rate, or to the intermediate steps of the effects sequence. The rate of media input can be measured in various ways, ranging from gross measures such as advertising dollars or gross rating points (GRPs) to measures that more closely approximate exposure such as reach at minimum effective frequency (effective reach).

Each measure is expressed as a rate for a particular time period. The time period can be weekly, monthly, or less often—depending on the corresponding rate at which the manager wants to measure (or has available) changes in sales or any other intermediate effect.

Advertising Dollars   The rate of overall expenditure on advertising is what most concerns senior management. The expenditure rate in relation to the rate of sales growth or decline provides an overall input-output evaluation. Advertising dollar-expenditure rate is an important measure but it is a gross measure of exposure from a causal perspective.

Gross Rating Points (GRPs)   The rate of GRPs achieved per time period also provides a gross measure of exposure. Total GRPs per week or month or for any other relevant time period, such as the purchase cycle duration, can be found by adding the *audience* (percent reach) figures for all vehicles[3] in which the ad was placed, that is, the total audience—repeated or not—for the total number of placements, in the time period. As explained in Chapter 16, GRPs take no account of how many exposures an individual receives and are simply a count of the (often repeated) exposures that are "out there" to be attended to.

First, GRP rate can be related to dollar-expenditure rate to see whether the advertising money is being spent "efficiently" (GRPs-per-dollar, over time periods). A high ratio means you're getting cheap media buys; a low ratio means that you're paying more than usual for each exposure. This index stops here; there's no reason "efficiency" (a ratio) should relate to "effectiveness" in terms of sales rate.

Second, GRP rate can be related directly to sales rate or to the rate achieved on intermediate measures. This provides a crude measure of the effectiveness of the media plan—crude because GRPs can be attained from many different individual audience-member exposure patterns. That is, a GRP figure can represent many alternative patterns of reach and frequency.

Reach at Minimum Effective Frequency (Effective Reach)   The rate of *target audience* reach at minimum effective frequency (see Chapter 16) is the most precise measure of exposure.

To measure target audience reach at minimum effective frequency, the manager needs to include direct media measurement in the tracking study market-survey questionnaire (see later in this chapter). Minimum effective frequency is calculated for the purchase cycle (Chapter 16) but *reach* at minimum effective frequency is a figure that can be translated to whatever time period has been used for the *other* tracking measures; or, alternatively, *they* can be taken at an interval corresponding with the purchase cycle. Either way, the equivalence of time period has to be made to use this measure of exposure in campaign evaluation.

If the rate of target audience reach at minimum effective frequency (effective reach) doesn't relate to the sales rate, then there's likely to be something wrong—not with the media plan but with either the advertising strategy or with its creative execution (either of which signals a major problem with earlier planning). Fortunately, tracking, since it traces the six-step effects chain, usually can isolate the location of the problem, as we will see with the remaining measures.

Processing Measures

Processing consists of the prospect's *immediate* responses to the ad (attention, learning, acceptance, emotional responses). Processing cannot be measured directly in a tracking study because interviewers can't "be there" when every exposure occurs. Instead, processing is measured *indirectly* in the tracking study in a very important way. Remember in the "laboratory" setting of ad testing, the ad is shown in isolation, out of its natural media context, with attention guaranteed by the test procedure. What ad testing misses out on is examining the ad's ability to be processed in the actual, competitive, real-world media environments[4] in which it is placed. In campaign evaluation, we have these environments. But we can't interview people immediately after they've been exposed, and certainly not after each of their exposures if there's more than one exposure per person.

So, in tracking, we measure *competitive attention indirectly* (which actually includes at least partial *processing*, because the respondent has to have *learned* in order to remember the ad when the interviewer calls). The more frequently used competitive attention measures are advertisement recognition, advertisement recall, and advertising category "cut-through."

Advertisement Recognition   In advertisement recognition, tracking study respondents are shown, or for radio, played, the ads from the campaign and asked whether they have seen or heard them before.[5] With answer categories of "yes," "not sure," and "no," only the "yes" answers should be counted as signifying recognition. Notice that the memory cue or stimulus is the *ad* itself and the response required is advertisement (not brand) recognition.

Advertisement recognition is a relatively easy response hardly at all diminished by interference (competitive learning) from whatever intervened between actual exposure and the re-exposure in the tracking study interview. Therefore it is a reasonably valid and reliable measure of whether in fact the target audience paid attention to each advertisement in the campaign.

Advertisement recognition is (1) partly a check on the *media plan*—whether each ad in fact reached the number of people that the plan called for; and (2) partly a check on the ad's ability to gain *attention* given that it reached those people. If you know that the media *vehicle* reached the number of people specified in the media plan, then the problem most likely is with the creative, specifically, its ability to gain attention in actual media environments. If so, the first corrective action should be a "show-and-tell" attention test.[6]

Advertisement Recall   A measure which demonstrates that an ad has been linked to the brand correctly during in-media processing is advertisement recall. Notice that the memory cue or stimulus is the *brand,* and the response is the ad. Recall of the ad's content provides evidence on the extent to which the brand's associated benefits came from the advertising and not elsewhere. It does not matter, ultimately, where they came from *except* as a check on the advertising's causality.

Day-after recall (DAR) should *not* be used for this purpose, unless the advertiser is prepared to pay for *multiple* DAR tests (see note 6). A far cheaper and more straightforward measure tied to the brand (memory cue or stimulus) rather than initially and prejudicially to the particular media vehicle (which is the initial memory cue in DAR) is that used by Colman and Brown.[7] The Colman-Brown measure is a two-stage measure, and we have improved the first stage by making it fit the appropriate advertising communication model:

1 *Show list of brands (if brand recall model) or pictures of brands (if brand recognition model).* Which of these brands have you seen or heard[8] advertised recently?

2 *For each brand named:* Please describe the advertisement or advertisements for this brand in as much detail as you can remember, and in particular, what the advertisement showed or said about the brand. *Probe thoroughly:* Tell me more about the advertisement. What else did it show or say?

Scoring for this measure (coding) is as follows. The respondent has to describe the advertisement, or each advertisement recalled for the brand, in *sufficient detail* to satisfy the coder that the advertisement was indeed seen or heard, and that the respondent is not guessing or describing some other brand's advertisement—hence the need for heavy probing during the second stage answer. Then, the recalled *content* of the advertisement or advertisements is classified into categories corresponding to the brand's benefits, to allow the advertising-caused inference to be made.

Again we stress that this is not day-after advertising recall (the common measure); DAR measures recall of a particular insertion of an ad, in a particular media vehicle, at a particular time. Rather, the appropriate measure is *general* advertising recall resulting from the *overall* media plan. Day-after recall and the general advertisement recall measure are not comparable and cannot be interchanged for interpretive purposes.

Category Advertising "Cut-Through" Whereas advertising recognition is proof that people attended to the ad (ad cue), and advertisement recall is proof that people processed the ad in relation to the brand (brand cue), what if people remember the ad but not the brand? This signals competitive, in-media processing failure, which happens often.

To detect this problem, the advertising "cut-through" measure is employed. We can't just ask people what advertising they remember, in general, because this question is too vague. Instead, we narrow down the recall task by giving them the *category* cue (for example, "fast-food restaurants"), and ask them what advertising they remember for this category of product. *Then* we ask them what *brand* was being advertised.

Cut-through should be tested for *each medium separately* (for example: for TV advertising, then for magazine advertising). This is to further narrow down the memory task and to curb the tendency for people to think that the question refers *only* to TV, as may happen if the question were to use the general term "advertising." Separate questions are needed for each advertising medium of interest.

Cut-through is then coded for adequate description of the advertisement's content *and* scored for correct or incorrect association of the brand with the advertisement. *Branded* cut-through is what is wanted; wrongly branded cut-through indicates the incidence of processing failure.

Communication Effects Measures

The communication effects measures in the tracking study should be *exactly* the same as the communication *objectives* measures used in the ad testing stage.

The advertising should be "post-tested" on the same communication measures on which it was "pre-tested." And, once again, to be valid, these measures must fit the advertising communication model for the brand, as explained in the previous chapter.

For *low involvement/transformational* communication models, we now include the brand attitude and brand purchase intention measures that were omitted (in favor of brand benefit beliefs) in ad testing. Brand attitude and brand purchase intention should emerge consciously if the campaign is working, and can now be measured.

There is one difference in the *order* of the measures. Brand awareness (brand recognition or brand recall) can now be measured *first,* preceded only by category communication effects if category need is an objective. There's no need for a delayed measure of brand awareness, because brand awareness has now had time to operate and must emerge first (before brand attitude) if purchase is to occur.

Target Audience Action Measures

The target audience action measures are the same as those reviewed in Chapter 4. Depending on the target audience, the campaign's action objectives could be trade or consumer behavior; purchase or purchase-related; and would be, specifically, trial, repeat or brand switching.

At this point, we have to think carefully about what is happening during the campaign (Table 20.1). With the exception of brand loyals and routinized favorable brand switchers, if the campaign is *successful,* the individuals who were in the target audience prior to the campaign will *move out* of that target audience. For example, new category users, if a target, should become category users, not stay NCUs. In fact, we want NCUs to enter our brand's franchise by becoming routinized favorable brand switchers, or better still, brand loyals.

This realization means that one index of the campaign's performance is *the changing incidence of prospect group membership itself.* For example, in a campaign aimed at new category users, the percent of consumers who are NCUs should get smaller; and in a campaign aimed at brand loyals, the percent of consumers who are BLs should *not* get smaller. (For simplification, Table 20.1 shows only five potential target audiences—the main four with a division

TABLE 20-1   WHAT HAPPENS TO PROSPECT GROUP MEMBERSHIP IF THE CAMPAIGN IS SUCCESSFUL?

Prior to campaign (that is, the target audience *for* the campaign)	Movement to final status if the campaign is successful
Brand loyals	→ Brand loyals (no change)
Routinized favorable brand switchers	→ Routinized favorable brand switchers (no change)
All *other* brand switchers Other-brand loyals New category users	→ Routinized favorable brand switchers *or* brand loyals

of the brand switcher group. A table by sub-groups, see Fig. 4.4 earlier, could show increases in status for all 12 sub-groups except single-brand loyals.)

So, unlike ad testing, we do *not* want to sample only the target audience. Rather, for tracking studies, we need a *random sample of the total potential audience* (for example, all adults for an adult-purchased consumer product, or all firms in the industry, for an industrial product). Target audience classification is done later, post-interview, so that the incidence of membership can be tracked as a percent of the *total* base of consumers.

Similarly, the action measures—percent trial, percent repeat, percent switching in versus out—must be taken on the total base. For example, if we mistakenly sampled only NCUs throughout the tracking study, trial would always be zero! Yet the campaign might be very successful because the base of NCUs is itself reducing relative to the total base. We'll add more on this in a moment in the methodology section of the chapter.

Sales or Market Share Measures

Sales measures and market share measures (relative sales in relation to the category or market, correctly defined) were described in Chapter 2. We can estimate sales by aggregating customer purchases, or measure sales directly from store audits, and so on. In Chapter 2, we explained why these alternative measures of sales may or may not give the same results.

Profit Measures

Profit measures were also described in Chapter 2. Profit can be tracked by substituting dollar contribution for dollar sales revenue, per period, and then subtracting the advertising expenditure per period. Although it is more usual to track only sales or market share, profit should be tracked as it is the "bottom line" measure of campaign effectiveness.

METHODOLOGY FOR TRACKING STUDIES

So far we have not indicated where the various measures come from (Table 20.2). By and large, the exposure (input) measures and the sales, market share,

TABLE 20-2   MEASUREMENT SOURCES BY STEP

1.	Exposure	Media audit (direct measurement, though, comes from the market survey)
2.	Processing	
3.	Communication effects	→ Market survey
4.	Target audience action	
5.	Sales or market share	Retail audit, factory withdrawals, etc.
6.	Profit	Company calculation

or profit measures (output) come from audit services or from company records. The measures for the middle steps—processing, communication effects, and target audience action—come from market surveys with consumers.

Market Survey Methodology

To diagnose the causality of advertising through every step, the most valid procedure is *panel* survey methodology. In a panel survey, the *same* consumers are interviewed in the benchmark (pre-campaign) wave and in each successive (during-campaign) wave. Unfortunately, this can prove to be *very* expensive and difficult to maintain.

Interviewing *separate samples* of consumers each time allows us only to relate *two* steps in the chain of effects and then only on an *aggregated* basis. We can relate exposure (for example, advertising dollars) to percent processing, or exposure to percent communication effects, or exposure to percent action, or exposure to sales (no survey needed), but we can't properly link processing to communication effects to action without tracking the same respondents.

To infer the causality of *how* the advertising worked (steps 2 through 4) panel methodology is best; practically, however, many companies settle for separate samples.

Market Survey Interview Methods

Tracking studies require personal (face-to-face) interviews because the interviewers have to show *ads* to respondents to measure processing (attention by the advertisement recognition method). Further, if the advertising communication model is a brand recognition model, the interviewers have to show pictures of *brands* or brand displays to respondents.

Telephone interviews can't be used unless we happen to be testing a radio campaign. We can play radio commercials over the phone, but we can't show TV or print ads over the phone. Note that this sole use of telephone interviewing for radio campaigns presumes a *brand recall* communication model, which radio campaigns would normally be using anyway.

Order of Measures in the Market Survey

The recommended order of measures in tracking study market surveys is shown in Table 20.3. Note that the measures of processing (2, 4, and 10) and exposure (11) and action (5) are interspersed with the measures of communication effects. This is to prevent order bias; that is, answers to early questions affecting or "giving away" answers to later questions.

The order-of-measures rationale can best be explained with the aid of a *simplified* set of questions for IBM PC's, a product and brand used in some of our ad testing examples in Chapter 19.

Category need ("Do you intend to buy a personal computer?") comes first, before any brands are asked about. For the same reason, category advertising

TABLE 20-3   TRACKING STUDY ORDER OF MEASURES IN THE MARKET SURVEY QUESTIONNAIRE

1. Category need*
2. Category advertising cut-through
3. Brand awareness:
    a. Brand recall*
    b. Brand recognition*
4. Advertisement recall
5. Action (reported purchase or purchase-related behavior)
6. Brand purchase intention
7. Brand attitude
8. Brand attitude benefit beliefs
9. Purchase facilitation*
10. Advertisement recognition
11. Profile variables (especially media exposure)

* If an objective.

cut-through ("What TV ads have you seen recently for personal computers?" "What magazine ads . . . .?") must be placed early in the sequence, because it stems from a category cue. Respondents are, however, asked to name the brand in the cut-through questions, so now it is appropriate to move to brand questions.[9]

Brand awareness may require brand recognition measurement, brand recall measurement, or both (*if* both are objectives of the campaign). If both, then *brand recall* ("What brands of personal computer come first to mind?") should precede *brand recognition* ("Which of these brands have you seen before?"), as the first is "unaided" whereas the second is "aided" in that the brands are shown to the respondent.

Advertisement recall ("What TV commercials have you seen recently for IBM Personal Computers?") is measured next. Even if we've measured brand recognition and thus "given" the respondent the brands, this doesn't matter, because advertisement recall is based on the brand-as-cue (see the Colman-Brown measure earlier).

Action measures are then taken. Depending on the action objectives, these may be purchase ("Which brand of personal computer do you have?") or purchase-related ("Which personal computer stores or retail outlets have you visited?"). Quite logically, brand purchase intention, which is intended action, is the next measure ("If you were going to buy a personal computer, how likely would you be to buy an IBM PC?").

Brand attitude ("Overall, how would you rank the IBM PC—the single best, and so on?") and then brand attitude benefit beliefs ("How does the IBM PC rate on low price, good performance, adequate service back-up, and so on?") are then measured, with their order based on the avoidance of having the respondent "compute" a new overall attitude from considering the questionnaire-provided benefit beliefs. Purchase facilitation (if an objective) would then follow *or,* if a minor objective, be incorporated into the benefit beliefs.

Advertisement recognition ("Have you seen this commercial on TV before?") occurs as the *last* processing measure—of in-media competitive attention—because we're now showing the respondent the ads (for example, the IBM "tramp" series for the IBM PC). To have shown the ads earlier would have biased every following measure.

Finally, profiling measures are taken. While these usually include demographics, the most important by far is the *direct media exposure measure* (see Chapter 16) in which respondents report (in the IBM PC example) which TV programs they watched and what magazines they read. In the panel method, media exposure is measured by having each panelist maintain a diary of TV viewing habits, readership of magazines, and so forth, and would *not* appear on the questionnaire. Without a diary, that is, using the questionnaire method alone, only types of TV programs or very recent exposure can be measured, although print media exposure can be reported from memory reasonably well.

Analysis of Market Survey Results

For a *causal* analysis, market survey results should be analyzed at the *individual* level. Ideally, again, this requires panel surveys with the same respondents interviewed at time t, time $t + 1$, time $t + 2$, through to the end of the tracking. At minimum, two waves with the same respondents (most often the benchmark wave and one follow-up wave) would be required.

The results are then arrayed into a series of "turnover" tables, as exemplified in Figure 20.1. Turnover tables track what happened to respondents from time t to time $t + 1$ and to successive time periods if surveyed—for example, whether exposure did or did not result in brand awareness, or whether brand attitude (given brand awareness) did or did not produce brand purchase intention—until all the steps of exposure → processing → communication effects → action are linked.

In the example in Figure 20.1, the pre- to post-turnover incidence for each cell indicates which diagnosis of causality is appropriate. If the campaign is

FIGURE 20.1   Turnover analysis for inferring causality in market survey results (example).

	Did not recognize brand at time $t + 1$	Recognized brand at time $t + 1$
Exposed at time *t*	(campaign not working)	(most of the *exposed* respondents should *end up in this cell*)
Not exposed at time *t*	(most of the *unexposed* repondents should be here)	(campaign not the cause of brand recognition)

working (here by increasing brand recognition), most (exposed) respondents should be in the top right-hand cell, indicating that (recent) exposure caused brand recognition. The lower right-hand cell shows the incidence of brand recognition due to *other* causes—such as advertising exposure prior to time t or to in-store exposure to the brand.

More precisely deterministic statistical techniques, such as cross-lagged correlation, can be applied to panel results. However, turnover analysis is simple for the manager to interpret, and it suffices for *reasonably* safe causal conclusions.

If, however, the market survey has employed separate samples rather than panel methodology, causal interpretation is rather unsafe. All that can be said with separate samples is that a certain *percent* of respondents showed brand awareness (or other processing or communication effects) at time t, another *percent* showed it at time $t + 1$, and so forth, and *simultaneously* in each time period a certain percent purchased. What we cannot safely conclude is that brand awareness (or other effects) at time t *caused* purchase at time $t + 1$ or in any other time period, because we haven't tracked the same individuals over time.

In practice, though, valid enough *inference* about sequential campaign effects can often be made from this less "scientific" survey procedure. The separate-sample method usually can detect any *major* problems with a campaign's progress through the six-step effects sequence.

Exposure-to-Sales Analysis

So far, we have assumed that the manager is interested in knowing completely *how* advertising works, through all six steps of the effects sequence. This requires market surveys with consumers and, ideally, panel methodology.

However, the manager, once convinced that a good understanding of causality has been gained, may then choose to track at a more general level *without* market surveys. This we call partial (aggregate) tracking because it jumps from step 1 to step 5 or 6. Most often, this consists of relating one of the *gross exposure* measures (advertising expenditure rate or GRP attainment rate) to an *aggregated* marketing objective measure (sales or market share, or profit).

This requires some form of direct input-output analysis. Such analysis may range from simply a crude comparison of advertising input trends with sales output trends, to a quantitative model of the observed relationship and thus predicted future relationship. Excellent quantitative models include BRANDAID and ADSTOCK, but these are beyond the mathematical scope of this book.[10]

APPLICATIONS OF TRACKING

There are five main applications of tracking studies, ranging from major to minor:

1 Determining why advertising is or is not working
2 Adjusting the budget

3 Adjusting the media plan
4 Adjusting the exposure ratio of individual ads in the pool
5 Making minor improvements in ads

Determining Why Advertising Is or Is Not Working

The most important application of tracking, at least initially, is to determine why the advertising campaign is or is not working (meeting its marketing goal). Until the campaign is actually launched, the manager has been operating only with the advertising plan—which, all things considered, is no more than a *hypothesis* about how the advertising is *expected* to work. Sophisticated managers will always want to test this hypothesis (through complete tracking, with panel methodology).

In reality, most advertising campaigns never have their plan's "hypothesis" tested. Direct response campaigns are a possible exception, but failure to test is true of most major media campaigns. Primarily this is because proper tracking is expensive, and difficult to analyze. But there's also another reason. If sales go up, the advertising agency often doesn't *want* the campaign fully evaluated, in case their campaign wasn't the cause! Conversely, if sales go down, the agency can rarely talk the client into funding a major tracking study that may absolve the agency (the advertising) as the cause. Either way, in reality, nothing is usually done. It takes a sophisticated *client manager* to initiate a proper tracking study.

Adjusting the Budget

Media budget adjustments, that is, increases or decreases in the rate of advertising spending, can be made without conducting market surveys. Aggregate input-output tracking—such as advertising-expenditure rate related to sales rate—is sufficient for this.

Adjusting the Media Plan

Gross adjustments of the media plan, such as increasing or decreasing GRPs in various *geographic* markets, requires only aggregate analysis as above.

However, *fine-tuning* of the media plan in terms of adjusting the reach and frequency to increase *reach at effective frequency,* requires market surveys and panel methodology. As we suggested in Part Seven, this is where the real answer lies as to why "half the money spent on advertising is wasted." Looked at it in this light, the money spent on *causal tracking research* is a very sound investment.

Adjusting the Exposure Ratio of Individual Ads in the Pool

Market surveys that include the processing measures, since these are individual-ad based, can use these results to adjust the exposure ratio of ads comprising the campaign's pool of ads.

The "winner" in ad testing, for example, may turn out not to be significantly more effective in campaign conditions than the "number two" ad. Their exposures could therefore be equalized. Or, a new winner may be found, or losers discovered, that should be up-weighted or down-weighted, respectively. For example, American Express adjusted the ratio of its "Do You Know Me" TV commercials (Robert Ludlum, Mel Blanc, Benny Goodman, and others) to reflect their apparent effectiveness within the campaign.

With continuous tracking, ratio adjustments can be made frequently, if necessary, to minimize "wearout," as explained later in this chapter.

Making Minor Improvements in Ads

The final and perhaps the most minor application of tracking research is to make small improvements in the creative content of particular advertisements while they are in the campaign. For example, a TV video "super" can be added to reinforce a benefit claim, or the audio can be re-recorded to mention the brand name more often. Print ads are even easier to change. Magazine ads and outdoor ads have quite a long insertion commitment to the media, meaning that adjustments cannot be made quickly. But changes in all other print and broadcast media can be made at short notice.

HOW OFTEN TO TRACK

We've left the discussion of one of the biggest decisions until now: how often to track the campaign. Only by understanding the purpose and methods of tracking can this decision correctly be made.

Essentially, there are three campaign considerations that determine the frequency and the type of tracking research that should be conducted (Table 20.4): initiation, change, and maintenance.

TABLE 20-4   HOW OFTEN TO TRACK AND WHAT TYPE OF TRACKING TO CONDUCT

Status of campaign	Frequency of tracking	Type of tracking
Initiation	Several purchase cycles* minimum	Complete causal: market surveys with panel methodology
Major change by competitor or in market	One purchase cycle* (two waves) initially, then several more if needed	Aggregate at first, then complete causal if serious problem
Maintenance	Monthly, with major review at mid-year and end-of-year planning period	Aggregate

* For long purchase cycle products, the tracking waves should be done *monthly*.

Campaign Initiation

When a new campaign is initiated, either a new brand's first campaign or a new strategy for an existing brand, the causality of the campaign's plan should be tested. This will require a complete set of measures, in market surveys using panel methodology, for a minimum of several purchase cycles.

All measures are needed. (It is even wise to include brand recall as well as brand recognition in case the new brand or strategy causes a change in the way the product is purchased. Although this is unlikely, both measures are inexpensive to include.) Use of lead indicator measures only, or less than complete measurement, will leave gaps in the causal chain. Total-market surveys with panel methodology should be used, with individual-level analysis.

To establish reliable causal inferences—and also because the new campaign, especially for a new brand, should be building rapidly—at least three to four purchase cycles should be tracked. Analysis is in terms of multiple turnover tables relating successive effects for successive (purchase cycle) time periods.

For campaign initiation for *long purchase cycle products,* monthly tracking intervals should be used rather than purchase cycle intervals. Most consumer durables and large industrial products fall into this classification. Whereas the monthly interval is arbitrary, it's a good starting point pending evidence that advertising in the category has substantial effects *only* over a longer period.

Major Change

Major change does not refer to a major change by the advertised brand, which would be classified as initiation in our table. Rather, it refers to major changes that occur (a) in a competitor's strategy or (b) in the market itself, such as a new government regulation, or a disaster as befell Tylenol in 1983. Any change likely to affect *our* brand's advertising performance should be tracked as soon as it occurs.

First, a quick and inexpensive *aggregate* assessment of the market should be made. Aggregate measures, notably sales and market shares, taken over one purchase cycle or one month apart for long purchase cycle products (two waves) should be enough to decide whether the change is serious and likely to continue (hence the two waves, to measure the trend). If a substantial effect on our brand's sales is forecast, then complete *causal* tracking should be resumed, again for several purchase cycles or several months as applicable. This second phase is to determine whether our brand will need to react with a new advertising strategy or even with a new marketing strategy—which would take the campaign back to initiation.

Maintenance Tracking

Certainly at the *aggregate* level, most often monitoring advertising expenditure rate and sales rate, maintenance tracking should be undertaken during the remaining periods of market "equilibrium." Aggregate data are easy to compile—the company usually *has* the necessary figures but managers neglect to *analyze* them.

This is where continuous data-review models such as ADSTOCK or BRANDAID come to the fore.[11] Graphic (not just numbers) reports or personal computer displays regularly signal whether the market is indeed in equilibrium and whether the company's advertising is proceeding as planned.

It is good management practice to schedule a major mid-year and end-of-year review in which client and agency are required to read and submit written comments on all available input, effects, and output trends, followed by a meeting. Regular reviews at minimum 6-month intervals serve to punctuate planning during maintenance periods.

These regular reviews will help managers to decide when the current advertising campaign has run its course. This leads to our final topic in campaign evaluation: wearout.

WHAT IS "WEAROUT"?

At a commonsense level, everyone knows what "wearout" is: when the advertising campaign is not working any more. But from a managerial perspective, diagnosing wearout, and correcting it, is far more complicated than this.

We will see that there actually are three possible conclusions to be drawn when the advertising campaign does not seem to be working any more:

1 Campaign obsolescence
2 Media plan slippage
3 Advertising wearout

To detect where the problem lies, and thus to draw the right conclusion and apply the right corrective actions, we need three types of audits which cover: the marketing plan (to check for campaign obsolescence); the media plan (to check for media plan slippage); and the advertisements themselves (to check for advertising wearout, that is, wearout of the creative executions themselves). The audits or checks should be conducted in the stated order, as explained next.

FIRST CHECK: MARKETING AUDIT

Before the manager can conclude that a sales decline is caused by advertising wearout, there are alternative causes to be considered. A complete *marketing audit* should be conducted because the problem may extend to the marketing plan rather than just the advertising plan. A marketing audit should be conducted *first* because, in a competitive market, the lead time for correction to stem the sales decline usually will be very short.

There are many reasons sales could decline without the brand's advertising having worn out in the conventional sense. They fall under three headings: changes in the brand's marketing mix, changes in a competitor's marketing mix, and changes in consumer values.

Changes in the Brand's Marketing Mix

A first set of reasons for a decline in sales, not due to advertising, is changes in (other) components of the brand's marketing mix. A change in product formulation or service, distribution, price, or promotion other than advertising could be the cause of the sales decline.

- If these changes have the effect of acting as purchase inhibitors, then the advertising strategy should be adapted to counter the inhibition. (See Chapter 6's discussion of purchase facilitation as a communication objective.) This is a minor correction within the same advertising plan.
- A major, deliberate change in the brand's marketing mix would, of course, call for a completely revised advertising plan.

New brands represent a special case. With new brands, a sales decline is often the result of the brand achieving its true repeat purchase incidence and rate; that is, high initial sales frequently represent the effect of a large incidence of trial purchases and an inflated purchase rate due to introductory deals, so that a drop-off occurs when less than 100 percent of the triers repeat, or when individual repeaters' rate of purchase without deals stabilizes to the brand's "true" repeat rate.[12]

- The true repeat effect for a new brand would not normally call for a change in advertising strategy, although it may signal an assessment of the promotion strategy if the repeat rate is too low (see Chapter 14's discussion of usage promotions).

Changes in a Competitor's Marketing Mix

A second set of reasons for a sales decline consists of changes in a competitor's marketing mix. A major new brand introduction, such as Aim toothpaste some years ago, can redefine the market and cause sales and market share declines for other brands. Or, a change in a competing brand's marketing mix, such as Colgate toothpaste's switch to a pump dispenser as an alternative package, can produce declines for other brands.

Under the heading of changes in a competitor's marketing mix we include changes in a competing brand's *advertising strategy* (target audience and communication objectives) but *not* changes in the competitor's *media* strategy *unless* the latter changes follow from a changed advertising strategy. Changes in a competitor's media strategy alone are discussed later.

- Changes in a competitor's *marketing mix other than advertising or promotion* that cause our brand's sales to decline generally call for a revised marketing plan and along with it a completely revised advertising plan.
- Changes in a competitor's *advertising (or promotion) strategy* that cause our brand's sales to decline can, more narrowly, often be countered by a change in our brand's creative (or promotion) strategy alone rather than a completely revised advertising plan.

An example of marketing plan revision would be the rush of many brands of personal computers to develop "IBM-compatibles" when IBM became the dominant competitor in the personal computer market. A revised marketing plan is necessary; a revised advertising plan alone would not counter this.

On the other hand, when Miller Beer changed its advertising strategy (target audience *and* creative strategy) to the "It's Miller Time" theme, which brought the Miller High-Life brand out of the doldrums in the beer market, rival Budweiser countered by simply revising its *creative* strategy to reflect even broader situational use than Miller's with the "When do *you* say Budweiser?" theme. Budweiser's counter-strategy suggested that a Bud is suitable at any time, not just after a hard day's work as Miller's advertising implied.

Changes in Consumer Values

A third set of reasons for a sales decline centers on changes in consumers' "tastes" or values, manifest in altered importance placed on the attributes (more accurately, the benefits) that consumers seek in a product category. The toothpaste market, for instance, underwent changes in consumers' benefit importance with the emergence of decay-prevention as a major consideration, and later the gel form of toothpaste emerged as a moderately important consideration for many consumers. Likewise, medically initiated sociocultural changes saw low tar emerging as a consumer benefit in the cigarette market, and low alcohol content or fewer calories emerging as consumer benefits in the beer market.

Changes in consumer values resulting in altered benefit importance weights (including the emergence of a new benefit which, by definition, previously had no importance) can be addressed in two ways.

- If the altered or new benefit threatens to *substantially re-partition* the market (see Chapter 2), then the usual response will be to quickly seek a product re-formulation, resulting in a change in the *marketing plan* that will enable our brand to compete successfully in the new sub-market (for example, Crest toothpaste also going to a pump dispenser form).
- Alternatively, an adequate response may be to revise the advertising strategy: the target audience and communication objectives. Our brand could focus on a more sharply defined target audience, such as the "old" category users, and try to boost the importance of a previous benefit in the brand attitude communication objective (for example, Ultra-brite continuing to go after the "cosmetic" segment when the fluoridated toothpastes entered).

Summary of External Causes

All of these "external" causes of a sales decline—changes in our brand's marketing mix, changes in a competitor's mix, or changes in the market itself via consumer-values changes—would be detected if the manager is conducting regular tracking research. Such changes call for a complete marketing or "situation audit" (see Chapter 18) in order to decide whether a revised *marketing* plan or, progressively less expensive, a revised *advertising* plan, advertising strategy, creative strategy, or promotion strategy is the appropriate solution.

Campaign Obsolescence Rather than "Wearout" With external causes of a sales decline, the assessment is that the current advertising campaign is *obsolete* rather than that the current campaign has "worn out" in the conventional meaning of the term. The conventional meaning of "wearout" is that the current campaign is failing to work up to expectation (failing to achieve the sales or market share goal) in the *absence* of external causes.

Only if the marketing audit establishes that external causes are not responsible for the sales decline can we then consider advertising wearout (as opposed to advertising obsolescence) to be the problem.

However, to isolate the exact internal cause or causes of advertising wearout, there is still further investigation to be done. We now know that the advertising *strategy* is still sound, but something could be wrong with the media plan, or with the way the creative executions are being scheduled in the media plan, or with the creative executions themselves. The best place to begin in detecting the internal cause or causes of wearout is with an audit of the media plan.

SECOND CHECK: MEDIA PLAN

Logically, with internal causes of wearout, the problem must be occurring in the exposure step (step 1) or the processing step (step 2) of the six-step effects sequence. This is because, if the advertising strategy is still appropriate, something must be breaking down in the steps *leading to* the communication objectives step (step 3) and target audience action step (step 4) that comprise the advertising strategy itself. We begin with exposure, by checking the media plan.

Changes in Vehicle Audiences

The pattern of exposures to the advertising could have changed because the delivery of the media plan itself has changed. Changes in media plan delivery are often obscured by the use of gross tracking indicators such as the amount spent on advertising or total GRPs (gross rating points). It is quite possible to be spending the same amount, say, each quarter or to be achieving the same level of GRPs, yet to have a substantial change occur in effective reach—the number of target audience individuals reached at the minimum effective frequency level.

Television programs, in particular, wax and wane in popularity and new programs and summer re-runs are remarkably unstable. But other media vehicles, too, are far less stable in their audience exposure than is commonly supposed. Total audience ratings do not provide the necessary data. As we have emphasized, the advertiser needs to know about exposure to the *target* audience, and this knowledge is not obtainable through total audience figures for media vehicles.

- The first check for internal causes of campaign wearout, therefore, should be to *update the direct matching survey* of the target audience's media exposure.
- For a brand using demographic or psychographic rather than direct matching, the ability to detect media plan "slippage" is considerably lessened by the indirect fix on the target audience. Nevertheless, a media plan check still is required, and this would be a good time to institute a direct matching survey (see Chapter 17). At the very least, a re-computation of the match between the demographic or psychographic target audience and vehicle audiences should be conducted.

"Maintenance" Plans

A related problem of exposure and media plan delivery occurs after a heavy initial burst of advertising for a new brand or for a new campaign. After the heavy initial burst, the advertising is often cut back to a "maintenance" level. But usually too little thought is given to what the maintenance plan actually delivers.

Again, gross statistics, such as "half the GRPs" (an especially common statistic) or "half the reach" or "half the average frequency" tell us nothing about what the plan is actually delivering. A so-called maintenance plan may look like it's achieving half the "impact" of the original plan but in fact it may be far below this, particularly if it drops nearly everyone below the minimum effective frequency level required in a purchase cycle (see also the technique of "pulsing," discussed at the end of the chapter).

There is also the question of *what* is being maintained by way of communication objectives. It is one thing, for example, to maintain a target audience of brand loyals with relatively low frequency advertising, but quite another to attempt to maintain a target audience of brand switchers with the same "maintenance" plan. Yet such distinctions rarely enter the evaluation of reduced media plans. Instead, all detailed consideration is buried in meaningless figures like GRPs, as though the target audience responds to advertising expenditure dispensed in any shape or form.

We have perhaps been unduly harsh in order to stress to the manager the importance of beginning the diagnosis of a wearout problem at the point at which it can first occur: exposure. Once the manager is satisfied that the delivery of the media plan has not changed in such a way as to alter exposure to the target audience in terms of effective reach per purchase cycle, then diagnosis of the remaining possible causes of wearout (which all reside in the processing step) can proceed.

To summarize, when internal campaign wearout is first signaled by a decline in sales in the absence of apparent causes outside the campaign, the manager should immediately request from the media planner a detailed accounting of the past and current delivery of the media plan. This accounting should be expressed in terms of the number of individuals reached in the purchase cycle (the purchase cycle should be checked, also, especially for new brands) at the minimum effective frequency level. If this figure has not changed, then exposure can be ruled out as a cause and the problem must reside in one or more of the processing responses to the ads themselves.

FINAL CHECK: THE ADVERTISEMENTS

Finally, we arrive at *advertising wearout* in the true sense of the term: that the *creative executions* are no longer meeting the sales objective even though the advertising strategy is correct and the media plan is sound. The problems could be in the processing responses of attention, learning, or acceptance, with the latter two including emotional responses. We will see that the solutions, interestingly, may require changes in the creative executions *or* changes in the media plan.

Attention Wearout

The first response in the processing of all advertisements is attention. Diminished attention to an advertisement, at the individual consumer level, after it has been processed several times, is a common cause of wearout.[13]

Diminished attention is particularly likely to affect campaigns in print media, where the easy response for the consumer is to turn the page. It is less a problem in broadcast media, and particularly TV, where the easy response is to watch or listen. Nevertheless, attention wearout can occur for an ad in any medium.

Slightly different advertising executions of the same advertising message strategy are the solution. Miller Lite was perhaps the first to do this on a comprehensive scale on TV, with its "ex-jock" pool of commercials, and Blue Nun was an early example on radio. But in print, where the attention-holding problem is severe, advertisers have been somewhat slower to use variations on a theme.[14] Exceptions include magazine ads for Kraft Singles, liquor brands such as Chivas Regal and Johnny Walker, and cigarette brands such as Kent and True, which operate with about 10 different executions of the same underlying message strategy. Figure 20.2 shows variations on a theme in the True campaign.

Learning (Interference) Wearout

Wearout alternatively can occur in the second response in processing: (rote) learning. As explained in Chapter 8, rote learning is necessary for two communication effects—*brand awareness,* in which the consumer must learn the connection between the category need and the brand, and *low involvement brand attitude,* in which the consumer must learn the connection between the brand and the main benefit or benefits representing the purchase motivation.

FIGURE 20.2   Examples of variations on a theme: Three True cigarette ads designed to increase brand recognition awareness. (Courtesy of Lorillard, U.S.A.)

Learning failure is very often due to prior attention failure, in which case it would be diagnosed in the foregoing attention analysis and the solution would be, as before, variations on a theme using new stimuli to regain attention.

However, learning failure also can occur in its own right due to *interference* from learning produced by competing brands. Interference can readily occur when one or more major competitors change their media schedule to attain

FIGURE 20.2   (Continued)

greater frequency against target audience individuals than previously; or change the ratio of ads in their pool, or even their advertising message execution slightly to achieve stronger associative learning of (the competitor's) brand awareness or brand attitude.

Changes in scheduling or changes in executional emphasis by a competitor can produce very significant interference effects.[15] An astute increase in

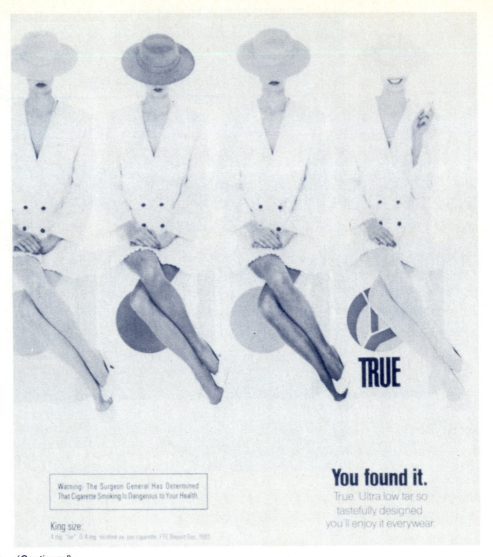

FIGURE 20.2   *(Continued)*

effective frequency, along the competitive lines suggested in Chapter 16, could find a brand dominating at the individual consumer level in terms of opportunities to learn the brand name as a top-of-mind response to the category need (brand recall) and simultaneously strengthening the connection between the brand and its benefit or benefits (brand attitude). Similarly, a brand chosen at the point of purchase (brand recognition) may increase its executional emphasis on package shots or improve its portrayal of benefits (brand attitude) and make large inroads on competitors—without altering its media expenditure or its advertising strategy at all.

Interference is the major problem that affects *recall* in learning, which underlies brand recall awareness and low involvement brand attitude. Interference is not, however, a very significant factor in *recognition* learning.[16]

We point out this distinction in the causes of recall unlearning (interference) and recognition unlearning (time-related decay) because the solutions to learning problems as causes of wearout depend on it in the following ways:

- If *brand recall* is the appropriate type of brand awareness communication objective for the brand, then *flighting* (see the final section of this chapter) is the best corrective tactic.
- However, if *brand recognition* is the objective, then flighting can be dangerous if too long a hiatus is placed between flights, instead, the normal *even schedule* (continuity) should be used.

A *conflict* therefore arises with brands that are noticed via *brand recognition* but chosen on the basis of *low involvement (recalled) brand attitude,* because brand recognition ideally requires an even schedule whereas low involvement brand attitude can benefit from flighting if interference is a problem.

The solution in the brand recognition/low involvement brand attitude case is to employ flighting but to ensure that there is only a relatively short delay between flights. Some evidence suggests that, for a new brand, the delay should be no longer than one month, though for an established brand, delays of up to three months may be tolerated.[17] Theoretically, too, the *less brand loyal* the target audience, the *shorter* the maximum delay that should be allowed in the schedule.

Acceptance (Over-exposure) Wearout

For higher risk purchase decisions, the brand is chosen via *high involvement brand attitude*—a considered decision in which *acceptance,* not just learning, of the advertising message is essential. Further, if *category need* is an objective (as for decidedly new products), or if *brand purchase intention* has to be induced (as for a brand that has a moderately favorable brand attitude but not a superior one), or if *purchase facilitation* has to be achieved (as for a brand that has poor distribution or a prohibitively high price), then acceptance of these elements by target consumers during processing is a further processing requirement.

In the high involvement situation, an advertiser would select an ad that initially (for example, in an advertising pre-test) produced acceptance responses to those elements relevant to the brand's communication objectives. However, the problem with acceptance-caused wearout is that the consumer's initial acceptance responses may, with over-exposure, turn negative.

For low risk purchase decisions in which the purchase motivation is *transformational,* likability of the ad is essential (see Chapter 9). Over-exposure can cause a previously liked ad to lose its appeal and even to become disliked after a while with continued exposures. Note that this process does not require counter-arguing, as in high involvement, but merely the loss of positive emotional response to the ad itself; of course, counter-arguing in the form of conscious rejection would also be fatal.

However, negative reactions are *most unlikely with print ads,* because the consumer can simply turn the page (for a magazine or newspaper ad), or look away (from a billboard or poster), or throw the ad away (direct mail). The wearout problem with print ads is almost certain to be attentional wearout, or possibly learning wearout caused by interference or delay, but not wearout due to over-exposure. A consumer is most unlikely to counter-argue with a print ad.

On the other hand, *broadcast ads are very susceptible to over-exposure* because consumers frequently do sit passively and attend to the ad. This is particularly true of television commercials, though less true of radio commercials because of radio's frequent use as a background medium. In fact, attitudinal wearout (negative shifts in attitude with repeated exposures) has been demonstrated *only* with television commercials and not with advertising in any other medium.[18]

The important question is: After how many exposures will an ad begin to provoke rejection responses? Some idea of an upper limit can be inferred from studies of new TV commercials by America's top agencies for brands known to be successful—that is, new commercials for established brands. Studies reviewed by Lukeman and Spielman using purchase intention measures and also Nielsen sales data suggest that 9 months is perhaps a caution period and 12 months a typical upper limit before a new commercial begins to lose its effectiveness.[19] These studies used time on air rather than number of exposures as the measure; however, we can infer that at a once-a-week rate, the typical consumer would see these commercials 35 to 50 times before the commercials wear out. For lesser commercials by lesser agencies, wearout is liable to occur much sooner. Also, for new advertisements for new brands, advertising performance should certainly be monitored well before 9 or 12 months have elapsed.

What corrective actions should be tried for advertising that has worn out due to over-exposure to, and rejection responses by, too many target audience consumers?

- If the advertising is *low* involvement/*informational, ignore* the rejection responses, as they are not relevant to this brand attitude strategy quadrant. If the advertising is *low* involvement/*transformational, drop the ad immediately,* as negative reactions are fatal in this quadrant.
- For *high* involvement brand attitude advertising, be it informational or transformational, the best solution is *variations on a theme.* The advertiser has to remove offending elements, or not present them as often, so as to delay wearout, and replace them with interesting elements. This means different advertisements must be used. A related and less expensive but less satisfactory solution which may work in the short run is to *rotate* the individual ads more often.
- A particular solution applies to target audiences who have fully learned (low involvement) or accepted (high involvement) a favorable brand

attitude[20]—these would be *brand loyals* or *routinized favorable switchers*—and this is to use *shorter ads*. Brief TV or radio commercials (10-second or 15-second spots) and smaller or reduced-copy print ads should serve to maintain brand awareness. Brand awareness should, in turn, "carry" the favorable brand attitude (by reminder) without providing actual attitude-relevant content. Over-exposure of loyal audiences to longer ads could fuel counter-argumentation and wearout.[21] Shorter ads should be used only for favorable target audiences. They are *not* suitable for other audiences whose communication effects are not at full strength.

Before assuming over-exposure is the cause, we again emphasize in campaign evaluation that the advertiser has to be alert for the other internal causes of wearout, including exposure slippage (which is *not* wearout but rather constitutes a problem with the media plan), attention, and learning. Also, it should be evident that the advertiser must not lose sight of the advertising communication model and particularly the brand attitude strategy. Remember the Charmin example: acceptance measures of processing would almost surely have suggested that the Mr. Whipple commercial had worn out early; however, acceptance was irrelevant to the low involvement/informational way in which this commercial worked.

FLIGHTING

Flighting—the massing of ads in bursts with complete gaps between the bursts—was recommended as a solution to competitive interference as a cause of wearout. Flighting is such a popular form of media scheduling that it deserves separate discussion.

When to Use Flighting

There are many, many brands whose success depends on minimizing interference; any brand for whom brand recall or low involvement brand attitude, or both, are objectives fits this category. For the same reason it works as a defensive media strategy against interference, flighting also can work as an offensive media strategy to increase a brand's sales response to its media expenditure.

Let us state clearly at the outset that the ideal media plan for the advertiser who can afford it is a high frequency schedule that swamps the competition in terms of learned communication effects and employs a relatively large and varied pool of ads to prevent wearout due to inattention or to rejection responses. This would be a continuous, even schedule, which would even ignore seasonal sales trends and simply out-advertise everyone else in the product category.

However, most advertisers cannot afford to out-advertise the competition, or at least not for sustained periods, and here's where flighting comes in. Several recent studies (notably those of Haley[22] and Simon[23]) have shown that it is more effective to flight advertising in bursts than to spend the same amount over a continuous period.

Both these studies advanced an essentially attention-based explanation. Simon's explanation, the better reasoned of the two, is stated in terms of Helson's adaptation-level theory.[24] Arguing that the presence of an ad is more likely to be noticed than its absence, Simon suggests that heavy bursts create an immediate sales response that then diminishes (is adapted to) because the ad loses attention. So you stop advertising—which few people notice—then burst heavily again to break the (now lower) attention level, which most people cannot fail to notice.

Whereas the attention explanation may be valid (neither study tests explanations), an equally likely explanation is that the heavy bursts are successful because, for a limited time, the advertising for the brand "dominates" other brands—that is, it reaches more target audience individuals at the competitively recommended minimum frequency level (see Chapter 16) during the purchase cycle.[25] The advertising may then lose attention, as Simon suggests, unless variations on a theme are used.

Flighted advertising seems worth trying for the advertiser who cannot afford a continuously heavy campaign with a large pool of varied ads. However, as Simon observes, there are several caveats with flighting as a media strategy:

- First, it is not recommended for new brands during initial launch advertising, which should be as heavy and continuous as possible, for at least several purchase cycles, because potential new triers are still entering the market.
- Second, the advertiser has to have the courage to live with a loss of sales during the hiatus periods when another brand has the opportunity to dominate.
- Third, the cyclical sales pattern caused by flighting can generate inventory problems and be disturbing to retailers (for the manufacturer's brand) or to manufacturers (if the retailer is doing the flighting).

For established brands with good retailer relations, flighting is worth trying.

Flighting versus Pulsing

The media planner must not lose sight of the fact that effective frequency is what counts—not just grossly planned increases and decreases in GRPs or advertising "weight." For example, flighting is often lumped together with pulsing; but as Kotler[26] points out, flighting is a completely on–completely off schedule, whereas pulsing employs a continuous low "maintenance" level of advertising with higher bursts interspersed on top of the maintenance level.

As we have argued earlier, so-called maintenance advertising may not maintain anything—unless by luck, or by design (which is unusual), it reaches *some* individuals at the effective frequency level. It would be better to turn the advertising off completely in the hiatus periods—that is, to employ flighting—and to throw all resources into the bursts.

The *distribution* of advertising in the bursts must be carefully calculated. The objective, as always, should be to reach as many target individuals as possible at (at least) the minimum effective frequency level. Also, if the communication objectives call for acceptance responses, then a maximum effective frequency for each ad (short of rejection-produced wearout) should be adhered to as well.

SUMMARY OF ADVERTISING WEAROUT SOLUTIONS

A summary of the causes of wearout and the respective solutions to these problems is presented in Table 20.5.

Omitted are the causes of sales declines that are not due to advertising wearout but *do* signal an advertising campaign's *obsolescence* because a new marketing or advertising plan will have to be devised. These are: (1) changes in other components of the brand's marketing mix; (2) changes in competitors' marketing mixes including their advertising strategy but not their media strategy alone; and (3) changes in consumer values, reflected in the altered importance of advertised benefits.

Another cause of sales decline omitted from the table is: (4) *slippage in the brand's media plan.* An update of the media plan to ensure that vehicles are selected to achieve the original effective reach goal is all that is required here. Again, this is not advertising wearout.

The final three causes of sales declines can legitimately be classified as *advertising wearout,* in that they represent a failure of the advertising in the absence of external causes—that is, in the absence of causes 1 to 4. The causes of advertising wearout are either: (5) attentional problems; (6) learning problems; or (7) acceptance problems. The manager must diagnose the problem correctly and should apply the solutions as indicated in Table 20.5.

TABLE 20-5   ADVERTISING WEAROUT: CAUSES AND SOLUTIONS

Cause of wearout	Corrective action
Attention—diminished attention (especially to print ads)	*Variations*—different executions of the same advertising message strategy, to hold attention
Learning—unlearning due to competitive interference (brand recall and *low involvement* brand attitude) or to too long a delay or hiatus in the media schedule (brand recognition)	*Flighting*—to offset competitive interference, but with a relatively short hiatus of one to three months maximum between flights
Acceptance—rejection responses (especially to broadcast ads) emerging with prolonged repetition; affects category need, *high involvement* brand attitude, *low involvement/ transformational* brand attitude, induced brand purchase intention, and purchase facilitation (when these are objectives)	*Variations*—different executions of the same advertising message strategy, to delay rejection of elements; *faster rotation* of existing ads, although this is only a short-term solution; also *shorter ads* for favorable target audience

Campaign evaluation, as we have seen, is not an easy task. Tracking studies can be expensive to conduct and difficult to analyze. Detection of advertising wearout also is difficult although the solutions are straightforward, once the right cause is detected. For the manager who is spending millions of dollars on advertising and promotion, however, campaign evaluation is a vital and necessary on-going and concluding aspect of advertising and promotion management.

NOTES

1 The fact that most advertising campaigns are not formally evaluated is reinforced in an interesting article by P.R. Klein and M. Tainiter, Copy Research validation: the advertiser's perspective, *Journal of Advertising Research,* 1983, *23* (5), 9–17. These investigators followed-up on 1165 TV commercials, from 412 campaigns, tested by the McCollum-Spielman testing service. Although many were very large budget campaigns, few were formally tracked.

In the study McCollum-Spielman's measure of *brand awareness* did not differentiate apparently successful from unsuccessful campaigns. We think we know why, as explained in the notes to Chapter 19. Their "clutter-awareness" procedure measures only brand *recall,* and not within a *category*-competitive context as in the real world.

However, McCollum-Spielman's various measures of *brand purchase intention* increase, including, where appropriate, semantic differential brand benefit belief increase, showed quite remarkable predictive validity. For commercials for which the percentage of individual test respondents showing an increase was below the norm for commercials in that product category, only 35 percent of the brands met or exceeded their sales objectives; for commercials above the norm, 88 percent of the brands met or exceeded their sales objectives (by managers' reports).

2 Again, defining media broadly to include promotion offer delivery as media (see Part Six).

3 For promotion offers, *audience* can be taken as the number of samples delivered, coupons distributed, and so on. These are equivalent conceptually to advertising vehicle GRPs.

Also, GRPs are expressed in *percent* rather than numbers. For example, a vehicle that reaches 3 percent of the target audience is thereby delivering 3 GRPs, as would three vehicles that each reach 1 percent of the target audience. Be careful! TV media planners often equate TV programs' *ratings* with GRPs; but ratings are the percent of U.S. households, excluding those few without TV sets, reached by the program, which obviously is far larger than *target audience* reach. Most of all, don't confuse TV programs' *share* percentages with GRPs; share is the percent of households *watching TV in that time period* who are tuned to a particular program, a much, much higher figure than either ratings or target audience reach. (GRPs originated with TV but are being used increasingly to refer to other media as well.) Because of the ease of misinterpretation, you can see why we prefer to work with *target audience numbers* rather than percentages such as GRPs.

4 Remember from Chapter 19 on ad testing that the attempt to create a competitive media environment in an *ad test* by exposing the ad in a "standard" media segment, such as a TV program or simulated magazine, with competing ads, is not a good solution. This represents a sample of size n = 1 from the *population* of media

environment*s* that the ad will actually face. For ad testing, the effort to be realistic causes more interpretive problems than it solves. Campaign evaluation is the place to test (to "post-test") whether the ad works in media.

5 Syndicated services offering advertisement recognition measures include: for TV commercials, Bruzzone Research Corporation (which mails out photoboards of TV commercials and has the questionnaires returned by mail); for radio commercials, Haug Associates (by phone); for magazine ads, Starch INRA Hooper (but *see note 6*); for newspaper ads and trade magazine ads, Starch Ballot, Readex, and Harvey Communication Measurement Service.

6 A suspected attention problem due to the creative execution not holding up in media is the one situation where day-after recall testing (for example, Burke, Gallup & Robinson, Mapes & Ross) makes sense because it is *known* that the respondents were exposed to the media vehicle (that is, the TV program). However, note that a valid test would require *multiple* DAR tests in a representative sample of programs used in the media plan, which becomes very expensive. Likewise, for magazine ads, the Starch recognition procedure is tied to a particular magazine, so diagnosis of creative attention for a magazine ad would require *multiple* Starch tests across a representative sample of magazines used in the media plan. Managers should hope that attention problems are sufficiently diagnosed in the ad testing phase—it's considerably cheaper!

7 S. Colman and G. Brown, Advertising tracking studies and sales effects, *Journal of the Market Research Society,* 1983, *25* (2), 165–183. Also G. Brown, Tracking studies and sales effects: a U.K. perspective, *Journal of Advertising Research,* 1985, *25* (1), 52–64.

8 If the campaign has used only one medium, or if the manager wants to track the campaign's advertising *by* media, the question can be narrowed accordingly, and in the latter case, repeated for each type of advertising—TV commercials, radio commercials, newspaper ads, and so on.

9 The astute observer will notice that brands mentioned in the category advertising cut-through measure will bias the next measure, brand recall (if an objective). However, this bias is far less serious than if brand recall were to come first.

10 J.D.C. Little, BRANDAID: A marketing-mix model, part 1: structure, *Operations Research,* 1975, *23* (4), 628–673. The ADSTOCK model is described in S. Broadbent, *Spending Advertising Money,* 3rd ed., London: Business Books, Ltd., 1979.

11 See note 10.

12 See especially: J.H. Parfitt and B.J.K. Collins, Use of consumer panels for brand share prediction, *Journal of Marketing Research,* 1968, *5* (2), 131–146; and J.D.C. Little, Aggregate advertising models: the state of the art, *Operations Research,* 1979, *27* (4), 629–667.

13 C.S. Craig, B. Sternthal, and C. Leavitt, Advertising wearout: an experimental analysis, *Journal of Marketing Research,* 1976, *13* (4), 365–372.

14 J.R. Rossiter, Visual imagery: applications to advertising, in A.A. Mitchell (Ed.), *Advances in Consumer Research: Vol 9,* Provo, UT: Association for Consumer Research, 1982, pp. 101–106.

15 Dramatic interference effects were demonstrated in a neatly designed experiment that varied the relative frequency (or "share of voice") of competitive advertising and also the creative effectiveness (or "reward value") of competing ads. Although a laboratory experiment, the conditions were quite similar to brand recall learning and low involvement brand attitude learning in the real world, where competitive interference and not time between exposures is postulated to be the "unlearning"

process. See L.A. Lo Sciuto, L.H. Strassmann, and W.D. Wells, Advertising weight and the reward value of the brand, *Journal of Advertising Research*, 1967, *7* (2), 34–38.

16 W.A. Wickelgren, *Learning and Memory*, Englewood Cliffs, NJ: Prentice-Hall, 1977, chapter 15.

17 For example, see: D.G. Clarke, Econometric measurement of the duration of advertising effect on sales, *Journal of Marketing Research*, 1976, *13* (4), 345–347; H. Simon, ADPULS: an advertising model with wearout and pulsation, *Journal of Marketing Research*, 1982, *19* (3), 352–363.

18 Some studies misleadingly suggest that counter-arguing is rarely a problem with broadcast commercials because their presentation lasts such a short time and then is supplanted immediately by another commercial or by the program. The evidence for minimal counter-arguing with broadcast commercials, however, has been based on *single-exposure* studies. With multiple exposures, as in the vast majority of actual campaigns, counter-arguing and consequent rejection clearly can occur. For the two viewpoints and evidence, see: P.L. Wright, Cognitive responses to mass media advocacy, in R.E. Petty, T.M. Ostrom, and T.C. Brock (Eds.), *Cognitive Responses in Persuasion*, Hillsdale, NJ: Lawrence Erlbaum Associates, 1981, pp. 263–282; and B.J. Calder and B. Sternthal, Television commercial wearout: an information processing view, *Journal of Marketing Research*, 1980, *17* (2), 173–186.

19 The Association of National Advertisers (A.N.A) convened a Television Workshop in New York on March 1, 1978, specifically to address the issue of wearout. Two of the presentation papers which proposed the interval of nine to twelve months for the life of the typical campaign here were: G. Lukeman, Wearout: how to spot it and what to do about it; and H. M. Spielman, What is the effect of repetition—"snowball" or wearout?

20 Note that the shorter ads recommendation is made for *low or high* involvement brand attitude, yet it is still designed to prevent acceptance wearout (solely a high involvement phenomenon). Brand loyals and routinized favorable brand switchers probably have moved to low involvement anyway in deciding to *re-purchase* the brand. The idea is to stop them from going back into high involvement (by reconsidering the purchase decision) through their irritation with the brand's advertising.

21 A recent test by the ABC network and the J. Walter Thompson agency of multiple 15-second commercials in a single pod or commercial break suggests an increased level of irritation as viewers realize there are more commercials. However, this presumes a major industry shift toward shorter commercials instead of selective use of them. Furthermore, the test audience was not analyzed for brand loyalty, to which our shorter-commercial recommendation applies. See L.G. Reiling, "Mixed spot lengths increase effects of the longer," *Marketing News*, April 26, 1985, p. 6.

22 R.I. Haley, Sales effects of media weight, *Journal of Advertising Research*, 1978, *18* (3), 9–18.

23 H. Simon, same reference as note 17.

24 H. Helson, *Adaptation-level Theory*, New York: Harper & Row, 1964.

25 "Dominance" has been conceptualized by some media theorists as a fourth strategic parameter—along with reach, frequency, and continuity—in the "media balloon" (see Chapter 15). In this four-parameter model, reach trades off against frequency, and dominance trades off against continuity, with all four "pulling" on the budget (see S. Broadbent, *Spending Advertising Money*, (3rd ed.) London: Business Books

Ltd., 1979). However, dominance already is accounted for in our approach in the *effective* frequency parameter: see the LC + 1 correction factor in Chapter 16.

26 P. Kotler, *Marketing Management: Analysis, Planning, and Control,* (4th ed.) Englewood Cliffs, NJ: Prentice-Hall, 1980, chap. 19.

DISCUSSION QUESTIONS

Although we recommended a project rather than discussion questions for Part Eight, below are some short-exercise questions for the three advertising research chapters.

20.1 Chapter 18: For McDonald's restaurants, prepare two summary advertising strategies aimed respectively at:
a Brand loyals
b Other-brand loyals

20.2 Chapter 18: Thinking carefully about probable target audience involvement and communication objectives, conduct a management judgment ad test of the Panadol advertisement in Figure 6.6.

20.3 Chapter 19: For the Chanel No. 5 bath lotion ad in Figure 9.7, write a memorandum to the research company listing, in order, the ad testing measures you believe would constitute a valid procedure for testing this ad. Explain your selection of measures and the recommended order of measurement.

20.4 Chapter 19: In recent years, Coca-Cola has primarily employed a brand recognition *and* brand recall/low involvement/informational and transformational advertising communication model. The two most recent campaigns, "It's the real thing," and "Coke is it!" seem transformational for brand loyals but informational (implied comparative) for brand switchers and other-brand loyals. In this complex situation, what specific measures would you recommend for testing these types of ads, and why?

20.5 Chapter 20: How can you prove that the target audience has been exposed to the ads in your campaign and, further, that the ads received at least initial attention?

20.6 Chapter 20: You have been running the same advertising campaign for 6 months. The rate of sales of your brand is starting to slow, and the other managers have recommended as the solution a fresh creative approach. What would be your recommendation?

20.7 Chapter 20: For magazine advertisements versus TV commercials, discuss the roles of attentional wearout and acceptance wearout, noting solutions in each of the four "cells" of your answer.

FURTHER READING

There are no good references for campaign evaluation or tracking studies as such. Instead, we have recommended some readings that assist in the analysis of tracking study results and then some readings on advertising wearout.

Leckenby, J.D. and Wedding, N. *Advertising Management: Criteria, Analysis and Decision Making.* Columbus, OH: Grid, 1982.

Chapters 7 and 8 of this book contain an excellent introductory explanation of why lagged advertising analysis is necessary to interpret the exposure-to-sales relationship. Chapter 8 also contains a simplified but helpful description of BRANDAID.

Fitzroy, P. *Analytical Models for Marketing Management*. New York: McGraw-Hill, 1976.

Very good, relatively easy to follow explanation of mathematical models in marketing. For advertising applications, see especially chapter 2 (consumer buying behavior) and chapter 7 (advertising strategy).

Lilien, G. and Kotler, P., *Marketing Decision Models: A Model-Building Approach*. New York: Harper & Row, 1983.

This is the best of the current textbooks on mathematical models for marketing decisions. This very detailed "how to do it" book covers basic to advanced models. Besides advertising models (chapter 14), the book is also noteworthy for its attention to sales promotion models (chapter 15). Probably advisable to read the Fitzroy text first, as the size of Lilien and Kotler is daunting!

Most articles on wearout fail to identify whether the responses that are "wearing out" are relevant to the brand's advertising communication objectives. The following articles were selected because they specify the processing response that is wearing out and illustrate our three types of advertising wearout.

Haley, R.I. Sales effects of media weight. *Journal of Advertising Research,* 1978, *18* (3), 9–18.

Attention wearout is the presumed process underlying the valuable case histories presented in this article. The author argues that constant media weight produces diminishing sales returns due to attention wearout.

Lo Sciuto, L.A., Strassman, L.H., and Wells, W.D. Advertising weight and the reward value of the brand. *Journal of Advertising Research,* 1967, *7* (2), 34–38.

Learning (interference) wearout is demonstrated in this well-designed series of laboratory experiments. Applies to brand recall and *low involvement* brand attitude learning.

Sawyer, A. Repetition, cognitive responses, and persuasion. In Petty, R.E., Ostrom, T.M., and Brock, T.C. (Eds.) *Cognitive Responses in Persuasion*. Hillsdale, NJ: Lawrence Erlbaum Associates, 1981, pp. 263–282.

Acceptance (over-exposure) wearout is carefully analyzed in this book chapter. Although not noted by the author, over-exposure only applies to *high involvement* brand attitudes, when the target audience counter-argues with the brand's benefit claims, and to low involvement/*transformational* advertising if the target audience begins to dislike the ad itself. It is not a problem for low involvement/informational advertising.

THE ADVERTISING AND PROMOTION PLAN

This appendix presents a managerial checklist for preparing the advertising and promotion plan. It presumes that you've read the book, and as such, has no explanatory text. Its purpose is to enable the manager to organize and summarize all that's been learned into an overall advertising and promotion plan that can be applied to any brand.

The reader should note that the six steps have been arranged into the manager's planning stages, with advertising and promotion offers considered separately. The plan's sections are:

A. Marketing objectives
B. Target audience action objectives
C. Communication objectives
D. Creative strategy
E. Promotion strategy
F. Media strategy
G. Managerial summary

For each sub-section of the plan, if the manager is sure the sub-section is based on sound research, the research box is checked; if not, the judgment box is checked.

A. MARKETING OBJECTIVES

research judgment

[ ]   [ ]

1. **Profit: how are advertising and promotion expected to contribute?**
   (Check all that apply and write in profit goal if known)

   • Maintain or increase price differential: A _____ P _____

   • Lower costs: A _____ P _____

- Increase sales volume (units): A ____   P ____
- Profit goal for period ____ (month/year) to ____ (month/year): $____

[ ]   [ ]   **2. Sales: what sales goal will yield the profit goal and what are advertising and promotion's expected contributions?**
(Write in)

- Current sales: units ____ $____
- Target sales at end of period: units ____ $____
- Expected contributions (overall budget): $ A ____ $ P ____

[ ]   [ ]   **3. Market share: if relevant in growth market**
(Write in)

- Market partitioning structure (diagram):

- Market (category) on which market share calculations are based: _____

  _____

- Market's annual growth rate: units ____ percent $____ percent
- Current market share: units ____ percent $____ percent
- Market share target (to yield sales target): units ____ percent $____ percent

---

B. TARGET AUDIENCE ACTION OBJECTIVES

research judgment

[ ]   [ ]   **1. Which households/companies/retailers are sales to come from?**
(Nominate one group per campaign, specifying sub-groups if applicable)

- New category users (trial)
- Brand loyals (use more)
- Brand switchers (buy more often)
- Other-brand loyals (convert)

[ ]   [ ]   **2. Who is the decision maker the advertising and promotion must reach?**
(Choose one or more roles per campaign and check target roles for advertising and promotion respectively)

- Initiator (proposes): A _____   P _____

- Influencer (recommends): A _____   P _____

- Decider (chooses): A _____   P _____

- Purchaser (buys): A _____   P _____

- User (uses): A _____   P _____

[ ]   [ ]   **3. What is the behavioral sequence model for the target audience?**
(Construct table)

	Stage 1	Stage 2	Stage 3	Stage 4
Roles at each stage				
Locations				
Timing				

4. What is the personal profile of the decision maker?
(Complete all)

[ ]   [ ]   - Current *and* target action frequency (and volume of purchase action)

[ ]   [ ]   - Media exposure patterns

[ ]   [ ]   - Demographics

[ ]   [ ]   - Psychographics

[ ]   [ ]   - Personality traits

[ ]   [ ]   - Likely personality state during media exposure

C. COMMUNICATION OBJECTIVES

research judgment

[ ]   [ ]   **1. Category need** (Choose one option)

- Omit

- Remind

- Sell

[ ]   [ ]   **2. Brand awareness** (Choose one option)

- Brand recognition (at p-o-p)

- Brand recall (prior to purchase)

- Both relevant

[ ]   [ ]   **3a. Brand attitude objective** (Choose one option)

- Create (new attitude)

- Increase (make present attitude more positive than it is)

- Modify (connect to new motivation)

- Maintain (current attitude)

- Change (from negative to positive)

[ ]   [ ]   **3b. Brand attitude strategy** (Explain selection of quadrant and the motivation, then list the brand attitude benefits)

- Brand attitude strategy quadrant (LI/I, LI/T, HI/I, HI/T) and why _____

_____

_____

- Motivation _____

[ ]   [ ]   - Benefits (including composition rule for benefits)

_____   _____

_____   _____

_____   _____

[ ]   [ ]   **4. Brand purchase intention** (Choose one option)

- Omit (soft-sell delayed)

- Generate (hard-sell immediate)

[ ]   [ ]   **5. Purchase facilitation** (Choose one option)

- Omit

- Incorporate in campaign (check those applicable):

product ____ price ____ distribution ____ selling ____ publicity ____

D. CREATIVE STRATEGY

research judgment

[ ]   [ ]   **1. Category need** (If an objective, list the benefit claims that are intended to "sell the category")

_____

_____

[ ]   [ ]   **2. Brand awareness** (describe how the brand is to be identified in the ad)

_____

_____

- General tactics checklist:

  brand awareness portrayal in ad matches consumer awareness response __

  category need-brand awareness contact time is sufficient _____

  unique execution in category _____

- Brand recognition checklist (if an objective):

  category need context for brand is clear _____

  brand awareness shows package _____

  brand name shown _____

  brand name heard _____

- Brand recall checklist (if an objective):

  main copy line associates category need with brand name _____

  main copy line is short _____

  main copy line is repeated _____

  personal reference explicit _____ or clearly implied _____

  bizarre execution _____

  jingle to be used (if broadcast)? _____

[ ]   [ ]   **3. Brand attitude** (List the benefit claim or claims verbatim for the brand and write "visual" after the benefit if it is a visual implied claim)

_____

_____

_____

_____

_____

_____

Describe emotion (for example, elation) or sequence of emotions (for example, disappointment → hope → relief) to be elicited by the ad in emotional portrayal of the motivation

_____

_____

- Low involvement/informational checklist (if applicable):

  problem-solution format _____

  1 or 2 benefits _____ or single group of benefits _____

  extreme claim or claims _____

- Low involvement/transformational checklist (if applicable):

  likable ad _____

  emotional execution unique to brand _____

  extreme but emotionally authentic claim _____

- High involvement/informational checklist (if applicable):

  correct emotional portrayal if early in product life cycle _____

  initial attitude taken into account _____

  claims are convincing (neither under-claimed nor over-claimed) _____

  refutational _____

  comparative _____

- High involvement/transformational checklist (if applicable):

  target audience will identify with product portrayal in ad _____

  emotional authenticity tailored to lifestyle groups within target audience

  _____

  transformational benefits are over-claimed _____

  informational benefits (if included) are convincing _____

[   ]   [   ]   **4. Brand purchase intention** (If hard-sell, identify reasons—for example, exhortational copy or promotion offer—to act immediately)

_____

_____

[   ]   [   ]   **5. Purchase facilitation** (If an objective, describe how the product, price, distribution, personal selling, or publicity barrier is addressed in the ad)

_____

_____

[   ]   [   ]   **6. Presenter(s) to be considered for ads?** (If so, complete the following for each potential presenter)

- Visibility: what percent of the target audience will immediately recognize the presenter _____

- Credibility (a) Expertise: (especially important for _low involvement/ informational_ and _high involvement/informational_ models). Describe nature of expertise ''hook'' to product

_____

_____

- Credibility (b) Objectivity: (especially important for _high involvement/ informational_ model). Describe presenter's reputation for honesty and objectivity

_____

_____

- Attraction (a) Likability: (especially important for _low involvement/ transformational_ model). Describe why the target audience likes or will like this presenter

_____

_____

- Attraction (b) Similarity: (especially important for _high involvement/ transformational_ model). Describe how the presenter is similar in lifestyle to the target audience

_____

_____

- Power: (relevant to *authority or fear appeals for hard-sell* brand purchase intention). Describe authoritative or commanding characteristics of presenter

_____

_____

[ ]   [ ]   **7. Campaign advertising units** (Complete this section in consultation with media strategy as regards continuity and wearout)

- Recommended advertising units (by medium) to be used throughout campaign period (Write in number of each unit required—for example, 2 × 30 seconds, 1 × full-page color, as applicable—and briefly justify if non-standard):

medium _____   units _____ _____ _____

medium _____   units _____ _____ _____

medium _____   units _____ _____ _____

E. PROMOTION STRATEGY

research judgment

[ ]   [ ]   **1. Is sales promotion to be used?** (Check)

Yes _____

No _____ (leave rest of this section blank)

[ ]   [ ]   **2. Trial promotion to be used?** (If yes, check offers to be used)

sampling _____   coupons _____

trade coupons _____   refund/rebate _____

bonus pack _____   direct price-off _____

warranty _____

- Describe how (each) promotion offer addresses:

brand awareness _____

brand attitude _____

purchase intention _____

[ ]   [ ]   **3. Usage promotion to be used?** (If yes, check offers to be used)

- Type of usage promotion

price-off _____   bonus pack _____

in/on pack _____   premium _____

contest _____   sweepstake _____

continuity program _____

- Describe how (each) promotion offer addresses:

brand awareness _____

brand attitude _____

purchase intention _____

[ ]   [ ]   **4. Promotion's fit with advertising** (Describe in a paragraph or two, with a flowchart if necessary, how the promotion plan fits the advertising plan, for example, intended "ratchet" effects)

- Joint A&P plan summary _____

_____

_____

_____

- A&P flowchart for period:

_____

[ ]   [ ]   **5. Expected profit contribution of promotion plan** (Give details in Appendix 1)

- Revenue $_____

- Cost $_____

- Profit $_____

F. MEDIA STRATEGY

research judgment

[ ]   [ ]

1. **Media selection** (Write in primary and secondary media selections and approximate percent of media budget for each. For secondary media, note purpose, for example, to boost specific communication objectives, imagery transfer, promotion, and so on)

   - Primary medium   _____ _____%

   - Secondary media   _____ _____% _____

                       _____ _____% _____

                       _____ _____% _____

[ ]   [ ]

2. **Minimum effective frequency** (Complete the following for each geographic market if plan differs by region, and for each target audience if more than one target)

   - Target audience purchase cycle for this product category ___months/days

   - Number of purchase cycles in planning period _____

   - MEF required for each purchase cycle in period

     ____ ____ ____ ____ ____ ____ ____ ____

[ ]   [ ]

3. **Effective reach** (Complete for each geographic market and target audience as applicable)

   - Estimated number of target audience consumers reached in each purchase cycle

     ____ ____ ____ ____ ____ ____ ____ ____

   - Probability of purchase when reached at MEF, for each purchase cycle if not constant

     ____ ____ ____ ____ ____ ____ ____ ____

[ ]   [ ]

4. **Media vehicles and ad units** (Make up an Appendix 2 in the following form for each purchase cycle in turn)

   - Purchase cycle # _____

• Vehicles	Unit(s)	Contribution to MEF	Cost
_____	_____	_____	_____
_____	_____	_____	_____

——————   ——————   ——————   ——————

——————   ——————   ——————   ——————

——————   ——————   ——————   ——————

- Effective reach of combined placements _____ × probability of purchase _____ × margin _____ = total revenue $_____ minus total cost of placements $_____ = profit $_____

[ ]   [ ]   **5. Continuity** (Take the perspective of the typical target audience member reached one or more times at MEF during the period and estimate how many times the individual will see each ad over the purchase cycles in the period)

- Ad 1 ____ ____ ____ ____ ____ ____ ____ ____ total ____

- Ad 2 ____ ____ ____ ____ ____ ____ ____ ____ total ____

- Ad 3 ____ ____ ____ ____ ____ ____ ____ ____ total ____

- Ad 4 ____ ____ ____ ____ ____ ____ ____ ____ total ____

- Total ____ ____ ____ ____ ____ ____ ____ ____ total ____

- MEF ____ ____ ____ ____ ____ ____ ____ ____

(Allow for any known special promotion activity in a particular purchase cycle)

[ ]   [ ]   **6. Wearout potential** (Estimate the number of exposures to the typical target audience member before each ad wears out then compare with totals in 5)

	Attention	Learning*	Acceptance
• Ad 1	_____	_____	_____
• Ad 2	_____	_____	_____
• Ad 3	_____	_____	_____
• Ad 4	_____	_____	_____

(* Insert largest competitor's frequency per purchase cycle that will cause major interference)

[ ]   [ ]   **7. Expected profit contribution of media plan** (Total from Appendix 2)

- revenue $_____

- cost $_____

- $ profit _____

G. MANAGERIAL SUMMARY

The foregoing detailed advertising and promotion plan is for operating managers. A managerial summary that can serve as a separate document should now be prepared, preferably no more than two pages long, for other executives. The summary should follow the same section headings as the main plan, showing the sequence of objectives and the strategies for meeting them.

- Title: brand and period
- Marketing objectives
- Target audience action objectives
- Communication objectives
- Creative strategy
- Promotion strategy
- Media strategy

Good summaries are hard to write. Remember the stand-alone requirement and the need for brevity for busy executives. Technical terminology should be translated or avoided and only the key numbers should be included. You should have several executives read the draft before it is cast in final form.

BASIC MEDIA OPTIONS

LEVELS OF MEDIA SELECTION

The media selection process incorporates selection decisions down three levels of media, from general to very specific (Figure B.1). This simple chart by no means does justice to the literally thousands of media options available to the manager. Its purpose is to designate the three levels of media selection that the manager must consider.

TELEVISION (Figure B.2)

TV Media Vehicles

At the broadest and cheapest level, an advertiser can make a *run-of-station* (ROS) buy. This means that the commercial may be inserted in or between any programs at any time, day or night, on any day of the week, at the TV station's discretion. The vehicle in this case is simply the TV network, for a national commercial, or a TV station, for a spot or a local commercial. A *national* commercial is a nationwide commercial placed by a national advertiser; since it must be placed on either the ABC, CBS, or NBC national networks, it is also known as a *network* commercial. A *spot* commercial is a local station commercial placed by a national advertiser. A *local* commercial is a local station commercial placed by a local advertiser.

Most advertisers will want somewhat more control over when the commercial is shown, so that they have a greater chance of reaching a specific rather than a general viewing audience. In this case, the media vehicle is a network or TV station buy by *daypart*. This means that the commercial is shown only at a particular time period during the day or evening. The commercial may be shown in or between any programs in that daypart. A fairly typical breakdown of TV dayparts is as follows: Monday to Friday early morning (7 AM–10 AM); Monday to Friday daytime (10 AM–4:30 PM); Monday to Friday early evening or "fringe" (4:30 PM–7:30 PM); Monday to Sunday prime time (7:30 PM–11 PM); Monday to Sunday late evening (11 PM–2 AM); weekend

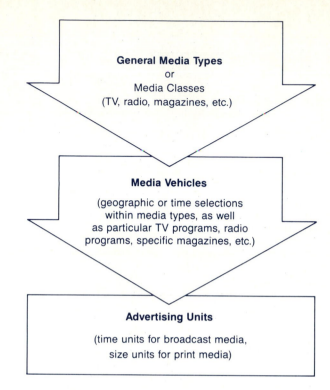

FIGURE B.1   Levels of media selection.

children's (7 AM–1 PM); and weekend sports (1 PM–7 PM); early evening news and late evening news are often regarded as dayparts also.

The most specific and expensive television media vehicle that an advertiser can buy is exact placement before, during, or following a particular TV *program*. For a premium price and with special negotiation, placement can be pinpointed to a particular location in a string or "pod" of commercials, such as first or last position in or adjacent to a particular program. This option is not often used and is not shown in the summary in Figure B.2.

TV Advertising Units

The standard advertising unit for TV is the 30-second (or :30) commercial. About 85 percent of all TV commercials are :30's. The next most frequent lengths are :60's, often used to introduce new brands, and :10's, or so-called "10-second ID's," often used in a brand awareness and brand attitude "reminder" role during or following the main campaign. Very long commercials include 5-minute and 9-minute "infomercials," which are being used increasingly on cable TV stations, and :120's, which are used mainly for direct response commercials, such as those for record albums or other products where a "complete sell" is attempted in the commercial. Odd lengths are used infrequently because TV stations find them awkward to schedule, although we are now seeing :15's or :45's "piggy-backed" by a *single* advertiser advertising *two* brands, such as two :15's in the timeslot normally occupied by one :30, or two :45's in the timeslot normally occupied by three :30's.

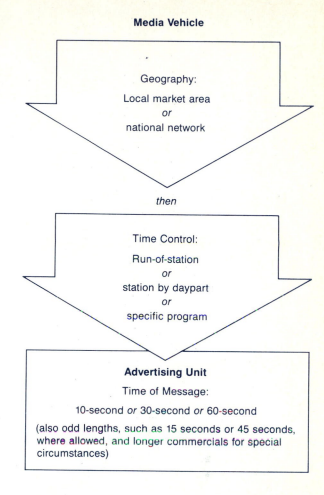

Media Vehicle

Geography:

Local market area
or
national network

then

Time Control:

Run-of-station
or
station by daypart
or
specific program

Advertising Unit

Time of Message:

10-second *or* 30-second *or* 60-second

(also odd lengths, such as 15 seconds or 45 seconds, where allowed, and longer commercials for special circumstances)

FIGURE B.2   Television media selection.

RADIO (Figure B.3)

Radio Media Vehicles

Radio media vehicles are similar to TV in terms of options—except that specific programs seldom are purchased as such. The radio media buyer can buy *run-of-station* (ROS) commercials, in which case the radio station is the media vehicle.

Alternatively, radio is purchased by *daypart*. Radio dayparts are similar to TV dayparts, with the addition of morning and afternoon "drivetime" (to reach automobile commuters on their car radios) and the absence of weekend children's time.

Radio vehicle buys are almost all spot or local buys because individual radio stations cover only local areas. There are no full-time national radio stations, unlike TV. However, multi-city coverage can be obtained through buying from radio networks, such as the Westinghouse Group, who own a string of stations in various cities across the nation, or by utilizing the TV networks' radio stations which are represented in most major cities. This multi-city approach is at best quasi-national as only one station is being purchased per city and any one radio station has relatively small coverage.

Media Vehicle

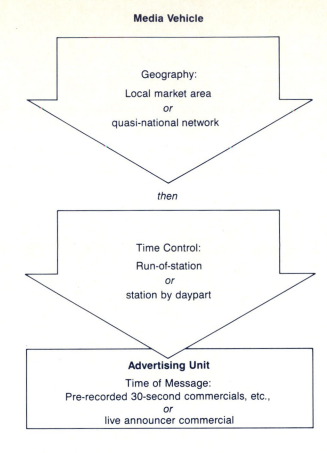

Geography:

Local market area

or

quasi-national network

then

Time Control:

Run-of-station

or

station by daypart

Advertising Unit

Time of Message:

Pre-recorded 30-second commercials, etc.,

or

live announcer commercial

FIGURE B.3   Radio media selection.

Radio Advertising Units

The advertising units for radio are identical to TV with the single but widely used exception of "live," announcer-read commercials that vary in length. Pre-recorded radio commercials are predominantly :30's with quite a few :60's and the occasional :45's or brief :15's or :10's.

MAGAZINES (Figure B.4)

Magazine Media Vehicles

The media vehicle for magazines is, for a basic media buy, the *magazine* itself—such as *TV Guide*, *Reader's Digest*, *National Geographic*, *Time*, *Newsweek*, *National Enquirer*, and *People*, to list the nation's seven most widely read magazines. Some magazines appear monthly, others are weekly vehicles. Many national magazines offer the advertiser *regional editions* to provide specific geographic coverage; also there are major-city magazines, such as *Chicago*, *Dallas*, and so on. Some magazines even offer *demographic editions*, such as *Time "Z"*, which claims that 100 percent of its circulation consists of households with incomes $40,000 and over.

Media Vehicle:

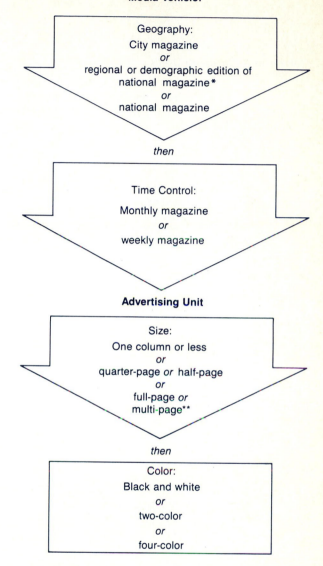

Geography:
City magazine
or
regional or demographic edition of
national magazine*
or
national magazine

then

Time Control:

Monthly magazine
or
weekly magazine

Advertising Unit

Size:
One column or less
or
quarter-page *or* half-page
or
full-page *or*
multi-page**

then

Color:
Black and white
or
two-color
or
four-color

* Business magazines are automatically demographic editions by
occupation or industry.

FIGURE B.4   Magazine media selection.   ** Including special inserts.

Occupational demographic coverage is provided by *business publications* and by *farm publications*. If these are magazines, space is sold as for general magazines. If these are newspaper or newsletter publications, space is sold as for newspapers as explained later.

For higher prices, media buyers can buy *particular section locations* as media vehicles within magazines, such as cover positions, or the first third of the magazine, or special inserts. These are very specific media vehicle options and are not shown in the summary figure.

Magazine Advertising Units

The advertising units for magazine advertisements are defined by two attributes: size and color. Magazine advertising space can be purchased in various *size* units, including multi-page, one-page (full), half-page, quarter-page, one-column or fractions of a column, and also as special inserts of various sizes. There are three basic *color* options, consisting of black and white (no color), two-color (black and white plus one color), or four-color (which produces a full-color effect resulting from the mixing of primary colors).

The most common unit in national magazines is one page, four-color (1P4C). Not shown in the figure is a further option known as "bleed," which refers to the ad extending to the edges of the page. Bleed units usually cost 15 percent more than regular non-bleed ads.

NEWSPAPERS (Figure B.5)

Newspaper Media Vehicles

As noted in Chapter 1, newspapers are the largest advertising medium overall—with TV, miscellaneous (not a single medium), direct mail, radio, general magazines, business publications, outdoor, and farm publications following, in that order. The media vehicle is the *newspaper itself*.

Most ads are placed *run-of-paper* (ROP), which means advertisers do not have position control within the paper. However, the paper's advertising editor will usually place the ad in an appropriate section of the paper, such as the business section, women's section, or entertainment section.

Newspapers are overwhelmingly used as *local* media vehicles. There is only one national newspaper of any substantial coverage, and that is essentially a business publication—the *Wall Street Journal*—although the *New York Daily News*, the *New York Times*, and *U.S.A. Today* are officially listed as national newspapers by the Audit Bureau of Circulations. None of these papers reaches more than about 2 million Americans.

Quasi-national coverage can be obtained through newspaper networks, such as Hearst papers or Knight-Ridder. But newspapers by and large are *local geographic vehicles* that cover particular cities, or particular suburbs, with the emergence of suburban newspapers.

Newspapers, as media vehicles, individually provide "daypart" coverage, in the gross sense that they are either *morning or afternoon* newspapers. First through late editions could also be considered as vehicles, although most newspaper ads are placed to run in all editions on a given day.

Newspaper Advertising Units

The advertising units for newspapers are similar to those for magazines: the two dimensions are size and color. Newspaper advertising *size* (space) is usually sold by

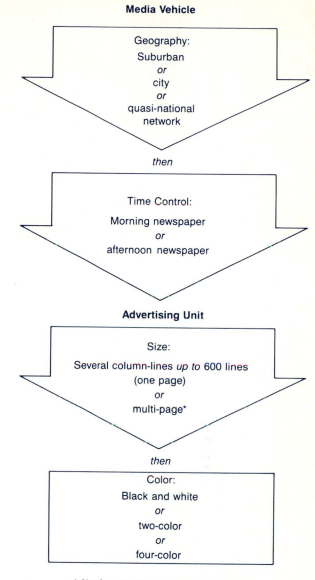

FIGURE B.5   Newspaper media selection.   * Also free-standing inserts or supplements.

the line, for smaller ads, and by page units for larger ads (a full-page newspaper ad is about 600 lines). Free-standing inserts or supplements also are quite common in newspapers, especially in Saturday or Sunday papers. *Color* options are black and white, two-color ads printed on newspaper, four-color ads printed on newspaper, and four-color ads as free-standing inserts. Color reproduction is much better in inserts than on newspaper stock.

DIRECT MAIL (Figure B.6)

Direct mailing pieces are simultaneously the media vehicle and the advertising unit. Advertising units for direct mail range from catalogs, to multi-page brochures, to "shopper" newspapers, to letters, to one-page flyers or handbills. As with other print units, the size and color options apply to direct mail, with the size options virtually unlimited.

OUTDOOR (Figure B.7)

Outdoor Media Vehicles

The media vehicles for outdoor advertising are quite varied—and not all are outdoors! They include outdoor billboards on highways or buildings; indoor billboards, as in airports or railway stations; smaller outdoor and indoor posters; and mobile outdoor vehicles such as display cards on the exterior of buses and taxis.

However, the main functional choice in outdoor media vehicles is *reading time*. If either the audience (for example, highway billboards) *or* the carrier (for example, taxi boards) is *mobile*, then reading time will be brief and the advertising content limited. But if the audience *and* carrier are *stationary* (for example, train or subway billboards, or cards inside buses or trains) so that reading time is prolonged, then the advertising content can be more detailed, much like a magazine or newspaper ad.

Outdoor Advertising Units

Outdoor advertising units differ from units in other media in that they are purchased as both space and time, rather like a combination of print and broadcast characteristics. The *size* or space units for billboards and larger posters are sheets, since each billboard ad is made up of continuous vertical sheets of paper of a standard size (except those

FIGURE B.6   Direct mail media selection.

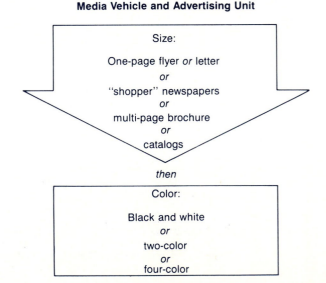

Media Vehicle and Advertising Unit

Size:

One-page flyer *or* letter
or
"shopper" newspapers
or
multi-page brochure
or
catalogs

then

Color:

Black and white
or
two-color
or
four-color

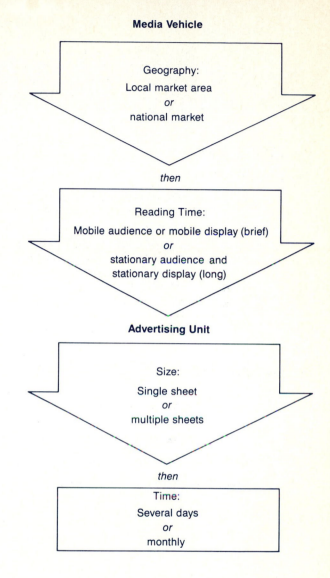

FIGURE B.7   Outdoor media selection.

painted, of course, but still to a standard size). Smaller posters and transit ads usually are single sheets or cards, with cost varying by square-inch area.

Outdoor ads are exposed over *time*, so the advertiser pays for a time unit as well. The time unit is typically 30 days (1 month), although shorter time units occasionally are available for special, limited duration announcements.

MISCELLANEOUS MEDIA (Figure B.8)

Miscellaneous or specialty media *altogether* constitute the third largest category of advertising although they are not, of course, a single medium.

Media Vehicle and Unit*

Timing in
Decision
Sequence:

Diffuse (e.g., t-shirts)

or

Point of purchase (e.g., p-o-p displays)

or

Point of use (e.g., calendars)

FIGURE B.8   Miscellaneous media selection.

* Units vary too widely to categorize and are virtually unique to the vehicle selected.

The largest sub-category of miscellaneous media is *point-of-purchase* (p-o-p) media. The vehicle range for p-o-p advertising is immense, as perusal of any large supermarket or variety store will reveal. *Calendars* would possibly be the next biggest sub-category. The average home has four calendars, three of which are in the kitchen. The average business person's office has two to three calendars, not counting personal diaries.[1]

There are all sorts of *other specialty vehicles*. They include shopping cart ads, airline ticket folders, magazine wrappers, egg cartons, shopping bags, T-shirts, sidewalk stenciling, VW "beetleboards," balloons and large inflatables, scoreboard ads, and laser beam "sky-writing" ads.[2] These unusual media should not be belittled. Many offer unique, inexpensive, and timely advertising delivery. Many are used by major advertisers, such as Chevrolet, Coca-Cola, Anheuser-Busch, McDonald's, and Kodak.

The main vehicle selection factor in miscellaneous media would be *timing within the decision sequence* (see Chapter 5's section on behavioral sequence models). Timing produces three main options: diffuse, point of purchase, and point-of-use.

Some specialty media are only *diffusely related* to the timing of the purchase decision; for example, a T-shirt with a Heineken logo that may be worn and seen in the early morning, when few people are ready to drink beer.

Timing at the actual *point of purchase* is a more time-controlled vehicle option. P-o-p vehicles are the final opportunity the advertiser has to influence a particular purchase decision. Specialty vehicles such as shopping carts, and scoreboard ads for items sold at the sports arena, could be classified as point-of-purchase timing, in addition to more conventional p-o-p displays.

Further timing control is offered by the realization that other specialty media are well-situated to influence *decisions to use* brands, away from the purchase situation itself. For example, a United Airlines office calendar may influence business trip flight selections toward United, or on-package recipes for Kraft cheese may influence usage of Kraft products in the kitchen.

IMPLICATIONS OF THE "NEW ELECTRONIC MEDIA"

In this appendix on media type selection we have as yet made no reference to the phenomenon that William Harvey,[3] in his influential *Media Science Newsletter*, refers to as the "New Electronic Media" (NEM). Although the NEM are being introduced through the medium of TV, they have significant implications for other media types, and for the entire process of media selection. We have written our chapters largely as if the NEM did not exist, because they have not as yet had a major influence on media planning.

What are the new electronic media? Harvey suggests the following "NEM segmentation" scheme for the nation's households:

I.	Non-NEM:	TV homes with no NEM equipment or services
II.	Basic NEM:	TV homes with any or all of the following:

- Basic cable TV
- Subscription TV
- Multi-point distribution service
- Direct broadcast satellite
- Video games

(but *none* of the next list)

III. Advanced NEM: TV homes with any or all of the following:

- Pay cable
- Videocassette recorder
- Videodisc player
- Picture phone
- Videotex
- Home computer
- Movies on demand
- Keyword video

Currently, about 60 percent of householders are in the non-NEM category; 22 percent have basic NEM; and 18 percent have advanced NEM. Projections are always hard to make, but Harvey predicts that the penetration of NEM will be rapid, so that the market will almost be reversed by 1990: about 60 percent will have advanced NEM, 20 percent basic NEM, and only 20 percent will be non-NEM.

The Impact of Basic NEM on Network and Local Television Stations

According to the above estimate, approximately 80 percent of households will have at least basic NEM access by 1990. The main characteristic of basic NEM is cable TV programs. Cable TV, mainly by showing almost-first-run movies, is already eating into conventional TV stations' share. The share of viewing households held by the three major networks during prime time, when most cable movies are shown, has already fallen to 80 percent. The networks' prime-time share is projected to decline to 60 percent by 1990.

However, because of U.S. population growth, the 60 percent projected prime-time share represents only a 5 percent loss in homes reached by the average prime-time network program. In 1980, just as cable TV was becoming a factor, the average prime-time network program reached 14.5 million households; in 1990, the average program is expected to reach 13.8 million households. Thus, in the medium-run, there is not any significant reason to modify TV buying practices.

The longer-run impact of cable TV is harder to predict. According to one scenario, which we believe to be the most likely, networks and local stations will hold about the same "mass" audience sizes as they do now, with just occasional "peel off" to cable movies. An alternative scenario is that cable programs might attract up to a third or even a half of all evening viewers. Under the latter scenario of major cable TV impact, there are disadvantages but compensating advantages for advertisers:

- TV media buying will become more complicated as the range of program vehicles expands, with increased costs to reach large audiences.
- However, the mass audience is likely to split into more selective audiences based on individual values and interests. And to the extent that this selectivity correlates with product attitudes, costs to reach *target* audiences should decline.
- TV is the most effective advertising medium overall, so the effectiveness of advertising should increase with more placements in the TV-based NEM.

The Impact of Basic NEM on Magazines

Cable TV offers not only movies but also "special interest" programming such as sports, news, and community activities. Thus, in the projected 80 percent of basic NEM households, TV will compete with magazines. If this scenario proves to be the dominant one, magazine media owners will suffer, but advertisers and media planners will benefit. "TV magazine" programs offer the *selectivity* of magazines with the *intrusiveness* (attention-holding capacity) of television. Also, the picture quality of TV will improve radically over the next 10 to 20 years, rivalling magazines' visual reproduction quality.[4] We should therefore witness:

- Greater use of TV as a secondary as well as a primary advertising medium (see Chapter 15 on primary and secondary media selection).

The Impact of Advanced NEM on Newspapers and the Yellow Pages

According to Harvey's estimate, by 1990, about 60 percent of households will have advanced NEM equipment. We believe this to be a high estimate for the following reason: The main characteristic of advanced NEM is the *interactive* "two-way" capacity it affords. Through picturephones, videotex, and home computers, TV's interactive usage would seem to be skewed initially toward higher education households, which would be well below 60 percent of households. We would estimate that about 20 percent of households at most, by 1990, will be using NEM regularly in this interactive mode.

For products with an educational and perhaps a professional income skew, the interactive TV audience will be substantial and attractive. As several commentators have noted, interactive use of TV will alter (this part of) the medium from an entertainment and news function to an information and transaction function (notably the "electronic newspaper" and also shopping via TV with telephone orders). The information and transaction functions have traditionally been provided by newspapers, for shopping ads and classifieds, and by specialized directories, such as the Yellow Pages. The implication is as follows:

- For reaching educated professionals, newspapers and the Yellow Pages will decline in coverage while the NEM will increase in coverage.

Summary of the "New Electronic Media"

The NEM *could* have profound implications for media selection as we know it. Television will assume more coverage in most individuals' personal media mix. Cable

TV will usurp some of the traditional media functions of "normal" non-cable TV, as well as reducing readership of magazines. Interactive TV will usurp some of the functions of newspapers and shopper information directories. Radio seems less likely to be affected although videodiscs pose some threat to in-home use of radio.

These predicted changes would seem to complicate and fragment the media buying process but, at the same time, promise more precise target audience reach. Furthermore, advertising should become more effective in the NEM, because, not only will NEM audiences be restricted to the most interested individuals, but also the attention-holding power of TV will cause even an undistinguished commercial to be processed.

Adoption of the NEM, especially the advanced NEM, involves major changes in work and leisure behavior patterns. Therefore, the extent of NEM's impact cannot be predicted with much accuracy. Media planners cannot afford to ignore the likely impact of the NEM—but these new media vehicles have not yet changed the media options for the great majority of media planners. The NEM at present could essentially be classified as "miscellaneous" media, an extension of the category just discussed. Of course, the next edition of this book may reflect an entirely different outlook on media selection because of the actual adoption or rejection of the various new electronic media.

NOTES

1 L.J. Haugh, "How calendars make promos a daily event," *Advertising Age*, December 7, 1981, p. 55.
2 "Media's stepchildren step up," *ad forum*, November 1981, pp. 14–16.
3 W. Harvey (author and publisher), *Media Science Newsletter*, June 16–30, 1981, *3* (5), whole issue and supplement, cited by permission.
4 Current TV pictures in the United States and Japan are composed of 525 lines; Europe and the United Kingdom have 625 lines. High definition TV (925 lines) is expected to become standard by the turn of the century.

AD UNIT MEF ADJUSTMENTS FOR INITIAL ATTENTION

It is worth adjusting the media plan's estimated contribution to the attainment of minimum effective frequency (MEF) per purchase cycle to allow for ad units when either of the following conditions applies:

- *Short campaigns that use non-standard units*—such as when an industrial advertiser announces a new product using a two-page spread in one or two issues of a trade magazine; or when a retailer runs short, shopper-reminder commercials on radio for one week in conjunction with a special sale.
- *Sustained campaigns in which non-standard units are used often*—such as when a corporate image advertiser employs 60-second TV commercials for a long period, or :60's interspersed equally with :30's; or when a consumer product advertiser runs a campaign consisting of 15-second TV commercials aimed at a favourable target audience.

With longer campaigns using mainly standard units with only the occasional variation to non-standard units, the contribution of the occasional variations to the already-calculated MEF figure is too small to be worth further adjustments. Completely standard-unit campaigns, of course, require no adjustment.

This appendix lists adjustments for non-standard advertising units in six major media: television, radio, newspapers, consumer magazines, industrial and business magazines, and outdoor. We list only the factors that make *at least 20 percent difference* (plus or minus 0.2) in their contribution to MEF. The adjustments reflect differences in *initial attention* generated by the physical characteristics of the advertising unit, such as length, size, and color.

For validity, and also for multi-media campaigns, it would be *ideal* to have an identical measure of initial attention to advertising units which is applicable across all media. This measure would be *advertisement recognition:* the minimum evidence that the audience paid attention to an ad (see Chapter 20 on campaign evaluation). In the past, advertisements in print media have used advertisement recognition, because it is easy for advertising research interviewers to show consumers a magazine or newspaper and ask which ads consumers recognize. Advertisements in broadcast media, however, used advertising recall prior to the development of videotape and audiotape recorders, and also more recently due to the technological inconvenience of operating this equipment in administering a broadcast advertisement recognition measure to consumers.[1] Outdoor advertisements have used neither measure, as we shall see.

The ad unit MEF adjustments are based on *advertising recall* for broadcast media and *advertisement recognition* for print media. Although these are by no means equivalent measures of initial attention,[2] they are the best adjustment factors we have available for the various media. They reflect relative differences from the "standard" unit in each medium and are better than intuitive adjustments or no adjustments at all.

TELEVISION

The recommended ad unit adjustment indices (contributions to MEF) for TV are shown in Table C-1.[3] Taking the 30-second commercial length as standard, we see that a 10-second commercial contributes 0.7 to MEF, which means that one-third the length gets about two-thirds of the attention of the standard commercial. The newer 15-second commercials (by interpolation, as not enough data are yet available on this length) contribute 0.8 to MEF. The 60-second commercial length exhibits a contribution of 1.2 to MEF. Commercials longer than 60 seconds are so perceptually distinctive and unusual on television that here we have made a judgment adjustment and indexed these at 2.0.

Another factor *not* adjusted for is position of the commercial in the commercial break. Contrary to popular opinion, this does not make a substantial difference to initial attention. While the first and last commercials in a break get a slight advantage, the difference in advertising recall is less than 5 percent (0.05 MEF). Similarly, position in in-program versus between-program breaks makes little difference.[4] Moreover, the vast majority of TV commercials are placed by daypart or by program and only very rarely by specific positions in a break (where the cost premium would be very high). Consequently, position in general is not worth adjusting for.

Radio

The recommended ad unit adjustment indices for radio commercials are shown in Table C-2. Although day-after advertising recall is sometimes used to test radio

TABLE C-1   ADJUSTMENTS (CONTRIBUTIONS TO MEF) FOR TELEVISION COMMERCIALS

Length (in seconds)	Index
120	2.0*
90	2.0*
60	1.2
30 (standard)	1.0
15	0.8†
10	0.7

* Judgment.
† Interpolation.

TABLE C-2   ADJUSTMENTS
(CONTRIBUTIONS TO MEF) FOR
RADIO COMMERCIALS

Length (seconds)	Index
60	1.2
30 (standard)	1.0
10	0.7

commercials, there are no norms available for units of differing lengths. Remembering that radio media vehicles are already weighted down by about one-half, we have then simply applied the TV commercial recall adjustment factors as being the best estimate of attention differences due to radio commercial length. The two most common variations from the standard 30-second length (apart from live announcer-read commercials) are 10-second and 60-second lengths, so only these are shown.

Newspapers

The recommended ad unit adjustment indices (contributions to MEF) for newspapers are shown in Table C-3. As mentioned earlier, the attention norms for print ads are based on advertisement recognition; specifically, the Starch advertisement recognition measure.[5]

There are two main adjustment dimensions for newspaper advertisements: size and color (Table C-3). First, in terms of size, taking a one-page ad as standard, we see that doubling the size, to a two-page ad, produces 50 percent higher probability of initial attention (1.5 exposures contributed to MEF), not double the attention or a 100-percent increase. The index, 1.5, is quite close to that predicted by the "square root law," an

TABLE C-3   ADJUSTMENTS (CONTRIBUTIONS TO MEF)
FOR NEWSPAPER ADVERTISEMENTS*

Size	Index†	
2 pages	1.5	
1 1/2 pages	1.2	
1 page (standard)	1.0	
1/2 page	0.9 ≈ 1.0	
1/4 page or smaller	0.7	
Color		
Black and white (standard)	1.0	
2-color	1.1 ≈ 1.0	
4-color	1.3	
Section	**Men**	**Women**
General news	1.0	1.0
Sports	1.0	0.5
Women's	0.6	1.0

* For products of general interest to both men and women.
†Multiply indices for multiple adjustment.

approximation originated by Daniel Starch which says that attention increases with the square root of size, that is, by $\sqrt{2} = 1.4$. However, for newspapers, this approximation breaks down for smaller ads, where we see that attention holds very well for half-page ads (0.9, which is less than 0.2 difference from 1.0 and therefore not worth adjusting for) and even one-quarter page or smaller ads (0.7, worth adjusting for). This higher-than-predicted attention for less-than-one-page ads is probably due to the tendency of newspaper readers to scan everything on the page, including smaller items, a habit reinforced by finding smaller news items of interest.

Second, in terms of color, taking black and white newspaper ads as standard, we see that the addition of *any* color increases attention. However, two-color ads (black and white plus *one* color) do not produce enough gain in attention (1.1 exposures contributed to MEF) to be worth adjusting for. Four-color ("full-color") advertisements increase attention by 30 percent (or 1.3 exposures contributed to MEF) and are worth adjusting for. With newspaper advertisements, the addition of full color in what is essentially a black and white medium[6] attracts greater attention.

A third adjustment dimension that sometimes may have to be applied for newspaper ads is section placement. Whereas men (71 percent) and women (69 percent) are equally likely to read newspapers on an average workday,[7] men are more likely to skip the women's section, and women are more likely to skip the sports section. General interest ads (for example, for cars, vacation trips, cigarettes) placed in the "cross-sex" section therefore are likely to suffer lower attention, as shown in the last panel of Table C-3. Of course, there is no reason other than editorial oversight that ads for "opposite sex" products would be placed in either the women's or the sports sections, so no norms are available for this eventuality.

Among the factors that do *not* make a difference in initial attention to newspaper advertisements are various page positions: left-hand page versus right-hand page (horizontally); above- versus below-the-fold (vertically); and outside versus "gutter" (side or bottom-of-page) positions. Many advertisers believe that right-hand pages gain more attention and many newspapers (and magazines—see next sections) charge a premium for this position; if so, cost savings can be obtained by using left-hand pages, as attention will not be affected.

Consumer Magazines

The recommended ad unit adjustments (contributed to MEF) for consumer magazines[8] are shown in Table C-4. Again, the two main adjustment dimensions are size and color. Looking ahead to a lower panel in the table, we see that Starch advertisement recognition norms provide exact readings for combinations of size and color, whereas with newspaper ads we had to multiply the two indices to estimate the combined effect. As can be seen, the multiplying method does very well. The actual results are all within 0.1 of the estimates that would be obtained from multiplication.

In terms of size, and taking a one-page consumer magazine ad as standard, we see that doubling the size (a two-page "spread") increases attention by about 30 percent (1.3 exposures contributed to MEF). This is a little below the prediction obtained by the square root law (1.4). Similarly, halving the size loses about 30-percent attention; a half-page ad contributes about 0.7 of an exposure to MEF, which is exactly the prediction made by the square root law. In round figures, an MEF of 4 can be achieved by four one-page ads or three two-page ads. Likewise, an MEF of 2 can be achieved by two one-page ads or three half-page ads. However, it must be realized that such comparisons *rarely are made*, because the target audience and communication objectives of different-sized ads—as explained earlier—generally are *different*.

TABLE C.4   ADJUSTMENTS (CONTRIBUTIONS TO MEF) FOR CONSUMER MAGAZINE ADVERTISEMENTS

Size	Index
2-page spread	1.3
1-page (standard)	1.0
½-page	0.7

Color	Index
4-color (standard)	1.0
2-color	0.6
Black and white	0.7

Size and Color

	½-page	1-page	2-page
4-color	0.8	1.0	1.3
2-color	0.5	0.7	0.8*
Black and white	0.6	0.8	0.9 ≈ 1.0

Position	Index
2nd cover	1.2
1st third	1.0
2nd third	1.0
3rd third	1.0
3rd cover	1.2
4th cover	1.3

* Estimate.

The ad-size effect works *within* magazines. For example, a full-page ad in *Life* magazine, which has a large page-size format, does not gain greater attention than a full-page ad in *Time* magazine, which has—relatively—a smaller page-size format. This is because readers tend to adjust the visual distance when reading, bringing *Time* closer to them than they would *Life*, so that the ad size on the retina (visual angle) is the same.[9] Thus, there is no advantage in advertising in larger magazines.

In terms of color, two interesting phenomena occur with consumer magazine ads. Four-color ads have now become standard in consumer magazines. Black and white ads, which used to be the standard, actually have decreased in attention from 10 years ago (0.8) to the present time (0.7) relative to full-color ads. Whereas this could be due to less creatively effective advertisers using black and white, this trend also counts against the belief that black and white ads will "stand out" in an all-color advertising environment.

The second interesting observation is that two-color ads fare slightly worse than no color at all. Perhaps two-color ads, in consumer magazines, are seen as "cheap" versions of four-color. Whatever the explanation, two-color ads are less well attended to (0.6 of an exposure contributed to MEF) than four-color ads.

Position in the magazine is another ad unit dimension long believed to be important by consumer advertisers. It turns out that only cover positions gain an advantage in attention, and then only to a maximum increase of 30 percent (1.3) on the outside of the back cover, with the two inside covers gaining 20 percent (1.2). Position within the magazine's *pages* makes a negligible difference (1.05 for the first third, 1.00 for the second third, and 1.01 for the final third: all shown as 1.0) and is *not* worth either seeking or adjusting for.

TABLE C.5 ADJUSTMENTS (CONTRIBUTIONS TO MEF) FOR INDUSTRIAL AND BUSINESS MAGAZINE ADVERTISEMENTS

Size	Index*
2-page	1.7
1-page (standard)	1.0
⅔-page	0.8
½-page	0.7
⅓-page	0.5
¼-page	0.4

Color	Index
4-color	1.4
2-color	1.2
Black and white (standard)	1.0

Position	Index
Cover (all 3 averaged)	1.3
Inside	1.0

Bleed	Index
Bleed	1.2
Non-bleed	1.0

Insert	Index
Ad with insert	1.3
No insert (run-of-press ad)	1.0

* Multiply indices for multiple adjustment.

A factor that does *not* make a difference in consumer magazines is left-hand page versus right-hand page position (just as in newspapers). With magazines, the belief that reading habits cause right-hand pages to gain "fuller" attention as pages are turned or flipped is not justified by relative attention scores.

Similarly, the "bleed" ad format, for which the advertiser pays extra because the ad runs to the edges of the page rather than being enclosed in magazines' normal white border, makes no difference to attention in consumer magazines.

Industrial and Business Magazines

Some changes from consumer magazines in terms of attention adjustments occur when advertising in industrial and business magazines.[10] The recommended ad unit adjustments (contributions to MEF) for industrial and business magazines are shown in Table C-5, beginning with the two main print ad dimensions of size and color.

The notable feature of the ad size adjustments is that double-page spreads in industrial and business magazines have a considerably greater effect on attention (1.7 exposures contributed to MEF) than in consumer magazines (1.3, earlier). This occurs possibly because the larger ads are more unusual in the industrial setting or because readers attribute more importance to advertisers who use larger ads. The attention loss with half-page ads (0.3, resulting in 0.7 MEF) is, however, identical in business and consumer magazines.

Color has a different effect in industrial and business magazine ads from its effect in other print media ads. In industrial and business magazine ads, we observe the "commonsense" effect: addition of one color to the black and white standard increases attention by 20 percent (1.2 MEF) and addition of full-color increases attention by 40 percent (1.4 MEF). This is in (slight) contrast to the idiosyncracies of color in other print media reported earlier, where the addition of one color in newspapers is insignificantly better (1.1), and one color in consumer magazines is insignificantly worse (0.6 versus 0.7) than no color at all.

The combined effect of size and color on attention to industrial and business ads has to be estimated by the multiplication method, as exact data are not available. As might be expected from the preceding individual factors, two-page, full-color ads are estimated to provide a very large increase in attention: 2.4 exposures contributed to MEF.

Other dimensions worth adjusting for in industrial and business magazine advertisements include, firstly, position in the magazine. Although individual cover position data are not available, cover positions, on average, contribute 1.3 to MEF.

In industrial and business magazines, but not consumer magazines, the bleed format adds a small but significant increment (1.2).

An in-ad coupon makes no significant difference to attention and hence is not shown in the table. However, a free-standing insert ad, or ads that incorporate such an insert, increase attention by 30 percent (1.3 MEF), as would be expected by the physical tendency for the magazine to open at the insert.

No data are available on left-hand versus right-hand page positions for industrial and business magazines. However, given the negligible effect of page side for newspapers and consumer magazines, our best estimate is that no adjustment should be made for page side in business publications.

Outdoor Ads

As we move away from the major media of TV, radio, newspapers, and magazines, research on advertising units becomes extremely scarce and incomplete. Outdoor media studies have been confined to billboards, for example, rather than the full range of outdoor and indoor posters, and inside and outside transit advertising.

A fairly common choice to be made in outdoor billboards is between the large 30-sheet size and the smaller 8-sheet size. An eye camera study by Perception Research Services using the simulated highway driving method found that the smaller size achieves, on average, 0.8 of the attention of the larger size.[11] However, other than following the widely demonstrated effect of ad size, adjustments for outdoor ads are very tentative as they undoubtedly depend on the context of surrounding outdoor ads, the mobile versus stationary relationship between viewers and the ad, and the viewing distance. At best, adjustments for outdoor would really be guesses. The best procedure is to make an assessment of ad size for the particular typical exposure context in which outdoor is planned, although, even here, the eye-camera study suggests that only large departures from average (in-context) size would make more than 20 percent difference in attention and therefore be worth adjusting for.

Miscellaneous and P-O-P Ads

Almost no information is available on advertising units' attention in miscellaneous media, including point-of-purchase displays. The overwhelming miscellany of options available suggests, again, that judgment in the exposure context is the only reasonable resort. Accordingly, we cannot provide any useful adjustment factors for miscellaneous and p-o-p ads.

Direct Mail

The fastest-growing medium, direct mail, also suffers from heterogeneity of options which makes standard adjustments impossible to provide. We may estimate that ads which form the whole of the mailing piece perform similarly regardless of size, because of the reader's natural tendency to adjust visual distance. About 80 percent of all direct mail is opened, contrary to the popular impression of "junk mail," so it is a high attention medium.

Ads *within* a mailing piece, such as in a catalog or a multi-ad flyer, should be subject to the same adjustments as consumer magazines (Table C-4) although this conclusion is by inference rather than being based on hard evidence.

NOTES

1 Bruzzone Research Company (BRC) offers an advertisement *recognition* measure for television commercials, in which photoboard versions of commercials with typed copy of the audio (like a comic strip) are presented to respondents. However, this service's use of a mail sample with questionable representativeness, plus the fact that norms are not available for different length commercials, make a good recognition adjustment for television unobtainable at present.

2 The relationship between advertisement recognition and advertisement recall is examined in detail in Chapter 20. To a fair extent they measure the same "memory for ads" factor, as demonstrated by R.P. Bagozzi and A.J. Silk, Recall, recognition, and the measurement of memory for print advertisements, *Marketing Science*, 1983, *2* (2), 95–134. Our contention is that the *relative* scores (and thus the index weights) for different advertising units should remain approximately the same despite differences in the memory measures used.

3 Adapted from Burke Marketing Research, Inc., *The Effect of Environmental and Executional Variables on Overall Memorability*, Cincinatti: Burke Marketing Research, Inc., 1979.

4 Again contrary to popular opinion, and somewhat surprisingly, Nielsen metered viewing data do *not* demonstrate that more channel switching takes place during commercials than during programs, which is the usual argument against between-program commercial positions. Also, with channel switching, the viewer is as likely to pick up a commercial on the new channel as to miss it on the old one, given that the switch is virtually instantaneous.

These results are confirmed by an independent study using meters, which found *less* switching of channels in between-program breaks (2 percent) than in during-program breaks (4 percent in daytime, 6 percent in prime time). The author of the latter study suggests that people switch to check other programs and avoid switching when they know commercials will be on the other channel. In any case, the attention loss due to position is negligible. See G.J. Eskin, Tracking advertising and promotion performance with single-source data, *Journal of Advertising Research*, 1985, *25* (1), 31, 33–39.

5 The Starch norms for newspaper advertisements were obtained from the following secondary sources: Newspaper Advertising Bureau, Inc., *The Audience for News-*

paper Advertising: Interest in Advertising and Shopping Behavior, New York: NAB, 1978, p. 13 (size); B. Stone, *Successful Direct Marketing Methods* (3rd ed.), Chicago: Crain Books, 1984, p. 174 (color); and D. Glauser, Newspaper advertising, *The Sunday Times Marketing Journal*, 1982, *3*, 2 (sex differences and page position).

6 These norms precede the appearance of America's first color newspaper, *USA Today*. As four-color pictorial content is the norm for such vehicles, it is possible that black and white ads and two-color ads, which would be unusual, may gain slightly greater attention than four-color ads, in color newspapers. In the absence of evidence, the safest procedure would be to index all ads at 1.0 for color newspapers, if they are used in the media plan.

7 The newspaper readership figures by sex are from Simmons Market Research Bureau (SMRB) 1979 surveys and were reported in E. Papazian (Ed.), *The Media Book 1980*, New York: The Media Book, Inc., 1980. They would *not* apply to more specialized newspapers with low opposite-sex *passalong* readership, such as *The Wall Street Journal*, for women, and probably suburban "shopper" newspapers, for men.

8 These are adapted from Starch advertising recognition norms (Noted scores) for 1980. Source: *Starch Tested Copy*, 1981, *6* (1), whole issue.

9 From a report by L. Weinblatt of The Pretesting Co., Inc., Fairlawn, NJ, appearing in: "Study disputes earlier findings," *Marketing News*, May 24, 1985, pp. 1, 38. The Pretesting Co. uses a miniature recorder clipped onto an eyeglasses frame to record attention via eye movements. This method, as contrasted with the more primitive headrest-plus-eye camera method, allows consumers to hold the magazine as they would normally when reading.

10 The industrial and business magazine attention data are 1978 and 1979 results taken from Carr Reports, published by Cahners Publishing Company, Boston (ca. 1983). The exact advertising recognition method used was not reported, although industrial and business magazines usually use a mail sample version of Starch scores. Thus, the adjustments should be internally applicable to advertising in this medium if not exactly comparable across media.

11 Study by Perception Research Services, Inc., Englewood Cliffs, NJ, reported in *Marketing News*, November 23, 1984, p. 12.

INDEXES

NAME INDEX

SUBJECT INDEX

COMPANY, PRODUCT, BRAND, AND PRESENTER INDEX